JOURNAL FOR THE STUDY OF THE NEW TESTAMENT
SUPPLEMENT SERIES
54

Executive Editor, Supplement Series
David Hill

JSOT Press
Sheffield

THE DEVELOPMENT OF EARLY CHRISTIAN PNEUMATOLOGY

with special reference to Luke–Acts

Robert P. Menzies

Journal for the Study of the New Testament
Supplement Series 54

To Joanne and Jessica,
the Love and Joy of my life

Copyright © 1991 Sheffield Academic Press

Published by JSOT Press
JSOT Press is an imprint of
Sheffield Academic Press Ltd
The University of Sheffield
343 Fulwood Road
Sheffield S10 3BP
England

Printed on acid-free paper in Great Britain
by
Billing & Sons Ltd
Worcester

British Library Cataloguing in Publication Data

Menzies, Robert Paul
    The development of early Christian pneumatology
    with special reference to Luke–Acts. (Journal for the
    study of the New Testament supplement series
    ISSN 0143-5108; no. 54)
    I. Title II. Series
    231.3

    ISBN 1-85075-306-7

CONTENTS

We often complain that Christian people at home have little zeal for the spread of the gospel. How can it be otherwise when our people are taught that the Holy Spirit is given, when they are taught to recognize him in their own souls, almost entirely as the sanctifier, the truth revealer, the strengthener, and in the church as the organizer and the director of counsels, whilst they are not taught in anything like the same degree that [the Spirit] is the spirit of redeeming love, active in them towards others, moving every individual soul to whom [the Spirit] comes and the church in which [the Spirit] dwells to desire and to labour for the bringing of all men everywhere to God in Jesus Christ?

—Roland Allen, 'The Revelation of the Holy Spirit in the Acts of the Apostles', *International Review of Missions* (April 1918)

ACKNOWLEDGMENTS

I would like to express my appreciation to the numerous people who, in a variety of ways, enabled me to write this book, originally penned as a PhD thesis at the University of Aberdeen. I am particularly indebted to the students and faculty of the Asia Pacific Theological Seminary (Baguio, Philippines), for the stimulus to undertake this project arose from my association with these friends and colleagues. The encouragement provided by this institution made my time of research at Aberdeen possible. For this I am most grateful.

Although the physical environment of Aberdeen is considerably different from that of Southeast Asia, I found the intellectual and spiritual climate to be equally enriching. I am especially thankful to have had the privilege of working under the supervision of Professor I. Howard Marshall, a man of incisive mind, gentle manner, and obvious enthusiasm for the study of the New Testament. I count myself doubly fortunate, for while at Aberdeen I had access to another gifted scholar, one with a special interest in the work of the Spirit, past and present, Max Turner. My fellow postgraduate students were also a major source of encouragement. Mike Nola helped a young 'rookie' feel at home. Conrad Gempf and Chuck Guth offered timely help when I encountered computer problems. And the 'lunch bunch' always provided food for thought. Although various individuals helped at the proof-reading stage, I owe a great debt to Gary Alan Long and Lynn Graham, both of whom took time from their busy schedules to read the entire manuscript. The fellowship and support of the Abbey Christian Fellowship were a constant source of strength. An Overseas Research Scholarship provided by the British Government lightened the financial load. Dr David Hill and the Sheffield Academic Press have kindly made the thesis available to a wider audience. Most of all, my wife Joanne joyfully sojourned with me, provided loving companionship, and paid most of the bills during the period of study. She also provided me with a beautiful daughter, who made life interesting and fun.

AB	Anchor Bible
AGAJU	Arbeiten zur Geschichte des Antiken Judentums und des Urchristentums
AnBib	Analecta Biblica
ANCL	Ante-Nicene Christian Library
AnGreg	Analecta Gregoriana
ANRW	*Aufstieg und Niedergang der römischen Welt*, ed. H. Temporini, W. Haase
ArBib	The Aramaic Bible
ASTI	*Annual of the Swedish Theological Institute*
ATANT	Abhandlungen zur Theologie des Alten und Neuen Testaments
AThD	Acta Theologica Danica
ATR	*Anglican Theological Review*
BamL	Bampton Lectures
BAR	Biblical Archaeology Review
BBB	Bonner biblische Beiträge
BeiHT	Beiträge zur historischen Theologie
BeiRT	Beiträge zur Religionstheologie
BETL	Bibliotheca Ephemeridum Theologicarum Lovaniensium
Bib	*Biblica*
BibT	*Bible Today*
BiKi	*Bibel und Kirche*
BJ	Bible de Jérusalem
BL	*Bibel und Leben*
BTB	*Biblical Theology Bulletin*
BTS	Biblisch-Theologische Studien
BWANT	Beiträge zur Wissenschaft vom Alten und Neuen Testament
BZ	*Biblische Zeitschrift*
BZNW	Beihefte zur Zeitschrift für die neutestamentliche Wissenschaft
CBQ	*Catholic Biblical Quarterly*
CBQMS	Catholic Biblical Quarterly Monograph Series
CGTC	Cambridge Greek Testament Commentary
CovQ	*Covenant Quarterly*
CTQ	*Concordia Theological Quarterly*
DL	*Doctrine and Life*
EE	*Der Evangelische Erzieher*
EHPR	Études d'Histoire et de Philosophie Religieuses
EJ	*Eranos Jahrbuch*
EKK	Evangelisch-Katholischer Kommentar
EQ	*The Evangelical Quarterly*

ErTS	Erfurter Theologische Schriften
ETL	*Ephemerides Theologicae Lovanienses*
EvTh	*Evangelische Theologie*
EWNT	*Exegetisches Wörterbuch zum Neuen Testament*, ed. H. Balz, G. Schneider
ExpTim	*Expository Times*
FRLANT	Forschungen zur Religion und Literatur des Alten und Neuen Testaments
FV	*Foi et Vie*
GCS	Die griechischen christlichen Schriftsteller der ersten drei Jahrhunderte
GNS	Good News Studies
Herm	Hermeneia
HM	Heythrop Monographs
HNT	Handbuch zum Neuen Testament
HNTC	Harper's New Testament Commentaries
HR	*History of Religions*
HTK	Herders Theologischer Kommentar
HTR	*Harvard Theological Review*
HTS	Harvard Theological Studies
IBS	*Irish Biblical Studies*
IDB	*The Interpreter's Dictionary of the Bible*
Int	*Interpretation*
ITQ	*Irish Theological Quarterly*
JANES	*Journal for Ancient Near Eastern Studies*
JBL	*Journal of Biblical Literature*
JETS	*Journal of the Evangelical Theological Society*
JJS	*Journal of Jewish Studies*
JL	Jordan Lectures
JSHRZ	Jüdische Schriften aus hellenistisch-römischer Zeit
JSNT	*Journal for the Study of the New Testament*
JSNTS	Journal for the Study of the New Testament Supplement Series
JSOT	*Journal for the Study of the Old Testament*
JSS	*Journal of Semitic Studies*
JTF	Jesuit Theological Forum
JTS	*Journal of Theological Studies*
Jud	*Judaica*
KEKNT	Kritisch-exegetischer Kommentar über das Neue Testament
KuD	*Kerygma und Dogma*
LCL	Loeb Classical Library
LD	Lectio Divina
LV	*Lumen Vitae*
MFSAAF	Meddelanden Från Stiftelsens för Åbo Akademi Forskningsinstitut
NCB	New Century Bible
NClarB	The New Clarendon Bible
Neo	*Neotestamentica*
NICNT	The New International Commentary on the New Testament

NICOT	The New International Commentary on the Old Testament
NIGTC	The New International Greek Testament Commentary
NovT	*Novum Testamentum*
NRT	*Nouvelle Revue Théologique*
NTA	Neutestamentliche Abhandlungen
NTD	Das Neue Testament Deutsch
NTS	*New Testament Studies*
NV	*Nova et Vetera*
OBO	Orbis Biblicus et Orientalis
OC	*One in Christ*
ÖTKNT	Ökumenischer Taschenbuchkommentar zum Neuen Testament
PA	Philosophia Antiqua
PGM	Papyri Graecae Magicae
PS	Patristica Sorbonensia
PTh	Le Point Théologique
PVTG	Pseudepigrapha Veteris Testamenti Graece
RB	*Revue Biblique*
RefR	*The Reformed Review*
Rel	*Religion*
RevRel	*Review for Religions*
RGG	*Religion in Geschichte und Gegenwart*, ed. K. Galling
RHPR	*Revue d'Histoire et de Philosophie Religieuse*
RNT	Regensburger Neues Testament
RQ	*Revue de Qumran*
RSR	*Revue des Sciences Religieuses*
RTP	*Revue de Théologie et de Philosophie*
RTR	*Reformed Theological Review*
SBF	Studium Biblicum Franciscanum
SBL	Society of Biblical Literature
SBLDS	Society of Biblical Literature Dissertation Series
SBLMS	Society of Biblical Literature Monograph Series
SBS	Stuttgarter Bibelstudien
SBT	Studies in Biblical Theology
Sem	*Semeia*
SH	Scripta Hierosolymitana
SJT	*Scottish Journal of Theology*
SJTOP	Scottish Journal of Theology Occasional Papers
SN	Studia Neotestamentica
SNT	Supplements to Novum Testamentum
SNTSMS	Society for New Testament Studies Monograph Series
SNTU	Studien zum Neuen Testament und seiner Umwelt
StANT	Studien zum Alten und Neuen Testament
StBT	Studia Biblica et Theologica
STDJ	Studies on the Texts of the Desert of Judah
StJud	Studia Judaica
StNT	Studien zum Neuen Testament
SubB	Subsidia Biblica
SUNT	Studien zur Umwelt des Neuen Testaments

SwJT	*Southwestern Journal of Theology*
Tarb	*Tarbiz*
TB	*Tyndale Bulletin*
TDNT	*Theological Dictionary of the New Testament*, ed. G. Kittel, G. Friedrich
Th	*Theology*
Them	*Themelios*
Théo	Théologie
THNT	Theologischer Handkommentar zum Neuen Testament
ThOP	Theology Occasional Papers
TJ	*Trinity Journal*
TNTC	Tyndale New Testament Commentaries
TPQ	*Theologisch-praktische Quartalschrift*
TRev	*Theologische Revue*
TU	Texte und Untersuchungen zur Geschichte der altchristlichen Literatur
TWAT	*Theologisches Wörterbuch zum Alten Testament*, ed. G.J. Botterweck, H. Ringgren
TWNT	*Theologisches Wörterbuch zum Neuen Testament*, ed. G. Kittel, G. Friedrich
UNDCSJCA	University of Notre Dame Center for the Study of Judaism & Christianity in Antiquity
VE	*Vox Evangelica*
VR	*Vox Reformata*
VT	*Vetus Testamentum*
VTSup	Vetus Testamentum Supplements
WBC	Word Biblical Commentary
WBKEL	Wissenschaftliche Beiträge zur kirchlich-evangelischen Lehre
WF	Wege der Forschung
WMANT	Wissenschaftliche Monographien zum Alten und Neuen Testament
WTJ	*Westminster Theological Journal*
WUNT	Wissenschaftliche Untersuchungen zum Neuen Testament
YJS	Yale Judaica Series
ZAW	*Zeitschrift für die alttestamentliche Wissenschaft*
ZKG	*Zeitschrift für Kirchengeschichte*
ZNW	*Zeitschrift für die neutestamentliche Wissenschaft*
ZTK	*Zeitschrift für Theologie und Kirche*

Chapter 1

INTRODUCTION

1. *The Task*

The following study is an attempt to reconstruct the development of early Christian pneumatology in the formative period from the church's inception up to the writing of Luke–Acts. The writings of Luke provide an excellent vantage point for surveying the pneumatological developments of this period. As a synoptic evangelist, Luke's pneumatological perspective can be elucidated through an analysis of the way in which he uses and modifies Mark and Q.[1] For this reason Luke's perspective can be easily compared with the pneumatology of the non-Pauline primitive church reflected in Matthew, Mark, and Q.[2] Furthermore, as a historian and theologian who chronicles the emergence of the early church, Luke discusses in considerable detail the nature of early Christian experience of the Spirit.[3] Thus Luke's perspective can be productively compared with the pneumatological insights of Paul. Since Luke and Paul offer relatively early and comprehensive treatments of pneumatic experience, the latter task is particularly significant for retracing developments in the formative period.

I shall begin this study by reviewing the significant contributions of a century of scholarship.[4] Each of the authors cited below, albeit in a

---

1. See the methodological comments in the introduction to Part II below.

2. See p. 18 n. 1 below on my use of the term 'primitive church'.

3. I shall capitalize the term 'Spirit' when it is used with reference to God's Spirit. This is simply a convenient way of distinguishing between references to spirit as a disposition of humans or created incorporeal beings and the Spirit of God; it does not necessarily imply personhood or independent existence.

4. Detailed summaries of past scholarship on the pneumatology of Paul and Luke respectively can be found in J.S. Vos, *Traditionsgeschichtliche Untersuchungen zur paulinischen Pneumatologie* (1973), pp. 1-25, and M.M.B. Turner, 'The Significance of Receiving the Spirit in Luke–Acts: A Survey of Modern Scholarship', *TJ* 2 (1981), pp. 131-58. On Luke see also F. Bovon, *Luc le théologien: vingt-cinq ans de recherches (1950–1975)* (1978), pp. 211-54. For this reason I shall limit the

variety of ways (some indirectly), deal with a question central to this inquiry: to what extent does Luke follow Paul in attributing soteriological significance to the gift of the Spirit? Put another way, to what extent does Luke, in a manner analogous to Paul, view reception of the Spirit as necessary for one to enter into and remain within the community of salvation: the source of cleansing (1 Cor. 6.11; Rom. 15.16), righteousness (Gal. 5.5; Rom. 2.29; 8.1-17; 14.17; Gal. 5.16-26), intimate fellowship with (Gal. 4.6; Rom. 8.14-17) and knowledge of God (1 Cor. 2.6-16; 2 Cor. 3.3-18), and ultimately, eternal life through the resurrection (Rom. 8.11; 1 Cor. 15.44f.; Gal. 6.8)? In view of the importance of this question for the task at hand, I shall categorize the principal authors discussed below according to their responses to this fundamental question. Three major categories emerge: those who emphasize the continuity between Luke and Paul at this point; those who emphasize discontinuity; and those holding mediating positions.

2. The Development of Early Christian Pneumatology:
A Survey of Modern Scholarship

2.1. Discontinuity

2.1.1. Hermann Gunkel. As early as 1868 B. Weiss, in his *Lehrbuch der biblischen Theologie des Neuen Testaments,* noted the distinctiveness of Paul's pneumatology as against that of the non-Pauline sector of the early church (*Urgemeinde*).[1] According to Weiss, the concept of 'der Geist als das gottgegebene Princip des neuen Lebens' was uniquely Pauline.[2] O. Pfleiderer, writing shortly after Weiss, came to similar conclusions in his lengthy work on Pauline theology, *Der Paulinismus.* Pfleiderer argued that the *Urgemeinde* viewed the Spirit essentially in Old Testament terms as the Spirit of revelation: a divine substance which, after coming upon humans, granted supernatural power and

---

scope of this review to the most significant contributions of the past and focus the discussion on the way in which they have dealt with the question outlined below.

1. B. Weiss and others such as O. Pfleiderer and H. Gunkel did not attempt to distinguish between the perspective of those communities represented by Matthew, Mark, and Q, and the perspective of Luke. For this reason they viewed Luke–Acts as a major resource for reconstructing the perspective of the non-Pauline early church. In the interest of precision, I shall refer to the non-Pauline early church (inclusive of Luke–Acts) as the *Urgemeinde*, and I shall refer to those early Christian communities within the *Urgemeinde* whose theological outlook is reflected in Matthew, Mark, and Q (excluding Luke–Acts) as the 'primitive church'.

2. B. Weiss, *Lehrbuch der biblischen Theologie des Neuen Testaments* (2nd edn, 1873), p. 216. See also pp. 338f., 413f., 454.

produced miracles. According to Pfleiderer Paul started from this conception, yet moved beyond it. For Paul, the Spirit was not simply the source of miraculous power, it was fundamentally the dynamic which shaped the entire Christian life:

> In short, the πνεῦμα is changed, in the mind of Paul, from an abstract, supernatural, ecstatic, Apocalyptic principle, to an immanent, religious, moral principle of the life of renovated humanity, to the nature of the καινὴ κτίσις.[1]

Although Weiss and Pfleiderer laid the groundwork, it was H. Gunkel who first devoted an entire monograph to the topic and initiated much of the modern discussion.[2] In *Die Wirkungen des heiligen Geistes*, first published in 1888, Gunkel offered detailed argumentation in support of his thesis that Paul, in light of his own experience, attempted to correct the pneumatology of the *Urgemeinde*, for whom 'war der Geist nur die Macht, welche bestimmte Wunder wirkt und größerer Wunder Bürge ist'.[3]

Emphasizing the essentially Jewish and experiential nature of the *Urgemeinde's* understanding of the Spirit, Gunkel began by posing the central question, 'an welchen Symptomen hat man im Urchristentum festgestellt, daß eine Erscheinung Wirkung des Geistes sei?'[4] According to Gunkel the answer was not to be found in the character of normal Christian behavior,[5] nor in relation to the purposes of God,[6] but rather in the mysterious and powerful nature of deeds which defied natural explanation.[7] Thus, according to Gunkel, the activity most characteristic of the gift of the Spirit in the *Urgemeinde* was glosso-

---

1. O. Pfleiderer, *Paulinism: A Contribution to the History of Primitive Christian Theology*, I (1877; orig. German edn, 1873), p. 200.

2. H. Gunkel, *Die Wirkungen des heiligen Geistes nach der populären Anschauung der apostolischen Zeit und nach der Lehre des Apostels Paulus* (1888). All references are from this edition unless otherwise stated. English references are from Gunkel, *The Influence of the Holy Spirit* (1979, trans. R.A. Harrisville and P.A. Quanbeck II).

3. *Die Wirkungen* (2nd edn, 1899), p. 89.

4. *Die Wirkungen*, p. 5. Gunkel criticized Pfleiderer for speaking of a doctrine of the Spirit, when for the early church the Spirit was a concrete and daily experience (p. 4).

5. *Die Wirkungen*, p. 9: 'Aber die gewöhnlichen religiösen Funktionen des einfachen Christen werden nicht als Gaben des heiligen Geistes empfunden'.

6. Gunkel rejects the suggestion put forth by Wendt, Pfleiderer, and others that the work of the Spirit is 'for special or definite divine purposes' (*Die Wirkungen*, pp. 16-17).

7. *Die Wirkungen*, p. 22.

lalia.[1] In glossolalia the mysterious and powerful character of the
Spirit was supremely displayed: 'Der Mensch ist bei der Glossolalie
von einer gewaltigen Macht überfallen, welche ihn völlig in Besitz
genommen hat'.[2]

This mysterious and powerful activity was not without theological
significance. Set against the background of first-century Judaism, these
marvelous manifestations were indications of the in-breaking of the
Kingdom of God: 'Wo Geist Gottes, da Reich Gottes...Das Auftreten
des Geistes ist der Anbruch der neuen Zeit, in welcher das Reich
Gottes kommt'.[3]

With this portrait of the *Urgemeinde* complete, Gunkel set out to
establish the uniqueness of Paul's understanding of the Spirit. Like the
Urgemeinde, Paul understood the Spirit to be the source of supernatural power. Yet Gunkel insisted that there were two significant differences in Paul's perspective. First, for Paul the supreme sign of the
gift of the Spirit was not limited to mysterious and powerful effects; it
entailed another essential ingredient: the divine purpose of the gift—
the edification of the Christian community.[4] For this reason Paul, in
contrast to the primitive church, held glossolalia in relatively low
esteem.[5] In this regard Paul was the first to emphasize the ethical
dimension of the gift of the Spirit.[6] Second, Paul viewed the Spirit not
simply as the source of sporadic and mysterious power, but as the
source of Christian life in its totality. Thus, for Paul, the Christian life
in its entirety was a sign of the presence of the eschatological
Kingdom:

> The community thus regards as pneumatic what is extraordinary in Chris-
> tian existence, but Paul what is usual; the community what is individual
> and unique, but Paul what is common to all; the community what abruptly
> appears, but Paul what is constant; the community what is isolated in
> Christian existence, but Paul the Christian life as such. And this yielded a
> totally different, infinitely higher evaluation of Christian conduct.[7]

Gunkel insisted that the source of Paul's unique insight into the
working of the Spirit was the personal experience of the Apostle.
Nothing else could adequately account for his new perspective. Arguing against H.H. Wendt, Gunkel denied that Paul had taken over from

1. Gunkel describes glossolalia as 'ekstatische Raserei' (*Die Wirkungen*, p. 21).
2. *Die Wirkungen*, p. 21.
3. *Die Wirkungen*, p. 59.
4. *Die Wirkungen*, p. 74.
5. *Die Wirkungen*, p. 72.
6. *Die Wirkungen*, p. 77.
7. *Die Wirkungen*, p. 82. ET from Gunkel, *The Influence*, p. 96.

the Old Testament 'seine Lehre von den sittlich-religiösen Wirkungen des πνεῦμα'.[1] In support of his position Gunkel sought to demonstrate that 'dem Judentum die Frömmigkeit des gewöhnlichen Mannes im allgemeinen nichts mit der רוח gemein zu haben schien'.[2] Gunkel acknowledged that there were instances where the Old Testament writers gave ethical significance to the Spirit, though he stressed that these were relatively rare.[3] According to Gunkel, the only true parallels to Paul were Pss. 51.13 and 143.10, yet the absence of similar references elsewhere proved his case.

Gunkel also rejected the view of Pfleiderer that Paul was influenced by the literature of hellenistic Judaism, particularly Wisdom. Although superficial similarities exist between the role of the Spirit in Paul's thought and that of wisdom/Spirit in Wisdom, the differences are dramatic: 'Weisheit lernt der Mensch, der Geist ergreift ihn'.[4]

The thesis advanced by J. Gloël, that Jesus and the first apostles acknowledged the ethical character of the work of the Spirit, was also summarily dismissed.[5] Gloël's thesis rested on texts from John, 1 Peter, and Acts. Gunkel responded by reversing the logic of Gloël's argument: John and 1 Peter were influenced by Paul. Gunkel had already dispensed with Gloël's interpretation of Acts in his portrait of the *Urgemeinde's* understanding of the Spirit. Although he acknowledged that the Spirit was not completely unrelated to the moral and religious sphere in Acts, Gunkel emphasized that the normal, ongoing religious life of the individual Christian was not a result of the gift of the Spirit. When ethical-religious conduct was attributed to the Spirit, it was simply a heightening of what was already present in the Christian. Thus, a connection to the moral and religious dimension of

---

1. *Die Wirkungen*, p. 85. See pp. 83-86 for arguments contra H.H. Wendt, *Die Begriffe Fleisch und Geist im biblischen Sprachgebrauch* (1878).

2. *Die Wirkungen*, p. 85.

3. *Die Wirkungen*, p. 10: 'Mit Ausnahme von Jes. 11,1.2; 28,6; 32,15ff.; Ez. 36,27 (vielleicht Sach. 12,10) Psalm 51,13; 143,10 werden unter den mannigfaltigen der berichteten Geisteswirkungen niemals solche genannt, welche in das Gebiet des Sittlichen oder Religiösen gehören'. H. Bertrams was at this point in agreement with Gunkel and restricted the number of OT texts which portrayed the Spirit as the source of moral and religious life even more sharply than Gunkel himself (*Das Wesen des Geistes* [1913], p. 46). More recently David Hill has written: 'Only once is moral renewal by the spirit desired by an individual for himself [Ps. 51.12-14]' (*Greek Words and Hebrew Meanings* [1967], p. 210).

4. *Die Wirkungen*, p. 87. Gunkel criticizes Pfleiderer's position put forth in *Das Urchristentum* (1887), pp. 86-88.

5. *Die Wirkungen*, p. 89. Gunkel criticized the viewpoint of J. Gloël expressed in *Der heilige Geist in der Heilsverkündigung des Paulus* (1888).

Christian life was not at the heart of the *Urgemeinde's* understanding of the Spirit—it was simply a by-product of a more fundamental perspective.[1] Gunkel concluded:

> Paul found ready-made the concept of the πνεῦμα as a wonder-working power, but on the basis of his experience, by which the Christian himself appeared to be the greatest miracle, he described the Christian life as an activity of the πνεῦμα in a completely original way.[2]

The sharpness with which Gunkel separated the pneumatology of Paul from that of the Judaism and the *Urgemeinde* which preceded him is striking. Certainly not all would allow Gunkel's wedge to be driven so deep. Indeed, his insistence that Paul was the first to give prominence to the ethical character of the Spirit has been widely challenged. On the basis of his examination of rabbinic texts F. Büchsel responded, 'Nach allen diesen Worten über den Geistbesitz der Frommen kann an dem sittlichen Charakter des Geistes kein Zweifel sein'.[3] More recently W.D. Davies concluded, 'The long-standing discussion as to whether Paul was the first to "ethicize" the Spirit can now be regarded, in light of the scrolls, as closed'.[4] It would appear that first-century Judaism was not as monolithic as Gunkel judged. This raises important questions concerning Gunkel's portrait of the *Urgemeinde*.

Gunkel can also be criticized for underestimating the degree to which the *Urgemeinde* identified the work of the Spirit with the purposes of God revealed in the ministry of Jesus. Luke identifies the work of the Spirit so closely with the mission of Jesus that it is 'the Spirit of Jesus' who directs the early missionaries (Acts 16.7). In this regard it is questionable whether Gunkel presents an adequate description of the *Urgemeinde's* criteria for identifying the work of the Spirit.[5]

These criticisms in no way detract from the genius and significance of Gunkel's work. Indeed, one can only wonder how Gunkel's views would have changed if he had access to the scrolls from Qumran or to the contributions redaction criticism has brought to our understanding of the synoptic gospels. Written in 1888, *Die Wirkungen* was remark-

---

1. *Die Wirkungen*, p. 9.
2. *Die Wirkungen*, p. 88. ET from Gunkel, *The Influence*, p. 102.
3. F. Büchsel, *Der Geist Gottes im Neuen Testament* (1926), p. 133.
4. W.D. Davies, 'Paul and the Dead Sea Scrolls: Flesh and Spirit', in *The Scrolls and the New Testament* (1958), p. 177.
5. Gunkel asserts that the Urgemeinde recognized the Spirit at work in events which were mysterious, powerful, somehow connected to the Christian community, not harmful to humans, effected by agents not unworthy of such a relationship to God (*Die Wirkungen*, p. 47).

able for its methodological sophistication and its insightful conclusions. Gunkel's emphasis on the significance of the Jewish background for understanding the pneumatology of the *Urgemeinde*, the eschatological nature of the Spirit as a sign of the presence of the Kingdom of God, and his suggestion of Pauline influence on John and 1 Peter, anticipated perspectives of a later era. His central thesis raised many issues which are still unresolved. In short, Gunkel set the agenda for the modern discussion.[1]

2.1.2. *Eduard Schweizer.*

E. Schweizer marks another significant milestone in the discussion concerning the development of early Christian pneumatology. His first essay treating the topic, an article published in the July 1952 issue of *Interpretation*, was followed by his contribution to the *TDNT* article on πνεῦμα in 1956.[2] Both essays attempt to distinguish Luke's pneumatology from that of the other synoptic evangelists and Paul.[3]

According to Schweizer, Matthew and Mark viewed the Spirit largely in Old Testament terms as the source of supernatural power for the performance of miracles. Thus they differed from the Old Testament perspective only in their emphasis on the presence of the Spirit in Jesus.[4] Yet this by itself did not communicate the true significance of Jesus, for he was not simply another pneumatic or spirit-inspired miracle worker. Therefore, whenever Matthew or Mark mentioned the Spirit it was in order to underline the uniqueness of Jesus as *the* eschatological deliverer.[5] However, the portraits they produced were not entirely clear on this point, for they did at times naïvely portray Jesus as a pneumatic.

Luke clarified this ambiguous picture. In his earthly life Jesus 'is not the object of the Spirit. . . He is Lord over the Spirit'.[6] As the exalted Lord he dispenses the Spirit to the eschatological community. In this way Luke stressed the distinctiveness of Jesus' experience of the Spirit as against that of the Old Testament prophets and the disciples.

---

1. The fact that an ET of *Die Wirkungen* was issued by Fortress Press (Philadelphia) in 1979 testifies to the lasting significance and relevance of this work.
2. E. Schweizer, 'The Spirit of Power: The Uniformity and Diversity of the Concept of the Holy Spirit in the New Testament', *Int* 6 (1952), pp. 259-78; and 'πνεῦμα', *TDNT*, VI, pp. 389-455.
3. Schweizer traces the development of the early church's thinking on the Spirit from the primitive pneumatologies of the primitive church (Matthew, Mark) and Luke to the more developed pneumatology of Paul.
4. 'πνεῦμα', p. 404; 'Spirit of Power', p. 260.
5. 'Spirit of Power', p. 264.
6. 'Spirit of Power', p. 265 and 'πνεῦμα', p. 405.

Luke differed from Matthew and Mark in another way. Schweizer asserted that Luke's pneumatology, more than the other evangelists', was shaped by 'the typically Jewish idea that the Spirit is the Spirit of prophecy'.[1] For this reason, in spite of Luke's special interest in the visible manifestations of the Spirit,[2] he never attributed miraculous healings or exorcisms to the Spirit. Rather, Luke always portrayed the Spirit as the source of inspired speech, such as glossolalia or preaching.[3]

According to Schweizer, Luke also went further than Matthew and Mark with reference to the bestowal of the Spirit. Whereas Matthew and Mark, consistent with the Old Testament, viewed the gift of the Spirit as limited to a specially chosen few, Luke understood that a new age had dawned: the Spirit had been given to all of God's people.[4] However, Luke remained relatively similar to the evangelists in his assessment of the significance of the gift. Betraying his indebtedness to Judaism, Luke understood the Spirit to be a supplementary gift, not necessary for salvation:

> The Spirit is, therefore, not the power which binds a man to God and transfers him into a state of salvation; it is a supplementary power which enables him to give form to his faith in the concrete activity of the proclamation of the gospel.[5]

Distinguishing his own position from that of Gunkel, Schweizer states that for Luke 'it would be wrong to ascribe only extraordinary religious effects to the Spirit'.[6] On the one hand παρρησία is attributed to the Spirit, on the other hand miracles are not. Yet Schweizer acknowledges that in Luke's perspective the Spirit is essentially 'the

---

1. 'πνεῦμα', p. 407; 'Spirit of Power', p. 266.

2. Schweizer attributes this interest in the visible manifestations of the Spirit to Luke's hellenistic background ('πνεῦμα', p. 407).

3. It is unfortunate that Schweizer's position has been obscured by a mistranslation. The English summary statement mistakenly includes a negative: 'Luke thus shares with Judaism the view that the Spirit is essentially the Spirit of prophecy. This does *not* prevent him from directly attributing to the πνεῦμα both the χαρίσματα ἰαμάτων on the one side and strongly ethical effects like the common life of the primitive community on the other' ('πνεῦμα', *TDNT*, VI, p. 409; italics are mine). Note the wording of the original German edition: 'Lukas teilt also mit dem Judentum die Anschauung, daß Geist im Wesentlichen Geist der Prophetie ist. Das hindert ihn, einerseits die χαρίσματα ἰαμάτων, andererseits stärker ethisch geprägte Wirkungen wie das Gemeinschaftsleben der Urgemeinde direkt auf das πνεῦμα zurückzuführen' ('πνεῦμα', *TWNT*, VI, p. 407).

4. 'Spirit of Power', p. 267; 'πνεῦμα', p. 410.

5. 'Spirit of Power', p. 268. See also 'πνεῦμα', p. 412.

6. 'πνεῦμα', p. 412.

extraordinary power which makes possible unusual acts of power'.[1]
This view has been modified by the Jewish tradition, which viewed the
Spirit as the source of prophetic inspiration, and by Christian tradition, which viewed the Spirit as a gift given to every member of the
new community.

Schweizer distinguishes sharply Paul's pneumatology from that of
Luke. For Luke, since the Spirit did not bestow salvation, it could only
function as a sign pointing to that which was yet to come. Yet for Paul
the Spirit was much more. The Spirit revealed the true significance of
the cross, and as such, bestowed salvation.

Paul's unique pneumatology was largely the result of the hellenistic
context in which he found himself. Schweizer asserted that hellenistic
society, in contrast to its Jewish counterpart, thought in terms of
superimposed spheres rather than detached aeons. The hellenist also
always thought of power in terms of substance. Therefore in the hellenistic world the Spirit could not be a sign of the age to come. It had
to be a substance from the heavenly sphere. This set the stage for
Paul's unique pneumatology, as well as that of the gnostics:

> If Jesus was the bringer of the Spirit, then He was the bearer of heavenly
> substance with which He endowed believers and united them with the
> heavenly world. A radical solution thus became possible for the first time.
> The point of the mission of Jesus was to bring the heavenly substance
> πνεῦμα into the world. Attachment to Jesus is attachment to this sub-
> stance of power, to the heavenly world. It is thus salvation itself.[2]

Paul, like the gnostic, adopted these hellenistic ideas, but unlike the
gnostic, he placed them in a uniquely Christian context. Both the gnostic and Paul understood the Spirit to be the means by which one is
transferred from the earthly world to the heavenly. But in contrast to
the gnostic, who viewed the Spirit as a heavenly substance inherent in
every one which could be rekindled by the redeemer myth, for Paul
the Spirit was separate from humans and revealed to them the
significance of the saving act of God in Christ.[3] Paul distinguished
himself from gnostic thought by focusing on the historical necessity of
the cross and resurrection and fusing these events together with the
bestowal of the Spirit.

In this way Paul also distinguished himself from Luke, for the Spirit
is now 'the decisive saving power which unites man with God, and thus

1. 'πνεῦμα', p. 412.
2. 'πνεῦμα', p. 416.
3. 'Spirit of Power', p. 273. See also 'πνεῦμα', p. 425.

bestows salvation upon him'.[1] This, according to Schweizer, constitutes the fundamental distinction between Luke and Paul. It is not the adoption of the ethical, nor the focus on the inner life; these are merely symptoms of a more basic distinction: '*pneuma* is now the power of God which brings a man to faith in the cross and resurrection of Jesus'.[2]

Although Schweizer accented the distinctiveness of Paul's pneumatology as Gunkel had before him, he advanced the discussion at significant points. First, building upon the work of H. von Baer, Schweizer emphasized the importance of the Jewish background for Luke's understanding of the Spirit in a unique way.[3] Arguing that Luke, more than the other synoptic writers, was influenced by the Jewish conception of the Spirit as the Spirit of prophecy, Schweizer distinguished Luke's pneumatology from that of Matthew and Mark on the one hand, and Paul on the other. In this way Schweizer was able to move beyond Gunkel. Schweizer's contention that late Judaism viewed the Spirit predominantly as the source of prophetic inspiration was undoubtedly correct; however, other perspectives existed as well.[4] Thus Schweizer has raised an important question: to what extent was Luke's understanding shaped by the Jewish conception of the Spirit as the Spirit of prophecy?

---

1. 'Spirit of Power', p. 272.
2. 'πνεῦμα', p. 432.
3. See §2.3.1 below for a discussion of H. von Baer. G.W.H. Lampe ('The Holy Spirit in the Writings of St. Luke', in *Studies in the Gospels* [1957], pp. 159-200) also noted the significance of the Jewish background (with its emphasis on the Spirit as the source of prophecy) for Luke's pneumatology. However, Lampe defined Luke's understanding of the Spirit of prophecy in broader terms (p. 162). In *The Seal of the Spirit* (1951), Lampe argued that Luke's distinctive emphasis on the gift of the Spirit (pp. 53, 65) as a (largely prophetic) enabling for missionary activity provided an explanation for the association of the gift with the laying on of hands rather than water baptism in Acts 8.14f.; 9.17. The former activity, argued Lampe, was a commissioning for service in the missionary enterprise (analogous to ordination) and bestowed special missionary charismata (pp. 72-78). According to Lampe, Luke also understood the Spirit to be active in the Christian in a more fundamental way. Lampe discussed this aspect of Luke's pneumatology more extensively in *God as Spirit: The Bampton Lectures, 1976* (1977), pp. 64-72.
4. J. Kremer argues that there were a variety of expectations in Judaism regarding the future bestowal of the Spirit (*Pfingstbericht und Pfingstgeschehen: Eine exegetische Untersuchung zur Apg 2,1-13* [1973], p. 84). Although the predominant expectation was that the end-time bestowal of the Spirit would result in a renewal of prophecy, Kremer asserts that at Qumran this bestowal of the Spirit was thought to result in moral renewal. See also M.A. Chevallier, *Souffle de Dieu* (1978), p. 62

Second, Schweizer argued that Luke carefully distinguished Jesus' experience of the Spirit from that of the Old Testament prophets and the disciples. Jesus was Lord of the Spirit. This is a theme which we shall meet again and with which I shall take issue.

Third, Schweizer shifted the focus in his treatment of Paul's pneumatology from the ethical dimension to the dimension of faith. The uniqueness of Paul's pneumatology is not to be found in the ethical dimension he added, rather it is found in his understanding of the Spirit as the power which generates belief. In this way Paul transformed the Spirit from a supplementary gift into that which is vital for salvation. Although this element was present in Gunkel's work, Schweizer represents a shift in focus.

Fourth, Schweizer argued that Paul's unique understanding of the Spirit resulted from hellenistic influence. This of course runs counter to Gunkel's insistence that Paul's uniqueness was solely the product of his personal experience. Schweizer can be criticized at this point for anachronistically attributing features exhibited in second-century gnostic material to the hellenistic world of the first century.[1]

2.1.3. David Hill. Employing the lexicographic method of the *TDNT*, D. Hill sought to uncover the significance of πνεῦμα for the various New Testament writers. The title of his work, *Greek Words and Hebrew Meanings*, suggests the major conclusion of his study: the New Testament usage of πνεῦμα is shaped by Judaism, not by Hellenism.[2]

Hill, like Schweizer before him, asserted that Luke's two-volume work was influenced largely by the prophetic character of the Jewish concept of the Spirit.[3] Building on this Jewish foundation, Luke portrayed the Spirit as the prophetic power which energized the missionary expansion of the church. The Spirit inspired the proclamation of the end-time prophets.

---

1. E. Brandenburger has argued that the origin of Paul's pneumatic mysticism is not to be found in hellenistic-gnostic influences, but rather in the dualistic wisdom of hellenistic Judaism (*Fleisch und Geist: Paulus und die dualistische Weisheit* [1968]).

2. D. Hill, *Greek Words and Hebrew Meanings. Studies in the Semantics of Soteriological Terms* (1967). In this regard Hill builds on the work of W.D. Davies who emphasized the Jewish character of Paul's theology, including his pneumatology (*Paul and Rabbinic Judaism. Some Rabbinic Elements in Pauline Theology* [1948], esp. pp. 177-226). See also O. Kuß, *Der Römerbrief* (1959), pp. 540-95; and L. Cerfaux, *The Christian in the Theology of Paul* (1967, French edn 1962), esp. p. 241. Kuß and Cerfaux note the significance of the Old Testament and Judaism for Paul's pneumatology, although for both his personal experience is of primary importance.

3. *Greek Words*, pp. 261-63.

According to Hill, Luke does not advance significantly beyond the Old Testament and Jewish perspective which viewed the Spirit as supplementary gift, a special endowment to fulfill a specific task. Hill notes that 'there is little reference in Acts to the presence of the Spirit as the inner principle of the believer's life or as an abiding gift within the Church's life'.[1]

In contrast, Paul grasped the broader dimensions of the Spirit's work. Rather than simply being the source of prophetic activity, the Spirit for Paul was the source of the entire Christian life, including the ethical dimensions. Hill downplays Paul's uniqueness at this point by emphasizing his indebtedness to Judaism:

> In ethicising the Spirit, Paul was not an innovator: he was emphasising what had been present in the Old Testament and what was implicit (though only rarely expressed) in later Jewish thought.[2]

Hill's work is significant in that, although he accents the differences between Luke and Paul in a manner similar to Schweizer, he underlines the Jewish character of the pneumatology of both Luke and Paul.[3] Like Schweizer, Hill maintains that for Luke the Spirit is the Spirit of prophecy. Yet Paul's uniqueness results not from his accommodation to the hellenistic context, but rather from his appropriation of themes present in the Old Testament and contemporary Judaism.

2.2. Continuity
2.2.1. *Friedrich Büchsel.* With *Der Geist Gottes im Neuen Testament* (1926), F. Büchsel added new impetus to the discussion. By stressing the relative homogeneity of the various pneumatologies represented in the New Testament, Büchsel offered an important alternative to Gunkel. If Gunkel was the father of the discontinuity perspective, Büchsel represents his counterpart for the continuity school.

According to Büchsel, the *Urgemeinde* viewed Jesus as the supreme *Pneumatiker*. Jesus became the *Pneumatiker par excellence* at his baptism. This perspective was shared by each of the synoptic evangelists. For although Matthew and Luke associated the Spirit with Jesus' birth, he was not yet driven by the Spirit, not yet filled with the Spirit, until

---

1. *Greek Words*, p. 264.
2. *Greek Words*, p. 270.
3. Although, as I have noted, he was by no means the first to argue this position, Hill presented this position within the context of a relatively comprehensive study of the pneumatology of the early church.

his baptism.[1] Only after his reception of the Spirit at his baptism did Jesus embark on his ministry of preaching and performing wonders.[2]

What was the significance of Jesus' reception of the Spirit, what did it mean to become a *Pneumatiker*? Büchsel answered this question by pointing to Jesus' unique awareness that he was the son of God: 'Jesu Geistbesitz ist Gottessohnschaft'.[3] Büchsel acknowledged that there was a difference between Jesus' self-understanding as Messiah and as the Son of God. Although both were mediated to Jesus by the Spirit at his baptism, Büchsel asserted that the emphasis was clearly on Sonship:

> Jesus' messianic consciousness was not the center-point of his self-understanding and effectiveness. He lived and died in devotion and obedience to God. That was of primary importance. Authority over the Jews and the world was always secondary. . . His messianic consciousness grew out of his filial relationship to God. Indeed, the latter gave the former uniqueness and depth.[4]

To be a *Pneumatiker* is to address God as Father. For this reason Büchsel denied that the *Urgemeinde* viewed the Spirit simply as miraculous power. On the contrary, the primitive church understood the Spirit to be the means by which man was brought into special relationship with God:

> One who receives the Spirit is brought into personal relationship with God. The recipient of the Spirit not only receives power for some special task, but also assurance that he is loved by God and the knowledge that he is God's son. The great difference which exists between power and a personal relationship with God is most evident in the account of Jesus' baptism.[5]

Similarly, Büchsel rejected Gunkel's suggestion that the Spirit had little ethical significance for the *Urgemeinde*. It was false to view the Spirit simply as the source of naked power, for the Spirit shaped the entire life of the supreme *Pneumatiker*, Jesus.[6]

Büchsel's analysis, as indicated, was based largely on the portrait of Jesus which emerged from the synoptic gospels. Jesus modeled what it meant to be a *Pneumatiker*, to experience the power of the Spirit. This

---

1. According to Büchsel this did not present a problem for Matthew or Luke: 'Jesus ist Gottes Sohn seit seiner Geburt, und er ist Gottes Sohn durch den Geistempfang bei seiner Taufe' (*Der Geist Gottes*, p. 165).
2. *Der Geist Gottes*, p. 149. See also pp. 220f.
3. *Der Geist Gottes*, p. 165.
4. *Der Geist Gottes*, p. 165. ET is my own.
5. *Der Geist Gottes*, p. 168. ET is my own.
6. *Der Geist Gottes*, pp. 182, 186-87, and especially p. 223.

was not without significance for the early church. Büchsel insisted that 'Die urchristlichen Gemeinden waren Gemeinden von Leuten, die alle in irgendeinem Maße *Pneumatiker* waren'.[1] Although Jesus' disciples had not received the Spirit during his earthly ministry,[2] Jesus promised that they would receive the pneumatic gift.[3] The subsequent reception of the Spirit by the early church shaped its existence as a community of *Pneumatiker*.

The early church's experience of the Spirit not only shaped its existence, but also exerted a tremendous influence on the documents of the New Testament which it produced. The Spirit provided the church with a theme that influenced the whole of the New Testament and gave it unity: 'Das Christentum des Neuen Testaments ist irgendwie pneumatische Frömmigkeit'.[4] The experience of the Spirit bound the early church together.

This is not to deny that Paul made a distinctive contribution. Yet, according to Büchsel, this contribution was not a radically new understanding of the Spirit. Paul was unique in two ways. First, in his epistles we have access, for the first time, to the self-reflection of a *Pneumatiker*.[5] That is, Paul, as no other New Testament writer, expressed what it meant to be a *Pneumatiker* from the perspective of personal experience. Second, Paul, by rejecting the necessity of obedience to the law, emphasized the significance of the Spirit in a new way. Paul placed the Spirit, as never before, at the center of the Christian life.[6] Yet this was simply a continuation, an extension of what was already present in the *Urgemeinde* before him; it does not represent a decisively new understanding of the Spirit. Indeed, possession of the Spirit meant essentially the same thing for the *Urgemeinde* as for Paul: 'Die Liebe Gottes ist ausgegossen in unser Herz'.[7]

Methodologically, Büchsel was significant for his emphasis on the Jewish origin of the early church's pneumatology;[8] this only a few

---

1. *Der Geist Gottes*, p. 230.

2. *Der Geist Gottes*, pp. 185ff.

3. Büchsel distinguishes between the gift of the Spirit as a special power to fulfil specific functions (for the apostles only) and the gift of the Spirit in the broader sense described above, granted to all (*Der Geist Gottes*, pp. 234-35).

4. *Der Geist Gottes*, pp. 228-29.

5. *Der Geist Gottes*, pp. 267f.

6. *Der Geist Gottes*, pp. 442-48.

7. *Der Geist Gottes*, p. 333.

8. *Der Geist Gottes*, pp. 200-201, 239-40, 252. Büchsel writes: 'Denn das Denken der Urgemeinde, auch der Geistgedanke der Urgemeinde, war am Alten Testament und der jüdischen Überlieferung orientiert' (p. 240).

years after Bousset and Leisegang.[1] But Büchsel's real contribution lay elsewhere. By maintaining that the Spirit was, above all, the source of sonship with God, the power which enabled the *Pneumatiker* to address God as Father, Büchsel was able to link the pneumatology of the *Urgemeinde* with that of Paul. Written in the wake of Pfleiderer and Gunkel, it is this focus on the continuity of the early church's understanding of the Spirit that makes Büchsel's voluminous work so significant. Although I shall criticize Büchsel's interpretation of Luke, there can be no doubt that his influence has been lasting.

2.2.2. James D.G. Dunn. The prolific pen of J. Dunn has, without question, exerted the greatest influence on recent discussion concerning the pneumatology of the early church. Dunn's initial major work, *Baptism in the Holy Spirit*,[2] was a two-pronged critique of Pentecostal and sacramental interpretations of the gift of the Spirit. Dunn asserted that, in the perspective of the early church, the gift of the Spirit was neither a *donum superadditum* received subsequent to conversion nor inextricably bound to water baptism; rather it was the 'chief element in conversion initiation'.[3] The enormous influence *Baptism in the Holy Spirit* had on subsequent discussion was reflected in the decision by Westminster Press in 1977 to reprint it as a 'classic'. Dunn's sequel, *Jesus and the Spirit*, has received equal acclaim.[4] The title is somewhat misleading, for in this book Dunn analyses the religious experience of both Jesus and the early church. These works, as well as other shorter essays by Dunn,[5] follow in the tradition of Büchsel by emphasizing the

1. H. Leisegang is briefly discussed in the section below on H. von Baer.
2. J.D.G. Dunn, *Baptism in the Holy Spirit: A Re-examination of the New Testament Teaching on the Gift of the Spirit in Relation to Pentecostalism Today* (1970).
3. *Holy Spirit*, p. 4.
4. *Jesus and the Spirit: A Study of the Religious and Charismatic Experience of Jesus and the First Christians as Reflected in the New Testament* (1975). A survey of reviews on *Jesus and the Spirit* indicates that it has been warmly received. The comments of E. Best are illustrative: 'The result is a massive contribution to an important subject in which interest has been created afresh by the rise of the neo-pentecostalist movement' (*SJT* 29 [1976], pp. 486-90, quote from p. 487). Note also the generally positive tone in the reviews by C.L. Mitton (*ExpTim* 87 [1976], pp. 161-62), J.L. Houlden (*JTS* 27 [1976], pp. 471-76), L.W. Hurtado (*JBL* 96 [1977], pp. 447-49), M.A. Chevallier (*RHPR* 57 [1977], pp. 120-21), D. Nineham (*Rel* 7 [1977], pp. 231-34).
5. See Dunn, 'Spirit-Baptism and Pentecostalism', *SJT* 23 (1970), pp. 397-407; 'Spirit and Kingdom', *ExpTim* 82 (1970), pp. 36-40; 'The Birth of a Metaphor: Baptized in the Spirit', *ExpTim* 89 (1977), pp. 134-38, 173-75; *Unity and Diversity in the New Testament: An Inquiry into the Character of Earliest Christianity* (1977), pp. 174-202.

underlying continuity which existed in the early church's experience and understanding of the Spirit.

Although Dunn's concerns are broader than the respective pneumatologies of Luke and Paul, he devotes considerable space, particularly in *Baptism in the Holy Spirit*, to Luke's understanding of the Spirit. Dunn argues that the gift of the Spirit for Luke, as for the early church as a whole, is that which makes a Christian truly Christian. The gift of the Spirit is the climax of conversion-initiation. The Spirit initiates believers into the new age and mediates to them the life of the new covenant.[1]

Dunn's case rests on three pivotal arguments. First, Dunn claims that Jesus' experience at the Jordan was not primarily an anointing for power; rather it marked his initiation into the new age.[2] Dunn, following in the steps of H. von Baer and H. Conzelmann, views Luke as portraying three distinct epochs in salvation history.[3] The decisive transition points are Jesus' Jordan experience and Pentecost. Each is said to be an initiation into the new age: Jordan for Jesus; Pentecost for the disciples.[4] Each is linked to the bestowal of the Spirit. For, as Dunn argues, the Spirit is the catalyst of the kingdom, the dynamic of the new age: 'Where the Spirit is there is the kingdom'.[5]

Dunn, like Büchsel, views Jesus' Jordan experience as the decisive point in his life. And with Büchsel, Dunn also sees Jesus' reception of the Spirit as more than simply an anointing with power. It is Jesus' entry into the new age and covenant. Dunn can even say that through his reception of the Spirit at the Jordan, Jesus entered into a 'newer and fuller phase of his messiahship and sonship'.[6] Yet Dunn is reluctant to say with Büchsel that Jesus' sense of sonship flowed from his reception of the Spirit. Spirit and sonship are two prominent aspects of Jesus' religious experience and both result from his Jordan experience,

1. *Holy Spirit*, pp. 23-32, 47-48. Cf. *Jesus and the Spirit*, p. 6; *Unity and Diversity*, p. 183.

2. *Holy Spirit*, p. 32: 'This "empowering for service" should not however be taken as the primary purpose of the anointing—it is only a corollary to it. The baptism in the Spirit, in other words, is not primarily to equip the (already) Christian for service; rather its function is to initiate the individual into the new age and to equip him for life and service in the new age and covenant'.

3. H. von Baer, *Der heilige Geist in den Lukasschriften* (1926); H. Conzelmann, *The Theology of St. Luke* (1961; German edn, 1953). However, it should be noted that these authors place the divisions between the epochs at different stages in Luke's narrative.

4. *Holy Spirit*, pp. 23-32, 40-41.

5. *Jesus and the Spirit*, p. 49. See also, 'Spirit and Kingdom', pp. 36-40.

6. *Holy Spirit*, p. 29.

but one cannot be said to have priority over the other; rather they are 'two sides of the one coin'.[1] In this regard Dunn is more sensitive to the difficulties Büchsel's view raises for Luke's Gospel. Indeed, he denies that Luke's account of Jesus' experience at the Jordan contradicts what Luke has already written in Luke 1 and 2.[2] Dunn resolves the apparent contradiction by focusing on Luke's scheme of salvation history. The experience of Jesus at the Jordan was 'not so much of Jesus becoming what he was not before, but of Jesus entering where he was not before—a new epoch in God's plan of redemption'.[3]

A second pivotal argument for Dunn is his claim that the Spirit is the essence and embodiment of the new covenant. This argument is particularly important for Dunn's interpretation of the gift of the Spirit at Pentecost. He asserts that Luke employs the term 'promise'[4] in the same sense as Paul to refer to the covenant promise of God to his people:

> Implicit here, therefore, is the thought of the Spirit as the new covenant fulfillment of the ancient covenant promise. The gift of the Spirit is now the means whereby men enter into the blessing of Abraham. . . It is very probable therefore that Luke also saw the Spirit as the essence and embodiment of the new covenant, as that which most distinguished it from the old.[5]

That Luke understood the Spirit to be the essence of the new covenant is confirmed by the fact that he presents the outpouring of the Spirit as taking place on the Feast of Pentecost. This is significant, insists Dunn, because 'Pentecost was more and more coming to be regarded as the feast which commemorated the lawgiving at Sinai'.[6] Pentecost was, for Luke, the giving of the new Torah. Thus Dunn emphasizes Luke's continuity with Ezek. 36.26; Jer. 31.33; and ultimately Paul.[7] Initiation into the new age involves incorporation into the new covenant: both are mediated through the Spirit.

The life of the new community, as well as that of the individual believer, is shaped by the Spirit. According to Dunn, the Spirit forms the corporate believers into the body of Christ, the church. Apostolic

---

1. *Jesus and the Spirit*, p. 66; see pp. 62-67.
2. *Holy Spirit*, p. 28.
3. *Holy Spirit*, p. 28.
4. τὴν ἐπαγγελίαν τοῦ πατρός (Lk. 24.49; Acts 1.4) and ἐπαγγελίαν (Acts 2.33, 38f.).
5. *Holy Spirit*, pp. 47-48.
6. *Holy Spirit*, p. 48. See also p. 49.
7. *Holy Spirit*, p. 48.

preaching and κοινωνία are a direct result of the activity of the Spirit. 'Luke's history at this point demonstrates Paul's doctrine.'[1]

A third pivot to Dunn's argument is his claim that, for Luke, 'the gift of' or 'to be baptized in' the Spirit always refers to an initiatory experience, the means by which one enters into the new age. For this reason Dunn argues that the Samaritans, Paul, and the Ephesians were not considered Christians by Luke before they received the gift of the Spirit.[2]

The picture of Luke's pneumatology which emerges is, indeed, very similar to that of Paul. Certainly there are differences. Dunn criticizes Luke for being 'crude' because 'he shares the enthusiasts' desire for tangibility'.[3] Luke's account also tends to be 'lop-sided' because it does not deal sufficiently with the broader aspects of the religious experience of the community: 'Nowhere is this lop-sidedness more evident than in his complete disregard for the experience of sonship'.[4] In contrast stands Paul, for whom the distinctive mark of the Spirit is his 'Christness'.[5] This was Paul's distinctive contribution, one born out of his personal experience.[6] Yet, in the final analysis, Dunn's work suggests an enormous amount of continuity between Paul and Luke on the Spirit: for the Spirit both initiates believer into the new age and mediates to him new covenant existence. Thus Dunn marks the unity rather than the diversity of their thought.

Dunn's influence has not been without warrant. He has put forth a carefully argued thesis which moves significantly beyond the earlier work of Büchsel in its sophistication. Dunn integrated a wide knowledge of modern scholarship with an appreciation for some of the difficulties of Büchsel's perspective. By setting Luke's pneumatology against the backdrop of his scheme of salvation history, Dunn shifted the focus from Büchsel's emphasis on 'sonship' to 'initiation into the new age'. Although I shall criticize the major tenets of Dunn's argument, one must acknowledge the significance of Dunn's achievement. He succeeded in raising the argument for continuity to a place of prominence in the modern discussion.

---

1. *Holy Spirit*, p. 51; cf. pp. 50-51.
2. *Holy Spirit*, pp. 55f. (Samaritans), 73f. (Paul), 83f. (Ephesians).
3. *Jesus and the Spirit*, p. 190.
4. *Jesus and the Spirit*, p. 191. See also *Unity and Diversity*, p. 181: 'Luke's understanding of the Spirit is that of an enthusiast'.
5. *Jesus and the Spirit*, pp. 301-42. See also *Unity and Diversity*, pp. 194-95.
6. *Jesus and the Spirit*, p. 201. See also *Unity and Diversity*, p. 190.

2.2.3. *Johannes S. Vos.* In *Traditionsgeschichtliche Untersuchungen zur paulinischen Pneumatologie* (1973), J.S. Vos provided support, albeit indirectly, to Dunn's thesis. Vos attempted to answer two related questions: what soteriological significance did the Spirit have for Paul? and how closely did he associate the work of the Spirit with the work of Christ?[1] Through an analysis of the Jewish background and relevant portions of Paul's epistles, Vos sought to distinguish pre-Pauline tradition from material which reflected Paul's distinctive thought. Of particular importance for this study is his conclusion that the primitive church shared with Paul the conviction that salvation was both the work of Christ and the work of the Spirit.

Evidence that the primitive church, did indeed, attribute salvation directly to the Spirit is elicited from three central texts: 1 Cor. 15.44ff.; Gal. 5.22f.; and 1 Cor. 6.11. Vos argues that these texts, all of which give stipulations for entrance into the Kingdom of God, reflect baptismal traditions of the primitive church.[2] This is particularly significant for these texts attribute a broad range of soteriological activity to the Spirit:

> In the three texts dealt with, every aspect of salvation—the cleansing, sanctification, and justification of the past, the upright life of the present, and the transformation of the future—is attributed to both Christ and the Spirit.[3]

Vos finds further support for this thesis in the literature of pre-Christian Judaism. On the basis of his examination of numerous Jewish texts,[4] Vos argues that pre-Christian Judaism frequently attributed soteriological functions to the Spirit: 'E. Schweizers These, der Geist erscheine im AT und "im ganzen Judt" nicht als heilsnotwendig, sondern als Kraft zu zusätzlichen Taten, ist unhaltbar'.[5] Therefore, reasons Vos, it is not surprising that the primitive church held similar beliefs.[6]

Vos seeks to uncover Paul's distinctive teaching by analysing texts which bear witness, not only to tradition which Paul has taken up, but also to the way in which Paul has reinterpreted this tradition. These

---

1. *Untersuchungen*, p. 25.
2. *Untersuchungen*, pp. 26-33.
3. *Untersuchungen*, pp. 32-33. ET is my own.
4. Vos cites numerous texts as attributing salvation directly to the Spirit: Ps. 51 (pp. 39-40); Ezek. 36.27 (pp. 41-43); Isa. 44.1-5 (pp. 43-45); 1QS 2.25b–3.12 (pp. 56-57); 1QS 3.13–4.26 (pp. 61-64); Wisdom (pp. 64-65); *Joseph and Aseneth* (pp. 69-70).
5. *Untersuchungen*, p. 77.
6. *Untersuchungen*, p. 77.

texts include Gal. 2.15–5.12, Rom. 1–8, and 2 Cor. 2.14–4.6. On the basis of this analysis Vos concludes that the primitive church and Paul viewed the entire life of the believer as a work of the Spirit. Salvation in all its dimensions flowed from the work of Christ and the Spirit. Vos writes:

> The entire life of the believer is considered to be a work of the Spirit: the believer's cleansing, sanctification, and justification; the life of sonship, freedom, and obedience; and the transformation into the image and glory of God.[1]

Yet Paul made several distinctive contributions. First, Vos argues that there was some fluidity in the way in which the primitive church related the work of the Spirit to the work of Christ. Prominence was given to the soteriological significance of Christ as the crucified one or as the resurrected one. In conjunction, the work of the Spirit was brought in relation to the work of Christ or separated from it. Paul, on the other hand, more than the community before him, tied together the work of Christ and the work of the Spirit.[2]

The second distinctive feature of Paul's pneumatology is an outgrowth of the first and of the polemic he waged against the Jewish nomists. Although both Paul and the primitive church viewed justification as a work of the Spirit, Paul, more than ever before, related justification to faith: 'Von der Christologie her versteht er das Werk des Geistes radikal als Schöpfung aus dem Nichts, und er bestimmt die Gerechtigkeit im Geist als Glaubensgerechtigkeit'.[3]

Third, Paul stressed, more than the tradition he received, the cosmic significance of the work of the Spirit. The redemptive work of the Spirit was not limited by national or social distinctions, rather it was a universal event which changed the very make-up of the cosmos.[4]

In spite of these distinctive elements, the amount of common ground Vos found between the primitive church and Paul is striking: both viewed the Spirit as the source of salvation in its broadest dimensions. In this regard Vos, like Dunn, emphasizeᴜ the continuity which existed between elements within the *Urgemeinde* and Paul. Yet through his tradition-historical analysis of relevant Pauline passages, Vos approached the question from a decidedly different angle. Rather than comparing the pneumatology of the Pauline epistles with that of other

---

1. *Untersuchungen*, p. 144. ET is my own.
2. *Untersuchungen*, pp. 86-87, 101, 117, 118-31; esp. summary statements on pp. 131, 145.
3. *Untersuchungen*, p. 145. See also pp. 85-88, 105-106, 107-15.
4. *Untersuchungen*, pp. 126-32, 145.

documents of the *Urgemeinde* (e.g. Matthew, Mark, Luke–Acts), Vos
sought to show the extent to which Paul's pneumatology had been
shaped by his predecessors. Herein lies Vos's major contribution to the
discussion.

Vos also criticized an important cornerstone of the discontinuity
school: Schweizer's analysis of Jewish pneumatology. Vos's treatment
of the Jewish documents highlighted their significance for the question
at hand, and, by virtue of his criticism of Schweizer, reopened discussion on the nature of Jewish pneumatology.

2.3. *Mediating Positions*
2.3.1. *Heinrich von Baer.* H. von Baer's *Der heilige Geist in den Lukasschriften* (1926) can be seen as a two-sided polemic against H.

Leisegang, who argued that the pneumatology of the early church
reflected widespread hellenistic influence,[1] and against the conclusions
of Gunkel described earlier. Yet von Baer's criticism led to a positive
contribution of his own. Noting Luke's interest in the work of the
Spirit and salvation history, von Baer asserted that the two themes are
interrelated: the Spirit is the driving force behind Luke's scheme of
salvation history. This focus on salvation history provided von Baer
with a distinctively Jewish background against which to set Luke's
pneumatology.

Anticipating the views of Hans Conzelmann, von Baer argued that
Luke divides salvation history into three distinct epochs.[2] In the first
epoch various figures, particularly John the Baptist, are endowed with
the Spirit of prophecy in order to announce the coming of the Messiah.[3] The second epoch is inaugurated at Jesus' birth, when 'der Geist
Gottes als Wesen des Gottessohnes in dieser Welt erscheint'.[4] The third
epoch begins with Pentecost, the point at which the Spirit begins to
work in the church.[5]

---

1. H. Leisegang, *Der Heilige Geist. Das Wesen und Werden der mystisch-intui-
tiven Erkenntnis in der Philosophie und Religion der Griechen* (1919); and *Pneuma
Hagion. Der Ursprung des Geistbegriffs der synoptischen Evangelien aus der
griechischen Mystik* (1922). For von Baer's critique of Leisegang, see *Der heilige
Geist*, pp. 13, 110, 138, 161; esp. pp. 112f., 131.

2. H. Conzelmann, *The Theology of St. Luke* (1961). Conzelmann acknowledges
his dependence on von Baer, if somewhat inadequately (see F. Bovon, 'Aktuelle
Linien lukanischer Forschung', in *Lukas in neuer Sicht* [1985], p. 10).

3. H. von Baer, *Der heilige Geist*, pp. 45-47.

4. *Der heilige Geist*, p. 49.

5. *Der heilige Geist*, pp. 92f.

Although von Baer sought to distinguish between the nature of the Spirit's activity in these epochs,[1] nowhere did he work out the distinctive features in detail. Rather than highlighting the distinctive aspects of the Spirit's work, von Baer tended to focus on the continuity which existed, particularly in the relationship between the Spirit and proclamation:

> A characteristic of Luke's writings, especially the book of Acts, is that the activity of the Spirit is always directly or indirectly related to the proclamation of the gospel.[2]

When von Baer writes that 'Der Pfingtsgeist ist der Missionsgeist',[3] he acknowledges that he is describing the work of the Spirit throughout Luke–Acts. This ambiguity concerning the nature of the Spirit's distinctive activity in the various epochs runs throughout von Baer's work. Here, then, is a fundamental tension which von Baer never resolves.

This tension is illustrated in von Baer's treatment of Jesus' experience at the Jordan. According to von Baer, Luke edits his sources in order to highlight the parallels between Jesus' experience of the Spirit at his baptism and that of the disciples at Pentecost. In each case the Spirit is primarily the power to preach the gospel.[4] Yet von Baer insists that the two events must be distinguished, for they lie 'in zwei verschiedenen Heilsepochen und mußten daher auch grundsätzlich nach verschiedenem Maßstabe beurteilt werden'.[5] Exactly how these events are to be distinguished is never clearly outlined.

The tension inherent in von Baer's work is nowhere more apparent than when he criticizes Gunkel's position.[6] In Acts 2, von Baer declares, we meet 'die sittlich erneuernde Kraft des Pfinstgeistes'.[7] Support for this statement is elicited from texts where the Spirit is cited as the source of joy (Acts 4.33), fear (Acts 2.43; 5.11), and unity (4.32).[8] Yet, as I have noted, von Baer also puts the accent elsewhere: 'Der Pfingstgeist ist der Missionsgeist'.

1. *Der heilige Geist*, pp. 4, 45, 57-58, 111.
2. *Der heilige Geist*, p. 103. ET is my own.
3. *Der heilige Geist*, p. 103.
4. *Der heilige Geist*, pp. 57-62, 98f.
5. *Der heilige Geist*, pp. 57-58.
6. *Der heilige Geist*, pp. 16-19, 100-102, 186-92.
7. *Der heilige Geist*, p. 188.
8. *Der heilige Geist*, pp. 188-90. In this regard von Baer's position is not unlike that of J.H.E. Hull. Although Hull acknowledges Luke's emphasis on the Spirit as power for proclamation, he also insists that 'Luke believed the Spirit to be the very

In short, von Baer's central thrust in *Der heilige Geist* was not to define the distinctive nature of the Spirit's activity in the various epochs of salvation history, but rather to show that the Spirit is the driving force behind Luke's scheme of salvation history. This, however, produces a certain tension in von Baer's work, one that is never resolved. On the one hand von Baer insists that the Spirit's activity is distinctive in each of the various epochs, but on the other hand he emphasizes the fundamental continuity which binds Luke's pneumatology and scheme of salvation history together. Similarly, von Baer asserts that the Spirit is the source of the moral-religious life of the believer, yet he acknowledges that it is fundamentally the power to proclaim the gospel. One is left with a sense of ambiguity.

In spite of the ambiguity present in von Baer's work, it is noteworthy for several reasons. First, von Baer argued persuasively against Leisegang for the Jewish origin of Luke's pneumatology. Second, his emphasis on the Spirit as the driving force in Luke's scheme of salvation history anticipated the work of Conzelmann and Dunn. Third, von Baer's criticisms of Gunkel, coupled with his emphasis on the Spirit as the *Missionsgeist*, gave new direction to the discussion concerning the nature of Luke's pneumatology and its relationship to Paul's. Although von Baer himself did not resolve the tension inherent in his work, he did attempt to forge a middle path between Gunkel on the one hand and Büchsel on the other.

2.3.2. Gonzalo Haya-Prats. Written at approximately the same time as Dunn's *Baptism in the Holy Spirit* and independent of it, G. Haya-Prats' *L'Esprit force de l'église* offered conclusions concerning Luke's pneumatology that differed dramatically from those of Dunn.[1] Whereas Dunn portrayed the gift of the Spirit as the climax of conversion-initiation, the source of new covenant existence, Haya-Prats argued that the Spirit was directly related to neither conversion nor salvation. Yet Haya-Prats was not content to restrict Luke's pneumatology as sharply as Gunkel or Schweizer had before him. The Spirit provided more than prophetic power. In this way Haya-Prats took up the tension in von Baer's work and sought to resolve it.

---

bond uniting every believer to Christ' (*The Holy Spirit in the Acts of the Apostles* [1967], p. 98. See also pp. 42, 45f., 143-68).

1. G. Haya-Prats, *L'Esprit force de l'église. Sa nature et son activité d'après les Actes des Apôtres* (1975). This work, originally written in Spanish and later published in French, shows no awareness of Dunn's work. Therefore it was probably written around 1970.

Haya-Prats argues that there are three discernible levels in the history of the composition of Acts. First, there existed a record of Pentecost. Second, Luke, the principal author of Luke–Acts, added to this record the accounts of Stephen, Ananias and Sapphira, and Philip, in order to build up gradually to two pericopes of central importance: the record of Cornelius and the Jerusalem Council. These two accounts, shaped by Luke's pen, show the Spirit's decisive intervention in the evangelization of the Gentiles. Third, the remaining sections of Acts were completed and amplified by a second redactor who attempted to imitate the style of Luke. Thus, Haya-Prats asserts that Acts consists of two distinct parts: one written by Luke, the principal author of Luke–Acts; the other produced by a later redactor.[1]

The various layers of tradition and the respective portions of Acts which they represent are distinguished by Haya-Prats according to the manner in which the Spirit's activity is described. Haya-Prats notes that in a number of passages the Spirit is described as working in co-operation with a human agent. The human agent is the subject of an action of which the Spirit is a complementary cause. Haya-Prats terms this mode of activity *influx complémentaire*.[2] However, in other passages the activity of the Spirit is emphasized so strongly that the role of the human agent all but disappears. The Spirit takes complete control, replacing the decisions and actions of the human agent. In these passages the Spirit is often the sole subject of an action. This mode of activity is termed *irruptions absorbantes*.[3] Haya-Prats argues that Luke's redaction in the first part of Acts is dominated by *influx complémentaire* activity. The second part of Acts, however, is characterized by *irruptions absorbantes*, and therefore attributed to a later redactor.[4] For this reason Luke's distinctive pneumatology emerges most clearly from the initial section of Acts and the Gospel of Luke. Above all, three passages stand out as central to Luke's theological concern: Jesus' baptism (Luke 3); the Jerusalem Pentecost (Acts 2); and the Gentile Pentecost (Acts 10).[5]

On the basis of his analysis of the initial portion of Acts, Haya-Prats asserts that Luke does not portray the gift of the Spirit as the climax of conversion-initiation. Three major arguments support Haya-Prats' thesis. First, Haya-Prats argues that Luke does not directly relate the gift of the Spirit to water baptism. Noting that the gift of the Spirit is

---

1. *Force*, pp. 73-82, 198.
2. *Force*, pp. 73-78.
3. *Force*, pp. 73-78.
4. *Force*, pp. 73-82.
5. *Force*, pp. 192-93, 203.

bestowed apart from (before or after) water baptism,[1] Haya-Prats characterizes the relationship as 'indépendance interne et directe'.[2] Second, Haya-Prats insists that in Luke's scheme initial faith does not result from the gift of the Spirit, rather this faith is a prerequisite for reception of the Spirit.[3] Third, according to Haya-Prats, the Spirit is the source of neither forgiveness nor progressive purification.[4] Rather, 'Luc attribue à Jésus toute l'œuvre du salut'.[5]

Positively, Haya-Prats argues that for Luke the Spirit is the source of special power which heightens (*réactivation extraordinaire*) certain aspects of the Christian life already present in the believer.[6] Generally the Spirit gives prophetic direction to the people of God[7] and in this way directs the unfolding plan of God's salvation in history.[8] Yet Haya-Prats distinguishes between two aspects of the Spirit's work: the *historique/kérygmatic* and the *eschatologique/fruitif*.[9] The *historique/ kérygmatic* dimension of the Spirit provides special power to proclaim the gospel. Haya-Prats limits this dimension to Jesus and the apostles.[10] The *eschatologique/fruitif* dimension of the Spirit, experienced by all believers, serves as a sign or guarantee of salvation. It is an

---

1. *Force*, pp. 130-38. On Pentecost see p. 57.

2. *Force*, p. 137.

3. *Force*, pp. 125-29, 130.

4. *Force*, pp. 122-25.

5. *Force*, p. 125. For this reason Haya-Prats, like Schweizer, does not attribute miracles of healing to the work of the Spirit (pp. 37ff., 147, 173). In contrast to Hull (*Acts*, pp. 139-42), Haya-Prats distinguishes between 'the Spirit of God' and 'the power of God'. The former is the source of prophetic activity, the latter works miracles of healing and exorcisms (p. 38).

6. *Force*, pp. 138-63. Haya-Prats acknowledges that the Spirit does, at times, have ethical significance for Luke. Yet he denies that the Spirit is the author of sanctification, for the Spirit merely heightens certain Christian characteristics already present in the believer and this is a special occurrence, not representative of ordinary Christian development (p. 147). Similarly, Haya-Prats denies that Luke attributes the religious life of the early church (Acts 2.42-47) to the Spirit (pp. 149-50).

7. *Force*, pp. 165-93. According to Haya-Prats, Luke's understanding of the Spirit is largely shaped by the OT. He sees little development in Jewish pneumatology during the intertestamental period and therefore views this body of literature as relatively insignificant.

8. *Force*, pp. 192-93.

9. *Force*, pp. 165-93, 206-207.

10. *Force*, pp. 69-70, 169-70, 174-75, 179, 182-83, 187, 193, 206-208. This dimension of the Spirit is, in a sense, also experienced by other members of the hierarchy, such as the seven; yet according to Haya-Prats, they are to be distinguished from the apostles in that they are chosen by the apostles, who remain the leaders of the expansion of the church (e.g. Peter in Acts 10). (See pp. 182-83, 207-208.)

anticipation of the fullness of salvation.[1] Haya-Prats supports these distinctions from his analysis of Lucan texts, particularly the three central passages mentioned previously: Luke 3; Acts 2; and Acts 10.

At his baptism, Jesus experienced the *historique/kérygmatic* dimension of the Spirit: he was anointed with power for his messianic mission. Yet this was not the 'promise of the Spirit'. Only at his exaltation did Jesus receive 'the promise of the Spirit'. This experience of the Spirit at his exaltation was quite different from what Jesus had previously experienced at the Jordan; for, as the Messianic King, he received 'the eschatological gift of the Spirit' and bestowed it on the people of God: Jews (Acts 2) and Gentiles (Acts 10).[2]

For this reason Haya-Prats insists that the *eschatologique/fruitif* dimension of the Spirit is most prominent at Pentecost.[3] The Spirit is received by the disciples as an anticipation of the fullness of salvation. Manifestations of this eschatological anticipation are inspired praise (glossolalia and prophecy) and joy. These manifestations testify that the recipients of the Spirit have been incorporated into the eschatological people of God. They signal the beginning of a new epoch, an end-time era in which salvation is offered to all. The *historique/kérygmatic* dimension of the Spirit is not wholly absent at Pentecost, but it is limited to the apostles.[4]

According to Haya-Prats, Luke highlights the parallels between Acts 2 and Acts 10 in order to emphasize their continuity. As in Acts 2, the *eschatologique/fruitif* dimension of the Spirit is most prominent in Acts 10: 'L'Esprit atteste que les païens sont sanctifiés par la foi en Jésus, sans avoir besoin de pratiquer la Loi de Moïse; ainsi est facilitée leur entrée massive dans l'Église'.[5]

Following von Baer, Haya-Prats views the Spirit in Luke–Acts as the driving force behind salvation history. However, in contrast to von Baer and Dunn, Haya-Prats sharply distinguishes between the work of Jesus and the Spirit in Luke's scheme: salvation is the work of Jesus;

---

1. See also K. Wurm, 'Rechtfertigung und Heil: eine Untersuchung zur Theologie des Lukas unter dem Aspekt "Lukas und Paulus"'(1978), p. 126: 'Wie für Paulus, so ist also auch für Lukas der Geist (sachlich, nicht expressis verbis) das "Angeld" (vgl. 2Kr 1,22; 5,5) des zukünftigen Heils'.

2. *Force*, pp. 69-70, 170-75. Haya-Prats indicates that the gift of the Spirit received by the disciples has a permanent or ongoing aspect: 'L'Esprit Saint est un don de la Promesse. Il s'agit d'un don permanent ou, plus exactement, d'une offre permanente qui se réalise chaque fois qu'une situation requiert l'assistance extraordinaire de l'Esprit' (p. 198).

3. *Force*, pp. 173-176, 185-89.

4. *Force*, p. 169. See also p. 138.

5. *Force*, p. 192. On Acts 10 see pp. 189-93.

the Spirit guides the historical development of salvation history. In this way Luke separated the work of the Spirit from conversion, sanctification, and salvation.[1] Thus, according to Haya-Prats, the Spirit neither initiates nor sustains the Christian life in Luke's scheme. In short, the Spirit is not the source of ordinary Christian existence.

It would appear that from Haya-Prats' perspective the pneumatologies of Luke and Paul are radically different. Yet we have seen that Haya-Prats distinguished between two aspects of the Spirit's work. Although Luke at times features the *historique/kérygmatic* dimension of the Spirit's work, the *eschatologique/fruitif* dimension represents the fundamental aspect of Luke's pneumatology.[2] Through his focus on the *eschatologique/fruitif* dimension of the Spirit, Haya-Prats found significant common ground between the pneumatologies of Luke and Paul, while at the same time maintaining that the Spirit for Luke was not the source of ordinary Christian existence. Although I shall question the validity of Haya-Prats' distinction between the *eschatologique/ fruitif* and *historique/kérygmatic* dimensions of the Spirit's activity, and particularly his insistence that the latter is limited to the apostles, Haya-Prats represents a significant alternative to the position espoused by Dunn.

2.3.3. *M.M.B. Turner*.

M. Turner's contribution to the current discussion comes in the form of a Cambridge PhD dissertation and several published essays.[3] Like Haya-Prats and von Baer, Turner approached the issue almost exclusively from the Lukan end. Turner's work resembled that of Haya-Prats in many ways. Following Haya-Prats, Turner criticized Dunn's thesis at a number of points, particularly Dunn's insistence that the gift of the Spirit initiated the believer into the new age.[4] Both argued that Luke did not simply equate the gift of the Spirit with salvation.[5] And Turner, like Haya-Prats, insisted that the gift of the Spirit for Luke offered more than simply power to

---

1. *Force*, pp. 201-202.
2. *Force*, p. 200.
3. M.M.B. Turner, 'Luke and the Spirit: Studies in the Significance of Receiving the Spirit in Luke–Acts' (1980). Other works of Turner related to the subject include: 'The Significance of Spirit Endowment for Paul', *VE* 9 (1975), pp. 56-69; 'Spirit Endowment in Luke–Acts: Some Linguistic Considerations', *VE* 12 (1981), pp. 45-63; 'Jesus and the Spirit in Lucan Perspective', *TB* 32 (1981), pp. 3-42; 'The Spirit of Christ and Christology', in *Christ the Lord* (1982), pp. 168-90; 'Spiritual Gifts Then and Now', *VE* 15 (1985), pp. 7-64.
4. 'Luke and the Spirit', pp. 148-55.
5. 'Luke and the Spirit', pp. 178-79.

proclaim the gospel.[1] Here, however, is where the paths of Turner and Haya-Prats diverge. Haya-Prats had argued that the gift of the Spirit had two aspects, neither of which related directly to ordinary Christian existence. Turner, on the other hand, insisted that for Luke the Pentecostal gift was the means of communication between the Lord and his disciples. Therefore the gift of the Spirit was, in Luke's perspective, essential for Christian existence (after Pentecost).[2] Turner and Haya-Prats sought to resolve the tension in von Baer's work and build a bridge between the schools of Gunkel and Büchsel. Whereas Haya-Prats' solution had more affinities with Gunkel's school, Turner identified more closely with Büchsel and his followers.

Through detailed analysis of relevant Lukan texts, Turner sought to answer the question: 'What activity (or nexus of activities) of the divine Spirit is being thought to be communicated to the disciple (or initiated in him) when he "receives the Spirit"?'[3] Turner's answer to this question is shaped largely by his assertion that Luke thought of the Spirit in terms of the Jewish Spirit of prophecy:

> In the Spirit of prophecy the early church had a concept which could readily be adapted to speak of its new sense of immediate awareness of God, and of communication with him, and, at the same time to refer to the charismatic character of much of its corporate worship.[4]

According to Turner, the essential function of the Spirit in Judaism, as the Spirit of prophecy, was to reveal God's message to his prophet. Criticizing Schweizer's position, Turner maintains that the Spirit as the power to preach the gospel 'bears little relationship to any "typical

---

1. 'Luke and the Spirit', pp. 159, 183-84.
2. See 'Spirit Endowment in Luke–Acts', p. 59; 'Jesus and the Spirit', p. 39; 'Spiritual Gifts', pp. 40-41; and 'Christology', pp. 180-81. Turner's thought appears to have undergone a process of development at this point. In 'Luke and the Spirit', Turner suggests that one need not personally receive the gift of the Spirit in order to live as a Christian in relationship to God: Christian existence can be maintained through responding to the charismata manifest through others (see p. 178 and esp. 184). He does however assert that the gift of the Spirit is received by each individual Christian after Pentecost (p. 159). In the subsequent essays cited above Turner seems to view reception of the gift as an essential element of individual Christian experience. Thus he maintains that it is the *sine qua non* of Christian existence (e.g. 'Spiritual Gifts', p. 41).
3. 'Luke and the Spirit', p. 35.
4. 'Luke and the Spirit', p. 134.

Jewish idea" of the Spirit of prophecy'.[1] The Old Testament and the literature of late Judaism[2] indicate, according to Turner, that:

> The proper sphere of activity of the Spirit of prophecy is thus not the imparting of charismatic character or authority in the delivery of a message, but usually in the prior revelation to the prophet of the content of the message to be delivered as an oracle, or preached about. Prophecy and preaching may overlap; but the activity of the Spirit of prophecy, and the Spirit's empowering of the preacher in his preaching, are complementary, not congruent roles.[3]

Turner interprets Luke as modifying and broadening this Jewish understanding. For Luke, the function of the Spirit of prophecy is varied: the Spirit grants wisdom, reveals the will of God, edifies the community through χαρίσματα, and inspires preaching and praise.[4] On the basis of his criticism of Schweizer, Turner also affirms that the Spirit is the source of miracles of healings and exorcisms.[5] The extent to which Luke, in Turner's perspective, has broadened the Jewish concept is seen most clearly in his understanding of the gift of the Spirit at Pentecost:

> Quite clearly, after the ascension, this gift promised by Peter is a *sine qua non* of Christian existence. The man who knows the presence of the Lord; who experiences Jesus speaking to him in his heart. . . any such man owes all this to the Spirit experienced as what Luke means by the Spirit of prophecy promised by Joel.[6]

In short, according to Turner the Spirit of prophecy is, for Luke, fundamentally 'the organ of communication' between God and humanity.[7]

---

1. 'Luke and the Spirit', p. 65.
2. Turner maintained that 'the Spirit of prophecy as understood by apocalyptic judaism, Qumran, rabbinic judaism, and even Philo, remains roughly within the guidelines of the OT concept' ('Luke and the Spirit', p. 66).
3. 'Luke and the Spirit', p. 66.
4. 'Spirit Endowment in Luke–Acts', p. 58: 'The referent of Joel's promise—the spirit of prophecy—had undergone some degree of evolution in the thinking of Judaism, and even more so in that of the earliest church; so that by the time Luke wrote, the range of charismata traced back to the Spirit of prophecy included not only those explicitly mentioned by Joel but also all manner of gifts of wisdom and guidance and, in addition, charismata of inspired speech'. Turner discusses this evolution of thought concerning the Spirit of prophecy in Judaism and modifications by the early Christians in 'Luke and the Spirit', pp. 66-67, 130-34, 178-80.
5. 'Luke and the Spirit', pp. 66-67, 139-46.
6. 'Spiritual Gifts', p. 41.
7. 'Spiritual Gifts', p. 40. See also 'Luke and the Spirit', p. 185, where Turner speaks of the Spirit as the 'organ of revelation' to the disciples.

Yet Turner, like Haya-Prats, distinguishes between the way in which the Spirit functions in Jesus' ministry and that of the disciples, between Jesus' experience of the Spirit at the Jordan and that of the disciples at Pentecost.

Turner asserts that Jesus' experience of the Spirit at the Jordan was essentially a prophetic anointing, an endowment of power to carry out his messianic duties.[1] Jesus' Jordan experience does not provide him with power for moral renewal or some new existential awareness of sonship. This resulted from Jesus' miraculous birth. At the Jordan, Jesus is anointed with power to fulfill his role as the eschatological herald, the end-time Moses, who announces and brings liberation to Israel.[2] Therefore, Turner argues that the primary function of the Spirit, as the Spirit of prophecy, is not to reveal divine messages to Jesus; rather, the Spirit empowers his word so that it can be revealed to others.[3] In short, Jesus receives the Spirit for others.

However, the experience of the disciples at Pentecost is not to be equated with that of Jesus at the Jordan. Speaking of the disciples, Turner writes, 'It would be hollow to assert that they receive the "same" Spirit [as Jesus]'.[4] Although, according to Turner, the disciples before Pentecost had already begun to experience the Spirit during the ministry of Jesus,[5] with the exalted Jesus' reception and subsequent bestowal of the Spirit on the disciples a new nexus of the Spirit's activity is unleashed:

> The gift of the Spirit is the means by which the now ascended Jesus can continue to bring the blessings of messianic ἄφεσις, or salvation, to his church, and through it to the world. Without such a gift there could be no christianity after the ascension except as a lingering memory of what had happened in Jesus' day. The Spirit of prophecy, as Luke understands it, is the vitality of the community both in its witness to Jesus and in its own religious life.[6]

In view of this distinction, Turner insists that the gift of the Spirit at Pentecost is not primarily an empowering for mission; this is 'merely one possible sphere... Luke places at least equal emphasis on the

---

1. 'Luke and the Spirit', pp. 53, 56-57, 73, 76, 81, 93, 158, 180f.

2. 'Luke and the Spirit', p. 85: Turner, on the basis of Lk. 4.1, 14 argues that Luke portrays Jesus as the eschatological Moses. See also 'Christology', pp. 176-79.

3. 'Luke and the Spirit', pp. 180-84.

4. 'Luke and the Spirit', p. 185. See also 'Jesus and the Spirit', pp. 28-33.

5. 'Luke and the Spirit', pp. 96-116; especially pp. 108-109, 115-16.

6. 'Luke and the Spirit', p. 159.

Spirit as the organ of revelation to the disciples'.[1] Whereas Jesus received the Spirit for others, the disciples received the Spirit, to a significant extent, for themselves.

Thus from Pentecost on, the Spirit enlivens the community, providing the link between the ascended Lord and his church. Yet this does not mean that Luke portrays the gift of the Spirit as the source of salvation *in toto*. Turner offers detailed criticism of Dunn's thesis that, for Luke, the gift mediates to its recipient the blessings of the new covenant to the believer. The gift of the Spirit is 'not the matrix of new covenant life, but an important element within it'.[2] On the basis of his analysis of Acts 8.4-24, Turner concludes:

> The very fact of the separation of baptism from receiving the Spirit here, and the characteristics of Luke's description, favour the view that he did not identify receiving the Spirit as the gift of messianic salvation itself, but as one particular nexus within it: the christian version of judaism's hope for the Spirit of prophecy.[3]

Turner, like Schweizer and Haya-Prats before him, emphasized the importance of the Jewish concept of the Spirit of prophecy for Luke's pneumatology. Yet through his criticism of Schweizer's analysis of the Spirit of prophecy in Judaism, and his description of Luke's modification of the concept, Turner raised new questions concerning the significance of this concept for Luke and offered a stimulating and new analysis of Luke's pneumatology. For Luke, the Spirit is neither the matrix of new covenant existence nor a *donum superadditum*. Rather the Spirit, as the Spirit of prophecy, is the means of communication between God and man: essential for Christian existence yet not identical with it.

3. *The Thesis*

The survey presented above has revealed that apart from the essays by Schweizer and Hill, which were by design general overviews and thus lacking in detailed argumentation, all of the major post-Gunkel studies have affirmed the relative homogeneity of the pneumatology of the early church. It is generally asserted that the soteriological dimension

---

1. 'Luke and the Spirit', p. 185.
2. 'Luke and the Spirit', p. 155. See pp. 148-55 for Turner's criticism of Dunn at this point. Turner writes: 'There is no evidence that Luke considers the application of atonement to be an operation of the Spirit falling within the nexus of activities designated by the expression "to receive the gift of the Holy Spirit"' (p. 153).
3. 'Luke and the Spirit', p. 170.

of the Spirit's activity which is so prominent in Paul's epistles was, to a significant extent, already an integral part of the pneumatology of the primitive church (Büchsel, Dunn, Vos). Furthermore, it is argued that this perspective exerted considerable influence on Luke. Thus Luke is said to have viewed the gift of the Spirit as the source of cleansing and moral transformation (Dunn, von Baer),[1] the essential bond which links the individual Christian to God (Turner), and a foretaste of the salvation to come (Haya-Prats).

In the following study I shall challenge these conclusions. I shall seek to establish that Paul was the first Christian to attribute soteriological functions to the Spirit and that this original element of Paul's pneumatology did not influence wider (non-Pauline) sectors of the early church until after the writing of Luke–Acts. Three interrelated arguments will be offered in support of this thesis.

In Part One I shall argue that soteriological functions were generally not attributed to the Spirit in intertestamental Judaism. The Spirit was regarded as the source of prophetic inspiration, a *donum superadditum* granted to various individuals so they might fulfill a divinely appointed task. The only significant exceptions to this perspective are found in later sapiential writings (1QH, Wisdom).

In Part Two I shall argue that Luke, influenced by the dominant Jewish perception, consistently portrays the gift of the Spirit as a prophetic endowment which enables its recipient to participate effectively in the mission of God. Although the primitive church, following in the footsteps of Jesus, broadened the functions traditionally ascribed to the Spirit in first-century Judaism and thus presented the Spirit as the source of miracle-working power (as well as prophetic inspiration), Luke resisted this innovation. For Luke, the Spirit remained the source of special insight and inspired speech. The important corollary is that neither Luke nor the primitive church attributes soteriological significance to the pneumatic gift in a manner analogous to Paul. Thus I shall distinguish Luke's 'prophetic' pneumatology from the 'charismatic' perspective of the primitive church on the one hand, and Paul's 'soteriological' understanding of the Spirit on the other.

In Part Three I shall argue, on the basis of my analysis of relevant Pauline texts, that the early Christian traditions used by Paul do not attribute soteriological functions to the Spirit, and that sapiential traditions from the hellenistic Jewish milieu which produced Wisdom provided the conceptual framework for Paul's distinctive thought. In this

---

1. See also J. Kremer, *Pfingstbericht*, pp. 177-79, 197, 219-220, 273; G.W.H. Lampe, *God a Spirit*, pp. 64-72; Hull, *Acts*, pp. 42, 45f., 53-55, 143-68.

way I hope to demonstrate that there were no Christian precursors to Paul at this point and that Paul's perspective represents an independent development.

Finally, by way of conclusion, I shall summarize my findings and draw out their implications for the development of early Christian pneumatology in the period from the inception of the church to the writing of Luke–Acts.

PART I

PNEUMATOLOGICAL PERSPECTIVES IN INTERTESTAMENTAL JUDAISM

INTRODUCTION

Articles and books extolling the virtues of Jewish studies for the interpretation of the New Testament are legion. The voluminous writings of Jacob Neusner, along with the productive pens of Geza Vermes and E.P. Sanders, have not only brought renewed interest and controversy to Jewish studies, they have also heightened the awareness of the field's significance for the study of the New Testament. Today everyone would affirm that 'Jesus was a Jew'.[1] The important corollary for this study is that the first Christians who thought through the significance of their experience of the Spirit did so in light of their Jewish background. Indeed, due to the early efforts of H. Gunkel, F. Büchsel, and H. von Baer, it is now recognized that Judaism provided the conceptual framework for the pneumatological reflection of Luke and Paul, as well as the primitive church before them. For this reason our inquiry into the development of early Christian pneumatology begins with a survey of the various pneumatological perspectives which were current in intertestamental Judaism.

In order to facilitate the analysis, I have arranged the sources into four groups: diaspora literature; palestinian literature; Qumran literature; and rabbinic literature. Although diaspora and palestinian sources can be distinguished on the basis of language and geography, the significance of these distinctions, as will become apparent, should not be overemphasized. Martin Hengel has established that from the middle of the third century BC 'Jewish Palestine was no hermetically sealed island in the sea of Hellenistic oriental syncretism'.[2] Clearly firm lines of demarcation cannot be drawn simply on the basis of language and geography.

---

1. G. Vermes, 'Jewish Studies and New Testament Interpretation', *JJS* 31 (1980), p. 1: 'It is, I am sure, no surprise to you, as it was to many readers of the great German biblical scholar Julius Wellhausen, at the beginning of this century, to hear that Jesus was not a Christian, but a Jew'. See also G. Vermes, *Jesus the Jew: A Historian's Reading of the Gospels* (1973).

2. M. Hengel, *Judaism and Hellenism*, I (1974), p. 312. See also Davies, *Paul*, pp. 1-16; and D.E. Aune, *Prophecy in Early Christianity and the Ancient Mediterranean World* (1983), p. 16.

Chapter 2

THE DIASPORA LITERATURE[1]

1. *The Septuagint*

With their tendency to translate רוח of the Hebrew scriptures with πνεῦμα, the LXX translators added new dimensions to the term. Whereas in Greek thought, with the notable exception of Stoicism, πνεῦμα was not usually associated with God and confined to such con-

---

1. The sources examined include those writings produced during the intertestamental period in regions outside of Palestine and written originally in Greek: Additions to Esther; additions to Daniel (i.e. The Prayer of Azarias, The Hymn of the Three Young Men, The History of Susanna, and Bel and the Dragon); The Prayer of Manasseh; The Epistle of Jeremiah; Demetrius; Eupolemus; Artapanus; Cleodemus; Philo the Epic Poet; Theodotus; Ezekiel the Tragedian; Aristobulus; *Sibylline Oracles* 3.98-808; Pseudo-Hecataeus; Pseudo-Phocylides; *2 Enoch; 3 Baruch; 3 Maccabees; 4 Maccabees; Letter of Aristeas*; Wisdom; the writings of Philo Judaeus; the writings of Flavius Josephus; the Alexandrian Text (K) of the Greek Old Testament (the LXX); *Treatise of Shem* (although *Treatise of Shem* was probably originally written in either Hebrew or Aramaic, I list it among the diaspora literature due to its provenance, which, according to J.H. Charlesworth, was probably Alexandria [*Old Testament Pseudepigrapha*, I, p. 475]); *Apocryphon of Ezekiel; Apocalypse of Zephaniah; Testament of Job; Ladder of Jacob; Prayer of Joseph; Orphica*; Fragments of Pseudo-Greek Poets; Aristeas the Exegete; Pseudo-Eupolemus. *Joseph and Aseneth* has been excluded from consideration due to its possible 2nd-century AD (or later) origin and evidence of Christian interpolations. See T. Holtz, 'Christliche Interpolationen in "Joseph und Aseneth"', *NTS* 14 (1967–8), pp. 482-97.

Subsections which focus on a single author are arranged (with the exception of Josephus) in chronological order. These works may be dated as follows: (1) LXX (3rd century BC). The *Letter of Aristeas* places the writing of the LXX during the reign of King Ptolemy II Philadelphus (284–247 BC). Although the legendary nature of the account is not to be disputed, the date of composition is likely close to the mark. (2) The writings of Josephus (c. 90 AD). This date is widely recognized and confirmed by Josephus' own hand. (3) Wisdom of Solomon (1st century BC). The dating of Wisdom remains a matter of dispute. Although Wisdom is generally placed in the 1st century BC, possible dates range from the mid-2nd century BC to the mid-1st century AD. (4) The writings of Philo (c. 25 BC). This date is commonly accepted and substantiated by autobiographical comments.

cepts as 'wind, breath, and air', in the LXX the association with divinity becomes quite common. Similarly, although the Greeks frequently alluded to prophetic inspiration, they rarely connected this inspiration with πνεῦμα.[1] However, in the LXX the πνεῦμα of God is routinely depicted as the source of prophetic inspiration. Indeed, apart from the inspiration of the Spirit, genuine prophecy is an impossibility.

For the translators of the LXX the characteristic activity of the Spirit was prophecy (e.g. Num. 11.25f.; 1 Kgdms 10.6f.; Ezek. 2.2f.). The close association between the Spirit and prophetic activity is particularly evident in two instances where πνεῦμα is inserted into the text although in the MT רוח is conspicuously absent:

1.   In Num. 23.7, just before Balaam utters his prophecy, the LXX inserts the phrase: καὶ ἐγενήθη πνεῦμα θεοῦ ἐπ' αὐτῷ.[2] The phrase ותהי עליו רוח אלהים does occur in the MT at 24.2 with reference to Balaam. Thus, the LXX translator has picked up this phrase and not only translated it as it appears in 24.2, but also inserted it into 23.7, showing his penchant for attributing prophecy to the Spirit.

2.   In Zech. 1.6, the word of the Lord came to Zechariah: πλὴν τοὺς λόγους μου καὶ τὰ νόμιμά μου δέχεσθε, ὅσα ἐγὼ ἐντέλλομαι ἐν πνεύματί μου τοῖς δούλοις μου τοῖς προφήταις. The phrase ἐν πνεύματί μου is absent from the MT and indicates how closely this particular translator associated prophetic inspiration with the Spirit.

In short, the concept of πνεῦμα is given broader definition through its association with רוח of the MT. Of primary importance for this study is the way in which various translators of the LXX equate prophetic inspiration with the activity of the Spirit.

2. *Diaspora Judaism: Various Texts*

Although the activity of the Spirit is not a prominent theme in much of the hellenistic Jewish literature of the intertestamental period, there are scattered references outside of Josephus, Philo, and Wisdom which deserve attention.

---

1. M. Isaacs, *The Concept of Spirit* (1976), p. 15. She notes as exceptions Euripides, *Fr.* 192, and Democritus, *Fr.* 18, where πνεῦμα plays a role in the inspiration of priests and poets; and the use of πνεῦμα with reference to divination in the descriptions of the Pythia at Delphi.
2. All texts of the LXX cited are from A. Rahlfs, *Septuaginta* (1979).

2.1. *The Spirit As the Source of Prophetic Inspiration*

When reference is made in this literature[1] to the divine πνεῦμα, it almost always appears as the source of prophetic activity (inspiring speech or granting special knowledge). For Aristobulus, prophecy and Spirit-inspiration are inextricably bound together. Eusebius records his claim that intelligent people 'marvel at the wisdom of Moses καὶ τὸ θεῖον Πνεῦμα, καθ' ὃ καὶ προφήτης ἀνακεκήρυκται'.[2] The κατά-clause indicates that Moses was proclaimed a prophet because of the marvelous activity of the Spirit in his life.

In The History of Susanna the story is told of how young Daniel, equipped with special insight and wisdom, was able to expose the treachery of two witnesses whose false testimony had condemned Susanna of adultery. The LXX attributes this special wisdom to an Angel, who gave a 'spirit of understanding' (πνεῦμα συνέσεως) to young Daniel (LXX, Sus. 45). However, Theodotion alters the LXX reading and attributes Daniel's special insight directly to the Holy Spirit. According to Theodotion, 'God stirred the Holy Spirit' (ἐξήγειρεν ὁ θεὸς τὸ πνεῦμα τὸ ἅγιον) already present in Daniel (Theodotion, Sus. 45).[3] There is no mention here of angelic mediation of the knowledge. Both angelic assistance (Dan. 9.21; 10.5) and the power of the Spirit (Dan. 4.9, 18; 5.11) are associated with the adult Daniel. Apparently the former tradition was picked up by the author of the LXX reading and the latter by Theodotion.[4]

One Greek manuscript of *Testament of Job* 43.2 attributes Eliphas's recital of a hymn to the inspiration of the Spirit.[5] Inspired praise is also associated with the Spirit in 48.3:

> She [Hemera] spoke ecstatically in the angelic dialect, sending up a hymn to God in accord with the hymnic style of the angels. And as she spoke ecstatically, she allowed 'The Spirit' to be inscribed on her garment.[6]

---

1. 'This literature' includes all those works cited as sources for diaspora Judaism in the introductory section, excluding those works dealt with separately: The LXX, Josephus, the works of Philo, and Wisdom.

2. Fragment 2 of Aristobulus in Eusebius, *Praeparatio Evangelica* 8.10.4; the text cited is from A.-M. Denis, *Fragmenta Pseudepigraphorum Quae Supersunt Graeca* (1970), p. 218.

3. Theodotion tends to add ἅγιον to πνεῦμα (see Sus 45; Dan. 4.8, 9, 18; 5.12; cf. Ps. 142.10 LXX).

4. This hypothesis is put forward by C.A. Moore, *Daniel, Esther, and Jeremiah: The Additions* (2nd edn, 1978), p. 108.

5. See R.P. Spittler, 'Testament of Job', in Charlesworth, *Pseudepigrapha*, I, p. 861 n. a on ch. 43. Spittler notes that manuscript P contains a reference to the Spirit here and in 51.2.

6. ET from Spittler, 'Testament of Job', p. 866.

We have seen that isolated diaspora texts, in a manner consistent with the translators of the LXX, present the Spirit as the source of prophetic activity. The only exceptions depict the divine πνεῦμα as the breath of God which gives physical life to all humans. Thus we read: 'the Spirit is a loan of God (θεοῦ χρῆσις) to mortals' (Pseudo-Phocylides 106).[1] 2 *Enoch* lists seven components of the human being. The seventh is 'his spirit from my [God's] spirit and from wind' (30.8).[2]

The lack of Spirit-references in other contexts indicates that experience of the Spirit was virtually identified with prophetic inspiration. Although Prayer of Manasseh 7b-15 is similar to Ps. 51.1-14 in both structure and content,[3] the text is silent concerning the Spirit. Psalm 51.11a, 'do not banish me', is paralleled in v. 13 of the Prayer, but Ps. 51.11b, 'do not take your Holy Spirit from me', is remarkably absent.

2.2. *Wisdom, the Law, and Reason: the Source of True Religion*
Esoteric wisdom can be associated with the inspiration of the Spirit in the diaspora literature (e.g. Theodotion, Sus. 45). However, at a more fundamental level wisdom is virtually identified with rational study of the Law. This is certainly the case in the definition of wisdom we read in *4 Macc.* 1.15-19:

> Reason, I suggest, is the mind making a deliberate choice of the life of wisdom. Wisdom (σοφία), I submit, is knowledge of things divine and human, and of their causes. And this wisdom, I assume, is the culture we acquire from the Law (αὕτη δὴ τοίνυν ἐστιν ἡ τοῦ νόμου παιδεία), through which we learn the things of God reverently and the things of men to our worldly advantage. The forms of wisdom consist of prudence, justice, courage, and temperance. Of all these prudence (φρόνησις) is the most authoritative, for it is through it that reason controls the passions (ἐξ ἧς δὴ τῶν παθῶν ὁ λογισμὸς ἐπικρατεῖ).[4]

In this text the source of wisdom is the instruction of the law (ἡ τοῦ νόμου παιδεία). The most significant outworking of wisdom is φρόνησις, for through 'prudence' the passions are controlled by rea-

---

1. ET from P.W. van der Horst, 'Pseudo-Phocylides', in Charlesworth, *Pseudepigrapha*, II, p. 578; Greek text from Denis, *Fragmenta Pseudepigraphorum Graeca*, p. 152.

2. ET from F.I. Andersen, '2 (Slavonic Apocalypse of) Enoch', in Charlesworth, *Pseudepigrapha*, I, p. 151. Extant manuscripts of 2 *Enoch* are only available in Slavonic, therefore the underlying Greek text is unavailable.

3. For the parallels between Prayer of Manasseh and Psalm 51 see Charlesworth, *Pseudepigrapha*, II, p. 630.

4. ET from H. Anderson, '4 Maccabees', in Charlesworth, *Pseudepigrapha*, II, p. 545.

son. Similarly the link between the law and the intellect (νοῦς) is made in 2.23, 'To the intellect he gave the Law, and if a man lives his life by the Law he shall reign over a kingdom that is temperate and just and good and brave'. Here again the virtues of wisdom result as the mind or intellect follows after the law.[1]

The entire book of *4 Maccabees* extols the triumph of reason over the passions. Eleazer, the seven sons, and their mother, all tortured and killed by Antiochus for not eating unclean food, are offered as examples of the triumph of reason over passion, of the victory of true religion centered on the law. The martyrs are vindicated, for resurrection is the ultimate reward of such a life (17.18; 18.18; 18.23).

According to the author of *4 Maccabees*, the source of true religion is the intellect informed by the Law rather than the illumination of the Spirit. Thus, while esoteric wisdom is attributed to the Spirit in the literature, sapiential achievement at a more fundamental level is associated with rational study of Torah, independent of Spirit-illumination.

2.3. *Sources of Miraculous Power*

Although prophetic activity is frequently attributed to the agency of the Spirit,[2] miraculous events not associated with inspired speech or special revelation are always attributed to other sources: angels, the name of God, and God himself. According to The Hymn of the Three Young Men, an angel of the Lord saved the Hebrew men from the heat of the furnace (LXX: Dan. 3.49). It is also an angel who carries Enoch away into the highest heaven (*2 En.* 67.2).

Artapanus attributes miraculous power to the will of God and the divine name. He records how Moses, who had requested the release of his people, was locked in prison by the king of Egypt. When night came, according to Eusebius's account, 'all of the doors of the prison opened of themselves' (*Pr. Ev.* 9.27.23). Clement of Alexandria, however, says the prison was opened at night 'by the will of God' (κατὰ βούλησιν τοῦ θεοῦ; *Stromata* 1.154.2).[3] Moses went to the palace of

---

1. See also 18.1-2.

2. Of course there are numerous instances where prophetic activity is recorded without reference to the Spirit. In the *Sibylline Oracles* descriptions of the prophetic state emphasize the compulsion of the prophet, but nowhere is this inspired or possessed state attributed to the Spirit of God (e.g. 3.295). See also Pseduo-Phocylides 129; Artapanus as cited in Eusebius, *Pr. Ev.* 9.27.21; and Theodotus as cited in *Pr. Ev.* 9.22.9. For dreams and visions see Ezekiel the Tragedian in the texts cited in *Pr. Ev.* 9.28-29 and Clement of Alexandria, *Stromata* 1.23.155f.; *Apocalypse of Zephaniah* 6.1; and *Ladder of Jacob* 1.3; 3.2.

3. ET from J.J. Collins, 'Artapanus', in Charlesworth, *Pseudepigrapha*, II, p. 901. Greek text from Denis, *Fragmenta Pseudepigraphorum Graecae*, p. 192.

the king and woke him. Frightened, the king ordered Moses to declare the name of the God who had sent him. Eusebius then records these climactic events:

> He bent forward and pronounced it [the divine name] into his ear. When the king heard it, he fell down speechless (ἀκούσαντα δὲ τὸν Βασιλέα πεσεῖν ἄφωνον) (*Pr. Ev.* 9.27.25).[1]

3. *Josephus*

When citing the Old Testament, Josephus retains the usage of πνεῦμα with reference to wind and breath. However, he is reluctant to employ πνεῦμα with reference to the spirit of humanity, and this usage virtually disappears.[2] When πνεῦμα refers to God, Josephus is much more apt to retain it, although he does prefer πνεῦμα θεῖον to the πνεῦμα θεοῦ of the LXX. Of special importance for this study is the significance Josephus attaches to πνεῦμα as the Spirit of God. Josephus has left us important clues concerning his own perception of the role of the Spirit of God through his alterations of the Old Testament text. To these clues I now turn.

3.1. *Additions of* πνεῦμα *to the LXX and/or MT*
On four occasions Josephus inserts πνεῦμα into texts where it is not present in the MT or the LXX, but is found in the immediate context. In *Ant.* 4.108, citing Num. 22.15f., Josephus introduces the idea that Balaam's ass was conscious of the πνεῦμα of God. The Spirit draws near to the ass and the ass then begins to speak with a human voice. Although the MT (24.2) and the LXX (23.7; 24.2) refer to the Spirit coming upon Balaam, neither speaks of the Spirit with reference to the ass. Josephus thus adds the idea that the speech of the ass, like the prophecy of Balaam, was inspired by the divine πνεῦμα. Similarly, in *Ant.* 4.119f., Josephus alters the MT and LXX reading of Num. 23.12 so that Balaam's prophetic speech is attributed to the πνεῦμα θεοῦ rather than to God.[3] Josephus's text emphasizes the passivity of Balaam

---

1. The text of Clement of Alexandria at this point is almost identical. Greek text is from Denis, *Fragmenta Pseudepigraphorum Graeca*, pp. 192-93. Cf. C.R. Holladay, *Fragments from Hellenistic Jewish Authors. I. Historians* (1983), p. 218.

2. Josephus usually replaces πνεῦμα as the spirit of humans with either a personal pronoun or ψυχή (E. Best, 'The Use and Non-Use of Pneuma by Josephus', *NovT* 3 [1959], pp. 219-20).

3. See F. Manns, *Le symbole eau-esprit* (1983), p. 149. This is the only instance where Josephus uses πνεῦμα θεοῦ; as noted above, he prefers the term πνεῦμα θεῖον.

and the compulsion of the Spirit. In *Ant.* 6.166, Josephus expands the account of the Spirit's transfer from Saul to David (1 Kgdms 16.13-14) by noting that David began to prophesy when the Spirit came upon him. And in an interpretative retelling of 1 Kgs 22.21-25, one of Josephus' characters declares, 'you shall know whether he is really a true prophet and has the power of the divine Spirit' (καὶ τοῦ θείου πνεύματος ἔχει τὴν δύναμιν; *Ant.* 8.408).[1]

In each addition cited above, the πνεῦμα of God is portrayed as the source of prophecy. This is even more striking when it is noted that in those passages where Josephus retains the biblical reference to the Spirit, all but one (*Ant.* 1.27 = Gen. 1.2) refer to the divine πνεῦμα as the source of prophetic inspiration.[2] However, Josephus never speaks of contemporary prophets as being inspired by the Spirit. He was undoubtedly convinced that prophecy inspired by the Spirit was a thing of the past.[3]

There is one addition of the divine πνεῦμα into an Old Testament context in which reference to the Spirit is wholly lacking. *Antiquities* 8.114 (1 Kgs 8.27-30) records Solomon's entreaty to the Lord, 'send some portion of your Spirit to dwell in the temple'. Josephus may have interpreted Solomon's request as a plea for the bestowal of the prophetic gift upon the temple priests. Or possibly, as Ernest Best suggests, Josephus replaced 'Shekinah', a term that would have been strange to Greeks, with πνεῦμα.[4]

3.2. *Omission and Interpretation of* πνεῦμα

Josephus not only adds references concerning God's πνεῦμα to Old Testament texts; he also omits such references, replacing them with interpretative comments. In a number of passages where the LXX

---

1. All citations from Josephus (English and Greek) are from H.J. Thackeray (ed.), *Josephus* (LCL, 1926-65).

2. Passages in which Josephus retains references to the πνεῦμα of God paralleled in the LXX or MT are: *Ant.* 1.27 (Gen. 1.2); *Ant.* 4.118 (Num. 23.7); *Ant.* 6.222 (1 Sam. 19.20); *Ant.* 6.223 (1 Sam. 19.23); *Ant.* 10.239 (Dan. 5.14—MT only). All these passages associate God's πνεῦμα with prophecy except *Ant.* 1.27 (Gen. 1.2). Best justifiably downplays the significance of this lone exception: 'with the exception of 1. 27 = Gen. 1.2 the divine πνεῦμα is thus connected with the gift of oracular or prophetic speech. . . In 1. 27 πνεῦμα plays no clear role; loyalty to such an important passage of Scripture demands its retention; a Greek could easily take it to mean "wind" or "breath"' ('Josephus', p. 223).

3. See Isaacs, *Spirit*, p. 49.; M.A. Chevallier, *Souffle de dieu: Le Saint-Esprit dans le Nouveau Testament* (1978), p. 73; W. Bieder, 'πνεῦμα', *TDNT*, VI, p. 375; Best, 'Josephus', p. 224.

4. Best, 'Josephus', p. 223.

explicitly speaks of the Spirit coming upon individuals, Josephus alters the text to say that they prophesied. Thus while in Judg. 13.25 we read of Samson 'the Spirit of the Lord began to stir him'; in *Ant.* 5.285 Josephus writes 'it was clear. . . that he was to be a prophet'. Similarly Joshua (*Ant.* 4.165 = Num. 27.18), Azariah (*Ant.* 8.295 = 2 Chron. 15.1), Zechariah (*Ant.* 9.168 = 2 Chron. 24.20), and Jahaziel (*Ant.* 9.10 = 2 Chron. 20.14) all prophesy.

It is noteworthy that Samson, who was endowed with special strength to defeat the Philistines, is called a prophet by Josephus (*Ant.* 5.285). Here Josephus used the term 'prophet' in a rather broad way. This usage appears to suggest that Josephus attributed the working of miracles and great exploits of strength to the Spirit. However, Josephus' omission of the Spirit in contexts where miracles and special exploits are mentioned indicates that this is not the case. According to Judg. 14.6, the Spirit of the Lord came upon Samson and enabled him to tear apart a lion. Yet in *Ant.* 5.287 no mention is made of the activity of the Spirit. Again in Judg. 14.19 Samson, inspired by the Spirit, is said to have killed thirty Philistines; the record of this story in *Ant.* 5.294 omits any reference to the Spirit. According to Judg. 15.14-15, the Spirit of the Lord enabled Samson to break his bonds and kill a thousand Philistines with the Jawbone of an ass. Yet in *Ant.* 5.301 the feat is attributed simply to θεοῦ συνεργίαν. Other exploits, such as the miraculous transportation of Elijah (*Ant.* 8.333 = 1 Kgs 18.12), the interpretation of dreams by Joseph (*Ant.* 2.87 = Gen. 41.38), and the special skills given to craftsmen (*Ant.* 3.200 = Exod. 28.3; 32.3; 35.31), although attributed to the Spirit in the LXX, are not explicitly connected with the divine πνεῦμα by Josephus.[1]

The omission of πνεῦμα in these texts indicates that Josephus viewed the Spirit exclusively as the source of esoteric wisdom and inspired speech. This perspective is consistent with the close association between the Spirit and prophecy we find elsewhere in Josephus' writings. For prophecy is the transmission of esoteric wisdom through inspired speech. Josephus' perspective also conforms to the general pattern of Jewish thought in the intertestamental period. The actions of the prophet were not limited to oracular prophecy by either Josephus (e.g. Samson, *Ant.* 5.285) or his contemporaries (*Ant.* 20.167-68; *Wars* 2.259). Indeed, Josephus ridicules leaders of revolutionary movements as 'false prophets' who promised to perform legitimating miracles (*Ant.* 20.168). Nevertheless, the Jewish authors of the period,

1. See Manns, *Symbole*, p. 147 n. 33; and Best, 'Josephus', pp. 224-25.

like Josephus, exhibit a remarkable reluctance to attribute miraculous deeds to the Spirit.[1]

4. *Wisdom of Solomon*

The author of Wisdom employs πνεῦμα with a variety of meanings. The term refers to breath or wind;[2] a permeating force which 'fills the world' and holds all things together (Wis. 1.7); the source of physical life; and the source of wisdom. The references to πνεῦμα which fall into the latter two categories shall form the basis of this analysis.

4.1. *Πνεῦμα as the Source of Physical Life*

As the source of physical life, πνεῦμα refers to a permanent gift which God grants to every human at creation. The author of Wisdom states that God's 'immortal Spirit' (τὸ ἄφθαρτον πνεῦμα) is in everyone (12.1). Thus he chastises the idol-maker, 'because he never came to know the God who shaped him, who inspired him with an active soul and breathed into him a living spirit' (πνεῦμα ζωτικόν; 15.11), and repudiates idolatry, for idols are made by a person 'who borrowed his spirit' (τὸ πνεῦμα δεδανεισμένος; 15.16).

4.2. *Πνεῦμα as the Source of Wisdom*

The author of Wisdom also identifies the Spirit of God with the wisdom of God. He uses the terms πνεῦμα and σοφία interchangeably (Wis. 1.4-7; 9.17), refers to the 'spirit of wisdom' (πνεῦμα σοφίας; 7.7; cf. 7.22), and describes wisdom as 'a breath of God's power' (ἀτμὶς. . . τῆς τοῦ θεοῦ δυνάμεως; 7.25). He also transfers functions normally reserved for the Spirit to wisdom. The Spirit is frequently cited in the diaspora literature as the source of special insight granted to leaders (*Amtscharisma*).[3] Nevertheless, in Wisdom this role is taken over by wisdom; wisdom made Joseph the ruler of Egypt (10.14) and enabled Moses to stand up to Pharaoh (10.16). Prophecy, elsewhere in the literature attributed to the inspiration of the Spirit, is also

---

1. Miracles are attributed to other sources, such as the δύναμις of God. After retelling the story of Elisha's death and burial, including the incident concerning the resurrection of the dead man who came into contact with Elisha's dead body (*Ant.* 9.182f. = 2 Kgs 13.20f.), Josephus notes that 'even after death he [Elisha] still had divine power' (ἔτι δύναμιν εἶχε θείαν; *Ant.* 9.183).

2. For πνεῦμα as breath see Wis. 2.3; 5.3; and 11.20. For πνεῦμα as wind or air see Wis. 5.11, 23; 7.20; 13.2; 17.18.

3. See for example Josephus, *Ant.* 6.166 (1 Kgdms 16.13-14) and Philo, *Gig.* 24 (Num. 11.17).

associated with wisdom (7.27; 11.1). It is therefore difficult to distinguish between πνεῦμα and σοφία. However, as R. Scroggs notes, several texts suggest that 'σοφία is more the content of revelation, while πνεῦμα is the means by which this content is revealed'.[1] Thus it appears that the identification of Spirit and wisdom in Wisdom should be seen principally in terms of function: wisdom is experienced through the Spirit.

The author of Wisdom clearly distinguishes the divine πνεῦμα, which all possess as the principle of life, from the Spirit of wisdom.[2] As the source of wisdom, the Spirit is granted only to those who humbly ask for it in prayer (7.7; cf. 8.20-21; 9.4). It is withheld from the impious (1.5).[3] The character of this pneumatic gift is given clearest expression in Solomon's prayer:

> Who has learned your will, unless you gave him wisdom, and sent your Holy Spirit from on high (ἔπεμψας τὸ ἅγιόν σου πνεῦμα ἀπὸ ὑψίστων)? In this way people on earth have been set on the right path, have learned what pleases you, and have been saved by wisdom (καὶ τῇ σοφίᾳ ἐσώθησαν) (Wis. 9.17-18).

I have noted that the Spirit is frequently cited in diaspora texts as the source of esoteric wisdom.[4] The perspective of Wis. 9.17-18 is unique in that every level of sapiential achievement, from the lowest to the highest, is attributed to the gift of the Spirit.[5] Indeed, apart from the illumination of the Spirit the will of God cannot be known. Thus the author of Wisdom views the gift of the Spirit as the essential source of moral and religious life. As such, it is necessary to possess the gift of the Spirit in order to attain salvation.[6] Although the σώζω of v.18

---

1. R. Scroggs, 'Paul: ΣΟΦΟΣ and ΠΝΕΥΜΑΤΙΚΟΣ', *NTS* 14 (1967), p. 50. Scroggs cites Wis. 1.4-7; 7.22f.; and particularly 9.17 in this regard.

2. G. Verbeke, *L'évolution de la doctrine du Pneuma* (1945), pp. 228-30.

3. J. Dunn, *Christology in the Making* (1980), p. 173: 'For all that the author of the Wisdom of Solomon uses the language of Stoicism, he has not the slightest thought of equating wisdom with some pantheistic ultimate reason'. On the differences between the pneumatological perspectives of Wisdom and Stoicism see J. Laporte, 'Philo in the Tradition of Biblical Wisdom Literature', in *Aspects of Wisdom in Judaism and Early Christianity* (1975), p. 119; Verbeke, *Pneuma*, pp. 225-27, 233-36; and Scroggs, 'ΠΝΕΥΜΑΤΙΚΟΣ', p. 48.

4. See for example Sus. 45 (Theodotion); Eusebius, *Pr. Ev.* 8.10.4; and Josephus, *Ant.* 8.408.

5. See Chapter 13 §1 below.

6. Vos writes: 'Die Weisheit, und damit die Gerechtigkeit, durch die man anteil am Heil bekommt, wird in der Sapientia Salomonis durchweg als Wirkung des göttlichen Geistes betrachtet' (*Untersuchungen*, p. 64).

may refer principally to physical preservation,[1] elsewhere immortality and authority over the nations are promised to the righteous and wise (Wis. 3.1-9; cf. 5.1-23).[2]

J.C. Rylaarsdam correctly notes that the author of Wisdom, through the identification of wisdom with Spirit, has transformed the concept of wisdom.[3] The important corollary is that this identification has also transformed the concept of the Spirit.[4] In contrast to his contemporaries discussed below, the author of Wisdom does not view the gift of the Spirit as a *donum superadditum* which enables prophets or sages to fulfill their divinely ordained task. Rather, the gift of the Spirit is the essential source of moral and religious life; and as such, it is a soteriological necessity.[5]

5. Philo

G. Verbeke notes that Philo, significantly influenced by hellenistic philosophy, employs the term πνεῦμα in four distinct ways.[6] Philo uses the term with reference to one of the four elements, air (*Gig.* 22);[7] an immaterial force which links material elements together

1. See Wis. 10.4; 14.4, 5; 16.7, 11; 18.5.
2. See also Wis. 6.18; 8.13, 17; 15.3.
3. J.C. Rylaarsdam, *Revelation in Jewish Literature* (1946), pp. 116-17: 'Thus, by interpreting the concept of Divine Wisdom as Spirit, the Wisdom of Solomon rendered inestimable service to the former; and, by transferring the functions of the Spirit to Wisdom, by making Wisdom the source of prophecy, and by affirming that Divine Wisdom came directly into human consciousness and experience, it assured to Divine Wisdom the same capacity of contemporaneity that was enjoyed by Spirit'.
4. G.T. Montague alludes to the impact of the wisdom tradition upon the theology of the Spirit: 'Enriched by the prophetic stream, wisdom brought to the theology of the spirit, long thought to be the peculiar gift of the prophet, an important relationship to the experiential, the daily living of God's revealed way, his wisdom. Paul, for example, would never have thought of praying that his readers be filled with the spirit of wisdom and discernment for daily living (Phil. 1.9; Col. 1.9-10; Eph. 1.15) had the way not been prepared by the wisdom tradition' (*The Holy Spirit: Growth of a Biblical Tradition* [1976], p. 110).
5. Vos, *Untersuchungen*, p. 65: 'Die inspirierte Weisheit, die früher nur besonderen Personen zu besonderen Anlässen zugebilligt wurde, ist jetzt im Rahmen des dualistischen Weltbildes heilsnotwendig'.
6. Verbeke, *Pneuma*, pp. 237-51.
7. See also *Ebr.* 106; *Cher.* 111; and *Op. Mund.* 29–30. The term is also used with reference to wind (*Op. Mund.* 41; *Abr.* 92) and breath (*Vit. Mos.* 1. 93; *Deus Immut.* 84). A. Laurentin argues contra Verbeke that Philo distinguishes between πνεῦμα and air, and does not view the former as an element ('Le Pneuma dans la doctrine de Philon', *ETL* 27 [1951], pp. 391-404). However, Verbeke's

(*Deus Immut.* 35-36);[1] the rational aspect of the human soul (*Leg. All.* 1.32f.); and prophetic inspiration (*Gig.* 24). I shall confine my analysis to the latter two usages mentioned.

5.1. *Πνεῦμα as the Rational Aspect of the Soul*

Philo states that the essence of the soul common to humans and animals is 'blood', but the essence of the 'intelligent and reasonable' (νοερᾶς καὶ λογικῆς) soul is πνεῦμα θεῖον (*Spec. Leg.* 4.123).[2] According to Philo, this divine πνεῦμα is breathed into every human soul at creation. It makes the mind (the νοῦς), which is the highest element of the soul, rational and capable of knowing God (*Leg. All.* 1.31-38).[3] Although the soul which allows the mind to be dominated by the desires of the body may, in some sense, die (*Leg. All.* 1.105-108),[4] the potential for immortality is resident in the divine gift of πνεῦμα, the mind or rational aspect of the soul, granted to every soul at creation.[5]

Philo, like the author of Wisdom, thus affirms that it is necessary to receive the gift of πνεῦμα in order to know the will of God and attain immortality. However, in contrast to the author of Wisdom, Philo

interpretation has been accepted by Bieder, 'πνεῦμα', p. 372; Hill, *Greek Words*, p. 223; and J. Davis, *Wisdom and Spirit* (1984), p. 54. See also M. Pulver, 'Das Erlebnis des Pneuma bei Philon', *EJ* 13 (1945), pp. 115f.

1. See also *Rer. Div. Her.* 242; and *Op. Mund.* 131.

2. All citations of Philonic texts (Greek and English) are from F.H. Colson and G.H. Whitaker, *Philo* (10 vols. and 2 suppl. vols.; LCL, 1929–1962).

3. See also *Op. Mund.* 135; *Det. Pot. Ins.* 80–90; *Plant.* 18–22; and *Congr.* 97. B.A. Pearson, 'Hellenistic-Jewish Wisdom Speculation and Paul' in *Aspects of Wisdom in Judaism and Early Christianity* (1975), p. 54: 'For Philo, man has within him, breathed into him by God, the capacity for knowing God and the higher truths of the universe'.

4. See also *Quaest. in Gen.* 1.16, 51; *Rer. Div. Her.* 52–57, 242–45; *Poster. C.* 39.

5. See *Leg. All.* 1.31-38, the references cited above, and the following secondary literature: A. Wolfson, *Philo* (1948), I, pp. 393-413; Verbeke, *Pneuma*, p. 242; Leisegang, *Der Heilige Geist*, pp. 76-102; Laurentin, 'Le Pneuma', p. 411; D.T. Runia, *Philo of Alexandria and the Timaeus of Plato* (1986), pp. 336-38; B.A. Pearson, *The Pneumatikos-Psychikos Terminology* (1973), pp. 18-21. Philo is not entirely consistent on this point (cf. *Leg. All.* 1.42, where Philo states that the less substantial πνοή rather than πνεῦμα is given to the earthly being at creation). However, as M.J. Weaver notes, 'that the πνεῦμα is sent to man at creation is more particularly Philo's view' ('Πνεῦμα in Philo of Alexandria' [1973], pp. 75-77, quote from p. 76; cf. T. Tobin, *The Creation of Man: Philo and the History of Interpretation* [1983], esp. pp. 128-29).

maintains that this gift has been given to all at creation.[1] This unique emphasis on the universality of the gift of the Spirit enables Philo to affirm the centrality of divine grace without forfeiting human responsibility.[2] Philo's perspective is given clear expression in *Leg. All.* 1.33f., where he seeks to explain 'why God deemed the earthly and body-loving mind worthy of the divine breath'. In his initial response Philo emphasizes God's gracious character: God loves to give good things to all, 'even those who are not perfect' (καὶ τοῖς μὴ τελείοις), thus 'encouraging them to seek and participate in virtue' (προκαλούμενος αὐτοὺς εἰς μετουσίαν καὶ ζῆλον ἀρετῆς). Philo then points to the important corollary: since all have the capacity to seek virtue, none without virtue can claim that God punishes them unjustly.

5.2. *Πνεῦμα as the Source of Prophetic Inspiration*
There is a sense in which the divine πνεῦμα is not the permanent possession of every human being.[3] As the source of prophetic inspiration,[4] the gift of the Spirit is reserved for a select group[5] and temporary in nature.[6] The recipient of the gift is granted special insight and persuasiveness of speech.

According to Philo, there are three types of knowledge:[7] knowledge ascertained through the senses by observation; knowledge that is attained through philosophical reflection;[8] and the highest form of knowledge, 'pure knowledge' (*Gig.* 22), which transcends reason.[9] 'Pure knowledge' is attained through an experience of Spirit-inspired prophetic ecstasy 'given only to a relatively few good and wise men'.[10] The ecstatic nature of this experience is frequently emphasized by

---

1. Isaacs, *Spirit*, p. 42: 'Philo seems to think that, as guide to right values, it [πνεῦμα] is the possession of all'.
2. Verbeke, *Pneuma*, pp. 243-44.
3. The relationship between the Spirit as the rational aspect of the soul (possessed by all) and the Spirit as the source of prophetic inspiration (possessed by only a few) is never clarified by Philo. See A.J.M. Wedderburn, *Baptism and Resurrection* (1987), pp. 272-73, and Chevallier, *Souffle*, p. 72.
4. For the term προφητικὸν πνεῦμα see *Fug.* 3 and *Vit. Mos.* 1.50, 277.
5. Thus Philo excludes the wicked from prophetic inspiration: 'the wicked may never be the interpreter of God or God-inspired [ἐνθουσιᾷ]' (*Rer. Div. Her.* 259).
6. See *Gig.* 20f.; *Quaest. in Gen.* 1.90; and *Deus Immut.* 2.
7. Davis, *Wisdom*, p. 52.
8. Davis notes that for Philo the ultimate source of philosophical reflection is the Law (*Wisdom*, p. 52).
9. *Gig.* 13f. Note also Wolfson, *Philo*, II, pp. 7-10.
10. Pearson, *Pneumatikos-Psychikos*, p. 45.

Philo.[1] He describes the prophetic state in terms of 'inspired frenzy' (θεοφορηθεῖσα; *Rer. Div. Her.* 69), 'divine intoxication' (θεία μέθη; *Leg. All.* 3.82)[2] and 'ecstasy' (ἔκστασις; *Rer. Div. Her.* 249, 265-66).

Philo gives numerous examples of the revelatory power of the Spirit of prophecy. Moses, the prophet *par excellence*,[3] is given special wisdom so that he can lead the nation (*Vit. Mos.* 2.40). When the children of Israel became despondent during their flight from the Egyptians, Moses gave them courage by prophesying their future deliverance (*Vit. Mos.* 2.246-52). Moses also issued prophetic words of guidance concerning the manna from heaven (*Vit. Mos.* 2.259f.) and the Sabbath (*Vit. Mos.* 2.263f.).

In *Gig.* 22 Philo declares that θεοῦ πνεῦμα is 'pure knowledge [ἀκήρατος ἐπιστήμη] which every wise man shares'. He supports the statement by citing two prooftexts from the Old Testament. A quotation from Exod. 31.2-3, 'God called up Bezaleel. . . and filled him with the divine spirit, with wisdom, understanding, and knowledge to devise in every work' (*Gig.* 23), is followed by an allusion to 'that spirit of perfect wisdom' (τοῦ πανσόφου πνεύματος ἐκείνου) which Moses imparted to the seventy elders (*Gig.* 24 = Num. 11.17).

The Spirit also enables the prophet to communicate the divine message with persuasive power.[4] Philo describes how the Spirit came upon Abraham and gave his words special persuasiveness (*Virt.* 216-19). The close association between the Spirit of prophecy and inspired speech is consistent with Philo's emphasis on the ecstatic nature of prophecy. In *Spec. Leg.* 4.49 Philo describes the prophet as a passive vehicle through which the Spirit speaks:

> For no pronouncement of a prophet is ever his own; he is an interpreter prompted by Another in all his utterances, when knowing not what he does he is filled with inspiration, as the reason withdraws and surrenders the citadel of the soul to a new visitor and tenant, the Divine Spirit which

1. Laporte, 'Philo', p. 119; Verbeke, *Pneuma*, pp. 252-53; Pulver, 'Das Erlebnis', pp. 127f.; and H. Lewy, *Sobria Ebrietas: Untersuchungen zur Geschichte der antiken Mystik* (1929), pp. 3-34.

2. See also *Fug.* 166; *Op. Mund.* 71; *Ebr.* 145f.

3. The prophetic Spirit may stay only a short while (*Gig.* 20), for humanity is flesh (*Gig.* 29). However, Moses was privileged to have the prophetic Spirit abide with him for a long time (*Gig.* 47). Cf. Artapanus (Eusebius, *Pr. Ev.* 9.27.23f.); Ezekiel the Tragedian (*Pr. Ev.* 9.29); *b. Yeb.* 49b; and *Sifra Lev.* 3b. For Moses as the eschatological prophet see R. Meyer, *Der Prophet aus Galiläa* (1970), p. 83; and Aune, *Prophecy*, pp. 124f.

4. On Philo's portrayal of the Spirit as the source of persuasive and eloquent speech see R.A. Horsley, 'Wisdom of Word and Words of Wisdom in Corinth', *CBQ* 39 (1977), pp. 225, 228, 235; and Davis, *Wisdom*, pp. 59, 62.

plays upon the vocal organism and dictates words which clearly express its prophetic message.[1]

It is possible, as Marie Isaacs suggests, that Philo limited the inspiration of the prophetic Spirit to the prophets of the biblical periods.[2] Although Philo speaks of prophetic inspiration as a contemporary reality,[3] he, like Josephus, never links contemporary prophecy to the inspiration of the Spirit.[4]

6. *Summary*

In the diaspora literature the Spirit of God almost always appears as the source of prophetic activity. As such, it inspires speech and grants esoteric wisdom. Sapiential achievement at a more fundamental level is attained through the study (unaided by the Spirit) of the Torah. The literature shows a general reluctance to associate the Spirit with miraculous deeds. Through the functional identification of Spirit and wisdom, the author of Wisdom breaks from his contemporaries and attaches soteriological significance to the pneumatic gift. He insists that the gift of the Spirit is the source of sapiential achievement at every level. Thus reception of the gift is necessary for one to know the will of God and attain immortality. Philo, with his conception of the Spirit as the rational element of the soul, offers the closest parallel to this perspective. However, in contrast to the author of Wisdom, Philo insists that this gift is granted to every human soul at creation. In Philo's perspective the pneumatic gift which is reserved for the pious is the Spirit of prophecy.

---

1. See also *Quaest. in Gen.* 3.9.
2. Isaacs, *Spirit*, p. 49. See also Wolfson, *Philo*, II, p. 54.
3. Philo claims that he has experienced prophetic inspiration (*Abr.* 35; *Migr. Abr.* 34f.; *Cher.* 27).
4. Isaacs suggests that an apologetic motive stands behind the reluctance of Philo and Josephus to speak of contemporary Spirit-inspired prophecy: 'They do not attribute this contemporary inspiration to the possession of the spirit. This they confine to the prophets of the biblical period. In so doing, they implicitly assert that the inspiration of the authors of scripture was qualitatively different from any subsequent insight' (*Spirit*, p. 49).

Chapter 3

THE PALESTINIAN LITERATURE[1]

1. *The Acquisition of Wisdom in Sirach*

For Ben Sira, the Law is the locus of wisdom.[2] The acquisition of wisdom is therefore inextricably linked to the study of the Law (6.37;

---

1. The sources examined include the following Jewish writings written in Palestine between 190 BC and AD 100, most of which were written in a Semitic language: *Jubilees*; *1 Enoch*; *Pseudo-Philo*; 1 Baruch; *Psalms of Solomon*; 1 Esdras; *4 Ezra*; Sirach; Tobit; Judith; 1 & 2 Maccabees (although 2 Maccabees was originally written in Greek, I include it among the Palestinian sources due to its close affinity to Palestinian Judaism; see R. Longenecker, *Paul: Apostle of Liberty* [1964], pp. 8, 12; and G. Stemberger, *Der Leib der Auferstehung* [1972], p. 8); *Testament of Moses*; *Life of Adam and Eve*; *The Lives of the Prophets*; *Eldad and Modad*; *More Psalms of David*; and *The Martyrdom of Isaiah*.

I have excluded the *Testaments of the Twelve Patriarchs* from examination in this section because they reflect a high degree of Christian influence. In the Testaments there are seven passages of importance which contain possible references to the Spirit of God: *T. Sim.* 4.4; *T. Lev.* 2.3; 18.7, 11; *T. Ben.* 9.3; *T. Jud.* 20.1f., 24.2. Of these seven passages, four (*T. Lev.* 18.7, 11; *T. Ben.* 9.3; *T. Jud.* 24.2) are undoubtedly of Christian origin. One (*T. Jud.* 20.1f.) parallels the 'two spirits' doctrine of 1QS 3.13–4.26 which I shall examine in the next chapter. The remaining two passages contain nothing distinctive.

Subsections which focus on a single author are arranged in chronological order. These works may be dated as follows: (1) Sirach (c. 180 BC). See G. Nickelsburg, *Jewish Literature between the Bible and the Mishnah* (1981), p. 55; and E. Schürer, *The History of the Jewish People* (1986), III, 1, p. 202; (2) *1 Enoch* (2nd century BC–1st century AD). *1 Enoch* is a composite work with many authors from a variety of periods. See E. Isaac, '1 (Ethiopic Apocalypse of) Enoch' in Charlesworth, *Pseudepigrapha*, I, pp. 6-7.

2. See Sir. 1.26; 3.22; 6.37; 15.1; 19.20; 21.11; 24.23; 33.3; 34.7f. E. Schnabel notes that the identification of law and wisdom 'which had been carried through most explicitly by Ben Sira was known, presupposed, implied and stated explicitly' by numerous other intertestamental writers (*Law and Wisdom from Ben Sira to Paul* [1985], p. 292). For Schnabel's detailed discussion of the identification of Law and wisdom in Sirach, see pp. 69-92. Note also Davis, *Wisdom*, pp. 9-16.

21.11; 15.1). However, Ben Sira can relate this nomistic wisdom[1] to the inspiration of the Spirit:

> He who devotes himself to the study of the law of the Most High will seek out the wisdom of all the ancients, and will be concerned with prophecies; he will preserve the discourse of notable men and penetrate the subtleties of parables; he will seek out the hidden meanings of proverbs and be at home with the obscurities of parables. He will serve among great men and appear before rulers; he will travel through the lands of foreign nations, for he tests the good and the evil among men. He will set his heart to rise early to seek the Lord who made him, and will make supplication before the Most High; he will open his mouth in prayer and make supplication for his sins. If the great Lord is willing, he will be filled with the spirit of understanding (πνεύματι συνέσεως ἐμπλησθήσεται); he will pour forth words of wisdom and give thanks to the Lord in prayer. He will reveal instruction in his teaching, and will glory in the law of the Lord's covenant (Sir. 39.1-8).

The term πνεύματι συνέσεως (39.6) undoubtedly refers to the wisdom which comes from the Spirit of God.[2] The anarthrous use of πνεῦμα is consistent with this claim. For in Sir. 48.24 we read that Isaiah looked into the future by means of a πνεύματι μεγάλῳ. Here the anarthrous πνεῦμα is clearly 'a circumlocution for the Spirit of God, the source of all true prophecy'.[3] Furthermore, the collocation of πνεῦμα and σύνεσις is frequently found in LXX with reference to wisdom imparted by the Spirit of God (Exod. 31.3; Deut. 34.9; Isa. 11.2). My judgment is confirmed by the context, which indicates that the Spirit of understanding is given in accordance with the will of the Lord (39.6a).

James Davis notes that in Sir. 38.24–39.11 three levels of sapiential achievement are delineated. The lowest level of sapiential achievement is achieved by those who work with their hands, farmers and craftsmen (38.25-34). A higher degree of wisdom is attained by the scribe who studies the law (39.1-5). The highest level of wisdom is reserved for the sage who receives the Spirit of understanding (39.6).[4] There-

---

1. Davis argues that the 'wisdom of the ancients' and 'prophecies' of v. 1 refer to the 'developing canonical corpus of prophecy and writings'; and vv. 2-3 speak of the 'haggadic' and 'halakic' interpretation of the law (*Wisdom*, pp. 17-18).
2. See Davis, *Wisdom*, pp. 20-22.
3. Davis, *Wisdom*, p. 164 n. 53.
4. Davis, *Wisdom*, pp. 16-21. H. Stadelmann distinguishes between 'der reguläre Schriftgelehrte' (Sir. 38.34c–39.5) and 'der inspirierte Schriftgelehrte' (Sir. 39.6-8; *Ben Sira als Schriftgelehrter* [1980], pp. 216-46). E. Schnabel, following G. Maier (*Mensch und freier Wille: Nach den jüdischen Religionsparteien zwischen Ben Sira und Paulus* [1971], p. 37) and H. Stadelmann (p. 234), states that the πνεύματι

fore, while Ben Sira attributes the highest level of sapiential achievement to the inspiration of the Spirit, he affirms that sapiential
achievement at a more fundamental level is attained exclusively
through the study of the Law.

The perspectives of Ben Sira and the author of *4 Maccabees* con-
verge at this point: both insist that wisdom can be attained by purely
rational means. This optimistic view of humanity's rational capacity is
reflected in Sir. 32.15: 'Study the Law and you will master it'. It is
also the presupposition upon which the call to responsible behavior is
based: 'If you wish, you can keep the commandments' (ἐὰν θέλῃς,
συντηρήσεις ἐντολάς; 15.15).

Ben Sira also portrays the gift of the Spirit as the source of inspired
speech. The scribe who is filled with the spirit of understanding 'will
pour forth words of wisdom' (αὐτὸς ἀνομβρήσει ῥήματα σοφίας;
39.6) and 'reveal instruction in his teaching' (αὐτὸς ἐκφανεῖ παιδείαν
διδασκαλίας αὐτοῦ; 39.8).[1] Enabled to see into the future by means
of spirit-inspiration, Isaiah is said to have revealed the hidden things to
come (48.25). Thus, according to Ben Sira, the Spirit endows the sage
or prophet with esoteric wisdom so that he can communicate it to
others.

2. *The Spirit in* 1 Enoch *and Jewish Apocalyptic*

2.1. *The Spirit and Divine Revelation*
References to the activity of the Spirit of God in *1 Enoch* are relatively rare.[2] Only three references to the divine Spirit are found in the
entire work (49.3; 62.2; 91.1), excluding the unusual passage in 99.16:
'He [God] will arouse the anger of his Spirit'.[3] Although the Ethiopic
texts refer to the Spirit in 99.16, the only extant Greek text of this passage, the *Chester Beatty* papryus (*1 En.* 97.6-104; 106f.), simply
refers to 'his anger' (τὸν θυμὸν αὐτοῦ).[4] In 91.1 the Spirit of God
appears as the source of prophetic activity: Enoch declares to his son,
Methuselah, 'a voice calls me, and the spirit is poured over me so that
I may show you everything that shall happen to you'.

σύνεσεως of 39.6 is 'not simply a professional characteristic feature of the scribe but
only a "gelegentliches donum superadditum"' (*Law and Wisdom*, p. 53).
   1. Cf. Sir. 24.30-34.
   2. For spirits of humans see 20.4f.; 22.3; 22.5; 22.7. For spirits of fallen angels
or evil spirits see for example: 15.8f.; 19.1. For the phrase 'Lord of the spirits' see
for example: 37.4; 38.2, 4, 6; 39.2, 7, 8, 9, 10, 12, 14; 40.2, 5, 6, etc.
   3. All texts from *1 Enoch* which are cited in English are from Isaac, '1 Enoch'.
   4. For the Greek text see M. Black, *Apocalypsis Henochi Graece* (1970), p. 40.

In 68.2 the 'power of the spirit' provokes the anger of the angel Michael on account of the severity of the judgment of the angels. Rather than a reference to the spirit of God, this phrase speaks of Michael's emotional state in terms of his spirit.[1] According to 70.2, Enoch was taken up in 'a wind (or spirit) chariot'. The phrase probably refers to a whirlwind rather than the Spirit of God. In 2 Kgs 2.11, a biblical passage which is quite similar to 70.2, Elijah is caught up 'in a whirlwind' (בסערה). However, a reference to the Spirit's activity cannot be ruled out entirely, for in 2 Kgs 2.16 the sons of the prophets speculate, 'perhaps the Spirit of the Lord has taken him up and cast him on some mountain'.[2]

The revelation of esoteric wisdom is, of course, a prominent theme in *1 Enoch*. However, in *1 Enoch* (and in Jewish apocalyptic in general)[3] the Spirit is rarely cited as a revelatory agent.[4] Although the divine Spirit is occasionally cited as the source of special revelation (49.3; 62.2; 91.1), these few references stand in stark contrast to the numerous occasions where special revelation comes by means of angelic messengers[5] or visionary experiences.[6]

2.2. *The Spirit and the Messiah*

There are numerous references in *1 Enoch* to the Messiah as a supernatural figure. Various names are given to the Messiah: 'the Elect One' (e.g. 49.2), 'the Son of Man' (e.g. 62.3), 'the Righteous One' (e.g. 53.6), and 'the Anointed One' (e.g. 52.4). In two passages (49.3; 62.2) the Messiah is said to be anointed with the Spirit.

---

1. R.H. Charles has suggested that the text originally read 'the power of my spirit' (*The Book of Enoch* [1912], p. 135).

2. See also 1 Kgs 18.12 where a servant of Ahab expects the Spirit of the Lord to carry Elijah away.

3. D.S. Russell, *The Method and Message of Jewish Apocalyptic* (1964), pp. 148, 158-164. Note for example the similar profusion of angelic activity and visionary experiences and relative lack of references to the Spirit in *Jubilees, Life of Adam and Eve*, and *4 Ezra*. (1) Angels—*Jubilees*: 1.27; 2.1; 4.21; 12.22; 12.27; 16.16f.; 17.11f.; 18.10; 41.24; *Life of Adam and Eve*: preface; 3.2; 6.2; 13.2.; 29.14; *4 Ezra*: 4.1; 5.31; 7.1; 10.29. (2) Visions/Dreams—*Jubilees*: 4.19; 14.1; 26.21; 29.7; 32.21f.; 41.24; *Life of Adam and Eve*: 2.2; *4 Ezra*: 9.38; 11.1; 13.1. Cf. references to the Spirit of God as the source of revelation: *Jub.* 25.14; 31.12; 40.5; *4 Ezra* 5.22; 14.22; no references in *Life of Adam and Eve*.

4. Russell, *Jewish Apocalyptic*, p. 160.

5. For angelic activity see 1.2; 10.11; 27.2; 43.4; 52.4; 54.4; 60.11, 24; 64.1; 71.2f.; 72.1; 74.2; 79.6; 80.1; 81.1; 82.7; 93.3; 108.5.

6. For visionary experiences see 1.2; 13.8f.; 37.1f.; 59.1; 83.1f.; 85.1f.; 86.1; 90.40f.

1 Enoch 49.3 describes 'The Elect One':

> In him dwells the spirit of wisdom, the spirit which gives thoughtfulness,
> the spirit of knowledge and strength, and the spirit of those who have
> fallen asleep in righteousness.

This text 'reproduces practically verbatim' Isa. 11.2;[1] a verse in which
the referent is clearly 'the Spirit of the Lord'. There can be little doubt
that the author of *1 Enoch* consciously borrows from Isa. 11.2 and
thus depicts the Messiah as one endowed with the Spirit of God.[2] In *1
En.* 49.3, as in Isa. 11.2, the Spirit provides the wisdom necessary to
rule and exercise judgment (49.4; cf. 51.3). *1 Enoch* 62.2 picks up Isa.
11.4 and continues to extol the power of 'the Elect One' to judge and
rule:

> The Lord of the Spirits has sat down on the throne of his glory, and the
> spirit of righteousness has been poured out upon him [the Elect One]. The
> word of his mouth will do the sinners in; and all the oppressors shall be
> eliminated from before his face.

In another Jewish writing with apocalyptic features, Psalms of
Solomon, the gift of the Spirit is again depicted as the means by which
the Messiah shall be endowed with special wisdom to rule
(*Amtscharisma*).[3] The Messiah will be 'powerful in the holy spirit
(δυνατὸν ἐν πνεύματι ἁγίῳ) and wise in the counsel of understanding, with strength and righteousness' (17.37). The connection between

1. M. Black, *The Book of Enoch* (1985), p. 212 (cf. Isa. 11:2: רוח חכמה ובינה רוח
עצה וגבורה). Black states that the last phrase, 'the spirit of those who have fallen
asleep', is problematic and may represent a corrupt text (pp. 213, 351). However,
Chevallier notes that there are two points at which *1 En.* 49.3 deviates from Isa. 11.2:
the phrase 'the Spirit of the Lord' has been dropped; and the phrase 'Spirit of knowledge and fear of the Lord' has been replaced by the phrase 'spirit of those who have
fallen asleep in righteousness'. On the basis of these alterations, Chevallier suggests
that the author of *1 En.* 49.3 did not want to portray the Messiah in subordinate terms
(*Le Messie*, p. 19).
2. Although Chevallier recognizes the dependence of *1 En.* 49.3 and 62.2 upon
Isa. 11.2f., he argues that these texts represent a different perspective: 'l'Esprit n'est
plus pour lui cette puissance mystérieuse que Dieu seul donnait, et qu'il ne donnait
qu'exceptionnellement' (*Le Messie*, p. 26). Chevallier's thesis is based largely on the
omission of 'the Spirit of the Lord' (Isa. 11.2) in *1 En.* 49.3. However the motivation for this omission is difficult to assess and may simply reflect stylistic concerns.
If, as Chevallier suggests, the omission was produced by a desire to eliminate subor-
dinationist language, then the omission says more about the author's concept of the
Messiah than his understanding of the Spirit.
3. All texts from *Psalms of Solomon* which are cited in English are from R.B.
Wright, 'Psalms of Solomon', in Charlesworth, *Pseudepigrapha*, II. Greek text from
A. Rahlfs, *Septuaginta* (1979).

the Messiah's wisdom and the gift of the Spirit is explicitly stated in *Pss. Sol.* 18.7. The coming Messiah will act 'in the fear of his God, in wisdom of spirit (ἐν σοφίᾳ πνεύματος), and of righteousness and of strength, to direct people in righteous acts, in the fear of God' (18.7).

1 Enoch and the *Psalms of Solomon* thus state that the Messiah will be endowed with wisdom by the Spirit of God so that he may rule effectively. Nowhere in Jewish intertestamental literature is it recorded that the Messiah will bestow the Spirit of God upon his followers.

2.3. *The Spirit and the Resurrection of the Dead*

In apocalyptic thought the resurrection, viewed in a variety of ways, becomes an important aspect of God's future salvation.[1] Although the Spirit of God is associated with the resurrection in Ezek. 37.14, one of the few Old Testament texts in which a future resurrection is described,[2] this association of Spirit and resurrection is strikingly absent in Jewish apocalyptic and the Jewish literature of the intertestamental period as a whole.[3]

Even though the exact nature of the resurrection depicted in the various parts of *1 Enoch* may be debated, it is clear that the resurrection of the body represents a prominent motif.[4] Resurrection also appears as a significant theme in *Psalms of Solomon*, 2 Maccabees, *4 Ezra*, Pseudo-Philo, and *Life of Adam and Eve*.[5] Yet as indicated above, the connection between resurrection and the Spirit of God, so prominent in Ezekiel 37, is not found in these writings.[6]

1. Montague, *Spirit*, p. 90. For the various ways in which the apocalyptic writers develop the concept of the resurrection, see Russell, *Jewish Apocalyptic*, pp. 369f.
2. Russell sees the apocalyptic development of the resurrection concept as stemming from Isa. 24–27; Ezek. 37 and Dan. 12. Although many scholars view Ezek. 37 as a symbolic reference to the restoration of the nation and as containing no doctrine of individual resurrection (e.g. Montague, *Spirit*, p. 90), Russell writes: 'The view taken here is that we have in this verse the first reference in Hebrew literature to the resurrection of the dead' (*Jewish Apocalyptic*, pp. 367f., quote from p. 378).
3. See D. Müller, 'Geisterfahrung und Totenauferweckung' (1980), pp. 111-32. Müller argues that *2 Bar.* 23.5 is the only text from the OT pseudepigrapha which (along with several rabbinic citations) portrays the Spirit of God as the agent of the resurrection. However *2 Bar.* 23.5 has been excluded from my analysis due to its late origin (2nd century AD).
4. Important passages in *1 Enoch* concerning the resurrection include: 22.13; 51.1; 61.5; 90.33; 100.5.
5. See for example *Pss. Sol.* 3.12; 14.10; 2 Macc. 7.8, 13, 23, 29; 14.46; *4 Ezra* 7.32; *Ps.-Philo* 3.10; 19.12; 25.7; 51.5; 64.7; *Life of Adam and Eve* 28.4; 41.3.
6. E. Sjöberg (in 'πνεῦμα', *TDNT*, VI, p. 385) cites 2 Macc. 7.23; 14.46; *Sib. Or.* 4.46, 189 as evidencing a link between eschatological renewal and the Spirit. But

3. *The Spirit and Prophetic Inspiration: Various Texts*

We have seen that the Spirit of God, when mentioned in Sirach and apocalyptic texts such as *1 Enoch*, is consistently portrayed as the source of esoteric wisdom and inspired speech. This tendency to identify the Spirit of God with prophetic inspiration is also characteristic of other Palestinian texts from the intertestamental period.[1]

References to the Spirit of God occur frequently in Pseudo-Philo.[2] In 9.10 we read that 'the Spirit of God came upon Miriam' and revealed to her in a dream that she would give birth to Moses. According to Ps.-Philo 18.10, although the prophet Balaam had been filled with the Spirit, when he prophesied for Balak it gradually departed from him.[3] After 'a holy spirit came upon Kenaz and dwelled in him', he prophesied in a state of ecstasy (28.6). Barak declares that the oracle which foretold the death of Sisera came from 'the Lord, who sent his Spirit' (31.9). Deborah, in the midst of her hymn of rejoicing, attributes her praise to the Spirit: 'But you, Deborah, sing praises, and let the grace of the holy spirit awaken in you, and begin to praise the works of the Lord' (32.14). In this text the locus of the Spirit's activity is not the revelation of special insight, but inspired utterance.

The Spirit also appears as *Amtscharisma* in Ps.-Philo 60.1: 'And in that time the spirit of the Lord was taken away from Saul'. It is debatable whether 62.2 speaks of the activity of the Spirit of God. D.J. Harrington translates the verse with spirit as an anarthrous noun: 'and

---

Müller responds: 'Die vier Stellen, die er [Sjöberg] (ausdrücklich als einzige) anführt, 2 Makk 7.23; 14.46; Sib IV,46.189, gehören, wie er selbst sieht, nicht hierher, weil sie nicht ausdrücklich vom Geist Gottes reden, sondern von der wiedergegebenen Lebenskraft der Menschen' ('Geisterfahrung', p. 111 n. 21). Müller states: 'Die Verbindung zwischen der endzeitlichen Erneuerung und der Geistbegabung ist in der apokryphisch-pseudepigraphischen Literatur so gut wie überhaupt nicht nachzuweisen' (p. 111). It is noteworthy that *4 Ezra* 6.26 and *Jub.* 1.22-25 describe the eschatological renewal in terms of Ezek. 36.26, but without reference to the Spirit of God.

1. W.R. Shoemaker ('The Use of רוח in the Old Testament, and of Πνεῦμα in the New Testament', *JBL* 23 [1904], pp. 39-40) and Hill (*Greek Words*, p. 220) emphasize the connection between wisdom and Spirit in the intertestamental literature.

2. Texts of Pseudo-Philo, also known by the Latin title *Liber Antiquitatum Biblicarum*, are extant in Latin only. All English texts cited are from D.J. Harrington, 'Pseudo-Philo', in Charlesworth, *Pseudepigrapha*, II.

3. See G. Vermes on the development of the Balaam-tradition in Num. 24.2 (LXX); Philo, *Vit. Mos.* 1.277; Josephus, *Ant.* 4.118; and Ps.-Philo 18 (*Scripture and Tradition in Judaism: Haggadic Studies* [1973], pp. 144-45, 173-75). Balaam's misuse of the prophetic gift is cited in the rabbinic literature as the reason God withdrew the prophetic gift from the Gentiles (*Num. R.* 20.1).

a spirit abided in Saul and he prophesied'. However in the Latin text 'spirit' can be interpreted either as a definite or indefinite noun. 1 Samuel 19.23, the biblical text upon which this passage is based, attributes Saul's prophecy to the Spirit of God. It is possible that Pseudo-Philo has tried to modify the text at this point in light of 60.1, deliberately avoiding a reference to the Spirit of God. Yet this is unlikely since the biblical text makes no such modification.

A number of other intertestamental writings depict the divine Spirit as the source of prophecy. Most of the manuscripts of *Jub.* 25.14, extant only in Ethiopic, record that Rebecca blessed Jacob after 'a spirit of truth descended upon her mouth'.[1] However manuscript C reads 'the Holy Spirit', indicating that this passage should be interpreted as a reference to the Spirit of God.[2] *Jubilees* 31.12f. records Isaac's Spirit-inspired blessing of Jacob's sons, Levi and Judah: 'The spirit of prophecy [*spiritus profetiae*] came down into his [Isaac's] mouth' (31.12). In *Jub.* 40.5 Pharaoh attributes Joseph's wisdom to the Spirit of the Lord.

It is recorded in *4 Ezra* 5.22f. that Ezra, having 'recovered the spirit of understanding [*spiritum intellectus*]' (5.22),[3] was once again able to speak to God. However, in light of 5.14, 'my [Ezra's] mind was troubled, so that it fainted', this reference probably refers to a restoration of Ezra's mental faculties. Nevertheless, in *4 Ezra* 14.22 the Holy Spirit is clearly depicted as the source of special insight. Ezra requests that the Holy Spirit (*spiritum sanctum*) be sent to him so that he can write all that has taken place in the world from the beginning (14.22).

The close association between the Spirit and prophetic activity is also highlighted by the author of the *Martyrdom of Isaiah*. In 1.7 the prophet Isaiah refers to 'the Spirit which speaks in me' (τὸ πνεῦμα τὸ λαλοῦν ἐν ἐμοί).[4] Isaiah's remarkable fortitude in the face of persecution is recounted in 5.14, where Isaiah, inspired by the Holy Spirit, prophesies until sawn in half.

The Lives of the Prophets attributes miracles to the biblical prophets (Jeremiah, 2.3f.; Ezekiel, 3.8f.; Elijah, 21.6; Elisha, 22.4).[5] Yet

---

1. ET from O.S. Wintermute, 'Jubilees' in Charlesworth, *Pseudepigrapha*, II.

2. R.H. Charles, *The Book of Jubilees* (1902), p. 158.

3. Latin text from B. Violet, *Die Esra-Apokalypse (IV. Esra)* (1910).

4. ET from M.A. Knibb, 'Martyrdom and Ascension of Isaiah', in Charlesworth, *Pseudepigrapha*, II. Greek text (1.8) is from Denis, *Fragmenta Pseudepigraphorum*, p. 107.

5. Miracles are also frequently attributed to angels. One of the central characters in Tobit is Raphael, an angel sent from God in response to prayer (3.16f.). Acting on

significantly these miracles are not performed in the power of the Spirit. Thus, while miracles are linked to prophets, the distinctive activity of the Spirit of God in relation to the prophet is revelation of the divine message and inspiration of its proclamation. Indeed, a survey of the Palestinian literature reveals that in only one instance is the Spirit described as the agent of miraculous activity not related to revelatory or speech functions. Pseudo-Philo 27.9-10 describes how the Spirit of God transformed Kenaz into a mighty warrior, enabling him to kill 45,000 Amorites (v.10):

> And Kenaz arose, and the Spirit of God clothed him, and he drew his sword . . . he was clothed with the Spirit of power and was changed into another man, and he went down to the Amorite camp and began to strike them down.

4. *Summary*

In the Palestinian literature surveyed, the Spirit consistently functions as the source of esoteric wisdom and inspired speech. The Spirit enables the sage to attain the heights of sapiential achievement, equips the Messiah with special knowledge to rule, and grants special insight to various servants of the Lord. The inspiration of the Spirit, whether it be in relation to the sage, Messiah, or servant, is almost always related to inspired speech. It is therefore apparent that the Palestinian authors viewed the Spirit as a *donum superadditum* granted to various individuals so that they might fulfill a divinely appointed task. The gift of the Spirit is not presented as a soteriological necessity: one need not possess the gift in order to live in right relationship to God and attain eternal life through the resurrection. The Spirit is not associated with the resurrection of the dead or the performance of miracles and feats of strength.[1]

---

behalf of God, Raphael restores Tobit's sight (11.14) and expels demons from Tobias' wife, Sarah (8.3). Similarly, in Pseudo-Philo angels are extensions of God's power on earth: guarding, fighting, inflicting judgment and punishment according to the divine will (Ps.-Philo 15.5; 24.3; 26.4; 27.10; 34.3; 38.3f.; 59.4; 61.8). In 2 Maccabees angels add supernatural clout to Jewish military endeavors (3.24; 12.22; 15.11). David attributes his salvation from the lion to angelic intervention in Psalm 153.5 (*5 Apoc. Syr. Pss.* 5).

1. As I have noted, the only exception is Ps.-Philo 27.9-10.

Chapter 4

THE QUMRAN LITERATURE[1]

The term רוח occurs frequently in the scrolls from Qumran and with diverse meanings.[2] It can refer to wind as in 1QH 1.10: 'Thou hast spread... the mighty winds (רוחות עוז) according to their laws'.[3] רוח is also used anthropologically, often with reference to the disposition or attitude of man. Thus in 1QM 11.10 we read that God 'will kindle the downcast of spirit (ונכאי רוח)' and make them mighty in battle.[4] However, רוח frequently refers to the totality of the human being. The author of 1QH 1.22 describes himself as 'a straying and perverted spirit (רוח התועה ונעוה) of no understanding'.[5] The scrolls' affinity to Jewish apocalyptic can be seen in the abundant references to supernatural spirits, both good and evil, created by God and active in the world of men. The angelic army which will fight with the righteous in the final battle are called 'the host of His spirits (צבא רוחיו)' in 1QM 12.9.

1. The sources examined include those texts contained in the third edition of Geza Vermes's convenient collection, *The Dead Sea Scrolls in English* (1987). The literature from Qumran was produced between c. 170 BC and AD 68.
2. K.G. Kuhn lists close to 150 references of רוח in his *Konkordanz zu den Qumrantexten* (1960). Surveys of the various usages have been provided by G. Johnston, ' "Spirit" and "Holy Spirit" in the Qumran Literature', in *New Testament Sidelights* (1960), pp. 27-42; W. Foerster, 'Der Heilige Geist im Spätjudentum', *NTS* 8 (1961-62), pp. 117-34; A. Anderson, 'The Use of "Ruah" in 1QS, 1QH, and 1QM', *JSS* 7 (1962), pp. 293-303; F. Nötscher, 'Heiligkeit in den Qumranschriften', *RQ* 2 (1960), esp. pp. 333-44; H. Ringgren, *The Faith of Qumran* (1963), pp. 87-93; D. Hill, *Greek Words*, pp. 234-41.
3. All English translations are from Vermes, *The Dead Sea Scrolls in English*. All Hebrew texts are from E. Lohse, *Die Texte aus Qumran* (1971) unless otherwise indicated. For רוח as 'wind' see also 1QH 6.23; 7.5, 23; CD 8.13; 19.25.
4. For further examples of this use of רוח see: 1QS 3.8; 8.3; 10.12, 18; 11.2; 1QH 2.15; 1QM 7.5; 11.10; 14.7.
5. Further examples include: 1QS 10.18; 1QH 3.21; 8.29; 13.13. At times it may appear that רוח indicates an essential part of man, such as the soul. However, Anderson notes that we can often 'regard the spirit, soul, flesh, etc., as expressions of the totality of man, although at times one aspect may receive a more special emphasis' (' "Ruah" ', p. 295).

Their foes shall be 'the host of Satan' and 'the spirits of wickedness' (רוחי רשעה; 1QM 15.14).[1] In the present study our primary focus will be directed to yet another category, those passages where רוח designates the Spirit of God. However, due to the ambiguous way the term רוח is often employed, there is some disagreement as to which texts should be included in this category. Disagreement also exists concerning the origin of the scrolls' pneumatology, particularly that of 1QS. Thus we begin with a discussion of the 'two spirits' in 1QS 3–4, a passage of importance for both debates.

1. The Two Spirits in 1QS 3–4

1QS 3.13–4.26 describes the conflict between two spirits which rages in every human. The outworking of this conflict shapes the behavior of each individual. Although the two spirits are named by a number of titles, the various terms, if not synonymous, are closely related.[2] The spirit of truth (רוח האמת; 1QS 3.19; 4.23), spirit of light (רוח אור; 1QS 3.25), prince of lights (שר אורים; 1QS 3.20), and the angel of [his] truth (מלאך אמתו; 1QS 3.24) rule the children of righteousness. The spirit of falsehood (רוח העול; 1QS 3.19; 4.9, 20, 23), spirit of darkness (רוח חושך; 1QS 3.25), and angel of darkness (מלאך חושך; 1QS 3.21) rule the children of darkness. The battle in the heart of every human rages until the final age, when God will destroy falsehood forever (1QS 4.18f.).

1.1. Dualism, Determinism, and the Two Spirits
There has been considerable disagreement as to the exact nature and function of these spirits. M. Burrows and K.G. Kuhn have emphasized the supernatural and cosmic character of the two spirits, and thus attributed a cosmic dualism of Persian origin to the scrolls.[3] In response, P. Wernberg-Møller has argued convincingly that the two spirits are human dispositions which are present equally in every person rather than opposing supernatural forces. Central to Wernberg-Møller's thesis is his observation that both spirits dwell in humans as

---

1. See also 1QH 7.29; 9.16; 10.8; 1QM 13.10.

2. For the terms as identical see Anderson, '"Ruah"', pp. 298-99; Davies, 'Flesh and Spirit', p. 171; Hill, *Greek Words,* p. 236. However, M. Treves distinguishes between the spirits and the angels/prince of lights ('The Two Spirits of the Rule of the Community', *RQ* 3 [1961], p. 450).

3. M. Burrows, *More Light on the Dead Sea Scrolls* (1958), p. 279; K.G. Kuhn, 'πειρασμός–ἁμαρτία–σάρξ im Neuen Testament und die damit zusammenhängenden Vorstellungen', *ZTK* 49 (1952), p. 206.

created by God.[1] Likening the two spirits to the rabbinic good and evil impulses, Wernberg-Møller asserts that according to 1QS 3–4 each individual must choose which spirit to follow. Thus he rejects the notion that the scrolls are characterized by cosmic dualism and show evidence of direct dependency on Persian sources.[2]

Wernberg-Møller is supported in his conclusions by M. Treves, who also views the two spirits as 'simply tendencies or propensities which are implanted in every man's heart'.[3] Noting that each individual is influenced by both spirits (1QS 3.24; 4.23) and that sin is voluntary (1QS 5.1, 8-10, 12), Treves states that the predestinarianism of the author of 1QS 'has been somewhat exaggerated. . . he does not appear to have diverged widely from the traditional Jewish views'.[4]

Although considerable disagreement still exists concerning the extent to which predestinarianism is present in 1QS,[5] the conclusions reached by P. Wernberg-Møller and M. Treves regarding the nature of the two spirits have received general acceptance. Their influence is reflected in the note of caution concerning the cosmic and supernatural character of the two spirits in subsequent studies by A. Anderson, D. Hill, and H.W. Kuhn.[6] Representative is Kuhn, who speaks of רוח in 1QS 3f. as

---

1. P. Wernberg-Møller, 'A Reconsideration of the Two Spirits in the Rule of the Community', *RQ* 3 (1961), p. 442: 'It is significant that our author regards the two "spirits" as created by God, and that according to IV, 23 and our passage [3.18f.] both "spirits" dwell in man as created by God (20). We are therefore not dealing here with a kind of metaphysical, cosmic dualism represented by the two "spirits", but with the idea that man was created by God with two "spirits"—the Old Testament term for "mood" or "disposition".'

2. Wernberg-Møller, 'Two Spirits', pp. 422f.

3. Treves, 'Two Spirits', p. 449.

4. Treves, 'Two Spirits', p. 451.

5. Anderson has criticized the view that the two spirits were present in equal measure in every man, arguing that if 'this were true then the final decision would always be with man'. According to Anderson, 'this is not the emphasis we find in the scrolls'. Anderson interprets the phrase בד בבד (1QS 4.16, 25) to mean 'proportionately' rather than 'in equal quantities' (contra Wernberg-Møller, 'Two Spirits', p. 433). Attempting to mitigate the argument from the OT use of the phrase (Exod. 30.34), he points to the general context of the passage and evidence from Cave 4 that describes humanity's spirit as composed of nine parts, with each part good or evil ('"Ruah"', p. 300). E.H. Merrill, *Qumran and Predestination* (1975), also maintains that predestinarian views are a significant part of the theology of 1QH.

6. Anderson, '"Ruah"', p. 299; H.W. Kuhn, *Enderwartung und gegenwärtiges Heil* (1966), pp. 121f.; and Hill, *Greek Words*, p. 236. See also J.L. Harter, 'Spirit in the New Testament: A Reinterpretation in Light of the Old Testament and Intertestamental Literature' (1965), pp. 60-61.

'das prädestinierte Sein oder "Selbst" des Menschen'.[1] As a result, caution has also been exercised in attributing the pneumatology of 1QS directly to Persian influences. It has been increasingly recognized that the pneumatology of the scrolls is not so different from that of the Judaism of its day.[2]

In view of the arguments presented by P. Wernberg-Møller and M. Treves, I conclude that the two spirits in 1QS are human dispositions. The doctrine of the two spirits was an attempt to reconcile the omnipotence of God with the mixed character of humanity. As the creator of all things, God has implanted in the heart of every human being the impulse (spirit) to do good and to do evil. Each individual must choose between the two impulses or spirits. The extent to which this choice is predetermined at creation by the allotment of the spirits is a point of continuing debate. Nevertheless, it is apparent that caution should be exercised in attributing to the scrolls on the basis of 1QS a rigid cosmic dualism and dependency on Persian (or gnostic) sources. The pneumatology of the scrolls is essentially Jewish.

1.2. *The Two Spirits and 1QH*

Having defined the two spirits as impulses within every human being, we must now examine the arguments put forward by W. Foerster that the spirit of truth in 1QS is identical to the Holy Spirit of 1QH.[3] Foerster cites numerous parallels between the functions attributed to the spirit of truth in 1QS and to the Holy Spirit in 1QH: the spirit of truth and the Holy Spirit 'enlighten the heart of humans' (1QS 4.2; 1QH 1.21; 12.11f.), instill fear into the hearts of men concerning the righteous deeds of God (1QS 4.2; 1QH 1.23; 9.23), bestow insight and understanding (1QS 4.3, 6; 1QH 6.35-37), and grant steadfastness (1QS 4.4; 1QH 2.7f., 25) and purity (1QS 4.5; 1QH 3.21; 6.8) of heart.

Several factors speak against Foerster's identification. First, it should be noted that none of the passages Foerster cites from 1QS explicitly names the spirit of truth as the subject of the action. On the contrary, all of the citations come from 1QS 4.2f. and refer to the various spirits which make up the counsel of the spirit of truth. Second, the parallels which Foerster cites are often superficial, exhibiting only a general conceptual correspondence. One would expect such similarities to exist between the activity of the Spirit of God and that of the good impulse in every human being. Third, in contrast to the Holy

---

1. Kuhn, *Enderwartung*, p. 122.
2. See Nötscher, 'Heiligkeit', pp. 343-44; Johnston, '"Spirit"', p. 29; Hill, *Greek Words*, p. 236; and Anderson, '"Ruah"', p. 303.
3. Foerster, 'Heilige Geist', pp. 129-31.

Spirit in 1QH, the two spirits in 1QS are created by God (3.13f.; 4.25). Fourth, the dualistic conflict between the two spirits in 1QS stands in sharp contrast to the sovereign action of the Holy Spirit in 1QH.

More problematic are the references to רוח in association with אמת and קודש in 1QS 3.6-7 and 4.21. F. Nötscher has argued that in these texts, the holy spirit and spirit of truth are identical and they describe a power granted by God which becomes active in humans for salvation.[1] This judgment is undoubtedly correct. But is this salvific power granted by God identified with the Spirit of God in each instance? And in light of Foerster's thesis we may ask: are the references to רוח קודש and רוח אמת in 1QS 3.6f. and 4.20f. to be equated with the רוח קודש of 1QH? I suggest that the spirits cited in 1QS 3.6f. and 4.20f. should not be identified with the Spirit of God; and that these spirits should therefore be distinguished from the רוח קודש of 1QH.

> For it is through the spirit of true counsel (רוח עצת אמת) concerning the ways of man that all his sins shall be expiated that he may contemplate the light of life. He shall be cleansed from all his sins by the spirit of holiness (וברוח קדושה) uniting him to His truth, and his iniquity shall be expiated by the spirit of uprightness and humility (וברוח יושר וענוה). And when his flesh is sprinkled with purifying water and sanctified by cleansing water, it shall be made clean by the humble submission of his soul (נפשו) to all the precepts of God (1QS 3.6-8).

The terms 'spirit of true counsel', 'spirit of holiness', and 'spirit of uprightness and humility' (1QS 3.6f.) all refer to the disposition of the individual:[2] in this instance, the inclination to adhere to the ordinances of the community. Thus, although רוח may emphasize the divine origin of this inclination or impulse, it does not refer to the Spirit of God. This judgment is suggested by the larger context, which, as we have noted, discusses the conflict between the two spirits or impulses which rages within every human. It is supported further by the way in which the references to רוח cited above, all of which are related to the individual's cleansing from sin, are paralleled with the disposition of the soul: 'it [his flesh] shall be made clean by the humble submission of his soul (נפשו) to all the precepts of God'. This conclusion is confirmed by

1. Nötscher, 'Heiligkeit', pp. 340-41: 'Der heilige Geist, auch Geist der Wahrheit oder der Treue genannt, ist die gottverliehene Kraft, die verbunden mit der eigene menschlichen Anstrengung die Heiligung bewirkt'. So also Ringgren, *The Faith of Qumran*, p. 89. Anderson sees this identification as a possibility ('"Ruah"', p. 301).

2. M.A. Knibb, *The Qumran Community* (1987), pp. 92-93.

the use of רוח קודש in 1QS 9.3,[1] a passage which refers to the readmission into the community of those who, due to inadvertent sin, have undergone two years of penance:

> When these become members of the Community in Israel according to all these rules, they shall establish the spirit of holiness (רוח קודש) according to everlasting truth. They shall atone for guilty rebellion and for sins of unfaithfulness that they may obtain loving kindness for the Land without the flesh of holocausts and the fat of sacrifice (1QS 9.3-4).

Here רוח קודש refers to the inclination to faithfully adhere to the ordinances of the community. This inner disposition rather than sacrifices shall effect atonement.[2]

> Then God will purify by his truth all the deeds of man and will refine for himself the frame of man, removing all spirit of injustice (רוח עולה) from within his flesh, and purifying him by the spirit of holiness (ברוח קודש) from every wicked action. And he will sprinkle upon him the spirit of truth (רוח אמת) like waters for purification (to remove) all the abominations of falsehood (in which) he has defiled himself through the spirit of impurity (ברוח נדה), so that the upright may have understanding in the knowledge of the Most High and the perfect of way insight into the wisdom of the sons of heaven (1QS 4.20-22).[3]

Again the context is instructive. This passage forms the climax of the entire 'two spirits' discussion. The 'spirit of holiness' and 'spirit of truth' are contrasted with the 'spirit of injustice' and 'spirit of impurity' which in the endtime will be rooted out of humankind. Thus, the time of conflict between the two spirits will come to an end, and the spirit of holiness and truth will dominate. Although the phrase 'sprinkle upon him' implies that the spirit of truth will be bestowed upon the faithful at the end, this imagery is metaphorical and merely describes the culmination of a battle which has been raging since creation: the complete victory of the spirit of truth over the spirit of falsehood, of the good impulse over the evil impulse.[4] This conclusion is confirmed by 1QS 4.26: 'He [God] has allotted them [the two spirits] to the children of men... that the destiny of all the living may be

---

1. See also the way in which רוח קודש is employed in CD 5.11; 7.4.
2. Knibb, *The Qumran Community*, p. 138.
3. ET from Knibb, *The Qumran Community*, p. 101.
4. Wernberg-Møller, 'Two Spirits', p. 423: 'The phraseology makes it plain that רוח is used in the sense in which it is employed in the Old Testament, namely as denoting the motive force in man which drives him to act in a certain way. The author's point of view is that perfection is at present, however desirable, not practicable, but it will be so when God will replace the "perverted" mind by a "true" and "holy" disposition.'

according to the spirit within [them at the time] of the visitation'. The parallels between 1QS 4.20-22 and the numerous rabbinic texts which speak of the endtime removal of the evil יצר lend further support to the thesis that the two spirits are impulses placed within every individual at creation.[1]

The contrast between the רוח קודש of 1QS 3–4 and that of 1QH becomes clear when it is recognized that in 1QH the term is never simply רוח קודש, but always רוח קודשך (your [God's] Holy Spirit).[2] Furthermore, it should also be noted that 1QS 4.20f. represents the only eschatological use of רוח in all of the Qumran literature.[3] On the basis of my rejection of Foerster's parallels, my examination of 1QS 3.6f. and 4.20f., and the considerations cited above, I conclude that the spirit of truth in 1QS 3–4 is not to be equated with the Holy Spirit of 1QH, the Spirit of God.[4]

1. See *Exod. R.* 15.6; 41.7; *Num. R.* 14.4; *Deut. R.* 6.14; *Midr. Ps.* 14.6; *Cant. R.* 1.2.4; *Eccl. R.* 2.1; 9.15.
2. The only possible exceptions are two occurrences of רוח found in 1QH 16.2-3. However, the text is damaged at this point and in both instances probably reads רוח קודשך (see the reconstructed text offered by Lohse, *Die Texte aus Qumran*, p. 162). Nötscher distinguishes between the spirit as a 'natürliche Gabe Gottes' and as a 'Heilsgabe Gottes': 'in diesem letzten Sinne [Heilsgabe] wird er mit Vorliebe, aber, wie es scheint, nicht immer und nicht ausschließlich, heiliger Geist genannt' ('Heiligkeit', pp. 337-38).
3. Foerster, 'Der Heilige Geist', p. 132; Davies, 'Flesh and Spirit', pp. 173, 177.
4. Unambiguous references to the Spirit of God are found in 1QH 7.6-7; 9.32; 12.12; 14.13; 16.2, 3, 7, 12; 17.26 (elsewhere in the scrolls: 1QS 8.16; CD 2.12; 4Q504 2 [frag. 4], 5; 1Q34bis 2.6-7). Other probable references to the Spirit of God include 1QH 12.11; 13.19; 16.9, 11. These judgments are supported by the conclusions of J. Pryke, who categorizes the uses of 'spirit' in the four main documents of Qumran (1QS; CD; 1QM; 1QH; '"Spirit" and "Flesh" in the Qumran Documents and Some New Testament Texts', *RQ* 5 [1965], p. 345). The only differences between the conclusions of Pryke and my own (excluding the references I have cited outside the four main documents) are: (1) Pryke's survey omits altogether 1QH 14.13 and 16.2, 3, 7, probably due to the corrupt nature of the text; and (2) Pryke lists 1QH 12.11 and 13.19, texts which I have listed as probable references to the Spirit of God, as references to the spirit of humanity; however he concurs with my judgment concerning 1QH 16.9. The reasons for my judgment concerning 1QH 12.11 and 13.19 will be discussed below.

2. *The Spirit and Wisdom*

The scrolls are the literary deposit of a 'wisdom community'.[1] Like Ben Sira, the authors of the scrolls identify wisdom with the law.[2] Nevertheless, they maintain that the wisdom of God remains inaccessible to those outside of the community (1QS 11.5-6). Wisdom is the exclusive possession of the community (CD 3.12-16; 1QS 5.11-12), for it cannot be apprehended by study alone. Divine illumination is required in order to attain wisdom,[3] and this revelatory gift is reserved for those within the community.

This pessimistic attitude toward humanity's ability to acquire wisdom apart from divine illumination is given clear expression in 1QH. God's ways and deeds are incomprehensible to humans (1QH 7.32), who are dust and creatures of clay (1QH 11.3). As spirits of flesh, they cannot understand God's wisdom (1QH 13.13, also 15.21).[4] However, the Hymns of 1QH also declare that the members of the community have overcome this deficiency through reception of the Spirit.

> And I know through the understanding
>   which comes from Thee,
> that in Thy goodwill towards [ashes
>   Thou hast shed] Thy Holy Spirit [upon me]
> and thus drawn me near to understanding thee (1QH 14.12b-13).

H.W. Kuhn has argued persuasively that 1QH 14.13 refers to the gift of the Spirit which is granted to every member upon entrance into the community.[5] The parallels between 14.12b-16 and 14.17-21a, particu-

---

1. See J.E. Worrell, 'Concepts of Wisdom in the Dead Sea Scrolls' (1968), pp. 120-54; M. Küchler, *Frühjüdische Weisheitstraditionen: zum Fortgang weisheitlichen Denkens im Bereich des frühjüdischen Jahweglaubens* (1979), pp. 88-113; Kuhn, *Enderwartung*, pp. 139-75; and more recently Schnabel, *Law and Wisdom*, pp. 190-206.

2. E. Schnabel, *Law and Wisdom*, pp. 206-26. See also Davis, *Wisdom*, pp. 31-40.

3. S. Holm-Nielsen, *Hodayot: Psalms from Qumran* (1960), p. 328: 'The holiness of the Holy Scriptures consists of their hiddenness and inaccessibility to "unenlightened" man; only he to whom the truth has been revealed by God has the possibility of realizing its actual significance; only he understands that the significance of the Scripture is to disclose the last times in which the community is living'.

4. Foerster accurately summarizes the content of 1QH: 'alles, was der Mensch vor Gott sein kann, alles, was er erkennt, und sein ganzer Wandel, ist nur möglich, wenn Gott ihm Einsicht und Kraft gibt' ('Heilige Geist', p. 128). Cf. M. Mansoor, *The Thanksgiving Hymns* (1961), pp. 58-62.

5. Kuhn, *Enderwartung*, pp. 131-32. See also Holm-Nielsen, *Hodayot*, p. 221.

larly the repetition of ואני ידעתי ('I know') and the verb נגש ('draw near'), demonstrate that these passages are closely related. Therefore, since the formula ובשבועה הקימותי על נפשי (literally, 'an oath I have placed on my soul') in 14.17 undoubtedly refers to a pledge made upon entrance into the community,[1] we may assume that this setting is also in view in 1QH 14.13. This judgment is confirmed by the fact that נגש is a *terminus technicus* for entrance into the community.[2] Thus, according to 1QH 14.12b-13, the gift of the Spirit enables every member of the community to draw near 'to the understanding of thee [God]' (לבינתך).

> And I know that man is not righteous
>> except through Thee,
> and therefore I implore Thee
>> by the spirit which Thou hast given [me]
>> to perfect Thy [favours] to Thy servant [for ever],
> purifying me by Thy Holy Spirit,
>> and drawing me near to Thee by Thy grace
>> according to the abundance of Thy mercies (1QH 16.11b-12).

1QH 16.11b-12 also refers to initiation into the community. The verb נגש is employed in 16.12. Furthermore, the formula ברוח אשר נתתה [בי] ('by the Spirit which thou hast given me') occurs frequently with reference to the Spirit as a gift given (suffix conjugation) upon entrance into the community.[3] Although wisdom terms are absent in this passage, the term ולהגישני ('to draw me near') implies the revelation of God's hidden wisdom (cf. 1QH 14.13).

> I, the Master (משכיל), know Thee (ידעתיכה), O my God,
>> by the spirit which Thou hast given to me,
> and by Thy Holy Spirit I have faithfully hearkened
>> to Thy marvelous counsel (לסוד פלאכה).
> In the mystery of Thy wisdom (ברז שכלכה)
>> Thou has opened knowledge (דעת) to me,
> and in Thy mercies
>> [Thou hast unlocked for me] the fountain of Thy might
>>> (1QH 12.11-13).

---

1. Kuhn, *Enderwartung*, p. 131. Cf. 1QS 5.7-11; CD 15.5-16; Josephus, *Wars* 2.139-42.
2. See 1QH 12.23; 14.13, 18, 19; 1QS 9.16; 11.13.
3. See Kuhn, *Enderwartung*, p. 130; and 1QH 12.11f.; 13.19. The use of the suffix conjugation which, in this instance, indicates completed action, emphasizes the association with entrance into the community. The fact that ברוח אשר נתתה [בי] is used synonymously with ברוח קודשך in 1QH 16.11b-12 (cf. 12.11-12) indicates that the former phrase, like the latter, refers to the Spirit of God.

> And I, Thy servant (עבדך),
>> I know (ידעתי) by the spirit which Thou hast given to me
>> [that Thy words are truth],
> and that all Thy works are righteousness,
>> and that Thou wilt not take back Thy word (1QH 13.18-19).

1QH 12.11-13 and 13.18-19 are also instructive. The formula ברוח אשר נתתה בי is found in both texts and sapiential terms abound. According to these Hymns, wisdom is attained through reception of the Spirit upon entrance into the community.

In accordance with the previous passages cited, the author of 1QH 9.32 places the reception of the Spirit in the past and parallels it with the revelation of 'certain truth' (אמת נכון):

> Thou hast upheld me with certain truth;
>> Thou hast delighted me with Thy Holy Spirit
>> and [hast opened my heart] till this day.

1QH 7.6-7 and 1QH 17.26 also place the reception of the Spirit in the past, although their contexts are imprecise and fragmentary, respectively. 1QH 16.2 and 3 are also fragmentary, but 16.6-7 is more revealing:

> Bowing down and [confessing all] my transgressions,
>> I will seek [Thy] spirit [of knowledge];
> cleaving to Thy spirit of [holiness],
>> I will hold fast to the truth of Thy Covenant,
> that [I may serve] Thee in truth and wholeness of heart,
>> and that I may love [Thy Name].

Although infinitives rather than finite verbs are found in 16.6-7, this is undoubtedly due to the declarative nature of the passage and does not contradict a past reception of the Spirit. This judgment is substantiated by the use of suffix conjugations in the verses prior to 16.6-7 and in 16.9, where discussion of the past event is again picked up: 'Thou... hast graced me with Thy spirit of mercy'. The revelation of God's truth is again linked to the gift of the Spirit received upon entrance into the community.

The texts cited above indicate that the Hymns from 1QH associate reception of the Spirit with entrance into the community. As an essential element of initiation into the community, the gift of the Spirit reveals the previously hidden wisdom of God to the recipient. Sapiential achievement at every level is dependent upon the reception of this gift. Indeed, reception of the gift enables one to know God and live within the community. Thus the Hymns of 1QH attribute soteriological significance to the gift of the Spirit.

It is possible that the Hymns of 1QH which attribute soteriological functions to the Spirit represent a late stage in the development of the community's pneumatology.[1] The pneumatological perspective of 1QH is decidedly different from 1QS, where the two spirits, in a manner analogous to the rabbinic good and evil יצר, appear as impulses placed within every individual at creation. The fact that the soteriological pneumatology so prominent in 1QH is virtually absent from the other Qumran writings lends further support to this hypothesis.[2] This evidence suggests that the pneumatology of Qumran underwent a process of development not unlike that which occurred within the Jewish wisdom tradition as a whole. The wisdom tradition displays an increasing pessimism toward humanity's ability to attain wisdom by purely rational means (study of the law unaided by the Spirit). The relatively optimistic anthropology of Sirach is replaced by more pessimistic appraisals of humans in 1QH and Wisdom. Similar developments can be traced within the scrolls. According to 1QS, the spirit of truth and the spirit of falsehood reside within each individual. Thus the individual appears to have some capacity, however small, to know God's will and respond accordingly. In contrast, 1QH presents humans as utterly incapable of attaining wisdom apart from the illumination of the Spirit. Thus the gift of the Spirit, previously viewed as the source of esoteric wisdom and inspired speech, becomes the source of sapiential achievement at every level. The process of development, both within the Qumran community and Jewish sapiential thought as a whole, culminates in the attribution of soteriological significance to the gift of the Spirit (Wisdom; 1QH).

3. *The Spirit and Prophetic Inspiration*

Consistent with their Jewish contemporaries, the authors of the scrolls portray the Spirit as the source of prophetic inspiration.[3] The link

---

1. A similar hypothesis of development, albeit for different reasons, is tentatively put forth by Davies: 'The source criticism of 1QS, and the other sectarian documents, has not been much attempted as yet, but it may well be that the section iii, 13ff., reflects an earlier "uncontaminated" stage in the history of the sect before Hellenistic influences had deeply colored its thought, while the psalms reflect a later stage when this had taken place' ('Flesh and Spirit', p. 165).

2. 4Q504 2 (frag. 4), 5 and 1Q34bis 2.6-7 also attribute soteriological functions to the Spirit.

3. Contra Ringgren, who writes: 'It should be pointed out that in Qumran there is also no reference to the spirit as the driving force in prophecy' (*The Faith of Qumran*, p. 90). For a more accurate appraisal see Nötscher, 'Heiligkeit', p. 338; and Johnston, ' "Spirit" ', pp. 36f.

between the Spirit and prophecy is made explicit in 1QS 8.16 and CD 2.12:

> This [path] is the study of the Law which He commanded by the hand of Moses, that they may do according to all that has been revealed from age to age, and the Prophets have revealed by His Holy Spirit (1QS 8.15-16).

> And in all of them He raised for Himself men called by name, that a remnant might be left to the Land, and that the face of the earth might be filled with their seed. And He made known His Holy Spirit to them by the hand of His anointed ones, and He proclaimed the truth [to them]. But those whom He hated He led astray (CD 2.11-13).

Although the text is badly damaged, it is likely that 1Q34bis 2.6-7 also associates the Spirit with divine revelation:

> And Thou didst renew for them Thy covenant [founded] on a glorious vision and on the words of Thy Holy [Spirit], on the works of Thy hands and the writing of Thy right hand, that they might know the foundations of glory and the steps towards eternity.

These texts are, of course, descriptions of the Spirit's activity in the distant past.[1] However, the inspiration of the Spirit is not limited to the prophets of the past. The title 'prophet' is never ascribed to the Teacher of Righteousness or other members of the community,[2] yet the scrolls suggest that the Spirit continued to grant esoteric wisdom to the wise in the community for the purpose of instruction.

These sages are most frequently designated by the term משכיל.[3] The various duties of the משכיל are set forth in 1QS 3.13-15; 4.22; and 9.12-20. Above all, the משכיל must 'instruct the upright in the knowl-

---

1. There are also references in the scrolls to a messianic figure endowed with the Spirit (1QSb 5.25; 11QMelch). These texts are similar in character to the texts from *1 Enoch* and *Psalms of Solomon* previously discussed (see Chapter 3 §2.2 above). Dunn has tentatively argued that the scrolls offer a close parallel to the idea that the Messiah would bestow the Spirit ('Spirit-and-Fire Baptism', *NovT* 14 [1972], pp. 89-91). However, his argument has been effectively refuted by Turner, 'Christology', pp. 181-83. Turner concludes: 'There are . . . no known pre-Christain references to the Messiah bestowing the Spirit' (pp. 182-83; see also C.F.D. Moule, *The Holy Spirit* [1978], pp. 38-39).

2. Aune, *Prophecy*, p. 133; H. Braun, *Qumran und das Neue Testament* (1966), II, p. 253; R. Leivestadt, 'Das Dogma von der prophetenlosen Zeit', *NTS* 19 (1973), pp. 297-98; G. Dautzenberg, *Urchristliche Prophetie: Ihre Erforschung, ihre Voraussetzungen im Judentum, und ihre Struktur im ersten Korintherbrief* (1975), p. 59. The term 'prophet' occurs in the Temple Scroll, but it is always associated with false prophecy (11QT 54.8f., 15; 61.2f.).

3. The title חכמי does occur (1QSa 1.28; 2.16), but it is less frequent and probably synonymous with משכיל.

edge of the Most High' (1QS 4.22). This knowledge is derived from an inspired interpretation of the law (1QS 9.17; 1QH 5.11).[1] That the Spirit is the source of this inspiration is clear from 1QH 12.11, where, as we have seen, the משכיל attributes his wisdom to the Spirit of God. Several texts allude to divinely inspired speech, although without explicit reference to the Spirit (1QH 1.27-29; 3.6-18; 7.11; 8.36; 11.12).

The inspiration of the Spirit, initially experienced upon entrance into the community, continued to be active in the member as he increased in purity and holiness. Holiness was closely associated with study and observance of the law.[2] Thus the community distinguished between various levels of sapiential achievement. All members of the community were ranked 'according to their understanding and deeds' (1QS 5.23-24).[3] The leaders of the community were to be perfect in holiness and wisdom (1QS 8.1f.).[4] Both attributes are associated with the inspiration of the Spirit throughout 1QH. The wise then, by definition, were those who experienced the Spirit in a particularly profound way. From their Spirit-inspired wisdom they were to instruct the community.

4. *Summary*

Although the Qumran community reserved the term 'prophet' for the biblical figures of the past, they clearly viewed the Spirit as active in their midst. The scrolls present the Spirit as the dynamic of the religious life of the community. The Spirit grants esoteric wisdom to the משכיל for the purpose of instruction and, according to 1QH, enables every member of the community to draw near to God. The pneumatological perspective of 1QH is, however, decidedly different from that of 1QS, where the two spirits, in a manner analogous to the rabbinic good and evil יצר, appear as impulses placed within every individual at creation. The Hymns of 1QH may represent a later stage in the community's reflection on the Spirit. They declare that the gift of the Spirit is the source of sapiential achievement at every level. For this reason, reception of the gift of the Spirit is necessary for one to know

---

1. E. Cothenet, 'Les prophètes chrétiens comme exégètes charismatiques de l'Écriture', in *Prophetic Vocation in the New Testament and Today* (1977), p. 87.
2. See Johnston, '"Spirit"', p. 36 and, on 1QH 3.6-18, M. Smith, 'What is Implied by the Variety of Messianic Figures?', *JBL* 78 (1959), pp. 66-72.
3. Davis, *Wisdom*, p. 42; and D. Flusser, 'The Dead Sea Scrolls and Pre-Pauline Christianity', in *Aspects of the Dead Sea Scrolls* (1967), p. 247.
4. See also 1QH 10.27.

God and live within the community of salvation. Thus the Hymns of 1QH, like Wisdom, attribute soteriological significance to the gift of the Spirit.

Chapter 5

THE RABBINIC LITERATURE[1]

1. *The Spirit and Prophetic Inspiration*

The Rabbis equated experience of the Spirit with prophetic inspiration.[2] The Spirit is consistently portrayed as the source of special insight and inspired speech throughout the rabbinic literature. Numerous rabbinic citations refer to various individuals 'seeing' or 'speaking in the Spirit'.[3] However, an important question must be addressed before the significance of this material for our inquiry can be properly assessed. Do these texts provide us with material valuable for reconstructing first-century Jewish perspectives on the Spirit? I shall seek to answer this question in the affirmative by demonstrating that rabbinic traditions which identify the Spirit with prophetic inspiration can be traced back to the pre-Christian era.

The Targum tradition also represents a rich source of information concerning Jewish perspectives on the Spirit. After some preliminary comments concerning the antiquity of the Targum tradition, I shall examine relevant texts from the various Targums.

1. The rabbinic literature examined includes portions from the Mishnah; the Tosefta; the Babylonian Talmud; the Jerusalem Talmud; the Tannaitic Midrashim; the Homiletic Midrashim; the *Midrash Rabbah*; *Midrash on Psalms*; *PRE*; *ARN*; and the Targums.

2. This judgment receives widespread support in the secondary literature: P. Schäfer, *Die Vorstellung vom heiligen Geist in der rabbinischen Literatur* (1972), p. 14; Strack–Billerbeck, *Kommentar*, II, p. 127; G.F. Moore, *Judaism in the First Centuries of the Christian Era: The Age of the Tannaim* (1927), I, p. 421; A. Marmorstein, *The Old Rabbinic Doctrine of God* (1927), p. 99; C.K. Barrett, *The Holy Spirit and the Gospel Tradition* (1947), p. 123; E. Ellis, '"Spiritual" Gifts in the Pauline Community', *NTS* 20 (1973–74), p. 131; Hill, *Greek Words*, p. 227; T. Marsh, 'Holy Spirit in Early Christian Thinking', *ITQ* 45 (1978), p. 106; E. Sjöberg, 'πνεῦμα', *TDNT*, VI, p. 382.

3. See the numerous texts cited by Schäfer, *Die Vorstellung*, pp. 151-57, 161.

1.1. *Early Rabbinic Tradition*

Although the rabbinic writings were compiled between AD 200 and 500, it is generally recognized that they contain traditions from the pre-Christian era.[1] However, these early traditions must be distinguished from those of a later era.[2] A methodology which will help us meet this objective has been proposed by Renée Bloch.[3] Bloch suggests that the antiquity of a tradition may be determined through a process of 'internal' and 'external comparison'. 'Internal comparison' involves tracing the development of a rabbinic tradition through the various stages which the documents containing the tradition represent. It is important to distinguish the primitive elements of the tradition from later additions or revisions. Jacob Neusner has offered some helpful guidelines for engaging in internal comparison.[4] Particularly noteworthy is Neusner's suggestion that related traditions be arranged into a logical sequence of development. 'External comparison' involves comparing rabbinic traditions, which are largely undated or dated inaccurately, with texts external to rabbinic Judaism 'which have at least an approximate date and in which the same traditions are found'.[5] With these methodological considerations in view, we turn to the rabbinic texts.

1.1.1. *T. Sot. 13.2.* A rabbinic lament over the cessation of prophecy is found in *t. Sot.* 13.2:

1. See for example J. Bowker, *The Targums and Rabbinic Literature* (1969), p. x; Longenecker, *Paul: Apostle of Liberty*, p. 5; R.F. Surburg, 'Rabbinical Writings of the Early Christian Centuries and New Testament Interpretation', *CTQ* 43 (1979), p. 273; G. Vermes, 'Jewish Studies', p. 12; M. McNamara, *Palestinian Judaism and the New Testament* (1983), p. 176; and more cautiously, E.P. Sanders, *Paul and Palestinian Judaism* (1977), pp. 59-60.

2. New Testament scholars have been criticized for 'massive and sustained anachronism in their use of Rabbinic sources' (P.S. Alexander, 'Rabbinic Judaism and the New Testament', *ZNW* 74 [1983], p. 244). See also S. Sandmel, 'Parallelomania', *JBL* (1962), p. 9; Sanders, *Paul*, p. 42; Vermes, 'Jewish Studies', pp. 7-8; J. Neusner, 'The Teaching of the Rabbis: Approaches Old and New', *JJS* 27 (1976), p. 32 and 'The History of Earlier Rabbinic Judaism: Some New Approaches', *HR* 16 (1977), pp. 220f.

3. R. Bloch, 'Methodological Note for the Study of Rabbinic Literature', in *Approaches to Ancient Judaism: Theory and Practice* (1978), pp. 56-61.

4. Neusner, 'The Teaching of the Rabbis', pp. 231-33.

5. Bloch, 'Methodological Note', p. 56.

When the latter prophets died, that is, Haggai, Zechariah, and Malachi, then the Holy Spirit came to an end in Israel. But even so, they made them hear [Heavenly messages] through an echo.[1]

The text clearly equates prophecy with the inspiration of the Spirit: the cessation of prophecy is the cessation of pneumatic experience. Furthermore, there are indications that *t. Sot.* 13.2 represents early tradition. As a Tannaitic document edited in the late third or early fourth century AD, the Tosefta comes from the earliest period of rabbinic redaction.[2] Internal criteria confirm the antiquity of the tradition contained in the text. External criteria suggest that the tradition originated in the pre-Christian era.

Internal Criteria

t. Sot. 13.2

משמת חגי זכריה ומלאכי נביאים האחרונים פסקה רוח הקודש מישראל ואף על פי כן היו משמיעין להן בבת קול

The passages which parallel *t. Sot.* 13.2 include:[3]

j. Sot. 9.13/14

משמתו נביאים חגי זכריה ומלאכי פסקה מהן רוח הקודש אף על פי כן משתמשין היו בבת קול

b. Sot. 48b

משמתו חגי זכריה ומלאכי נסתלקה רוח הקודש מישראל ואף על פי כן היו משתמשין בבת קול

b. San. 11a

משמתו נביאים האחרונים חגי זכריה ומלאכי נסתלקה רוח הקודש מישראל ואף על פי כן היו משתמשין בבת קול

b. Yom. 9b

משמתו נביאים האחרונים חגי זכריה ומלאכי נסתלקה רוח הקודש מישראל ועדיין היו משתמשין בבת קול

The striking similarities between these texts indicate that they are dependent upon related traditions. However, the texts differ at significant points and a comparison of these differences is revealing. While *t. Sot.* 13.2 and *j. Sot.* 9.13/14 employ פסקה with reference to

---

1. ET by J. Neusner, *Sota* 13.3 (Heb. text: 13.2), in *Nashim* (1979), *The Tosefta*, III.

2. Schürer, *History*, I, p. 77. Cf. Bowker, *The Targums*, pp. 62-63.

3. The Hebrew text of *t. Sot.* 13.2 is from M.S. Zuckermandel, *Tosefta* (1882). The Hebrew text of *j. Sot.* 9.13/14 is from תלמוד ירושלמי (Wilna: Romm, 1926). Texts for *b. Sot.* 48b, *b. Sanh.* 11a, and *b. Yom.* 9b are from L. Goldschmidt, *Der Babylonische Talmud*. Other parallel texts are *Cant. R.* 8.9.3 and *Yalq.* בשלח §261. However, both of these works were edited at a relatively late period (*Cant. R.*: 7th–8th century; Yalqut: 13th century) and tend to draw upon already existing traditions (see Schürer, *History*, I, p. 99 [*Yalqut*]; Bowker, *The Targums*, p. 83 [*Cant. R.*]).

the departure of the Holy Spirit from Israel/them respectively, the three texts from the Babylonian Talmud employ נחלקה. However, all three citations from the Babylonian Talmud agree with *t. Sot.* 13.2 against the Jerusalem Talmud in their use of רוח הקודש מישראל rather than מהן רוח הקודש. Thus, at significant points of disagreement, the texts of the Jerusalem (*j. Sot.* 9.13/14) and Babylonian Talmuds (*b. Sot.* 48b; *b. Sanh.* 11a; *b. Yom.* 9b) agree with *t. Sot.* 13.2. This fact suggests that the Jerusalem and Babylonian Talmuds are dependent upon the earlier tradition contained in *t. Sot.* 13.2.[1]

This judgment receives further support from an analysis of the immediate context of *t. Sot.* 13.2 and the parallel texts. Each of the passages cited above, with the exception of *b. Yom.* 9b,[2] record a message uttered by the בת קול in the midst of a gathering of the wise in Jericho:

> 'There is among you a man who is worthy to receive the Holy Spirit
> (יש כאן אדם שראוי כרוח הקודש), but the generation is unworthy of such an
> honor'. They all set their eyes upon Samuel the Small. At the time of his
> death what did they say? 'Woe for the humble man, woe for the pious
> man, the disciple of Hillel the Elder!' (*t. Sot.* 13.4).[3]

The parallel texts in the Babylonian Talmud (*b. Sot.* 48b, *b. Sanh.* 11a) replace the רוח הקודש of *t. Sot.* 13.4 with שכינה. The use of שכינה rather than רוח הקודש is characteristic of the Babylonian Talmud and probably represents a later redaction.[4] This suggests that the Babylonian Talmud has altered the early tradition preserved in *t. Sot.* 13.4.

---

1. Schäfer, *Die Vorstellung*, p. 95.
2. *B. Yom.* 9b does not follow the other parallel passages at this point and represents an independent redaction of several traditions. *J. Sot.* 9.17 contains a significant variation from the other texts cited. In *j. Sot.* 9.17 the בת קול declares that 'two among you' (in contrast to the singular, 'a man' in *t. Sot.* and parallels) are worthy of the *Bath Kol* and then names Hillel as one of the two: ויצאת בת קול ואמרה להן יש ביניכם שנים ראוין לרוח הקודש והלל הזקן אחד מהן.
3. Samuel the Small is from the second generation Tannaim (AD 90–130; H.L. Strack, *Introduction to the Talmud and Midrash* [1931], p. 112).
4. See Schäfer, *Die Vorstellung*, pp. 93, 97, 142; A.M. Goldberg, *Untersuchungen über die Vorstellung von der Schekhinah in der frühen rabbinischen Literatur* (1969), pp. 219-24. For an opposing opinion see J. Abelson, *The Immanence of God in Rabbinic Literature* (1912), p. 379. Abelson tentatively sugggests that the rabbis originally preferred to use שכינה rather than רוח הקודש while the latter term was employed by Jewish Christians. When the break between Christianity and Judaism became clear, the use of רוח הקודש was deemed more acceptable. However, the later redactional insertion of שכינה alongside or as a replacement for רוח הקודש is to be preferred over Abelson's theory due to (1) numerous early references to רוח הקודש in the

The rabbinic discussion concerning the dating of the withdrawal of the Holy Spirit and the cessation of prophecy follows a logical progression of thought. By placing *t. Sot.* 13.2 within this logical sequence, it is possible to uncover further evidence for the relative antiquity of the tradition underlying this text. *T. Sot.* 13.2 dates the withdrawal of the Holy Spirit from the death of Haggai, Zechariah, and Malachi. This statement contradicts another strand of rabbinic tradition which associates the withdrawal of the Holy Spirit with the destruction of the first temple,[1] for Haggai, Zechariah, and Malachi lived in the post-exilic period after the destruction of the first temple.

Two attempts to resolve this apparent contradiction are recorded in *Pesikta de Rabbi Kahana* 13,14:

> As Benjamin was the last of the tribes, so was Jeremiah the last of all the prophets. Did Haggai, Zechariah, and Malachi not prophesy after him? Rabbi Eleazar and Rabbi Samuel bar Nachman: R. Eleazar said: They shortened (קיערי) his [Jeremiah's] prophecy. R. Samuel bar Nachman said: The commission to prophesy to them was already laid in the hands, the hands of Haggai, Zechariah, and Malachi.[2]

With the term קיערי ('shortened'), Rabbi Eleazar states that Haggai, Zechariah, and Malachi were dependent on the prophecy of Jeremiah. Rabbi Eleazar is thus able to associate the post-exilic prophets with the period before the destruction of the first temple and reconcile the two apparently contradictory traditions concerning the withdrawal of the Holy Spirit and the cessation of prophecy. Rabbi Samuel bar Nachman resolves the problem in a different manner. He argues that the post-exilic prophets had already received their prophecies or prophetic commissions in the time of Jeremiah, i.e. before the destruction of the first temple: they *only proclaimed* their prophecies after the first temple was destroyed.[3] These attempts at reconciliation indicate that the two conflicting views were already firmly established at a relatively early date.[4] Thus, in light of *PRK* 13,14, *t. Sot.* 13.2 must be placed in

---

literature of intertestamental Judaism, and (2) the unique way in which the terms are employed in the Babylonian Talmud (cf. Goldberg, *Untersuchungen*, p. 467).

1. Rabbinic citations which link the withdrawal of the Holy Spirit with the first temple include: *Lam. R. Proem* 23; *Eccl. R.* 12.7.1; *Num. R.* 15.10.

2. The Hebrew text of *PRK* 13,14 is from B. Mandelbaum, *Pesikta de Rab Kahana* (1962), p. 238. ET is my own.

3. Schäfer, *Die Vorstellung*, p. 96.

4. R. Samuel bar Nachman and R. Eleazar (ben Pedath) may be placed in the early part of the 4th century AD (see Bowker, *The Targums*, p. 369; Strack, *Introduction*, pp. 124-25).

the earliest period of the development of rabbinic thought on this matter.

External Criteria. Outside the rabbinic literature we search in vain for exact parallels to *t. Sot.* 13.2. Nevertheless, 1 Macc. 4.46, 9.27, and 14.41 reflect the conviction that the age of prophecy had ceased.[1] These texts bear witness to the existence of a tradition concerning the cessation of prophecy in the early part of the first century BC.[2] This external witness, coupled with the internal criteria detailed above, suggests that *t. Sot.* 13.2 represents a tradition which originated in the pre-Christian era.

1. Thus Marmorstein asserts that the author of 1 Maccabees must have been familiar with the view that the Holy Spirit vanished with the last prophets (*Studies in Jewish Theology* [1950], pp. 123-24). See also Ps. 74.9; Zech. 13.2-6; Josephus, *Apion* 1.41; 2 *Bar.* 85.1-3. The Mishnah (*m. Sot.* 9.12, 15) also presupposes concepts similar to those expressed in *t. Sot.* 13.2. R. Meyer argues that John Hyrcanus fills the role of the prophet expected in 1 Macc. 4.46; 14.41 ('προφήτης', *TDNT*, VI, p. 816). However, the lack of explicit textual support for his position and the fact that the Spirit is never attributed to John speak against Meyer's thesis.

2. Nickelsburg dates 1 Maccabees between 104 and 63 BC (*Jewish Literature*, p. 117); Schürer, *History*, III, p. 181: 'The first decades of the first century BC appear to be the most probable period of composition'. R. Meyer has given classic expression to the thesis that prophecy remained active in Judaism through the second temple period ('προφήτης', pp. 818-28; see also Aune, *Prophecy*, p. 103; and G. Krodel, 'The Functions of the Spirit in the Old Testament, the Synoptic Tradition and the Book of Acts', in *The Holy Spirit in the Life of the Church* [1978], p. 16). Meyer cites numerous instances of prophetic activity within this period. In light of this evidence, E.E. Urbach has argued that rabbinic references to the cessation of prophecy were directed against Christian claims to the Spirit of prophecy and therefore are later additions ('?מתי פסקה הנבואה' ['When Did Prophecy Disappear?'], *Tarb* 17 [1945-46], pp. 1-11). However, Schäfer (*Die Vorstellung*, pp. 143-46), Davies (*Paul*, pp. 209-15), and Hill (*New Testament Prophecy* [1979], pp. 33-37) have argued that isolated instances of prophetic activity do not jeopardize the antiquity of the rabbinic teaching. This judgment is supported by my survey of the literature as well as the texts from 1 Maccabees cited above: some texts speak of the present activity of the Spirit, but on a level not to be equated with the prophetic inspiration of the past (Sirach, Qumran, Philo, Wisdom; cf. Davies, 'Reflections on the Spirit in the Mekilta', p. 98; Marmorstein, *Jewish Theology*, pp. 122-44; and Abelson, *The Immanence of God*, p. 260). Other texts speak of ongoing prophetic activity, yet never attribute this activity to the inspiration of the Spirit and thus carefully distinguish between the prophecy of the past and that of the present (Josephus, Philo, Rabbis). In view of this evidence, Schäfer's hypothesis must be judged more tenable than Urbach's: 'Es fragt sich, ob man mit Urbach in der rabbinischen These unbedingt eine Antwort auf die Polemik der Kirchenväter sehen muß und nicht ebensogut umgekehrt die Polemik der Kirchenväter als Reaktion auf die jüdische Auffassung vom hl. Geist verstehen kann' (*Die Vorstellung*, p. 144).

1.1.2. ARN A.34. A commentary on the mishnaic tractate *Pirke Aboth, Aboth de Rabbi Nathan (ARN)* offers important insight into rabbinic perspectives on the Spirit:

> By ten names was the Holy Spirit called, to wit: parable, metaphor, riddle, speech, saying, glory, command, burden, prophecy, vision *(ARN A.34).*[1]

There is a striking coherence in the ten names given for the Holy Spirit in *ARN* A.34: virtually all of the names are related to phenomena characteristic of prophetic inspiration. The majority of the names are directly related to aspects of speech.[2] The Spirit is also associated with special revelation (vision), and explicitly cited as the source of prophecy.

In several of the texts which parallel *ARN* A.34 the term 'Holy Spirit' is replaced with 'Prophecy' (e.g. *ARN* B.37; *Gen. R.* 44.6; *Cant. R.* 3.4).[3] These texts do not refer to the Holy Spirit. *Cant. R.* 3.4 serves as an example of this variation in the tradition:

> There are ten expressions denoting prophecy: vision, prophecy, preaching, speaking, saying, commanding, burden, poetry, riddle.[4]

A third variation in the tradition is found in *MHG* Gen. 242:

> With ten names prophecy is named: 'seeing' as it is said 'is the Seer here?' (1 Sam. 9.11); 'watching' as it is said 'I have appointed you a watchman' (Ezek. 3.17 and 33.7); 'proverb' as it is said 'the proverbs of Solomon' (Prov. 1.1); 'interpretation' as it is said 'my interpreters are my friends' (Job 16.20);[5] 'the Holy Spirit' as it is said 'take not your Holy Spirit from me' (Ps. 51.13);[6] 'prophecy' as it is said 'I will raise up a prophet for them' (Deut. 18.18); 'vision' as it is said 'the vision of Isaiah the son of Amoz' (Isa. 1.1); 'oracle' as it is said 'the oracle which Habakkuk saw' (Hab. 1.1); 'sermon' as it is said 'do not preach against the house of Isaac'

---

1. ET from J. Goldin, *The Fathers according to Rabbi Nathan* (1955).
2. Schäfer, *Die Vorstellung*, p. 19, writes of *ARN* A.34: 'Die Gleichsetzung von "hl. Geist" und "Prophetie" ist in diesem Text eindeutig. Der Begriff "hl. Geist" wird auf die verschiedenen Ausformungen der prophetischen Rede eingeschränkt.'
3. For a more comprehensive list of texts see Schäfer, *Die Vorstellung*, p. 19.
4. ET is from M. Simon, 'Song of Songs', *The Midrash Rabbah* (1977), IV.
5. This text may provide insight into the problematic phrase in Job 16.20 (מליצי רעי). *MHG* Gen. 242 supports the translation of the NIV ('My intercessor is my friend') against that of the Good News Bible ('My friends scorn me').
6. MT Ps. 51.13; ET Ps. 51.11. Although Schäfer indicates that he has used Margulies's text, he attaches an erroneous biblical reference to 'Holy Spirit' at this point in his German translation (Deut. 18.18 rather than Ps. 51.11). He appears to have skipped over the line dealing with 'prophecy' and then incorrectly attributed the biblical reference, Deut. 18.18, to 'Holy Spirit'. This would also account for the fact that Schäfer lists nine rather than ten names (*Die Vorstellung*, p. 19).

(Amos 7.16); 'riddle' as it is said 'son of man speak a riddle' (Ezek. 17.2).[1]

Reversing the roles of the terms 'Holy Spirit' and 'prophecy' found in *ARN* A.34, *MHG* Gen. 242 lists רוח הקדש as a name for נבואה. The biblical text which *MHG* Gen. 242 cites as support for the identification of the Spirit with prophecy, Ps. 51.11 (MT Ps. 51.13), is particularly striking. This text is frequently interpreted by modern exegetes with reference to the Spirit as the source of the moral-religious life.[2] Yet, according to *MHG* Gen. 242, the Spirit of Ps. 51.11 is the Spirit of prophecy. Thus *MHG* Gen. 242 gives us valuable insight into how extensively the gift of the Spirit was identified with prophetic inspiration by the rabbis.

Internal Criteria. The tradition of the 'ten names' has been preserved in three variant forms represented by *ARN* A.34, Songs 3.4, and *MHG* Gen. 242. How are we to assess the development of this tradition? In terms of final redaction, *ARN* A is to be dated earlier than *Midrash Rabbah* and *Midrash Haggadol*.[3] Although *ARN* A, in its present form, belongs to the post-Talmudic period, all of the rabbis whom it cites belong to the age of the Mishna and it 'may be considered as Tannaitic in substance'.[4] The question of the relationship between *ARN* A and *ARN* B is relevant, in that they represent two of the variant forms of this tradition. Although this question has not yet received a definitive answer, some feel that *ARN* A represents an earlier (if less faithful) version of a lost proto-*ARN*.[5] If we are allowed to borrow a criterion from textual criticism in our analysis of the literary relationship of these texts, 'the harder reading is to be preferred', *ARN* A.34 would undoubtedly be selected as the more primitive version. We can visualize later redactors altering the text to read 'prophecy' rather than 'Holy Spirit' for contextual reasons. However, it is more difficult to

---

1. Hebrew text is from Mordecai Margulies, *Midrash Haggadol on the Pentateuch: Genesis* (1947), p. רמב (242). ET is my own.

2. See for example, Gunkel, *Die Wirkungen*, p. 10; Hill, *Greek Words*, p. 210; and W. Kaiser, 'The Promise of God and the Outpouring of the Holy Spirit: Joel 2.28-32 and Acts 2.16-21', in *The Living and Active Word of God* (1983), p. 122.

3. Schürer places *Midrash Haggadol* in the 13th century AD and *Cant. R.* in the 7th or 8th century AD (*History*, I, pp. 93, 95). See also Bowker, *The Targums*, for the relative late origin of *Midrash Haggadol* (p. 72 n. 4) and *Midrash Rabbah* (pp. 77f.; esp. Songs, p. 83).

4. Schürer, *History*, I, p. 80. See also Goldin, *The Fathers* (1955), p. xi; and Bowker, *The Targums*, p. 88.

5. See Goldin, *The Fathers*, p. xxii.

speculate why a redactor would do the reverse, particularly in light of the fact that *ARN* A.34 is the only text which preserves the tradition in this way. It is also possible that the inclusion of 'Holy Spirit' as one of the names for prophecy in *MHG* Gen. 242 is an accommodation to the early tradition preserved in *ARN* A.34 and its alteration by later redactors. Therefore, it is most probable that *ARN* A.34 represents an early tradition, one upon which the other parallel texts are dependent.[1]

External Criteria. There are no texts outside the rabbinic literature which parallel *ARN* A.34. Nevertheless, as we have seen, numerous texts throughout the intertestamental period associate the Spirit with prophetic inspiration in a manner similar to *ARN* A.34. It is therefore quite probable that this tradition cited by the rabbis of the Tannaitic period originated in the pre-Christian era.

1.2. *The Targums*

It is generally recognized that the Targums 'embody ancient exegetical traditions'.[2] Thus, although the nature of the development of the Targum tradition remains a matter of dispute,[3] most scholars agree that the Targums constitute an invaluable source for reconstructing first-century Jewish thought.[4] I shall therefore assess the significance of the Targums for this inquiry into Jewish perspectives on the Spirit.

---

1. Schäfer writes: 'Die Fassung der ARN version A Kapitel 34 is mit großer Wahrscheinlichkeit ursprünglich und gehört in die tannaitische Zeit' (*Die Vorstellung*, p. 20).
2. Vermes, *Scripture and Tradition*, p. 177. Note also R. Le Déaut, *The Message of the New Testament and the Aramaic Bible (Targum)* (1982), p. 25: 'We can, with some degree of confidence, consider that the targumic sources on the whole represent an exegetical tradition which is at least contemporary to Christ'.
3. P. Kahle (*The Cairo Geniza*, 2nd edn [1959]) and A. Diez Macho ('The Recently Discovered Palestinian Targum: Its Antiquity and Relationship with the other Targums', VTSup 7 [1959], pp. 222-45) have argued for the priority of the Palestinian Targum tradition (*CN, Frag. Targ.*, and *Targ. Ps.-J.*), particularly its primary representative, *CN*. This view has been contested by Schäfer ('Die Termini "Heiliger Geist" und "Geist der Prophetie" in den Targumim und das Verhältnis der Targumim zueinander', *VT* 20 [1970], pp. 304-14) and A.M. Goldberg ('Die spezifische Verwendung des Terminus Schekhinah in Targum Onkelos als Kriterium einer relativen Datierung', *Jud* 19 [1963], pp. 43-61; and *Untersuchungen* [1969]). Both Schäfer and Goldberg argue for the relative antiquity of TO.
4. I refer to the Targums of the Pentateuch (*CN, TO, Targ. Ps.-J., Frag. Targ.*) and *Targum Jonathan (TJ)* to the Prophets. The Targums on the Writings are, on the whole, considered to be of later origin (Aramaic fragments of Job have, however, been discovered at Qumran). For this reason I shall limit the inquiry to the Targums of the Pentateuch and Prophets. For a survey of recent trends see McNamara, *Pales-*

1.2.1. *The Targums of the Pentateuch*

Codex Neofiti. In *CN*, apart from the references to the Spirit in connection with creation,[1] the Spirit of God is almost always designated by the term רוח קודשה.[2] The only occurrence of רוח נבואה is found in the margin of Exod. 2.12. *CN* Exod. 31.3 also contains a reference to רוח דנבי ('spirit of a prophet') which may be a corruption of רוח נבואה ('Spirit of prophecy'). In each of these occurrences רוח קודשה appears as the source of prophetic inspiration.

The pneumatological perspective of *CN* is particularly apparent in those texts where the MT text has been significantly modified. Jacob's flight from Laban to the hill country of Gilead is described in Gen. 31.21. *CN* adds in the margin this explanatory note: 'because he had seen in the holy spirit (ברוח קודשא) that liberation would be effected there for Israel in the days of Jephthah of Gilead'.[3] According to *CN* Gen. 42.1, Jacob saw 'in the holy spirit' (ברוח קודשא) that corn was being sold in Egypt. The margin of *CN* Exod. 2.12 gives justification for Moses' murder of the Egyptian: '[Moses saw] in the holy spirit (ברוח קודשא) the two worlds and behold, there was no proselyte destined to arise from that Egyptian; and he smote the Egyptian and buried him in the sand'.[4] *CN* Num. 11.28 records that Joshua, in response to the prophesying of Eldad and Medad, asked Moses to 'withhold the holy spirit from them' (מנע מנהון רוח קודשה). In each of these additions to the MT by *CN*, the Spirit is the source of special revelation or inspired speech.

---

tinian Judaism, pp. 211-17. Note also P. Seidelin, 'Der 'Ebed Jahwe und die Messiasgestalt im Jesajatargum', *ZNW* 35 (1936), p. 195; Bowker, *The Targums*, p. 19; Diez Macho, 'Palestinian Targum', p. 236; Schürer, *History*, I, pp. 102, 104-105; Le Déaut, *Aramaic Bible (Targum)*, pp. 24-28; Kahle, *The Cairo Geniza*, p. 208, writes: 'In the Palestinian Targum of the Pentateuch we have in the main material coming from pre-Christian times which must be studied by everyone who wishes to understand the state of Judaism at the time of the birth of Christianity'.

1. See *CN* Gen. 1.2; 2.7. For the connection in *CN* Gen. 2.7 between the Spirit as the source of human life and the source of speech see M. Wojciechowski, 'Le don de l'Esprit Saint dans Jean 20.22 selon Targ. Gn. 2.7', *NTS* 33 (1987), pp. 289-92.

2. Or similar expressions (רוח דקדש; ברוח קודשא). See Gen. 31.21 (M); 41.38; 42.1; Exod. 2.12 (M2); 35.31; Num. 11.17, 25 (2×), 26, 28, 29; 14.24; 24.2; 27.18. This list includes the marginal readings in Gen. 31.21 and Exod. 2.12. Exod. 2.12 has two marginal readings (M1: ברוח נבואה; M2: ברוח קודשא).

3. The Aramaic text of *CN* is from Diez Macho, *Neophyti I* (6 vols., 1968). An ET is provided by M. McNamara and M. Maher in the same work.

4. This is the reading of M2. M1 reads: '[Moses looked] in a spirit of prophecy in this world and in the world to come and he saw and behold, there was no innocent man to go forth from him and he smote the Egyptian and buried him in the sand'.

Targum Onkelos. This Targum explicitly states what is implied in the redaction of *CN*: the Spirit of God is 'the Spirit of prophecy' (רוח נבואה).[1] The only exception is a reference to רוח קודשא in *TO* Gen. 45.27. J.P. Schäfer has questioned the authenticity of this reading.[2] Regardless of which reading is to be preferred, in *TO* Gen. 45.27 the Spirit functions as the Spirit of prophecy, revealing to Jacob the veracity of the message brought to him that Joseph lives. The *TO* frequently translates the רוח אלהים of the MT with רוח נבואה. Two examples are listed below.[3]

Gen. 41.38:

MT	בו	רוח אלהים	איש אשר
TO	מן קדם יוי ביה	דרוח נבואה	גבר

Num. 27.18:

MT	בו	רוח	איש שאר	
TO	נבואה ביה	דרוח	גבר	

These redactions in *TO* represent further evidence of the tendency in the Targum tradition to equate the activity of the Spirit with prophetic inspiration.[4]

Targum Pseudo-Jonathan. This Targum reflects the terminology characteristic of both *CN* and *TO*, using the term רוח קודשא 15 times and the term רוח נבואה 11 times.[5] For *Targ. Ps.-J.*, like *CN*, רוח קודשא is the source of prophetic inspiration. Particularly noteworthy are the numerous texts into which *Targ. Ps.-J.* inserts the term רוח קודשא which do not parallel *CN*. One example is *Targ. Ps.-J.* Gen. 27.5,

1. See *TO* on Gen. 41.38; Exod. 31.3; 35.31; Num. 11.25, 26, 29; 24.2; 27.18. Aramaic texts are from A. Sperber, *The Bible in Aramaic. I. The Pentateuch according to Targum Onkelos* (1959). The MSS which contain 'Spirit of prophecy' in the texts above are: MS Socin 84; MS Solger 2; the First Biblia Rabbinica, Venice 1515/17; the Second Biblia Rabbinica, Venice 1524/25; Biblia Hebraica, Ixar 1490. The reading in Exod. 35.31 is supported by all the MSS cited above except MS Socin 84.

2. Sperber appears to view this as the original reading and he is supported by *MHG* Gen. 767. However, Schäfer points to *PRE* ch. 38 (p. 89b) as evidence that the reading 'Spirit of prophecy' might be original. *Targ. Ps.-J.* also reads 'Spirit of prophecy'. See Schäfer, 'Das Verhältnis', p. 307.

3. See also Schäfer, *Die Vorstellung*, pp. 23, 26.

4. Cothenet, 'Les prophètes chrétiens', p. 90 n. 51: 'C'est le signe que pour le judaïsme la principale manifestation de l'Esprit réside dans la parole prophétique'.

5. רוח קודשא: Gen. 6.3; 27.5, 42; 30.25; 31.21 (= *CN*); 35.22; 37.33; 43.14; Exod. 31.3 (= *CN*); 33.16; Deut. 5.21; 18.15, 18; 28.59; 32.26. רוח נבואה: Gen. 41.38 (= *TO*); 45.27; Exod. 33.16; 35.31 (= *TO*); Num. 11.17, 25 (= *TO*), 26 (= *TO*), 28, 29 (= *TO*); 24.2 (= *TO*); 27.18 (= *TO*).

which states that Rebecca was enabled by the Holy Spirit to hear the words Isaac spoke to Esau:

MT	יצחק אל־עשו	בדבר	ורבקה שמעת
CN	כד מלל יצחק עם עשו		ורבקה שמעת
TPsJ	כד מליל יצחק עם עשו	ברוח קודשא	ורבקה שמעת[1]

The Fragment Targum. As in *CN*, the *Frag. Targ.* generally uses the term רוח קודשה rather than רוח נבואה. However, רוח נבואה does appear in *Frag. Targ.* Num. 11.28:

> And Joshua son of Nun, Moses' attendant, from among the youths, spoke up and said: 'My master, Moses, stop the prophetic spirit from them (פסוק מנהון רוח נבואה)'.[2]

Furthermore, only five occurrences of רוח קודשה can be found in *Frag. Targ.*,[3] and of these five occurrences, two are unique to *Frag. Targ.* in relation to *CN*: Gen. 27.1 and Gen. 37.33. According to *Frag. Targ.* Gen. 27.1, Isaac was capable of being deceived by Jacob because 'he was old and his eyes were too dim to see' (with the MT) and furthermore, because 'the holy spirit departed from him'. In *Frag. Targ.* Gen. 37.33 the entire sense of the biblical passage is changed. Upon seeing Joseph's torn tunic, rather than assuming the worst (as in the MT), Jacob responds:

> It is my son's garment; a wild beast has not devoured him nor has my son been killed at all; however, I see through the holy spirit that an evil woman stands opposite him, the wife of Potiphar (*Frag. Targ.* Gen. 37.33).

In the texts unique to *Frag. Targ.* there is no change from *CN* in the way the activity of the Holy Spirit is perceived: the Spirit is the source of special revelation and inspiration. Although the Targums of the Pentateuch refer to the Spirit of God with different terms and in different contexts, they all agree on a fundamental point: the Spirit of God is the Spirit of prophecy.

---

1. The Aramaic text of *Targ. Ps.-J.* is from M. Ginsburger, *Pseudo-Jonathan* (1903).
2. Contra Schäfer, 'Das Verhältnis', p. 308: 'Im Fragmententargum. . . der Terminus "Geist der Prophetie" wird nicht verwendet'. The Aramaic text and ET is from M.L. Klein, *The Fragment-Targums of the Pentateuch according to their Extant Sources* (2 vols.; 1980). Only one MS contains the Targum on Num. 11.28: MS Paris-Bibliothèque nationale Hébr. 110, folios 1-16.
3. Gen. 27.1; 37.33; 42.1 (= *CN*); Exod. 2.12 (= *CN*); Num. 11.26 (= *CN*).

1.2.2. *Targum Jonathan to the Prophets. Targum Jonathan* modifies the Spirit-terminology of the MT in a variety of ways.[1] References to the Spirit of God in the MT are often translated רוח נבואה in *Targum Jonathan*.[2] According to *TJ* 1 Sam 10.10, 'the Spirit of prophecy (רוח נבואה) from before the Lord resided upon [Saul] and he sang praise in their midst'.[3] So also *TJ* Isa. 61.1 reads: 'The Spirit of prophecy (רוח נבואה) from before the Lord Elohim is upon me'.[4]

The prophetic character of pneumatic experience is presupposed in three other texts from the Targum of Isaiah. Compare the following texts from *TJ* Isaiah with their counterparts in the MT:

MT Isa. 40.13   Who has understood the spirit of the Lord (רוח־יהוה)?

TJ Isa. 40.13   Who hath directed the holy spirit (רוח קדשא) in the mouth of all the prophets (בפום כל נבייא)?

MT Isa. 63.11   Where is he who set his Holy Spirit (רוח קדשו) among them?[5]

TJ Isa. 63.11   Where is he who caused the word of his holy prophets (מימר נביי קודשיה) to dwell among them?

MT Isa. 59.21   This is my covenant with them, says the Lord, My Spirit (רוחי), who is on you, and my words (דברי) that I have put in your mouth will not depart from you.

TJ Isa. 59.21   This is my covenant with them, saith the Lord; my holy spirit (רוח קדשי) which is upon thee, and the words of prophecy (ופתגמי נבואתי) which I have put in thy mouth, shall not depart from thy mouth.

In the Targum of Ezekiel the phrase 'the hand of the Lord' (MT: יד־יהוה) is frequently altered to 'the Spirit of prophecy' (רוח נבואה).[6] Compare, for example, *TJ* Ezek. 1.3, 'the Spirit of prophecy (רוח

---

1. Aramaic texts are from A. Sperber, *The Bible in Aramaic II: The Former Prophets according to Targum Jonathan* (1959); and *The Bible in Aramaic III: The Latter Prophets according to Targum Jonathan* (1962). ETs are from: S.H. Levey, *The Targum of Ezekiel* (1987); D.J. Harrington and A.J. Saldarini, *Targum Jonathan of the Former Prophets* (1987); J.F. Stenning, *The Targum of Isaiah* (2nd edn, 1953).

2. See for example *TJ* Judg. 3.10; 1 Sam. 10. 6, 10; 19.20, 23; 2 Sam. 23.2; 1 Kgs 22.24; 2 Kgs 2.9; Isa. 61.1; Ezek. 11.5.

3. The MT reads: והצלח עליו רוח אלהים ויתנבא בתוכם.

4. The MT reads: רוח אדני יהוה עלי.

5. A similar alteration occurs in *TJ* Isa. 63.10. רוח is frequently translated with מימר in the Targum of Isaiah: see *TJ* Isa. 4.4; 28.6; 30.28; 34.6; 48.16; 59.19; 63.10, 11, 14.

6. See *TJ* Ezek. 1.3; 3.22; 8.1; 40.1. Compare also *TJ* Ezek. 3.14, 'and a prophecy from before the Lord overwhelmed me', with the biblical text: 'and the strong hand of the Lord upon me'.

נבואה) from before the Lord rested upon (Ezekiel)', with the biblical text: 'the hand of the Lord (יד־יהוה) was upon (Ezekiel)'. In texts where prophetic inspiration is not in view, references to the Lord's hand, 'my hand' (MT: ידי), are rendered 'my power' (גבורתי).[1] In texts from the former prophets which speak of miraculous (non-prophetic) deeds, such as Samson's exploits, 'the Spirit of the Lord' (MT: רוח יהוה) is often rendered 'Spirit of power' (רוח גבורא).[2] However, רוח נבואה is occasionally found in texts where we would expect to find רוח גבורא (e.g. *TJ* Judg. 3.10; *2* Kgs 2.9). These texts, along with the modifications of *TJ* Ezekiel and *TJ* Isaiah cited above, indicate that the redactors of *TJ* tended to associate the Spirit exclusively with prophetic inspiration.

2. *The Spirit and the Age to Come*

Several passages in the Hebrew Scriptures anticipate a universal outpouring of the Spirit over the house of Israel in 'the last days'.[3] In the following section I shall examine how these biblical passages were interpreted by the Rabbis and discuss the relevance of the rabbinic evidence for reconstructing eschatological expectations in first-century Judaism.

2.1. *The Eschatological Bestowal of the Spirit*
The expectation of an endtime outpouring of the Spirit is found in a number of rabbinic texts. Although the rabbis maintained that the Spirit had departed from Israel due to her sin,[4] they looked forward to the day when the Spirit would once again come upon her people.[5] This eschatological outpouring of the Spirit is generally interpreted in light of Joel 3.1f. (MT) as a restoration of the Spirit of prophecy.[6] *MHG* Gen. 140 and *Num. R.* 15.25 are representative of this perspective:

---

1. See *TJ* Ezek. 6.14; 13.9; 14.9, 13; 25.7, 13, 16; 39.21. This practice is not limited to *TJ* Ezekiel: see for example *TJ* Josh. 4.24; Jer. 6.12; 15.6; 16.21; 51.25.
2. See for example *TJ* Judg. 11.29; 13.25; 14.6, 19; 15.14; 1 Sam. 16.13, 14. See also 1 Sam. 11.6, where 'the Spirit of God' is rendered 'Spirit of power'.
3. Num. 11.29; Joel 3.1f.; Ezek. 36.27; 37.14; 39.29; Isa. 44.3; Zech. 12.10.
4. See the texts cited by Schäfer, *Die Vorstellung*, pp. 103-11, esp. *MHG* Gen. 135, 139f.; *MHG* Exod. 438; *Ruth R. Proem* 2; *Sif. Deut.* §173.
5. Schäfer, *Die Vorstellung*, p. 143: '"Aufhören" zu einem bestimmten Zeitpunkt und "Wiederkehr" in der Endzeit sind die beiden Pole eines geschichtstheologischen Schemas, das ohne Zweifel für viele Rabbinen maßgebend war'.
6. See *MHG* Gen. 139f.; *Num. R.* 15.25; *Deut. R.* 6.14; *Lam. R.* 4.14; *Midr. Ps.* 14.6, 138.2. *Ag. Ber.* §23.2 clearly refers to a restoration of the Spirit of prophecy, but without reference to Joel 3.1.

The Holy Spirit, as in Scripture: 'I will raise up prophets from your sons' (Amos 2.11). But because they sinned, he departed from them, as it is written: 'Also, her prophets find no vision from the Lord' (Lam. 2.9). But one day the Holy One will bring him back to Israel, as it is written: 'And afterward, I will pour out my Spirit on all flesh, and your sons and daughters will prophesy' (Joel 3.1) (*MHG* Gen. 140).

The Holy One, blessed be He, said: 'In this world only a few individuals have prophesied, but in the World to come all Israel will be made prophets', as it says: 'And it shall come to pass afterward, that I will pour out my spirit upon all flesh, and your sons and your daughters shall prophesy, your old men', etc. (Joel 3.1). Such is the exposition given by R. Tanhuma, son of R. Abba (*Num. R.* 15.25).[1]

Ezekiel 36.26 is frequently cited with reference to the age to come. However, it is usually interpreted as a prophecy concerning the end-time removal of the evil יצר (impulse), and, in this regard, almost always without reference to the activity of the Spirit.[2] A notable exception is *Tan. add.* to חקת:

Concerning this the Wise say: The one who does not look at another's wife, the evil impulse (יצר הרע) has no power over him. In the World to come the Holy One, blessed be He, will take the evil impulse from us and place in us his Holy Spirit (רוח קדשו), as it is written: 'I will remove the heart of stone from your flesh and I will put my Spirit in you' (Ezek. 36.26f.).[3]

Numerous texts cite Ezek. 36.26 independent of any reference to the evil יצר. These texts are also remarkably silent concerning the activity

1. Hebrew text of *MHG* Gen. 140 is from M. Margulies, *Midrash Haggadol on the Pentateuch, Genesis*, p. 140. ET is my own. ET of *Num. R.* 15.25 is from J.J. Slotki, 'Numbers' in vol. III of *The Midrash Rabbah*.

2. *Exod. R.* 15.6; 41.7; *Num. R.* 14.4; *Deut. R.* 6.14; *Cant. R.* 1.2.4; *Eccl. R.* 9.15; *Midr. Ps.* 14.6. For example *Exod. R.* 41.7 reads: 'God then said to Moses: "In this world they made idols because of the Evil Inclination in them, but in the millennium I will uproot from them the Evil Inclination and give them a heart of flesh", as it says, "And I will take away the stony heart from out of your flesh, and I will give you a heart of flesh" (Ezek. 36.26)'. Jer. 31.33 is also cited in conjunction with the hope that the evil יצר would be removed in the age to come: *Cant. R.* 1.2.4; *Eccl. R.* 2.1.

3. Hebrew text is from S. Buber, *Midrasch Tanchuma* (1885). ET is my own. *Num. R.* 17.6 also refers to the Spirit by quoting from Ezek. 36.27 as does *Tan. add.* to חקת. However Num. 17.6 lacks the editorial comment, ויתן בקרבנו רוח קדשו, which is unique to *Tan. add.* to חקת.

of the Spirit: they usually refer to the endtime transformation of the heart without alluding to the Spirit.[1]

My judgment that the rabbis generally interpreted the eschatological outpouring of the Spirit as a restoration of the Spirit of prophecy (Joel 3.1f.) is confirmed by *Deut. R.* 6.14 and *Midr. Ps.* 14.6. These texts speak of the age to come with reference to both Ezek. 36.26 and Joel 3.1. In each instance, the transformation of the heart alluded to in Ezek. 36.26 is presented as a prerequisite for the eschatological bestowal of the Spirit, which is interpreted in light of Joel 3.1 as an outpouring of the Spirit of prophecy.[2]

In *Deut. R.* 6.14 the future eradication of the evil יצר is linked to Ezek. 36.26 and cited as a precondition for the endtime restoration of the divine presence (שכינה). The rabbis commonly believed that experience of the Spirit was dependent upon the immanence of the שכינה.[3] Therefore, Joel 3.1 is offered as scriptural proof that in the age to come the שכינה shall be restored to Israel.

> God said: 'In this world, because there are amongst you slanderers, I have withdrawn My divine Presence (שכינתי) from amongst you', as it is said, 'Be Thou exalted, O God, above the heavens' (Ps. 52.12). 'But in the time to come, when I will uproot the Evil Inclination from amongst you', as it is said, 'And I will take away the stony heart out of your flesh' (Ezek. 36.26), 'I will restore My Divine Presence (שכינתי) amongst you'. Whence this? For it is said, 'And it shall come to pass afterward, that I will pour out My Spirit upon all flesh', etc. (Joel 3.1); 'and because I will cause My Divine Presence (שכינתי) to rest upon you, all of you will merit the Torah, and you will dwell in peace in the world', as it is said, 'And all children shall be taught of the Lord; and great shall be the peace of thy children' (Isa. 44.13) (*Deut. R.* 6.14).[4]

Midrash on Psalm 14.6 also refers to the transformation of Israel's heart (Ezek. 36.26) as a precondition for the eschatological bestowal of the Spirit of prophecy (Joel 3.1f.).

> Another comment: David spoke the first time in behalf of the Master, the Holy One, blessed be He, who said: 'Oh that they had such a heart as this always, to fear Me, and keep My commandments' (Deut. 5.25); and he spoke the second time in behalf of the disciple Moses who said: 'Would that all the Lord's people were prophets' (Num. 11.29). Neither the words

---

1. See *b. Suk.* 52a; *Gen. R.* 34.15; *Num. R.* 15.16; *Cant. R.* 6.11.1; *Eccl. R.* 1.16. By way of contrast, the following texts refer to the activity of the Spirit with reference to Ezek. 36.26f.: *b. Ber.* 31b; *b. Suk.* 52b; *Num. R.* 9.49; *Midr. Ps.* 73.4.

2. Cf. Turner, 'Luke and the Spirit', p. 150.

3. See *b. Yom.* 9b, *Ag. Ber.* §23.2, and Schäfer, *Die Vorstellung*, pp. 140-43.

4. ET is from J. Rabinowitz, 'Deuteronomy' in *The Midrash Rabbah*. Hebrew text is from S. Liebermann, *Midrash Debarim Rabbah* (1940).

of the Master nor the words of the disciple are to be fulfilled in this world, but the words of both will be fulfilled in the world-to-come: The words of the Master, 'A new heart also will I give you and ye shall keep Mine ordinances' (Ezek. 36.26), will be fulfilled; and the words of the disciple, 'I will pour out My spirit upon all flesh; and your sons and daughters shall prophesy' (Joel 3.1), will also be fulfilled (*Midr. Ps.* 14.6).[1]

A large group of texts refer to the eschatological bestowal of the Spirit in general terms.[2] These texts offer little information concerning the Spirit's future function. However, in view of the evidence cited above and the general tendency of the rabbis to identify the Spirit with prophetic inspiration, one may assume that these texts are harmonious with the perspective of *MHG* Gen. 140 and *Num. R.* 15.25: the eschatological outpouring of the Spirit signifies the restoration of the prophetic gift.

Although many of the texts cited above were edited at a relatively late date,[3] the following factors suggest that they bear witness to traditions which accurately reflect aspects of the hope of first-century Judaism.[4] First, 1QS 3.13–4.26 offers an early parallel to the rabbinic texts which speak of the end-time eradication of the evil יצר in light of Ezek. 36.26. The conceptual similarities between 1QS 3–4 and the relevant rabbinic texts are apparent; and the term יצר appears in 1QS 4.5.[5] Second, in view of the antiquity of the tradition concerning the withdrawal of the Spirit and biblical texts such as Num. 11.29 and Joel 3.1f., it is highly probable that traditions similar to those found in *MHG* Gen. 140 and *Num. R.* 15.25 were current in the first century. Indeed, although it is quite likely that these traditions were often suppressed in the post-Christian era for polemical reasons,[6] it is difficult to imagine why rabbis of this later period would create such traditions

1. ET is from W.G. Braude, *The Midrash on Psalms* (1959).

2. See *MHG* Gen. 135; *Num. R.* 15.10; *Cant. R.* 1.1.11; *Pes. R.* 1b; *Lam. R.* 3.138. See for example *Cant. R.* 1.1.11: 'R. Johanan said in the name of R. Aha who had it from R. Simeon b. Abba: Let us recite songs and praises to Him who will one day cause the holy spirit to rest upon us, let us sing before Him many songs'.

3. For example, *Midrash Haggadol* was compiled in the 13th century AD (Schürer, *History*, I, p. 93). Note however Schäfer's judgment concerning *MHG* Gen. 140 (cited above): 'Der Midrasch ist in der vorliegenden Form wahrscheinlich relative spät, doch wurden ohne Zweifel ältere Traditionen verwandt' (*Die Vorstellung*, p. 108).

4. So also Davies, *Paul*, p. 216.

5. 1QS 4.4f. refers to 'a spirit. . . of holy intent (ביצר קודש)'. On the relationship between the יצר in the scrolls and the rabbinic יצר see B. Otzen, 'יצר', *TWAT*, III, p. 839. Cf. Jub. 1.20-25.

6. See Kremer, *Pfingstbericht*, pp. 81-82.

in light of Christian claims. However, the silence of the non-rabbinic intertestamental literature concerning a universal outpouring of the Spirit of prophecy may indicate that this expectation was a peripheral element in the hope of first-century Judaism.[1]

2.2. *The Spirit and the Resurrection*

The rabbis occasionally associate the Holy Spirit with the resurrection in the age to come. These citations generally fall into one of two categories: texts which refer to the 'chain' saying of R. Phineas b. Jair;[2] and texts which cite Ezek. 37.14.[3]

The 'chain' of R. Phineas b. Jair is found in the earliest strata of the rabbinic literature, the Mishnah:

> R. Phineas b. Jair says: Heedfulness leads to cleanliness, and cleanliness leads to purity, and purity leads to abstinence, and abstinence leads to holiness, and holiness leads to humility, and humility leads to the shunning of sin, and the shunning of sin leads to saintliness, and saintliness leads to [the gift of] the Holy Spirit, and the Holy Spirit leads to the resurrection of the dead. And the resurrection of the dead shall come through Elijah of blessed memory. Amen (*m. Sota* 9.15).[4]

The initial part of the 'chain' (up to and including 'saintliness leads to [the gift of] the Holy Spirit') portrays the Spirit as a gift presently available to the pious individual. The latter part of the 'chain' ('the Holy Spirit leads to the resurrection of the dead') describes the Spirit as an eschatological gift granted to the nation.[5] How can these disparate conceptions of the Spirit (contemporary–individual/eschatological– national) be reconciled? P. Schäfer suggests a possible solution.[6] He postulates that the initial part of the 'chain'[7] represents the original form of a tradition which originated in mystical circles outside of

---

1. See Hill, *New Testament Prophecy*, pp. 35-36 and Chevallier, *Le Messie*, p. 105. Of course expectations which centered on a prophetic or messianic figure endowed with the Spirit undoubtedly played a prominent role in the hopes of first-century Judaism (see Chapter 3 §2.2 above).

2. See *m. Sota* 9.15; *b. 'Abod. Zar.* 20b; *Yalq. Isa.* §503; *j. Sheq.* 3.4; *Cant. R.* 1.1.9 and the various other texts cited by Schäfer, *Die Vorstellung*, pp. 118f.

3. *Gen. R.* 14.8; 96 (MSV); 96.5; *Exod. R.* 48.4; *Cant. R.* 1.1.9; *Midr. Ps.* 85.3; *Pes. R.* 1.6. In the 'chain' of *Cant. R.* 1.1.9, Ezek. 37.14 is cited as the prooftext for the statement, 'the Holy Spirit leads to the resurrection of the dead'.

4. Strack places R. Phineas b. Jair in the 4th generation of the Tannaim (c. 180 AD) (*Introduction*, p. 117). ET is from H. Danby, *The Mishnah* (1933).

5. Schäfer, *Die Vorstellung*, p. 120.

6. Schäfer, *Die Vorstellung*, pp. 120-21.

7. That is, from the beginning up to and including 'and saintliness leads to [the gift of] the Holy Spirit'.

orthodox Judaism. The latter part of the 'chain'[1] was inserted later to accommodate the 'chain' to the orthodox perspective (withdrawal of the Spirit in the past/return in the age to come).

Schäfer's hypothesis is not entirely convincing. Although there is some textual support for his suggestion that the reference to Elijah is secondary,[2] the crucial phrase which links the Spirit to the resurrection is found in all of the parallel texts. Furthermore, a number of other texts refer to the Spirit as a reward for piety.[3] Since these texts were not expunged or altered by the rabbis, I am hesitant to view *m. Sota* 9.15 as the product of such activity.

There is an alternative solution, one that is not dependent on hypothetical redactional activity. F. Büchsel argued that when the rabbis spoke of the Spirit as a reward for pious living, they did not imply that contemporary experience of the Spirit was possible.[4] Rather, they were using language descriptive of the age to come for the purpose of moral exhortation in the present. Thus Büchsel interprets the Spirit-references in the 'chain' as descriptions of the ideal future.[5] In this way Büchsel provides a satisfying solution to the problem posed by the text. The temporal contradiction is resolved, for both statements concerning the Spirit refer to that which will be experienced in the age to come. The individual and national dimensions of the text are also reconciled, for the purpose of the text is to provide moral exhortation: the text affirms that the piety of the individual leads to the future redemption of the nation. This redemption is described in terms of the

---

1. That is: 'The Holy Spirit leads to the resurrection of the dead. And the resurrection of the dead shall come through Elijah of blessed memory.' See Schäfer, *Die Vorstellung*, p. 121.

2. *'Abod. Zar.* 20b and *Yalq. Isa.* §503 omit the part which speaks of Elijah: 'And the resurrection of the dead shall come through Elijah of blessed memory'.

3. The Holy Spirit is cited as a reward for: 'obedience to the law' (*Mech.* 113f.); 'learning and doing [the law]' (e.g. *Lev. R.* 35.7; *b. Ber.* 17a); 'good works' (*Num. R.* 10.5; *Ruth R.* 4.3); 'the proclamation of the Torah' (*Cant. R.* 1.1.8f.); 'devotion to Israel' (*Num. R.* 15.20); 'study of the Torah' (*Eccl. R.* 2.8.1). These and other texts are cited by Schäfer, *Die Vorstellung*, pp. 127-33.

4. Büchsel, *Der Geist Gottes*, pp. 128-29. Büchsel correctly notes that 'der heilige Geist ist nicht die Kraft, sondern der Lohn der echten Frömmigkeit' (p. 131).

5. Büchsel, *Der Geist Gottes*, p. 131: 'Wird hier von Idealen oder von Realitäten gesprochen? Mir ist sehr zweifelhaft, daß dieser Kettenspruch Realitäten, Tatsachen, die im Leben jedes wahrhaft Frommen vorliegen, beschreiben will. Wahrscheinlich will er nichts sein als eine Aufforderung, eine Verheißung für das ernste sittliche Streben. So wenig die Totenauferstehung schon Besitz der Frommen ist, so wenig scheint mir der heilige Geist schon Besitz der Frommen.'

future resurrection, which is associated with the eschatological gift of the Spirit.

The second group of texts relate the Spirit to the resurrection by drawing upon Ezek. 37.14.[1] Several of these texts repeat a tradition dealing with the fate of the righteous who die outside of Israel.[2] Ezekiel 37.12f. is a crucial element in the tradition because it associates the resurrection with 'the land of Israel' (Ezek. 37.12). The phrase, ונתתי רוחי בכם (Ezek. 37.14), however, plays a relatively minor role. This is particularly apparent in *Pes. R.* 1.6, where the phrase is interpreted in light of Isa. 42.5 as a reference to the restoration of the 'breath' (נשמה) of life.

> 'And His land shall make expiation for His people' (Deut. 32.43). Does this statement mean that the righteous outside the Land will lose out? No! Why not? Because, as R. Eleazar, citing R. Simai, went on to say, God will make underground passages for the righteous who, rolling through them like skin bottles, will get to the Land of Israel, and when they get to the Land of Israel, God will restore their breath to them, as is said, 'He that giveth breath unto the people upon it, and spirit to them that go through it' (Isa. 42.5). As a matter of fact, in Ezekiel there is an explicit verse on this point: 'You shall know that I am the Lord when I open your graves' (Ezek. 37.13), 'and bring you into the Land of Israel' (Ezek. 37.12). In that hour, 'I will put My spirit in you, and ye shall live' (Ezek. 37.14). You thus learn that in the days of the Messiah the dead of the Land of Israel are to be [at once] among the living; and that the righteous [dead] outside the Land are to get to it and come to life upon it (*Pes. R.* 1.6).[3]

Ezekiel 37.14 does not appear to have exerted significant influence on rabbinic eschatological expectations. The texts which refer to Ezek. 37.14 are few and relatively late. Furthermore, when Ezek. 37.14 is cited in the literature, it is often ancillary to Ezek. 37.12. The 'chain' of R. Phineas b. Jair (*m. Sota* 9.15) indicates that the Spirit was, in some quarters, associated with the resurrection at a relatively early date. However, in view of the virtual silence on this matter in the non-rabbinic sources of the intertestamental period,[4] one must conclude that the Spirit of God was generally not associated with the resurrection in first-century Judaism.

---

1. *Gen. R.* 14.8; 96 (*MSV*); 96.5; *Exod. R.* 48.4; *Midr. Ps.* 85.3; *Pes. R.* 1.6.
2. *Pes. R.* 1.6; *Gen. R.* 96.5; cf. *Gen. R.* 96 (*MSV*).
3. ET of *Pes. R.* 1.6 is from W.G. Braude, *Pesikta Rabbati: Discourses for Feasts, Fasts, and Special Sabbaths* (1968).
4. See Chapter 3 §2.3 above.

3. *Summary*

We have seen that early rabbinic tradition identifies the Spirit as the source of prophetic inspiration. The ancient exegetical traditions contained in the Targums also tend to associate the Spirit exclusively with prophetic inspiration. This pneumatological perspective is reflected in the eschatological expectation of the rabbis. According to the rabbis, the Spirit had departed from Israel due to her sin; however, in the age to come the Spirit would once again come upon her people. This eschatological outpouring of the Spirit is generally interpreted in light of Joel 3.1f. as a restoration of the Spirit of prophecy. By way of contrast, Ezek. 36.26f. is usually interpreted as a prophecy concerning the endtime removal of the evil יצר, and most frequently without reference to the activity of the Spirit. Indeed, the eradication of the evil יצר is presented as a prerequisite for the end-time bestowal of the Spirit of prophecy. These expectations are probably rooted in early tradition, although they may represent a peripheral element in the hopes of first-century Judaism. Ezekiel 37.14 did not exert much influence on rabbinic conceptions of the age to come. Thus, one may conclude with some confidence that the Spirit of God was generally not associated with the resurrection in first-century Judaism.

CONCLUSION

The literature of intertestamental Judaism consistently identifies experience of the Spirit with prophetic inspiration. The Spirit enables the sage to attain the heights of sapiential achievement, equips the Messiah with special knowledge to rule, and grants insight to the prophet of the Lord. The inspiration of the Spirit, whether it be in relation to the sage, Messiah, or prophet, is almost always related to inspired speech. However, the literature shows a general reluctance to associate the Spirit with miraculous deeds. The man or woman endowed with the Spirit may perform miracles, but these works of wonder are usually not attributed to the Spirit. Furthermore, contemporary experience of the Spirit was deemed either an impossibility or less profound in nature than that of the past. The outlook for the future was more positive. Although Jewish expectations centered on the appearance of a prophetic or messianic figure endowed with the Spirit, an eschatological bestowal of the Spirit of prophecy probably constituted an aspect of the Jewish hope. Thus I conclude that the Jews of the pre-Christian era generally regarded the gift of the Spirit as a *donum superadditum* granted to various individuals so that they might fulfill a divinely appointed task. The gift of the Spirit was not viewed as a soteriological necessity: one need not possess the gift in order to live in right relationship to God and attain eternal life through the resurrection. Indeed, the gift of the Spirit was generally not associated with the resurrection of the dead.

The only exceptions to the perspective outlined above are found in sapiential writings. The wisdom tradition displays an increasing pessimism toward man's ability to attain wisdom by purely rational means (study of the law unaided by the Spirit). The relatively optimistic anthropology of Sirach is replaced by more pessimistic appraisals of man in Wisdom and 1QH. In these texts, the gift of the Spirit, previously viewed as the source of esoteric wisdom and inspired speech, is presented as the source of sapiential achievement at every level. Thus the developments within the sapiential tradition culminate in the attribution of soteriological significance to the gift of the Spirit.

PART II

THE PROPHETIC PNEUMATOLOGY OF LUKE

INTRODUCTION

My goal in the following section is to uncover Luke's distinctive pneumatology. The method of analysis employed is redaction-critical. I shall examine relevant passages in Luke–Acts in an effort to detect Luke's 'creative contribution in all its aspects' to the tradition concerning the work of the Spirit which he transmits.[1] I shall not assume Luke's theological perspective is revealed only in his modification of received sources;[2] thus my concern will include Luke's selection, as well as his arrangement and modification of received material.

I accept the two-document hypothesis as axiomatic.[3] Therefore, I have assumed that Luke knew Mark and a written source Q. Although Markan priority has been subjected to severe criticism of late, it still remains, in my opinion, the best solution to a complex problem.[4] Similarly, while recognizing that questions related to Q are equally com-

---

1. S.S. Smalley, 'Redaction Criticism', in *New Testament Interpretation* (1977), p. 181. See also the definition of R.H. Stein, 'What is Redaktionsgeschichte?', *JBL* 88 (1969), p. 54.

2. In his article 'Shifting Sands: The Recent Study of the Gospel of Luke' (in *Interpreting the Gospels*, 1981), C.H. Talbert notes dissatisfaction with redaction-critical approaches which focus exclusively on modification of tradition: 'It has been asked whether Lucan theology should be sought only in the places where the evangelist differs from tradition instead of also in the areas where he reproduces tradition with little or no change' (pp. 210-11). Similarly, Smalley chides those who 'assume that the special contribution of the evangelists can be discovered only when they depart from their received sources, or do not depend on them at all, rather than when they reproduce them without alteration' ('Redaction Criticism', p. 187). See also J.B. Tyson, 'Source Criticism of the Gospel of Luke', in *Perspectives on Luke–Acts* (1978), p. 39, and R.C. Tannehill, *The Narrative Unity of Luke–Acts: A Literary Interpretation* (1986), esp. vol. I, p. 6.

3. B.H. Streeter, *The Four Gospels: A Study in Origins* (1924).

4. For a relatively recent and good defense see G.M. Styler, 'The Priority of Mark', Excursus 4 in Moule, *The Birth of the New Testament* (3rd edn, 1981), pp. 285-316. See also I.H. Marshall, 'How to Solve the Synoptic Problem: Luke 11:43 and Parallels', in *The New Testament Age* (1984), II, pp. 313-25 and the conclusions of J.A. Fitzmyer, 'The Priority of Mark and the "Q" Source in Luke', in *Jesus and Man's Hope*, I, (1970), p. 162.

plex, I have concluded that it represents (at least partially) a written source utilized by both Matthew and Luke.[1]

The separation of tradition from redaction is more difficult in Acts than in Luke's Gospel since we are unable to reconstruct with the same degree of certainty any of the sources employed by the author.[2] I reject, however, the notion that due to a lack of source material Luke produced Acts in a manner entirely different from his Gospel. In spite of notable claims to the contrary,[3] the conditions for the formation of tradition were not unfavorable in apostolic times.[4] In the formation of Acts, like his Gospel, Luke used a variety of written (and perhaps oral) sources.[5] It is, however, generally impossible to determine to what extent Luke's narrative is based on traditional material.[6] Nevertheless, since Luke 'is not satisfied with transcribing his sources' but 'rewrites the text by putting the imprint of his vocabulary and style everywhere',[7] Acts remains an invaluable source for determining Luke's distinctive pneumatological perspective.

1. See Lk. 3.7-9 = Mt. 3.7-10 and the conclusions of G. Fee, 'A Text-Critical Look at the Synoptic Problem', *NovT* 22 (1980), p. 23.

2. J. Dupont, *The Sources of Acts: The Present Position* (1964), pp. 166-67.

3. M. Dibelius, *Studies in the Acts of the Apostles* (1956), pp. 2f. and E. Haenchen, *The Acts of the Apostles* (1971), pp. 81-90.

4. J. Jervell, *Luke and the People of God: A New Look at Luke–Acts* (1972), pp. 19-39 and *The Unknown Paul. Essays on Luke–Acts and Early Christian History* (1984), pp. 13-25, 68-95. See also W.W. Gasque, 'Did Luke Have Access to Traditions about the Apostles and the Early Christians?', *JETS* 17 (1974), pp. 45-48.

5. See for example M. Hengel, 'Zwischen Jesus und Paulus', *ZTK* 72 (1975), p. 157; R. Glover, '"Luke the Antiochene" and Acts', *NTS* 11 (1964–65), pp. 97-106; R.A. Martin, 'Syntactical Evidence of Aramaic Sources in Acts I–XV', *NTS* 11 (1964–65), pp. 38-59; and the summary of major source theories in F. Hahn, 'Der gegenwärtige Stand der Erforschung der Apostelgeschichte', *TRev* 82 (1986), p. 181.

6. Dupont, *Sources*, p. 88.

7. *Sources*, p. 166.

Chapter 6

PROPHECY RENEWED:
THE INFANCY NARRATIVES (LUKE 1.5–2.52)

1. *Source Criticism*

Attempts at reconstructing the sources behind the initial chapters of
Luke's Gospel have produced limited and rather varied conclusions.[1]
Raymond Brown has emphasized Luke's creative hand,[2] while others,

---

1. For a summary of the history of source criticism on this section see H.H.
Oliver, 'The Lucan Birth Stories and the Purpose of Luke–Acts', *NTS* 10 (1964),
pp. 202-26 and I.H. Marshall, *The Gospel of Luke: A Commentary on the Greek
Text* (1978), pp. 45-49. Of course sources are unnecessary if one views the infancy
narratives as the creations of Matthew and Luke. Some have suggested this, arguing
that the infancy narratives were not meant to be taken as historical accounts, rather
they are of another genre altogether: Midrash (Midrash, although often loosely
defined, usually designates a creative and free commentary on Scripture which was
common in late Judaism). However, this categorization of the infancy narratives has
been severely criticized, for 'es sich hier nicht um aktualisierende Erklärung der
Schrift handelt; vielmehr werden die Ereignisse um die Geburt Jesu mit Hilfe der
Schrift meditierende ins Licht gerückt' (G. Schneider, 'Jesu geistgewirkte Empfängnis (Lk 1,34f)', *TPQ* 119 [1971], p. 108). H. Schürmann also rejects Midrash as an
appropriate designation for Lk. 1–2. According to Schürmann, Lk. 1–2 is closer to
Haggadah, which involves the exposition of events rather than Scripture. See Schürmann, *Traditionsgeschichtliche Untersuchungen zu den synoptischen Evangelien*
(1968), p. 202. Other critics of the Midrash label include R. Laurentin, *Les évangiles
de l'enfance du Christ* (1982), pp. 57-58, J. Fitzmyer, *The Gospel According to
Luke I–IX* (1981), pp. 308-309, and R.T. France, 'Scripture, Tradition, and History
in the Infancy Narratives of Matthew', in *Gospel Perspectives*, II (1981), pp. 243ff.

2. Brown rejects the idea that Luke utilized a 'Baptist' or 'Marian' source. In his
opinion, Luke received only a modicum of traditional material: the names of John the
Baptist's parents, a tendency to compare the conception of Jesus to the conception of
Old Testament salvific figures by the use of an annunciation pattern, the notion of the
virginal conception of Jesus, plus various elements of ch. 2. From this, Luke created
two diptychs: one containing the annunciation accounts of John and Jesus (1.5-25
and 1.26-45, 56); the other containing the birth-circumcision-naming accounts for
John and Jesus (1.37-66, 80 and 2.1-12, 15-27, 34-40). To this finished literary unit
Luke then added four pre-Lukan canticles: the Magnificat (1.46-55); the Benedictus

such as Stephen Farris have argued for a more substantial core of traditional material behind Luke's account.[1] The issue is a complicated one: does Luke 1–2 reflect the 'translation Greek' of originally Semitic sources or a skillful imitation of Septuagint style on the part of the author? Brown despaired of reaching a conclusion on stylistic grounds, and therefore his conclusions were reached purely on the basis of content and thought pattern.[2] Farris, however, utilizing criteria developed by Raymond Martin for distinguishing between translation Greek and original Greek, has argued persuasively on the basis of style that Luke 1 and 2 are based largely on Semitic sources.[3] Attempts to reconstruct these sources have not produced any assured results.[4] Indeed, the problem at this point in time appears unsolvable. Since my primary concern is with isolated portions of the non-hymnic sections of Luke 1–2, it will be sufficient to note the following points. First, the linguistic evidence, as Farris has shown, indicates that in all probability Luke's use of traditional material reaches beyond the hymnic material.[5] Second, although Luke probably drew upon traditional material for the narrative portions of Luke 1–2, these sections, in their final forms, have been significantly shaped by Luke. Luke has selected, organized, and modified the traditional material at his disposal. By

---

(1.67-79); the Gloria (2.13-14); and the Nunc Dimittis (2.28-33). In this second stage Luke also added the pre-Lukan account of the boy Jesus in the Temple. Brown also feels that 2.41-51 stems from a popular tradition of pre-ministry marvels which are attested in Jn 2.1-11 and the apocryphal literature. See Raymond E. Brown, 'Luke's Method in the Annunciation Narratives of Chapter One', in *Perspectives on Luke–Acts* (1978), pp. 126-38; Brown, *The Birth of the Messiah: A Commentary on the Infancy Narratives in Matthew and Luke* (1977), esp. pp. 247f.; and M.R. Mulholland, 'The Infancy Narratives in Matthew and Luke—of History, Theology and Literature. A Review Article of Raymond E. Brown's Monumental *The Birth of the Messiah*', *BAR* 7 (1981), pp. 46-59, esp. p. 56.

1. See Stephen C. Farris, 'On Discerning Semitic Sources in Luke 1–2', in *Gospel Perspectives*, II (1981), pp. 201-38 and Farris, *The Hymns of Luke's Infancy Narratives: Their Origin, Meaning and Significance* (1985).

2. Brown, The *Birth of the Messiah*, p. 246.

3. See Farris, 'Sources', pp. 201-38 and *Hymns*, pp. 50-66. Farris is supported in this judgment by Laurentin (*Les évangiles*, p. 45). On the basis of style, F. Gryglewicz comes to similar conclusions regarding the Hymns of Luke. See F. Gryglewicz, 'Die Herkunft der Hymnen des Kindheitsevangeliums des Lucas', *NTS* 21 (1975), pp. 265-73.

4. Schürmann's assessment of the present situation is accurate: 'Die Traditionsgeschichte von Lk 1–2 liegt trotz aller scharfsinnigen Untersuchungen immer noch im Dunkel sich widersprechender Hypothesen' (*Das Lukasevangelium*, I [1969], pp. 143-44).

5. See also Marshall, *Commentary on Luke*, pp. 46-49.

comparing the text of Luke 1–2 with Luke's literary style and theological perspective reflected throughout his two-volume work, I believe it is possible, at least with regard to those sections which refer to the activity of the Spirit, to distinguish between tradition and Lukan redaction. In light of these considerations I conclude that we have in chs. 1 and 2 material which provides important insight into Luke's unique perspective on the Spirit.

2. *Various Texts*

The theme of fulfillment is central to the infancy narratives of Luke. Providing commentary on the narrative portions of the text, the canticles proclaim that the promises of God find their fulfillment in the events of Luke 1–2.[1] Indeed, from the beginning a sense of anticipation is created as the reader enters into the world of pietistic Judaism. He is introduced to a host of righteous characters: Zechariah and Elizabeth are δίκαιοι ἀμφότεροι ἐναντίον τοῦ θεοῦ (1.6); Mary is κεχαριτωμένη (1.28); Simeon is δίκαιος καὶ εὐλαβής (2.25); Anna is a προφῆτις (2.36). These devout figures are dedicated to the law (1.59; 2.21-22) and the Temple cult (1.9; 2.27, 37). The atmosphere is permeated with a sense of joy (χαρά, 1.14; 2.10; χαίρω, 1.14, 28, 58; ἀγαλλίασις, 1.14, 44; ἀγαλλιάω, 1.47; σκιρτάω, 1.41). These twin themes of piety and joy highlight the sense of expectation which is generated by angelic visitations and prophecy and which culminates in the births of the precursor and the Messiah.

A leading role in this drama of fulfillment is played by the Spirit. The silence of spirit-inspired prophetic activity to which the intertestamental literature attests is shattered at the very outset of the narrative, and pneumatic inspiration constitutes a recurring motif. In 1.13f. the angel Gabriel announces to Zechariah that his wife Elizabeth will bear a son, John. Of John it is written: πνεύματος ἁγίου πλησθήσεται ἔτι ἐκ κοιλίας μητρὸς αὐτοῦ (1.15).[2] Here the Spirit is depicted as the impetus of John's prophetic ministry. This judgment is confirmed by the immediate context: John will go before the Lord

---

1. In *Proclamation from Prophecy and Pattern: Lucan Old Testament Christology* (1987) D.L. Bock notes that Lk. 1–2 are 'saturated with references to fulfilled promise without explicitly pointing to specific passages grounded in OT texts' (p. 88). Thus he argues that 'proclamation from prophecy' is a more accurate description of Luke's scheme than the popular 'proof from prophecy'.

2. Although the phrase ἔτι ἐκ κοιλίας μητρὸς αὐτοῦ may mean either 'while yet in his mother's womb' or 'from birth', in light of Lk. 1.41-44 the former meaning is to be preferred.

ἐν πνεύματι καὶ δυνάμει Ἠλίου (1.17). John's unique reception of the Spirit while still in the womb points to John's special status and role: he is 'more than a prophet' (7.26, 28) and 'shall go before the Lord' (1.17).[1]

The use of πίμπλημι in conjunction with the anarthrous usage of πνεῦμα ἅγιον in v. 15 and the collation of πνεῦμα and δύναμις in v. 17 indicate that these phrases are to be attributed to Luke.[2] The use of πίμπλημι with the Spirit is characteristic of Luke (Lk. 1.41, 67; Acts 2.4; 4.8, 31; 9.17; 13.9, 52). Although πίμπλημι is also found in conjunction with the Spirit in the LXX (Exod. 28.3; 31.3; 35.31; Deut. 34.9; Wis. 1.7; A of Sir. 48.12), the frequency is rather low when compared with Luke.[3] The anarthrous usage of πνεῦμα ἅγιον in v. 15 is clearly 'einen lukanischen Vorzugsterminus'.[4] Similarly, the combination of πνεῦμα and δύναμις is also common to Luke (Lk. 1.35; 4.14; Acts 1.8; 10.38; cf. Lk. 24.49; Acts 6.3-8),[5] although again this usage is not entirely unique (1QH 7.6f.).[6] It is significant that the phrases πνεύματος ἁγίου πλησθήσεται ἔτι ἐκ κοιλίας μητρὸς αὐτοῦ in v. 15 and ἐν πνεύματι καὶ δυνάμει Ἠλίου in v. 17 can be omitted from the text without significantly altering the flow of thought. On the whole, the evidence suggests that these phrases are to be attributed to Luke. Although it is quite possible, indeed I suggest likely, that Luke had access to traditional material concerning John's miraculous birth by the aged Elizabeth, I conclude that Luke has placed the references to the Spirit (1.15, 17) in the narrative in order to emphasize the pneumatic and prophetic character of John's ministry and to strengthen the links between John and Jesus.

---

1. W. Grundmann, *Das Evangelium nach Lukas* (1961), p. 51.

2. P.L. Kjeseth argues that this passage is traditional on the grounds that Luke tends to limit the Spirit to Jesus ('The Spirit of Power' [1966], p. 89). This argument must be rejected in light of the frequent references to the Spirit's activity in Lk. 1–2.

3. Although acknowledging that the phrase 'filled with the Spirit' may have been present in Luke's source, J. Fitzmyer notes that 'this detail could be a Lukan redactional modification of the source, made by Luke to stress the Spirit-guided activity of John's prophetic role' (*Luke I–IX*, p. 319).

4. Schneider, 'Jesu geistgewirkte Empfängnis', p. 109. The anarthrous usage occurs with the following frequency: Matthew, 3×; Mark, 1×; Luke, 8×; John, 2×; Acts, 16×.

5. Schneider ('Jesu geistgewirkte Empfängnis', p. 110) and L. Legrand ('L'Arrière-plan néotestamentaire de Lc. 1,35', *RB* 70 [1963], p. 163) point to the combination of πνεῦμα with δύναμις as an indication of Lukan redaction.

6. The wording of 1.17 is motivated by considerations discussed in Chapter 6 §3 concerning Luke's usage of πνεῦμα and δύναμις. It may also reflect the desire on the part of Luke to parallel John with Jesus (1.35).

Luke 1.41 states that upon meeting Mary, Elizabeth ἐπλήσθη πνεύματος ἁγίου and pronounced an inspired blessing upon her and the child she would bear. The phrase ἐπλήσθη πνεύματος ἁγίου occurs again in Lk. 1.67 with reference to Zechariah. The close association between the activity of the Spirit and prophecy is made explicit in this introductory formula: 'Zechariah was filled with the Holy Spirit and prophesied (ἐπροφήτευσεν)'. This usage of προφητεύς in 1.67 parallels that of ἀνεφώνησεν κραυγῇ μεγάλῃ in 1.42. Thus in Lk. 1.41 and 1.67 the Spirit acts as the Spirit of prophecy, inspiring prophetic speech. Luke's penchant for using πίμπλημι with the Spirit, the parallels between 1.41 and 1.67, and the introductory role of the phrases lead us to conclude that Luke is responsible for at least the phrase ἐπλήσθη πνεύματος ἁγίου in v. 41 and v. 67.[1] Luke highlights the Spirit's role in the prophetic activity of Elizabeth and Zechariah, as well as John.[2]

A cluster of references to the Spirit appear in Lk. 2.25-27 with reference to Simeon. After a description of Simeon's piety we read: καὶ πνεῦμα ἦν ἅγιον ἐπ' αὐτόν (2.25). The following verses define more precisely how the Spirit functioned in the life of Simeon. In v. 26 the Spirit is cited as the source of special revelation: ἦν αὐτῷ κεχρηματισμένον ὑπὸ τοῦ πνεύματος τοῦ ἁγίου that he would live to see the Messiah. The phrase καὶ ἦλθεν ἐν τῷ πνεύματι εἰς τὸ ἱερόν (v. 27) refers to the state of inspiration which not only led Simeon into the temple, but which also led to his spontaneous outburst of praise. Thus in 2.25-27 the Spirit functions as the Spirit of prophecy, granting special revelation, guidance, and inspiring speech.

The separation of source material from Lukan redaction is exceedingly difficult in these verses. The issue is irrelevant if Luke created the story in its entirety, but as I have suggested, this is unlikely. If vv. 25-27 reflect traditional material as I suspect, it is quite possible that Luke has influenced its present form. Even if a written source forms the basis of vv. 25-27, it would not have been difficult for Luke to have altered this source by inserting the three references to the Spirit. The phrase καὶ πνεῦμα ἦν ἅγιον ἐπ' αὐτόν is not integral to the flow of thought and could easily have been added to the end of v. 25. Similarly, ὑπὸ τοῦ πνεύματος τοῦ ἁγίου of v. 26 and ἐν τῷ πνεύματι of v. 27 can be deleted (and thus added) without the sense

---

1. Fitzmyer concludes that Lk. 1.67 is 'undoubtedly redactional' (*Luke I–IX*, p. 382).

2. Laurentin (*Les évangiles*, p. 216) describes the pneumatic experiences of John, Elizabeth, and Zechariah as 'une triple Pentecôte, puisque Luc caractérise cet événement par le même formule [as in Acts 2.4 and 4.31]'.

of the verses being altered. This of course does not constitute proof that Luke added these phrases to an existing source. However, in light of Luke's interest in the Spirit elsewhere in the infancy narratives and throughout Luke–Acts I suggest this as a plausible hypothesis. Although the linguistic evidence by itself is unconvincing, it does lend credibility to my hypothesis of Lukan redaction in v. 25 and v. 27. The unusual construction of πνεῦμα-verb-ἅγιον (2.25) is found in Acts 1.15, and ἐπί with πνεῦμα is frequently employed by Luke (Lk. 4.18; Acts 1.8; 2.17; 10.44, 45; 11.15; 16.6).[1] The verb of motion with ἐν τῷ πνεύματι (2.27) finds parallels in Lk. 4.1 and 4.14, material which is clearly Lukan.

In a manner similar to Simeon, the prophetess Anna speaks over the child in the Temple (2.36f.). There is no allusion to the activity of the Spirit here. This silence concerning the Spirit may be the result of two factors. First, whether it be due to a lack of source material or his own literary purpose, Luke does not record the content of Anna's inspired message. This contrasts sharply with the experience of Elizabeth, Mary, Zechariah, and Simeon.[2] Second, the activity of the Spirit is implicit in the reference to Anna as a προφῆτις. I suggest that since Luke did not record Anna's inspired words, he refrained from alluding to the Spirit's activity in a direct way, choosing simply to name her as a prophetess. Although this is conjecture, it fits the general pattern of the infancy narratives where the Spirit inspires oracles transcribed by Luke.

From this analysis of the passages cited above it is evident that Luke not only has a special interest in the Holy Spirit, but also that his understanding of the Spirit is inextricably related to prophetic phenomena. This conclusion is not dependent on any specific source theory. Those who argue for a minimal amount of traditional material behind Luke's infancy narratives will have no difficulty in accepting my conclusions. However, I have attempted to demonstrate that this conclusion is also compatible with the view that Luke did have access to a considerable amount of traditional material, largely in the form of written sources. Indeed, we can go a step further. Although my case is advanced if these hypotheses regarding Luke's modification of source material in the infancy narratives are accepted, the conclusion stated above is not dependent upon them. Regardless of whether Luke is responsible for the Spirit-references in the infancy narratives or

---

1. Lk. 4.18 and Acts 2.17 are quotations from the OT.
2. The reference to John the Baptist in 1.15 is in the future tense. However, it would appear that his filling is accompanied by the prophecy of Elizabeth (1.41f.) and his leaping in the womb.

whether they are to be attributed to his sources, the fact that he has chosen this material is in itself an indication of his theological *Tendenz*.[1] Clearly, in each of the passages cited above the Spirit functions as the source of prophecy. However, there is one exception to this otherwise uniform pattern. To this exception I now turn.

3. *Birth by the Spirit (Luke 1.35)*

Luke 1.35 records Gabriel's explanation to Mary concerning how the miraculous birth is to take place:

Πνεῦμα ἅγιον ἐπελεύσεται ἐπὶ σέ,
καὶ δύναμις ὑψίστου ἐπισκιάσει σοι.

The passage poses a problem. If Luke, consistent with the Judaism of his day, understands the Spirit as the Spirit of prophecy, how can he attribute creative functions to the Spirit? Not only is this description of the Spirit's activity unique to Luke, but it is also quite uncommon to the Jewish thought-world of Luke's day.[2] In light of these considerations the question cannot be overlooked:[3] what does this passage tell us of Luke's understanding of the activity of the Spirit? By way of response I shall examine the traditional basis of the passage, the role this passage plays in the Jesus–John parallels which are so central to the structure of Luke's narrative, and the significance of the parallelism in v. 35.

In his 'Jesu geistgewirkte Empfängnis (Lk. 1,34f)', G. Schneider has argued persuasively on the basis of style that Luke 'hat 1,34f von sich aus formuliert'.[4] It is equally clear that, although the infancy

---

1. Laurentin notes that one of the striking differences between the infancy narratives of Matthew and Luke is that while Matthew focuses solely on Christ, Luke attaches great importance to the activity of the Spirit as well (*Les évangiles*, p. 541).

2. See Davies, *Paul*, pp. 189-90. Legrand poses the problem in this way: 'Ce rôle de l'Esprit en Lc. 1,35 pose un problème. Le Judaïsme contemporain du Nouveau Testament ne semble pas s'être intéressé beaucoup au thème de l'Esprit créateur, tel qu'il apparaît en Lc. 1,35' ('L'arrière-plan néotestamentaire de Lc. 1,35', p. 177). The attempt by Leisegang (*Pneuma Hagion*, pp. 14-71) to trace Luke's account to Hellenistic mystery religions has been discredited by both von Baer (*Der Heilige Geist*, pp. 112-23) and Barrett (*Gospel Tradition*, pp. 10-14).

3. Oliver's criticism of Schweizer is appropriate: 'Schweizer's article is the poorer because it fails to show how the idea of the Spirit in the nativity stories relates to the overall activity of the Spirit. The minor reference to Luke 1.35 in connection with Matt. 1.18 is inadequate' ('The Lucan Birth Stories', p. 225).

4. Schneider, 'Jesu geistgewirkte Empfängnis', p. 110, see pp. 109-10 for his discussion of the Lukan characteristics of Lk. 1.34-35. See also Schneider, 'Lk

narratives of Luke and Matthew represent independent accounts, they are both based upon a tradition that connected Jesus' miraculous conception to the activity of the Spirit (Mt. 1.18, 20). This tradition then forms the basis of Luke's reference to the Spirit in 1.35, which in its present form reflects Luke's hand.[1]

Luke's decision to include in his Gospel the tradition concerning the Spirit's creative role in Jesus' conception was probably influenced by his desire to draw parallels between John and Jesus. Indeed, the Jesus–John parallels form the basis of the structure of Luke's narrative: John is the precursor, Jesus the Messiah.[2] As we have seen, John was 'filled with the Spirit' while yet in his mother's womb. It would only be natural for Luke to include traditional material which shows the superiority of Jesus.[3]

There is also evidence that through his formulation of v. 35, Luke has attempted to minimize the contrast between the creative role of the Spirit in the tradition and his own prophetic understanding of the Spirit. First, G. Schneider notes that Luke does not connect the Spirit to the conception process as explicitly as Matthew. Whereas Matthew directly relates the Spirit's activity to the one who has been conceived (τὸ γεννηθέν, aorist passive, Mt. 1.20) in Mary's womb, Luke simply refers to the one who is born (τὸ γεννώμενον, present passive, Lk. 1.35).[4] Second, Luke does not attribute the birth of Jesus exclusively to the activity of the Spirit. With the phrase καὶ δύναμις ὑψίστου ἐπισκιάσει σοι Luke adds another dimension to the tradition.

1,34.35 als redaktionelle Einheit', *BZ* 15 (1971), pp. 255-59. In basic agreement with Schneider's conclusions are: Legrand, 'L'arrière-plan néotestamentaire de Lc. 1,35', p. 188; Brown, *The Birth of the Messiah*, p. 301; and Schürmann, *Lukasevangelium*, I, pp. 49f.

1. Schneider sees an oral tradition behind the two accounts ('Jesu geistgewirkte Empfängnis', p. 110). See also Legrand, 'L'arrière-plan néotestamentaire de Lc. 1,35', p. 190.

2. See Brown, *The Birth of the Messiah*, p. 250: 'All the analyses agree that Luke intended to show parallels between JBap and Jesus'. See also Laurentin, *Structure et Théologie de Luc I–II* (1964), pp. 42-43; Schürmann, *Untersuchungen*, p. 199; and P. Minear, *To Heal and to Reveal* (1976), p. 99.

3. Schweizer, 'The Spirit of Power', p. 263: 'The story is, in fact, told by Luke so that it surpasses the story of the birth of the Baptist'. See also Chevallier, *Le Messie*, p. 86.

4. Schneider, 'Jesu geistgewirkte Empfängnis', p. 112. Although Schneider speculates that this indicates Luke's account is closer to the tradition than Matthew's since the tendency was to speak more and more in biological terms (he cites Apocrypha as evidence), this need not be the case. One can say that the evidence indicates Luke is more reserved in the manner in which he relates the Spirit to the creative process.

Although this phrase is often ignored as a redundant piece of synonymous parallelism,[1] Luke's usage of δύναμις elsewhere suggests this addition is theologically motivated.

E. Schweizer has pointed out that Luke nowhere attributes exorcisms or miracles of healings to the work of the Spirit. Certainly Schweizer is right when he notes that according to Lk. 12.10 'the Spirit is no longer the power of God manifested in exorcisms' (Mk 3.29), but 'the power of God manifested in the inspired utterance of the witnesses of Jesus'.[2] Luke's insertion of ἐν δακτύλῳ θεοῦ (Lk. 11.20) in lieu of Q's ἐν πνεύματι θεοῦ (Mt. 12.28),[3] despite his interest in the Spirit, is striking and points in a similar direction. This makes Luke's omission of ἰάσασθαι τοὺς συντετριμμένους τῇ καρδίᾳ in Lk. 4.18f. (Isa. 61.1, LXX) all the more significant. It is to be noted that although Luke describes Stephen as 'a man full of the Holy Spirit' (Acts 6.3), he prefaces the comment that Stephen 'did great wonders and miraculous signs' with the appellation, 'a man full of God's grace and δύναμις' (Acts 6.8). It can also be argued that Luke attributes the blinding of Elymas in Acts 13.11 to the χεὶρ κυρίου so that the action of the Spirit on Paul described in Acts 13.9 has an exclusively prophetic sense. Similarly, in light of this Lukan tendency I would argue that the longer reading of Acts 8.39 is the more original: πνεῦμα ἅγιον ἐπέπεσεν ἐπὶ τὸν εὐνοῦχον, ἄγγελος δὲ κυρίου ἥρπασεν τὸν Φίλιππον.[4] If this is the case Philip is 'snatched away' by an angel of the Lord, not by the Holy Spirit. Consistent with the general tendency in the writings of intertestamental Judaism, Luke takes great care not to associate the Spirit directly with the broader dimensions of the miraculous, such as healings and exorcisms; rather he limits reference regarding the direct agency of the Spirit to prophetic activity: the Spirit is the source of special revelation and inspired speech.

---

1. See for example Barrett, *Gospel Tradition*, p. 76.
2. Schweizer, 'πνεῦμα', p. 407. See also Haya-Prats, *Force*, pp. 37-44.
3. See Chapter 9 §3 below for an analysis of this text.
4. As I.H. Marshall notes, 'This [the shorter ending] is an abrupt ending to the story, and it is considerably eased by a longer form of the text. . . Although the MS evidence for the longer text is weak, it could be original' (*The Acts of the Apostles* [1980], p. 165). For a discussion on the manuscript evidence see B. Metzger, *A Textual Commentary on the Greek New Testament* (2nd edn, 1975), pp. 360-61. The manuscript evidence is inconclusive since it is quite possible that the longer reading is absent in the other manuscripts due to accidental omission.

Luke does, however, attribute healings and exorcisms to the δύναμις of God (Lk. 4.36; 5.17; 6.19; 8.46; 9.1; Acts 4.7; 6.8).[1] Luke's redactional employment of δύναμις in Lk. 9.1 (cf. Mk 6.7) is particularly instructive, for here the disciples are granted δύναμις to expel demons and heal the sick even though they have not yet received the Spirit. This would appear to indicate an important distinction between Luke's use of δύναμις and πνεῦμα. The question becomes more complicated, however, when it is recognized that Luke can use the two terms together with little apparent distinction, as is the case in Lk. 1.35 (Lk. 1.17; 4.14; 24.49; Acts 1.8; 10.38). Are the terms synonyms for Luke or is a distinction intended? Certainly the evidence cited above would point to a nuanced usage of these terms on the part of Luke, but what of the passages where the terms occur together?

John's ministry, in Lk. 1.17, is described in terms of Elijah's: καὶ αὐτὸς προελεύσεται ἐνώπιον αὐτοῦ ἐν πνεύματι καὶ δυνάμει Ἠλίου. In 4.14 of his Gospel Luke writes that Jesus returned to Galilee ἐν τῇ δυνάμει τοῦ πνεύματος, clearly a redactional addition of Luke. In Lk. 24.49 the disciples are told to wait in Jerusalem until they are clothed with ἐξ ὕψους δύναμιν, a reference to the gift of the Spirit. This is made explicit by Acts 1.8: ἀλλὰ λήμψεσθε δύναμιν ἐπελθόντος τοῦ ἁγίου πνεύματος ἐφ᾽ ὑμᾶς. Finally, in Acts 10.38 Peter declares of Jesus: ἔχρισεν αὐτὸν ὁ θεὸς πνεύματι ἁγίῳ καὶ δυνάμει. These passages indicate that for Luke, the Holy Spirit is the source of 'power'. However, they do *not* indicate that the two terms are merely synonyms.[2] Close examination reveals that Luke uses these terms in a highly nuanced way. In each of the cases cited above Luke uses δύναμις in relation to πνεῦμα in order to describe the source of both prophetic activity and miracles of healing or exorcisms. That is to say that when Luke uses the terms δύναμις and πνεῦμα together he has in mind a combination of prophetic speech *and* miracles of healing and exorcisms, rather than the separate activities which are normally associated with πνεῦμα and δύναμις respectively. In Lk. 1.17 Luke likens John's ministry to that of Elijah, an Old Testament figure known for 'power of miracles *and* his gift of the prophetic spirit, both of which were passed on to Elisha' (2 Kgs 2.15).[3] Luke 4.14 is a redactional insertion on the part of Luke describing the means by which Jesus proclaimed the good news (4.15f.) *and* performed exorcisms

---

1. Note that the references to δύναμις in Lk. 4.36; 6.19; 9.1, and probably Acts 10.38 are redactional.
2. Schweizer, 'πνεῦμα', p. 407; Haya-Prats, *Force*, pp. 37-44; A. George, 'L'Esprit Saint dans l'œuvre de Luc', *RB* 85 (1978), p. 516.
3. Brown, *The Birth of the Messiah*, p. 261. The italics in the quotation are mine

(4.33f.) and miracles of healing (4.40) in Galilee. Luke 24.49 and Acts 1.8 are Lukan descriptions of the means by which the disciples became witnesses, a role which included proclaiming the gospel (Peter, Acts 2.14) *and* healing the sick (Peter, Acts 3.1). In these passages it is by virtue of its relationship to πνεῦμα that δύναμις can refer to a broad range of activities including prophetic speech as well as exorcisms and miracles of healing. Each of these passages is programmatic and refer to the means by which God enables a broad range of activities to take place. Similarly, Acts 10.38 is a panoramic description in retrospect: Peter summarizes the entire earthly ministry of Jesus (ὃς διῆλθεν εὐεργετῶν καὶ ἰώμενος πάντας) and the means by which it was accomplished. Therefore, I conclude that although Luke can speak of πνεῦμα as the source of δύναμις, the two terms are not synonymous. Each produces a specific nexus of activities and when Luke refers to both a broader range of activities is envisioned.

It may at first appear strange that Luke can speak of the Spirit as the source of 'power' and yet take great care not to associate the Spirit directly with healings and exorcisms. However, this is remarkably consistent with what we have found in the intertestamental literature: the prophet is a being of the Spirit and may work miracles, but these miracles are not attributed directly to the Spirit.[1] For Luke, as for intertestamental Judaism, the Spirit inspires prophetic activity. For this reason, although miracle-working power may find its origin in the Spirit of God, miracles are carefully distanced from the Spirit (e.g. Lk. 11.20). Luke frequently maintains this distance through his nuanced use of δύναμις.

Luke's use of πνεῦμα and δύναμις can be shown as follows:

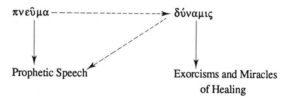

Luke's highly nuanced usage of πνεῦμα and δύναμις supports my contention that he has crafted the parallel statements in v. 35 in order to accomodate the traditional account of the Spirit's creative role in the birth of Jesus with his own prophetic understanding of the Spirit.

---

1. Josephus is particularly close to Luke at this point. Josephus alters his sources in order to distance the Spirit from non-prophetic miraculous activity (see Chapter 2 §3.2 above) and he corrolates δύναμις with πνεῦμα in a manner analogous to Luke (*Ant.* 8.408).

Consistent with his usage elsewhere, in v. 35 Luke associates δύναμις with the πνεῦμα of the tradition because he has in mind a broad range of activities. The divine intervention alluded to in v. 35 is the source of Mary's miraculous pregnancy and her inspired proclamation in 1.46f.

The connection between the promise of the Spirit's presence in v. 35 and Mary's utterance in vv. 46f. can hardly be questioned. All three of the canticles attributed to men or women are proclaimed under the influence of the Spirit's activity (Zechariah—the Benedictus; Elizabeth and Mary—the Magnificat;[1] Simeon—the Nunc Dimittis), and the only major adult character who is not brought into direct relationship with the Spirit, Anna, does not utter an oracle. Furthermore, references to the appellation ἅγιον link v. 35 with the Magnificat (v. 49).

The wording of the parallel stichs in v. 35 coincides nicely with the thesis that Luke emphasizes here the prophetic role of the Spirit and the creative role of δύναμις. The ἐπέρχομαι[2] + ἐπί construction with πνεῦμα ἅγιον in the first stich parallels the reference to the Pentecostal outpouring of the Spirit in Acts 1.8. This would suggest prophetic phenomena, not supernatural creation. A verb more likely to speak of divine creation for Luke, ἐπισκιάζω, appears in the second stich in relation to δύναμις ὑψίστου. Although there is no evidence that would suggest ἐπισκιάζω is descriptive of procreation,[3] it does refer to the presence of God in a very personal and immediate way (Exod. 40.35).

In short, I have argued that Luke attributes the miraculous birth of Jesus to the the activity of the Spirit because this accurately reflected early Christian tradition and it suited his structural scheme of paralleling John with Jesus. However, Luke sought to minimize the contrast between the creative role of the Spirit in the tradition and his own prophetic understanding of the Spirit. He accomplished this task by modifying the tradition, which associated the Spirit with biological conception in an explicit manner (cf. Mt. 1.20). Luke's principal

---

1. This might explain the transition from Elizabeth to Mary in the Magnificat (1.46). At any rate, the textual evidence in 1.46 supports Μαριάμ rather than 'Elizabeth' as the original reading. See Brown, *The Birth of the Messiah*, pp. 334-35 for a discussion of the textual evidence.

2. ἐπέρχομαι is Lukan (Lk. 11.22; 21.26; Acts 1.8; 8.24; 13.40; 14.19). It occurs only twice elsewhere in the NT (Eph. 2.7 and Jas 5.1).

3. The suggestions along this line by Leisegang, *Pneuma Hagion*, pp. 25f. have been largely rejected. See for example Grundmann, *Lukas*, p. 58 and Marshall, *Commentary on Luke*, p. 70.

alteration involved the insertion of a reference to δύναμις paralleling πνεῦμα into the narrative. Consistent with his usage elsewhere, this association of δύναμις with πνεῦμα enabled Luke to relate the activity of the Spirit to Mary's prophetic proclamation and in a less direct way to the miraculous birth.

4. The Pneumatology of the Pre-Lukan Tradition

This analysis of Lk. 1.35 has confirmed my findings in the other portions of the infancy narratives: Luke's understanding of the Spirit is inextricably related to prophetic activity. However, it has also shed light on the pneumatology reflected in the pre-Lukan tradition. The tradition reflected in Lk. 1.35 indicates that the primitive church spoke of the activity of the Spirit in broader terms than Luke. It was not reluctant to attribute miraculous events, such as the virgin birth of Jesus, exorcisms, or healings directly to the intervention of the Spirit. This judgment is confirmed by Mt. 12.28 = Lk. 11.20 and Mk 3.29 = Lk. 12.10. While the pneumatology of the primitive church may be designated charismatic, that of Luke is more specifically prophetic.

The distinction between the charismatic pneumatology of the primitive church and the prophetic pneumatology of Luke is due on the one hand to the influence which Jesus exerted on the primitive church.[1] The experience and teaching of Jesus shaped the primitive church's understanding of the Spirit of God as the source of miracle-working power. I have already noted how infrequently miraculous events are attributed to the Spirit of God in intertestamental Judaism. The difference between the perspective of Jesus and that of Judaism is illustrated with reference to exorcism. While Jesus claimed to cast out demons by 'the Spirit of God',[2] there is not a single text in the Old Testament or in the Jewish literature of the intertestamental period which attributes the exorcism of demons to the agency of the Spirit.[3] One of the many strengths of James Dunn's *Jesus and the Spirit* is the stress which it places on the uniqueness of Jesus' consciousness of the Spirit.[4] This

---

1. See Chapter 9 §3 and § 4 below.

2. On πνεύματι θεοῦ of Mt. 12.28 (= Lk. 11.20) as the original reading of Q see Chapter 9 §3 below. Note also Mt. 12.31-32; Mk 3.28-30; and Lk. 12.10.

3. See Chapter 9 §4.3 below.

4. Dunn, *Jesus and the Spirit*, p. 53. E.P. Sanders argues that Mt. 12.28 does not constitute compelling evidence that Jesus interpreted his exorcisms as a sign of the present inbreaking of the Kingdom of God or that he possessed a unique self-understanding (*Jesus and Judaism* [1985], pp. 133-41, 157-58). Sanders fails to recognize

uniqueness is most evident in Jesus' claim to perform exorcisms and miracles by the Spirit of God.[1]

On the other hand, the distinction results from the way in which Luke has appropriated and yet kept distinct (as outlined above) two spheres of thought: the traditional Jewish understanding of πνεῦμα θεοῦ as the source of prophetic inspiration and the hellenistic understanding of δύναμις as miracle-working power. Whereas Jesus and the primitive church viewed the divine πνεῦμα as the direct agent of prophetic inspiration and miracle-working power,[2] Luke, as we have seen, described the former in terms of πνεῦμα and the latter in terms of δύναμις. In short, the primitive church, following in the footsteps of Jesus, broadened the perceived functions of the Spirit of God so that it was viewed not only in traditional Jewish terms as the source of prophetic power, but also as miracle-working power. Luke, on the other hand, retained the traditional Jewish understanding of the Spirit as the Spirit of prophecy and, with the term δύναμις, incorporated a hellenistic mode of expression to speak of miracle-working power. While δύναμις may be mediated through the Spirit (thus the phrase ἐν τῇ δυνάμει τοῦ πνεύματος, Lk. 4.14), the former rather than the latter is understood to be the divine potency by which miracles are wrought.

The antiquity of the tradition reflected in Lk. 1.35, and thus its significance for the primitive church, has been questioned. Two arguments against the antiquity of this tradition have been put forth; both view it as reflecting a late stage in the development of the early church's christology. First, H. Schürmann insists this tradition must be late since it is not found in Mark or the Pauline epistles.[3] However, this argument from silence is not compelling, particularly when the purposes of Mark or Paul may have precluded their incorporation of

---

the uniqueness of Jesus' reference to the Spirit of God as the agent of his exorcisms (Mt. 12.28).

1. Contra G. Burge, *The Anointed Community: The Holy Spirit in the Johannine Tradition* (1987), p. 65: 'To be a potent bearer of the Spirit in exorcism did not differentiate Jesus from other exorcists and magicians'.

2. See Chapter 9 §4.3 below.

3. Schürmann, 'Die geistgewirkte Lebensentstehung Jesu', in *Einheit in Vielfalt* (1974), p. 158. See also the similar conclusion of Schneider, 'Jesu geistgewirkte Empfängnis', p. 105. For a summary of the arguments against the historicity and early nature of the tradition concerning Jesus' conception by the Spirit see U. Wilckens, 'Empfangen von Heiligen Geist, geboren aus der Jungfrau Maria—Lk 1,26-38', in *Zur Theologie der Kindheitsgeschichten: Der heutige Stand der Exegese* (1981), pp. 62-64.

this material.[1] Second, there is the commonly-held theory that the early church progressively 'read back' the christological moment (the moment at which Jesus became the Son of God indicated by formulations centering on the terms 'Spirit', 'power', and 'Son of God') originally associated with Jesus' resurrection into his earthly ministry (transfiguration and baptism) and then into the account of his birth.[2] A key weakness in this theory is that there is little evidence that the pre-Pauline church viewed the Spirit as the source or power of Jesus' resurrection. Thus, the initial link in the chain is broken. Romans 1.3f. is often cited in support of this notion, but the actual wording of the pre-Pauline formula is disputed. H. Schlier, for example, does not place the Holy Spirit in the original formula, although he does view it as pre-Pauline.[3] The latter judgment I shall question. This theory has also been criticized on other grounds: the exegetical evidence does not support the contention that the primitive church understood the resurrection of Jesus as the moment at which Jesus became the Son of God.[4] In light of these considerations the view of I.H. Marshall is to be preferred:

> May it not be the case that the early church regarded the resurrection as confirmation of an already-existent status rather than as the conferring of a new status? We would suggest that this is a more accurate exegesis of the relevant texts.[5]

The affirmation of Jesus' miraculous birth by the Spirit reflected in Lk. 1.35 is undoubtedly pre-Lukan and there is no convincing reason for rejecting it as an early tradition of the primitive church.

5. The Theological Homogeneity of Luke–Acts

Having reached these conclusions concerning the nature of Luke's pneumatology as reflected in the infancy narratives, the question must now be asked how significant this material is for understanding Luke's

1. See D. Guthrie, *New Testament Theology* (1981), pp. 368-69.
2. For a good summary of this position see Brown, *The Birth of the Messiah*, pp. 29-32, 135-37.
3. H. Schlier, 'Zu Röm 1,3f', in *Neues Testament und Geschichte* (1972), pp. 207-18.
4. Marshall, *The Origins of New Testament Christology* (1976), pp. 119-20. See also Laurentin, *Les évangiles*, pp. 52-54. R.H. Fuller has argued that the birth traditions took shape 'as the expression not of a retrojected Son of God, but of a Son of David Christology' ('The Conception/Birth of Jesus as a Christological Moment', *JSNT* 1 [1978], p. 39).
5. Marshall, *Christology*, p. 120.

pneumatology as a whole. Certainly Hans Conzelmann's outright dismissal of the significance of the infancy material for ascertaining Luke's theological perspective is to be rejected.[1] Yet what are we to make of his *heilsgeschichtlich* scheme with three distinct epochs? Can the infancy material be fitted into this scheme, or does it represent an insurmountable challenge to the validity of Conzelmann's approach?

Representatives of the former position include H.H. Oliver, who used the infancy material to support Conzelmann's conclusions with only minor modifications,[2] and W.B. Tatum, who arrived at similar conclusions by attempting to contrast the work of the Spirit in Luke 1–2 with the operation of the Holy Spirit elsewhere in Luke–Acts.[3] Tatum's article merits special attention since it centers on the work of the Spirit.

According to Tatum, Luke 'uses the birth narratives to characterize that period in salvation history before the ministry of Jesus as the Epoch of Israel'.[4] In support of this claim Tatum attempts to distinguish between the work of the Spirit in the three epochs of *Heilsgeschichte*: the epoch of Israel, the epoch of Jesus' ministry, and the epoch of the church. In spite of these divisions Tatum notes that the Spirit functions as the Spirit of prophecy in Luke 1–2 (epoch of Israel) *and* in Acts 2f. (epoch of the church). The only distinction is that what was formerly limited to a few chosen individuals in the epoch of Israel is universally available in the epoch of the church.[5] This leads Tatum to conclude that 'the prophetic Spirit in the nativity stories recalls the role of the Spirit in the past history of Israel'.[6] Although this may be true, Tatum ignores the fact that the renewed activity of the prophetic Spirit, once prominent in the past history of Israel, is itself an indicator of the dawning of the messianic age.[7] Far from designating the

---

1. Talbert, 'Shifting Sands', p. 202: 'Conzelmann's work on Luke ignored the first two chapters and did not treat them as integral to the Gospel. The response to this position has been unanimously negative.'

2. Oliver, 'The Lucan Birth Stories', pp. 202-26.

3. W.B. Tatum, 'The Epoch of Israel: Luke I–II and the Theological Plan of Luke–Acts', *NTS* 13 (1966–67), pp. 184-95.

4. Tatum, 'The Epoch of Israel', p. 190.

5. 'The Epoch of Israel', p. 191.

6. 'The Epoch of Israel', p. 191.

7. E. Ellis, *The Gospel of Luke* (1974), pp. 28-29. Laurentin argues that Luke's reference to the angel Gabriel, in light of Dan. 9.21, is a sign that the messianic age has come (*Luc I–II*, p. 46). Schürmann also points out the eschatological signs which appear in Lk. 1–2: angels, phenomena of nature, etc. (*Untersuchungen*, p. 203). See also Kjeseth's criticism of Conzelmann's view that for Luke the Spirit is no longer an eschatological gift ('The Spirit of Power', p. 106).

events of Luke 1–2 as a 'period of preparation',[1] the activity of the prophetic Spirit marks the decisive transition in God's plan for the restoration of his people.[2] Indeed, the profusion of prophetic activity inspired by the Spirit characterizes Luke 1–2 as a drama of fulfillment. The content of the prophets' proclamation reveals the true significance of the events related in the narrative. Thus, both the *form* and the *content* of prophecy herald the message: God is *now* fulfilling his promises of old. Only by ignoring the eschatological significance of the restoration of the gift of Spirit and the prophecy which it produces can Tatum attempt to separate Luke 1–2 from the rest of Luke–Acts.

Tatum also argues that the Spirit-motif in Luke 1–2 sets John apart from Jesus and places the former in the epoch of Israel.[3] Tatum's argument rests on his attempt to distinguish between the prophetic function of the Spirit in Luke 1–2 and the messianic function of the Spirit in the epoch of Jesus' ministry. This distinction is based on three observations: first, during his ministry Jesus is the sole bearer of the Spirit, this is in striking contrast to the profusion of the Spirit's activity elsewhere; second, while the passive forms of πληρόω (frequently used in Luke 1–2) suggest intermittent association, Jesus' relation to the Spirit (πλήρης, Lk. 4.1) intimates a more permanent connection; third, following Schweizer, Tatum suggests that Jesus is no longer a Man of the Spirit, but is now Lord of the Spirit. It should be noted, however, that Tatum's initial point does not further his argument. The limitation of the Spirit to Jesus during his ministry does not indicate that the function of the Spirit has changed. Indeed, I shall argue that the Spirit in relation to Jesus continues to function as the source of special revelation and inspired speech.[4] Tatum's second point is mitigated by the fact that πλήρης πνεύματος ἁγίου is not applied exclusively to Jesus (Lk. 4.1), but is also a description used of various disciples in the epoch of the church (Acts 6.3, 5; 7.55; 11.24), an epoch in which by Tatum's own admission the Spirit functions as the Spirit of prophecy. The contrast Tatum attempts to draw between the intermit-

---

1. Ellis, *Luke*, p. 193.

2. Continuity between the pneumatology of Lk. 1–2 and the rest of Luke–Acts is affirmed by the linguistic evidence. Von Baer (*Der heilige Geist*, p. 54), Brown (*The Birth of the Messiah*, p. 243), and Schneider ('Jesu geistgewirkte Empfängnis', pp. 107-108) point out the lexical and stylistic similarities which exist between the references to the Spirit in Lk. 1–2 and Acts.

3. The fact that the births of both John and Jesus are announced as 'good news' (εὐαγγελίζομαι, 1.19; 2.10) should call for caution at this point.

4. As Minear notes, this view is completely compatible with what we find in Lk. 1–2: 'It is the kinship in prophetic vocation that the birth stories, with their unique kind of witness, so deftly articulate' (*To Heal*, p. 97).

tent or temporary character of the experiences of the Spirit recorded in Luke 1–2 and the permanent character of Jesus' experience of the Spirit breaks down when it is recognized that for John the gift of the Spirit of prophecy was permanent (Lk. 1.15, 76; 20.6) and, although the references to Jesus are less conclusive, in Acts the gift of the Spirit was clearly repetitive for the disciples (Acts 2.4; 4.8, 31).[1] Tatum's third point is also dubious. Luke 4.1, 14 will not support the claim that Jesus is 'no longer a Man of the Spirit, but is now Lord of the Spirit',[2] and, in any event, what is at issue here is not the function of the Spirit, but the status of Jesus and his relationship to the Spirit.

In short, Tatum does point to superficial differences in the activity of the Spirit in various stages of Luke's work: reference to the Spirit's activity is limited to Jesus during the period of his earthly ministry and the Spirit, as never before, is universally available in Acts. However, Tatum fails to demonstrate that these epochs mark a transformation in the *function* of the Spirit. In each epoch the Spirit functions as the Spirit of prophecy. This fact and the eschatological significance of the Spirit's return suggest that Luke's pneumatology does not support a rigid three-epoch interpretation of Luke's scheme of *Heilsgeschichte*; on the contrary, Luke's pneumatology emphasizes the fundamental continuity which unites his story of fulfillment.

Recent trends in Lukan scholarship have confirmed this judgment by demonstrating the theological homogeneity of Luke–Acts. P. Minear has argued persuasively that it is only by ignoring the infancy narratives that Conzelmann can put forth his thesis.[3] According to W.C.

---

1. R. Stronstad (*The Charismatic Theology of St. Luke* [1984], p. 4) criticizes attempts to distinguish between a temporary gift of the Spirit in Lk. 1–2 and a permanent gift of the Spirit in Acts. He points out that for John the gift of the Spirit of prophecy was permanent and for the disciples in Acts the gift was repetitive. The point is equally valid for Tatum's proposed distinction. It should also be noted that the caricature of OT figures as having only an intermittent association with the Spirit cannot be pressed too far. Moses, for example, received a permanent endowment of the Spirit (Num. 11.17f.). Concerning the permanent nature of Moses' experience of the Spirit see Hill, *Greek Words*, p. 209. Haya-Prats's comments on the gift of the Spirit are instructive: 'Il s'agit d'un don permanent ou, plus exactement, d'une offre permanente qui se réalise chaque fois qu'une situation requiert l'assistance extra-ordinaire de l'Esprit' (*Force*, p. 198).

2. See Chapter 8 §2 below. Note also Bovon, *Luc le théologien*, p. 226.

3. P.S. Minear, 'Luke's Use of the Birth Stories', in *Studies in Luke-Acts* (3rd edn, 1978), p. 121. See also Tannehill, *The Narrative Unity of Luke-Acts*, I, pp. 21f. and J. Borremans, 'The Holy Spirit in Luke's Evangelical Catechesis: A Guide to Proclaiming Jesus Christ in an Secular World', *LV* 25 (1970), pp. 287-89, esp. p. 288 n. 2.

Robinson, a theme that unites the ministry of Jesus with that of the church is Luke's depiction of both in terms of 'a journey'. Both Jesus and the early church travel 'the way of the Lord'.[1] I.H. Marshall has emphasized the continuity which exists between Luke and Acts with regard to christological, soteriological, and eschatological themes.[2] G. Braumann views persecution as a theme which unites Luke's two-volume work.[3] E. Lohse has presented 'promise and fulfillment' as a connecting thread which runs throughout Luke–Acts.[4] Therefore, it would appear that Martin Hengel gives voice to a consensus in Lukan scholarship when he writes:

> The argument introduced by H. Conzelmann and often repeated since then, that Luke divides history up into three periods, was certainly attractive, but nevertheless misleading. . . In reality, the whole double work covers the one history of Jesus Christ, which also includes the interval between resurrection and parousia as the time of his proclamation in the 'last days' (Acts 2.17), and which Luke clearly distinguishes from the epoch of the old covenant as the time of the messianic fulfilment of the prophetic promises.[5]

This conclusion confirms my conviction that the Spirit-material in Luke 1–2 is of vital importance for understanding Luke's pneumatology as a whole. Since Luke–Acts is 'one history of Jesus Christ', the material in the infancy narratives cannot be seen in isolation from the rest of Luke's two-volume work.[6] Distinctions between the pneumatology of Luke 1–2 and the rest of Luke–Acts based on a rigid three-epoch scheme of Luke's *Heilsgeschichte* must be rejected.

1. W.C. Robinson, *Der Weg des Herrn* (1964).
2. I.H. Marshall, *Luke: Historian and Theologian* (1970); see also Marshall, 'Luke and His "Gospel"', in *Das Evangelium und die Evangelien* (1983), esp. pp. 300-301.
3. G. Braumann, 'Das Mittel der Zeit', *ZNW* 54 (1963), pp. 117-45.
4. E. Lohse, 'Lukas als Theologe der Heilsgeschichte' (1953), in *Die Einheit des Neuen Testaments* (1973).
5. M. Hengel, *Acts and the History of Earliest Christianity* (1979), p. 59. See also S.G. Wilson, *The Gentiles and the Gentile Mission in Luke–Acts* (1973), pp. 59-67; U. Busse, *Das Nazareth-Manifest Jesu* (1977), pp. 84-93; and Hahn, 'Der gegenwärtige Stand der Erforschung der Apostelgeschichte', p. 183.
6. This conclusion presents difficulties for the thesis put forth by Dunn in *Baptism in the Holy Spirit*. As M. Green notes: 'It is a weakness in Dunn's useful book *Baptism in the Holy Spirit* that he sweeps aside these dozen or so references to the Spirit in the first three chapters of Luke and insists that the Kingdom did not come until the baptism of Jesus. In fact, Luke could hardly go to greater lengths in stressing that the Age to Come dawned with Jesus' birth' (*I Believe in the Holy Spirit* [1975], p. 58).

Chapter 7

THE BAPTIST'S PROPHECY (LUKE 3.16)

1. *The Original Form of the Prophecy*

John's prophecy concerning the coming Spirit-baptizer is presented in variant forms in Mark and Q:

Mk 1.8: αὐτὸς δὲ βαπτίσει ὑμᾶς ἐν πνεύματι ἁγίῳ.

Q–Lk. 3.16-17 = Mt. 3.11-12: αὐτὸς ὑμᾶς βαπτίσει ἐν πνεύματι ἁγίῳ καὶ πυρί. οὗ τὸ πτύον ἐν τῇ χειρὶ αὐτοῦ διακαθᾶραι τὴν ἅλωνα αὐτοῦ καὶ συναγαγεῖν τὸν σῖτον εἰς τὴν ἀποθήκην αὐτοῦ, τὸ δὲ ἄχυρον κατακαύσει πυρὶ ἀσβέστῳ.

Although the history of interpretation has produced a variety of views concerning the original form of John's prophecy,[1] several factors indicate that the tradition presented in Q faithfully represents the Baptist's original words. First, the Q version is to be preferred over that of Mark. Mark's omission of καὶ πυρί and the winnowing metaphor (Lk. 3.17 = Mt. 3.12) can be easily reconciled with his intent to present the εὐαγγελίου Ἰησοῦ (Mk 1.1).[2] However, it is unlikely that this aspect of the prophecy would have been inserted into Q had it not originated from John, for the prophesied judgment does not find its fulfillment in the narratives of the gospels or Acts. The argument that καὶ πυρί represents a 'Christian pesher-ing to the Pentecostal fulfillment'[3] cannot be sustained in view of the note of judgment already present in the context of Q (Mt. 3.7-10, 12; Lk. 3.7-9, 17).[4] Second, attempts to reduce the original scope of the Baptist's

---

1. For a survey of the various views see J. Dunn, 'Spirit-and-Fire Baptism', *NovT* 14 (1972), pp. 81-92.
2. See for example Chevallier, *Le Messie*, p. 55.
3. Ellis, *Luke*, p. 89.
4. Fitzmyer also affirms there is no evidence of Christian peshering here (*Luke I–IX*, p. 473).

prophecy to a 'baptism of fire'[1] must be rejected: there is no textual
evidence for this view and it necessitates 'a considerable degree of
development of the tradition within a comparatively short period'.[2]
Third, there are no convincing reasons to reject the Q version as an
authentic witness to the Baptist's prophecy.[3] Although the purported
parallels to the Baptist's prophecy which J. Dunn has adduced from the
Qumran scrolls cannot be accepted,[4] the Baptist should be allowed a
certain degree of creativity. We would expect as much from a prophet.
Nevertheless, the extent of his creativity need not be overstated. I shall
argue that when the Baptist's prophecy, as faithfully represented in Q,
is correctly interpreted, it is harmonious with messianic and
pneumatological views current in the Judaism of John's day.

2. *The Original Meaning of the Prophecy*

Just as there have been a variety of views regarding the original form
of the prophecy, so also have interpretations of the prophecy been
numerous and varied. Yet acceptance of the authenticity of the Q form
of the prophecy narrows the field considerably. One of the most
widely accepted interpretations of the prophecy has been put forth by
J. Dunn, an advocate of the authenticity of the Q version.[5] Dunn
asserts that the phrase βαπτίσει ἐν πνεύματι ἁγίῳ καὶ πυρί refers to
a single baptism which, from the perspective of the Baptist, was to be
experienced by all.[6] In this 'one purgative act of messianic judgment'
the Spirit and fire function together as agents of both cleansing and

---

1. Leisegang, *Pneuma Hagion*, pp. 72-80; von Baer, *Der heilige Geist*, pp. 161-
63; R. Bultmann, *The History of the Synoptic Tradition* (1968), p. 246; J.M. Creed,
The Gospel According to Luke (4th edn, 1953), p. 54; T.W. Manson, *The Sayings
of Jesus* (2nd edn, 1949), pp. 39-41; V. Taylor, *The Gospel According to Mark*
(1952), p. 157.

2. E. Best, 'Spirit-Baptism', *NovT* 4 (1960), p. 239. Note also the objection to
this thesis raised by Büchsel: 'Sein [John's] Messias ist nicht nur Richter' (*Der Geist
Gottes*, p. 144).

3. See the arguments by Marshall, *Commentary on Luke*, pp. 145-48 and Dunn,
'Spirit-and-Fire Baptism', pp. 86-92 and *Holy Spirit*, pp. 9-10.

4. Dunn, *Holy Spirit*, pp. 9-10 and 'Spirit-and-Fire Baptism', pp. 89-92. My
own study of the scrolls has confirmed the objections to this view offered by Best,
'Spirit-Baptism', p. 237. See my comments on this subject in Chapter 7 §2 below.
As I have noted in Chapter 3, the references which speak of the Spirit as a gift of the
Messiah from *T. Levi* 18.6-8 and *T. Jud.* 24.2-3 are to be viewed as Christian inter-
polations.

5. Dunn, *Holy Spirit*, pp. 8-22 and 'Spirit-and-Fire Baptism', pp. 81-92.

6. *Holy Spirit*, pp. 11-13.

destruction. Of particular importance for this study is Dunn's claim that the Spirit is 'purgative and refining for those who had repented, destructive... for those who remained impenitent'.[1] This leads Dunn to conclude that 'for the repentant it (the Spirit-and-fire baptism) would mean a refining and purging away of all evil and sin which would result in salvation and qualify to enjoy the blessings of the messianic kingdom'.[2]

Dunn's thesis has a number of attractive features. Unlike several other theories, Dunn's interpretation is not dependent on a hypothetical reconstruction of the text. He accepts as original and accounts for a baptism ἐν πνεύματι ἁγίῳ καὶ πυρί. Dunn's interpretation also attributes both positive and negative dimensions to the baptism. This dual understanding of the prophecy is necessary if one is to account for its positive treatment by Mark and Luke, and its negative portrayal by Matthew.[3] However, as attractive as Dunn's thesis is and as skill-fully as it is presented, it must be rejected in light of *religions-geschichtlich* and contextual considerations.

First, let us address the *religionsgeschichtlich* question. Dunn por-trays the Spirit as an agent which cleanses the repentant (individuals) of Israel and in this way initiates them into the messianic kingdom. Dunn adduces parallels for this understanding of the Spirit from the Qumran scrolls (1QS 3.7-9; 4.21; 1QH 16.12; 7.6; 17.26; frag. 2.9, 13) and from various Old Testament passages. He attaches particular importance to Isa. 4.4, which may well have been 'in the Baptist's mind'.[4] However, neither the Qumran literature nor Isa. 4.4 supports Dunn's case.

Several factors speak against the appropriateness of reading John's prophecy against the background provided by the scrolls of Qumran. I have already suggested that the references to 'spirit' in 1QS 3–4 refer to a disposition of man, not to the Spirit of God. And, although the Hymns do contain references to the cleansing work of the Spirit of God, these references are not related to judgment, as is clearly the case in Q. On the contrary, they refer to a gift of the Spirit which is given upon entrance into the covenant community. There is no hint of a dual aspect of the Spirit's work, encompassing both purification and destruction, in these passages. Furthermore, while the Hymns speak of

---

1. *Holy Spirit*, p. 13.
2. *Holy Spirit*, p. 14.
3. See Chapter 7 §3 below.
4. J. Dunn, *Holy Spirit*, p. 12. This suggestion was originally made by G.W.H. Lampe, 'The Holy Spirit in the Writings of St. Luke', in *Studies in the Gospels* (1957), p. 162. For Dunn's comments on the Qumran references see pp. 9-10.

the cleansing of the individual, I shall argue that the Baptist's prophecy refers to the cleansing of Israel *by the separation of the righteous from the wicked*.[1] As we have seen, in Dunn's reading of the prophecy the Spirit functions to purify the individual and initiate him into the messianic kingdom. This aspect of his interpretation may fit well with the Hymns of Qumran, but it does not coincide with the Baptist's prophecy, as contextual considerations discussed below indicate.

Isaiah 4.4 cannot be adduced in support of Dunn's thesis, for this text does not refer to the inner renewal or moral transformation of the individual. Rather, the text refers to the cleansing of the nation through the removal of the wicked.[2] Isaiah 4.3 names the 'holy' as 'those who are left in Zion'. Thus the reference in Isa. 4.4 to cleansing by means of 'a spirit of judgment and a spirit of fire' refers to the cleansing of the righteous remnant by means of separation from the wicked: while the former are established in Jerusalem, the latter are driven out. My analysis is supported by the Targum to Isa. 4.3-4:

> And it shall come to pass that he that shall be left shall return to Zion, and he that hath kept the law shall be established in Jerusalem, holy shall he be called; everyone that is written down for eternal life shall see the consolation of Jerusalem: when the Lord shall have removed the pollution of the daughters of Zion, *and carried off from the midst of her the spillers of innocent blood that are in Jerusalem*, by the word of judgment and by the word of his final decree.[3]

Contextual considerations confirm that the future baptism of which John prophesied involved a sifting of Israel, not the inner purification of the individual. This is the thrust of the winnowing metaphor of Q (Lk. 3.17 = Mt. 3.12), with its vivid threshing imagery. Threshing involved tossing the grain into the air with the aid of a wheat shovel (πτύον). This was done so that the wind might separate the grain from the chaff.[4] The double meaning of רוח/πνεῦμα as 'Spirit' and 'wind'

---

1. Best, 'Spirit-Baptism', p. 237. R. Pesch is right to question the validity of 1QS 4.20-22 as a parallel to John's prophecy: 'Von einer eschatologischen Reinigung durch den Geist (vgl. z.B. 1QS 4,20-22) war in der Gerichtspredigt kaum die Rede' (*Das Markusevangelium*, I [1976], p. 85; so also Manns, *Le Symbole*, p. 266). Yet Pesch is wrong to reject outright the possibility of a reference to eschatological purification. The difficulty arises when this eschatological purification is interpreted as the inner transformation of the individual, an activity attributed to the Spirit of God in the Hymns of Qumran, not in 1QS 4.20-22.

2. Chevallier, *Souffle*, pp. 100-101. As J.D.W. Watts notes, 'the necessary "purge" envisioned in Chaps 1 and 3' is the referent of Isa. 4.4 (*Isaiah 1–33* [1985], p. 50).

3. ET from J.F. Stenning, *The Targum of Isaiah* (italics are mine).

4. See Isa. 41.16; Jer. 4.11; Marshall, *Commentary on Luke*, p. 148.

may well have been in the mind of the Baptist and later picked up by the Synoptists,[1] although this is not essential for my interpretation. According to the Q metaphor, after its separation from the grain, the chaff was to be consumed by fire. The metaphor then clearly suggests that the future baptism would include aspects of cleansing and destruction. Yet we can go further: the metaphor also specifies what kind of cleansing the baptism would effect. The cleansing envisioned is not the purification or moral transformation of the individual, as Dunn suggests; rather, it involves a cleansing of Israel by means of separation: the righteous (grain) shall be separated from the unrighteous (chaff). This then is the work of the Spirit prophesied by the Baptist: separation. The 'fire' is the destructive wrath of God which will consume the unrighteous. Thus the baptism ἐν πνεύματι ἁγίῳ καὶ πυρί which John prophesied was to be a deluge of messianic judgment which all would experience.[2] All would be sifted and separated by a powerful blast of the Spirit of God: the unrighteous would be consumed in fire, and in this way the righteous remnant would be gathered together and the nation purified.[3]

---

1. F.J. Foakes-Jackson and K. Lake, *The Beginnings of Christianity*, IV, p. 238. It is possible that John uttered רוח (winnowing fork) knowing that both the concept of winnowing and the sound of the word itself, so similar to רוח, would evoke images of the previously mentioned Spirit of God.

2. In 'The Meaning of the Verb "to Baptize"' (EQ 45 [1973], pp. 130-40) Marshall argues persuasively that in Mk 1.8 and parallels βαπτίζω should be translated 'deluge', 'flood', or 'drench' with the Spirit.

3. The grammatical significance of the single ἐν governing two dative nouns connected by καί should not be over emphasized. On the basis of this grammatical construction Dunn asserts that the 'future baptism is a single baptism in Holy Spirit and fire, the ἐν embracing both elements' (Holy Spirit, p. 11). However, for exceptions to this usage in Luke–Acts see: Lk. 2.52 (variant); 10.13 = Mt. 11.21; 21.25, 34; 24.19; 24.44; Acts 7.22; 16.2; 26.20. The omission rather than repetition of a preposition before phrases connected by καί is common in the NT and is particularly characteristic of Luke and Matthew. Out of 111 opportunities Luke repeats the preposition only 25 times (22.5%). Out of 35 opportunities Matthew repeats the preposition only 11 times (31.4%). Compare this usage with Mark (10 out of 26; 38.5%); John (8 out of 15; 53.3%); Romans/1 Corinthians (14 out of 24; 58.3%); Ephesians (6 out of 16; 37.5%); Pastorals (4 out of 24; 16.6%); Revelation (24 out of 38; 63.2%). See Nigel Turner, *A Grammar of New Testament Greek*, III (1963), p. 275. Yet it must be noted that I speak not of two separate baptisms, one of Spirit for the repentant and one of fire for the unrepentant; rather, I speak of a single act of judgment which includes two elements: sifting and destruction. All are sifted, not simply the righteous; and, although only the unrighteous are destroyed by fire, this is the means by which the righteous are purified.

This reading of the text not only does justice to the immediate context, it also has a number of other attractive features.

First, it solves the *religionsgeschichtlich* problem mentioned above. The functions attributed to the Spirit in this interpretation of the Baptist's prophecy are entirely consistent with messianic and pneumatological views current in Judaism. Isaiah 4.4 refers to the Spirit of God as the means by which Israel shall be sifted and cleansed;[1] and, as we have already noted, a number of intertestamental texts describe the Messiah as charismatically endowed with the Spirit of God so that he may rule and judge (e.g. *1 En.* 49.3; 62.2). Several texts tie these two concepts together. Perhaps most striking is *Ps. Sol.* 17.26-37, a passage which describes how the Messiah, 'powerful in the Holy Spirit' (17.37), shall purify Israel by ejecting all aliens and sinners from the nation. Isaiah 11.2, 4, which is echoed in *1 En.* 62.2 and 1QSb 5.24-25, declares that the Spirit-empowered Messiah will slay the wicked 'with the breath of his lips' (רוח שפתיו)[2]. Against this background it is not difficult to envision the Spirit of God as an instrument employed by the Messiah to sift and cleanse Israel. Indeed, the texts cited above suggest that when John referred in metaphorical language to the messianic deluge of the Spirit, he had in mind Spirit-inspired oracles of judgment uttered by the Messiah (cf. Isa. 11.4), blasts of the Spirit which would separate the wheat from the chaff. However, we search in vain for a reference to a messianic bestowal of the Spirit which purifies and morally transforms the individual. I have already noted that references to the soteriological activity of the Spirit during the intertestamental period are exceedingly rare and limited to a minor strand within the wisdom tradition.

Second, this interpretation renders attempts to read John's prophecy as a baptism in 'wind and fire' superfluous.[3] John likens the activity of the Spirit to the sifting force of a powerful wind, but this in itself is an insufficient reason to deny him a direct reference to the Holy Spirit.

---

1. Note also Ps. 1.4-5 and Job 15.30.

2. Note how 1QSb 5.24-25 and *1 En.* 62.2 compress and bring together the language of Isa. 11.2 and 11.4. Chevallier notes the significance of Isa. 11.2, 4 for John's prophecy (*Le Messie*, p. 70). Isaiah 27.8f. and 30.28 also refer to the רוח of God in similar terms, as a 'blast of the Spirit/breath of God', although here the theme of judgment rather than sifting seems to be most prominent. See Montague, *Spirit*, p. 38.

3. Proponents of this view include R. Eisler, *The Messiah Jesus and John the Baptist* (1931), pp. 274-79; Barrett, *Gospel Tradition*, p. 126; Schweizer, 'πνεῦμα', p. 399 and *The Holy Spirit* (1980), pp. 52-53; Chevallier, *Le Messie*, pp. 56-57; Grundmann, *Lukas*, p. 105; Best, 'Spirit-Baptism', pp. 240-43.

Textual evidence for the omission of ἅγιος is lacking,[1] and thus proponents of the 'wind and fire' view are forced to speculate that John's words were reinterpreted by the church at a very early stage.

Third, this interpretation fits well with the subsequent and varied usage of the text by the synoptic writers. To this point I now turn.

3. *The Use and Interpretation of the Prophecy in the Early Church*

The omission of καὶ πυρί, coupled with the τοῦ εὐαγγελίου Ἰησοῦ Χριστοῦ of Mk 1.1 and the absence of any mention of judgment or wrath, indicates that Mark interpreted John's preaching and prophecy largely in positive terms. The form of Mark's account (Mk 1.8), so similar to Acts 1.5; 11.16, probably reflects the conviction that the prophecy was fulfilled, at least in part, at Pentecost.[2] However, Mark's purpose in relating the Baptist's prophecy is essentially christological:[3] the prophecy serves to point to the unique status of Jesus as the Spirit-baptizer. Therefore, Mark fails to elaborate further on the nature of the prophecy's fulfillment. For more specific information we shall have to turn elsewhere.

Matthew's account of the Baptist's preaching in Mt. 3.7-12 corresponds more closely to Q than to that of Luke in Lk. 3.7-18.[4]

---

1. The evidence for the omission of ἅγιος is exceedingly weak (MSS 63, 64; Tert.; Aug.; Clem. Alex.). The variant readings in these MSS can be explained as an attempt to state more explicitly the connection between the πνεῦμα of v. 16 and the winnowing metaphor of v. 17. Thus Fitzmyer is justified when he writes: 'The omission . . . is scarcely evidence of the more original Lucan text' (*Luke I–IX*, p. 473).

2. Turner, 'Luke and the Spirit', p. 50. Perhaps the Pentecost fulfillment (cf. Lk. 24.49; Acts 1.8) of the prophecy is alluded to in the promise of Mk 13.11. As N. Petersen notes, this passage represents 'the story-time fulfillment of the Baptist's prediction' (*Literary Criticism for New Testament Critics* [1978], p. 70). J.E. Yates (*The Spirit and the Kingdom* [1963]) puts forth the thesis that, according to Mark and Q, the Baptist's prophecy was accomplished in the ministry of Jesus. The objections to this position are numerous and significant. They have been chronicled by Hill (*Greek Words*, pp. 245-246) and more extensively by Turner, 'Luke and the Spirit', pp. 49-52. A pivot to Yates's argument is his insistence that the Acts account, in which the Spirit is portrayed as an endowment, is incompatible with the notion of the Spirit as an agent of sifting and cleansing (see pp. 5, 12, 13, 23, 40). However, as my comments below demonstrate, the Acts account is completely compatible with that of Mark and Q.

3. J. Shelton, *'Filled with the Holy Spirit': A Redactional Motif in Luke's Gospel* (1982), p. 26.

4. Manson, *Sayings*, pp. 253-54; W. Wink, *John the Baptist in the Gospel Tradition* (1968), p. 18. Contra Schürmann, *Lukasevangelium*, I, p. 169.

Although Lk. 3.10-15 cannot be attributed to Luke on stylistic grounds and is likely to represent traditional material, it probably came from a source other than Q.[1] This judgment is supported by Luke's summary of John's preaching recorded in Lk. 3.18, a verse which is clearly from Luke's hand.[2] The εὐηγγελίζετο τὸν λαόν of Lk. 3.18 indicates that Luke interpreted John's preaching, particularly his prophecy concerning the coming baptizer, in a predominantly positive way. Thus it is probable that Luke inserted Lk. 3.10-15, traditional material from another source which emphasized and illustrated the concept of repentance, into the narrative of Q (Mt. 3.7-12 = Lk. 3.7-9, 16-17) in order to separate the negative pronouncement of judgment in Lk. 3.7-9 = Mt. 3.7-10 from John's prophecy of the coming baptizer. In this way Luke created a context appropriate for his positive appraisal of the Baptist's prophecy. Matthew, on the other hand, following the Q version more closely, retains and possibly heightens[3] the emphasis on the negative and judgmental aspect of John's preaching. Addressed to the 'Pharisees and Sadducees', the prophecy serves as a warning against the rejection of Jesus: to reject Jesus is to reject the Messiah and future judge; it will inevitably result in the judgment of God and destruction. Therefore, Matthew (following Q) frames the Baptist's prophecy in largely negative terms, featuring destructive judgment, Luke emphasizes its positive elements: the sifting and purification of the righteous remnant.

Yet this raises an interesting question: If Luke interpreted the Baptist's prophecy in a predominantly positive way and thus sought to emphasize this aspect of the prophecy in his account, why did he follow the Q version with its reference to καὶ πυρί (Lk. 3.16 = Mt. 3.11) and the πυρὶ ἀσβέστῳ of the winnowing metaphor? Presuming that Luke had the Markan and Q versions before him, it is indeed

---

1. Luke has clearly edited his source, as the ὄχλοι of 3.10 corresponds to the ὄχλοις of 3.7. The fact that Lk. 3.10-15 refers to questions offered by various groups of people, rather than simply 'Pharisees and Sadducees', is another indication that this section has been inserted by Luke. Although the phrase πολλοὺς τῶν Φαρισαίων καὶ Σαδδουκαίων (Mt. 3.7) is likely redactional, it probably reflects a reference to 'Pharisees' in Q. In Mt. 16.1/Mk 8.11 and Mt. 16.6/Lk. 12.1 Matthew inserts 'Pharisees and Sadducees' for 'Pharisees'.

2. Verses 18-20 are 'strongly Lucan in language' (Marshall, *Commentary on Luke*, p. 149).

3. The phrase πολλοὺς τῶν Φαρισαίων καὶ Σαδδουκαίων (Mt. 3.7) is probably redactional.

striking that Luke follows Q in Lk. 3.16-17.[1] The question becomes even more pressing when we remember that Luke refers only to a Spirit-baptism in Acts 1.5 and 11.16.[2] What was so significant about the Q account that, in spite of these incongruities with his own view, Luke chose to follow it?

The answer to this question is found in the importance Luke attached to the winnowing metaphor of Q. For Luke, the winnowing metaphor was essential if the true significance of the future Spirit-baptism was to be recognized. The winnowing metaphor specified that the deluge of Spirit, initiated by the Messiah, would *sift* the people of Israel. This thought of *sifting* is vital to Luke's interpretation of the bestowal of the Spirit on the disciples at Pentecost: 'John baptized with water, but in a few days, you will be baptized with the Holy Spirit. . . But you

---

1. Luke clearly has a christological motive in mind, as Lk. 3.15 indicates. But if this were his only motive, the Markan account would have served that purpose most admirably.

2. Dunn argues that Luke omits the reference to 'fire' in Acts 1.5 because Jesus has already undergone a baptism of fire on the cross on behalf of his disciples (*Holy Spirit*, pp. 42-43; see also 'The Birth of a Metaphor—Baptized in the Spirit (Part 1)', pp. 137-38). Through this baptism of fire Jesus 'drains the cup of wrath which was the portion of others' (p. 43). The baptism which Jesus bestows on his disciples is thus no longer a baptism of Spirit and fire, but now only of Spirit (Acts 1.5). Dunn supports this contention by pointing to Lk. 12.49f., which he interprets in light of Lk. 3.16. However, an examination of Lk. 12.49f. indicates that it cannot bear the weight of Dunn's argument. Contrary to Dunn's thesis, Lk. 12.49 does not state that Jesus shall take upon himself the 'fire' of judgment; rather, that he came to 'pour it out on the earth'. This is a clear reference to the 'eschatological conflagration' (Conzelmann, *The Theology of St. Luke*, p. 109). The verses which follow in the pericope (12.50-53) speak of the events which precede and foreshadow the coming judgment. The phrase, βάπτισμα δὲ ἔχω βαπτισθῆναι, which appears in 12.50 is a metaphorical reference to the deluge of suffering which Jesus shall experience on the cross and, as such, is unrelated to the baptism prophesied by John. Verses 51-53 describe the separation of good from evil (and the division which it causes) which shall occur before the destruction of the wicked by fire. It is possible that the 'fire' of judgment is interpreted by Luke (and perhaps the redactor of Q) as referring to both this preliminary sifting process and the final act of fiery judgment itself. However, since the process of separation described in vv. 51-53 seems to precede the kindling of the 'fire' alluded to in 12.49 (note the use of ἤδη in 12.49), the 'fire' of 12.49 is probably understood simply as a reference to the final judgment. The verses which follow (12.54-59) develop further the theme of imminent and inescapable judgment. The evidence thus suggests that Luke omits 'fire' in Acts 1.5, not because 'Jesus has exhausted the fire which was kindled upon him' (Dunn, *Holy Spirit*, p. 43) on the cross, but because the final act of judgment, the destruction of the wicked by fire, did not find its fulfillment at Pentecost. Note also the critique of Dunn's position offered by Turner, 'Luke and the Spirit', p. 153.

will receive power when the Holy Spirit comes on you; and you will be my witnesses' (Acts 1.5, 8). Just as John prophesied that the Spirit would sift and separate, so also Luke understood the Pentecostal bestowal of the Spirit to be the means by which the righteous remnant would be separated from the chaff (cf. Lk. 2.34f.). John did not specify how this sifting would occur, alluding to the Spirit's role in the coming apocalypse only in very general terms; however, in light of Pentecost, Luke interprets the Spirit empowered mission and preaching of the disciples to be the means by which this sifting occurs.[1] For this reason the Q version, with its winnowing metaphor, was of vital importance to Luke. It pointed to the decisive role which the Spirit would play in the early church: as the source of the supernatural guidance of the mission of the church and its inspired proclamation of the gospel, the Spirit was the catalyst of the Christian mission and, as such, an instrument of *sifting*.

Thus, in Luke's perspective, John's prophecy finds initial fulfillment at Pentecost and continuing fulfillment in the Spirit-empowered mission of the church. However, the final act of separation, the destruction of the unrighteous in the fire of messianic judgment, still awaits its fulfillment. While it is likely that John viewed the sifting activity of the Spirit and the consuming activity of the fire as different aspects of one apocalyptic event, Luke has separated these aspects chronologically in view of the ongoing mission of the church.

I am now in a position to summarize these conclusions and assess their implications for my argument. John declared that a deluge of messianic judgment was coming: the righteous would be separated from the wicked by a powerful blast of the Spirit of God, and the latter would be consumed by fire. In this way the righteous remnant would be gathered together and the nation purified.

Mark and Luke, in their respective accounts, emphasize the positive aspect of the prophecy: the sifting out of the righteous remnant. Therefore, they do not hesitate to associate John with the εὐαγγέλιον (Mk 1.1; Lk. 3.18). Luke clearly interprets the sifting activity of the Spirit of which John prophesied to be accomplished in the Spirit-directed mission of the church and its Spirit-inspired proclamation of the gospel (Acts 1.5, 8; 11.16). Thus the mission of the church anticipates the final act of messianic judgment. Although Mark does not

---

1. J. Jervell, *Luke and the People of God: A New Look at Luke–Acts* (1972), p. 49: 'Above all, he [Luke] wants to describe what happened to Israel through the Christian missionary preaching. The picture is clear: Israel has not rejected the gospel, but has become divided over the issue.' See also D.L. Tiede, 'The Exaltation of Jesus and the Restoration of Israel in Acts 1', *HTR* (1986), p. 283.

elaborate on the nature of the prophecy's fulfillment, he probably interpreted the prophecy in a similar manner.

Matthew emphasizes the negative and judgmental aspect of John's preaching. Matthew, like Mark, is not interested in pointing to the future fulfillment of the prophecy in the mission of the church, although he undoubtedly was aware of this perspective. Rather his interest centers on the christological significance of the prophecy and the didactic purpose it serves.

Of particular importance for this study is the light that John's prophecy, and its subsequent use in the synoptic gospels, sheds on the pneumatological perspective of John the Baptist, the primitive church, and Luke. According to John, the Spirit of God was the means by which the Messiah would sift and judge Israel. If, as the parallels from the intertestamental literature suggest, John had Spirit-inspired oracles of judgment in mind at this point, then his perspective on the Spirit is not so different from that of Luke. For Luke, interpreting John's prophecy as a reference to the Spirit-empowered mission of the church, highlights the prophetic aspects of the Spirit's activity: the Spirit, in guiding the mission of the church, grants special insight, and, as the impetus behind the proclamation of the gospel, inspires speech. In view of the similarities between Mark's account and Acts 1.5 and 11.16, it would appear that the viewpoint of the primitive church is accurately reflected in Luke's interpretation. Thus 'Spirit and fire baptism', as prophesied by John and as interpreted by the early church, refers neither to the means by which the individual is purified nor to an event which initiates one into the the blessings of the messianic kingdom. John's prophecy, particularly as interpreted by Luke, attributes prophetic rather than soteriological functions to the Spirit.

Chapter 8

JESUS AND THE SPIRIT:
THE PNEUMATIC ANOINTING (LUKE 3–4)

Luke not only affirms that Jesus was begotten by the Spirit, he also declares that the coming Spirit-baptizer was himself anointed with the Spirit (Lk. 3.22; 4.18; Acts 10.38). This leads us to a question of central importance: what significance does Luke attach to Jesus' pneumatic anointing? Can we affirm with F. Büchsel that Jesus became uniquely aware of God as Father through his reception of the Spirit at the Jordan? And, in light of the preceding discussion and the texts to be examined, how are we to evaluate J. Dunn's claim that the primary purpose of Jesus' anointing at Jordan was not to empower him for his messianic ministry, but rather to initiate him into the new age and covenant? Certainly the positions of Büchsel and Dunn represent a direct challenge to my thesis that Luke understands and consistently portrays the activity of the Spirit in prophetic categories. These questions then provide the impetus for the analysis of the Spirit-passages in Lk. 3.21-22; 4.1, 14, 16f. While the description of Jesus' pneumatic anointing accounts for only one extended sentence in Luke's Gospel (3.21-22), the significance which Luke attaches to this event can be seen only in light of the context into which he has placed it.

1. Jesus' Pneumatic Anointing (Luke 3.21-22)

1.1. Source Criticism
I begin this analysis of the baptism pericope by addressing the pressing source-critical question: was Luke's account of Jesus' baptism influenced by another written source (Q) or are the features peculiar to Luke to be attributed simply to his alteration of Mark? A comparison of the synoptic accounts of Jesus' baptism reveals two minor agreements of Luke with Matthew against Mark: first, Matthew and Luke use forms of ἀνοίγω rather than Mark's σχιζομένους with reference to the opening of heaven; and second, while Mark has the Spirit descending εἰς αὐτόν, Matthew and Luke agree with ἐπ' αὐτόν. These

minor agreements probably reflect coincidental redaction rather than traces of Q.[1] Matthew and Luke often tone down the forceful language of Mark[2] and on several occasions replace a Markan εἰς with ἐπί or ἐν.[3]

The strongest argument that Q did contain an account of Jesus' baptism is found in the structure of Q itself, not in the minor agreements of Matthew and Luke against Mark.[4] An account of Jesus' baptism would serve to link the ministry of John with that of Jesus and provide a suitable introduction to the temptation narrative, which presupposes the divine sonship of Jesus.[5] However, if such an account did exist, it has not exerted much visible influence on Matthew or Luke. The deviations from the Markan text peculiar to Matthew and Luke reflect their respective interests and styles, not an underlying text.[6] In light of these considerations it appears unlikely that Luke's account of Jesus' baptism (Lk. 3.21-22) was influenced by a written source other than Mk 1.9-11.

1.2. *Lukan Redaction*
Luke has made a number of changes to the Markan text. However, several of these alterations reflect literary or stylistic motivations, rather than a particular theological *Tendenz*. We should not overemphasize the significance of Luke's movement of John's imprisonment forward in his narrative (Lk. 3.20; Mk 6.17), nor of his omission of any explicit reference to John the Baptist in the baptismal account.[7] By

1. So also Fitzmyer, *Luke I–IX*, p. 479; G.O. Williams, 'The Baptism in Luke's Gospel', *JTS* 45 (1944), pp. 31-33.

2. See for example Mk 1.43 and the alterations in Mt. 8.4 and Lk. 5.14. However, this kind of alteration may also reflect the influence of Q, as in the case of Mk 1.12 (ἐκβάλλω): Mt. 4.1 (ἀνάγω) = Lk. 4.1 (ἄγω).

3. See Mk 4.7, 18; 11.8 and parallels. Williams, 'The Baptism', pp. 31-32.

4. L.E. Keck, 'The Spirit and the Dove', *NTS* 17 (1970), pp. 58-59.

5. Schürmann, *Lukasevangelium*, I, p. 197; Marshall, *Commentary on Luke*, p. 150.

6. For example note the language characteristic of Matthew in Mt. 3.15 (πληρῶσαι πᾶσαν δικαιοσύνην) and the clearly Lukan addition of προσευχομένου in Lk. 3.21.

7. Conzelmann (*The Theology of St Luke*, p. 21) has argued that Luke placed the account of John's imprisonment (Mk 6.17f.) at this point in the narrative (Lk. 3.20) and omitted any reference to John at Jesus' baptism because John and Jesus belong to different eras in Luke's scheme of salvation history. However, this thesis, like Conzelmann's entire three-epoch scheme, has been subjected to severe criticism and must be rejected (see Oliver, 'Lucan Birth Stories', p. 217 and Minear, 'Birth Stories', p. 123). If Luke's redactional activity in Lk. 3.20f. was motivated by theological interests, the suggestion of S.G. Wilson that Luke intended 'to damp down

concluding the story of John's ministry before beginning that of Jesus', Luke was able to bring out the parallels between John and Jesus more clearly, particularly the fate of the prophet which they would share.[1] Moreover, while the addition of σωματικῷ εἴδει emphasizes the objective character of the descent of the Spirit, this merely heightens what was already present[2] or, if L.E. Keck is correct,[3] what Luke believed to have been present in the Markan text. The replacement of Mark's εἶδεν by the ἐγένετο construction may also be due to Luke's desire to emphasize the objective character of the event, but it probably simply reflects stylistic concerns,[4] as with Luke's addition of τὸ ἅγιον to the Markan τὸ πνεῦμα.

More significant are Luke's alterations of the events surrounding Jesus' reception of the Spirit: unlike Mark, Luke has Jesus receive the

excessive veneration of John by the Baptist sect' is much more plausible than the *heilsgeschichtlich* hypothesis of Conzelmann ('Lukan Eschatology', *NTS* 16 [1970], p. 332; cf. Williams, 'The Baptism', pp. 34-38 and Robinson, *Weg des Herrn*, p. 19). See also Robinson's critique of the evidence Conzelmann cites for his thesis from Luke's redaction of Markan geography, evidence which Robinson describes as 'brüchig' (pp. 10f.). Certainly too much should not be read into the omission in Lk. 3.21 of the Markan geographical notes. With regard to Lk. 16.16, although the linguistic and grammatical evidence is indecisive, in light of Lk. 3.18 and considerations alluded to above, it is most improbable that Luke intended to exclude John from the era in which the gospel is preached (see Marshall, *Luke: Historian and Theologian*, p. 146; Minear, 'Birth Stories', p. 122; and F. Bovon, 'Aktuelle Linien lukanischer Forschung', in *Lukas in neuer Sicht* [1985], p. 22).

1. G. Braumann argues that John's arrest in Lk. 3.20 is not motivated by the desire to separate the ministry of John from that of Jesus, rather it is intended to foreshadow the fate of Jesus and of his church ('Das Mittel der Zeit', *ZNW* 54 [1963], p. 125). According to Braumann, persecution is a theme which unites John, Jesus, and the church. See also Marshall, *Commentary on Luke*, pp. 148-49 and Schürmann, *Lukasevangelium*, I, p. 184.

2. H. Greeven, 'περιστερά', *TDNT*, VI, pp. 63-72, esp. n. 59.

3. Keck maintains that Mark's ambiguous rendering of an original adverbial phrase was later misinterpreted and given an adjectival meaning ('The Spirit and the Dove', pp. 41-67, esp. pp. 63-67).

4. The εἶδεν of Mk 1.10 probably refers to a visionary 'seeing' and 'seeing' is often associated by Luke with visionary phenomena. Yet the significance of this fact is mitigated by Luke's usage of θεωρέω rather than εἶδεν in visionary contexts (e.g. Acts 7.56; 9.3; 10.11). That Luke speaks of an objective, rather than visionary event, is suggested by his insertion of σωματικῷ εἴδει; however, for arguments to the contrary see Turner, who asserts that Luke understood Jesus' experience as a private vision ('Luke and the Spirit', p. 212 n. 78). It is true that the reality of an event for Luke is in no way diminished by its visionary character (Acts 7.56; 9.3; 10.11; 22.17f.).

Spirit after his baptism,[1] while praying. Luke is not concerned to draw connections between Jesus' water baptism and his reception of the Spirit.[2] Indeed, what was of central importance to Luke was not Jesus' baptism; rather, his reception of the Spirit, occasioned by prayer. For this reason Luke has transformed an account of Jesus' baptism into an account of Jesus' reception of the Spirit.

These changes, as striking as they may be, represent a shift in emphasis rather than specific content.[3] The elements which provide the interpretative clues necessary for uncovering the significance of Jesus' pneumatic anointing are essentially the same in Mark as in Luke. I refer to the phenomena which accompany Jesus' reception of the Spirit: the dove metaphor and, more significant, the declaration of the heavenly voice.

1.3. The Significance of Jesus' Pneumatic Anointing

The enigmatic dove. A number of interpretations regarding the significance of the dove have emerged, but none is entirely satisfactory.[4] Some have sought to link the symbol of the dove with the establishment of the new covenant by relating the περιστερά of the

---

1. It is possible that (1) βαπτισθέντος could refer to action simultaneous with ἐν τῷ βαπτισθῆναι and (2) both could refer to action simultaneous with the present participle προσευχομένου and the descent of the Spirit upon Jesus (thus the verse is rendered by Turner: 'At the time when the whole people were baptized, and when Jesus too was baptized—and while he was actually praying—heaven opened. . .' ['Luke and the Spirit', p. 211 n. 77]). However, the second option is improbable due to the change in the tenses of the participles (aorist participle: βαπτισθέντος; present participle: προσευχομένου; see Dunn, *Holy Spirit*, p. 33; Bovon, *Luc le théologien*, p. 251) and Luke's usage of the articular aorist infinitive with the dative elsewhere (e.g. Lk. 2.27, 19.15; see also F. Blass and A. Debrunner, *A Greek Grammar of the New Testament* [1961], §404; and M.A. Chevallier, 'L'Apologie du baptême d'eau à la fin du premier siècle: introduction secondaire de l'etiologie dans les récits du baptême de Jesus', *NTS* 32 [1986], p. 535). The first option remains likely. Thus my translation reads: 'After all the people and Jesus had been baptized, while he was praying. . .'

2. The reception of the Spirit is associated with prayer, not water baptism (see also Lk. 11.13; Acts 1.14; 4.31; 8.15).

3. The key exception is the emphasis on prayer, a motif which runs throughout Luke's Gospel (5.16; 6.12; 9.18, 28f.; 11.1; 22.41; 23.46) and Acts as well (see the preceding note).

4. For a survey and critique of the various options, see F. Lentzen-Deis, *Die Taufe Jesu nach den Synoptikern* (1970), pp. 170-83; Keck, 'The Spirit and the Dove', pp. 41-57. I shall limit my discussion to those which have a direct bearing on the topic at hand.

baptismal account with Noah's dove.[1] Yet these attempts prove unconvincing, for Noah's dove is nowhere connected to the Spirit.[2] Others, linking the baptismal dove to the creative activity of God in Gen. 1.2, have interpreted the symbol as pointing to a new creation.[3] Rabbinic tradition seemingly supports this viewpoint when it speaks of the movement of the Spirit over the primaeval chaos in terms of the fluttering of a dove.[4] However, the chief and fatal weakness of this theory is that in the rabbinic sources cited the dove is not a symbol of the Spirit, rather the point of comparison 'is the motion of the Spirit and the movement of a dove'.[5] For this reason the dove is not integral to the comparison; as the text from *Gen. R.* 2.4 indicates, the comparison can be made with any bird.[6]

Perhaps the most convincing view has been put forth by L.E. Keck,[7] who maintains that Mark's ὡς περιστεράν reflects an original adverbial reference to the descent of the Spirit which, due to its ambiguity,[8] was later misinterpreted and given adjectival significance. While this interpretation does justice to the rabbinic parallels which compare the movement of the Spirit to that of a dove, it is questionable whether a natural reading of Mk 1.10 supports such an interpretation.[9] Given the enigmatic nature of the reference to the dove, we shall be on firmer ground if we look to the declaration of the heavenly voice for a basis from which to interpret the Spirit's role at Jordan.[10]

1. Von Baer, *Der heilige Geist*, p. 58; suggested as a possibility by Lampe, *Seal*, p. 36.

2. Keck, 'The Spirit and the Dove', p. 49.

3. Barrett cautiously points in this direction (*Gospel Tradition*, pp. 38-39). Dunn, attempting to support his thesis that Jesus' reception of the Spirit at the Jordan marks his initiation into the new covenant, points to this view and the view cited above as possibilities (*Holy Spirit*, p. 27).

4. While the Ben Zoma tradition of *Gen. R.* 2.4 refers simply to a bird, an allusion to a dove is found in the Babylonian Talmud's version of the Ben Zoma story (*b. Hag.* 15a).

5. Keck, 'The Spirit and the Dove', p. 52.

6. See also Marshall, *Commentary on Luke*, p. 153.

7. Keck, 'The Spirit and the Dove', pp. 41-67, esp. pp. 63-67.

8. According to Keck, this was the result of translating the phrase from Aramaic to Greek.

9. Greeven writes: 'Both authors and readers knew enough of the general descent of the divine breath not to need an image for this. The reference is obviously to the visible manifestation which has to be expressed' ('περιστερά', *TDNT*, *VI*, p. 68 n. 58). See also E. Haenchen, *Der Weg Jesu* (1966), p. 53.

10. Chevallier writes: 'Cette colombe reste un rappel impitoyable à l'humilité exégétique' (*Souffle*, p. 120); see also Lentzen-Deis, *Die Taufe Jesu*, p. 182 and S. Gero, 'The Spirit as a Dove at the Baptism of Jesus', *NovT* 18 (1976), p. 17.

The heavenly declaration. The declaration of the heavenly voice consists of two stichs: the first reminiscent of Ps. 2.7; the second of Isa. 42.1.[1]

σὺ εἶ ὁ υἱός μου ὁ ἀγαπητός
ἐν σοὶ εὐδόκησα

In view of the royal character of Psalm 2 and the reference to messianic judgment (Mk 1.7-8) in the immediate context, it is virtually certain that Mark understood σὺ εἶ ὁ υἱός μου ὁ ἀγαπητός as a reference to Jesus as the Messiah-King.[2] However, it is possible that in this instance υἱός signifies more: that Jesus was the Messiah because he stood in unique filial relationship to God.[3] Since few would deny that during his earthly ministry Jesus related to God as Father in a relatively unique way,[4] it is quite possible that the reference to υἱός would have been understood in this way.[5] In view of Lk. 1.35 and 2.49, this is almost certainly the case for Luke. Whether or not on the basis of this passage we can attribute Jesus' messianic status to his filial relation to God, it is clear that the declaration identifies Jesus as the Messiah-King. The addition of the second stich, drawn from Isa. 42.1, is significant in that it brings the concept of the Servant of Israel together with that of the royal Messiah. Jesus is thus identified by the heavenly voice as the Servant-Messiah. It is noteworthy that both figures, the Servant of Isa. 42.1 and the Davidic Messiah of Ps. 2.7, are enabled by the Spirit to carry out their respective tasks.[6]

Of course the christology presented by the heavenly voice is not the primary concern here; we are chiefly concerned with the implications

---

1. Although it is generally recognized that Ps. 2.7 and Isa. 42.1 form the basis of the divine declaration (for a dissenting voice see M.R. Mansfield, *'Spirit and Gospel' in Mark* [1987], p. 27), one cannot rule out other sources of influence (I.H. Marshall, 'Son of God or Servant of Yahweh? A Reconsideration of Mark 1.11', *NTS* 15 [1968–69], p. 335). Most problematic is the source and significance of ἀγαπητός. While the term may stem from a Jewish understanding of Ps. 2.7 (see the Targum on Ps. 2.7) or simply from Isa. 42.1, other possibilities, such as Bock's suggestion that the term stems from Isa. 41.8 (in association with Isa. 42.1), cannot be ruled out. For a discussion of the various options see Bock, *Proclamation*, pp. 99-105; and Marshall, 'Son of God', pp. 326-36. My acceptance of ἀγαπητός as an adjective of 'my son' rather than as a separate title follows the UBS text.

2. Bock, *Proclamation*, p. 104.

3. Marshall, *Christology*, p. 117.

4. J. Jeremias, *The Prayers of Jesus* (1967), pp. 11-67.

5. This is particularly true if Gen. 22.2f. forms part of the background to the saying. This is suggested as a possibility by Marshall, 'Son of God', pp. 334-35.

6. See Isa. 11.1-2; Isa. 42.1. G.R. Beasley-Murray, 'Jesus and the Spirit', in *Mélanges Bibliques* (1970), p. 474.

the divine declaration holds for the relationship between christology and pneumatology. The pressing question remains: what light does the heavenly declaration shed on the significance of Jesus' pneumatic anointing?

The reference to υἱός has encouraged F. Büchsel to speak of Jesus' pneumatic anointing in adoptionistic terms: 'Jesu Geistbesitz ist Gottes-sohnschaft'.[1] Although Büchsel acknowledged that 'Jesus ist Gottes Sohn seit seiner Geburt',[2] he asserted that through his pneumatic anointing at Jordan Jesus' sonship is perfected and completed.[3] According to Büchsel, Jesus' experience at Jordan marked the beginning of a new and deeper existential awareness of God as Father. Similarly, J. Dunn, while acknowledging that Jesus is Messiah and Son from birth, declares that 'there is also a sense in which he only becomes Messiah and Son at Jordan'.[4] For Dunn this means that at the River Jordan the Spirit initiates Jesus into the new age and covenant.

How are we to evaluate such claims? Does Jesus in some sense become Son and Messiah at the Jordan? Does the Spirit provide Jesus with a new awareness of God as Father and/or initiate him into the new age and covenant? I suggest that the evidence points in a different direction. The divine declaration does not designate Jesus' reception of the Spirit as the beginning, in any sense, of his sonship or messiahship. On the contrary, through his reception of the Spirit Jesus is equipped for his messianic task. We may speak of the Jordan event as signalling the beginning of Jesus' messianic ministry, but not of his messiahship.

This judgment is supported by the form of the citation from Ps. 2.7. The word order of the septuagintal reading, Υἱός μου εἶ σύ, has been altered in the Markan tradition to σὺ εἶ ὁ υἱός μου. The shift in word order suggests that the declaration was understood as the identification of Jesus as the υἱός of God, rather than as confirming the bestowal of the status of sonship upon Jesus.[5] If the tradition had intended to signify Jesus' adoption or his entrance into a new dimension of sonship by quoting from Ps. 2.7, it would have been natural to include the latter part of the verse as well: ἐγὼ σήμερον γεγέννηκά σε.[6] That the voice

1. Büchsel, *Der Geist Gottes*, p. 165.
2. *Der Geist Gottes*, p. 166.
3. *Der Geist Gottes*, p. 167.
4. Dunn, *Holy Spirit*, p. 28.
5. E. Lohmeyer, *Das Evangelium des Markus* (1959), p. 23.
6. H. Ervin, *Conversion-Initiation and the Baptism in the Holy Spirit* (1984), p. 11. The textual evidence for the inclusion of this phrase in the Lukan text is extremely weak and undoubtedly secondary. See Metzger, *A Textual Commentary*, p. 136 and Marshall, *Commentary on Luke*, p. 155.

merely identifies an already existing status is also suggested by the repetition of the declaration (οὗτός ἐστιν ὁ υἱός μου) on the mount of transfiguration (Mk 9.7 and par.).

Further support for my rejection of an adoptionistic reading of the text is found in the messianic conceptions which form the background to the heavenly declaration. As noted above, the Spirit equips both the Servant of Israel (Isa. 42.1) and the Davidic Messiah (Isa. 11.1) for their respective tasks. Reference to the Spirit as the source of the Servant-Messiah's special status or unique standing before God is conspicuously absent in these texts.[1] The correlation of the messianic concepts associated with the Servant of the Lord and the Davidic Messiah together with the anointing of the Spirit suggests divine empowering, not divine adoption.[2]

If it is unlikely that Mark interpreted the Jordan event as Jesus' adoption,[3] in light of the infancy narratives (Lk. 1.35; 2.49), it is virtually certain that Luke did not. Not only is a divine begetting precluded by Lk. 1.35, but Jesus is well aware of his unique relationship to God as Father long before the Jordan event (Lk. 2.49). Moreover, when the eschatological nature of Luke 1–2 is recognized and Conzelmann's rigid *heilsgeschichtlich* scheme is discarded, it cannot be maintained that Jesus' baptism is the *pivot* of salvation history—the point at which Jesus enters into the new age.[4] The evidence suggests that neither Büchsel nor Dunn has adequately explained the significance of Jesus' pneumatic anointing at the Jordan.

This is not to deny that the Jordan event represents a significant event in salvation history; indeed, this is suggested by the heavenly declaration and the events which accompany it. Furthermore, it is equally clear that Jesus' experience at the Jordan represents a new beginning. However, in view of the discussion above, I conclude that the Jordan event represents the inauguration of Jesus' messianic task, not the beginning of his sonship or messiahship. Similarly, the heavenly declaration, as a confirmation of Jesus' existing status, constitutes

---

1. It is significant that Lentzen-Deis, in his massive work *Die Taufe Jesu*, rejects the creative activity of the Spirit (as in Gen. 1.2 and in the eschatological sense of new creation as in Isa. 32.15; 44.3; Ezek. 36.26; 37.1-14) as forming a suitable background to Jesus' reception of the Spirit at Jordan (see pp. 135f.).

2. Hill, *Greek Words*, p. 244; G.R. Beasley-Murray, *Baptism in the New Testament* (1962), p. 61; and I. de la Potterie, 'L'onction du Christ: Étude de théologie biblique', *NRT* 80 (1958), p. 235.

3. For a critique of the tenuous foundations on which 'read back' christologies are built see Marshall, *Commentary on Luke*, p. 151; note also Marshall, *Christology*, pp. 118-20.

4. Contra Dunn, *Holy Spirit*, pp. 24-32.

Jesus' call to begin his messianic mission.[1] The important corollary for this study is that Jesus' pneumatic anointing, rather than being the source of his unique filial relationship to God or his initiation into the new age, is the means by which Jesus is equipped for his messianic task.[2] That this is indeed how Luke interprets Jesus' pneumatic anointing is confirmed by his redactional activity in Lk. 4.1, 14, 16f., to which I shall now turn.[3]

2. The Redactional Bridge: Luke 4.1, 14

2.1. Luke 4.1

Each of the synoptic authors preface their accounts of Jesus' temptation with reference to the Spirit:

Mt. 4.1:   Τότε ὁ Ἰησοῦς ἀνήχθη εἰς τὴν ἔρημον ὑπὸ τοῦ πνεύματος.
Mk 1.12:   Καὶ εὐθὺς τὸ πνεῦμα αὐτὸν ἐκβάλλει εἰς τὴν ἔρημον.
Lk. 4.1:   Ἰησους δὲ πλήρης πνεύματος ἁγίου ὑπέστρεψεν ἀπὸ τοῦ Ἰορδάνου, καὶ ἤγετο ἐν τῷ πνεύματι ἐν τῇ ἐρήμῳ.

Luke probably had access to two written sources at this point, Mark and Q. The fundamental function of the verse, for which the reference to the Spirit is of particular importance, is the same in each of the synoptic gospels: it serves to link the account of Jesus' temptation with

---

1. So also Hill, *New Testament Prophecy*, p. 48. While the account of Jesus' anointing has only superficial similarities to the 'prophetic call form' (see A. Feuillet, 'Vocation et mission des prophètes, baptême et mission de Jésus. Étude de christologie biblique', *NV* 54 [1979], pp. 22-40; N. Habel, 'The Form and Significance of the Call Narratives', *ZAW* 77 [1965], pp. 297-323; G. Meagher, 'The Prophetic Call Narrative', *ITQ* 39 [1972], pp. 164-77; T.Y. Mullins, 'New Testament Commission Forms, Especially in Luke–Acts', *JBL* 95 [1976], pp. 603-14; B.J. Hubbard, 'Commissioning Stories in Luke–Acts: A Study of their Antecedents, Form and Content', *Sem* 8 [1977], pp. 103-26) and significant divergences (Chevallier, *Souffle*, p. 84; R.F. Collins, 'Luke 3.21-22, Baptism or Anointing', *BibT* 84 [1976], p. 825), this merely reflects Jesus' unique status.

2. See also Jeremias, *New Testament Theology*, p. 52; Hill, *New Testament Prophecy*, p. 48; C.H. Talbert, *Literary Patterns, Theological Themes, and the Genre of Luke–Acts* (1974), pp. 117-18; B. Aker, 'New Directions in Lucan Theology: Reflections on Luke 3:21-22 and Some Implications', in *Faces of Renewal* (1988), pp. 110-11; H.D. Hunter, *Spirit-Baptism: A Pentecostal Perspective* (1983), pp. 72-73; and de la Potterie, 'L'onction', pp. 225-52.

3. The significance of Lk. 4.1, 14, 16f. for interpreting Lk. 3.21-22 cannot be disputed. See Lentzen-Deis, *Die Taufe Jesu*, p. 147; Collins, 'Luke 3.21-22, Baptism or Anointing', p. 828; Tannehill, *The Narrative Unity of Luke–Acts*, I, p. 58; and M. Dömer, *Das Heil Gottes* (1978), pp. 61-62. Luke heightens the connection between Lk. 3.22 and 4.18 through his use of ἐπί.

that of his baptism. While Luke retains the essential content of his sources, he significantly alters the form in which it is presented. Two alterations are particularly striking: first, Luke has inserted the phrase Ἰησοῦς δὲ πλήρης πνεύματος ἁγίου;[1] and second, rather than following the constructions of Mark or Q (Mt.), Luke states that Jesus ἤγετο ἐν τῷ πνεύματι ἐν τῇ ἐρήμῳ.[2]

E. Schweizer has made much of Luke's redaction here. On the basis of these two alterations he concludes:

> Luke, then, avoids the idea that the Spirit stands over Jesus. The OT view of the power of God coming upon men does not satisfy him. Jesus becomes the subject of an action in the Holy Spirit. He is not a pneumatic, but the Lord of the πνεῦμα.[3]

However, Schweizer has surely exaggerated the significance of these alterations. The similarities between the description of Jesus in 4.1 and that of John in 1.15, 17[4] and Simeon in 2.25, 27[5] should warn us against reading too much into the wording here. While it is true that πλήρης πνεύματος ἁγίου is not found prior to Lk. 4.1, the phrase is used of disciples in Acts[6] and therefore is not unique to Jesus. This is all the more significant when it is realized that Luke uses ἐπλήσθη/σαν πνεύματος ἁγίου to describe the experience of the disciples in Acts, as well as that of John, Elizabeth, and Zechariah in the infancy narratives.[7] Certainly the distinction between πλήρης πνεύματος ἁγίου and ἐπλήσθη/σαν πνεύματος ἁγίου should not be overemphasized. Although the latter, as the aorist tense dictates, describes a momentary experience, the effects can be long lasting (e.g. Lk. 1.15; Acts 4.31). And the former, as Acts 7.55 indicates, can refer to a spe-

---

1. The use of πλήρης is common to Luke (Lk. 5.12; Acts 6.3, 5, 8; 7.55; 9.36; 11.24; 13.10; 19.28), and the use of πλήρης with πνεῦμα undoubtedly reflects Luke's hand (Acts 6.3, 5; 7.55; 11.24). Note also Luke's use of πνεῦμα with πίμπλημι (Lk. 1.15, 41, 67; Acts 2.4; 4.8, 31; 9.17; 13.9).

2. In view of Lk. 2.27 and particularly 4.14 this alteration can be attributed to Luke with a high degree of confidence.

3. Schweizer, 'πνεῦμα', pp. 404-405.

4. πνεύματος ἁγίου πλησθήσεται. . . προελεύσεται ἐνώπιον αὐτοῦ ἐν πνεύματι (Lk. 1.15, 17).

5. πνεῦμα ἦν ἅγιον ἐπ' αὐτόν. . . καὶ ἦλθεν ἐν τῷ πνεύματι εἰς τὸ ἱερόν (Lk. 2.25, 27).

6. See the general reference in Acts 6.3 and the references to Stephen (Acts 6.5; 7.55) and Barnabas (Acts 11.24).

7. John: 1.15 (future passive); Elizabeth: 1.41; Zechariah: 1.67. See H.L. Drumwright, 'The Holy Spirit in the Book of Acts', *SwJT* 17 (1974), p. 5.

cial and momentary state of inspiration.[1] The only real distinction that can be made is that πλήρης πνεύματος ἁγίου implies the prior experience designated by the phrase ἐπλήσθη πνεύματος ἁγίου. This explains why Luke describes only Jesus, Stephen, and Barnabas as πλήρης πνεύματος ἁγίου: the phrase ἐπλήσθη πνεύματος ἁγίου, while used to describe the experience of most of the major characters in Luke–Acts, is never related to these three. In Lk. 4.1 the phrase signifies that Jesus, as one who has been filled with the Spirit at Jordan, has constant access to the Spirit of God who provides what is required (either special knowledge or the ability to communicate God's message effectively) at each moment of need. There is a remarkable consistency which runs throughout Luke's two-volume work: whether it be Simeon, Jesus, Stephen, or Paul, the terms used to describe the Spirit's work and the action it inspires are similar. Therefore, it is highly improbable that the description of Jesus as πλήρης πνεύματος ἁγίου signifies any change in Luke's perspective concerning the way in which the Spirit functions.

The differences which exist between Luke's ἤγετο ἐν τῷ πνεύματι ἐν τῇ ἐρήμῳ and the corresponding phrases in Mk 1.12 and Mt. 4.1 can hardly bear the weight that Schweizer's conclusion demands. Although Schweizer contends that 'Jesus becomes the subject of an action in the Holy Spirit',[2] Luke's ἤγετο is a passive nonetheless, and whether ἐν τῷ πνεύματι is taken as a dative of agency or sphere, Luke's construction portrays Jesus as subordinate to the Spirit.[3] While Luke's construction certainly softens Mark's τὸ πνεῦμα αὐτὸν ἐκβάλλει εἰς τὴν ἔρημον, it is difficult to see how it differs significantly from Matthew's Ἰησοῦς ἀνήχθη εἰς τὴν ἔρημον ὑπὸ τοῦ πνεύματος. The distinctions become all the more blurred when it is recognized that Luke can use ὑπὸ τοῦ πνεύματος and ἐν τῷ πνεύματι as functional equivalents. According to Luke, Simeon was instructed by the Spirit (ὑπὸ τοῦ πνεύματος τοῦ ἁγίου, Lk. 2.26) and, in the immediate context, Luke states that Simeon ἦλθεν ἐν τῷ πνεύματι εἰς τὸ ἱερόν.[4] This suggests that Luke's ἤγετο ἐν τῷ

---

1. Contra Schweizer, 'πνεῦμα', p. 405 n. 463. See Acts 19.28 for an example where πλήρης with a noun other than πνεῦμα (θυμός) designates a state of temporary duration.

2. Schweizer, 'πνεῦμα', p. 405.

3. Fitzmyer, *Luke I–IX*, p. 514. Chevallier claims that according to Luke Jesus is led into the desert by God, while according to Matthew the Spirit is the agent (*Souffle*, p. 124). While this is a possibility, it does not alter the fact that Jesus is subordinate to the Spirit.

4. This point is made by Turner, 'Luke and the Spirit', p. 82.

πνεύματι ἐν τῇ ἐρήμῳ is a slightly modified form of Q, and that the alterations were made by Luke for purely stylistic reasons.

While it is difficult to see any theological *Tendenz* in Luke's alteration of Q, his decision to follow Q over Mark may reflect his prophetic understanding of the Spirit. Mark's account, with its emphasis on compulsion (ἐκβάλλει), implies that the Spirit led Jesus in a physical way, rather than by special revelation. Q on the other hand avoids the more physical connotations of Mark. Thus Luke is quite content to follow Q, for there is nothing in Q's account incompatible with his prophetic understanding of the Spirit: the Spirit, by means of special revelation, provides special guidance.

If we reject Schweizer's thesis, how shall we account for Luke's insertion of Ἰησοῦς δὲ πλήρης πνεύματος ἁγίου into the text? A single reference to the Spirit would have been sufficient to link the account of Jesus' baptism with that of his temptation. Luke appears to have something special in mind with this added or second reference to the Spirit. I suggest that with the insertion of this phrase Luke has consciously edited his source in order to emphasize the fact that Jesus' experience at Jordan was the moment at which he 'was filled with the Spirit'. In this way Luke was able to bring out the continuity between Jesus' experience of the Spirit and that of the early church.[1] The insertion of ἐπλήσθη πνεύματος ἁγίου at Lk. 3.21-22 would have necessitated a radical departure from his source and Luke, as the text indicates, was reluctant to do so. However, with the insertion of Ἰησοῦς δὲ πλήρης πνεύματος ἁγίου at 4.1, a more convenient place for such an insertion, Luke was able to make the same point: just as Jesus was empowered by the Spirit at the Jordan, so it was also for the early church at Pentecost and beyond; and so it must be for the church to which Luke writes. This hypothesis not only explains why Luke has inserted a phrase which otherwise appears awkward and redundant, but it also does justice to the remarkable continuity in Spirit-terminology which exists throughout Luke's two-volume work. In short, rather than pointing to the uniqueness of Jesus' experience of the Spirit, Luke's description of Jesus as πλήρης πνεύματος ἁγίου indicates that he regarded Jesus' experience at the Jordan as the moment at which 'he was filled with the Spirit'—the moment at which Jesus, like the early church, was empowered to carry out his divinely appointed task.

---

1. The link to Pentecost would have been quite obvious, for the disciples were 'filled with the Spirit' (ἐπλήσθησαν πνεύματος ἁγίου) at Pentecost (Acts 2.4). Of course the parallels are not exhausted with Pentecost.

2.2. Luke 4.14

While Lk. 4.14-15 has customarily been viewed as the product of Luke's free redaction of Mk 1.14, H. Schürmann asserts that the tradition-history of this pericope is more complex.[1] Schürmann maintains that Lk. 3.1–4.44 is based on an account of the beginning of Jesus' ministry preserved in Q. This 'Bericht vom Anfang' contained two major sections: the first section undergirds Lk. 3.3-17, 4.1-13; the second section, analogous to, yet independent of, Mk 1.14-39 (6.1-6), lies behind Lk. 4.14-44. According to Schürmann, Lk. 4.14-16, which forms the *Eingangstor* of Luke's narrative, is a composite of the major structural elements of the second section of the *Bericht* and thus cannot be attributed solely to Lukan redaction of Mark[2]

Schürmann's thesis is vulnerable at a number of points. If Q did contain a *Bericht* such as this, we would expect to find more prominent traces of its influence in Matthew than actually exist. Would Matthew, with his interest in portraying Jesus as the fulfillment of Old Testament expectations, pass over an account of Jesus' self-referential *pesher* of Isa. 61.1? It is possible, but highly improbable. Even more telling is J. Delobel's critique of the heart of Schürmann's hypothesis.[3] On the basis of his detailed analysis of Lk. 4.14-16, Delobel concludes that the linguistic features of Lk. 4.14-16 can be most adequately explained as Lukan redaction of Mk 1.14f.[4]

The weakness of Schürmann's hypothesis is clearly seen in his analysis of v. 14a.[5] Schürmann puts forth three arguments in support of a pre-Lukan source: first, the apparent agreement of Mt. 4.12

---

1. Schürmann, 'Der "Bericht vom Anfang"—Ein Rekonstruktionsversuch auf Grund von Lk 4,14-16', in *Untersuchungen* (1968), pp. 69-80; see also Schürmann's 'Zur Traditionsgeschichte der Nazareth-Perikope Lk 4,16-30', in *Mélanges Bibliques* (1970), pp. 187-205.

2. Schürmann argues that the influence of Q can be seen in the parallels which exist between Luke and Matthew: Lk. 4.1a = Mt. 4.12 (Mk 1.14); Lk. 4.14b = Mt. 9.26 (Mk 1.28); Lk. 4.15 = Mt. 13.54a (Mk 1.39a); Lk. 4.16 = Mt. 4.13 (Mk 6.1). For discussion of these points see ' "Bericht vom Anfang" ', pp. 71-79.

3. Schürmann acknowledges that his entire hypothesis rests on his interpretation of Lk. 4.14-16 (' "Bericht vom Anfang" ', p. 70).

4. J. Delobel, 'La rédaction de Lc., IV, 14-16a et le "Bericht vom Anfang" ', in *L'Évangile de Luc* (1973), pp. 203-23.

5. Schürmann, ' "Bericht vom Anfang" ', pp. 70-71. The unusual form Ναζαρά (Lk. 4.16; Mt. 4.13) cannot bear the weight of Schürmann's hypothesis, as Fitzmyer correctly notes: 'Schürmann has tried to argue that the form Ναζαρά points to a source distinct from Mark (most likely 'Q'), but he then has to include the preceding Matthean episode (at least what = Luke 4:13-15, 17)—which is highly unlikely' (*Luke I–IX*, p. 530).

(ἀνεχώρησεν) with Luke (ὑπέστρεψεν) against Mk 1.14 (ἦλθεν); second, the transitional nature of v. 14a, which indicates that the verse originally served as both a conclusion to the temptation narrative and an introduction to a variant account of the exorcism at Capernaum (Mk 1.21-28; Lk. 4.31-37); and third, the previous point is supported by the reference to δύναμις in Lk. 4.14, which points to the Capernaum account (Lk. 4.36: ἐξουσίᾳ καὶ δυνάμει). Regarding the first point, Delobel points out that ἀναχωρέω is common to Matthew and ὑποστρέφω is clearly a Lukanism.[1] When this linguistic evidence is coupled with the recognition that the two terms have different nuances, the apparent agreement between Matthew and Luke disappears. The second and third points also fail to convince. In view of Luke's usage of δύναμις with πνεῦμα elsewhere, it is almost certain that the occurrence of δύναμις in Lk. 4.14 is redactional.[2] Similarly, since the term does not occur in Mark's account at 1.27, it is equally certain that its inclusion in Lk. 4.36 is the result of Lukan redaction.[3] Luke inserts the reference to δύναμις in v. 14a in order to anticipate the account of Jesus' expulsion of the demon at Capernaum (4.31-37). Indeed, Luke's statement that Jesus returned to Galilee ἐν τῇ δυνάμει τοῦ πνεύματος points forward to the preaching of Jesus in Nazareth (4.15, 18f.) and to the exorcism in Capernaum. Consistent with his prophetic understanding of the Spirit, Luke refrains from introducing Jesus' ministry in Galilee with reference to the Spirit only, such as in 4.1 (πλήρης πνεύματος ἁγίου),[4] for the ministry in Galilee includes both inspired preaching (4.15, 18f.) and an exorcism (4.36).[5] Schürmann correctly emphasized the connection between Lk. 4.14 and 4.36; he was wrong, however, to attribute this connection to pre-Lukan

---

1. Delobel, 'La rédaction de Lc., IV, 14-16a', p. 210: ἀναχωρέω—Matthew, 10×; Mark, 1×; Luke–Acts, 2×; John, 1×; ὑποστρέφω—Luke–Acts, 32×; the rest of the NT, 3×.

2. Contra J. Jeremias, *Die Sprache des Lukasevangeliums* (1980), pp. 38, 119. See Chapter 6 §3 above.

3. This conclusion is supported by T. Schramm's analysis of Lk. 4.31-44: 'Alle Abweichungen von der Mk-Vorlage in Lk 4,31-44 sind als spezifisch luk Redaktionsleistungen möglich und daher am besten als solche anzusehen. Der Einfluß einer Überlieferungsvariante auf Lk scheint ausgeschlossen' (*Der Markus-Stoff bei Lukas* [1971], p. 90; for his analysis see pp. 85-91).

4. This, in spite of the fact that πλήρης πνεύματος ἁγίου in 4.14 would have made the link with 4.1 more obvious.

5. For a more detailed discussion of Luke's use of πνεῦμα and δύναμις see Chapter 6 §3 above.

tradition. The evidence suggests that the connection was made by Luke himself.[1]

Luke's redactional activity in 4.14 not only plays an important introductory role, as noted above, but it also concludes the temptation narrative and, as such, provides valuable insight into Luke's unique understanding of the temptation account.[2] Luke's redaction in 4.14 complements his earlier insertion in 4.1 and together these alterations form a redactional bridge which enables Luke to highlight the unique pneumatic significance which he attaches to the temptation account. Luke alone tells us that Jesus entered the desert πλήρης πνεύματος ἁγίου (4.1), equipped by the Spirit for his messianic task, and that after the temptation he left as he had entered: ἐν τῇ δυνάμει τοῦ πνεύματος (4.14). This has encouraged some to conclude that for Luke, the Spirit is the power by which Jesus overcomes the temptings of the devil.[3] However, this conclusion is improbable. Luke gives no indication that the Spirit enabled Jesus to overcome the temptation. As the repetition of γέγραπται ὅτι indicates,[4] Jesus was supported in his victory over the devil by his commitment to Scripture. Therefore, any connection to the Spirit must be inferred from the context. That this is not Luke's intention is indicated by his usage elsewhere: the Spirit is never portrayed as the direct cause of a decision to orient one's life toward God. The Spirit may provide guidance (as in 4.1) which ultimately leads to the fulfillment of God's plan, but the Spirit is never the direct source of one's obedience to God. I suggest that there is a more adequate interpretation of the data, consistent with Luke's overall theological scheme. Luke's redactional activity in 4.1, 14 indicates not that the Spirit is the source of Jesus' obedience; rather, that Jesus' obedience is the source of his continuing relationship with the Spirit. In Luke's perspective, when Jesus enters into the desert his commitment to his messianic task is tested and thus also his worthiness to be a man of the Spirit, for the purpose of the Spirit is to enable Jesus to carry out his messianic task. Because Jesus remained committed to his task,

1. So also Delobel, 'La rédaction de Lc., IV, 14-16a', p. 211.
2. It is generally recognized that Lk. 4.14a concludes the temptation narrative and introduces the section which follows (4.16-44). See Delobel, 'La rédaction de Lc., IV, 14-16a', pp. 210-11; Schürmann, ' "Bericht vom Anfang" ', p. 71.
3. See J. Dupont, *Les Tentations de Jésus au Désert* (1968), pp. 49-50; U. Busse, *Das Nazareth-Manifest Jesu: Eine Einführung in das lukanische Jesubild nach Lk 4,16-30* (1977), p. 19; Fitzmyer, *Luke I–IX*, p. 513; Schürmann, *Lukasevangelium*, I, p. 216; Turner, 'Luke and the Spirit', pp. 84-85; M. Miyoshi, *Der Anfang des Reiseberichts Lk. 9,51–10,24: Eine redaktionsgeschichtliche Untersuchung* (1974), p. 136; and Beasley-Murray, *Baptism*, p. 61.
4. See Lk. 4.4, 10. Cf. v. 12: ὅτι εἴρηται.

he returned to Galilee ἐν τῇ δυνάμει τοῦ πνεύματος.¹ Thus, Luke's perspective is not unlike that of the rabbis, who held that the gift of the Spirit was given only to the worthy and that the Spirit departed from those who failed to remain worthy.² For Luke, the Spirit gives significance to Jesus' temptation.³

The redactional bridge also enables Luke to maintain the pneumatic thrust of his narrative and emphasize the connections between Jesus' pneumatic anointing and his sermon at Nazareth.⁴ That Luke intends to draw parallels between the two accounts is substantiated by his movement of the Nazareth pericope (Lk. 4.16f.) forward in his narrative (cf. Mk 6.1-6)⁵ and by his use of ἐπί in 3.22 and 4.18.⁶ The significance of these connections will be explored in the next section.

3. *The Sermon at Nazareth (Luke 4.16-30)*

The Nazareth pericope (4.16-30) not only sheds light on Luke's understanding of Jesus' pneumatic anointing, but it stands as the cornerstone of Luke's entire theological program.⁷ This conclusion is universally accepted⁸ and stems from two observations: first, Luke

---

1. Note the contrast with Saul, who as the King of Israel was endowed with the Spirit of God (1 Sam. 10.6, 10; 11.6), yet as a result of his disobedience, the Spirit departed from him (1 Sam. 16.14).
2. See Chapter 5 §1.1.1 and §2.1 above for relevant rabbinic citations.
3. So also Stronstad, *Charismatic Theology*, p. 41.
4. Dupont, *Les Tentations*, p. 49; R.C. Tannehill, 'The Mission of Jesus according to Luke 4.16-30', in *Jesus in Nazareth* (1972), pp. 68-69; W. Eltester, 'Israel im lukanischen Werk und die Nazarethperikope', in *Jesus in Nazareth* (1972), p. 136.
5. Lk. 4.23, which presupposes prior miracles in Capernaum, indicates that the position of the account has been altered by Luke.
6. Schürmann, 'Zur Traditionsgeschichte der Nazareth-Perikope', p. 191; Busse, *Das Nazareth-Manifest Jesu*, p. 17.
7. Grundmann, *Lukas*, p. 107: 'Die Perikope ist Eckstein seiner heilsgeschichtlichen Theologie'.
8. See for example: von Baer, *Der heilige Geist*, p. 63; Bovon, 'Aktuelle Linien', p. 34; Busse, *Das Nazareth-Manifest Jesu*, p. 28; H.J. Cadbury, *The Making of Luke–Acts* (1927), p. 189; Chevallier, *Le Messie*, p. 76; B. Chilton, 'Announcement in Nazara: An Analysis of Luke 4.16-21', in *Gospel Perspectives*, II, (1981), p. 150; H.J.B. Combrink, 'The Structure and Significance of Luke 4:16-30', *Neo* 7 (1973), p. 39; Eltester, 'Israel', p. 135; Fitzmyer, *Luke I–IX*, pp. 526, 529; D. Hill, 'The Rejection of Jesus at Nazareth (Lk 4.16-30)', *NovT* 13 (1971), p. 161; E. Lohse, 'Missionarisches Handeln Jesu nach dem Evangelium des Lukas', in *Die Einheit des neuen Testament* (1973), p. 164; Marshall, *Commentary on Luke*, p. 178; M. Rese, *Alttestamentliche Motive in der Christologie des Lukas* (1969), p. 143; Shelton, 'Filled with the Spirit', p. 239; W. Schmeichel, 'Christian

alters Mark's chronology in order to place this pericope at the outset of Jesus' ministry; second, the pericope combines the major theological themes of Luke–Acts: the work of the Spirit, the universality of the gospel, the grace of God, and the rejection of Jesus. For this reason the passage is invaluable for this inquiry into Luke's pneumatology,[1] and more specifically, into the significance Luke attaches to Jesus' pneumatic anointing.

3.1. *Tradition and Redaction in Luke 4.18-19*
While I have rejected Schürmann's hypothesis that a pre-Lukan 'Bericht vom Anfang', preserved in Q, forms the basis of Lk. 4.14f.,[2] this does not necessarily lead to the conclusion that Lk. 4.16-30 is the product of Luke's redaction of Mk 6.1-6. On the contrary, it is highly probable that Luke, in writing the account, has drawn upon traditional material other than Mk 6.1-6. Jesus undoubtedly taught in the synagogue at Nazareth; while we have no other record of the content of his preaching at Nazareth, the general thrust of the passage accords well with what we know of his teaching elsewhere (Lk. 7.22 = Mt. 11.5).[3]

Prophecy in Lukan Thought: Luke 4:16-30 as a Point of Departure', in *Society of Biblical Literature 1976 Seminar Papers* (1976), p. 294; R.B. Sloan, *The Favorable Year of the Lord* (1977), p. 1; Tannehill, 'The Mission of Jesus', p. 51; and P.F. Esler, *Community and Gospel in Luke–Acts* (1987), pp. 34, 164.

1. The connections between the Nazareth pericope (4.16f.) and the account of Pentecost (Acts 1–2) have been noted by: Chevallier, *Le Messie*, p. 76; George, 'L'Esprit Saint', pp. 506, 515; Busse, *Das Nazareth-Manifest Jesu*, pp. 99, 101, 118; Shelton, 'Filled with the Spirit', pp. 239, 298; Tannehill, *The Narrative Unity of Luke–Acts*, I, p. 57; and Chilton, 'Announcement in Nazara', pp. 151, 161. Note Chilton's (p. 151) criticism of Schmeichel's view that Luke aborts the Spirit-motif, so prominent in the early part of the Gospel, at 4.18 in favor of a prophetic rejection motif introduced in Lk. 4.22-30 ('Christian Prophecy in Lukan Thought', pp. 293-304). In a more general way the connections between the mission of Jesus and that of the church are stressed by D.L. Tiede, *Prophecy and History in Luke–Acts* (1980), p. 55; Lentzen-Dies, *Die Taufe Jesu*, pp. 35 (Jesus' baptism and Pentecost), 285; and D.P. Moessner, '"The Christ Must Suffer"', *NovT* 28 (1986), p. 223. Key points of similarity between the Nazareth pericope and the account of Pentecost include the following: both are programmatic accounts, located at the beginning of the respective missions of Jesus and the church, which refer to the activity of the Spirit; both point to the fulfillment of OT prophecies (Lk. 4.16f.–Isa. 61.1-2; Acts 2–Joel 3.1f.); both foreshadow the subsequent mission to the Gentiles; and both foreshadow the opposition and resistance which will be faced.

2. So also Fitzmyer, *Luke I–IX*, p. 527; contra C. Tuckett, 'Luke 4,16-30, Isaiah and Q', in *Logia: Les Paroles de Jésus—The Sayings of Jesus* (1982), pp. 343-54.

3. In light of 11 Q Melch, Jesus' application of Isa. 61.1 to himself is not at all surprising. On the relationship between 11 Q Melch and Lk. 4.18f. see Turner, 'Luke and the Spirit', pp. 67-71; Hill, 'The Rejection of Jesus', p. 179.

It is not improbable that an account of such an event circulated among the early Christians and, indeed, there are numerous linguistic features which indicate that Luke's account is based on traditional material other than Mk 6.1-6.[1] However, when one attempts to move beyond these general conclusions, the questions of tradition and history become numerous and exceedingly complex.[2] Fortunately, since our concern centers on the quotation from Isaiah in Lk. 4.18-19, we can justifiably narrow the initial discussion to the following source-critical question: to what extent does the quotation from Isaiah in Lk. 4.18-19 represent traditional material?

The question is a difficult one, for since the text is taken almost verbatim from the LXX, we cannot rely on linguistic evidence for indications of Lukan redaction. However, since the citation in Lk. 4.18-19 diverges from Isa. 61.1-2 (LXX) at several points, it may be possible to determine whether these alterations point to a particular theological *Tendenz* and, if so, whether the *Tendenz* corresponds to distinctive aspects of Luke's theological program expressed elsewhere.

An analysis of Lk. 4.18-19 reveals close adherence to the Septuagint text of Isa. 61.1-2, with a number of striking divergences:[3]

---

1. Chilton argues that ἐν ταῖς συναγωγαῖς αὐτῶν (4.15) and Ναζαρά (4.16) reflect traditional material ('Announcement in Nazara', pp. 161f.) and Jeremias suggests the βιβλίον of 4.17, 20 is one among many traditional words in the account (*Die Sprache*, pp. 121-28). Thus Schürmann cautions against viewing Lk. 4.16-30 as the product of Lukan redaction of Mark ('Zur Traditionsgeschichte der Nazareth-Perikope Lk 4,16-30', p. 205). See also A. Strobel, 'Die Ausrufung des Jobeljahres in der Nazarethpredigt Jesu: Zur apokalyptischen Tradition Lc 4.16-30', in *Jesus in Nazareth* (1972), p. 30.

2. For a summary of these issues see Marshall, *Commentary on Luke*, pp. 177-80.

3. The punctuation of the text is disputed. On the basis of Luke's interpretation of the quotation in Lk. 4.43, I have followed the LXX and put a stop after με in order to make εὐαγγελίσασθαι dependent on ἀπέσταλκεν (see Marshall, *Commentary on Luke*, p. 183). In contrast, the UBS text places a stop after πτωχοῖς and in this way makes εὐαγγελίσασθαι dependent on ἔχρισεν. Following the UBS scheme, Turner argues that for Luke, Jesus was anointed with the Spirit to act, and this concept was more prominent in his mind than the notion that Jesus had the Spirit as a result of his anointing ('Luke and the Spirit', p. 217 n. 105). However, this argument fails to recognize that in the punctuation scheme I have adopted above, the Spirit-anointing is paralleled with ἀπέσταλκέν and is thus portrayed as the source of each of the activities described (see Combrink, 'Structure', pp. 29-30). Regardless of which punctuation scheme is followed, the text portrays the Spirit as the source behind the various activities described.

Luke 4.18-19	Isaiah 61.1-2 (LXX)
Πνεῦμα κυρίου ἐπ᾽ ἐμέ,	Πνεῦμα κυρίου ἐπ᾽ ἐμέ,
οὗ εἵνεκεν ἔχρισέν με·	οὗ εἵνεκεν ἔχρισέν με·
εὐαγγελίσασθαι πτωχοῖς	εὐαγγελίσασθαι πτωχοῖς
ἀπέσταλκεν με.	ἀπέσταλκέν με.
	ἰάσασθαι τοὺς συντετριμμένους τῇ καρδίᾳ
κηρύξαι αἰχμαλώτοις ἄφεσιν	κηρύξαι αἰχμαλώτοις ἄφεσιν
καὶ τυφλοῖς ἀνάβλεψιν	καὶ τυφλοῖς ἀνάβλεψιν
ἀποστεῖλαι τεθραυσμένους ἐν	ἀποστεῖλαι τεθραυσμένους ἐν
ἀφέσει,	ἀφέσει, [Isa. 58.6]
κηρύξαι ἐνιαυτὸν κυρίου δεκτόν	καλέσαι ἐνιαυτὸν κυρίου δεκτὸν καὶ ἡμέραν ἀνταποδόσεως.

As the comparison above indicates, the citation in Lk. 4.18-19 deviates from the text of Isa. 61.1-2 (LXX) at four points: the phrase ἰάσασθαι τοὺς συντετριμμένους τῇ καρδίᾳ has been omitted; an excerpt from Isa. 58.6 (LXX), ἀποστεῖλαι τεθραυσμένους ἐν ἀφέσει, has been inserted in the quotation; the καλέσαι of the LXX has been altered to κηρύξαι; the final phrase of the LXX (καὶ ἡμέραν ἀνταποδόσεως), which refers to divine retribution, has been omitted.

It has already been indicated that the historicity of the general outline of Luke's account need not be doubted:[1] Jesus entered into the synagogue in Nazareth, read from the scroll of Isaiah (61.1-2), applied the passage to himself, and encountered resistance. Luke's account is generally consistent with the format of the ancient synagogue service. After the recitation of the *Shema* (Deut. 6.4-9; 11.13-21) and prayers, including the *Shemoneh Esreh*, a passage from the Pentateuch was read (*seder*), and this was followed by a reading from the Prophets (*haphtara*).[2] The *seder* and *haphtara* were followed by the singing of a psalm, and then came the sermon, introduced by an introductory reading (*petitha*) chosen from the Prophets or Writings.[3] The choice of the *haphtara* was somewhat flexible, with verbal and thematic links to the *seder* usually guiding the choice.[4] Although a fixed lectionary was developed for the *haphtara*, it is generally accepted that the lec-

1. So also Hill, 'The Rejection of Jesus', pp. 161-80, esp. p. 179.
2. While the *seder* was usually at least twenty-one verses, the *haphtara* was often around ten verses. The Targum was read after the completion of three verses.
3. C. Perrot, 'Luc 4, 16-30 et la lecture biblique de l'ancienne Synagogue', *RSR* 47 (1973), pp. 324-40, esp. pp. 329-30; P. Billerbeck, 'Ein Synagogengottesdienst in Jesu Tagen', *ZNW* 55 (1965), pp. 143-61; Marshall, *Commentary on Luke*, p. 181.
4. Perrot, 'Synagogue', pp. 331-32. Perrot also notes that the *haphtara* usually started from a point within the section that was opened.

tionary system was not operative before the destruction of the temple.[1] This would have allowed Jesus to read from the text of his choosing, as Luke's account suggests. It is quite possible then that Lk. 4.18-19 represents a condensed form of the *haphtara*, which would have extended to at least Isa. 61.9.[2]

However, the historicity of the event notwithstanding, it is unlikely that the variant form of Isa. 61.1-2 found in Lk. 4.18-19 stems from Jesus himself. It is difficult to imagine a synagogue reader taking such liberties with the text.[3] Particularly striking is the insertion of the phrase from Isa. 58.6 into the text of Isa. 61.1-2; for, although skipping verses was permissable in the *haphtara*, it is unlikely that such a rearrangement of the text would have been tolerated (*m.Meg.* 4.4; *t.Meg.* 4.19).[4] I am, therefore, justified in concluding that it is improbable that Jesus, during the course of the *haphtara* in a synagogue service, inserted Isa. 58.6c into the text of Isa. 61.1-2 and made the other alterations to Isa. 61.1-2 recorded in Lk. 4.18-19. The question which remains is, of course, whether the interpretative reproduction of the *haphtara*, in the form in which it is presented in Lk. 4.18-19,[5] stems

---

1. L. Morris, *The New Testament and Jewish Lectionaries* (1964), pp. 11-34; L. Crockett, 'Luke IV. 16-30 and the Jewish Lectionary Cycle: A Word of Caution', *JJS* 17 (1966), pp. 13f.; J. Heinemann, 'The Triennial Lectionary Cycle', *JJS* 19 (1968), pp. 41-48; Sloan, *The Favorable Year*, p. 30; J. Kodell, 'Luke's Gospel in a Nutshell (Lk 4:16-30)', *BTB* 13 (1983), p. 17; Busse, *Das Nazareth-Manifest Jesu*, pp. 109-10; B. Reicke, 'Jesus in Nazareth—Lk 4,14-30', in *Das Wort und die Wörter* (1973), p. 48.

2. Perrot, 'Synagogue', p. 327.

3. Perrot, 'Synagogue', p. 327.

4. On the strength of *t. Meg.* 4.19, P. Billerbeck argues that it was forbidden to jump backwards in the *haphtara* (Strack–Billerbeck, *Kommentar*, IV, p. 167). This leads Busse to conclude: 'Das Mischzitat kann in dieser Form nie in einem Synagogengottesdienst verlesen worden sein' (*Das Nazareth-Manifest Jesu*, pp. 109-10). While Reicke's suggestion that Jesus altered the text as a demonstration of his prophetic authority is possible, it is improbable ('Jesus in Nazareth', pp. 48-49). Chilton argues that the mixed text is traditional on the basis of a similar reading in the Old Syriac NT. He writes: 'The authorship of Jesus would explain how, despite its divergence from the LXX, this tradition is still available in the Old Syriac Gospels, and to a lesser extent in the Greek text of Luke' ('Announcement in Nazara', p. 164). However, Chilton's argument has been criticized by Bock. Noting that the character of the Old Syriac NT is generally dependent on the Western text, Bock concludes that the Old Syriac version is a corruption of the original text and not a dominical reading. For Bock's detailed argumentation see *Proclamation*, pp. 107-108.

5. This is not to deny that Jesus actually read from Isa. 61.1-2 in the synagogue at Nazareth or that he applied its fulfillment to this act; indeed, it has been indicated that there is no reason to deny the historicity of this event. It is also possible that Jesus read from a number of OT passages, for the *haphtara* could be drawn from more than

from Luke or is carried over from pre-Lukan tradition. As I have indicated, this question can only be answered on the basis of an analysis of the alterations of the text from Isaiah and the theological motivations which have produced them. To this task we now turn.

The omission of ἰάσασθαι τοὺς συντετριμμένους τῇ καρδίᾳ. It is often suggested that Isa. 61.1d has been omitted in order to make room for the insertion of Isa. 58.6c.[1] If structural concerns motivated the omission, it is of little use in determining whether the quotation stems from pre-Lukan tradition or Luke's final redaction, for such concerns could have influenced the text at either stage. However, the weakness of this hypothesis becomes evident when it is recognized that the structural elements of the passage have been used to explain why Isa. 61.1d has been omitted *and* why the phrase must have been included in the original reading of the text.[2] In view of the ambiguous nature of the arguments from structure and the varied conclusions they have produced, it is unlikely that structural elements played a significant role in the omission of Isa. 61.1d.

Much more probable is the view put forth by M. Rese that Luke omits Isa. 61.1d because of his prophetic understanding of the Spirit:

one passage (*m. Meg.* 4.4; Strack–Billerbeck, *Kommentar*, IV, p. 167). As D. Seccombe notes, 'What lies behind Luke's account could, therefore, be more complex than meets the eye' (*Possessions and the Poor in Luke–Acts* [1982], p. 47). It is, however, unlikely that the text as it appears in Lk. 4.18-19 was read by Jesus during the course of the *haphtara* in a synagogue service. Luke 4.18-19, 21 serves as an interpretive summary of Jesus' reading and sermon.

1. Busse, *Das Nazareth-Manifest Jesu*, p. 34; R. Morgenthaler, *Die lukanische Geschichtsschreibung als Zeugnis: Gestalt und Gehalt der Kunst des Lukas* (1949), I, pp. 84-85; Turner, 'Luke and the Spirit', p. 70. H. Ringgren suggests the alterations indicate that Luke quoted the text from memory ('Luke's Use of the Old Testament', *HTR* 79 [1986], p. 229). However, as R. Albertz notes, this is exceedingly improbable, since the citation corresponds so closely to the LXX where it is not modified ('Die "Antrittspredigt" Jesu im Lukasevangelium auf ihrem alttestamentlichen Hintergrund', *ZNW* 74 [1983], p. 185).

2. For the former view see Busse and Turner cited above; for the latter view see Reicke, 'Jesus in Nazareth', pp. 48-49. Reicke acknowledges the weakness of the textual support for the inclusion of Isa. 61.1d in the original text of Lk. 4.18-19 (While A, Θ, Ψ, and the majority text tradition include the phrase, Sinaiticus, B, D, L, W, and Ξ omit it. It is difficult to image a copyist omitting the line; its insertion, however, can be explained as assimilation to the LXX.). His conclusion is based largely on the structure of the passage. By way of contrast, Combrink ('Structure', p. 35) has argued that the structure of the passage confirms the conclusion of Rese, who, following Schweizer, asserts that Luke omitted Isa. 61.1d because he viewed the Spirit as the Spirit of prophecy.

'Durch die Streichung will Lk. sichern, daß der Geist des Herrn als prophetischer Geist und nicht als wunderwirkende Macht aufgefaßt wird'.[1] This conclusion accords well with my analysis of Luke's redactional activity elsewhere and offers a plausible explanation of an omission which is otherwise extremely difficult to explain. However, Rese's conclusion has been criticized by M. Turner, who offers three objections.[2]

First, noting that the reference to healing in Isa. 61.1d is metaphorical, Turner argues that Luke's 'alleged predilection for the concept of the Spirit of prophecy' does not provide a motive for its omission.[3] However, the force of this objection is mitigated by the special significance which Luke attaches to ἰάομαι. The metaphorical usage of the term in Isa. 61.1d notwithstanding, ἰάομαι is used frequently by Luke (Luke, 11×; Acts, 4×; cf. Matthew, 4×; Mark, 1×; John, 3×) and as a *terminus technicus* for the miraculous healings of Jesus.[4]

Second, Turner claims that the insertion of Isa. 58.6c adds a new element to the quotation, one that is incompatible with Luke's purported prophetic understanding of the Spirit. According to Isa. 58.6c, Jesus not only proclaims ἄφεσις, but effects it through acts of power, such as healing and exorcisms: 'This broader concept of "setting the afflicted at liberty" has nothing to do with the activities of the Spirit of prophecy'.[5] However, it is by no means certain that this is how Luke interpreted Isa. 58.6c. Indeed, each of the other three infinitival phrases in 4.18-19 refer to preaching, a point which is emphasized through the alteration of καλέσαι (LXX) to κηρύξαι:

a. εὐαγγελίσασθαι πτωχοῖς
b. κηρύξαι αἰχμαλώτοις ἄφεσιν
   καὶ τυφλοῖς ἀνάβλεψιν
c. ἀποστεῖλαι τεθραυσμένους ἐν ἀφέσει
d. κηρύξαι ἐνιαυτὸν κυρίου δεκτόν.

---

1. Rese, *Alttestamentliche Motive*, p. 214; see also pp. 144-45, 151-52.
2. Turner, 'Luke and the Spirit', pp. 60-67.
3. 'Luke and the Spirit', p. 61. See also Tuckett, 'Luke 4,16-30', p. 348 n. 28.
4. Lentzen-Deis, *Die Taufe Jesu*, p. 147 n. 206 and Miyoshi, *Reiseberichts*, p. 135 n. 79.
5. Turner, 'Luke and the Spirit', p. 62. This criticism is primarily directed at Rese's claim that Luke has inserted Isa. 58.6c into the quotation from 61.1-2 because he understood it to refer to the forgiveness of sins which the Spirit of prophecy inspires Jesus to proclaim (see Rese, *Alttestamentliche Motive*, p. 146). However, the implications of this objection for Rese's conclusion regarding the omission of Isa. 61.1d are obvious.

The passage as it stands undeniably emphasizes preaching as the most prominent dimension of Jesus' mission.[1] That this motif is characteristic of Luke is evident in Lk. 4.44, where he retains Mark's reference to preaching, but omits his reference to exorcisms. This indicates that Luke probably understood ἀποστεῖλαι τεθραυσμένους ἐν ἀφέσει as the effect of Jesus' preaching ministry.[2] It is quite likely that the insertion of Isa. 58.6d was made as a result of the verbal linkage which ἄφεσις provides with the preceding phrase (see b. above) and that these stichs (b. and c.) were viewed as presenting a unified message: Jesus effects salvation through his Spirit-inspired proclamation.[3] The fact that Luke elsewhere portrays miracles of healings and exorcisms as a vital part of Jesus' ministry of liberation is irrelevant to the present discussion.[4] The point is that Luke, in 4.18-19 and throughout his two-volume work, does not relate these activities directly to the work of the Spirit.[5] As I have noted, this theological *Tendenz* is unique to Luke.

---

1. The specific elements of the preaching named in Isa. 61.1f., such as 'release of the captives' and 'recovery of sight to the blind', are employed by Luke as metaphors which speak of the eschatological liberation effected by Jesus' proclamation, of which a primary element is 'forgiveness of sins'. On καὶ τυφλοῖς ἀνάβλεψιν as metaphor see Seccombe, *Possessions*, pp. 59-61.

2. Beasley-Murray fails to recognize that the liberation referred to in the metaphorical language of the quotation, including the phrase from Isa. 58.6c, may be enacted by the Spirit-inspired proclamation of Jesus. For this reason he incorrectly contrasts the proclamation of liberation with the actual process of liberation itself, the prophet of the new age with its agent: 'The preacher is said to possess authority "to set at liberty those who are oppressed", and not simply to proclaim liberty to them. The preacher is therefore more than a prophet of the new age; he is its agent. The anointing of the Spirit, accordingly, must be viewed as more than the gift of prophetic utterance; it is equipment for eschatological action, as in Mt. 12.28' ('Jesus and the Spirit', p. 472).

3. Bock notes that 'a prophetic picture (Isa. 61) is joined to a liberation portrait (Isa. 58)' (*Proclamation*, p. 109). It would be more accurate to say that a liberation portrait (Isa. 58) has been inserted into a prophetic picture (Isa. 61). The emphasis in 4.18-19 clearly falls on the prophetic functions which Jesus assumes.

4. For the important role which miracles play in Luke's portrayal of Jesus' minsitry see O. Betz, 'Jesu Evangelium vom Gottesreich', in *Das Evangelium und die Evangelien* (1983), pp. 61-63.

5. This point is missed by J. Shelton when he writes: 'Attempts to attribute its [Isa. 58.6c] absence to the redactional activity of Luke fall short when one realizes that the same Isaianic passage was used by Jesus in the Q material (7.22f.) to assert His messiahship in relation to healings' ('Filled with the Spirit', p. 245). The key distinction between Lk. 7.22f. and 4.18-19 is that the latter contains a direct reference to the Spirit, the former does not. There is an element of truth in C.-P. März's assertion that for Luke 'Verkündigung und Machttat fallen nicht als zwei verschiedene

Third, and perhaps most significantly, Turner challenges the basis upon which Rese's conclusion rests: Schweizer's claim that 'Luke adopts the typically Jewish idea that the Spirit is the Spirit of prophecy'.[1] Turner maintains that, as the source of Jesus' inspired preaching, the Spirit 'bears little relationship to any "typical Jewish idea" of the Spirit of prophecy'.[2] Turner argues that, according to the Old Testament and the writings of intertestamental Judaism, the role of the Spirit in relation to prophet was not to impart power and authority in the delivery of the message; rather, prior to and independent of the proclamation of the message, the Spirit revealed the content of the message which was to be delivered. In short, Turner asserts that the Jews viewed the Spirit of prophecy as the organ of revelation rather than the source of inspired speech.

It is extremely doubtful, however, whether the distinction Turner makes between the Spirit's role as the agent of revelation and as the source of inspired speech would have been recognized by the Jews of antiquity. Undoubtedly this distinction was alien to rabbis, who commonly described the prophet simply as one who 'speaks in the Holy Spirit' (מדבר ברוח הקודש). Indeed, by definition the prophet was not simply a man who received revelation; he was the mouthpiece of God. Revelation and proclamation go hand in hand, and both are attributed to the Spirit.[3] While some passages focus on the Spirit's role in the revelatory act, others, such as Isa. 61.1, focus on the prophet's Spirit-inspired utterance.[4] Generally, to emphasize one aspect of the prophetic event is to imply the other.[5]

Dinge auseinander, sondern Jesu Wort als Erfüllungsgeschehen umfaßt beides' (*Das Wort Gottes bei Lukas. Die lukanische Worttheologie als Frage an die neuere Lukas-forschung* [1974], p. 39). Certainly Jesus' proclamation is closely associated with his miracles and indeed, at times, effects them. However, it should be noted that Luke does not always portray miracles as the effect of the word of Jesus (e.g. Lk. 6.19) and Luke never directly relates the Spirit to the miracle-producing word (e.g. Lk. 4.36). For Luke, Jesus' proclamation is the word of the Spirit; his miracles are, at times, produced by a word of power.

1. Turner, 'Luke and the Spirit', pp. 62-67.
2. Turner, 'Luke and the Spirit', p. 65.
3. This is stated with particular clarity in the 'ten names given to the Holy Spirit' recorded in *ARN* A.34 and alternatively in the variant traditions, the 'ten names given to prophecy'. See Chapter 5 §1.1.2.
4. See for example: Num. 23.7 (LXX); *Frag. 2* of Aristobulus, Eusebius, *Prae. Ev.* 8.10.4; *Ps.-Philo* 62.2; Josephus, *Ant.* 6.166; and the alterations which Josephus makes to the LXX (*Ant.* 4.165 = Num. 27.18; *Ant.* 8.295 = 2 Chron. 15.1; *Ant.* 9.168 = 2 Chron. 24.20; *Ant.* 9.10 = 2 Chron. 20.14).
5. Note the close relationship between revealed wisdom and inspired speech in Sir. 39.6 and *1 En.* 62.2.

Numerous other texts indicate that the distinction proposed by Turner was not maintained. Ecstatic prophecy, such as that recorded in Num. 11.25f., is a case in point.[1] In light of passages such as Num. 24.2f.,[2] 1 Sam. 10.10, and Joel 3.1f. (LXX), it cannot be maintained that other, less enthusiastic forms of prophetic speech, were deemed uninspired by the Spirit of God. Indeed, Philo declares the very thing that Turner denies: the Spirit endowed Abraham's words with special persuasive power (*Virt.* 217).[3]

A decisive objection to Turner's criticism is that Luke himself made the connection. He explicitly describes Spirit-inspired speech as prophetic activity in the infancy narratives and Acts 2.17 (cf. 2.4f.);[4] and the idea is implicit in Lk. 4.18f. (Isa. 61.1).[5] Indeed, where else could these notions have come from if Luke's conception of the Spirit as the source of inspired speech was not influenced by Judaism? Turner's response that Luke owes much more to 'such messianic ideas as are found in Isa. 11.4, or to relatively characteristic christian concepts' than to the Jewish concept of the Spirit of prophecy is no alternative.[6] We have already noted how messianic and prophetic functions merge in intertestamental Judaism,[7] and there can be little doubt that these 'Christian concepts' were shaped by Judaism.

If, on the one hand, Turner incorrectly exaggerates the Jewish emphasis on the Spirit as the source of revelation to the exclusion of the Spirit's role in the inspiration of the prophetic message, Schweizer, on the other hand, heightens the apparent difference between the Jew-

---

1. See also Philo, *Spec. Leg.* 4.49; *Leg. All.* 3.82; *Rer. Div. Her.* 249, 265-66; *Ps.-Philo* 28.6. As Aune notes, the 'emphasis on the articulation of oracular speech while in a state of inspiration, though rare in the OT (cf. Balaam in Num. 23-24), is more frequent in early Judaism' (*Prophecy*, p. 270).

2. See also Josephus on Num. 22.15f. (*Ant.* 4.108) and on Num. 23.12 (*Ant.* 4.119f.).

3. See Chapter 2 §5.2, Note also *T. Job* 43.2, 48.3; *Ps.-Philo* 32.14; and *Jub.* 25.14, 31.12f.; where the Spirit is cited as the source of inspired praise or blessing; and *Mart. Isa.* 5.14, which states that Isaiah, inspired by the Spirit, prophesied until sawn in half.

4. Thus J. Panagopoulos writes: 'Prophetie ist also bei Lukas mit dem verkündigten Evangelium von Jesus Christus gleichzusetzen' ('Die urchristliche Prophetie: Ihr Charakter und ihre Funktion', in *Prophetic Vocation in the New Testament and Today* [1977], p. 13).

5. The connection is explicitly expressed in the Targum of Isaiah, which reads: ' The spirit of prophecy [רוח נבואה] from before the Lord Elohim is upon me' (text of Isa. 61.1 from J.F. Stenning, *The Targum of Isaiah* [1953]).

6. Turner, 'Luke and the Spirit', p. 66.

7. Indeed, Isa. 11.4 speaks of inspired speech. This point is emphasized in the Targum to Isa. 11.4.

ish understanding of the Spirit and that of Luke by failing to emphasize that, according to Luke, the Spirit is the source of both inspired
speech and special revelation, and that often the two functions merge.
This is true for Jesus (Lk. 10.21), as well as the early church (Lk.
12.12). Indeed, it is difficult to make rigid distinctions at this point.

In short, it is inaccurate to distinguish sharply between the purported Jewish view of the Spirit as the source of revelation and Luke's
understanding of the Spirit as the means by which a previously understood message is powerfully proclaimed, for both descriptions are
caricatures.

Having reviewed the evidence, I have found Turner's criticisms of
Rese's position to be untenable at each point. Perhaps the weakest link
in Turner's argument against Rese is his inability to present a plausible
alternative.[1] I have already noted the inadequacy of arguments based
on structure. On this basis I conclude that Luke was responsible for the
omission of Isa. 61.1d in Lk. 4.18 and that the motivation for this
alteration came from Luke's prophetic understanding of the Spirit.
This conclusion accords well with Luke's redactional activity elsewhere and offers a plausible explanation of an omission which is otherwise extremely difficult to explain.

The insertion of Isaiah 58.6c (LXX): ἀποστεῖλαι τεθραυσμένους ἐν
ἀφέσει. We noted above that the insertion of Isa. 58.6c was probably
made as a result of the verbal linkage which ἄφεσις provides with the
preceding phrase. M. Rese suggests that the linkage was made by Luke
because he interpreted ἄφεσις to refer to the forgiveness of sins which
Jesus, inspired by the Spirit, proclaimed.[2] On the other hand, M.
Turner, building on the work of R. Sloan, asserts that the linkage was
motivated by jubilary concerns.[3] In contrast to Sloan, Turner argues
that Luke does not develop jubilary themes elsewhere and therefore
concludes that the linkage of Isa. 61.1f. with 58.6 points to the traditional origin of the quotation.[4] While Turner's hypothesis is plausible,
several factors indicate that the insertion is to be attributed to Luke.
First, although Luke does not develop jubilary themes elsewhere,[5] he

---

1. Turner, 'Luke and the Spirit', p. 70.
2. Rese, *Alttestamentliche Motive*, p. 146.
3. 'Luke and the Spirit', p. 70; Sloan, *The Favorable Year*, pp. 39-40.
4. 'Luke and the Spirit', pp. 67-71.
5. Turner's criticism of Sloan is justified: '[Sloan] fails to distinguish distinctively
jubilee language from more general redemption-language, and thus tends to press all
uses of εὐαγγελίζομαι, ἄφεσις, ἀφίημι—and even contexts where forgiveness is
implied (cf. 120)—into the service of his thesis that Jesus' ministry is characterized as

does display special interest in the term ἄφεσις (Luke, 5×; Acts, 5×; cf. Matthew, 1×; Mark, 2×), generally understood as 'release from sins'.[1] Second, Turner's suggestion that Isa. 58.6 was linked with Isa. 61.1-2 in order to heighten a distinctive jubilee emphasis is unconvincing.[2] There is no evidence of such a linkage in the literature of intertestamental Judaism[3] and, although Isa. 61.1-2 employs the picture of the jubilee as a 'metaphorical expression of the eschatological salvation of God',[4] it is by no means certain that the jubilary motif is emphasized in other parts of Luke's narrative (4.16-30), whether traditional or redactional.[5] This indicates that the linkage of Isa. 61.1f.

a jubilee year' ('Luke and the Spirit', p. 226 n. 177). See also Turner's essay, 'The Sabbath, Sunday, and the Law in Luke/Acts', in *From Sabbath to Lord's Day* (1982), pp. 99-157, where he argues that Luke does not have a distinctive Sabbath theology, and Tannehill, *The Narrative Unity of Luke–Acts*, I, p. 68.

1. Of the ten occurrences of ἄφεσις in Luke–Acts, excluding the two occurrences in Lk. 4.18-19, all are related to 'sins' (e.g. ἄφεσις ἁμαρτιῶν). For Luke's emphasis on ἄφεσις and the forgiveness of sins see Tannehill, 'The Mission of Jesus', pp. 70-71. Luke's emphasis on the contiguous aspects of the missions of John, Jesus, and the early church is clearly evident in his use of ἄφεσις: in three passages unique to Luke, John the Baptist (Lk. 1.77), Jesus (Lk. 4.18), and the disciples (24.47) are all commissioned to proclaim ἄφεσις.

2. Turner, 'Luke and the Spirit', p. 70. See also Sloan, *The Favorable Year*, pp. 39-40.

3. This is the case, even though one might expect such a linkage in 11Q Melch. Perrot asserts that Isa. 58.6 was read on the Day of Atonement and that this provides the link to Isa. 61.1f., since the Day of Atonement marked the beginning of the jubilee ('Synagogue', pp. 332f.). However, there is no evidence that Isa. 58.6 was associated with the Day of Atonement in NT times (see Seccombe's criticism of Perrot's thesis in *Possessions*, pp. 48-49). Indeed, since it is unlikely that a lectionary system governing the *haphtara* was operative in the 1st century, arguments based on lectionary tables must be viewed with extreme caution.

4. Sloan, *The Favorable Year*, pp. 162-63; see also pp. 171-72 where Sloan argues (contra Yoder, *The Politics of Jesus* [1972]) for an eschatological-metaphorical interpretation of jubilee imagery rather than a legal-concrete one. For similar conclusions see M. Rodgers, 'Luke 4.16-30—A Call for a Jubilee Year?', *RTR* 40 (1981), pp. 72-82 and Seccombe, *Possessions*, pp. 54-56.

5. A. Strobel points out several allusions to jubilee imagery in the broader content of 4.16-30, none of which is convincing. (1) Strobel asserts that the emphasis on the present fulfillment of the prophecy (4.21) accords well with jubilary chronology. Strobel argues that Jesus' ministry began in a jubilee year (AD 26–27) and this forms the background to the citation ('Die Ausrufung', pp. 38-50, esp. pp. 42-50); however, as Marshall notes, this suggestion is hard to fit into the chronology of the Jesus' ministry (*Commentary on Luke*, p. 184). (2) Strobel claims that Jesus' return to his hometown (4.14) echoes Lev. 25.10 (LXX) (p. 41). This interpretation undoubtedly reads too much into Luke's alteration of Mark, particularly in light of Lk. 2.39. And, as I have noted, Lk. 4.14 is to be attributed to Luke, not pre-Lukan tradition. (3)

with Isa. 58.6 was made by Luke and, not in order to heighten a distinctive jubilary emphasis, but rather as a result of his interest in ἄφεσις as a description of the liberating power of Jesus' preaching, of which an important aspect was forgiveness of sins.[1] Third, this conclusion is confirmed by the text's correlation with another motif of Luke: the duplication of a word in Old Testament quotations, such as ἄφεσις and ἀποστέλλω in 4.18, is characteristic of Lukan style.[2]

The alteration of καλέσαι (LXX) to κηρύξαι. Since Luke never uses καλέω in reference to preaching, it is quite probable that this alteration reflects his emphasis on preaching as the pre-eminent activity inspired by the Spirit.[3] However, noting that the preference for κηρύσσω is not unique to Luke, D. Bock maintains that 'the change points as firmly to a traditional source as it does to Luke'.[4] Nevertheless, the force of Bock's point is lessened by Luke's frequent duplication of words in quotations from the Old Testament. Thus the alteration of καλέσαι (LXX) to κηρύξαι corresponds to Luke's handling of Old Testament citations elsewhere and strongly suggests that the alteration reflects Luke's hand.[5]

Strobel notes that the extension of the famine from three (1 Kgs 17.21) to three-and-a-half years suggests an awareness of apocalyptic chronology (pp. 40-41). This does indicate that Luke had contact with a tradition (like Jas 5.17) concerning the drought influenced by the stereotyped length of distress in apocalyptic literature. It does not, however, show a special affinity to jubilee concepts. See Fitzmyer, who writes: 'This apocalyptic detail is meaningless in the Lucan account, the evangelist has simply inherited it' (*Luke I–IX*, p. 538).

1. Tannehill notes that although the context speaks of release for 'prisoners' and the 'oppressed', and does not refer directly to release of sins, 'when these phrases are no longer applied to physical imprisonment, they leave considerable room for interpretation. . . in the light of the importance to Luke of the "release of sins", this must be an important aspect of what he had in mind when he chose to emphasize the word ἄφεσις' ('The Mission of Jesus', p. 71).

2. Note the repetition of κηρύξαι (Lk. 4.18, 19 = Isa. 61.1-2); ἐν ταῖς. . . ἡμέραις (Acts 2.17, 18 = Joel 3.1f.); καὶ προφητεύσουσιν (Acts 2.17, 18 = Joel 3.1f.); ἔργον (Acts 13.41, 2× = Hab. 1.5); σου (Lk. 7.27 = Mal. 3.1). See Shelton, 'Filled with the Spirit', p. 251.

3. So also Rese, *Alttestamentliche Motive*, p. 146.

4. Bock, *Proclamation*, p. 106. None of the evangelists uses καλέω with reference to preaching, and κηρύσσω is used frequently by the other evangelists as well: Luke, 8×; Matthew, 9×; Mark, 12×.

5. So also T. Holtz, *Untersuchungen über die alttestamentlichen Zitate bei Lukas* (1968), p. 40.

The omission of καὶ ἡμέραν ἀνταποδόσεως *(LXX)*. It is debatable whether any particular theological interest should be attached to this omission for, strictly speaking, it does not represent an alteration of the LXX. Nevertheless, the quotation is broken off abruptly in the middle of a sentence.[1] Thus, while a number of factors may have influenced the length of the quotation, it is quite likely that the phrase was omitted from the citation in order to stress the grace of God.[2] While this emphasis on the salvific dimension of Jesus' work may have been taken over from tradition, it is equally compatible with Luke's perspective,[3] and therefore indecisive in determining whether the quotation stems from a traditional source or Luke's hand. However, in view of the conclusions cited above, it is most probable that the entire quotation, as it stands in Lk. 4.18-19, reflects Luke's redactional stamp.[4]

3.2. *Conclusion: The Significance of Luke's Redaction in Luke 4.18-19*

Having examined the alterations of Isa. 61.1-2 (LXX) in Lk. 4.18-19, I am now in a position to summarize my conclusions and assess their significance for Luke's pneumatology and, more specifically, his understanding of Jesus' pneumatic anointing.

The historicity of the general outline of events in Luke's account (4.16-30) need not be questioned for the linguistic data indicates that the account is based on traditional material other than Mk 6.1-6. Nonetheless, it is evident that Luke has made at least two decisive alterations to the traditional material available to him. First, he has moved the account forward in the chronology of his Gospel. Second, he has altered the wording of the quotation from Isa. 61.1-2. While the pre-Lukan tradition in all probability portrayed Jesus' preaching at Nazareth as centering on Isa. 61.1-2, it is highly unlikely that the quotation as it stands in Lk. 4.18-19 is traditional. As a result of my analysis of the text I have concluded it is highly probable that: the phrase ἰάσασθαι τοὺς συντετριμμένους τῇ καρδίᾳ was omitted by Luke due to his distinctive prophetic pneumatology; due to the verbal linkage which ἄφεσις provides with the preceding phrase, Luke inserted Isa. 58.6c (ἀποστεῖλαι τεθραυσμένους ἐν ἀφέσει) into the text of

---

1. J. Jeremias, *Jesus' Promise to the Nations* (1958), p. 45.

2. Grundmann, *Lukas*, p. 121; K. Giles, 'Salvation in Lukan Theology (1)', *RTR* 42 (1983), p. 12.

3. Rese, *Alttestamentliche Motive*, pp. 152-53.

4. So also Tannehill, 'The Mission of Jesus', pp. 64, 66; contra C. Tuckett, 'Luke 4,16-30', pp. 346-50.

Isa. 61.1-2 in order to emphasize the liberating power of Jesus' Spirit-inspired preaching; Luke is responsible for the alteration of καλέσαι (LXX) to κηρύξαι—this change, while reflecting Luke's emphasis on preaching as the pre-eminent activity inspired by the Spirit, is due principally to stylistic concerns. I have also concluded that it is quite likely that Luke omitted the final phrase of Isa. 61.2a (καὶ ἡμέραν ἀνταποδόσεως) in order to emphasize the salvific dimension of Jesus' work.

The profound implications which these conclusions have for this inquiry into Luke's understanding of Jesus' pneumatic anointing cannot be missed. First, by moving the Nazareth pericope forward in the chronology of his Gospel, Luke links the account with that of Jesus' reception of the Spirit at the Jordan and, as a result, highlights the significance of Jesus' pneumatic anointing for his entire ministry. The quotation from Isaiah, which plays such a prominent role in the narrative, defines with precision the significance which Luke attaches to Jesus' pneumatic anointing: Jesus' reception of the Spirit at the Jordan was the means by which he was equipped to carry out his messianic mission.[1] Second, by altering the text of Isa. 61.1-2 (LXX), Luke brings the quotation into conformity with his distinctive prophetic pneumatology and thus highlights preaching as the primary product of Jesus' anointing and the pre-eminent aspect of his mission.[2] While the activity of the Spirit is generally portrayed in prophetic terms (i.e. as the source of inspired speech) in Isa. 61.1-2,[3] through his redactional activity Luke has heightened this aspect of the text. Indeed, according to Luke, the Spirit-inspired preaching of Jesus effects salvation.[4] This

---

1. This conclusion, as noted above, is substantiated by Acts 10.38.

2. After noting that Luke often portrays Jesus as a prophet, P.J. Achtemeier points out that 'such hints are not, however, carried through in any systematic, or even perfunctory way, when Luke makes use of his miracle tradition' ('The Lukan Perspective on the Miracles of Jesus: A Preliminary Sketch', in *Perspectives on Luke–Acts* [1978], p. 166). I suggest this phenomenon is due to Luke's understanding of prophetic activity and the Spirit by which it is inspired. Although the prophet may perform miracles, they are not his primary function and therefore they are not directly attributed to the Spirit.

3. As we have noted, the Targum of Isaiah reads: 'The spirit of prophecy (רוח נבואה) from before the Lord Elohim is upon me'.

4. That salvation is manifest in Jesus' preaching is indicated not only by 4.18-19, but also by Jesus' words in 4.21: ἐν τοῖς ὠσὶν ὑμῶν (Rese, *Alttestamentliche Motive*, p. 147). Although perhaps it would be inaccurate to say that for Luke preaching is the exclusive means (apart from healings and exorcisms) by which salvation is effected, it is significant that in 4.18-19 Luke emphasizes preaching as the pre-eminent work of the Spirit and consciously omits any direct reference to healing.

assessment of Luke's pneumatology is entirely consistent with his christology—Luke, more than any of the other synoptic evangelists, views Jesus' entire ministry,[1] as well as his 'anointing' (as Lk. 4.18-19 indicates),[2] in prophetic terms. In short, my analysis of Lk. 4.18-19 has confirmed the conclusions from the previous analysis of Lk. 3.21-

Perhaps this emphasis on the salvific character of Jesus' preaching accounts for the lack of emphasis he places on the salvific character of Jesus' death (so also Hill, *New Testament Prophecy*, p. 158).

1. Luke often depicts people reacting to Jesus as a prophet (Lk. 7.16, 39; 9.8, 19; 24.19; Acts 2.30). Jesus refers to himself as a prophet (Lk. 4.24) and he accepts the fate of a prophet (Lk. 11.49-50; 13.33). Jesus is explicitly identified as the prophet-like-Moses in Acts 3.22; 7.37 and perhaps this identification is also suggested in Luke's portrayal of Jesus' childhood (Isaacs notes the parallels to Philo's depiction of Moses' childhood [*Spirit*, p. 130]), in Lk. 9.35 (Deut. 18.15: αὐτοῦ ἀκούετε), in Lk. 10.1 (Num. 11.25: commissioning of the 70), in 11.20 (Exod. 8.19: δάκτυλος), and in the attribution of τέρατα καὶ σημεῖα to Jesus in Acts 2.22; 4.30 (cf. Acts 7.36). For Luke's unique emphasis on Jesus' prophetic role see Lentzen-Deis, *Die Taufe Jesu*, pp. 272, 285; Minear, *To Heal*, pp. 102-47; Aune, *Prophecy*, p. 155; Schmeichel, 'Christian Prophecy in Lukan Thought', pp. 293-304, esp. pp. 293-94; P.E. Davies, 'Jesus and the Role of the Prophet', *JBL* 64 (1945), p. 243; Stronstad, *Charismatic Theology*, pp. 43-45; R.J. Dillon, *From Eye-Witness to Ministers of the Word: Tradition and Composition in Luke 24* (1978), pp. 117-27, 131-32, 140-41; and Tannehill, *The Narrative Unity of Luke–Acts*, I, pp. 96-99, 286-89. There is no conflict between this emphasis and that of Jesus as the royal Messiah, for 'ultimately, the concepts of the eschatological prophet and the Messiah merge' (Marshall, *Commentary on Luke*, p. 183; cf. *Luke: Historian and Theologian*, p. 127; see also Meyer, *Der Prophet aus Galiläa*, pp. 18-31, esp. 23, 26; F. Hahn, *The Titles of Jesus in Christology* [1969], p. 364; and W. Meeks, *The Prophet-King: Moses Traditions and the Johannine Christology* [1967], pp. 100-256). In his article 'Jesus the Christ' (*NTS* 8 [1961–62], pp. 101-16), W.C. van Unnik cites numerous Jewish texts which connect the Spirit with the anointing of both kings and prophets. Particularly striking are those texts which describe the king, upon being anointed with the Spirit, as prophesying (1 Sam. 10.1f., 9f.; *Ant.* 6.8.2 on 1 Sam. 16.13). On the merging of these elements in Lk. 4.18f. see Bock, *Proclamation*, pp. 110-11; Tuckett, 'Luke 4,16-30', p. 346; and Tiede, *Prophecy*, p. 46.

2. This conclusion is also supported by Lk. 4.23-24. As Marshall notes: 'In Is. 61 the anointing is clearly that of a prophet (cf. 1 Ki. 19:16; CD 2:12; 6:1; 1 QM 11:7), and in view of 4.23 the same motif should be seen here' (*Commentary on Luke*, p. 183). Indeed, in Lk. 3.21-22, the allusion to Isa. 42.1 indicates that the anointing, even in the tradition, should not be seen in exclusively regal Messianic categories. Lentzen-Deis writes: 'Der jesajanische Gottesknecht von Jes 42 trägt weitgehend "prophetische" Züge im Gegensatz zu einer rein irdisch nationalen Messiashoffnung' (*Die Taufe Jesu*, p. 158). For the prophetic character of Lk. 4.18-19 see also J. Kodell, 'Luke's Gospel', p. 17; Sloan, *The Favorable Year*, pp. 68-73; Turner, 'Luke and the Spirit', pp. 73-74; Shelton, 'Filled with the Spirit', p. 248; and Miyoshi, *Reiseberichts*, p. 135.

22 and 4.1, 14: according to Luke, Jesus' pneumatic anointing, rather than the source of his unique filial relationship to God or his initiation into the new age, was the means by which Jesus was equipped to carry out his divinely appointed task. Thus Luke's portrayal of Jesus' pneumatic anointing, which anticipates the experience of the early church,[1] is consistent with his prophetic pneumatology.

---

1. See Chapter 8 §2.1 above.

Chapter 9

JESUS AND THE SPIRIT: THE PNEUMATIC SAYINGS

Several texts in Luke–Acts, apart from Lk. 4.18-19, relate sayings of Jesus pertaining to the Holy Spirit. In the following chapter I shall examine these texts as they occur in Luke–Acts and assess their significance for Luke's pneumatology.

1. *The Spirit-Inspired Exultation (Luke 10.21)*

Luke follows his account of the return of the seventy (two) with material drawn from Q (10.21-24).[1] The pericope records Jesus' joyful expression of thanksgiving to the Father, who, through Jesus, has revealed 'things hidden from the wise' to the disciples. This inspired exultation is followed by a pronouncement to the disciples: they are indeed 'blessed', for they are the favored recipients of God's revelation. Of particular importance for this study is the way in which Luke introduces Jesus' initial words of praise in Lk. 10.21b:

> Mt. 11.25b: ἀποκριθεὶς ὁ Ἰησοῦς εἶπεν
> Lk. 10.21b: ἠγαλλιάσατο ἐν τῷ πνεύματι τῷ ἁγίῳ καὶ εἶπεν[2]

---

1. The two passages are linked by the temporal phrase in v. 21a: Ἐν αὐτῇ τῇ ὥρᾳ.

2. The MSS contain several variant readings at this point: 1. ἐν τῷ πνεύματι τῷ ἁγίῳ (א; D; L; Ξ; 33; 1241; it); 2. τῷ πνεύματι τῷ ἁγίῳ (P75; B; C; K; Θ; f¹; 1424; it^aur; vg); 3. ἐν τῷ πνεύματι (P45); 4. τῷ πνεύματι (A; W; Δ, Ψ). Variants 3 and 4 can be dismissed as secondary. Metzger points out that 'the strangeness of the expression "exulted in the Holy Spirit" (for which there is no parallel in the Scriptures)' may have led to the omission of τῷ ἁγίῳ from P45; A; W; Δ; Ψ (*A Textual Commentary*, p. 152). Marshall notes that Lukan usage elsewhere (Lk. 2.27; 4.1; Acts 19.21) cannot be cited in support of variant 3 since in Lk. 2.27 and 4.1 'the adjective ἅγιος is missing because the full phrase has just been used' (*Commentary on Luke*, p. 433). The external evidence clearly favors variants 1 and 2. Although it is difficult to distinguish between these two options, the judgment of the UBS committee in favor of variant 1, based on the Septuagint's frequent use of ἀγαλλιᾶσθαι with a preposition (ἐν or ἐπί), is to be preferred.

A comparison of Lk. 10.21b with Mt. 11.25b reveals that Matthew preserves the original introductory phrase of Q, which Luke has decisively altered.[1] The verb ἀγαλλιάω and its cognate noun, ἀγαλλίασις, are characteristic of Luke;[2] and, as I have already established, Luke frequently alters his sources in accordance with his pneumatological interests.[3] Thus it is clear that Luke has replaced the ἀποκριθείς of Q with a phrase more to his liking: ἠγαλλιάσατο ἐν τῷ πνεύματι τῷ ἁγίῳ.

In assessing the significance of Luke's redaction it is important to define with precision the action signified by the verb ἀγαλλιάω. In the LXX ἀγαλλιάω, which is usually found in Psalms and the poetic portions of the Prophets, denotes spiritual exultation which issues forth in praise to God for his mighty acts.[4] The subject of the verb is not simply ushered into a state of sacred rapture; he also 'declares the acts of God'.[5] The close association between ἀγαλλιάω and the utterance of inspired words of praise is illustrated in the phrase, καὶ ἠγαλλιάσατο ἡ γλῶσσά μου (Ps. 15.9, LXX; quoted in Acts 2.26),[6] and in Ps. 94.1 (LXX), where the verbs ἀγαλλιασώμεθα and ἀλαλάξωμεν are employed as synonyms:[7]

> Δεῦτε ἀγαλλιασώμεθα τῷ κυρίῳ,
> ἀλαλάξωμεν τῷ θεῷ τῷ σωτῆρι ἡμῶν.

In the New Testament the verb is used in a similar manner.[8] The linkage between ἀγαλλιάω and the declaration of the mighty acts of God is particularly striking in Luke–Acts.[9] The verb describes the joyful praise of Mary (Lk. 1.47), Jesus (Lk. 10.21), and David (Acts 2.25) in response to God's salvific activity in Jesus. That ἀγαλλιάω in Lk. 10.21b refers to the declaration of words of praise is confirmed by

1. S. Schulz, *Q: Die Spruchquelle der Evangelisten* (1972), p. 213.
2. Miyoshi, *Reiseberichts*, p. 121. Seven out of the sixteen occurrences in the NT of ἀγαλλιάω (NT, 11×; Luke–Acts, 4×) and ἀγαλλίασις (NT, 5×; Luke–Acts, 3×) are found in Luke–Acts (on Luke's usage see W.G. Morrice, *Joy in the New Testament* [1984], pp. 20-21).
3. See the discussion of the data presented by C.S. Rodd ('Spirit or Finger', *ExpTim* 72 [1960-61], pp. 157-58) in Chapter 9 §2 below.
4. R. Bultmann, 'ἀγαλλιάομαι', *TDNT*, I, p. 19; Morrice, *Joy*, p. 20.
5. R. Bultmann, 'ἀγαλλιάομαι', p. 20.
6. Note also Ps. 125.2 (LXX) where a similar expression is used.
7. See also (LXX): Pss. 5.12; 9.2-3; 34.27; 91.5; 95.11; 96.1; Isa. 12.6; 25.9; 61.10.
8. R. Bultmann, 'ἀγαλλιάομαι', p. 20; Morrice, *Joy*, p. 21.
9. The linkage is made explicit in three out of four occurrences of the verb (Lk. 1.47; 10.21; Acts 2.25). The only exception is Acts 16.34.

the Semitic structure of the verse, which parallels ἀγαλλιάω with εἶπεν.[1] Luke's addition of the instrumental phrase,[2] ἐν τῷ πνεύματι τῷ ἁγίῳ, in Lk. 10.21b is consistent with the usage of ἀγαλλιάω cited above: the praise of Mary and Jesus is uttered under the inspiration of the Spirit (Lk. 1.35; 10.21), and David is described as a prophet (Acts 2.30). Indeed, Jesus' experience of the Spirit in 10.21b parallels that of the leading figures in the infancy narratives and the disciples in Acts.[3] In short, for Luke the phrase ἠγαλλιάσατο ἐν τῷ πνεύματι τῷ ἁγίῳ καὶ εἶπεν was an appropriate way of describing prophetic activity:[4] it signified the Spirit-inspired declaration of the acts of God. Thus Luke's alteration of Q in Lk. 10.21b, which emphasized the pneumatic and prophetic character of Jesus' declaration, reflects Luke's unique interpretation of the event and his distinctive prophetic pneumatology.

2. *Encouragement to Pray for the Spirit (Luke 11.13)*

Luke 11.1-13 forms a section devoted to Jesus' teaching on prayer. The section begins with a disciple's request for instruction on how to pray (11.1), which Jesus answers in the form of a model prayer (11.2-4)[5] and parabolic teaching concerning the willingness and certainty of

---

1. So also Shelton, 'Filled with the Spirit', p. 374. On the Semitic character of the verse see Manson, *Sayings*, p. 79. Note the Semitic parallelism in Matthew's construction: ἀποκριθεὶς ὁ Ἰησοῦς εἶπεν.

2. Turner acknowledges that in Lk. 10.21 the phrase ἐν τῷ πνεύματι τῷ ἁγίῳ designates the cause of Jesus' rejoicing, but he asserts that the phrase refers principally to the Spirit's work in the disciples. Their report of the Spirit's work in their own ministry was the indirect cause of Jesus' rejoicing ('Luke and the Spirit', p. 87). This hypothesis assumes much, particularly in view of the fact that Luke nowhere associates the Spirit with the disciples of Jesus during his ministry and that he regularly describes the Spirit as the direct source of inspired speech.

3. Haya-Prats, *Force*, pp. 152-53; Shelton, 'Filled with the Spirit', p. 373; Miyoshi, *Reiseberichts*, p. 137.

4. Strack–Billerbeck, *Kommentar*, II, p. 176: 'ἠγαλλιάσατο ἐν τῷ πνεύματι τῷ ἁγίῳ = im Geist prophetischer Rede'. See also Barrett, *Gospel Tradition*, pp. 101-102. Perhaps the rabbinic rule that 'the Holy Spirit rests only on a joyful man' (*j. Suk.* 5.55a, 54) stems from the association of joy and the Holy Spirit found in Ps. 51.13-14 (MT; 50.13-14, LXX).

5. The variant reading in 11.2, ἐλθέτω τὸ πνεῦμα σου τὸ ἅγιον ἐφ' ἡμᾶς καὶ καθαρισάτω ἡμᾶς, is undoubtedly secondary. The external evidence is weak: the reading is preserved in two minuscule manuscripts (700; 162), is quoted by Gregory of Nyssa and Maximus of Turin, and alluded to by Tertullian. Furthermore, while the variant can easily be accounted for as a liturgical adaptation of the original form of the Lord's prayer, it is difficult to imagine why this reading, if original, would have been 'supplanted in the overwhelming majority of the witnesses by a concept originally

God's response (11.5-13). The section concludes by comparing the heavenly Father with an earthly counterpart: 'If you then, who are evil, know how to give good gifts to your children, how much more will the heavenly Father give the Holy Spirit to those who ask him!' (11.13). This concluding comparison, with its reference to the Holy Spirit, warrants examination.

The similarities in wording between Lk. 11.9-13 and Mt. 7.7-11 indicate that the passage stems from Q. However, there is a crucial difference: Mt. 7.11b has ἀγαθά rather than the πνεῦμα ἅγιον of Lk. 11.13b.[1] There can be little doubt that Matthew's ἀγαθά represents the original wording of Q.[2] Matthew follows his sources closely with reference to the Spirit: he never omits a reference to the Spirit which is contained in his sources and he never inserts πνεῦμα into Markan or Q material. Luke, on the other hand, inserts πνεῦμα into Q material on three occasions (Lk. 4.1; 10.21; 11.13) and into Markan material once (Lk. 4.14).[3] These data suggest that Luke, rather than Matthew, has altered Q. This conclusion is confirmed by the awkwardness of Luke's construction: the insertion of πνεῦμα ἅγιον breaks the

---

much more Jewish in its piety' (Metzger, *A Textual Commentary*, p. 156). And, as G. Schneider notes, 'die "Reinigung", die der Geist Gottes bei den Betern dieser Bitte bewirken soll, entspricht nicht der theologischen Konzeption des Lukas, sondern dürfte aus Ez 36, 22-32 LXX herausgelesen sein' ('Die Bitte um das Kommen des Geistes im lukanischen Vaterunser (Lk 11,2 v.1)', in *Studien zum Text und zur Ethik des Neuen Testaments* [1986], p. 370). In the same article, G. Schneider evaluates the scholarly discussion of the variant reading in the modern era. He concludes that the reading was produced by a post-Lukan redactor (p. 371).

1. There are several variant readings, but the external evidence for πνεῦμα ἅγιον is strong (P75; ℵ; C; L; X; Θ; Ψ) and the other variant readings can be explained as assimilation with Matthew (Metzger, *A Textual Commentary*, p. 158).

2. Barrett, *Gospel Tradition*, pp. 126-27; Schulz, *Q*, p. 162; W. Ott, *Gebet und Heil: Die Bedeutung der Gebetsparänese in der lukanischen Theologie* (1965), pp. 107-108; Schweizer, 'πνεῦμα', p. 409; Manson, *Sayings*, p. 81; Fitzmyer, *Luke X–XXIV*, pp. 915-16; Grundmann, *Lukas*, p. 235; Ellis, *Luke*, p. 164; Büchsel, *Der Geist Gottes*, p. 190; von Baer, *Der heilige Geist*, p. 150.

3. See Rodd, 'Spirit or Finger', pp. 157-58. Marshall's assertion that 'it has been argued convincingly by C.S. Rodd that Luke has no greater predilection for adding references to the Spirit in the body of his Gospel than Matthew' (*Commentary on Luke*, pp. 475-76; see also p. 470) misses Rodd's point: Rodd demonstrates that 'Matthew keeps close to his sources and never in the passages examined adds references to the Holy Spirit. On the other hand, Luke both adds such references, and deletes them' ('Spirit or Finger', p. 158). Thus, while Rodd demonstrates the plausibility of Luke's deletion of a reference to the Spirit in Q (e.g. Lk. 11.20), his argument also establishes how unlikely it is that Matthew would have made such a deletion in Lk. 11.13b = Mt. 7.11b.

parallelism of the *a minore ad maius* argument which links the δόματα ἀγαθά given by earthly fathers (Lk. 11.13a = Mt. 7.11a) with the ἀγαθά given by the heavenly Father (Lk. 11.13a = Mt. 7.11a).[1]

Having established that the πνεῦμα ἅγιον of Lk. 11.13b is redactional, the significance of this alteration for Luke's pneumatology must now be assessed. Three observations will be made.

First, Luke's alteration of the Q form of the saying anticipates the post-resurrection experience of the church.[2] This is evident from the fact that the promise that the Father will give πνεῦμα ἅγιον to those who ask begins to be realized only at Pentecost.[3] By contemporizing the text in this way, Luke stresses the relevance of the saying for the post-Pentecostal community to which he writes.[4]

---

1. Schulz, *Q*, p. 162. However, Marshall notes that 'the form in Matthew could be a generalizing one, made in order to assimilate the second part of the saying to the first' (*Commentary on Luke*, p. 470).

2. Fitzmyer, *Luke X–XXIV*, p. 916; Ellis, *Luke*, p. 164; Stronstad, *Charismatic Theology*, p. 46.

3. On the basis of Luke's redaction in Lk. 11.13b, Turner asserts: '[Luke] considers that the Spirit was a present possibility to some of Jesus' hearers, one which they could experience in answer to prayer, at least as a power to be used against the demonic, if not also as a power at the center of their being guarding them against the attacks of evil powers (11.24-6)' ('Luke and the Spirit', p. 115; see also pp. 96-116). Turner distinguishes between the disciples' experience of the Spirit during the ministry of Jesus and their reception of the gift of the Spirit at Pentecost. The former is 'the power which effects release from Satan's domination' (p. 116); the latter includes a broader range of functions. Turner maintains that the Spirit as 'the power which effects release from Satan's domination' is experienced by the disciples during Jesus' ministry in two ways: (1) in the proclamation of Jesus; (2) in the power over Satan (notably in exorcisms) which the disciples exercise in the missions of the twelve and seventy (p. 110). Point (1) need not be denied. Indeed, Turner is convincing when he argues that the circle of disciples, and those beyond the circle who believed Jesus' preaching, experience 'the life of the kingdom' during Jesus' ministry. However, as the power of Jesus' proclamation, the Spirit is experienced only in an indirect way by the disciples. Turner goes beyond the evidence when he suggests that during the ministry of Jesus the Spirit is at work through the disciples themselves as the power by which demons are exorcized. The distinction between the disciples' pre-Pentecostal, mediated experience of the Spirit in the proclamation of Jesus, and the activity of the Spirit through Jesus and the post-Pentecostal church is clear and consistently maintained by Luke. Undoubtedly he has the latter in mind in Lk. 11.13b since the former is never articulated as such by Luke and is merely a corollary of the latter.

4. Contra Schuyler Brown, '"Water Baptism" and "Spirit-Baptism" in Luke–Acts', *ATR* 59 (1977), pp. 135-51, esp. pp. 150-51. Brown argues that by detaching the gift of the Spirit from the rite of Christian initiation, Luke could restrict the gift

to the early period of the church. Brown's argument rests on four points: (1) Luke's representation of the Pentecost event indicates that he had limited knowledge of glossolalia and thus suggests that the practice had died out in his community some time before the writing of Acts (also Conzelmann, *Acts*, pp. 15, 159-60); (2) The gift of the Spirit is always related to the mission of the church and, since this is the responsibility of the apostles (Acts 1.8), they (and their representatives) are the sole recipients of the gift; (3) Acts 20.29-30 suggests that the Lukan community was threatened by heretical doctrine, therefore Luke affirmed apostolic authority over the individual's possession of the Spirit; (4) Luke has historicized Mark's apocalyptic discourse and therefore he is writing in a period after the church had successfully withstood the Jewish persecution. Although the church still faced persecution from Rome, Luke had no interest in cultivating an enthusiasm for martyrdom. Thus Lk. 11.13 and 12.10-12 are directed solely to apostles and their associates in the initial period of the church. However, Brown's argument can be questioned. (1) Acts 10.46 and 19.6 suggest that Luke was acquainted with the practice of glossolalia (see J. Dupont, 'The First Christian Pentecost', in *The Salvation of the Gentiles* [1979], pp. 46f.). Luke's account in Acts 2.4f., whether motivated by theological concerns or early tradition (note the claims made by various modern-day charismatics that contemporary glossolalia has, on numerous occasions, taken the form of an utterance in a foreign language unkown to the speaker; e.g. M. Kelsey, *Speaking with Tongues* [1965], pp. 152-57, 162f.; J.L. Sherrill, *They Speak with Other Tongues* [1965], pp. 13f.; H. Ervin, '*These Are Not Drunken as Ye Suppose*' [1968], pp. 127-28; D. and R. Bennett, *The Holy Spirit and You* [1971], pp. 91f. As Dunn notes, 'If such claims can be made with such conviction in the twentieth century, it is more readily conceivable that they were made at the time of the first Christian Pentecost' [*Jesus and the Spirit*, p. 151]), does not invalidate this evidence. (2) The apostles in Acts 1.8 are representative of the entire church and Luke does not elsewhere limit the gift of the Spirit to the apostles (see Chapter 10 §1 below). (3) Brown's assumption, that a concern for heresy led Luke to restrict the Spirit to the apostles, is based on an exaggerated representation of the conflict between Spirit and institution in the early church. Although Paul faced the spectre of heresy and disputes concerning his apostolic authority, he still affirmed the validity of pneumatic experience (e.g. 1 Corinthians). More recently Mansfield has put forth the thesis that 'Mark's concept of Gospel (content and authority) was shaped in part by the challenge of ecstatic pneumatic prophets who appealed directly to the revelation of the Spirit of Christ for truth and authority in the church (cf. 13:10–11, 22)' (*Mark*, p. 18). It is doubtful whether Mk 13.22 will bear the weight of Mansfield's thesis concerning the challenge of 'ecstatic pneumatic prophets' and, in any case, this insists that Mark responded by associating the Spirit with 'Gospel', thus affirming the validity of contemporary pneumatic experience within proper limits. (4) Brown's suggestion that Luke wrote to a church which had successfully withstood the Jewish persecution is based on a tenuous estimation of the significance of πρὸ δὲ τούτων πάντων in Lk. 21.12. It is unlikely that the passage (Lk. 21.12) refers exclusively to the early days of the church (Marshall, *Commentary on Luke*, p. 767). These substantial points of criticism aside, Brown's thesis is ultimately unconvincing because it does not adequately account for Luke's redactional activity in Lk. 11.13 (would Luke modify the text if the alteration had no relevance for his readers?) and the universal language in Acts 2.17f. and 2.38.

Second, the context indicates that the promise is made to disciples (Lk. 11.1).[1] Thus Luke's contemporized version of the saying is directed to the members of the Christian community.[2] Since it is addressed to Christians, the promise cannot refer to an initiatory or soteriological gift.[3] This judgment is confirmed by the repetitive

---

1. Beasley-Murray, *Baptism*, p. 119 and B. Aker, 'New Directions', pp. 118-19.

2. As I.H. Marshall notes, there were undoubtedly a number of concerns which, in varying degrees, influenced Luke's two-volume work ['Luke and His "Gospel"', pp. 289-308]. In light of Luke's interest in the mission of the church it would not be surprising if one of the aims Luke had in mind when he wrote Luke–Acts was to pen a missionary manifesto—a work which would offer theological and methodological direction for the ongoing Christian mission (e.g. support the validity of the mission to the Gentiles; emphasize the necessity of the Spirit's enabling). E. Lohse suggests that in his *Reisebericht* (Lk. 9.51–18.14) Luke presents Jesus as a model missionary who, in his Spirit-empowered ministry to the Samaritans, anticipates the church's pneumatic anointing at Pentecost and subsequent mission to the Gentiles: 'Damit aber hat Lukas in dem Leben des irdischen Jesu bereits den Weg vorgezeichnet, den nach seiner Auferstehung und Erhöhung seine Jünger, ausgerüstet mit der Kraft des Heiligen Geistes, nehmen sollten' ('Missionarisches Handeln', p. 174; see pp. 165-77 and 'Theologe der Heilsgeschichte', p. 161). For similar emphases see Minear, *To Heal*, pp. 81-147; Hill, *New Testament Prophecy*, p. 158; E. Haenchen, 'The Book of Acts as Source Material for the History of Early Christianity' in *Studies in Luke–Acts* (1966), p. 278; and R. Maddox, *The Purpose of Luke–Acts* (1982), p. 187. My suggestion is supported by the recognition that Luke–Acts is addressed principally to the Christian community (see Maddox, *Purpose*, pp. 12-15, 180-81; E. Franklin, *Christ the Lord: A Study in the Purpose and Theology of Luke–Acts* [1975], p. 46; Esler, *Community*, pp. 25f.).

3. Montague, *Spirit*, pp. 259-60. Thus Lk. 11.13b indicates that Luke does not simply equate the presence of the Spirit with the presence of the Kingdom. For this reason Dunn's affirmation, based on Lk. 11.13 and Lk. 12.31f., that 'the Kingdom and the Spirit are alternative ways of speaking about the disciples' highest good' needs modification ('Spirit and Kingdom', p. 38). Note also S. Smalley, who, following Dunn writes: 'Luke's theological understanding, moreover, is such that he also views the activity of the Spirit among men and the arrival of the kingdom of God as aligned if not synonymous. Where the Spirit is, there is the kingdom' ('Spirit, Kingdom, and Prayer in Luke–Acts', *NovT* 15 [1973], p. 68). While Smalley has correctly emphasized the close relationship between Spirit, kingdom, and prayer in Luke–Acts, the nature of this relationship, particularly between Spirit and kingdom, needs clarification, for the two are not synonymous: the former is the means by which the latter is proclaimed and thus made available to the world. E. Franklin correctly notes that 'the Spirit. . . is neither a substitute for, nor an embodiment of the Kingdom' ('The Ascension and the Eschatology of Luke–Acts', *SJT* 23 [1970], p. 198). For Luke, the Kingdom is present, above all, in Jesus (O. Merk, 'Das Reich Gottes in den lukanischen Schriften', in *Jesus und Paulus* [1973], pp. 201-20).

character of the exhortation to pray:[1] prayer for the Spirit (and, in light of the promise, we may presume this includes the reception of the Spirit) is to be an ongoing practice. The gift of πνεῦμα ἅγιον to which Luke refers neither initiates one into the new age, nor is it to be received only once;[2] rather, πνεῦμα ἅγιον is given to disciples and is to be experienced on an ongoing basis.

Third, Luke's usage elsewhere indicates that he viewed the gift of πνεῦμα ἅγιον in 11.13b as an endowment of prophetic power. On two occasions in Luke–Acts the Spirit is given to those praying;[3] in both the Spirit is portrayed as the source of prophetic activity. Luke alters the Markan account of Jesus' baptism so that Jesus receives the Spirit after his baptism while praying (Lk. 3.21). As we have noted, this gift of the Spirit, portrayed principally as the source of Jesus' proclamation (Lk. 4.18-19), equipped Jesus for his messianic task. Later, in Acts 4.31 the disciples, after having prayed, 'were all filled with the Holy Spirit and spoke the word of God boldly'. Again the Spirit given in response to prayer is the impetus behind the proclamation of the word of God.

To sum up, through his redactional activity in Lk. 11.13b, Luke encourages post-Pentecostal disciples to ask for the gift of the Spirit which, for Luke, meant open access to the divine πνεῦμα—the source of power which would enable them to be effective witnesses for Christ (Lk. 12.12; Acts 1.8) by providing what was required in time of need, whether it be special knowledge or the ability to powerfully proclaim the gospel in the face of persecution.

3. *ἐν δακτύλῳ θεοῦ (Luke 11.20)*

Luke's account of the Beelzebub Controversy stems from Q, as the close correspondence with Matthew's text indicates (Lk. 11.14-

---

1. Note for example the repetitive force of ὅταν προσεύχησθε, λέγετε (11.2) and the continuous action implicit in the present indicative active verbs in 11.10: λαμβάνω, εὑρίσκω.

2. Büchsel notes the repetitive character of the exhortation (*Der Geist Gottes*, pp. 189-90). So also Montague, *Spirit*, pp. 259-60.

3. Acts 8.15, 17 represents the only instance in Luke–Acts, apart from the two texts discussed above, where reception of the Spirit is explicitly associated with prayer. However here the Spirit is bestowed on the Samaritans in response to the prayer of Peter and John. While the situation in Acts 8.15, 17 is not a true parallel to Lk. 11.13b, as we shall see, in Acts 8.15f. the Spirit is portrayed in prophetic terms (see Chapter 11 §2.2 below). Prayer is implicitly associated with the reception of the Spirit at Pentecost (Acts 1.14; 2.4). Here also the gift of the Spirit is presented as a prophetic endowment (see Chapter 10 below).

23 = Mt. 12.22-30). However, in Lk. 11.20 there is a significant deviation from its Matthean counterpart:

Lk. 11.20:   εἰ δὲ ἐν δακτύλῳ θεοῦ [ἐγὼ] ἐκβάλλω τὰ δαιμόνια,
ἄρα ἔφθασεν ἐφ᾽ ὑμᾶς ἡ βασιλεία τοῦ θεοῦ.
Mt. 12.28:   εἰ δὲ ἐν πνεύματι θεοῦ ἐγὼ ἐκβάλλω τὰ δαιμόνια
ἄρα ἔφθασεν ἐφ᾽ ὑμᾶς ἡ βασιλεία τοῦ θεοῦ.

The question as to which evangelist preserves the original reading of Q has been much discussed. While it has been customary to view Luke's δακτύλῳ θεοῦ as original,[1] a number of more recent works suggest that this judgment should be reassessed[2] and, as the following points indicate, an analysis of the evidence supports this claim:

(A) In view of their use of πνεῦμα elsewhere, it is more likely that Luke deleted the reference contained in Q than that Matthew added the term to the tradition. As we have noted, Matthew follows his sources closely with reference to the Spirit, never omitting a reference to πνεῦμα which is contained in Mark and/or Q. Luke, on the other hand, feels free to alter his sources: not only does he add πνεῦμα to his sources; he is also willing, when inclined, to omit the term (Lk. 20.42 = Mk 12.36).[3]

(B) The fact that Matthew's version includes the phrase ἡ βασιλεία τοῦ θεοῦ rather than his customary ἡ βασιλεία τῶν οὐρανῶν suggests 'that Matthew has hurried over the Q version of Mt. 12.28 without stopping to modify it as he

---

1. T.W. Manson, *The Teaching of Jesus* (1952), p. 82 and *Sayings*, p. 86; Barrett, *Gospel Tradition*, p. 63; and J.L. Leuba, 'Der Zusammenhang zwischen Geist und Tradition nach dem Neuen Testament', *KuD* 4 (1958), p. 236.

2. Rodd, 'Spirit or Finger', pp. 157-58; J.E. Yates, 'Luke's Pneumatology and Luke 11.20', in *Studia Evangelica II* (1964), pp. 295-99; R.G. Hamerton-Kelly, 'A Note on Matthew XII.28 Par. Luke XI. 20', *NTS* 11 (1964–65), pp. 167-69; Dunn, *Jesus and the Spirit*, pp. 45-46; Turner, 'Luke and the Spirit', p. 88; J.-M. Van Cangh, ' "Par l'esprit de Dieu—par le doigt de Dieu" Mt 12,28 par. Lc 11,20', in *Logia* (1982), pp. 337-42. However, note the conclusion by Fitzmyer: 'Luke has undoubtedly preserved "the finger of God" in v. 20 from "Q" ' (*Luke X–XXIV*, p. 918). A number of other more recent works also view Luke's 'finger of God' as original: G. Schneider, *Das Evangelium nach Lukas, Kapitel 11-24* (1977), p. 266; J. Ernst, *Das Evangelium nach Lukas* (1977), p. 375; E. Schweizer, *Das Evangelium nach Matthäus* (1973), p. 186.

3. Note also Lk. 21.15 = Mk 13.11; however, Luke includes a variant of this tradition which does refer to the Holy Spirit (Lk. 12.12). See Rodd, 'Spirit or Finger', pp. 157-58 and Yates, 'Luke's Pneumatology and Luke 11.20', pp. 295-99.

normally would have done'.[1] When the phrase ἡ βασιλεία τοῦ
θεοῦ appears in his source material, Matthew normally alters
it to ἡ βασιλεία τῶν οὐρανῶν.[2]

(C) In the Q account of the Beelzebub Controversy the saying (Lk.
11.20 = Mt. 12.28) is followed by Jesus' statement concerning
blasphemy against the Holy Spirit (Mt. 12.32 = Lk. 12.10).[3]
This suggests that Matthew's πνεύματι θεοῦ formed part of
the text of Q;[4] for, as the editorial comment in Mk 3.30 indi-

---

1. Dunn, *Jesus and the Spirit*, p. 45. See also Rodd, 'Spirit or Finger', p. 158.

2. Note for example Mt. 4.17; 5.3; 8.11; 10.7; 11.11f.; 13.11, 31, 33; 19.14, 23.
The only exception to this practice, other than Mt. 12.28, is Mt. 19.24. See Dunn,
Jesus and the Spirit, p. 45.

3. See §4.1 below for evidence supporting the claim that Mt. 12.12-32 reflects the
original order of Q.

4. As Yates notes, the authenticity of Matthew's πνεύματι θεοῦ has also been
questioned on the basis of an unstated assumption: the term was unlikely to have been
used by Jesus ('Luke's Pneumatology and Luke 11.20', p. 295). However, the
blasphemy saying (Mt. 12.31-32; Mk 3.28-29; Lk. 12.10) shows that this assumption is without basis. On the historicity of the blasphemy saying see Marshall, *Commentary on Luke*, pp. 516-19; Dunn, *Jesus and the Spirit*, pp. 49-52; Fitzmyer,
Luke X–XXIV, p. 962; D. Aune, 'Magic in Early Christianity', in *ANRW* II 23.2,
p. 1532. (1) M.E. Boring suggests that the saying was created by the early church: a
reference by Jesus to universal forgiveness was taken up by a Christian prophet in a
situation where Christians were charged with blasphemy because of their claim to
have the Holy Spirit. Boring acknowledges that the reference to blasphemy against
the Spirit is pre-Markan (for it is in all three versions of the saying), but he argues that
it is a creation of the early church nonetheless: 'The saying. . . comes from the
early Palestinian church, not from the historical Jesus, to whom such exaltation of the
spirit, denial of forgiveness on theological grounds, and use of the form "sentences of
holy law" were all foreign' ('The Unforgivable Sin Logion Mark III 28-29/Matt XII
31-32/Luke XII 10: Formal Analysis and History of the Tradition', *NovT* 18 [1976],
pp. 276-77). Thus Boring concludes that only the initial part of the saying (his pre-
Markan reconstruction: ἀφεθήσεται πάντα τὰ ἁμαρτήματα τοῖς υἱοῖς τῶν
ἀνθρώπων; perhaps also ὅσα ἐὰν βλασφημήσωσιν) was uttered by Jesus, the rest
of the saying was created by the early church (p. 277). Note, however, that of the
three reasons Boring cites for rejecting the bulk of the saying as authentic, the first
two are dubious and the third is irrelevant (even if the form of the saying suggests that
it was reformulated by the early church, this does not indicate to what extent the saying reflects the original words of Jesus: Boring suggests that the statement of universal forgiveness is the only authentic part of the saying, but this judgment is not based
on any form-critical criteria). Boring's method and conclusions have been severely
criticized by Hill, *New Testament Prophecy*, pp. 181-85 and Aune, *Prophecy*,
pp. 241-42. (2) Noting that exorcisms were not attributed to the agency of the Spirit
of God in Judaism (see §4.3 below), Leisegang postulates that the original form of
the blasphemy contrasted 'blasphemy against God' with the unforgivable 'blasphemy
against the Holy Name'. A similar saying circulated in hellenistic circles which con-

cates, the 'blasphemy saying' is unintelligible apart from this prior reference to πνεῦμα.[1]

(D) A plausible motive for Matthew's alteration of the text is lacking. Although it has been suggested that Matthew altered the text in order to avoid an anthropomorphism,[2] C.S. Rodd points out that Matthew had no special aversion to anthropomorphic expressions.[3] Indeed, as J. Dunn notes, it is improbable that Matthew would have altered 'finger of God' to 'Spirit of God' in view of the fact that his interest in drawing parallels between Moses and Jesus is much more prominent than his interest in the Spirit.[4]

(E) We need not search long for a plausible motive for Luke's alteration of 'Spirit of God' to 'finger of God':[5] the alteration

---

trasted blasphemy against the earthly Jesus (Son of Man) with blasphemy against the Holy Spirit, the latter a reference to prophetic inspiration. The similarity of the logia led to Mark's replacement of ἅγιον ὄνομα with ἅγιον πνεῦμα. Matthew picked up Mark's altered form of the saying and placed it at the climax of the Beelzebub Controversy alongside the hellenistic saying (thus the two forms of the saying in Mt. 12.31-32). In view of this saying, Matthew altered the original reading of ἅγιον θεοῦ in the expulsion saying (Mt. 12.28) to πνεῦμα θεοῦ. Luke had access to both the hellenistic version and the Jewish version (in its pre-Markan form: ἅγιον ὄνομα) of the 'blasphemy saying'. He picked up the former and placed it in an appropriate setting (12.10); the latter he rejected as unintelligible to his hellenistic audience. This concern for his hellenistic audience also led him to replace the reference to ἅγιον θεοῦ in the expulsion saying (Lk. 11.20) with δακτύλῳ θεοῦ (*Pneuma Hagion*, pp. 107-108). However, Leisegang's hypothesis is unconvincing: (a) there is no evidence for the existence of a pre-Markan form of the saying which referred to 'blasphemy against the Holy Name'; (b) if this form of the text did exist, it is unlikely that Mark would have altered it (Leisegang's scenario at this point is tenuous); (c) the so-called 'hellenistic form' of the saying was undoubtedly in Q, and, as I shall argue, Matthew rather than Luke has retained its original context; (d) Leisegang's hypothesis is based on the unacceptable assumption that a rigid distinction existed between the thought-worlds of Judaism and Hellenism.

1. Note also how in Lk. 12.10, Luke alters the meaning of the blasphemy saying by changing the context. This is possible because the meaning of the blasphemy saying is dependent on the way in which πνεῦμα is employed in the context.

2. Manson, *Teaching of Jesus*, p. 82.

3. In support of his judgment, Rodd cites Mt. 5.34 and 6.4, two anthropomorphisms found only in Matthew ('Spirit or Finger', p. 158).

4. Dunn, *Jesus and the Spirit*, p. 45.

5. The significance of the distinction between the use of 'finger of God' and 'Spirit of God' in this context should not be minimized in view of the fact that the Spirit of God is never portrayed as the agent of exorcism in the OT or in the literature of intertestamental Judaism (see §4.3 below). Indeed, Jewish and Lukan pneumatological perspectives suggest that in this context 'Spirit of God' is not merely a synonym

is consistent with and motivated by his distinctive prophetic pneumatology.[1] We have already noted Luke's reluctance to associate the Spirit directly with activities which do not correspond to strictly prophetic categories (e.g. exorcisms and miracles of healing) and his willingness to alter his sources accordingly, whether by adding (1.35; 4.14) or deleting material (4.18). That Luke's alteration in Lk. 11.20 was indeed motivated by pneumatological concerns is confirmed by Luke's movement of the blasphemy saying from its original context in Q (Mt. 12.32) to Lk. 12.10.[2] To this modification of Q we now turn.

of, nor interchangeable with, 'finger of God' (contra Beasley-Murray, 'Jesus and the Spirit', p. 469; Hamerton-Kelly, 'A Note', pp. 168-69).

1. Yates argues that Luke alters 'Spirit of God' to 'finger of God' because he could not conceive of the Spirit as the subject or agent of an action. According to Yates, for Luke, the Spirit never acts through Jesus (or men filled with the Spirit) directly upon others. The Spirit is an endowment, not an agent ('Luke's Pneumatology and Luke 11.20', pp. 297-99). Yate's description of Luke's pneumatology and his proposed motivation for the alteration is ultimately unconvincing, for Luke depicts the Spirit as an agent on numerous occasions: Lk. 2.27; 4.1 (as we have seen, the significance of Luke's redaction at this point should not be overemphasized); Acts 8.29; 10.19; 11.12; 13.2, 4; 16.6, 7; 20.22, 23, 28. Haya-Prats attempts to distinguish between various layers of tradition in Luke–Acts based on the different ways in which the Spirit is described (whether the Spirit is the agent of an action or simply a complementary cause) and thus he attributes the second part of Acts to a later redactor (*Force*, pp. 73-82; see the summary in Chapter 1 §2.3.2 above). This hypothesis is highly improbable, especially since it does not adequately account for Acts 8.29; 10.29; and 11.12. Thus the majority of the passages cited above cannot be attributed to a later redactor. These passages then establish that Luke can speak of the Spirit acting through men filled with the Spirit directly upon others. In short, the distinction between the Spirit as agent and endowment is not consistently maintained by Luke. The distinction between Luke's pneumatology and that of the primitive church is not found in his reluctance to view the Spirit as an agent (the Spirit is the agent of inspired speech), but rather in his reluctance to portray the Spirit as the agent of miracles of healing and exorcisms.

2. Dunn suggests that Luke altered 'Spirit of God' to 'finger of God' as a result of his 'clear and distinctive Exodus typology' (*Jesus and the Spirit*, p. 46; see also Van Cangh, ' "Par l'esprit" ', pp. 339-41, who attributes the alteration to Luke's Moses typology as well as his distinctive pneumatology). While Luke's interest in drawing parallels between Moses, the leader of Israel's Exodus, and Jesus, who as the first to rise from the dead is the leader of the new Exodus, need not be doubted (so J. Mánek, 'The New Exodus in the Books of Luke', *NovT* 2 [1958], p. 21; see also C.F. Evans, 'The Central Section of St. Luke's Gospel', in *Studies in the Gospels* [1957], pp. 37-53) and may have influenced his use of 'finger of God' in 11.20 (see Exod. 8.19; Deut. 9.10) A. Deissmann in *Light from the Ancient East* [1910], pp. 308-309 notes the use of δάκτυλος τοῦ θεοῦ in a binding charm), it cannot be

4. 'Blasphemy Against the Spirit' and Fearless Witness (Luke 12.10, 12)

4.1. The Context of the Saying in Q

Jesus' saying concerning blasphemy against the Holy Spirit circulated in two variant forms preserved by Mark and Q. A comparison of the synoptic accounts reveals that Matthew records both traditions, inserting the Q saying into the one preserved by Mark (Mt. 12.31-32),[1] while Luke, predominantly following Q, conflates the two accounts:[2]

Matthew 12.31	Mark 3.28-29
Διὰ τοῦτο λέγω ὑμῖν πᾶσα	Ἀμὴν λέγω ὑμῖν ὅτι πάντα
ἁμαρτία καὶ βλασφημία	
ἀφεθήσεται τοῖς ἀνθρώποις,	ἀφεθήσεται τοῖς υἱοῖς τῶν ἀνθρώπων
	τὰ ἁμαρτήματα καὶ αἱ βλασφημίαι
	ὅσα ἐὰν βλασφημήσωσιν·
ἡ δὲ τοῦ πνεύματος βλασφημία	ὃς δ' ἂν βλασφημήσῃ εἰς τὸ πνεῦμα τὸ ἅγιον,
οὐκ ἀφεθήσεται	οὐκ ἔχει ἄφεσιν εἰς τὸν αἰῶνα,
	ἀλλὰ ἔνοχός ἐστιν αἰωνίου ἁμαρτήματος

Matthew 12.32	Luke 12.10
καὶ ὃς ἐὰν εἴπῃ λόγον κατὰ	καὶ πᾶς ὃς ἐρεῖ λόγον εἰς
τοῦ υἱοῦ τοῦ ἀνθρώπου,	τὸν υἱὸν τοῦ ἀνθρώπου,
ἀφεθήσεται αὐτῷ·	ἀφεθήσεται αὐτῷ·
ὃς δ' ἂν εἴπῃ κατὰ τοῦ πνεύματος τοῦ ἁγίου,	τῷ δὲ εἰς τὸ ἅγιον πνεῦμα βλασφημήσαντι
οὐκ ἀφεθήσεται αὐτῷ	οὐκ ἀφεθήσεται.
οὔτε ἐν τούτῳ τῷ αἰῶνι οὔτε ἐν τῷ μέλλοντι.	

The important corollary for this study is that the Q form of the blasphemy saying is preserved, at least in part, by Matthew and Luke;

cited as the primary motivation behind Luke's deletion of 'Spirit of God'. Apart from the fact that Luke appears to show more interest in the Spirit than in an Exodus typology, Dunn's proposed motivation does not account for Luke's movement of the blasphemy saying from its original location in Q (Mt. 12.32) to Lk. 12.10. A plausible motive for Luke's alteration of Lk. 11.20 must also account for this modification of Q as well.

1. The comparison follows that of R. Holst ('Re-examining Mk 3.28f. and Its Parallels', *ZNW* 63 [1972], pp. 122-24), who notes that although the Greek Synopses (Aland; Huck-Greeven) parallel Mt. 12.32 with Mk 3.29, such a view requires a complicated mingling of the Markan and Q material by Matthew. Holst suggests a simpler solution: 'Matthew has simply inserted a Q saying into a Markan saying' (p. 122). Thus the ὃς δ' ἂν of Mk 3.29a is not to be paralleled with Mt. 12.32b. It is merely a linguistic coincidence. Matthew simplifies the Markan saying and, by using the indicative, has eliminated the ὃς δ' ἂν of Mk 3.29a. The ὃς δ' ἂν of Mt. 12.32 reflects the original wording of Q, which Luke has altered by adding πᾶς and changing the subjunctive to the indicative.

2. While Lk. 12.10 is primarily drawn from Q, the εἰς τὸ ἅγιον πνεῦμα βλασφημήσαντι is influenced by Mark. So also Schramm, *Markus-Stoff*, p. 46.

yet in different contexts. In Matthew's Gospel the saying forms part of the Beelzebub Controversy (Mt. 12.22f.), while in Luke the saying is sandwiched between an exhortation to fearlessly confess Christ before men (Lk. 12.2-9) and a promise of the Spirit's assistance in the face of persecution (Lk. 12.11-12). This raises a crucial question: which evangelist has preserved the original context of the Q saying? Three points are relevant.

(A) The blasphemy saying in Lk. 12.10 fits awkwardly into the Lukan context. While the statement in v. 9, 'he who denies me [the Son of Man] before men will be denied before the angels of God', stands in sharp contrast to v. 10, 'everyone who speaks a word against the Son of man will be forgiven',[1] the thematic links between vv. 2-9 and vv. 11-12 are strong.

(B) The context which Matthew provides for the saying is appropriate from a historical and literary perspective: the saying is a fitting response to the charge that Jesus cast out demons by the prince of demons (Mt. 12.24) and there is no reason to doubt its historicity.[2] That Matthew does indeed provide the correct historical context for the saying is confirmed by Mark (Mk 3.22-30).[3] We have already noted that the reference to the Spirit in Mt. 12.28 links the blasphemy saying to that which precedes and makes the passage intelligible.[4] The context is essential for the interpretation of the saying. Indeed, as the analysis of Lk. 12.10 will reveal, if the context of the saying is altered, the meaning is changed. This leads to the third point.

(C) It is unlikely that Q would have preserved the saying in the Lukan context, since this would have altered the original meaning of the saying.

The evidence thus suggests that Luke has taken the blasphemy saying (Lk. 12.10 = Mt. 12.32) from its original context in Q (and Mark) and placed it in another block of Q material (Lk. 12.2-9, 11-12).[5] In

---

1. Marshall, *Commentary on Luke*, p. 510.
2. Dunn, *Jesus and the Spirit*, p. 52.
3. Note C.E.B. Cranfield, who argues that Mark presents the saying in its proper historical context (*The Gospel According to Saint Mark* [5th edn, 1977], p. 139).
4. See Chapter 9 §3, point (C) above.
5. So also A. Loisy, *L'Évangile selon Luc* (1924), p. 344 and Lampe, 'The Holy Spirit', p. 190; contra H. Schürmann ('Zur Traditions- und Redaktionsgeschichte von Mt 10,23', in *Untersuchungen* (1968), pp. 150-55) and Marshall (*Commentary on Luke*, p. 156) who posit that Luke's account represents the original setting of the saying in Q on the basis of the catchword connection between 'Son of Man' (12.9.

order to evaluate the significance of this alteration we must examine the meaning of the saying as it occurs in the context of Q/Mark and Luke.

4.2. The Meaning of the Saying in the Contexts of Q/Mark and Luke
In both Q and Mark the saying forms part of the Beelzebub Controversy (Mt. 12.22-30, 32; Mk 3.20-33). It is recorded as Jesus' response to the charge that he casts out demons by the prince of demons (Mt. 12.24; Mk 3.22). In this context the meaning is clear: to 'blaspheme against the Holy Spirit' is to attribute to the agency of Satan the exorcisms which Jesus performs by the Holy Spirit.[1] The Spirit is thus the means by which Jesus casts out demons.

The saying in its Lukan context has been subject to a variety of interpretations; but scholarly opinion is generally divided between two options, both of which view the saying as directed to the early church.

---

10) and 'Holy Spirit' (12.10, 12). See also Hans-Theo Wrege, 'Zur Rolle des Geisteswortes in frühchristlichen Traditionen (Lc 12,10 parr.)', in *Logia* (1982), pp. 373-77, note esp. p. 374. It has been questioned whether Lk. 12.11-12 should be attributed to Q. It is possible to view Mt. 10.19-20 and Lk. 12.11-12 as separate redactional variants of Mk 13.11, with Lk. 21.14-15 representing another variant form of the saying (either drawn from L or the result of Luke's redaction of Mark) employed in order to avoid repetition. Luke 12.11-12 has been thoroughly reworked by Luke, for Lukanisms abound (note especially εἰσφέρω [Luke, 4×; Acts, 1×; cf. Matthew, 1×; Mark, 0×]; συναγωγή [Luke, 15×; Acts, 19×; cf. Matthew, 9×; Mark, 8×]; ἀπολογέομαι [Luke, 2×; Acts, 6×; cf. Matthew, 0×; Mark, 0×] [so also Jeremias, *Die Sprache*, p. 214]; and δεῖ [Luke, 18×; Acts, 22×; Matthew, 8×; Mark, 6×]); and Mt. 10.19-20 shows a great deal of correspondence with Mk 13.11. However, the phrase μὴ μεριμνήσητε πῶς ἢ τί, which occurs in both Mt. 10.19 and Lk. 12.11 presents a major obstacle to this view. Although the Lukan text is disputed at this point, μὴ μεριμνήσητε πῶς ἢ τί has strong external support. It is possible that D preserves the original reading (μὴ προμεριμνᾶτε πῶς) (favored by E. Klostermann, *Das Lukasevangelium* [1975], p. 135 and G.D. Kilpatrick, 'The Greek New Testament Text of Today and the Textus Receptus', in *The New Testament in Historical and Contemporary Perspective* [1965], p. 192): μεριμνήσητε and ἢ τί can be explained as assimilation to Matthew. However, internal evidence can also be adduced to argue against the originality of D: προμεριμνᾶτε can be explained as assimilation to Mark and the omission of ἢ τί as a scribal refinement (avoiding needless repetition of the phrase) (Metzger, *A Textual Commentary*, p. 160; Marshall, *Commentary on Luke*, p. 520). Therefore the weight of the textual evidence favors μὴ μεριμνήσητε πῶς ἢ τί as the original reading. On this basis I conclude that Lk. 12.11-12 represents a saying from Q (Schulz, *Q*, p. 442; Schürmann, 'Mt 10,23', pp. 150-55) which has been heavily reworked by Luke and conflated with Mk 13.11 by Matthew. Luke probably preserves the original context of Q at this point since the thematic link with 12.2-9 is strong.

1. Cranfield, *Mark*, p. 141.

One views 'blasphemy against the Spirit' as an offense committed by the opponents of the Christian mission. The saying is thus a word of comfort to the disciples: those who reject their message will not be forgiven.[1] The other interpretation sees in 'blasphemy against the Spirit' an offense committed by Christians: it is their failure to heed the voice of the Spirit and bear witness to Christ in the face of persecution.[2]

The second interpretation is to be preferred: Lk. 12.8-9 indicates that the saying should be viewed as a warning to disciples;[3] and the first view fails to account adequately for the Son of Man/Spirit distinction in 12.10.[4] Although it is possible to argue, as does G. Bornkamm, that 'blasphemy against the Son of Man' refers to the pre-Pentecostal denial of Jesus, which, in contrast with 'blasphemy against the Spirit', is forgivable since it is only after Pentecost that the true identity of Jesus is made known,[5] as Marshall notes, there is no distinction of tenses in v. 10 to support this suggestion.[6] The Son of Man/Spirit distinction is easily accounted for by the second interpretation: 'blasphemy against the Son of Man' refers to the unbeliever's rejection of Jesus; 'blasphemy against the Spirit' is committed by the believer who rejects the inspiration of the Spirit and denies Christ in the face of persecution.[7]

1. K. H. Rengstorf, *Das Evangelium nach Lukas* (1937), p. 155; Chevallier, *Souffle*, p. 131.

2. Von Baer, *Der heilige Geist*, p. 138; Schweizer, 'πνεῦμα', p. 407 n. 483; Lampe, 'The Holy Spirit', pp. 190-91; Kjeseth, 'The Spirit of Power', p. 123; and A.A. Trites, *The New Testament Concept of Witness* (1977), p. 182.

3. See Schweizer, who notes that vv. 8f. are 'undoubtedly addressed to disciples' as is the βλασφημεῖν of Acts 26.11 ('πνεῦμα', p. 407).

4. I.H. Marshall, 'Hard Sayings—VII. Lk 12.10', *Th* 67 (1964), p. 65.

5. G. Bornkamm, *Jesus of Nazareth* (1960), p. 212 (n. 1 of ch. 8).

6. Marshall, 'Hard Sayings', p. 66. Marshall suggests that the saying in Luke means essentially what it does in Matthew: 'clear and witting blasphemy against the evident working of the Spirit. . . is contrasted with unwitting blasphemy against the Son of man' (p. 67; see also the similar judgment in *Commentary on Luke*, p. 519). This interpretation, however, does not harmonize well with the context (the phrase εἰς τὸ ἅγιον πνεῦμα βλασφημήσαντι in v. 10 should be interpreted in light of the promise of the Spirit's assistance in the face of persecution in v. 12, particularly since the connection between the Spirit and courageous witness is so prominent in Luke–Acts), renders Luke's alteration of Q meaningless, and, as we have seen, is inconsistent with Luke's distinctive pneumatology.

7. For Luke, 'the denial of the Son of Man before men' in v. 9 corresponds to 'the blasphemy against the Spirit' in v. 10. Barrett, following the lead of patristic interpretations and A. Fridrichsen ('Le péché contre le Saint-Esprit', *RHPR* III [1923], pp. 367-72), argues that 'blasphemy against the Son of man means pre-ban-

This examination of the blasphemy saying has revealed that in Luke's version the Spirit functions in an altogether different manner than in that of Q and Mark. No longer the power to exorcise demons, the Spirit is the means by which the disciples bear witness to Jesus in the face of persecution.[1]

4.3. The Significance of Luke's Alteration of Q

I am now in a position to summarize these findings and assess their significance for Luke's pneumatology. Luke has decisively altered the account of the Beelzebub Controversy in Q (Mt. 12.22-30, 32 = Lk. 11.14-23; 12.10) at two points. He has (1) replaced πνεύματι θεοῦ (Mt. 12.28) with δακτύλῳ θεοῦ (Lk. 11.20) and (2) taken the blasphemy saying (Lk. 12.10 = Mt. 12.32) from its original setting and inserted it into a block of Q material (Lk. 12.2-9, 11-12)[2] containing exhortations to bear witness to the Son of Man. Both alterations are consistent with and motivated by Luke's distinctive prophetic pneumatology. By replacing πνεύματι θεοῦ with δακτύλῳ θεοῦ Luke eliminated a reference which attributed Jesus' exorcisms to the agency of the Spirit. By altering the context of the blasphemy saying Luke was able to alter the function which it ascribed to the Spirit: no longer the power to exorcise demons, in its Lukan context the Spirit is the means by which the disciples courageously bear witness to Jesus in the face of persecution.[3] In short, while the redactors of Q, Mark, and Matthew

---

tismal sin, remitted in baptism; blasphemy against the Holy Spirit means post-baptismal sin, for which there is no remission' (*Gospel Tradition*, p. 106). However, this interpretation fails to account for the Lukan context, which emphasizes bearing witness to Christ in the face of persecution (12.8-9; 11-12). Citing *Didache* 11.7 ('Do not test or examine any prophet who is speaking in the Spirit, for every sin shall be forgiven, but this sin shall not be forgiven'), Barrett does acknowledge that 'in some quarters at least, the Q saying may have had a more specific reference. . . to many Christians (though not to St Paul) one of the supreme manifestations of the Holy Spirit in the Church was the gift of prophecy, allied to that of tongues' (p. 107).

  1. Schweizer, 'The Spirit of Power', p. 266; George, 'L'Esprit Saint', p. 519; Leisegang, *Pneuma Hagion*, p. 108.

  2. Schürmann argues that Mt. 10.23 formed the ending of a block of Q material which undergirds Lk. 12.2-12. Thus, according to Schürmann the Q block was comprised of Lk. 12.2-12 + Mt. 10.23 ('Mt 10,23', pp. 150-55). While I must differ with Schürmann regarding the inclusion of v. 10 in this block of Q material, his hypothesis concerning Mt. 10.23 is not substantially affected by its omission. Although there is no textual evidence to support the existence of Mt. 10.23 in Q, the connections between Mt. 10.23 and Lk. 12.9,11-12 are striking. The hypothesis concerning Mt. 10.23 is an intriguing possibility.

  3. E. Schweizer, 'πνεῦμα', p. 405: 'Luke here removes the saying about the sin against the Holy Ghost from its Marcan context because he cannot possibly see the

attribute Jesus' exorcisms to the agency of the Spirit, Luke avoids the concept by modifying the tradition.

Luke's modification of the Q account of the Beelzebub Controversy highlights the distinctiveness of his prophetic pneumatology in relation to the charismatic pneumatology of the primitive church, and it reveals how closely Luke's understanding of the Spirit conforms to pneumatological perspectives current in Judaism. There is not a single text in the Old Testament or in the Jewish literature of the intertestamental period which attributes the exorcism of demons to the agency of the Spirit.[1]

decisive manifestation of the Spirit in the exorcisms of the pneumatic Jesus'. See also Leisegang, *Pneuma Hagion*, p. 107.

1. Leisegang, *Pneuma Hagion*, p. 101: 'Nirgends ist hier [OT and Jewish intertestamental literature] irgendwo die Rede von einer Dämonenaustreibung durch den heiligen Geist'. The earliest account of an exorcism in the Jewish literature is found in Tob. 6.15-19; 8.2-3, where prayer to God and magical techniques result in the expulsion of the demon, which is bound by the angel Raphael. Josephus records two accounts of the expulsion of demons. In the first, David is said to have driven away evil spirits from Saul with his music (*Ant.* 6.166-8). In the second, a method of exorcism attributed to Solomon, to whom 'God granted knowledge of the art used against demons' (*Ant.* 8.45) is recounted: '[Eleazar] put to the nose of the possessed man a ring which had under its seal one of the roots prescribed by Solomon, and then, as the man smelled it, drew out the demon through his nostrils, and, when the man at once fell down, adjured the demon never to come back into him, speaking Solomon's name and reciting the incantations which he had composed' (*Ant.* 8.46-47; see also PGM 94.17-21). References to the expulsion of demons are more frequent in the rabbinic literature; however, the Spirit is never mentioned in these accounts: see Strack–Billerbeck, *Kommentar*, IV, pp. 501-35. Thus Schweizer writes: 'The fact that the Spirit of God is not mentioned by the Rabbis as one of the many means of driving out demons shows how different was their approach' ('πνεῦμα', p. 398). From the scrolls of Qumran note 1Q GA 20.29. For secondary literature discussing Jewish accounts of exorcisms see Barrett, *Gospel Tradition*, pp. 53-59; Vermes, *Jesus the Jew*, pp. 61-69; D.L. Tiede, *The Charismatic Figure as Miracle Worker* (1972), pp. 187-94; H.C. Kee, *Medicine, Miracle and Magic in New Testament Times* (1986), pp. 21-26; Hull, *Hellenistic Magic and the Synoptic Tradition* (1974), pp. 31, 63-65; Bultmann, *Synoptic Tradition*, pp. 231-32; W. Heitmüller, 'Im Namen Jesu' (1903), pp. 138-54. On Jewish demonology in general see H. van der Loos, *The Miracles of Jesus* (1965), pp. 339-61; W. Foerster, 'δαίμων', *TDNT*, II, pp. 10-16; E. Langston, *Essentials of Demonology. A Study of Jewish and Christian Doctrine: Its Origin and Development* (1949), esp. pp. 35-59, 105-44; O. Böcher, *Dämonenfurcht und Dämonenabwehr: Ein Beitrag zur Vorgeschichte der christlichen Taufe* (1970), pp. 161-319. Early pagan accounts of exorcisms include Lucian, *The Lover of Lies*, 16, 17, 31 and Philostratus, *Life of Apollonius*, 2.4; 3.38; 4.10, 20, 25. Notice also that miracles of healing are not directly associated with the Spirit in the OT (thus the healings performed by Elijah [1 Kgs 17.19-24] and Elisha [2 Kgs 4.33-35, 5.10-15, 6.18-20] are attributed to the intervention of God in response to prayer and various complementary acts, but never

Exorcisms are wrought by God in response to prayer. While a prominent feature of such prayers is the evocation of the divine name,[1] reference to the Spirit of God is strikingly absent.[2]

I have suggested that the reasons for the difference in outlook at this
point between the early church on the one hand and that of Judaism
and Luke on the other are twofold:[3] (1) the primitive church, following in the footsteps of Jesus, broadened the perceived functions of the
Spirit of God so that it was viewed not only in traditional Jewish terms
as the source of prophetic power, but also as miracle-working power.[4]

---

to the agency of the Spirit [see also Gen. 20.17; Num. 12.13-15; 2 Kgs 20.5; Kee,
Medicine, pp. 9-20]) or in intertestamental Judaism. On healing by means of prayer
see *b. Ber.* 34b; *b. Hag.* 3a (see also Strack–Billerbeck, *Kommentar*, II, pp. 2-10;
IV, p. 771).

1. Thus Origen writes: 'It is certain, however, that the Jews trace their genealogy
back to the three fathers, Abraham, Isaac, and Jacob. And the names of these individuals possess such efficacy, when united with the name of God, that not only do those
belonging to the nation employ in their prayers to God, and in the exorcising of
demons, the words, "God of Abraham, and God of Isaac, and God of Jacob" [ὁ
θεὸς Ἀβραάμ, καὶ ὁ θεὸς Ἰσαάκ, καὶ ὁ θεὸς Ἰακὼβ] but so also do almost all
those who occupy themselves with incantations and magical rites' (Contra *Celsus*
4.33 [see also 5.45; Justin Martyr, *Dialogue with Trypho*, 85.3], trans. F. Crombie,
Origen contra Celsum, in ANCL 23; Greek text from Migne, *Patrologia Graec-Lat.*).
Origen's remarks find confirmation in the magical papyri: see for example PGM
4.1180f., 1220f., 1230f., 3015f., 3070f.; 5.115f., 475f. (texts from *Papyri Graecae
Magicae: Die griechischen Zauberpapyri*, ed. K. Preisendanz [1928]). Note also
PGM 3.120 where entreaty to the gods is said to be made in 'the Hebrew tongue'. On
the use of the divine name in prayer for the expulsion of demons and other miraculous
acts see the sources cited in the note above, especially Heitmüller, 'Im Namen Jesu',
pp. 138-54; Hull, *Hellenistic Magic*, p. 31. Note also F. Preisigke, 'Die Gotteskraft
der frühchristlichen Zeit' (1922), in *Der Wunderbegriff im Neuen Testament* (1980),
pp. 228f.; M. Simon, *Verus Israel* (1986), pp. 343-44; and D. Aune, 'Magic',
pp. 1545-49.

2. A text from the 'Great Paris Magical Papyrus' records a prayer of this kind
which, having been influenced by Christian practice, does include a reference to the
Spirit. In order to drive out demons one is to stand behind the possessed person
(olive branches are to be laid in front of him) and say over his head: 'Hail, God of
Abraham; hail, God of Isaac; hail, God of Jacob; Jesus Chrestos, the Holy Spirit, the
Son of the Father, who is above the Seven, who is within the Seven. Bring Iao
Sabaoth; may your power issue forth from him, NN, until you drive away this
unclean daimon Satan, who is in him' (PGM 4.1230f.; ET from H.D. Betz (ed.), *The
Greek Magical Papyri in Translation: Including the Demotic Spells* [1986]). Note also
P5a; P5b; P10; P12; and P15 in *Papyri Graecae Magicae*, II (ed. K. Preisendanz;
1931).

3. See Chapter 6 §4 above.

4. The attitude of Jesus and the primitive church toward miracles remains essentially Jewish. In *Medicine, Miracle and Magic in New Testament Times*, Kee argues

Thus the Spirit was envisioned as the agent of exorcism. (2) Luke, on the other hand, retained the traditional Jewish understanding of the Spirit as the Spirit of prophecy and, with the term δύναμις, incorporated a hellenistic mode of expression to speak of miracle-working power.[1] Therefore, while δύναμις may be mediated through

persuasively against the claims that (1) the miracles stories were 'developed by the early Christians as they moved out into the hellenistic world and away from the original Jewish matrix' (*Medicine*, pp. 75-79; contra M. Dibelius, *From Tradition to Gospel* [1971], pp. 70-104, esp. pp. 99-101 and Bultmann, *Synoptic Tradition*, pp. 209-44, esp. pp. 239-41) and (2) that the miracles of Jesus show strong affinities to hellenistic magic (*Medicine*, pp. 112-21; contra Morton Smith, *Jesus the Magician* [1978] and Hull, *Hellenistic Magic*). Kee concludes: 'The role of Jesus as healer was by no means an accommodation of an itinerant preacher-prophet to hellenistic culture, but was in direct continuity with the Old Testament prophetic understanding of what God was going to do in the New Age, for the salvation of his people and for the healing of the nations'. See also Vermes, *Jesus the Jew*, pp. 20-26, 58-82 and Aune, 'Magic', pp. 1507-57. While Aune views magic and religion as inextricably intertwined, he concludes that the title of 'messianic prophet' rather than 'magician' is most appropriate to Jesus (p. 1539). Jesus' unique understanding of the Spirit of God as the means by which he cast out demons may be a reflection of his interpretation of Isa. 61.1-2.

1. Hull argues persuasively that the background for Luke's usage of δύναμις is not found in Jewish conceptions of prophetic power, but rather in the hellenistic idea of magical *mana* (*Hellenistic Magic*, pp. 105-14). It is significant that for Luke ' "power" is not a metaphor but is that reality which carries the actual potency of the spirit world into our world' (p. 105). O. Schmitz ('Der Begriff δύναμις bei Paulus', in *Festgabe für Adolf Deissmann* [1927], pp. 157-58) distinguishes between two conceptions of δύναμις: (1) the hellenistic view (common in Diaspora Judaism) of δύναμις as a magical substance; and (2) the traditional Jewish (OT) view of 'power' as an attribute of the living God who acts in history to accomplish his will. Whereas the Hellenist (Jew or otherwise) understood δύναμις as a concrete entity with independent existence, for the Jew whose perspective was determined more exclusively by the OT, δύναμις was a metaphor for divine action and inseparable from God. While Matthew and Mark generally reflect the traditional Jewish view of 'power', (there is a notable exception: Mk 5.30), the hellenistic view is common to Luke–Acts (see Mk 5.30 = Lk. 8.46, Lk. 6.19; Acts 5.15; 19.12). According to Schmitz, Paul's usage of δύναμις reflects little hellenistic influence (p. 160). Schmitz asserts that Paul was able to emphasize the non-substantial and traditional Jewish character of δύναμις by associating it with πνεῦμα. Although δύναμις invades the objective world, it (as the link with Spirit indicates) always designates divine activity and is never separated from God (p. 161). In contrast to Paul, Luke distinguishes more clearly between δύναμις and πνεῦμα. Thus, while Matthew, Mark, and Paul reflect the traditional Jewish understanding of δύναμις, Luke's usage of the term is more distinctively hellenistic. On Luke's use of δύναμις see also Kee, *Medicine*, p. 115 and Grundmann, 'δύναμαι', pp. 300-301.

πνεῦμα (as in Lk. 4.14), the former rather than the latter is the divine agent by which exorcisms are wrought.[1]

5. *The Pre-Ascension Promise (Luke 24.49; Acts 1.4-5, 8)*

Luke 24.47-49 and Acts 1.4-8 present parallel accounts of Jesus' pre-ascension commission to the disciples.[2] Both accounts are decidedly Lukan in style,[3] and together they provide an important thematic link which unites Luke's two-volume work.[4] These facts indicate that Luke has carefully crafted both accounts in order to further his literary and theological aims. Nevertheless, the extent of Luke's literary activity at this point should not be overestimated.[5] A comparison with Mt. 28.16-30 and Jn 20.21-23 suggests that these Lukan pericopes are based on a

---

Although Preisigke correctly describes the δύναμις which heals the woman in Lk. 8.43f. as 'stoffliche Gotteskraft', it is difficult to accept his judgment that the πνεῦμα which fills the Christian or which is received through the laying on of hands is a 'göttliche Fluidum' ('Die Gotteskraft der frühchristlichen Zeit', pp. 210-47). The background for these (and other similar) NT statements concerning the πνεῦμα of God is not to be found in the Egyptian cult of Amon-Re (pp. 214f.), but rather in the Scriptures of Judaism. The language is thus metaphorical.

1. See Lk. 4.33-37 = Mk 1.23-28; Lk. 6.17-20a = Mk 3.7-13a; Lk. 9.1 = Mk 6.7; Acts 10.38. It is significant that the references to δύναμις in Lk. 4.36, 6.19, 9.1 (and I suspect Acts 10.38) are redactional.

2. J.F. Maile, 'The Ascension in Luke–Acts', *TB* 37 (1986), p. 39.

3. J. Kremer, *Pfingstbericht*, p. 180 and 'Die Voraussagen des Pfingstgeschehens in Apg 1,4-5 und 8: Ein Beitrag zur Deutung des Pfingstberichts' in *Die Zeit Jesu* (1970), pp. 146-47; U. Wilckens, *Die Missionsreden der Apostelgeschichte* (3rd edn, 1974), p. 56; R.J. Dillon, *From Eye-Witness to Ministers of the Word: Tradition and Composition in Luke 24* (1978), p. 220; R.H. Fuller, *The Formation of the Resurrection Narratives* (1972), pp. 117-19; J. Finegan, *Die Überlieferung der Leidens- und Auferstehungsgeschichte Jesu* (1934), p. 91 n. 5; G. Lohfink, *Die Himmelfahrt Jesu: Untersuchungen zu den Himmelfahrts- und Erhöhungstexten bei Lukas* (1971), p. 276; Fitzmyer, *Luke X–XXIV*, pp. 1578-82; J. Roloff, *Die Apostelgeschichte* (1981), p. 17. Particularly important for this inquiry is the phrase ἡ ἐπαγγελία τοῦ πατρός (Lk. 24.49; Acts 1.4), which, as Jeremias notes (*Die Sprache*, p. 322), is Lukan. The term ἐπαγγελία is characteristic of Luke (Luke, 1×; Acts, 8×; cf. Matthew, 0×; Mark, 0×; John, 0×) and the repetition of the phrase in Lk. 24.49 and Acts 1.4 confirms its Lukan pedigree. Note also the Lukan collocation of πνεῦμα and δύναμις (implicit in Lk. 24.49; explicit in Acts 1.8).

4. Jesus' pre-ascension commission to the disciples forms the end of Luke's Gospel and the beginning of Acts. This literary overlapping is clearly intended to emphasize the continuity between the Gospel and Acts. See Talbert, *Literary Patterns*, p. 60.

5. For example see the unwarranted conclusion of Bultmann, *Synoptic Tradition*, p. 286, 'vv. 44-49 is obviously in its entirety a literary production of Luke'.

core of traditional material.[1] The specific content of this traditional material and the extent to which it has influenced Luke's account is exceedingly difficult, if not impossible, to ascertain. For my purposes it will be sufficient to point out the significance of these parallel accounts for Luke's literary and theological program.

5.1. *The Renewal of 'Israel's' Prophetic Calling to the World*

Jesus' commission to the disciples recorded in Lk. 24.47-49 is set in the broader context of his explication of Scripture (24.44-49). After a preliminary statement concerning the necessary fulfillment of all scriptural prophecies pertaining to himself (24.44), Jesus explains to the disciples that his passion and resurrection were prophesied in Scripture and thus essential elements of the divine plan (24.46). In v. 47 Jesus indicates that the mandate of scriptural prophecy includes the future mission of the church: καὶ κηρυχθῆναι ἐπὶ τῷ ὀνόματι αὐτοῦ μετάνοιαν εἰς ἄφεσιν ἁμαρτιῶν εἰς πάντα τὰ ἔθνη— ἀρξάμενοι ἀπὸ Ἰερουσαλήμ (24.47).[2] The scriptural basis for this assertion is probably Isa. 49.6, which is cited in Paul's sermon in Pisidian Antioch (Acts 13.47) and alluded to elsewhere in Luke–Acts (Lk. 2.32; Acts 1.8; 26.23; perhaps 28.28).[3] By accepting the vocation of Israel to be a prophet commissioned to bring 'light to the nations' and 'salvation to the ends of the earth' (Isa. 49.6),[4] the disciples actively participate in the fulfillment of Old Testament prophecy.

The conceptual background of Isa. 49.6 is also prominent in the parallel version of the commission recorded in Acts 1.4-8. Jesus'

---

1. Marshall, *Commentary on Luke*, pp. 903-904; V. Taylor, *The Passion Narrative of St Luke: A Critical and Historical Investigation* (1972), pp. 112-14.
2. J. Wellhausen (*Das Evangelium Lucae* [1904], pp. 140-41) argues that κηρυχθῆναι should be treated as a Hebrew infinitive with the force of a jussive and thus interpreted as a command from Jesus independent of scriptural prophecy. However, this view is grammatically unsound (citing J.M. Creed, *St. Luke*, p. 301, Marshall notes that 'this interpretation would require the reading ἐπὶ τῷ ὀνόματί μου' [*Commentary on Luke*, p. 906]) and, in view of Luke's tendency to anchor the mission to the Gentiles in OT prophecy (especially Isa. 49.6; see Lk. 2.29-35, Acts 13.47, 26:23), it is highly improbable.
3. See D.L. Tiede, 'The Exaltation of Jesus', pp. 285-86. See also Franklin, *Christ the Lord*, pp. 120-21.
4. The task outlined in Lk. 24.47 is described as the proclamation of 'repentance' (μετάνοιαν). J.-C. Basset notes that this term is 'cher aux prophètes' ('Dernières paroles du ressuscité et mission de l'eglise aujourd'hui (à propos de Mt 28, 18-20 et parallèles)', *RTP* 114 [1982], p. 362). According to Luke, John (Lk. 3.3), Jesus (Lk. 5.32), and the disciples all proclaim a message of 'repentance'.

commission is again set in the context of instruction (Acts 1.2f.),[1] although the instruction is not explicitly tied to Scripture as in Lk. 24.44f. His command to wait in Jerusalem for ἡ ἐπαγγελία τοῦ πατρός (Acts 1.4) is followed by a question from the disciples: 'Lord, are you at this time going to restore the Kingdom to Israel?' The question is a literary device which anticipates possible misconceptions and thus calls for further clarification.[2] Jesus' response is intended to challenge the disciples' narrow expectation of a restoration limited to the faithful of Israel:[3] καὶ ἔσεσθέ μου μάρτυρες... ἕως ἐσχάτου τῆς γῆς (Acts 1.8; cf. Isa. 49.6). Echoing the words and concepts of Isa. 49.6,[4] Jesus declares that God's promises are indeed being fulfilled; however, 'the promise of God's reign is not simply the restoration of the preserved of Israel, but the renewal of the vocation of Israel to be a light to the nations to the ends of the earth'.[5]

5.2. ἡ ἐπαγγελία τοῦ πατρός *(Luke 24.49; Acts 1.4)*

The disciples are able to assume this collective prophetic vocation to which they have been called only after they have received ἡ ἐπαγγελία τοῦ πατρός. Luke makes the point in both pre-ascension accounts by recording Jesus' command to the disciples to remain in Jerusalem until they have received ἡ ἐπαγγελία τοῦ πατρός (Lk. 24.49; Acts 1.4). The reason for the delay is made explicit: the reception of 'the promise' will result in the disciples being 'clothed with power from on

---

1. The syntax of Acts 1.2 is ambiguous: διὰ πνεύματος ἁγίου may qualify either ἐντειλάμενος τοῖς ἀποστόλοις or οὓς ἐξελέξατο. Haenchen opts for the latter alternative, 'This is Luke's way of making the Apostles' authority plain to the reader' (*Acts*, p. 139). But in view of the context, which centers on the teaching of Jesus, and Luke's emphasis on the Spirit as the source of inspired speech, the former view is more probable (see Shelton, 'Filled with the Holy Spirit', pp. 434-37 and Guthrie, *New Testament Theology*, p. 536 n. 68). In either case the Spirit functions as the source of prophetic inspiration.

2. As D. Hill ('The Spirit and the Church's Witness: Observations on Acts 1:6-8', *IBS* 6 [1984], pp. 16-17) notes, this literary device is found frequently in Luke–Acts: Lk. 1.34; 7.23; 22.24; Acts 2.37; 7.1; 17.19.

3. Jesus' response deals with the problem of 'the eschatological near-expectation', but, as Haenchen notes, this problem is linked 'with a second problem: "Is the kingdom restricted to Israel?"' (*Acts*, p. 143).

4. The phrase ἕως ἐσχάτου τῆς γῆς occurs in Isa. 8.9; 48.20; 49.6; 62.11; cf. 45.22 (LXX). The link between Acts 1.8 and Isa. 49.6 is affirmed by D. Seccombe, 'Luke and Isaiah', *NTS* 27 (1981), pp. 258-59 and Tiede, *Prophecy*, pp. 59-60, 'The Exaltation of Jesus', p. 285.

5. Tiede, 'The Exaltation of Jesus', p. 286.

high' and thus enable them to become effective 'witnesses' (Lk. 24.48-49;[1] Acts 1.8).[2]

---

1. In Lk. 24.49 ἀποστέλλω should be understood as a futuristic present (Blass and Debrunner, *A Greek Grammar*, p. 168). The force of δὲ is continuative rather than adversative.

2. Von Baer notes the parallels between the Spirit's anointing of Jesus at the Jordan and the promise of the Spirit which enables the disciples to bear witness for Christ *(Der heilige Geist*, p. 85). Haya-Prats also recognizes that Jesus was empowered for his mission through his reception of the Spirit at the Jordan. However, Haya-Prats distinguishes between this 'historique/kérygmatic' work of the Spirit at the Jordan and the promise of the Spirit which Jesus received at his exaltation and poured out upon the disciples on the day of Pentecost (Acts 2.33). The 'promise' is principally an anticipation of the fullness of salvation (the 'eschatologique/fruitif' work of the Spirit) rather than an enduement of power *(Force*, p. 174-75; see Chapter 1 §2.3.2 above). Haya-Prats interpretation of the 'promise' is vulnerable at a number of points. (1) Above all, Haya-Prats's interpretation fails to do justice to Lk. 24.49 and Acts 1.8: the 'promise' is an endowment of power which enables the disciples to become effective witnesses. Haya-Prats's attempt to limit this aspect of the promise to the apostles cannot be substantiated exegetically. The Pentecostal bestowal of the Spirit is not limited to the apostles (the πάντες of Acts 2.4 refers to the 120 of the preceding verses) and elsewhere Luke does not limit the 'historique/ kérygmatic' dimension of the Spirit to the apostles (e.g. Stephen, Acts 6.5, 8f.; Philip, Acts 6.3, 8.5f.; Apollos, Acts 18.25). The evidence suggests that 'Luke regards the Eleven as representing the whole community when the promise is made to them' (R.N. Flew, *Jesus and His Church* [1960], pp. 106-107). (2) Haya-Prats's interpretation also fails to adequately account for the striking parallels which exist between the descent of the Spirit on Jesus at the Jordan and on the disciples at Pentecost. That Pentecost is for the disciples what the Jordan was for Jesus can hardly be questioned (for the literary parallels see Talbert, *Literary Patterns*, p. 16). Particularly striking is the fact that Luke interprets the Jordan and Pentecost events with reference to OT texts, both of which (Isa. 61.1-2, cf. Targum of Isa. 61.1-2 and Joel 3.1f.) describe the prophetic activity of the Spirit. These two objections might also be raised against Turner's attempt to distinguish between Jesus' anointing at the Jordan and that of the disciples on the day of Pentecost. For Turner, Jesus' reception of the Spirit at his exaltation (Acts 2.38) signals the beginning of a new nexus of the Spirit's activity. The Pentecostal Spirit is understood by Luke to be the organ of revelation between God and man. No longer is the Spirit primarily the power to bear witness; it is now the *sine qua non* of Christian existence. Whereas Jesus received the Spirit principally for others, at Pentecost the disciples receive the Spirit largely for themselves (see 'Luke and the Spirit', pp. 182-84 and Chapter 1 §2.3.3 above). In a manner similar to Haya-Prats, Turner has failed to do justice to the description of the 'promise' from Luke's own hand and the striking literary parallels which link the Jordan event with Pentecost. Indeed, only by ignoring Lk. 24.49 and Acts 1.8 can Haya-Prats and Turner escape the force of the thesis put forward by M.A. Chevallier: 'La communication de l'Esprit saint au peuple eschatologique est interprétée chez Luc comme la source d'un témoignage en vue de donner à l'Eglise sa dimension

Luke identifies this source of prophetic power, ἡ ἐπαγγελία τοῦ πατρός, with the gift of the Spirit which was initially bestowed upon the disciples at Pentecost. (1) A comparison of Lk. 24.48-9 with Acts 1.8 reveals that ἡ ἐπαγγελία τοῦ πατρός (Lk. 24.49) and ἅγιον πνεῦμα (Acts 1.8) are used interchangeably to describe the source of power which would enable the disciples to fulfill their role as 'witnesses' (μάρτυρες). (2) In Acts 1.4-5 ἡ ἐπαγγελία τοῦ πατρός is presented as the fulfillment of John's prophecy concerning the messianic deluge of the Spirit. We have already noted that, according to Luke, John's prophecy of a messianic deluge of the Spirit which would sift and separate the just from the unjust found its initial fulfillment in the Pentecostal bestowal of the Spirit and the proclamation which it inspired.[1] That Luke views Pentecost (Acts 2.4) as the fulfillment of the Baptist's prophecy follows from the temporal phrase in Acts 1.5 (οὐ μετὰ πολλὰς ταύτας ἡμέρας).[2] (3) Acts 2.33 states what is implicit in the narrative: at Pentecost (Acts 2.4) Jesus poured out on the disciples the ἐπαγγελίαν τοῦ πνεύματος τοῦ ἁγίου λαβὼν παρὰ τοῦ πατρός.

Does Luke provide any clues concerning why he chooses to speak of the gift of the Spirit as ἡ ἐπαγγελία τοῦ πατρός? We have noted that Luke views the gift of the Spirit given to the disciples at Pentecost as a fulfillment of John's prophecy concerning the messianic deluge of the Spirit, but it is unlikely that this prophecy would have prompted Luke to speak of the gift as 'the promise of the Father'.

In Acts 1.4 Jesus indicates that he has spoken of 'the promise of the Father' to the disciples on a prior occasion, but this ambiguous reference offers little by way of explanation concerning the origin of the term. Since Lk. 24.49 and Acts 1.4 record the same address from different perspectives,[3] Jesus' remark must refer to one of two prior statements regarding the Spirit (if recorded by Luke): Lk. 11.13 or 12.12. Neither passage connects the promise of the Spirit to an Old

---

universelle' ('Luc et l'Esprit Saint à la Mémoire du P. Augustin George (1915–1977)', *RSR* 56 [1982], p. 5).

1. See Chapter 7 §3 above. Kremer correctly notes that 'durch diese "Taufe" [in the Spirit, Acts 1.5] werden die Jünger für ihre Aufgabe in der Endzeit gerüstet. Auf die sonst in der Urkirche mit dem Begriff "Taufe" verbundenen Wirkungen des Geistempfangs (z.B. Neuschöpfung, Heiligung, Gotteskindschaft, Unterpfand der ewigen Herrlichkeit) wird in keiner Weise hingewiesen' (*Pfingstbericht*, p. 190; cf. 'Die Voraussagen', pp. 167-68).

2. Schneider, *Die Apostelgeschichte*, I, p. 201.

3. I.H. Marshall, 'The Significance of Pentecost', *SJT* 30 (1977), p. 350.

Testament text, although Lk. 11.13 affirms that the gift of the Spirit is given by the Father.

The only Old Testament text cited by Luke which adequately accounts for his use of the term 'the promise of the Father' with reference to the gift of the Spirit is Joel 3.1-5a (LXX; Acts 2.17-21).[1] Several factors suggest that this passage has indeed motivated Luke's usage of the term. First, we have noted that according to Luke 'the promise of the Father' was received by the disciples at Pentecost (Acts 2.4, 33). Luke interprets this event in light of Joel 3.1f. (Acts 2.17-21).[2] Second, Luke's desire to emphasize that the promise comes from the Father explains his insertion of λέγει ὁ θεός into the Joel text in Acts 2.17. Third, Peter's speech in Acts 2 concludes with a call to repent, be baptized, and receive the gift of the Spirit (Acts 2.38). In his closing words, Peter affirms that ὑμῖν γάρ ἐστιν ἡ ἐπαγγελία καί... ὅσους ἂν προσκαλέσηται κύριος ὁ θεὸς ἡμῶν (Acts 2.39). The final refrain echoes the words of Joel 3.5a (quoted in Acts 2.21), thus the promise is tied linguistically and contextually to the Joel citation. Although the ἐπαγγελία of Acts 2.39 includes both the Spirit of prophecy (Joel 3.1; Acts 2.17) and salvation (Joel 3.5a; Acts 2.21), whereas ἡ ἐπαγγελία τοῦ πατρός in Lk. 24.49 and Acts 1.4; 2.33 refers exclusively to the gift of the Spirit of prophecy, the connection to the Joel citation is clear. In Acts 2.39 Luke extends the range of the promise envisioned to include the promise of salvation offered in Joel 3.5 (as well as the promise of the Spirit of prophecy in Joel 3.1) because the audience addressed are not disciples. Consistent with Lk. 24.49, Acts 1.4, and 2.33, the promised gift of the Spirit in Acts 2.38 refers to the promise of Joel 3.1, and thus it is a promise of prophetic enabling granted to the repentant.[3] The promise of Acts 2.39, like the

1. E. Lohse, 'Die Bedeutung des Pfingstberichtes im Rahmen des lukanischen Geschichtswerkes', in *Die Einheit des Neuen Testaments* (1973), p. 188.

2. This judgment remains valid even if Luke's account of Peter's speech is heavily dependent on traditional material. It is quite possible, as Talbert suggests, that Luke has designed his narrative so that Jesus' teaching concerning the Father's promise of the Spirit (Lk. 24.49; Acts 1.4) parallels Peter's interpretation of the Pentecost event in light of Joel 3.1 (Acts 2.16-21). Talbert suggests that this literary pattern was produced in order 'to ground the disciples' teaching in the instruction of Jesus' (*Literary Patterns*, p. 97). While this suggestion may be accurate, it should be noted that it does not further our knowledge concerning the extent to which the sayings reflect traditional material or represent historical events.

3. Lake and Cadbury, *The Beginnings of Christianity*, IV, p. 26. P. Tachau correctly notes that 'bei Paulus kennzeichnet der Geist die gesamte Existenz des Christen und beschreibt das neue Sein der Gläubigen (vgl. etwa Röm 8,11; Gal 5,25), bei Lukas ist er eine zusätzliche Gabe (vgl. Apg. 2,38), die allerdings Voraussetzung für

promise of Jesus in Acts 1.8, points beyond 'the restoration of the preserved of Israel': salvation is offered (Joel 3.5), but the promise includes the renewal of Israel's prophetic vocation (Joel 3.1).[1]

This brief summary of the relevant passages has revealed that ἡ ἐπαγγελία τοῦ πατρός (Lk. 24.49, Acts 1.4; cf. 2.33) and ἡ ἐπαγγελία with reference to the Spirit (Acts 2.38f.) find their origin in Joel 3.1 (LXX): ἐκχεῶ ἀπὸ τοῦ πνεύματός μου ἐπὶ πᾶσαν σάρκα, καὶ προφητεύσουσιν. J. Dunn's attempt to interpret the Lukan promise of the Spirit (Lk. 24.49; Acts 1.4; 2.33, 38f.) against the backdrop of Gen. 17.7-10, Ezek. 36.25f., and Jer. 31.33f. ignores the evidence from Luke's own hand, and thus his description of the gift of the Spirit as 'the means whereby men enter into the blessings of Abraham' and 'the essence and embodiment of the new covenant' must be questioned.[2] For Luke the promise with reference to the Spirit refers to the gift of the Spirit of prophecy promised in Joel 3.1. This promise, which is initially fulfilled at Pentecost (Acts 2.4), mediates the δύναμις necessary for the disciples to take up their prophetic vocation. It is important to note that Luke's use of δύναμις in Lk. 24.49 and Acts 1.8 is consistent with my description of his usage elsewhere: δύναμις is mediated by the Spirit but not equivalent to it; and, in conjunction with the Spirit, δύναμις designates the ability to perform a broad range of activities (inspired speech and miracles of healing/exorcisms).[3]

die Verkündigung der Kirche ist' ('Die Pfingstgeschichte nach Lukas. Exegetische Überlegungen zu Apg. 2,1-13', *EE* 29 [1977], p. 101).

1. Kjeseth, 'The Spirit of Power', p. 134, 'The gift of the spirit of power is given, not to restore the Kingdom to Israel, but to send out witnesses to the end of the earth'.

2. Dunn, *Holy Spirit*, pp. 47-48. Lampe also interprets the Lukan promise of the Spirit against the backdrop of 'many passages of the Old Testament in which the action of the Spirit is portrayed under the imagery of cleansing, healing and life-giving water. . .' ('The Holy Spirit', p. 162; cf. *God as Spirit*, p. 65). So also F.F. Bruce, 'The Holy Spirit in the Acts of the Apostles', *Int* 27 (1973), pp. 170-71; *The Acts of the Apostles: The Greek Text with Introduction and Commentary* (1951), p. 98; Kaiser, 'The Promise of God', p. 120; Hull, *Acts*, pp. 42, 45; and D. Carson, *Showing the Spirit* (1987), pp. 153-54. By way of contrast note the conclusion of Kremer: 'Aus der Verwendung des Ausdrucks "Verheißung" folgt aber nicht, daß Lukas Pfingsten als die Erfüllung der im Alten Bund gegebenen Verheißung des Neuen Bundes und somit das Pfingstgeschehen als den neuen Bundesschluß verstanden hat' (*Pfingstbericht*, p. 182). See also the critique of Dunn's position put forward by Turner, 'Luke and the Spirit', pp. 148-159 and the relevant comments of Stronstrad, *Charismatic Theology*, pp. 56-57.

3. L. O'Reilly, *Word and Sign in the Acts of the Apostles* (1987), pp. 16-17. See also Chapter 6 §3 above.

Chapter 10

THE DISCIPLES AND THE SPIRIT:
THE PROPHETIC GIFT (ACTS 2)

The importance of Pentecost for this inquiry into Luke's distinctive
pneumatology can hardly be exaggerated. Strategically placed at the
outset of his second volume, Luke's account of the Pentecostal
bestowal of the Spirit occupies a central place in his theological plan[1]
and thus serves as an interpretative key to Luke's understanding of the
Spirit's work in the church.

In spite of its obvious importance for Luke's pneumatology and
numerous studies on the topic, considerable disagreement continues to
exist concerning the significance which Luke attaches to the Pentecostal
gift. In the introductory survey we noted two particularly significant
interpretations of the Pentecostal gift. First, J. Dunn speaks for many
when he asserts that the Pentecostal bestowal of the Spirit is the means
by which the disciples enter into the new age and experience the
blessings of the new covenant.[2] Thus Dunn insists that the disciples'
reception of the Spirit at Pentecost 'is primarily initiatory, and only
secondarily an empowering'.[3] Second, while denying that the Pentecostal gift of the Spirit mediates the blessings of the new covenant *in
toto*, G. Haya-Prats and M. Turner, albeit in different ways, also argue
that the gift of the Spirit is not primarily an endowment of power for
mission.[4] According to Haya-Prats the Spirit is received by the disciples at Pentecost principally as an anticipation of the fullness of salva-

---

1. W. Grundmann, 'Der Pfingstbericht der Apostelgeschichte in seinem theologischen Sinn', in *Studia Evangelica, II* (1964), p. 587; Kremer, *Pfingstbericht*, p. 213;
Dörner, *Das Heil Gottes*, p. 139.
2. See Dunn, *Holy Spirit*, pp. 38-54; Lampe, 'The Holy Spirit', p. 162; cf. *God
as Spirit*, p. 65; Büchsel, *Der Geist Gottes*, pp. 234-35; Bruce, 'The Holy Spirit',
pp. 170-72; F.D. Bruner, *A Theology of the Holy Spirit: The Pentecostal Experience
and the New Testament Witness* (1970), p. 214.
3. Dunn, *Holy Spirit*, p. 54.
4. See Chapter 1 §2.3.2 and §2.3.3 above.

tion.[1] For Turner the Pentecostal gift is, above all, the organ of revelation to each disciple and, as such, it is the *sine qua non* of Christian
existence.[2] Whereas Jesus received the Spirit for others, at Pentecost
the disciples receive the Spirit largely for themselves.[3]

My own research points to conclusions which are decidedly different
from those presented above. In attempting to put forth the thesis that
Luke consistently portrays the Spirit as the source of prophetic activity
(inspiring speech and granting special insight), I have thus far analysed
several passages which are crucial for an accurate assessment of Luke's
understanding of the Pentecostal bestowal of the Spirit. I have argued
that Luke interprets the sifting and separating activity of the Spirit of
which John prophesied (Lk. 3.16) to be accomplished in the Spirit-
directed and Spirit-empowered mission of the church. Thus John's
prophecy finds its initial fulfillment in the Pentecostal bestowal of the
Spirit. I have also asserted that the Spirit came upon Jesus at the Jordan
in order to equip him for his messianic task (Lk. 3.22; 4.18f.). The
striking parallels between Jesus' pneumatic anointing at the Jordan and
that of the disciples at Pentecost suggest that Luke interpreted the latter
event in light of the former: Pentecost was for the disciples what the
Jordan was for Jesus.[4] The logical corollary is that at Pentecost the
Spirit came upon the disciples in order to enable them to be effective
witnesses. Finally, I have affirmed that for Luke the 'promise' with
reference to the Spirit (Lk. 24.49; Acts 1.4, 2.33, 38f.) refers to the
gift of the Spirit of prophecy promised by Joel. This 'promise', ini-

---

1. Haya-Prats, *Force*, pp. 173-76, 185-89.
2. Turner, 'Luke and the Spirit', pp. 159 and 'Spiritual Gifts', pp. 40-41.
3. 'Luke and the Spirit', pp. 182-84.
4. Talbert lists four literary features which Luke duplicates in order to tie Jesus'
anointing at the Jordan with that of the disciples at Pentecost: (1) both Jesus and the
disciples are praying; (2) both accounts place the descent of the Spirit after prayer; (3)
both accounts record a physical manifestation of the Spirit; (4) in both accounts the
respective ministries of Jesus and the disciples begin with a sermon which is thematic
of what follows, appeals to the fulfillment of prophecy, and speaks of the rejection of
Jesus (*Literary Patterns*, p. 16). See also Hill, *New Testament Prophecy*, p. 95;
Minear, *To Heal*, p. 136; Stronstad, *Charismatic Theology*, pp. 51-52; I. de la Potterie, 'L'onction du Christ', *NRT* 80 (1958), p. 238; von Baer, *Der heilige Geist*,
p. 85; F. Hahn, 'Sendung des Geistes: Sendung der Jünger', in *Universales Christentum angesichts einer pluralen Welt* (1976), p. 93; O'Reilly, *Word and Sign*,
p. 30; Dunn, *Holy Spirit*, p. 40; W. Russell, 'The Anointing with the Holy Spirit in
Luke–Acts', *TJ* ns 7 (1986), pp. 47-63; and Chapter 8 §2.1 above. On the connections between the Nazareth pericope (Lk. 4.16f.) and the Pentecost account (Acts 2)
see Chapter 8 §3 above.

tially fulfilled at Pentecost, enables the disciples to take up the prophetic vocation to the nations to which they have been called.

The picture which emerges from my conclusions outlined above is remarkably clear: according to Luke, the Spirit, understood to be the source of prophetic activity, came upon the disciples at Pentecost in order to equip them for their prophetic vocation (i.e. for their role as 'witnesses'). The disciples receive the Spirit, not as the source of cleansing and a new ability to keep the law, not as a foretaste of the salvation to come, nor as the essential bond by which they (each individual) are linked to God; indeed, not primarily for themselves. Rather, as the driving force behind their witness to Christ, the disciples receive the Spirit for others.[1] If my exegesis is correct, the gift of the Spirit is principally an endowment of power for mission, and thus the interpretations put forth by Dunn, Haya-Prats, and Turner need modification. In the following chapter I shall seek to demonstrate that these conclusions are harmonious with Luke's account of that first Christian Pentecost recorded in Acts 2.

1. *Pentecost: The Event Described (Acts 2.1-13)*

Luke's account of the Pentecostal outpouring of the Spirit recorded in Acts 2.1-13 is undoubtedly based on traditional material[2] and, in spite of numerous difficulties in the text, the historicity of the event which it describes need not be doubted.[3] The account has been subjected to

---

1. I. Broer, 'Der Geist und die Gemeinde: Zur Auslegung der lukanischen Pfingstgeschichte (Apg 2,1-13)', *BL* 13 (1972), p. 282.

2. Broer, 'Der Geist', pp. 276-77; Tachau, 'Pfingstgeschichte', pp. 92-93; Kremer, *Pfingstbericht*, pp. 259-67; A.T. Lincoln, 'Theology and History in the Interpretation of Luke's Pentecost', *ExpT* 96 (1984–85), p. 209; Grundmann, 'Pfingstbericht', p. 585. Contra Haenchen, *Acts*, pp. 172-75.

3. See Dunn, *Jesus and the Spirit*, pp. 135-56; Marshall, 'Pentecost', pp. 360-65. Haenchen's contention that the account is a fictitious literary production created by Luke (*Acts*, pp. 172-75) is extreme. However, the extent to which the account is a record of what actually happened is subject to widespread discussion. For example, Krodel states that 'the account is not a realistic narrative which conveys to us what actually happened' ('Functions', p. 31) and C.A. Evans argues that Luke's account has been significantly influenced by Joel. Luke gleaned from Joel 'not only additional relevant content and vocabulary, but clues as to how the narrative should develop' ('The Prophetic Setting of the Pentecost Sermon', *ZNW* 74 [1983], pp. 148-50). Lincoln suggests that Luke has taken over traditions and 'reworked and reinterpreted them to create his own history-like narrative' ('Theology and History', p. 209). Although the discussion continues, Dunn and Marshall have argued persuasively that Luke's account bears witness to a historical event of tremendous significance for the expansion of the church.

detailed source analysis.[1] Although the numerous attempts to reproduce the sources underlying Luke's account have failed to produce any conclusive results,[2] they have shown that the account reflects Luke's literary style and therefore has been significantly shaped by Luke himself.[3] As such, the Pentecost account is a good example of Luke's literary method: he is both a historian who utilizes traditional material and a theologian who skillfully shapes and interprets it.

The account itself poses numerous problems for the interpreter, but the main points of the narrative may be reconstructed as follows. A band of disciples numbering about 120 (Acts 1.15)[4] gathered together in 'the upper room' of a house (Acts 2.1-2; cf. 1.13).[5] Here the disci-

1. See Tachau, 'Pfingstgeschichte', pp. 88-92 for a summary and evaluation of the source-critical issues. Broer, 'Der Geist', pp. 267-69, 271-73 and Schneider, *Die Apostelgeschichte*, I, pp. 243-47 survey the various attempts' to reconstruct the sources behind the pericope.

2. See Tachau, 'Pfingstgeschichte', p. 89; Broer, 'Der Geist', p. 276-77; and the conclusions of Kremer, *Pfingstbericht*, pp. 259-67.

3. Broer, 'Der Geist', p. 270; Lohse, 'Die Bedeutung', p. 183, 190; N. Adler, *Das erste christliche Pfingstfest: Sinn und Bedeutung des Pfingstberichtes Apg. 2,1-13* (1938), pp. 32f.

4. The πάντες of 2.1 refers to the 120 mentioned in Acts 1.15 and not simply the apostles: (1) this is the most natural reading of πάντες, since the 120 are present in the preceding verses; (2) this conclusion is supported by the repetition of ἐπὶ τὸ αὐτὸ in 1.15 and 2.1; (3) the potentially universal character of the gift is stressed in 2.17 and 2.39; therefore it would be strange if any of the disciples present were excluded from the gift at Pentecost; (4) more than twelve languages are recorded to have been heard, implying more than twelve were present. See Dunn, *Holy Spirit*, p. 40; Marshall, 'Pentecost', pp. 352-53; Broer, 'Der Geist', p. 281; Kremer, *Pfingstbericht*, p. 215; Schneider, *Die Apostelgeschichte*, I, p. 247. Note, however, Dupont's attempt to limit the 'all' of Acts 2.1 to the apostles and the additional persons mentioned in Acts 1.14 ('Christian Pentecost', pp. 37-38). The number 120 is an approximation, as the ὡσεί of 1.15 indicates. Marshall notes that the inclusion of the number was not without significance: 'in Jewish law a minimum of 120 Jewish men was required to establish a community with its own council; in Jewish terms the disciples were a body of sufficient size to form a new community' (*Acts*, p. 64).

5. The upper room (Acts 1.13) is to be preferred over the temple (Lk. 24.53) as the referent of οἶκον in Acts 2.2: (1) Luke almost always calls the temple the τὸ ἱερόν; (2) Luke uses οἶκος with reference to the temple (Acts 7.47) only when the context makes its meaning clear. See Haenchen, *Acts*, p. 168; Marshall, 'Pentecost', p. 353; Kremer, *Pfingstbericht*, p. 104. Lohse's objection that 'eine so große Menge jedoch könne nur im Tempel Platz gefunden haben' ('Die Bedeutung', p. 179; see also M. Bachmann, *Jerusalem und der Tempel* [1980], p. 167) is arbitrary. Jews and Christians renovated private homes for use by the religious community and such renovations often included the creation of a large meeting hall through the removal of walls separating adjoining rooms (see the evidence collected by L.M. White, 'Domus Ecclesiae—Domus Dei: Adaptation and Development in the Setting for the Early

ples were 'all filled with the Holy Spirit' (ἐπλήσθησαν πάντες πνεύματος ἁγίου); an experience which was accompanied by heavenly signs (ἦχος ὥσπερ φερομένης πνοῆς βιαίας and γλῶσσαι ὡσεὶ πυρός) and produced inspired speech (Acts 2.3-4). A crowd composed of diaspora Jews (and thus ἀπὸ παντὸς ἔθνους τῶν ὑπὸ τὸν οὐρανόν) currently residing in Jerusalem[1] assembled[2] in amazement, for they heard the disciples miraculously declaring 'the mighty acts of God' (τὰ μεγαλεῖα τοῦ θεοῦ) in each of their own native languages (Acts 2.5-12).[3] The diversity of the nationalities represented by the

Christian Assembly' [1982]). The excavation of a private dwelling at Dura-Europos (Syria) offers a particularly good example of this sort of activity. Through the removal of a dividing wall the Christians were able to create a large hall (7.35–7.60 m long and 4.22 m wide) accessible to the community (see C.H. Kraeling, *The Christian Building, The Excavations at Dura-Europos*. Final Report VIII.2 [1967], Plan IV and V). Certainly large rooms were not unknown to the home-owners of Jerusalem: N. Avigad has unearthed a mansion in the Jewish Quarter of Jerusalem (destroyed by fire in 70 AD) containing a large meeting hall (11 m long and 6.5 m wide) capable of accommodating 120 adults (N. Avigad, *Discovering Jerusalem* [1984], pp. 95-103). It is also possible that the large gathering was not confined to one room of the house. A former colleague at the University of Aberdeen, Brad Blue, notes that the ἐπὶ τὸ αὐτό of v. 15 could refer to an entire level or complex of rooms in a building rather than the single ὑπερῷον of v. 13 and that this interpretation is supported by the phrase ἐπλήρωσεν ὅλον τὸν οἶκον in Acts 2.2.

1. The phrase εἰς Ἰερουσαλὴμ κατοικοῦντες Ἰουδαῖοι (2.5, 14) suggests that the crowd of Jews consisted of residents of Jerusalem and not pilgrims temporarily staying in Jerusalem in order to observe the Feast of Pentecost. The apparent contradiction with 2.9 (οἱ κατοικοῦντες τὴν Μεσοποταμίαν) and 2.10 (οἱ ἐπιδημοῦντες Ῥωμαῖοι) is resolved when it is understood that the list refers to the various Jews of the Diaspora now living in Jerusalem by reference to their country of origin (Kremer, *Pfingstbericht*, pp. 148-149). The beginning portion of Peter's speech in 2.14, Ἄνδρες Ἰουδαῖοι καὶ οἱ κατοικοῦντες Ἰερουσαλὴμ πάντες, is a case of synonymous parallelism rather than a reference to two distinct groups (Haenchen, *Acts*, p. 178).

2. That the disciples left the house to meet the crowd is implicit in the narrative.

3. Luke's description of the event makes it clear that in this instance λαλεῖν ἑτέραις γλώσσαις refers to intelligible human languages and not unintelligible glossolalia found elsewhere in Acts (10.46; 19.6) and 1 Corinthians (12–14). See J. Dupont, *Nouvelles études sur les Actes des Apôtres* (1984), p. 197; O'Reilly, *Word and Sign*, p. 39; Carson, *Showing the Spirit*, p. 80; Turner, 'Spiritual Gifts', pp. 17-23; Krodel, 'Functions', p. 31; Kremer, *Pfingstbericht*, p. 119. T.L. Wilkinson has argued the impossible position that 'tongues-speech' in Acts and 1 Corinthians always refers to communication in intelligible human languages ('Tongues and Prophecy in Acts and 1st Corinthians', *VR* 31 [1978], pp. 1-20). For a criticism of this position see C.G. Williams, 'Glossolalia as a Religious Phenomenon: "Tongues" at Corinth and Pentecost', *Rel* 5 (1975), pp. 16-32. Williams goes on to argue that the 'tongues-speech' described in Acts 2 was originally, as that

crowd, and so also the miraculous character of the disciples' speech, is highlighted by the *Völkerliste* of Acts 2.9-11a. The crowds' mixed response to this dramatic event (Acts 2.12-13) sets the stage for Peter's speech.

Several features of the narrative have important implications for this inquiry.

1. Consistent with his usage elsewhere, in his Pentecost account Luke portrays the gift of the Spirit as the source of prophetic inspiration. The immediate result of the Spirit's activity is inspired speech. As we noted, the disciples miraculously declare 'the mighty acts of God' (τὰ μεγαλεῖα τοῦ θεοῦ) in the various languages spoken by the representatives of the *Völkerliste* (Acts 2.9-11). A comparison of 2.4b (καθὼς τὸ πνεῦμα ἐδίδου ἀποφθέγγεσθαι αὐτοῖς) with 2.14a (καὶ ἀπεφθέγξατο αὐτοῖς) indicates that Luke also understood Peter's sermon to be inspired by the Spirit.[1]

---

of Acts 10, 19 and 1 Corinthians 12–14, glossolalia and not xenolalia. Arguing that a language miracle was not necessary for communication since all would have spoken Aramaic and/or Greek (so also H.W. Beyer, 'ἕτερος', *TDNT*, II, pp. 702f.), Williams states that Luke, seeking 'to emphasize the role of the Spirit as the power guiding the missionary expansion of the Church' (p. 25), interpreted the phenomenon as xenolalia. Yet, as Marshall points out, this objection is not as weighty as it appears, 'Although the audience was Jewish, the various groups from the Diaspora would still have had their own languages, and the declaration of the gospel would come to them more significantly in their own tongues' ('Pentecost', p. 361). More problematic is the response by some in the crowd recorded in 2.13, 'They have had too much wine', for it implies that some did not understand the inspired speech of the disciples. Attempts to resolve this dilemma by postulating an editorial merging of two sources, one featuring glossolalia and the other, xenolalia (F. Spitta, *Die Apostelgeschichte, ihre Quellen und deren geschichtlicher Wert* [1891], pp. 22-60; and more recently Grundmann, 'Pfingstbericht', p. 585), must be judged unsuccessful (see the objections of Broer, 'Der Geist', pp. 271-273; Lohse, 'Die Bedeutung', p. 183; K. Haacker, 'Das Pfingstwunder als exegetisches Problem', in *Verborum Veritas* [1970], p. 130; and Wilson, *The Gentiles*, pp. 125-26). Perhaps the problem is not so acute, since 'the accusation of drunkenness would have been made by anybody who did not understand the languages other than his own which were being spoken, and also by anybody who wanted to deride the bold speaking of the disciples' (Marshall, 'Pentecost', p. 361). In any event, the 'tongues-speech' which Luke envisions in Acts 2.4f. involves the miraculous speaking of intelligible human languages, previously unknown by the speakers.

1. Broer, 'Der Geist', p. 281 and Shelton, '"Filled with the Holy Spirit" and "Full of the Holy Spirit": Lucan Redactional Phrases', in *Faces of Renewal* (1988), p. 104 n. 15. The verb ἀποφθέγγομαι occurs only three times in the NT (Acts 2.4, 14; 26.25). The rarity of its usage heightens the parallelism between 2.4 and 2.14.

2. Luke's account highlights the missiological significance of the Pentecostal gift. By skillfully integrating the *Völkerliste* into his narrative, Luke stresses what is central in the narrative:[1] the gift of the Spirit enables the disciples to communicate with people 'from every nation under heaven' (Acts 2.5).[2] The product of this divine gift should not be understood simply as praise directed to God. It is, above all, proclamation.[3] This is suggested by the language miracle and confirmed by the content of the inspired speech, τὰ μεγαλεῖα τοῦ θεοῦ (Acts 2.11).[4] In the Septuagint τὰ μεγαλεῖα is usually connected with verbs of proclamation and, as such, is addressed to people.[5] One may thus affirm with H. von Baer that 'der Pfingstgeist ist der Missionsgeist'.[6]

3. Luke's use of the phrase ἐπλήσθησαν πάντες πνεύματος ἁγίου (Acts 2.4) with reference to the disciples at Pentecost indicates that their experience was not unlike that of John, Elizabeth, Zechariah, or Jesus.[7] Whether it be John in his

---

1. Whether or not the *Völkerliste* stems from early tradition, ancient lists such as the astrological list of Paul of Alexandria (see Kremer, *Pfingstbericht*, p. 157), or Luke himself, the point is valid. For there can be little doubt that Luke has carefully constructed the narrative as it currently stands.

2. Hill, *Greek Words*, p. 260; G. Schille, *Die Apostelgeschichte des Lukas* (2nd edn, 1984), p. 101; Dömer, *Das Heil Gottes*, p. 157. J. Dupont ('La nouvelle Pentecôte (Ac 2, 1-11)' in *Nouvelles études* (1984), pp. 195-96) stresses the significance of the phrase ('from every nation under heaven') and the *Völkerliste* for the universal mission of the church and therefore concludes: 'Dans l'instant où l'Esprit saisit les apôtres, l'Eglise s'est trouvée en face de sa mission universelle' (p. 196).

3. Contra Turner (*Spiritual Gifts*, p. 17; 'Luke and the Spirit', p. 133), Haya-Prats (*Force*, pp. 169-70) and R. Pesch (*Die Apostelgeschichte (Apg 1-12)* [1986], p. 107), who view the inspired speech of Acts 2.4f. as praise and not proclamation.

4. Kremer, *Pfingstbericht*, pp. 143-44.

5. Kremer (*Pfingstbericht*, p. 144) cites Tob. 11.15 (A, B); Pss. 104/105.1 (S); Sir. 17.8, 10; 33 [36].8; 2 Macc. 3.34. Note also that the inspired utterances in the infancy narratives are generally given in the 3rd person (Lk. 1.46-55, 67-75; 2.33-35) and, if given in the 2nd person are usually directed to people, not to God himself (Lk. 1.42-45, 76-79). The one exception, Simeon's outburst of praise in Lk. 1.29-32, should probably be understood as both praise and proclamation. This judgment is suggested by the summary of Anna's prophetic activity in Lk. 2.38 which brings both elements together: καὶ αὐτῇ τῇ ὥρᾳ ἐπιστᾶσα ἀνθωμολογεῖτο τῷ θεῷ καὶ ἐλάλει περὶ αὐτοῦ πᾶσιν τοῖς προσδεχομένοις λύτρωσιν Ἰερουσαλήμ.

6. Von Baer, *Der heilige Geist*, p. 103.

7. See Chapter 8 §2.1 above concerning the relationship between the phrase πλήρης πνεύματος ἁγίου, descriptive of Jesus in Lk. 4.1, and ἐπλήσθη πνεύματος ἁγίου.

mother's womb, Jesus at the Jordan, or the disciples at Pentecost, the Spirit comes upon them all as the source of prophetic inspiration, and as such, empowers them to carry out their divinely appointed tasks. Although the phrase ἐπλήσθη/σαν πνεύματος ἁγίου is descriptive of an experience which produces an inspired state of rather short duration (resulting in inspired speech) and which is clearly repetitive,[1] the experience so designated also has a more permanent dimension.[2] This is most evident from the experiences of John (1.15), Jesus, and Paul (9.17); each of whom received the Spirit when they were 'filled with the Spirit' as an initial and lasting endowment which equipped them for their respective ministries. Luke's usage suggests that the divine activity designated by the phrase ἐπλήσθη/σαν πνεύματος ἁγίου[3] involves a permanent promise of pneumatic assistance (either special knowledge or power of speech) for each moment of need.[4] The momentary and repetitive instances of inspiration linked to the phrase represent specific and concrete realizations of this promise. It is therefore appropriate to speak of the disciples' pneumatic anointing at Pentecost as the moment at which they, like Jesus at the Jordan, were equipped with prophetic power for the mission which lay ahead (Lk. 24.49; Acts 1.8).

1. See Acts 4.8, 31; 13.9 (cf. 9.17); note also 13.52.
2. Marshall, *Luke: Historian and Theologian*, p. 201.
3. Luke can speak of the Pentecostal outpouring of the Spirit in a variety of ways, all of which designate the same experience (e.g. Acts 1.4—τὴν ἐπαγγελίαν τοῦ πατρός; 1.8—ἐπελθόντος τοῦ ἁγίου πνεύματος ἐφ' ὑμᾶς; 2.4—ἐπλήσθησαν... πνεύματος ἁγίου; 2.17—ἐκχεῶ... πνεύματός μου; 2.38—τὴν δωρεὰν τοῦ ἁγίου πνεύματος; 10.47—τὸ πνεῦμα τὸ ἅγιον ἔλαβον; 11.15—ἐπέπεσεν τὸ πνεῦμα τὸ ἅγιον ἐπ' αὐτούς; 11.17—τὴν... δωρεὰν ἔδωκεν αὐτοῖς. See Dunn, *Holy Spirit*, pp. 70-72.
4. Haya-Prats, *Force*, p. 198. Contra Turner, 'Luke and the Spirit', p. 157, 'A normally continuous spiritual state entered by πνεύματος πλησθῆναι is not to be deduced here [Acts 2.4]: Luke does not use the expression as a direct equivalent for τὸ ἅγιον πνεῦμα λαμβάνειν'. Turner's attempt to distinguish between the force of πλησθῆναι πνεύματος ἁγίου and λαμβάνειν πνεῦμα ἅγιον must be rejected since Luke uses both terms with reference to the same Pentecostal experience (see the preceding note and Dunn, *Holy Spirit*, p. 71).

2. *Pentecost: The Event Interpreted (Acts 2.14-21)*

Luke's narrative continues with an account of Peter's interpretation of the Pentecostal event (2.14-21). Responding to those from the crowd who charged that the inspired disciples 'had drunken too much wine', Peter declares that, far from the antics of inebriated men, the dramatic event of which they are witnesses is, in reality, a fulfillment of Joel 3.1-5a: ἀλλὰ τοῦτό ἐστιν τὸ εἰρημένον διὰ τοῦ προφήτου Ἰωήλ (Acts 2.16).[1] The text of Joel 3.1-5a is then cited with a few modifications:[2]

---

1. The name Ἰωήλ is not found in D. Although it is possible that the name is secondary, the omission is perhaps best explained as scribal error: the name 'had fallen out accidently from the Western text' (Metzger, *A Textual Commentary*, p. 294).

2. There are numerous textual problems associated with the quotation. (1) In v. 17 the reading of ἐν ταῖς ἐσχάταις ἡμέραις is attested by ℵ; A; D; and most of the other manuscripts. The reading preserved in B, μετὰ ταῦτα, should be regarded as a scribal attempt to bring the original text in conformity with the Septuagint (see Bock, *Proclamation*, pp. 160-61). (2) The reading ὁ θεός in v. 17 is supported by ℵ; A; B; and most of the other manuscripts. The alternative reading κύριος is found in D and E. G. Kilpatrick has argued that the tendency was to change κύριος to θεός since the former is ambiguous and may mean God or Christ ('An Eclectic Study of the Text of Acts', in *Biblical and Patristic Studies in Memory of Robert Pierce Casey* [1963], pp. 65-66; see also 'Some Quotations in Acts', in *Les Actes des Apôtres* [1979], p. 96). However, Metzger notes there is 'no evidence that such a tendency as Kilpatrick suggests operated in the case of codex Bezae' (*A Textual Commentary*, p. 296) and Bock queries, 'If the reference was ambiguous, why are there no efforts to substitute Jesus for the variant?' (*Proclamation*, p. 342). It is also possible that D has modified the original text to bring it into conformity with 2.34 (note the omission of the article in both instances). Since the internal evidence is not decisive and the external evidence strongly favors ὁ θεός, it is most probable that ὁ θεός represents the original reading. (3) E. Epp has argued persuasively that in v. 17 several variant readings attested by D reflect a theological tendency characteristic of the Western text (a heightening of the universalism of Luke) and are therefore secondary: D reads πάσας σάρκας rather than πᾶσαν σάρκα attested by most manuscripts; D alters the first two occurrences of the pronoun ὑμῶν to αὐτῶν and omits the last two occurrences of the pronoun altogether (*The Theological Tendency of Codex Bezae Cantabrigiensis in Acts* [1966], pp. 66-70). (4) The external evidence indicates that several variant readings in v. 18 supported by D are secondary: D omits μου after δούλους and δούλας, the phrase ἐν ταῖς ἡμέραις ἐκείναις, and the phrase καὶ προφητεύσουσιν. (5) Two variant readings in vv. 19 and 20 can also be dismissed as secondary: in v. 19, D omits αἷμα καὶ πῦρ καὶ ἀτμίδα καπνοῦ, probably because this phrase does not find explicit fulfillment in the narrative; in v. 20 the phrase καὶ ἐπιφανῆ is lacking in D and ℵ, probably the result of parablepsis (see Metzger, *A Textual Commentary*, p. 298). (6) Two insertions in v. 20 are probably the result of efforts to improve the style of the original text: ἤ is placed after πρίν in B

Acts 2.17-21/Joel 3.15a

Καὶ ἔσται ἐν ταῖς ἐσχάταις ἡμέραις, λέγει ὁ θεός,————————[μετὰ ταῦτα καὶ]
ἐκχεῶ ἀπὸ τοῦ πνεύματός μου ἐπὶ πᾶσαν σάρκα,
καὶ προφητεύσουσιν οἱ υἱοὶ ὑμῶν καὶ αἱ θυγατέρες ὑμῶν,
καὶ οἱ νεανίσκοι ὑμῶν ὁράσεις ὄψονται,————————————— Inverted
καὶ οἱ πρεσβύτεροι ὑμῶν ἐνυπνίοις ἐνυπνιασθήσονται·======[ἐνύπνια]
καί γε ἐπὶ τοὺς δούλους μου καὶ ἐπὶ τὰς δούλας μου ἐν ταῖς ἡμέραις ἐκείναις⌉
ἐκχεῶ ἀπὸ τοῦ πνεύματός μου,
καὶ προφητεύσουσιν.
καὶ δώσω τέρατα ἐν τῷ οὐρανῷ ἄνω καὶ σημεῖα ἐπὶ τῆς γῆς κάτω,   Insertions
    αἷμα καὶ πῦρ καὶ ἀτμίδα καπνοῦ·
ὁ ἥλιος μεταστραφήσεται εἰς σκότος καὶ ἡ σελήνη εἰς αἷμα
    πρὶν ἐλθεῖν ἡμέραν κυρίου τὴν μεγάλην [καὶ ἐπιφανῆ].
καὶ ἔσται πᾶς ὃς ἂν ἐπικαλέσηται τὸ ὄνομα κυρίου σωθήσεται.

The tradition-history of the passage, as with the Speeches in Acts generally, is problematic. However, whether one follows M. Dibelius in viewing the speeches in Acts as 'inventions of the author'[1] or, under the influence of F.F. Bruce, insists that the Speeches are 'condensed accounts of speeches actually made',[2] the significance of Peter's pesher[3] of the Joel citation for Luke's pneumatology cannot be missed.

and M (contra ℵ; A; C; D; Ψ); τήν is placed before ἡμέραν in A; Ψ; M (contra ℵ; B; D).

1. M. Dibelius, *A Fresh Approach to the New Testament and Early Christian Literature* (1936), p. xv; see also 'The Speeches in Acts and Ancient Historiography', in *Studies in the Acts of the Apostles* (1956), pp. 138-85. The impact Dibelius has had on the study of the speeches in Acts is illustrated by the opening words of E. Schweizer's article on the subject, 'Ever since Martin Dibelius' essay about this subject, it has been more and more widely recognized that the speeches are basically compositions by the author of Acts who, to be sure, utilized different kinds of material for particular passages' ('Concerning the Speeches in Acts', in *Studies in Luke–Acts* [1966], p. 208). Dibelius's influence is reflected in Haenchen's *Acts*, Wilckens's *Missionsreden*, and R.F. Zehnle's *Peter's Pentecost Discourse: Tradition and Lukan Reinterpretation in Peter's Speeches of Acts 2 and 3* (1971).

2. F.F. Bruce, 'The Speeches in Acts: Thirty Years After', in *Reconciliation and Hope* (1974), p. 53, see also pp. 53-68. Note also W.W. Gasque, 'The Speeches of Acts: Dibelius Reconsidered', in *New Dimensions in New Testament Study* (1974), pp. 232-50.

3. In *pesher* interpretation the author brings out the contemporary relevance of a particular text by pointing to its fulfillment in current events. As a method of biblical exegesis common in certain sectors of first-century Judaism—most notably in the Qumran community—*pesher* took the form of 'this is that' (or 'that is this', where the OT quotation is followed by its interpretation). Note the 'this is that' form of Acts 2.16: τοῦτό ἐστιν τὸ εἰρημένον διὰ τοῦ προφήτου Ἰωήλ. See R. Longenecker,

For, whether by creation or selection, modification, and arrangement of received tradition, Luke has placed his unique stamp on the text. One is therefore justified in assuming that Peter's *pesher* of Joel 3.1-5a was central for, though not necessarily the result of, Luke's understanding of the Pentecostal bestowal of the Spirit.

The judgment stated above encourages us to move beyond the broader and more complex questions of tradition and history pertaining to Peter's speech in Acts 2 and to focus attention on the source-critical question immediately relevant to this study: are the various modifications to Joel 3.1-5a (LXX) which are reflected in Acts 2.17-21 to be attributed to Lukan redaction or early Christian tradition? In an effort to answer this question I shall examine Acts 2.17-21 seeking to determine what theological concerns (if any) have motivated modifications to the Joel text and whether these modifications reflect any literary and/or theological tendencies which suggest that they are the product of Lukan redaction.

(1) *The alteration of* μετὰ ταῦτα *to* ἐν ταῖς ἐσχάταις ἡμέραις *in v. 17.* E. Haenchen has argued that the ἐν ταῖς ἐσχάταις ἡμέραις of v. 17 'steht in Spannung zu der Haltung des Lukas'.[1] According to Haenchen Luke was not of the opinion that the *Endzeit* had broken in with Pentecost and the church, therefore the phrase must be judged as a secondary emendation. But, as F. Mußner has demonstrated, neither μετὰ ταῦτα nor ἐν ταῖς ἐσχάταις ἡμέραις stands in tension with Luke's eschatology, for both readings place Pentecost in 'the last days' *before* the Day of the Lord.[2]

Biblical Exegesis in the Apostolic Period (1975), p. 43, see also pp. 38-45, 70-75 and E. Ellis, *Luke*, pp. 7-8.

1. E. Haenchen, 'Schriftzitate und Textüberlieferung in der Apostelgeschichte', *ZTK* 51 (1954), p. 162.

2. F. Mußner, 'In den letzten Tagen (Apg 2,17a)', *BZ* 5 (1965), pp. 263-65. See also Wilckens, *Missionsreden*, pp. 33, 225-26; Kremer, *Pfingstbericht*, p. 171 n. 14; Rese, *Alttestamentliche Motive*, pp. 51-52; and Bock, *Proclamation*, p. 161. Consistent with his thesis (developed in *The Theology of St. Luke*) that Luke's two-volume work is shaped by a concern to deal with the delay of the *parousia*, H. Conzelmann asserts that the formula ἐν ταῖς ἐσχάταις ἡμέραις has become stereotyped and 'spricht nicht mehr Naherwartung aus' (*Die Apostelgeschichte* [1963], p. 29). However, Conzelmann's central thesis has been almost universally rejected by recent scholarship (see W.W. Gasque, 'A Fruitful Field: Recent Study of the Acts of the Apostles', *Int* 42 [1988], p. 118) and his judgment concerning ἐν ταῖς ἐσχάταις ἡμέραις is a product of this erroneous approach. In accordance with the eschatological perspective of Joel, Luke uses ἐν ταῖς ἐσχάταις ἡμέραις to refer to a period of God's gracious intervention which immediately precedes the Day of the Lord. Therefore the phrase as used by Luke is not irreconcilable with a *Naherwartung*. Indeed, A.J. Mattill has argued persuasively that Luke did not abandon the

Haenchen is not alone in exaggerating the eschatological import of this alteration. Pointing to the ἐν ταῖς ἐσχάταις ἡμέραις of v. 17, J. Dunn asserts that for the disciples Pentecost represents the decisive pivot of the aeons, the point at which they enter into 'the last days'.[1] However, as I have already established, Luke considered the time of messianic fulfillment to have begun with Jesus' miraculous birth and the other events chronicled in the infancy narratives.[2] It follows that the entire ministry of Jesus is carried out in 'the last days'.[3] Therefore, although the Pentecostal bestowal of the Spirit, as an event of the prophesied *Endzeit*, constitutes irrefutable proof that 'the last days' have arrived, it is one in a series of such events and does not mark the beginning of 'the last days'.[4]

The phrase ἐν ταῖς ἐσχάταις ἡμέραις does not alter the eschatological perspective of the Joel text nor does it signify that Pentecost ushers in the new age; rather, it clarifies what with μετὰ ταῦτα could only be gleaned from the broader context of Joel: the Pentecostal bestowal of the Spirit is an event of the *Endzeit*, that period of God's deliverance which precedes the Day of the Lord. Thus, while the alteration highlights the eschatological significance of the Joel prophecy and its Pentecostal fulfillment, it does not represent a significant contribution to or departure from the original text of Joel. We have noted that the eschatological perspective of the text is harmonious with the theology of Luke. However, since the alteration merely reflects a perspective already present in the text of Joel, it cannot be termed distinctively Lukan. For this reason theological considerations do not provide an adequate basis on which to make a judgment concerning the traditional or Lukan origin of the alteration.

I turn now to arguments of style. Noting that ἐν ταῖς ἐσχάταις ἡμέραις appears nowhere else in Luke's two-volume work, D. Bock

---

Naherwartung (*Luke and the Last Things* [1979]; see also the judgment of R.P. Martin, 'Salvation and Discipleship in Luke's Gospel', *Int* 30 [1976], p. 373).

1. Dunn, *Holy Spirit*, pp. 46-47; see also von Baer, *Der heilige Geist*, p. 92.
2. See Chapter 6 above.
3. A. Weiser, *Die Apostelgeschichte. Kapitel 1–12* (1981), p. 92: 'Lukas will mit seiner Änderung des Joel-Textes aber nicht etwa sagen, daß nun das Ende eintrete; sondern für ihn ist die ganze Zeit seit Jesu Wirken bereits "Endzeit", deren Ende aber unberechenbar bleibt'. This judgment finds confirmation from Luke's citation of Joel 3.1-5a if, as Weiser suggests, the τέρατα and σημεῖα of 2.19 include the 'signs and wonders' which God worked through Jesus (*Die Apostelgeschichte. Kapitel 1–12*, p. 92; see point 6 below for a discussion of this issue).
4. Turner, 'Luke and the Spirit', p. 154.

suggests that the phrase stems from tradition.[1] However, although the phrase is indeed unique to Luke, a close parallel occurs in the following verse: ἐν ταῖς ἡμέραις ἐκείναις (Acts 2.18 = Joel 3.2). We have already noted Luke's penchant for duplicating words and phrases in quotations from the Old Testament.[2] Thus ἐν ταῖς ἐσχάταις ἡμέραις (Acts 2.17), as a slightly modified duplicate of ἐν ταῖς ἡμέραις ἐκείναις (Acts 2.18),[3] corresponds to Lukan style and is to be attributed to his hand.

(2) *The insertion of* λέγει ὁ θεός *in v. 17.* The original sense of the Joel citation remains unaltered by the insertion of λέγει ὁ θεός.[4] As with the alteration discussed above, λέγει ὁ θεός merely clarifies what is evident from the broader context of Joel:[5] the promise of Joel 3.1-5a originates with God himself.[6] While insertions of this type are not uncommon in Old Testament quotations cited by New Testament authors,[7] we may presume the redactor deemed it important that the promise of Joel be attributed directly to God. A motive for the insertion may be found in Luke's previous reference to the Pentecostal gift of the Spirit as ἡ ἐπαγγελία τοῦ πατρός (Lk. 24.49, Acts 1.4). Through the insertion of λέγει ὁ θεός the redactor, now identified as Luke,[8] was able to emphasize that the promise of Joel 3.1-5a was indeed ἡ ἐπαγγελία τοῦ πατρός.

---

1. Bock, *Proclamation*, p. 161; see also Holtz, *Untersuchungen*, p. 8. Noting that ἐν ταῖς ἐσχάταις ἡμέραις is not characteristic of Luke but common in the post-apostolic church, Holtz argues that the phrase is not original.

2. See Chapter 8 §3.1 above. Note the repetition of κηρύξαι (Lk. 4.18, 19 = Isa. 61.1-2); ἐν ταῖς. . . ἡμέραις (Acts 2.17-18 = Joel 3.1f.); καὶ προφητεύσουσιν (Acts 2.17-18=Joel 3.1f.); ἔργον (Acts 13.41, 2× = Hab. 1.5); σου (Lk. 7.27 = Mal. 3.1). On Luke's fondness of double expressions see R. Morgenthaler, *Die lukanische Geschichtsschreibung als Zeugnis: Gestalt und Gehalt der Kunst des Lukas* (2 vols.; 1948). For Morgenthaler's discussion on Acts 2.17f. see I, p. 88.

3. The parallelism between ἐν ταῖς ἐσχάταις ἡμέραις (Acts 2.17) and ἐν ταῖς ἡμέραις ἐκείναις (Acts 2.18) is heightened by the occurrence of ἐκχεῶ ἀπὸ τοῦ πνεύματός μου and καὶ προφητεύσουσιν following each phrase. While the repetition of ἐκχεῶ ἀπὸ τοῦ πνεύματός μου is original to the text of Joel, the duplication of καὶ προφητεύσουσιν is Lucan.

4. Rese, *Alttestamentliche Motive*, p. 49.

5. Note the ἐγὼ κύριος ὁ θεὸς ὑμῶν of Joel 2.27 and the εἶπεν κύριος of Joel 3.5b.

6. Holtz points out that such clarification is necessary because of the introduction in Acts 2.16 which attributes the saying to Joel (*Untersuchungen*, p. 6).

7. See Acts 7.6, 49; Rom. 12.19; 1 Cor. 14.21; 2 Cor. 6.17.

8. I have already noted that the phrase ἡ ἐπαγγελία τοῦ πατρός is Lukan (see Chapter 9 §5 above). The connection with ἡ ἐπαγγελία τοῦ πατρός is thus a clear

(3) *Stylistic modifications in v. 17.* Two alterations have been motivated by stylistic concerns and as such they are of little consequence for this study. The transposition of the lines which begin with καὶ οἱ νεανίσκοι ὑμῶν and καὶ οἱ πρεσβύτεροι ὑμῶν was perhaps motivated by the desire to place 'young men' (rather than 'old men') directly after the reference to 'sons' and 'daughters'.[1] The use of the dative ἐνυπνίοις rather than the accusative ἐνύπνια of the Septuagint[2] defies explanation since the verb ἐνυπνιάζομαι normally takes the accusative.[3] Presumably the dative was preferred by the redactor.

(4) *The insertion of γε and μου (2x) in v. 18.* It is generally recognized that the double insertion of μου in v. 18 alters the original meaning of Joel 3.2.[4] The δοῦλοι and δοῦλαι of Joel 3.2 represent yet another segment of Jewish society to whom the Spirit will be given and thereby add to the series of examples which illustrate the promise of Joel 3.1: ἐκχεῶ ἀπὸ τοῦ πνεύματός μου ἐπὶ πᾶσαν σάρκα.[5] However, with the insertion of μου in Acts 2.18 these terms no longer refer to literal slaves nor to an additional group which will receive the Spirit.[6] In Acts 2.18 the terms become religious metaphors which include and give further definition to the groups previously mentioned.[7] The transformation of 'slaves' into 'servants of God' highlights what is implicit in the text of Joel: the gift of the Spirit is given

---

indication that λέγει ὁ θεός stems from Luke's hand. Indeed, even if ἡ ἐπαγγελία τοῦ πατρός represents traditional material, the literary linkage suggests that λέγει ὁ θεός was inserted into the Joel citation by the author of Luke–Acts. Bock states that evidence from style may be adduced in support of the traditional origin of the insertion. He asserts that although the insertion of λέγει ὁ θεός in Acts 2.17 is similar to introductory formula found in Acts 2.25, 34, it is unique in Luke–Acts in that 'it is encased inside the quotation rather than preceding it' (*Proclamation*, p. 344 n. 25). However, Acts 7.7 and 7.49 provide examples which indicate that this phenomenon is not limited to Acts 2.17.

1. Schneider, *Die Apostelgeschichte*, I, p. 268.

2. Bock (*Proclamation*, p. 162) argues persuasively against Holtz's contention that the dative represents the original reading of the LXX (*Untersuchungen*, pp. 9-10).

3. Holtz, *Untersuchungen*, p. 9. The only other occurrence of the verb in the NT is in Jude 8, where as a participle and the subject of the sentence it occurs without a direct object. Acts 2.17 records the only occurrence of ἐνύπνιον in the NT.

4. See for example Haenchen, *Acts*, p. 179 and 'Schriftzitate', p. 161; Schneider, *Die Apostelgeschichte*, I, p. 268; Conzelmann, *Acts*, p. 20; Kremer, *Pfingstbericht*, p. 172; Roloff, *Die Apostelgeschichte*, p. 53.

5. L.C. Allen, *The Books of Joel, Obadiah, Jonah and Micah* (1976), p. 99; H.W. Wolff, *Joel and Amos* (1977), p. 67.

6. Haenchen, *Acts*, p. 179 and 'Schriftzitate', p. 161.

7. Conzelmann, *Acts*, p. 20.

only to those who are members of the eschatological community of salvation.[1] The motive for such redactional activity was undoubtedly a desire to emphasize that the disciples of Jesus, as recipients of the Spirit of prophecy, are indeed members of this community. The insertions also highlight the pneumatological perspective of the redactor: membership in the community of salvation is not dependent on the gift of the Spirit; rather, the former is a presupposition for the latter.[2] The Spirit of prophecy is given to those who already are the servants of God. This perspective accords well with the pneumatology of early Judaism, the primitive church, and Luke. As such, it does not provide sufficient criteria on which to judge the ultimate origin of the insertions.

T. Holtz has argued that the γε and double μου of v. 18 are not redactional, for they do not represent alterations to the text of Joel. Holtz suggests that the text of the Septuagint which Luke employed was, at this point, similar to Codex Alexandrinus and thus the terms were simply carried over by Luke from the Seputagint.[3] Central to Holtz's argument is his contention that the phrase καί γε is conceptually incompatible with the change in perspective occasioned by the double insertion of μου. According to Holtz the intensive καί γε, rendered as 'sogar' ('even'), fits well with the unexpected promise directed specifically to slaves in Joel 3.2; but it is irreconcilable with the less exceptional and broader prophecy concerning servants of God in Acts 2.18.[4]

Holtz's thesis is, however, vulnerable at several points. First, καί γε is characteristic of Luke. Luke uses γε more frequently than any other gospel writer[5] and the two—possibly three—occurrences of καί γε in the New Testament are found in Luke–Acts.[6] Second, in Acts 2.18 καί

1. Roloff, *Die Apostelgeschichte*, p. 53.
2. Contra Dunn, *Holy Spirit*, p. 22: 'The baptism in the Spirit was not something distinct from and subsequent to entry into the Kingdom; it was only by means of the baptism in Spirit that one could enter at all'. This conclusion is consistent with the theological perspective expressed throughout Luke–Acts: initial faith, forgiveness, and progressive purification are not products of the gift of the Spirit (see Haya-Prats, *Force*, pp. 121-29; Bovon, 'Aktuelle Linien', p. 23). Note also Ervin's criticism of Dunn's thesis in light of Acts 2.18 (*Conversion-Initiation*, p. 2).
3. Holtz, *Untersuchungen*, pp. 10-11.
4. Holtz, *Untersuchungen*, p. 10.
5. Matthew, 4×; Mark, 0×; Luke, 8×; John, 1×; Acts, 4×.
6. The phrase occurs in Acts 2.18; 17.27; and variant readings of Lk. 19.42. The omission of the phrase in Lk. 19.42 is supported by א; B; D; Θ; L; 579. Witnesses supporting the inclusion of the phrase are: A; Ψ; K; W; Δ; Π; f1; f13. The UBS text supports the omission of the phrase, but gives its preferred reading a C rating.

γε should be rendered 'indeed' rather than 'sogar' ('even') as Holtz suggests. In Acts 17.27 καί γε simply confirms the statement which follows (that God is near) and is most accurately translated in English as 'indeed'.[1] Therefore in Acts 2.18 καί γε need not imply, as the translation 'even' suggests, that the prophecy which follows is distinct from and more exceptional than those which precede.[2] If, as in Acts 17.27, the phrase simply confirms the statement which follows and is rendered 'indeed', then Holtz's purported contradiction disappears. Even if Holtz is right and the verse does contain a genuine contradiction, he is left with the problem of explaining its occurrence in the Septuagint.[3] Third, the critical editions of the Septuagint agree that the γε and double μου readings of the Alexandrian text group represent late additions.[4] The Alexandrian text has a tendency to adopt readings from citations in the New Testament[5] and thus the occurrence

---

1. Haenchen, *Acts*, pp. 524, 515.

2. Note the translation of Acts 2.18 offered by Lake and Cadbury, *The Acts of the Apostles* (1933; *The Beginnings of Christianity*, IV), pp. 21-22, 'Yes, and on my slaves and on my handmaids in those days I will pour out my spirit' (see also the RV). Similarly the verse in *La Bible en français courant* (Alliance Biblique Universelle, 1987) reads, 'Oui, je répandrai de mon Esprit sur mes serviteurs et mes servantes en ces jours-là, et ils prophétiseront'. Compare also the translation of Acts 2.18 given in *Das Neue Testament* (rev. Elberfelder Übersetzung; Wuppertal: R. Brockhaus Verlag, 1985), 'und sogar auf meine Knechte und auf meine Mägde werde ich in jenen Tagen von meinem Geist ausgießen, und sie werden weissagen', with Luther's rendering, 'und auf meine Knechte und auf meine Mägde will ich in jenen Tagen von meinem Geist ausgießen, und sie sollen weissagen', or the translation offered in *Hoffnung für alle. Das Neue Testament* (Basel: Brunnen, 1983), 'Allen Männern und Frauen, die mir dienen, will ich meinen Geist geben, und sie werden in meinem Auftrag reden'. Whereas *Das Neue Testament* renders καί γε 'und sogar', the editions of Luther and *Hoffnung für alle. Das Neue Testament* offer different—and I suggest at this point more accurate—translations.

3. Holtz is not unaware of the problem. He suggests that it is more likely that the contradiction resulted from an illogical scenario of manuscript emendation (i.e. the manuscript which originally contained the γε later added the μου, while the manuscript which omitted the γε failed to add the μου) than from intentional modifications made by a single redactor. See *Untersuchungen*, p. 11 n. 2.

4. See J. Ziegler (ed.), *Duodecim prophetae. Septuaginta Vetus Testamentum Graecum*, XIII (Göttingen, 1967), pp. 41, 43, 235 (Joel 3.2); A. Rahlfs (ed.), *Septuaginta*, p. 522 (Joel 3.2); see also Wolff, *Joel and Amos*, p. 56. The witnesses which support the omission of γε and double μου from Joel 3.2 include W; B (retains the initial μου); S or ‬א; and V; A and Q are the major witnesses which include the terms.

5. Ziegler (ed.), *Duodecim prophetae*, XIII, p. 43. By way of example Ziegler cites the Alexandrian text of Hos. 10.8 which follows Lk. 23.30 against the other principal manuscripts.

of γε and double μου in the Alexandrian text group may be attributed to assimilation with Acts 2.18. I conclude therefore that the insertions in Joel 3.2 are redactional and, on the basis of style, that they stem from Luke.

(5) *The insertion of* καὶ προφητεύσουσιν *in v. 18.* Although Holtz and Haenchen have suggested that the καὶ προφητεύσουσιν of v. 18, reduplicated from v. 17, crept into the text of the LXX through scribal error,[1] stylistic and theological considerations provide conclusive evidence that the insertion is the result of Lukan redaction.[2] The insertion, as a reduplication of καὶ προφητεύσουσιν in v. 17, is consistent with Luke's penchant for duplicating words and phrases in quotations from the Old Testament noted above. Theologically the insertion is also significant. It serves to emphasize that the gift of the Spirit produces prophetic inspiration. The corollary is that the disciples, as recipients of the gift, are not inebriated men—they are eschatological prophets proclaiming the word of God.[3] This emphasis on the gift of the Spirit as the source of prophetic inspiration is characteristic of Luke.[4]

(6) *The insertion of* ἄνω, σημεῖα, *and* κάτω *in v. 19.* The collocation of σημεῖα and τέρατα formed by the insertion is characteristic of Luke[5] and thus confirms the Lukan origin of the alteration.[6] The

---

1. Holtz, *Untersuchungen*, pp. 11-12 and (more tentatively) Haenchen, *Acts*, p. 179 n. 4.

2. Schneider (*Die Apostelgeschichte*, I, pp. 268-69), Kremer (*Pfingstbericht*, p. 172), and Schweizer ('πνεῦμα', p. 408) all recognize the Lukan character of the insertion. Bock affirms that the phrase does not stem from the LXX, but concludes that 'it may be traditional or Lucan' (*Proclamation*, p. 162).

3. Bock, *Proclamation*, p. 162. Note also O'Reilly, *Word and Sign*, p. 89, 'We conclude that the preaching of the gospel in Acts is understood by Luke as an essentially prophetic activity'.

4. Schneider, *Die Apostelgeschichte*, I, pp. 268-69; Kremer, *Pfingstbericht*, p. 172; Schweizer, 'πνεῦμα', p. 408; Chevallier, 'Luc et l'Esprit', p. 10. This conclusion is of course substantiated by the exegesis of relevant texts from Luke–Acts offered above. Note also Acts 19.6.

5. The collocation of σημεῖα and τέρατα occurs in the NT as follows: Matthew, 1×; Mark, 1×; John, 1×; Acts, 9× (Acts 2.19, 22, 43; 4.30; 5.12; 6.8; 7.36; 14.3; 15.12); the rest of the NT, 4×. The terms appear together outside the NT and with considerable frequency in the LXX (see K.H. Rengstorf, 'σημεῖον', *TDNT*, VII, pp. 206-207, 239-43 and Holtz, *Untersuchungen*, p. 13 n. 3). In view of the high frequency with which Luke uses the phrase in proportion to the other NT writers, one may assume that it represents one of Luke's many Septuagintalisms. Note also that the phrase occurs in introductory (Acts 5.12; 6.8) and summary statements which are generally recognized as Lukan (Acts 2.43; 14.3; 15.12).

precise referent of the τέρατα ἐν τῷ οὐρανῷ ἄνω and σημεῖα ἐπὶ τῆς γῆς κάτω is difficult to determine. The miracles of Jesus,[1] the cosmic signs accompanying the crucifixion,[2] the phenomena which accompanied the Pentecostal outpouring of the Spirit,[3] the miracles of the disciples,[4] and the cosmic portents associated with the Day of the Lord[5] are all viable possibilities. Luke probably had a combination of these events in mind when he penned the verse.

I.H. Marshall suggests that τέρατα designates the cosmic portents which shall herald the end of the world, while σημεῖα alludes to the gift of tongues and healing miracles recorded throughout Acts.[6] This proposal accounts for the ἄνω and κάτω of v. 19 and accords well with the immediate context of the citation (vv. 19b, 20), but it is incompatible with the numerous occasions in Acts where the disciples are cited as performing both σημεῖα and τέρατα.[7] Luke's usage of τέρατα καὶ σημεῖα as a technical term for charismatic activity suggests that the distinctions between τέρατα ἐν τῷ οὐρανῷ ἄνω and σημεῖα ἐπὶ τῆς γῆς κάτω should not be pressed too far. For Luke the principal purpose of ἄνω and κάτω is not to distinguish between two spheres of divine intervention (heaven and earth), but rather to

---

6. Schneider, *Die Apostelgeschichte*, I, p. 269; Kremer, *Pfingstbericht*, pp. 172-74; Rese, *Alttestamentliche Motive*, p. 49; (more tentatively) Holtz, *Untersuchungen*, pp. 12-13. Bock asserts that since the theological significance of the alteration is difficult to evaluate, the source of the insertion, whether traditional or Lukan, cannot be determined (*Proclamation*, p. 163). This judgment, however, ignores the frequent collocation of σημεῖα and τέρατα in Acts.

1. G. Stählin, *Die Apostelgeschichte* (1936), pp. 42, 44-45; Wilckens, *Missionsreden*, p. 33; G. Lüdemann, *Das frühe Christentum nach den Traditionen der Apostelgeschichte* (1987), p. 51.

2. F.F. Bruce, *The Acts of the Apostles* (1951), p. 90; Rese, *Alttestamentliche Motive*, p. 54.

3. Roloff, *Die Apostelgeschichte*, p. 53; Montague, *Spirit*, pp. 285-86.

4. Weiser, *Die Apostelgeschichte. Kapitel 1–12*, p. 92. With reference to 'signs', Haenchen writes, 'man denkt an die Wundertaten der Apostel' ('Schriftzitate', p. 161). The 'signs' however cannot be limited to the apostles: 'signs and wonders' are also attributed by Luke to 'servants' of God (Acts 4.29-30); Barnabas (Acts 14.3; 15.2); and Stephen (Acts 6.8). Thus H.K. Nielsen concludes: 'Die Heilungstätigkeit der Apostelgeschichte zufolge nicht speziell an das Apostolat gebunden war' (*Heilung und Verkündigung* [1987], p. 167). Nielsen however rejects a connection between the τέρατα and σημεῖα of Acts 2.19 and the miracles of healing performed by the disciples (p. 170).

5. Schneider, *Die Apostelgeschichte*, I, p. 269; Bock, *Proclamation*, p. 167; Kremer, *Pfingstbericht*, pp. 172-74.

6. Marshall, *Acts*, p. 74.

7. See Acts 2.43; 4.30; 5.12; 6.8; 14.3; 15.12.

emphasize the universal character of the 'signs and wonders'—they are portents that cannot be overlooked.[1] So also τέρατα and σημεῖα do not refer to two specific and distinctive types of miraculous acts; rather, together they refer to a single series of divine acts—events such as the miracle of Pentecost, the healings recorded in Acts, and the cosmic portents to come—which anticipate the near arrival of the Day of the Lord. In view of the reference to τέρασι καὶ σημείοις in v. 22, it is virtually certain that the semantic range of the collocation in v. 19 also includes the miracles of Jesus,[2] and it may embrace the miraculous events accompanying Jesus' supernatural birth as well.[3] The theological significance of the insertions is now evident. Through his redactional activity in v. 19 Luke was able to link the miraculous events associated with Jesus (v. 22) and his disciples (vv. 3-11, 43) together with the cosmic portents listed by Joel (vv. 19b-20) as 'signs and wonders' which mark the end of the age. In this way Luke stresses the imminence of the Day of the Lord: the miracles in Luke–Acts are precursors of those cosmic signs which shall signal the Day of the Lord.

---

1. Schneider, *Die Apostelgeschichte*, I, p. 269 n. 47: 'Die Zufügung von ἄνω and κάτω verdeutlicht, daß die Zeichen überall und unübersehbar geschehen'. This judgment finds confirmation in the flexibility of Luke's language concerning the sphere in which σημεῖα or τέρατα occur. Luke 21.26 refers to 'σημεῖα [not τέρατα] in the sun, moon, and stars'. The Spirit at Pentecost comes as a wonder ἐκ τοῦ οὐρανοῦ (Acts 2.2) manifested in the signs on earth of γλῶσσαι ὡσεὶ πυρός and miraculous speech (2.3-12) (Montague, *Spirit*, p. 286). Note also Lk. 21.11 where the σημεῖα to come are described as ἀπ' οὐρανοῦ.

2. Weiser, *Die Apostelgeschichte. Kapitel 1–12*, p. 92. Bock raises two objections against this semantic extension: (1) the signs follow the outpouring of the Spirit, 'thus this sequence excludes the references to Jesus or to the crucifixion'; (2) 'the exposition as a whole does not connect these signs done by Jesus [v. 22] with the Spirit as the Joel quote does' (*Proclamation*, p. 346 n. 43). Concerning point (1) it must be stated that there is no reason to assume that Luke felt the various eschatological events described in Joel 3.1-5a needed to occur in the order given in the text. As we have noted, the evidence from his own hands indicates otherwise. In response to point (2) one need only point out that the quotation from Joel does not connect the outpouring of the Spirit with the various signs described in 2.19-20. Although from Luke's perspective the 'signs and wonders' of Acts 2.19 undoubtedly include the Spirit-inspired speech at Pentecost, they designate a much broader spectrum of activities, the rest of which (including the interpretation which Bock proposes for 'signs and wonders': cosmic signs heralding the end) have no connection with the Spirit of prophecy.

3. For a discussion of the eschatological significance of Lk. 1–2 see Chapter 6 above. Note also Lk. 2.12, καὶ τοῦτο ὑμῖν τὸ σημεῖον, although here σημεῖον refers to the lowly and unspectacular circumstances of Jesus' birth.

Having examined the various alterations and determined their Lukan origin, we are now in a position to assess the significance of the modified quotation of Joel 3.1-5a for Luke's understanding of the Pentecostal bestowal of the Spirit. Three points emerge.

(1) *The Spirit of Pentecost is the Spirit of prophecy.* Luke's insertion of καὶ προφητεύσουσιν in v. 18 emphasizes what is otherwise evident from his use of Joel 3.1-5a as the hermeneutical key for the miracle of Pentecost: the Spirit comes upon the disciples as the source of prophetic inspiration. Indeed, the Joel passage explicitly declares what can be deduced from a survey of Luke–Acts: the Spirit, as the Spirit of prophecy, produces inspired speech—intelligible and unintelligible (10.46; 19.6)[1]—and grants special insight, often through visions and revelatory dreams.[2] While the Pentecost event centers on inspired

---

1. Luke, unlike Paul, regards 'tongues' as a special type of prophecy (Turner, 'Luke and the Spirit', p. 132; Carson, *Showing the Spirit*, p. 141). O'Reilly, *Word and Sign*, p. 57: 'For Luke tongues and prophecy are not nearly so distinct as they are for Paul, because for him tongues can be intelligible (Acts 2) and prophecy can be an expression of ecstatic praise'.

2. Of the 59 references to the Spirit of God in Acts, 36 are unequivocally linked to prophetic activity. Although the distinction between the two activities listed below is at times arbitrary since they often overlap, Luke's usage in Acts may be conveniently summarized as follows: the Spirit is the agent of inspired speech (1.8, 16; 2.4, 14, 17, 18, 33; 4.8, 25, 31; 5.32; 6.10; 7.51; 9.31; 10.44, 45; 13.9; 18.25; 19.6; 28.5) and special revelation through which he directs the mission of the church (1.2; 7.55; 8.29; 10.19; 11.12, 28; 13.2, 4; 15.28; 16.6, 7; 19.21; 20.22, 23; 21.4, 11). On the basis of this analysis of the Pentecost account and the important passages discussed in the following chapter, one may affirm that the connection between the Spirit and prophetic activity is implicit in the remaining 23 references (1.5; 2.38; 5.3, 9; 6.3, 5, 10; 8.15, 17, 18, 19, [39]; 9.17; 10.38, 47; 11.15, 16, 24; 13.52; 15.8; 19.2, 12; 20.28). Four groups of texts are often cited as proof that Luke viewed the Spirit as the source of the religious and ethical life of the Christian (see for example von Baer, *Der heilige Geist*, pp. 188-90; Bovon, *Luc le théologien*, p. 232; and Dunn, *Holy Spirit*, pp. 50-51); however, these texts are consistent with the affirmation made above. (1) Acts 2.42-47. As Haya-Prats notes (*Force*, pp. 150-56), there is no indication that Luke considered the diverse aspects of community life mentioned in this summary (so also 4.31-36; 5.11-16) to be the direct result of the Spirit's activity. (2) Acts 5.1-11. Luke's narrative at this point presupposes that the Spirit of prophecy is operative in Peter; thus he is aware of the deception perpetrated by Ananias and Sapphira and describes it as an offense against the Spirit (5.3, 9). Although here the Spirit undoubtedly influences the religious and ethical life of the Christian community, the Spirit does so as the Spirit of prophecy, giving voice to special revelation which in turn directs the actions of the various constituents of the church. The gift of Spirit is never presented as the direct and principal source of moral transformation in the individual; rather, it remains for Luke a prophetic *donum superadditum* which directs the community (indirectly through the prophet) in special instances. (3) Acts

speech, visions and dreams are cited as manifestations of the prophetic gift (2.17) and they appear regularly throughout the narrative in Acts. This indicates that for Luke the value of the Joel passage as an interpretative key is not limited to the manifestation of the Spirit on the day of Pentecost, but extends to those pneumatic events described in the subsequent sections of Acts.[1]

For Luke, the Spirit of prophecy is a gift given exclusively to the people of God. The gift does not produce faith, it is given to faith. Nor can it be said that the gift is the means by which one is justified before God, for a heart for God is the precondition rather than the result of the prophetic gift. This is the clear implication of Luke's use of the Joel text and particularly his insertion of γε and μου (2×) in v. 18. Attempts to interpret the gift of the Spirit prophesied by Joel in light of Ezekiel's promise of cleansing from moral defilement and a new heart for God (Ezek. 36.25f.)[2] have no basis in either the text of Luke–Acts or in prevailing Jewish expectations concerning the eschatological bestowal of the Spirit. My survey of relevant passages from the Jewish literature[3] revealed that the promise of Ezekiel was generally not related to the eschatological bestowal of the Spirit. Rather, Ezek. 36.26 was usually interpreted as a prophecy concerning

6.3, 5, 10; 11.24. The description of the deacons as πλήρεις πνεύματος καὶ σοφίας and Stephen and Barnabas as πλήρης πίστεως καὶ πνεύματος ἁγίου and πλήρης πνεύματος ἁγίου καὶ πίστεως respectively indicates that these men were endowed with the prophetic gift (an *Amtscharisma* vital for the fulfillment of their calling) through which they received special wisdom and confidence. This Spirit-inspired wisdom and faith enabled Stephen (6.10) and Barnabas (11.23-24) to speak authoritatively. Pointing to the ὅτι which connects 11.23 with v. 24, Shelton writes, 'Why does Luke call Barnabas "full of the Holy Spirit and faith?"'. . . because of his exhortation' ('Lucan Redactional Phrases', pp. 83-84, quote p. 84; see also Haya-Prats, *Force*, pp. 142-47, esp. p. 146: 'La sagesse et la foi des sept et en particulier de Philippe (et aussi de Barnabé) ont un sens essentiellement kérygmatique'). (4) Acts 13.52. The χαρά in this instance is remarkable and attributed to the Spirit because it is experienced in the face of persecution (Acts 13.50; 14.19f.). Here, as in Acts 4.31, the Spirit comes upon a persecuted band of disciples in order to equip them with boldness for the task of mission (cf. Acts 13.49). Luke probably penned Acts 13.52 with the promise of Lk. 12.12 in mind. This conclusion not only accords well with the immediate context, but it is suggested by Luke's use of πίμπλημι with the Spirit, which elsewhere in Acts is always associated with an endowment of power for mission resulting in inspired speech (2.4; 4.8, 31; 9.17; 13.9; cf. Lk. 1.41, 67). The parallels between this summary statement and that of Acts 4.31 are particularly striking.

1. Kremer, *Pfingstbericht*, p. 172.
2. See the literature cited Chapter 9 §5.2 above.
3. For my discussion on the various texts see Chapter 5 §2.1 above.

the endtime removal of the evil יצר (impulse), and most frequently without any reference to the activity of the Spirit.[1] The eschatological bestowal of the Spirit, when it appears in the literature, is generally interpreted in connection with Joel 3.1f. as a restoration of the Spirit of prophecy.[2] The hope is frequently expressed that the Spirit of prophecy, withdrawn from Israel due to past sin, will be restored in greater measure in the age to come.[3] Righteousness remains the precondition for the restoration of the prophetic gift. On the two occasions when the promises of Ezekiel and Joel are brought together (*Deut. R.* 6.14; *Ps. R.* 14.6), the transformation of Israel's heart (Ezek. 36.26) is cited as a prerequisite for the eschatological bestowal of the Spirit, which is interpreted in light of Joel 3.1f. as an outpouring of the Spirit of prophecy.

The purpose of the prophetic gift, explicitly stated in Lk. 24.49 and Acts 1.8, is to equip the disciples with power for the mission which lay ahead. This judgment finds confirmation in Luke's citation of Joel, which equates the proclamation of the word of God with prophetic speech.[4] Indeed, the fruit of the prophetic gift is consistently portrayed throughout Acts as the driving force behind the ongoing mission of the church.[5] The Spirit gives the disciples boldness and persuasive power

---

1. See for example *Exod. R.* 15.6, 41.7; *Num. R.* 14.4; *Deut. R.* 6.14; *Midr. Ps.* 14.6; *Cant. R.* 1.2.4; *Eccl. R.* 9.15.

2. See for example *MHG* Gen. 139f.; *Num. R.* 15.25; *Deut. R.* 6.14; *Lam. R.* 4.14; *Midr. Ps.* 14.6, 138.2. Although the texts cited here and above are late (3rd century AD and later), I mention them for two reasons. First, as G. Vermes notes, we are not operating in an ideal situation—our access to relevant source material is limited ('The Impact of the Dead Sea Scrolls on the Study of the New Testament', *JJS* 27 [1976], p. 116). The texts cited represent the earliest available witnesses concerning Jewish interpretation of Joel 3.1f. and Ezek. 36.26 in the post-canonical era. Thus, those wishing to interpret Joel 3.1f. in light of Ezek. 36.26 or link the latter text to Jewish expectations concerning the eschatological bestowal of the Spirit must bear the burden of proof. Second, it is quite likely that these texts bear witness to early traditions and accurately reflect Jewish thought in the first century. See Chapter 5 §2.1 above.

3. See Schäfer, *Die Vorstellung*, pp. 89-115.

4. O'Reilly, *Word and Sign*, pp. 86-89; Panagopoulos, 'Die urchristliche Prophetie', pp. 12-13.

5. Acts 9.31 demonstrates that the words of παράκλησις delivered by Spirit-inspired προφῆται to members of the Christian community cannot be separated from the Christian mission to the world: καὶ τῇ παρακλήσει τοῦ ἁγίου πνεύματος ἐπληθύνετο (on Acts 9.31 see Hill, *New Testament Prophecy*, pp. 102-103). Prophetic inspiration in Acts is always given principally for the benefit of others (not the recipient of the Spirit) and ultimately for the expansion of the church. Therefore Broer is justified when he writes: 'Die Gemeinde erhält den Geist nicht für sich

in their proclamation of the word of God[1] and provides direction, frequently through visions and dreams, for the expanding mission.[2]

(2) *The Spirit of Pentecost is universally available to the people of God.* By applying Joel 3.1f. to Pentecost, Luke asserts that Moses' wish for a bestowal of the Spirit of prophecy upon πάντα τὸν λαὸν κυρίου (Num. 11.29)—reaffirmed as a hope for the age to come in later Jewish tradition[3]—had found initial fulfillment in the Pentecostal gift. Although the πᾶσαν σάρκα of Joel 3.1 refers to ' "everybody" in Israel'[4] and Luke probably intended Peter's words to be understood initially along similar lines,[5] it is evident that Luke understood the promise to extend ultimately to the Gentiles who were incorporated into the people of God (Acts 10.44f.; 11.15f.). According to Luke the community of faith is, at least potentially, a community of prophets; and, it was his expectation that this potential would be realized in the church of his day (Lk. 11.13; 12.10-12; Acts 2.38-39) as it had been in the past (e.g. Acts 2.4; 19.6).[6] Once the exclusive possession of an elite

selbst, nicht zu ihrer eigenen Erbauung, vielmehr zum Zeugnisablegen für Jesus vor der Welt. Der Geist, den die Gemeinde erhält, ist Geist der Mission' ('Der Geist', p. 282).

1. Von Baer, *Der heilige Geist*, pp. 102-104. See Acts 4.13, 31; 5.32; 6.10; 9.31; 13.9, 52. Note Hill's observation that miracle-working is distinguished from prophecy in Acts (2.17f., 43; 5.12-16; 10.34, 40; 19.11f.; *New Testament Prophecy*, p. 108).

2. See Acts 7.56; 9.10f.; 10.3f.; 16.9f.; 18.9f.; 22.17f.; 23.11. Stephen's vision in Acts 7.55f. (cf. 16.9f.) is explicitly linked to the Spirit. Guidance is often attributed directly to the Spirit: Acts 8.29; 10.19; 11.12, 28; 13.2, 4; 15.28; 16.6, 7; 19.21; 20.22, 23, 28; 21.4.

3. Though, as we have seen, this hope was generally linked to Joel 3.1f.

4. Wolff, *Joel and Amos*, p. 67; see also Allen, *Joel, Obadiah, Jonah and Micah*, p. 98.

5. Haenchen, *Acts*, p. 179: 'Luke. . . does not yet intend Peter to proclaim the gift of the Spirit to all men, for that would be anticipating the decisive turning-point of the Cornelius episode (10.44f.; 11.18)'.

6. Contra (1) E. Käsemann's thesis that Luke, as a representative of *Frühkatholizismus*, has institutionalized the Spirit and thereby domesticated the pneumatology of the early church ('Amt und Gemeinde im Neuen Testament', in *Exegetische Versuche und Besinnungen* [1970] I, pp. 109-34; 'Geist und Geist-gaben', *RGG* 3 [1958], II, pp. 1272-79; and 'The Cry for Liberty in the Worship of the Church', in *Perspectives on Paul* (1971), pp. 122-24); and (2) Brown's assertion that 'by detaching the gift of the spirit from the rite of Christian initiation, Luke is able to restrict this gift to the early period of the church, allowing in later periods only the spirit's continuing guidance of the church through the decisions of its leaders, who safeguard the apostolic tradition' ('"Water Baptism"', pp. 135-51, quote from p. 149; see my critique of Brown's thesis on p. 213 n. 2). The judgment of Hengel is to be preferred: 'As far as Luke is concerned, both his enthusiastic conception of

group within the covenant community, the Spirit of prophecy is now, in the last days, universally available to the people of God.[1]

The view advocated above has not received universal acceptance from the scholarly community. Pointing to Luke's description of a special group within the church as προφῆται, many have rejected the notion that Luke viewed the church as a community of prophets.[2] However, this objection fails to account for the flexibility with which the terms προφῆται and προφητεύειν were used in the early church.[3] Paul, for example, refers to a special group of προφῆται (1 Cor. 12.29), yet 'clearly expected that other members of the assembly other than the prophets would be inspired to prophesy (cf. 14.5, 24, perhaps 31)'.[4] And Luke's usage is considerably more flexible than Paul's. Thus, it appears that Luke's designation of various individuals as προφῆται, while implying that these individuals exercise the prophetic gift in a more regular and perhaps profound way than others in the community,[5] does not invalidate the claim that Luke expected each

---

the Spirit and his understanding of the ministry of the church, which at least outside Jerusalem still did not have any hierarchical structure, fail to match the label ["early catholicism"]' (*Acts*, p. 64). See W.G. Kümmel's summary of the 'early catholic' interpretation of Luke and his telling criticism of this position in 'Lukas in der Anklage der heutigen Theologie', *ZNW* 63 (1972), pp. 149-65. Note also the criticisms offered by Leon Morris, 'Luke and Early Catholicism', *WTJ* 35 (1973), pp. 121-36 and I.H. Marshall, ' "Early Catholicism" in the New Testament', in *New Dimensions in New Testament Study* (1970), pp. 217-31.

1. Stronstad, *Charismatic Theology*, p. 59: 'With the outpouring of the Holy Spirit upon the disciples, the age of the prophethood of all believers has dawned'. See also Turner, 'Luke and the Spirit', pp. 130-34 and Hill, *New Testament Prophecy*, pp. 96-97.

2. Flew, *Jesus and His Church*, p. 105; Lampe, *God as Spirit*, pp. 66-69; Jervell, *The Unknown Paul*, pp. 103-104.

3. Panagopoulos, 'Die urchristliche Prophetie', p. 17: 'Die Prophetie als Funktion der Kirche beinhaltet und verkündigt das Evangelium von Jesus Christus. Dabei wird nicht immer genau zwischen allen Gläubigen als Trägern des Geistes und den einzelnen Propheten unterschieden; die Grenzen sind meistens fließend.' See also J. Reiling, 'Prophecy, the Spirit and the Church', in *Prophetic Vocation* (1977), p. 67; H. Kraft, 'Vom Ende der urchristlichen Prophetie', in *Prophetic Vocation* (1977), p. 168; E. Ellis, 'Prophecy in the New Testament Church—And Today', in *Prophetic Vocation* (1977), p. 51 and 'The Role of the Christian Prophet in Acts', in *Apostolic History and the Gospel* (1970), p. 62; D. Hill, 'Prophecy and Prophets in the Revelation of St. John', *NTS* 18 (1972), pp. 411-13 and *New Testament Prophecy*, p. 99; Turner, 'Luke and the Spirit', p. 131.

4. Dunn, *Jesus and the Spirit*, p. 281. See also Carson, *Showing the Spirit*, pp. 117-18 and G. Fee, *The First Epistle to the Corinthians* (1987), pp. 685, 695.

5. Hill, *New Testament Prophecy*, pp. 99, 108.

member of the church to receive the Spirit as the Spirit of prophecy and, as such, to become prophets.[1]

(3) *The Spirit of Pentecost is an eschatological sign.* Luke's application of the Joel text to Pentecost—and particularly his alteration of μετὰ ταῦτα to ἐν ταῖς ἐσχάταις ἡμέραις (Acts 2.17)—highlights the eschatological significance of the Pentecostal gift. The Pentecostal deluge of the Spirit, as an event of the *Endzeit*, is proof that the period immediately preceding the Day of the Lord ('the last days') has indeed arrived. The miracle of Pentecost does not, however, mark the beginning of the *Endzeit*. Rather, it is one in a series of 'signs and wonders' (Acts 2.19) which extends from the miraculous events associated with the birth and ministry of Jesus to the cosmic portents yet to come and heralds the imminent arrival of the Day of the Lord.

3. *Pentecost: A New Sinai?*

Jacques Dupont gives voice to a perception held by many when he describes Pentecost as 'un nouveau Sinaï'.[2] According to this popular line of interpretation, striking points of correspondence between the Pentecost account and Jewish Sinai traditions suggest that Luke and the early Christians viewed the Pentecostal outpouring of the Spirit as the promulgation of a new law and the establishment of a new covenant.[3] Three interrelated arguments are generally offered in support of this conclusion. It is asserted that: (1) by the time Luke penned Acts Pentecost was regarded as a feast commemorating the giving of the law on Sinai;[4] (2) the Pentecost account contains numerous literary allusions

---

1. So also Turner, 'Luke and the Spirit', pp. 130-34 and C.M. Robeck, 'The Gift of Prophecy in Acts and Paul, Part I', StBT 5 (1975), pp. 29-30, 35.

2. Dupont, 'La nouvelle Pentecôte', p. 193, see pp. 193-95.

3. Dupont, 'La nouvelle Pentecôte', p. 195. See also Dunn, *Holy Spirit*, pp. 48-49; Hull, *Acts*, pp. 53-55; Lampe, *God as Spirit*, p. 68; W.L. Knox, *The Acts of the Apostles* (1948), p. 86; O'Reilly, *Word and Sign*, pp. 18-29; R. Le Déaut, 'Pentecost and Jewish Tradition', *DL* 20 (1970), pp. 250-67. Dupont and Lampe speak of the gift of the Spirit as a superior substitution for the law, while Knox and Le Déaut describe the Spirit as a new law. Hull and Dunn prefer to speak of the Spirit as the power of the new law of Christ rather than as the new law itself. So also Pesch: 'Das Feuer des Geistes ist der mit Pfingsten gegebene Ermöglichungsgrund der Erfüllung der Tora' (*Die Apostelgeschichte [Apg 1-12]*, p. 113).

4. See the literature cited above, especially Le Déaut, 'Jewish Tradition', pp. 250-67. Note also J. Potin, *La fête Juive de la Pentecôte* (1971), pp. 301-302 and Haya-Prats, *Force*, pp. 188-189. Haya-Prats interprets Pentecost against the backdrop of Sinai, but argues that Luke does not view the Spirit as a substitute for the law. Rather, for Luke, the Spirit testifies that faith has replaced the law for converts from

to Sinai traditions and therefore was shaped with this event in mind;[1] (3) Acts 2.33 is based on Ps. 67.19 (LXX) and should be interpreted in light of the Psalm.[2] Whereas the rabbis interpreted Ps. 67.19 with

paganism. Luke does however present the gift of the Spirit 'comme le don annonçant la constitution du nouveau peuple de Dieu, de même que la Loi du Sinaï annonçait celle de l'ancien' (p. 189). Grundmann argues that the Pentecost account was influenced by the associations of the feast with the renewal of the covenant, but is more cautious with regard to specific links to Sinai and the law ('Pfingstbericht', pp. 592-93).

   1. See Le Déaut, 'Jewish Tradition', pp. 263-66; Knox, *Acts*, pp. 81-84; Otto Betz, 'Die Proselytentaufe der Qumransekte und die Taufe im Neuen Testament', *RQ* 1 (1958–59), p. 227, 'The Eschatological Interpretation of the Sinai-Tradition in Qumran and in the New Testament', *RQ* 6 (1967), p. 93, and 'φωνή', *TDNT*, IX, p. 296; Pesch, *Die Apostelgeschichte (Apg 1-12)*, pp. 101-102; Lüdemann, *Das frühe Christentum*, pp. 47-48; Dupont, 'La nouvelle Pentecôte', pp. 194-95 and 'Christian Pentecost', pp. 39-45. Pointing to the similarities between Acts 2.1-13 and the Sinai traditions (particularly Philo, *Dec.* 33, 46), Dupont writes, 'It is quite easy for us to believe, therefore, that Luke's description of Pentecost in Acts would have reminded Jewish readers of that spectacular scene on Sinai. By alluding in his Pentecost episode to several very well known features of that scene, such as the "resounding noise" which is also a "sound", Luke establishes a parallelism between the two events. In this way he subtly suggests that the first Christian Pentecost is a repetition of the original theophany of Sinai which was commemorated by the Jewish feast of Pentecost' ('Christian Pentecost', p. 40). So also Maddox, noting Philo's midrash on Exod. 19 and the rabbinic tradition describing the division of the divine word at Sinai into seventy languages, writes, 'All this suggests an interpretation of the Pentecost-event as a re-enactment of God's coming to Israel to establish the Sinai-covenant, so that the new covenant of the end-time is hinted at' (*Purpose*, p. 138). Schweizer asserts that the Pentecost account was 'strongly influenced' by Sinai traditions in the pre-Lukan stage ('πνεῦμα', p. 411). Turner ('Christology', p. 178) and Kremer (*Pfingstbericht*, pp. 238-52) reject any direct literary dependence between Luke and the Sinai traditions, yet affirm that elements of Pentecost account show contact with such traditions. Dunn (*Holy Spirit*, p. 49; cf. *Jesus and the Spirit*, pp. 140-41), while affirming that a link exists, rejects the notion that the Sinai traditions have 'powerfully moulded' the Pentecost account. Similarly, Hull states that Luke had the giving of the law in mind when he wrote Acts 2, yet asserts that the account was based on historical facts and not primarily theologically determined (*Acts*, pp. 53-55, 78-79). Adler concludes: 'Die Erzählung vom Sprachenwunder steht unter dem Einfluß der jüdischen Sage von den wunderbaren Ereignissen bei der Gesetzgebung am Berge Sinai, die entweder unbewußt auf die Entwicklung der Pfingsterzählung eingewirkt hat, order bewußt in der Erzählung der Apg nachgebildet worden ist' (*Pfingstfest*, pp. 36-37).

   2. F.H. Chase, *The Credibility of the Book of the Acts of the Apostles* (1902), p. 151; H.J. Cadbury, 'The Speeches in Acts', in *The Beginnings of Christianity*, V, pp. 408-409; Knox, *Acts*, pp. 85f.; G. Kretschmar, 'Himmelfahrt und Pfingsten', *ZKG* 66 (1954-55), pp. 216, 218; Le Déaut, 'Jewish Tradition', pp. 260-262; B. Lindars, *New Testament Apologetic* (1961), pp. 42, 51-59; T.

reference to Moses who, at Sinai, ascended into heaven to receive the Torah in order that he might give it to men, in Acts 2.33 the Psalm is applied to Jesus who ascended to the right hand of God, received the Spirit, and poured it out on the disciples. Thus the gift of the Spirit is viewed as the essence of the new covenant and the new law—an interior law, written on the heart (Jer. 31.33; cf. Ezek. 36.26).[1]

This line of interpretation is admittedly incompatible with my assessment of Luke's understanding of the Pentecostal gift. Yet how strong are the arguments adduced in support of the position outlined above? Did Luke really intend to present Pentecost as a new Sinai?

3.1. *Pentecost as a Feast Commemorating the Giving of the Law at Sinai*

The term 'feast of Weeks' (חג שבעות) referred to the period of seven weeks during which the grain was harvested (Deut. 16.9f.)[2] and, more specifically, to the festival day culminating this period on which the first-fruits of the wheat harvest (i.e. the cereal offering, Lev. 23.17f.) were offered by the people to the Lord.[3] The date of this festival day was established as the fiftieth day (seven weeks and a day) after the sheaf offering (Lev. 23.9f.) was presented by the priest to God on behalf of the people.[4] Thus the festival became known among Greek

---

Dupont, 'Ascension du Christ et don de l'Esprit d'après Acts 2,33', in *Nouvelles études* (1984), pp. 199-209; Turner, 'Christology', pp. 176-79.

1. This line of interpretation is followed by Knox, *Acts*, pp. 85f.; Le Déaut, 'Jewish Tradition', pp. 260-62, 266; Kretschmar, 'Himmelfahrt', pp. 209-53 and Dupont, 'Ascension', pp. 199-209. Turner however accepts the link between Ps. 67.19 and Acts 2.33, yet interprets the gift of the Spirit as the Spirit of prophecy promised in Joel 3.1f.—not as the essence of the new covenant and new law ('Christology', pp. 179-181; cf. 'Luke and the Spirit', pp. 151-152). And although B. Lindars argues that Acts 2.33 is based on Ps. 67.19, his concern is to trace the development of this tradition in the thought of the early church and not to draw out the parallels with Sinai traditions.

2. See also Exod. 34.22; Num. 28.26; 2 Chron. 8.13.

3. Thus the feast was also known as the 'feast of harvest' (Exod. 23.16) and the 'day of firstfruits' (Num. 28.26).

4. The calculation of this date became a matter of dispute between the Pharisees and the Boethusians (a group of Sadducees). The dispute centered on the interpretation of the term 'Sabbath' in Lev. 23.15-16. The Pharisees interpreted the 'Sabbath' in question as a reference to the first day of the Passover feast (celebrated as a Sabbath), and thus counted 50 days from Nisan 15. Thus the festival day fell on the same day of the week as Nisan 16. The Boethusians, however, understood the 'Sabbath' of Lev. 23.15 to refer to the first weekly Sabbath after the Passover, and thus the festival day always fell on a Sunday. The method of computation advocated by the Pharisees appears to have dominated in the 1st century. See J.C. Rylaardsdam. 'Feast

speaking Jews as 'the day of Pentecost' (ἡ ἡμέρα τῆς πεντηκοστῆς).[1] As such, Pentecost was a festival of harvest.

The feast ultimately became associated with the giving of the law at Sinai. This is implied by R. Jose b. Chalaphta (c. 150 AD)[2] and R. Eleazar (c. 270 AD),[3] who place the giving of the law on the day of Pentecost,[4] and confirmed by the lectionary (triennial) cycle which normally called for the Decalogue to be read on Pentecost. However, this evidence is late and of little value for reconstructing Jewish attitudes toward the feast before the destruction of the temple.[5] The transformation of the feast from a harvest festival to a festival commemorating the law was undoubtedly given impetus through the destruction of the temple.[6] Without the temple the rituals of sacrifice so central to the harvest feast could no longer be performed.[7] New

of Weeks', *IDB*, IV, p. 826; Kremer, *Pfingstbericht*, pp. 12-14; Marshall, 'Pentecost', p. 348 n. 1; and S. Safrai, *The Jewish People in First Century* (1976), II, pp. 892-93.

1. See Tob. 2.1; 2 Macc. 12.32; Philo, *Dec.* 160; *Spec. Leg.* 2.176; Josephus, *Ant.* 3.252; 13.252; 14.337; 17.254; *War* 1.253; 2.42; 6.299; Acts 2.1; 20.16; 1 Cor. 16.8.

2. *S. 'Ol. R.* 5: 'The Israelites immolated the Passover lamb in Egypt on the fourteenth of Nisan and it was a Thursday . . . The third month, the sixth day of the month, the Ten Commandments were given to them, and it was a sabbath day' (cited from Le Déaut, 'Jewish Tradition', pp. 256-57).

3. *B. Pes.* 68b: 'It [the feast of Weeks] is the day on which the Torah was given'.

4. Le Déaut, 'Jewish Tradition', pp. 259-60. Le Déaut notes that 'an old text of the Palestinian Targum, found in Cairo, explicitly indicates Exodus 19:1–20:23 as a reading for the "feast of weeks" ' (p. 260).

5. The lectionary system was not operative until after the destruction of the temple (note also Kremer, *Pfingstbericht*, p. 21: 'Die Lesung von Ex 19-20 hatte ursprünglich beim Neujahrsfest ihren festen Platz und wurde vermutlich erst später mit dem Pfingstfest verbunden') and the rabbinic texts clearly stem from this later period (R. de Vaux, *Ancient Israel: Its Life and Institutions* [1961], p. 495: 'The idea that it [the feast of Pentecost] commemorated the day on which the Law was given on Sinai was not accepted by the Rabbis until the second century of our era'. Note also Strack–Billerbeck, *Kommentar*, II, p. 601: 'Die spätere Meinung, daß das Fest zum Andenk an die sinaitische Gesetzgebung gefeiert werde, läßt sich quellenmäßig erst seit dem 2. nachchristl. Jahrh. nachweisen').

6. E. Lohse, 'πεντηκοστή', *TDNT*, VI, pp. 48-49 and 'Die Bedeutung', p. 186; Rylaarsdam, 'Feast of Weeks', p. 827; Kremer, *Pfingstbericht*, pp. 18-19; B. Noack, 'The Day of Pentecost in Jubilees, Qumran, and Acts', *ASTI* 1 (1962), p. 80.

7. Note also Noack, 'The Day of Pentecost', p. 80: 'The dwelling of Israel in its own country was the natural condition for attaching any meaning to an agricultural festival; when Israel was exiled in AD 70 and again permanently in 135, that condition

practices and emphases would have emerged out of necessity; and, in view of the Pharisees' emphasis on the law, it is only natural that the reading of the Decalogue and the commemoration of its revelation at Sinai became prominent features of the feast.[1]

What evidence is there that Pentecost had been transformed into a festival commemorating the giving of the law at Sinai by the time of Luke's writing? *Jubilees* portrays the feast as a harvest festival (22.1; 6.21-22) and, more significantly, as a ceremony for the renewal of the covenant made to Noah (6.1-20). However, the connections between the feast and the giving of the law at Sinai are minor (1.1; 6.19) and based on the perception of Sinai as a renewal of the Noahic covenant.[2] Indeed, while the feast is emphatically linked to the covenants made with Noah (6.1-20) and Abraham (15.1-24), a similar emphasis with regard to the giving of the law at Sinai is lacking.

The liturgical practice of the Qumran community included an annual[3] ceremony of covenant renewal (1QS 1.8–2.18), but associations with the feast of Pentecost remain obscure.[4] On the basis of the

did not exist any more, except in the comparatively rare cases of Jews still inhabiting the land of their forefathers—many of them, it is true, were Rabbis'.

1. Potin puts forth the hypothesis that after the destruction of the Temple the Pharisees, who originally commemorated the giving of the law on the feast of Trumpets, moved the celebration of the law (including the reading of the Decalogue) to the feast of Pentecost. Why was this change in the liturgical calendar made? Potin argues that before the destruction of the temple the feast of Pentecost had become known as a feast of the covenant and, perhaps, given national and patriotic significance. Therefore, the Pharisees sought to emphasize the importance of the law by placing the law at the center of the nation's celebration and renewal of the covenant (*La fête Juive*, pp. 139-40).

2. Potin, *La fête juive*, pp. 128, 135. Potin contrasts the perspective of *Jubilees*, which focuses on the covenant, with the rabbinic emphasis on the law (pp. 131-32). See also Noack, 'The Day of Pentecost', pp. 85-86; Kretschmar, 'Himmelfahrt', p. 229; Schneider, *Die Apostelgeschichte*, I, p. 246 n. 34; and Conzelmann, *Acts*, p. 16 n. 25.

3. Note the translation of 1QS 2.19 offered by P. Wernberg-Møller and G. Vermes: 'Thus they shall do, year after year' (P. Wernberg-Møller, *The Manual of Discipline Translated and Annotated with an Introduction* [1957], p. 24; Vermes, *The Dead Sea Scrolls in English*, p. 63). This translation, in contrast to that of T.H. Gaster (*The Scriptures of the Dead Sea Sect* [1957], p. 51: 'The following procedure is to be followed year by year'), indicates that the preceding instructions (1QS 1.8–2.18) form part of an annual ceremony.

4. No date is given for the ceremony in the scrolls which have been published to date, although J.T. Milik states that unpublished evidence from the *Damascus Document* (4QDb) places the ceremony in the same month as Pentecost (*Ten Years of Discovery in the Wilderness of Judaea* [1959], p. 117). See also Kremer, *Pfingstbericht*, p. 17 and A. Jaubert, *La notion d'alliance dans le Judaïsme aux*

community's use of *Jubilees* and 'oath terminology'[1] in the *Damascus Document* and the *Community Rule*, Roger Le Déaut concludes that the feast of שבעות was celebrated by the community as a feast of the covenant.[2] Although this suggestion is supported by the community's probable adoption of the solar calendar of *Jubilees*,[3] it has not been substantiated by evidence from the scrolls.

The evidence from *Jubilees* and the scrolls of Qumran establishes that in some sectarian circles the feast of Pentecost was, by the mid-second century BC, celebrated as a harvest festival *and* a feast of covenant renewal. However, this evidence does not indicate that the feast of Pentecost was viewed more specifically as a festival commemorating the giving of the law at Sinai. While it is possible that the linkage of the feast with a ceremony for covenant renewal led to the later associations with Sinai,[4] such a linkage does not demonstrate that these later associations occurred prior to the destruction of the temple.[5] And, even more significant, several factors indicate that the sectarian observance of Pentecost as a feast of covenant renewal was not indicative of general practice in first-century Judaism.[6] Josephus and Philo know nothing of the feast as either a festival of covenant renewal

abords de l'ère Chrétienne (1963), p. 215. Note, however, the judgment of Conzelmann: 'It cannot be proved that the festival involved a covenant renewal, and in view of the order of festivals in 1QS 1, the argument from silence is convincing' (*Acts*, p. 16).

1. The unpointed שבעות can be read as either 'weeks' or 'oaths'.
2. Le Déaut, 'Jewish Tradition', pp. 254-56.
3. See S. Talmon, 'The Calendar Reckoning of the Sect from the Judaean Desert', in *Scripta Hierosolymitana IV: Aspects of the Dead Sea Scrolls* (1967), pp. 177-79; Jaubert, *La notion d'alliance*, p. 90; Manns, *Symbole*, p. 110; and Vermes, *The Dead Sea Scrolls in English*, pp. 43-44. Note, however, the more cautious appraisal of Sanders (as well as the literature he cites): 'I am not competent to judge whether or not the calendars are identical or only similar, and it is not clear that enough evidence exists to allow the decision to be made' (*Paul*, p. 385).
4. See for example Potin, *La fête juive*, pp. 139-40. It is possible that this linkage was also facilitated by 2 Chron. 15.10-12 and Exod. 19.1: the former text places the renewal of the covenant under Asa in the third month of the fifteenth year of his reign; the later text places the events of Sinai in the third month after the exodus from Egypt.
5. See Rylaarsdam, 'Feast of Weeks', p. 827.
6. The unique and sectarian nature of the Qumran community's celebration of the feast of Weeks is illustrated in the peculiar liturgical calendar of the Temple Scroll (11QT). The feast of First-fruits or Weeks is divided into three different feasts (the feasts of New Wheat, New Wine, and Oil), each separated by an interval of fifty days (cf. 11 QT, cols. 18-24). See Y. Yadin, *The Temple Scroll: The Hidden Law of the Dead Sea Sect* (1985), pp. 91-96.

or a celebration of the Torah.[1] In fact, Philo connects the giving of the law with the feast of Trumpets.[2] Similarly, the New Testament shows no awareness of the feast as a remembrance of the covenant or Sinai. The allusions to the feast in the New Testament consistently draw upon imagery taken from the harvest festival.[3] And the rabbis offer decisive proof that at least as late as the early second century AD the association of the law with Pentecost was open to dispute.[4]

My conclusions may be summarized as follows: (1) Pentecost was not celebrated as a festival commemorating the giving of the law at Sinai at the time of Luke's writing; (2) While Pentecost was regarded as a feast of covenant renewal in some sectarian circles during the first century, the feast was generally celebrated simply as a harvest festival in the Judaism of this period; (3) It is therefore illegitimate to assume that the mere mention of τὴν ἡμέραν τῆς πεντηκοστῆς (Acts 2.1) would have evoked images of Moses, Sinai, or the covenant renewal ceremony in the minds of Luke's readers.

3.2. *Acts 2.1-13: Literary Allusions to Sinai traditions?*

Numerous passages have been cited in support of the contention that Luke was influenced by Sinai traditions when he penned the Pentecost account.[5] The most prominent of these include texts from Philo (*Dec.* 32–36, 44–49; *Spec. Leg.* 2.188-89), *Targ. Ps.-J.* on Exod. 20.2, and several rabbinic legends (e.g. *b. Shab.* 88b).[6] The texts from Philo and *Targ. Ps.-J.* contain imagery similar to that employed by Luke in Acts 2.1-4 and the rabbinic legends refer to a language miracle at Sinai

---

1. For texts that indicate the feast was viewed as a harvest festival see Philo, *Spec. Leg.* 2.176-87; *Dec.* 160; and Josephus, *Ant.* 3.252-57. Note also Tob. 2.1: ἐν τῇ πεντηκοστῇ τῇ ἑορτῇ, ἥ ἐστιν ἁγία ἑπτὰ ἑβδομάδων.

2. *Spec. Leg.* 2.188.

3. As Rylaarsdam ('Feast of Weeks', p. 828) notes, the NT allusions are 'in terms of the symbolic meaning of the sacrificial loaves as first fruits (Rom. 8:23; 11:16; 1 Cor. 15:20, 23)'.

4. In *b. Yom.* 4b R. Jose the Galilean and R. Akiba discuss whether or not the Torah was proclaimed on the day of the feast of Weeks. As Noack notes, 'this would seem to indicate that, at the time of Trajan or even Hadrian, this was still a matter for contention among the Rabbis' ('The Day of Pentecost', p. 81). Note also the comment of Milik, *Ten Years of Discovery*, p. 117: 'Later Jewish tradition was divided, some placing this event [the giving of the law at Sinai] on the first of the month, but the majority on the Feast of Weeks'.

5. See the literature cited on p. 269 n. 1. Note also Kremer's survey of the various Sinai traditions in *Pfingstbericht*, pp. 238-53.

6. For a more complete listing of the rabbinic legends see Strack–Billerbeck, *Kommentar*, II, pp. 604-605.

which is often paralleled with the miraculous speech of the disciples in Acts 2.5-13.

How significant are these parallels? Do they suggest that Luke has consciously shaped his Pentecost account in light of these or similar Sinai traditions? In assessing the significance of these texts for Luke's literary activity in Acts 2.1f. one must be mindful of the cautions voiced by S. Sandmel in his helpful article, 'Parallelomania'.[1] Sandmel offers three comments which are particularly relevant for this inquiry. First, he notes that similarities may reflect a shared milieu rather than direct literary dependence. For this reason it is imperative not only to isolate the parallels between Acts 2.1f. and the various Sinai traditions, but also to determine the parameters of the milieu in which these parallels are found. Indeed, a crucial yet often ignored question must be addressed: are the parallels between Acts 2.1f. and the texts from Philo and *Targ. Ps.-J.* unique to Sinai traditions or are they representative of a broader milieu? Second, Sandmel notes that distinctions are often more important than similarities. As one compares Acts 2.1f. with the various Sinai traditions, it is important to be alert to distinctions as well as to similarities. Third, Sandmel warns against anachronistically reading late rabbinic citations as 'persuasive parallels' for the New Testament documents. This warning serves to remind us of the tenuous nature of the purported parallels between Acts 2.1f. and the rabbinic legends. Is there any support for the assumption that these legends are based on first-century traditions? With these cautionary words and questions in mind, I shall examine the texts cited above and assess their significance for the tradition-history of Acts 2.1-13.

3.2.1. *Language/Imagery Parallels: Philo and Targum Pseudo-Jonathan.* In *Dec.* 33 Philo describes the declaration of God at Sinai as 'an invisible sound in the air' (ἦχον ἀόρατον ἐν ἀέρι) which changed into 'flaming fire' (πῦρ φλογοειδές) and sounded forth like 'breath through a trumpet' (πνεῦμα διὰ σάλπιγγος). Indeed, Philo indicates in *Dec.* 46 that the divine voice (φωνή) came out of the midst of this heavenly fire (ἀπ' οὐρανοῦ πυρός) for the flame was transformed into the language (φλογὸς εἰς διάλεκτον) of the people present. We read in *Spec. Leg.* 2.189 that this 'blast of the trumpet' reached to the 'ends of the earth' (ἐν ἐσχατιαῖς κατοικοῦντας).

The images of wind and fire are also associated with the word of God delivered at Sinai in *Targ. Ps.-J.* on Exod. 20.2:

---

1. Sandmel, 'Parallelomania', pp. 1-13.

The first word (דבירא קדמאה), as it came forth from the mouth of the Holy One, whose Name be blessed, was like storms (כזיקין), and lightnings (כברקין), and flames of fire (כשלהוביין דינור), with a burning light on His right hand and on His left. It winged its way through the air of the heavens (באויר שמיא), and was made manifest unto the camp of Israel, and returned, and was engraven on the tables of the covenant that were given by the hand of Mosheh.[1]

These descriptions of the word of God in terms of wind and fire from heaven are quite similar to aspects of Luke's Pentecost account. At Pentecost the Spirit's coming is associated with the sound of wind from heaven (ἐκ τοῦ οὐρανοῦ ἦχος ὥσπερ φερομένης πνοῆς βιαίας) and the imagery of fire (γλῶσσαι ὡσεὶ πυρός). The immediate result is inspired speech (λαλεῖν ἑτέραις γλώσσαις) in the languages (διαλέκτῳ) of those present. Indeed, a number of the terms utilized by Philo with reference to the Sinai event are also found in Acts 2.1f.: ἦχον, πῦρ, πυρός, πνεῦμα, φωνή, οὐρανοῦ, διάλεκτον, κατοικοῦντας.

These similarities should not obscure the significant differences which exist between the Lukan account and the Sinai traditions of Philo and *Targ. Ps.-J.*[2] In contrast to the Sinai traditions, Luke associates the Spirit rather than the voice of God with the wind and fire imagery. In Luke's account these metaphors are not directly related to the language miracle. It is particularly significant that neither Philo nor *Targ. Ps.-J.* refers to the voice of God at Sinai being transformed into *different* languages as in the miracle of Pentecost.[3]

---

1. ET from J.W. Etheridge, *The Targums of Onkelos and Jonathan Ben Uzziel on the Pentateuch* (1968); Aramaic text from M. Ginsburger, *Pseudo-Jonathan*.

2. Kremer, *Pfingstbericht*, pp. 245-48.

3. As noted above, in *Dec.* 46 Philo describes the transformation of the heavenly flame into the language of the people present. The text reads: φωνὴ δ' ἐκ μέσου τοῦ ῥυέντος ἀπ' οὐρανοῦ πυρὸς ἐξήχει καταπληκτικωτάτη, τῆς φλογὸς εἰς διάλεκτον ἀρθρουμένης τὴν συνήθη τοῖς ἀκρωμένοις, ᾗ τὰ λεγόμενα οὕτως ἐναργῶς ἐτρανοῦτο, ὡς ὁρᾶν αὐτὰ μᾶλλον ἢ ἀκούειν δοκεῖν ('Then from the midst of the fire that streamed from heaven there sounded forth to their utter amazement a voice, for the flame became articulate speech in the language familiar to the audience, and so clearly and distinctly were the words formed by it that they seemed to see rather than hear them' [LCL]). That Philo has in mind here a single language is evident from (1) his use of the singular form of διάλεκτος (εἰς διάλεκτον) without qualification (cf. ἤκουον εἷς ἕκαστος τῇ ἰδίᾳ διαλέκτῳ λαλούντων αὐτῶν, Acts 2.6) and (2) the context, which indicates that the 'audience' is restricted to the people of Israel. Reference to the universal scope of the divine oracle is found only in *Spec. Leg.* 2.189. Here the giving of the law is described as a 'trumpet blast' reaching to the 'ends of the earth' and no reference is made to the transformation of the sound into language.

Indeed, according to Philo the words are not so much heard as they are seen (*Dec.* 46f.). The lightning-motif present in the accounts of Philo and *Targ. Ps.-J.* is entirely absent in Acts 2.1f. Similarly, the trumpet blast metaphor so prominent in Philo's description of the Sinai event (cf. Heb. 12.18f.) is without parallel in Luke's account. Philo of course connected the giving of the law with the feast of Trumpets (*Spec. Leg.* 2.188-89), not Pentecost.

In spite of these important differences the collocation of terms such as 'wind', 'fire', 'heaven', 'language, word, or voice' in each of the texts suggests that they stem from a similar milieu. However, as we noted above, it is important to determine the parameters of this shared milieu. It is often assumed that these parallels indicate Luke's account has been influenced by Sinai traditions. Yet this assumption is valid only if the collocation of terms outlined above is unique to Sinai traditions. Evidence from numerous Jewish texts reveals that this is not the case. The following texts are unrelated to the giving of the law at Sinai, yet they contain the terms and imagery common to Acts 2.1f. and the Sinai traditions:[1]

1. In the sixth vision of *4 Ezra* (13.1f.) Ezra sees a divine figure whom he likens to 'wind' (*ventus*) and associates with 'clouds from heaven' (*nubibus caeli*; 13.3). The figure's 'voice' (*vox*) is compared to 'fire' (*ignem*; 13.4). From his mouth issue forth 'streams of fire' (*fluctum ignis*), from his lips 'flaming breath' (*spiritum flammae*), and from his tongue (*lingua*) 'a storm of sparks' (*scintillas tempestatis*; 13.10).[2]

2. In Ch. 14 of *1 Enoch* the author describes his visionary transport by the 'winds' (ἄνεμοι) into 'heaven' (οὐρανόν; 14.8-9). There he encountered a wall surrounded by 'tongues of fire' (γλῶσσαι τοῦ πυρός; 14.9, 10). Passing through the wall and a house of fire, Enoch entered into a second house built entirely of 'tongues of fire' (14.15). In this house of fire stood a fiery throne and upon this throne sat 'the Great Glory' (14.18-20). From this dazzling throne, engulfed with fire,

---

1. See also the imagery employed in Exod. 3.2 (fire/voice); Exod. 13.21; 14.24; Num. 14.14 (cloud/fire); 1 Kgs 19.11-12 (fire/wind); Job 37.2-5 (thunder/lightning/voice); Ezek. 1.25-28 (voice/fire); Dan. 7.9-14 (fire/cloud/languages); 1 Thess. 1.7 (heaven/fire).

2. ET from Metzger, 'The Fourth Book of Ezra' in Charlesworth, *The Old Testament Pseudepigrapha*, I, p. 551; Latin text from the edition of Violet, *Die Esra-Apokalypse (IV. Esra)*, pp. 366f.

came the voice of God: 'Come near to me, Enoch, and to my holy Word' (14.25).[1]

3.   2 Samuel 22.8-15 contains a graphic and visionary description of the Lord's intervention on David's behalf. With 'fire' (πῦρ) flaming from his mouth, the Lord 'parted the heavens' (ἔκλινεν οὐρανούς) and came down (22.9-10). Soaring on the 'wings of the wind' (πτερύγων ἀνέμου; 22.11), 'the voice [φωνήν] of the Most High resounded'. This divine declaration is likened to thunder (22.14) and the 'rebuke of the Lord' to a 'blast of the breath of his anger' (πνοῆς πνεύματος θυμοῦ αὐτοῦ; 22.16).

4.   Isaiah 66.15f. records a prophecy of eschatological judgment and restoration: 'See, the Lord is coming with fire (πῦρ), and his chariots are like a whirlwind (ὡς καταιγίς); he will bring down his anger with fury, and his rebuke with flames of fire (φλογὶ πυρός; 66.15)'. Then the Lord will 'gather all nations and tongues' (πάντα τὰ ἔθνη καὶ τὰς γλώσσας) (66.18).

These texts indicate that the terms shared by Luke, Philo, and Jonathan Ben Uzziel are not unique to Sinai traditions but characteristic of theophanic language in general.[2] This fact and the notable differences between Acts 2.1f. and the texts of Philo and *Targ. Ps.-J.* suggest that Luke's Pentecost account was not influenced by these or similar Sinai traditions.[3] The similarities between Luke's Pentecost account and the Sinai traditions of Philo and Jonathan Ben Uzziel are best explained by their common acquaintance with the language of Jewish theophany.

3.2.2. The Language Miracle Parallel: b. Shabbat 88b. Representative of the rabbinic Sinai legends cited as parallels to Acts 2.5-11 are two

---

1. ET from E. Isaac, '1 Enoch', pp. 20-21; Greek text from the edition of Black, *Apocalypsis Henochi Graece*, pp. 28-29. In the final phrase cited ('my holy Word') Isaac's translation follows the Ethiopic text. The Greek text, however, reads: τὸν λόγον μου ἄκουσον.

2. Conzelmann, *Acts*, p. 16; Schneider, *Die Apostelgeschichte*, I, pp. 246-47; Kremer, *Pfingstbericht*, p. 245, 248.

3. So also Lohse concludes: 'One can hardly accept as valid any attempt to establish a connection with the Sinai tradition on the basis of Acts 2. Reference has often been made to the elaboration of the Sinai story by Philo in *Dec.* 32–49. But this account does not mention Pentecost and is simply a development of the OT narrative' ('πεντηκοστή', p. 49 n. 33). See also Lohse, 'Die Bedeutung', pp. 185-86; Wilson, *The Gentiles*, p. 127; and Schneider, *Die Apostelgeschichte*, I, p. 246 n. 34.

traditions recorded in the Babylonian Talmud (*b. Shab.* 88b).[1] With reference to the divine declaration at Sinai, Rabbi Jochanan (d. 279 AD) is quoted as saying: 'Every single word that went forth from the Omnipotent was split up into seventy languages'. A similar tradition from the school of Rabbi Ishmael (d. 135 AD) is also cited: 'Just as a hammer is divided into many sparks, so every single word that went forth from the Holy One, blessed be He, split up into seventy languages'.[2]

These descriptions of the miraculous division of the divine word into seventy languages bear some resemblance to the language miracle of Acts 2.5-13. The key parallel is the communication of a divine oracle in different languages. Yet this similarity can hardly be cited as proof that Luke's account was influenced by these rabbinic traditions. Given the contexts of Sinai (divine oracle) and Pentecost (inspired speech) and the respective writers' interest in the universal significance of the events which they describe, it is not surprising that a parallel of this nature is found in these accounts.

Apart from the superficial parallel outlined above, these texts have little in common. In the rabbinic legends the oracle is delivered by God himself; in Luke's account it is transmitted by Spirit-inspired disciples. The rabbinic legends speak of individual words being divided into different languages, a concept completely foreign to Luke's account. And of course the number of language groups represented by Luke's *Völkerliste* is considerably less than the seventy cited in the rabbinic legends. These differences demonstrate the improbability of any direct link between Luke's account and the rabbinic Sinai legends.[3]

The theory that Luke was influenced by these rabbinic legends can also be questioned on the grounds that it anachronistically reads Acts 2 in light of rabbinic texts from a later era.[4] Although it is possible that

---

1. ET from H. Freedman *Shabbath*, II, (1938) in I. Epstein (ed.), *The Babylonian Talmud*, p. 420.

2. R. Jochanan: כל דיבור ודיבור שיצא מפי הגבורה נחלק לשבעים לשונות; cf. with the tradition of R. Ishmael: כל דיבור שיצא מפי הקדוש ברוך הוא נחלק לשבעים לשונות. Hebrew text from *Der Babylonische Talmud*, ed. L. Goldschmidt, I, p. 522.

3. Note the introduction given to these and other similar rabbinic Sinai legends in the *Kommentar* of Strack and Billerbeck: 'Man hat das Sprachenwunder der Pfingstgeschichte mehrfach als legendarisches Gegenstück zu gewissen Sagen hinstellen wollen, mit denen die alte Synagoge die sinaitische Gesetzgebung ausgeschmückt hat. Zum Beweis, wie wenig berechtigt diese Meinung ist, lassen wir die betreffenden Ausschmückungen hier folgen' (II, p. 604). So also Kremer concludes: 'Die unübersehbaren Unterschiede verbieten es auch hier, eine literarische Abhängigkeit zu folgern' (*Pfingstbericht*, p. 251).

4. Lohse, 'πεντηκοστή', p. 49 n. 33 and 'Die Bedeutung', p. 185.

these texts reflect traditions which stem from the first century, support for such an assumption is lacking. Indeed, an analysis of the Sinai accounts produced in the first century of our era[1] suggests that the tradition concerning the division of the divine voice into seventy languages was a later development. Neither Philo nor Josephus shows an awareness of this tradition. The tradition's absence from Philo's Sinai account is particularly striking since his emphasis on the universal dimension of the divine oracle (*Spec. Leg.* 2.189) points toward the necessity of such a view. It would appear that Philo represents a stage in the progressive development of the Sinai tradition which was a necessary antecedent to the tradition concerning the seventy languages. It is therefore unlikely that the tradition cited in *b. Shab.* 88b was widely known at the time of Luke's writing.

Having completed the examination of the relevant texts from Philo, *Targ. Ps.-J.*, and the Babylonian Talmud, I am now in a position to summarize my findings. The similarities and differences between Acts 2.1f. and the Sinai traditions of Philo and *Targ. Ps.-J.* suggest that these accounts represent two independent textual traditions produced by authors who were familiar with the language of Jewish theophany. The often cited parallels between Luke's account and the rabbinic legends are more apparent than real and, in all probability, these legends belong to a later era. The evidence thus indicates that Luke was not influenced by these or similar Sinai traditions when he penned his Pentecost account. This judgment precludes the more radical claim that Luke consciously shaped his account in order to present Pentecost as a 'new Sinai'.[2]

3.3. *Acts 2.33: Moses Typology and Associations with Psalm 67.19 (LXX)?*

The assertion that Luke (or the tradition he utilized) portrays the gift of the Spirit in Acts 2.33 as the essence of the new covenant is founded on two suppositions: (1) Acts 2.33, as Eph. 4.8, is based on Ps. 67.19

---

1. Philo, *Dec.* 32–36; 44–49; *Spec. Leg.* 2.188-189; Josephus, *Ant.* 3.79-80, 90; cf. Heb. 12.18-21.

2. It is difficult to follow the logic of those who, on the one hand deny that Luke's Pentecost account has been significantly shaped by the Sinai traditions, yet on the other hand continue to insist that Luke intended to present the bestowal of the Spirit at Pentecost as the giving of the new Torah (e.g. Dunn, *Holy Spirit*, pp. 48-49; Hull, *Acts*, pp. 53-55, 78-79). Although I have argued that neither assumption is valid, it would appear that the former assumption is a necessary presupposition for the latter. Would Luke's audience have interpreted the Pentecost event in light of the giving of the law at Sinai unless Acts 2.1-13 was significantly shaped by the Sinai traditions?

(LXX); (2) Acts 2.33 represents a Christian counterpart to rabbinic exegesis of Psalm 67[1] and, as such, presents the bestowal of the Spirit as a gift which supersedes the Torah.[2] In the following section I shall examine the validity of these suppositions.

Proponents of the view that Acts 2.33 is based on Ps. 67.19 (LXX)/Eph. 4.8 generally analyse the verse in the following manner.[3] The words τήν τε ἐπαγγελίαν and τοῦτο ὃ ὑμεῖς [καὶ] βλέπετε καὶ ἀκούετε are judged Lukan and therefore regarded as additions to the Psalm citation. So also τοῦ πνεύματος τοῦ ἁγίου and ἐξέχεεν are to be attributed to Lukan redaction since they have been imported from the Joel citation (2.17). Pointing to the version of Ps. 67.19 recorded in Eph. 4.8, Barnabas Lindars suggests that ἔδωκεν originally stood in the place now taken by the redactional ἐξέχεεν.[4] The phrase τῇ δεξιᾷ οὖν τοῦ θεοῦ can also be dismissed as redactional, for it anticipates Ps. 110.1 in Acts 2.35. We are therefore left with ὑψωθείς and λαβὼν παρὰ τοῦ πατρός. These words, taken in conjunction with the reconstructed ἔδωκεν and the ἀνέβη of v. 34, are thus offered as evidence that Ps. 67.19 forms the basis of the text (see diagram).

Eph. 4.8: διὸ λέγει,

⎡Ἀναβὰς εἰς ὕψος ⎤ᾐχμαλώτευσεν αἰχμαλωσίαν,⎤ ⎡ἔδωκεν⎤ ⎡δόματα⎤ τοῖς ⎡ἀνθρώποις.⎤

Psalm 67.19: ⎡ἀνέβης εἰς ὕψος ᾐχμαλώτευσας αἰχμαλωσίαν, ἔλαβες δόματα ἐν ἀνθρώπῳ,⎤

Acts 2.33f.: τῇ δεξιᾷ οὖν τοῦ θεοῦ ⎡ὑψωθείς⎤

τήν τε ἐπαγγελίαν⎤ τοῦ πνεύματος τοῦ ἁγίου ⎡λαβὼν⎤ παρὰ τοῦ πατρὸς

⎡ἐξέχεεν⎤τοῦτο ὃ⎤ὑμεῖς [καὶ] βλέπετε καὶ ἀκούετε.

οὐ γὰρ Δαυὶδ ⎡ἀνέβη⎤εἰς τοὺς οὐρανούς. . .

In spite of the obvious differences between Acts 2.33 and Ps. 67.19 (LXX)/Eph. 4.8, this ingenious proposal appears plausible at first sight. Yet after detailed examination, the tenuous nature of each of the proposed verbal links becomes apparent. First, ὑψωθείς hardly constitutes a genuine parallel to the phrase ἀνέβης εἰς ὕψος (Ps. 67.19).[5] And R. O'Toole argues persuasively that the covenant which underlies the

---

1. The Targum of Ps. 68.19 (MT) reads: 'You have ascended to heaven, that is Moses the prophet. You have taken captivity captive, you have learned the words of the Torah, you have given them as gifts to men'. For the rabbinic exegesis of the Psalm see Strack–Billerbeck, *Kommentar*, III, pp. 596-98.

2. See the literature cited on p. 270 nn. 1, 2, especially Dupont, 'Ascension', pp. 199-209.

3. See Lindars, *Apologetic*, pp. 42-44, 51-59; Dupont, 'Ascension', pp. 199-209; and Turner, 'Christology', pp. 176-79.

4. Lindars, *Apologetic*, p. 54.

5. Wilckens, *Missionsreden*, p. 233.

Lukan Pentecost is not that of Sinai but the promise made to David in
2 Sam. 7.12-16. According to O'Toole, since Luke's entire argument
in Acts 2.22-36 is based on the promises made to David, ὑψωθείς is
best explained by the Davidic tradition in Psalm 88 (cf. Ps. 117.16;
Isa. 52.13).[1] Second, as D. Bock correctly notes, when the method
employed above to separate redactional elements from Luke's underlying source in Acts 2.33 is consistently applied to the entire verse,
ἀνέβη and λαβὼν παρὰ τοῦ πατρός are also seen to be redactional.
The term ἀνέβη appears frequently in Luke–Acts (27×) and in the
general context (Acts 1.13). The promise of the Father (τοῦ πατρός)
is alluded to in Lk. 24.49 and Acts 1.4. We are thus left with λαβών
which occurs frequently in Luke–Acts (51×) and is 'naturally used to
describe the movement of the promise of the Spirit from the initiating
sender. . . to the mediating dispenser'.[2] Third, the suggestion that
ἔδωκεν originally stood behind ἐξέχεεν is pure conjecture.

The evidence suggests that Acts 2.33 was not influenced by Psalm
67. All the elements of the verse 'are traceable within the Lucan narrative',[3] the key term from Psalm 67, δόματα, is lacking, and Luke's
argument focuses on the promises made to David, not Moses.[4] The
absence of any reference to Moses, the law, or the covenant in Acts 2
speaks decisively against this proposal and the other two previously
discussed.[5] While Acts 2.33 clearly signifies that the Pentecostal
outpouring of the Spirit constitutes irrefutable proof that Jesus has
been exalted to the right hand of God,[6] this proof does not consist of a

---

1. R.F. O'Toole, 'Acts 2:30 and the Davidic Covenant of Pentecost', *JBL* 102
(1983), pp. 245-58.
2. Bock, *Proclamation*, p. 182. See also the judgment of Wilckens, *Missionsreden*, p. 233: 'λαβών muß keineswegs aus Ps 68(67),19 ἔλαβες δόματα erklärt
werden, vielmehr spielt Lukas an Lk 24,49; Acts 1,8 an. Vor allem spricht gegen
Duponts These, daß Act 2,34 zur Begründung von 2,33 Ps 110(109),1 zitiert wird.'
3. Bock, *Proclamation*, p. 182.
4. O'Toole, 'Davidic Covenant', pp. 245-58.
5. Broer, 'Der Geist', p. 282; Chevallier, *Souffle*, p. 175; Tachau, 'Pfingstgeschichte', p. 88; Bock, *Proclamation*, p. 181; O'Toole, 'Davidic Covenant',
p. 246; P.H. Menoud, 'La Pentecôte lucanienne et l'histoire', *RHPR* 42 (1962),
p. 144; Noack, 'The Day of Pentecost', pp. 90-91; de Vaux, *Ancient Israel*,
p. 495; Kremer, *Pfingstbericht*, pp. 239-40; Conzelmann, *Acts*, p. 16; Haenchen,
Acts, pp. 172, 174; Franklin, *Christ the Lord*, p. 98; Marshall, 'Pentecost',
pp. 364-65; Dömer, *Das Heil Gottes*, pp. 152-53. Similarly, suggestions that Luke
(or the tradition which he utilized) presents Pentecost as a reverse of Babel have no
foundation in the text. So also Broer, 'Der Geist', p. 283 n. 115; Tachau,
'Pfingstgeschichte', p. 88; Franklin, *Christ the Lord*, p. 98.
6. Turner highlights the christological significance of Acts 2.33 and justifiably so
('Christology', pp. 168-90). The text is particularly striking in view of the fact that

powerful pneumatic transformation of the recipient's ethical life. Rather, the proof is an irruption of Spirit-inspired prophetic activity which is visible to all.

Even if the improbable hypothesis outlined above could be established, serious objections to the thesis that Acts 2.33 represents a Christian counterpart to rabbinic exegesis of Psalm 67 and, as such, presents the gift of the Spirit as the essence of the new covenant would remain. For even if this rabbinic exegetical tradition dates back to the first century, it is by no means evident that the Christian interpretation of the Psalm is dependent upon it. Barnabas Lindars, for example, argues that the association of the Psalm with Moses in the Targum tradition and the application of the Psalm to Christ in the early church (Eph. 4.8) represent independent developments.[1] Furthermore, in the one clear reference to Ps. 67.19 in the New Testament, Eph. 4.8, the 'gifts' (δόματα) which Jesus gives are not associated with the new covenant or an internal law written on the heart, rather they are gifts of (spirit-enabled) ministry (e.g. apostles, prophets, etc.).

This examination of the various arguments adduced in support of the claim that Luke (or the tradition he utilized) presents Pentecost as a 'new Sinai' has revealed that they are each deficient at crucial points. The evidence suggests that Luke neither shaped the Pentecost account with Sinai traditions in mind nor unconsciously used material significantly influenced by them. The Pentecost account indicates that Luke did not view the gift of the Spirit as the power of the new law of Christ. According to Luke, the Spirit of Pentecost is the source of prophetic inspiration and, as such, the Spirit of mission.

---

there are 'no known pre-Christian references to the Messiah bestowing the Spirit' ('Christology', pp. 182-83). To speak of Jesus bestowing the Spirit is to attribute to Jesus the prerogative of God.

1. Lindars, *Apologetic*, pp. 52-53.

Chapter 11

THE DISCIPLES AND THE SPIRIT:
THE PROPHETIC COMMUNITY

1. *Introduction*

I have argued that a careful analysis of the Pentecost narrative supports the thesis that Luke consistently portrays the Spirit as the source of prophetic power (producing special insight and inspired speech) which enables God's servants to fulfill their divinely appointed tasks. In Acts these servants are the disciples of Jesus and their ultimate task is to bear witness to the gospel of Jesus Christ unto the ἐσχάτου τῆς γῆς (1.8). In the following chapter I shall examine texts from Acts relevant to this inquiry hitherto not (or only briefly) discussed and attempt to demonstrate that in Luke's perspective the Christian community is, by virtue of its reception of the Spirit, a prophetic community empowered for a missionary task.

The agenda for this chapter has been set by numerous attempts to establish a direct and necessary link between the gift of the Spirit and Christian initiation in Acts. Two contemporary New Testament exegetes are representative of this broad stream of scholarship: J. Dunn and J. Kremer. Both Dunn and Kremer argue that a thorough examination of Acts reveals that for Luke, the Spirit is more than simply the source of prophetic power. Dunn asserts that for Luke 'the one thing that makes a man a Christian is the gift of the Spirit'.[1] Kremer contends that in several texts, most notably in Acts 2.38, by virtue of its close relationship to water baptism, the gift of the Spirit is presented as the 'Mittel der Errettung und des Lebens' and not principally as the source of prophetic power.[2] In order to evaluate the validity of

1. Dunn, *Holy Spirit*, p. 93; see pp. 90-102 for a summary of Dunn's argument that Luke presents the gift of the Spirit as the most important of the three elements normally associated with Christian-initiation (repentance, water-baptism, and the gift of the Spirit).

2. Kremer, *Pfingstbericht*, p. 197; see also pp. 177-79, 197, 219-20, 273. Although Kremer acknowledges that in the Pentecost account (Acts 2.1-13; cf. vv. 14-17) and elsewhere in Luke–Acts, Luke portrays the gift of the Spirit as the

these conclusions I shall examine each of the texts pertinent to the discussion as they occur in Acts: Acts 2.38; 8.4-25; 9.17-18; 10.44-48 (cf. 11.15-17; 15.8-10); 18.24-28; 19.1-7.

2. Christian Initiation and the Gift of the Spirit in Acts

2.1. Acts 2.38

It is often asserted that the collocation of repentance, baptism, and the promise of the Spirit in Acts 2.38 demonstrates that Luke,[1] like Paul and John, viewed reception of the Spirit as a necessary element in Christian initiation.[2] Acts 2.38 is thus offered as proof that for Luke the gift of the Spirit is the 'bearer of salvation', much more than a prophetic endowment.[3] Yet does Acts 2.38 support such a conclusion? The evidence suggests otherwise.

I have already noted that contextual considerations speak decisively against the interpretation outlined above. Consistent with Lk. 24.49, Acts 1.4, and 2.33, the promised gift of the Spirit in Acts 2.38 refers to the promise of Joel 3.1, and thus it is a promise of prophetic enabling granted to the repentant.[4]

---

source of prophetic activity, he insists that the gift involves more than this: 'Diese einengende Darstellungsweise schließt aber nicht aus, daß der Geistempfang nach Lukas noch andere Aspekte besitzt' (p. 220). Indeed, according to Kremer, the Pentecostal gift of the Spirit is the source of the 'eigentliche Leben der urkirchlichen Gemeinde' (p. 177).

1. Since Luke has placed his unique stamp upon the text either through creation of material or selection, modification, and arrangement of received tradition, I am justified in assuming that the text reflects his perspective. See my brief comments in Chapter 10 §2 on the problematic tradition-history of Peter's speech.

2. For example J. Giblet writes: 'As is seen particularly at the end of Peter's discourse on the day of Pentecost, Christian initiation is a single act which consists essentially of three elements: conversion. . . baptism in the name of Jesus Christ. . . the gift of the Holy Spirit' ('Baptism in the Spirit in the Acts of the Apostles', *OC* 10 [1974], p. 171). And with reference to the gift of the Spirit in Acts 2.38, B. Sauvagant affirms: 'Ce don accordé par Dieu est le facteur décisif de la conversion au christianisme' ('Se repentir, être baptisé, recevoir l'Esprit, Actes 2,37 ss.', *FV* 80 [1981], p. 86). Similar sentiments are offered by Dunn, *Holy Spirit*, pp. 90-92. The necessary connection between the gift of the Spirit and Christian initiation is also presupposed by those who argue that the gift is given through baptism: e.g. von Baer, *Der heilige Geist*, pp. 170f.; Beasley-Murray, *Baptism*, pp. 107f.; Haenchen, *Acts*, p. 184; Conzelmann, *Acts*, p. 22; Lüdemann, *Das frühe Christentum*, p. 52.

3. Dunn, *Holy Spirit*, p. 92; note also the position espoused by Kremer cited above (*Pfingstbericht*, pp. 177, 197).

4. See Chapter 9 §5.2 above.

Furthermore, the collocation of baptism and reception of the Spirit in Acts 2.38 tells us little about the nature of the pneumatic gift. While it may indicate that for Luke the rite of water baptism is normally accompanied by the bestowal of the Spirit,[1] Luke's usage elsewhere suggests that even this conclusion may be overstating the case. There is certainly nothing in the text which lends credence to Kremer's contention that the Spirit is presented here as the 'Mittel der Errettung und des Lebens'.[2] Kremer would be on more solid ground if it could be established that the text presupposes an inextricable bond between water baptism and forgiveness of sins on the one hand and reception of the Spirit on the other. Yet this conclusion is clearly unwarranted. Since Luke fails to develop a strong link between water baptism and the bestowal of the Spirit elsewhere, and regularly separates the rite from the gift (Lk. 3.21f.; Acts 8.12f.; 9.17f.; 10.44; 18.24),[3] the phrase καὶ λήμψεσθε τὴν δωρεὰν τοῦ ἁγίου πνεύματος should be interpreted as a promise that the Spirit shall be 'imparted to those who are already converted and baptized'.[4] In any case, the most that can be gleaned from the text is that repentance and water baptism are the normal prerequisites for reception of the Spirit,[5] which is promised to every believer.

---

1. See for example Roloff, *Die Apostelgeschichte*, p. 61; Haenchen, *Acts*, p. 184; and Schneider, *Die Apostelgeschichte*, I, p. 277.

2. Kremer, *Pfingstbericht*, p. 197. Note Turner's word of caution, 'When it is asserted that Acts 2.38 proves that the Spirit is bestowed by baptism, and that this in turn has implications for the meaning of the gift itself which make it impossible to restrict the function of the Spirit to the Spirit of prophecy, exegesis has been forsaken for dogmatic reasons' ('Luke and the Spirit', p. 160).

3. Note also that the terms employed by Luke with reference to the reception of the Spirit are not baptismal terms (see J. Ysebaert, *Greek Baptismal Terminology: Its Origins and Early Development* (1962), pp. 61-62, 266-68).

4. Schweizer, 'πνεῦμα', p. 412. Although the καὶ λήμψεσθε (future tense) construction is ambiguous (e.g. Sauvagant, 'Se repentir', p. 86; Haya-Prats, *Force*, p. 136; Beasley-Murray, *Baptism*, p. 107), the judgment offered by S. Brown is compelling, 'Surely it is preferable to interpret the passage in accordance with all the other texts which we have considered and to understand the words "you shall receive" to point to an event subsequent to baptism' (' "Water-Baptism" ', p. 144). On the distinction between the rite of baptism and the bestowal of the Spirit in Acts 2.38 see Bovon, *Luc le théologien*, p. 251; Haya-Prats, *Force*, pp. 136-38; F.J. Leenhardt, *Le baptême chrétien, son origine, sa signification* (1946), pp. 37-38; Ysebaert, *Baptismal Terminology*, p. 267; J. Coppens, 'L'imposition des mains dans les Actes des Apôtres' in *Les Actes des Apôtres* [1979], pp. 429-30; and M. Barth, *Die Taufe: ein Sakrament?* (1951), pp. 141-45.

5. Pesch, *Die Apostelgeschichte (Apg 1–12)*, p. 271: 'Die Taufe ist nach 2,38 Bedingung des Geistempfangs (vgl. auch 19,5f.), aber Gott ist nicht an diese Bedin-

The evidence outlined above also highlights the improbable nature of Dunn's claim that in Acts 2.38 Luke portrays the gift of the Spirit as a necessary and climactic element in Christian initiation.[1] As we have seen, this claim ignores important aspects of the immediate context; and, as I shall establish, it is inconsistent with Luke's usage elsewhere, most notably in Acts 8.12f.

Luke undoubtedly viewed reception of the Spirit as a normal and important experience in the life of every Christian. Acts 2.38 suggests that repentance and water baptism constitute the normal prerequisites for receiving the Spirit and it may suggest that Luke viewed water baptism as the normal occasion for reception of the pneumatic gift. However, these conclusions cannot be adduced to support the assertion that Luke viewed the Spirit as 'the bearer of salvation' and, as such, a necessary element in Christian initiation. On the contrary, they are completely compatible with my contention that Luke portrays the Spirit as a prophetic enabling granted to those already converted. Indeed, the importance which Luke attaches to the gift of the Spirit does not bear witness to the purported integral role which it plays in conversion; it is a reflection of Luke's conviction that the church is a prophetic community with a missionary task.[2]

2.2. *Acts 8.4-25*

Acts 8.4-25 provides a real problem for those who argue that for Luke reception of the Spirit is a necessary element in Christian initiation. The narrative indicates that the Samaritans believed the preaching of Philip and were thus baptized by him (v. 12), yet they did not receive the Spirit until some time later (v. 15-17). The implications of this account for Luke's understanding of the Spirit are apparent. Since Luke considered the Samaritans to be Christians (i.e. converted) before they received the Spirit, it can hardly be maintained that he understood the Spirit to be either the 'Mittel der Errettung' or the 'one thing that makes a man a Christian'.

Those advocating a necessary link between reception of the Spirit and baptism/Christian initiation have attempted to mitigate the force of this text in a variety ways. It has been argued that the separation of the gift of the Spirit from the rite of baptism in Acts 8.4f. does not represent historically reliable tradition; rather, the problematic text is the

gung gebunden (vgl. 10, 44-48)'. See also O. Glombitza, 'Der Schluß der Petrusrede Acta 2:36-40: Ein Beitrag zum Problem der Predigten in Acta', *ZNW* 52 (1961), p. 117.

1. Dunn, *Holy Spirit*, pp. 90-92.
2. Schweizer, 'πνεῦμα', p. 413 and 'The Spirit of Power', p. 268.

result of Luke's modification of his source material. This argument has generally taken one of two forms. It is claimed that Luke, either by conflating two originally independent sources,[1] or embellishing a traditional story originally about Philip's ministry in Samaria (including Simon's conversion) with fabricated material concerning Peter and John,[2] separated the gift from the baptismal rite and thus divided what in reality formed 'one indissoluble whole'.[3]

These theories have been severely criticized and must be judged improbable.[4] In any event, while offering possible explanations concerning how the narrative came to exist in its present form, these theories fail to deal with the crucial question concerning the implications of the text for Luke's pneumatology. It is unreasonable to assume that a man of Luke's editorial capabilities was unable to shape this account

---

1. O. Bauernfeind, *Die Apostelgeschichte* (1939), pp. 124-25; D.-A. Koch, 'Geistbesitz, Geistverleihung und Wundermacht: Erwägungen zur Tradition und zur lukanischen Redaktion in Act 8.5-25', *ZNW* 77 (1986), pp. 64-82. Both Bauernfeind and Koch assert that Luke conflated two sources, a record of the missionary activity of Philip and a report concerning the confrontation between Simon and Peter. According to Koch, the sources were conflated in order to emphasize the success of Philip's missionary activity and to link the new community to Jerusalem (p. 78). See also E. Schweizer, 'Die Bekehrung des Apollos, Apg 18,24-26', in *Beiträge zur Theologie des Neuen Testaments: Neutestamentliche Aufsätze* (1955–1970), p. 79; and C.K. Barrett, 'Light on the Holy Spirit from Simon Magus', in *Les Actes des Apôtres* (1979), p. 293.

2. Dibelius, *Studies*, p. 17; Conzelmann, *Acts*, pp. 62f.; Haenchen, *Acts*, pp. 307-308; E. Käsemann, 'Die Johannesjünger in Ephesus', in *Exegetische Versuche und Besinnungen*, I (1960), pp. 165-66. According to Haenchen, Luke inserted the tradition (which had already gone through an extensive process of development) describing Philip's ministry in Samaria (including Simon's conversion) into his narrative concerning the apostles' ministry in Samaria in order to show the superiority of Christian miracles over contemporary magical practices. Käsemann, followed by Conzelmann, argued that Luke modified the traditional account of Philip's ministry in Samaria in order to present an idealized picture of a church unified under the authority of Jerusalem. In this way Luke sought to defend the church of his day against heretics: 'Lukas hat Geschichte übermalt und konstruiert, um die Una sancta apostolica gegenüber dem Zugriff der Gnostiker und Häretiker seiner Tage zu verteidigen' (Käsemann, 'Die Johannesjünger', p. 168). See my summary of Käsemann's thesis in Chapter 11 §2.5 below.

3. Haenchen, *Acts*, p. 308.

4. For criticism of source theories see Pesch, *Die Apostelgeschichte (Apg 1–12)*, p. 271; Beasley-Murray, *Baptism*, pp. 115-17; Dunn, *Baptism*, pp. 60-62. Lampe calls recourse to the two-source theory of composition of the Samaritan account a 'desperate expedient' (*Seal of the Spirit*, p. 69). Note also J.D.M. Derrett, 'Simon Magus (Act 8.9-24)', *ZNW* 73 (1982), p. 53. For criticism of Käsemann's thesis see my comments in Chapter 11 §2.5.

without contradicting his own pneumatology.[1] Luke does not limit the bestowal of the Spirit to apostles (cf. 9.17).[2] And, even if he did intend to establish a link between the new community and Jerusalem, Luke's description of events in Antioch (Acts 11.22-24) indicates that he could have made the point without attributing the bestowal of the Spirit to the representatives of Jerusalem. The inescapable conclusion is that Luke simply did not feel that the text as it stands posed a problem. This judgment is confirmed by the fact that the 'problem' passage (vv. 14-17) is filled with themes and language characteristic of Luke.[3]

Others have sought to ease the tension by describing the course of events narrated in Acts 8.4f. as a unique exception necessitated by a new and decisive turning-point in the mission of the church: the Spirit was withheld until the coming of the apostles from Jerusalem in order to demonstrate to the Samaritans 'that they had really become members of the Church, in fellowship with its original "pillars"'.[4] Yet this view faces a number of serious objections. First, there is little reason to assume that this instance represents a unique exception, either historically or for Luke. Nothing in the text itself supports such a view[5] and, as we have noted, Luke regularly separates the gift from the rite.[6] Second, the explanation offered for this purported exception is highly improbable. It is unlikely that the Samaritans would need any further assurance of their incorporation into the church after baptism. And, in similar decisive turning-points the assurance of incorporation into the church (as well as the reality itself) is not dependent on contact with representatives of Jerusalem (Acts 8.26f.; 9.17f.; 18.24f.) or their

---

1. So also Turner, 'Luke and the Spirit', p. 161.
2. K. Giles, 'Is Luke an Exponent of "Early Protestantism"? Church Order in the Lukan Writings (Part 1)', *EQ* 54 (1982), p. 197; Marshall, *Acts*, p. 157; and Dunn, *Holy Spirit*, pp. 58-60.
3. Koch, 'Geistbesitz', pp. 69-71; Turner, *Luke and the Spirit*, p. 161.
4. Lampe, *Seal*, p. 70. Similar views are espoused by Chevallier, *Souffle*, pp. 201-202; Bruner, *Holy Spirit*, pp. 175-76; Ewert, *The Holy Spirit in the New Testament* (1983), pp. 119-20; Green, *Holy Spirit*, pp. 138-39; Marshall, *Acts*, pp. 153, 157; and R.F. O'Toole, 'Christian Baptism in Luke', *RevRel* 39 (1980), pp. 861-62.
5. J. Dunn, '"They Believed Philip Preaching (Acts 8.12)": A Reply', *IBS* 1 (1979), p. 180.
6. S. Brown, '"Water-Baptism"', pp. 143-44; Derrett, 'Simon Magus', p. 53. The responses offered by Haenchen, 'the few cases in Acts when reception of the Spirit is separated from baptism are justified exceptions' (*Acts*, p. 184), Hull, 'exceptions only prove the rule' (*Acts*, p. 119), and Brunner, 'the Spirit is temporarily suspended from baptism here "only" and precisely to teach . . . that suspension cannot occur' (*Holy Spirit*, p. 178) are hardly compelling.

bestowal of the Spirit to the newly converted (Acts 11.22-24).[1] Nevertheless, even if this theory is accepted, the 'problem' posed by the text is not eradicated.[2] For however exceptional the event may have been (historically and for Luke), we must still account for Luke's carefully crafted interpretation of this event. Indeed, Luke's account betrays a pneumatology decidedly different from Paul or John, neither of whom could conceive of baptized believers being without the Spirit.[3]

Fully aware that the implications for Luke's pneumatology which emerge from the two positions outlined above are incompatible with their respective attempts to tie reception of the Spirit to conversion-initiation (Dunn) and baptism (Beasley-Murray) in Luke–Acts,[4]

1.　See Dunn, *Holy Spirit*, pp. 62-63 and Beasley-Murray, *Baptism*, pp. 117-18. Lampe also acknowledges that the hypothesis outlined above does not adequately account for all of the evidence and therefore modifies his thesis: 'We must, however, look a little further than this [the hypothesis outlined above] for our explanation, for, although this hypothesis may account for the events at Samaria, it will not help us to explain the imposition of hands by Ananias upon St. Paul, nor that which he himself administered to "certain disciples" at Ephesus' (*Seal*, p. 70). Therefore, Lampe suggests that Luke's distinctive emphasis on the gift of the Spirit as an enablement for missionary activity (pp. 53, 65) provides an additional key for understanding Luke's association of the gift with the laying on of hands rather than water baptism. According to Lampe, the former rite was a commissioning for service in the missionary enterprise (analogous to ordination) and bestowed special missionary charismata (pp. 70-78). Lampe's suggestion is affirmed by F.F. Bruce, *Commentary on the Book of Acts* (1954), pp. 182-83.

2.　This is certainly the case if it is claimed that the reception of the Spirit merely assures the Samaritans that they have already been incorporated into the church (see Lampe, *Seal*, pp. 69-70; Dunn [*Holy Spirit*, p. 62 n. 33], citing Lampe, *Seal*, p. 72, notes, however, that there is some ambiguity on this point). If it is asserted that the Samaritans were not *actually* incorporated into the church until their reception of the Spirit, then one must still explain the phenomenon of conversion apart from the Spirit. In any case, this view is irreconcilable with the baptism of the Samaritans recorded in Acts 8.12 (see Dunn, *Holy Spirit*, pp. 62-63; Beasley-Murray, *Baptism*, p. 118).

3.　Coppens, 'L'imposition des mains', p. 430; Hull, *Acts*, pp. 107-108; Weiser, *Die Apostelgeschichte. Kapitel 1–12*, p. 203; Turner, 'Luke and the Spirit', p. 169; Lampe, *Seal*, pp. 53, 65, 70-78.

4.　In a response to criticisms of his position ('Reply', pp. 177-83), Dunn readily acknowledged that his interpretation of the Samaritan incident was influenced by his conviction that 'Luke shared the regular view among the major NT writers that it is the gift of the Spirit which constitutes a Christian' (p. 178). Beasley-Murray introduces his argument by claiming that Luke's 'theology was such that he would have taken it for granted that the Spirit worked in the lives of these people for their salvation' (*Baptism*, p. 118).

J. Dunn and G.R. Beasley-Murray offer alternative interpretations of Acts 8.4-25.

Beasley-Murray argues that Luke 'regarded these Christians as not without the Spirit but without the spiritual gifts that characterized the common life of the Christian communities'.[1] According to Beasley-Murray the πολλὴ χαρά of Acts 8.8 implies that the Samaritans received the Spirit when they were baptized, and the anarthrous use of πνεῦμα ἅγιον in Acts 8.15f. suggests that apostles imparted spiritual gifts, not the Spirit himself. Neither of these arguments commends itself. The πολλὴ χαρά of Acts 8.8 results from the exorcisms and healings performed by Philip; it does not imply possession of the Spirit.[2] Nor can a neat distinction be made between τὸ πνεῦμα τὸ ἅγιον and πνεῦμα ἅγιον: they are equivalent titles.[3] However, the decisive objection against Beasley-Murray's thesis is Luke's explicit statement in v. 16: the Spirit 'had not yet fallen on any of them'.[4]

Dunn seeks to establish that the Samaritans were not really Christians before they received the Spirit. He maintains that their 'initial response and commitment was defective' and that Luke 'intended his readers to know this'.[5] The following arguments are produced in support of this claim: (1) Luke's description of Philip as preaching τὸν

---

1. Beasley-Murray, *Baptism*, p. 119; see pp. 118-20 for his argument. Similar views are espoused by J.E.L. Oulton, 'The Holy Spirit, Baptism, and Laying on of Hands in Acts', *ExpTim* 66 (1955), pp. 236-40; M. Gourges, 'Esprit des commencements et esprit des prolongements dans les Actes: Note sur la "Pentecôte des Samaritains" (Act., VIII, 5-25)', *RB* 93 (1986), pp. 376-85; and many others from the Reformed school who follow the lead of J. Calvin, *The Acts of the Apostles 1–13* (ed. D.W. & T.F. Torrance, 1965), pp. 235-36.

2. Turner, 'Luke and the Spirit', p. 168. Turner, citing as examples Lk. 13.17 and 19.37, notes that 'such joy is frequently mentioned as the response to God's various saving acts throughout Luke–Acts'. Expanding on Beasley-Murray's argument, Oulton argues that similarities in the descriptions of the life of the Samaritan community (Acts 8. 5-13) and that of Jerusalem converts after Pentecost (Acts 2.41-47) suggest that the Samaritans possessed the Spirit before the arrival of the apostles ('The Holy Spirit', p. 238). However, this argument fares no better than Beasley-Murray's, for Luke fails to associate the Spirit with either of these descriptions of community life.

3. See Dunn, *Holy Spirit*, pp. 56, 68-70; M. Turner, 'Luke and the Spirit', pp. 167-68. As Dunn aptly puts it, 'The true formula is not πνεῦμα ἅγιον = charismata (alone), but πνεῦμα ἅγιον = Holy Spirit + charismata, or more precisely, the Holy Spirit bringing and manifesting his coming and presence by charismata' (p. 56).

4. Dunn, *Holy Spirit*, p. 56; Marshall, *Acts*, p. 157; F. Bovon, *Luc le théologien*, pp. 247, 249-50, 252.

5. Dunn, *Holy Spirit*, p. 63; for his argument see pp. 63-68.

Χριστόν *simpliciter* (v. 5) and τῆς βασιλείας τοῦ θεοῦ (v. 12) suggests that the Samaritans understood Philip's message in terms of their
own nationalistic expectations of the Messiah and the kingdom he was
to bring—expectations already 'roused to near fever-pitch' by the
magician Simon. For the former phrase 'is always used in Acts of the
Messiah of pre-Christian expectation' and the latter, when preached to
non-Christians, always refers to the 'Kingdom of Jewish expectations'.[1] (2) The Samaritans' response to Simon betrays a predilection
for magic and a general lack of discernment. Luke indicates that their
response to Philip was equally shallow through his use of προσέχω, a
term descriptive of the Samaritan response to both Philip and Simon
(vv. 6, 10f.). (3) Since πιστεύειν with the dative object usually
signifies intellectual assent, the phrase ἐπίστευσαν τῷ Φιλίππῳ (rather
than πιστεύειν εἰς or ἐπὶ κύριον) reveals that the Samaritan response
was simply an assent of the mind and not reflective of genuine faith.
(4) The comparison between the clearly defective experience of Simon
and that of the other Samaritans (vv. 12-13) demonstrates that they
'all went through the form but did not experience the reality'.[2]

Dunn's hypothesis has been subjected to intense criticism and must
be rejected in view of the evidence.[3] Indeed, none of the arguments
outlined above can be sustained. (1) There is nothing in Luke's account
which would suggest that Philip's message was either deficient or misunderstood. On the contrary, Philip is presented as one of the group
alluded to in Acts 8.4 who went about 'preaching the word'
(εὐαγγελιζόμενοι τὸν λόγον). Since τὸν λόγον embodies the content

---

1. Quotations from Dunn, *Holy Spirit*, p. 64.
2. Dunn, *Holy Spirit*, p. 66. I have omitted reference in my summary to the comments put forth by Dunn in sections (e) and (f) of the chapter under discussion (*Holy
Spirit*, pp. 66-67) for they do not further his argument: the former presupposes the
point in question (for Luke 'possession of the Spirit was the hallmark of the Christian') and the latter, building on the assumption that the Samaritans' initial response
was defective, merely offers a hypothesis concerning why this might have been the
case (due to the animosity which existed between Samaritans and Jews they lacked
assurance that they were really accepted into the Christian community).
3. See for example E.A. Russell, '"They Believed Philip Preaching" (Acts
8.12)', *IBS* 1 (1979), pp. 169-176; Turner, 'Luke and the Spirit', pp. 163-67;
Ervin, *Conversion-Initiation*, pp. 25-40; Marshall, *Acts*, p. 156; Ewert, *Holy Spirit*,
pp. 118-19; H.D. Hunter, *Spirit-Baptism: A Pentecostal Alternative* (1983), pp. 83-
84; Giles, 'Church Order (Part 1)', p. 197; O'Toole, 'Christian Baptism', p. 861;
Green, *Holy Spirit*, p. 138; Carson, *Showing the Spirit*, p. 144; Russell, 'The
Anointing', pp. 60-61; Stronstad, *Charismatic Theology*, pp. 64-65.

of the kerygma (cf. Acts 2.41; 6.2; 8.14),[1] it is quite evident that Luke understood Philip's preaching, variously described (vv. 5, 12), to be 'kerygmatic in the full sense'.[2] And there is nothing in the phrases ἐκήρυσσεν αὐτοῖς τὸν Χριστόν (v. 5) and εὐαγγελιζομένῳ περὶ τῆς βασιλείας τοῦ θεοῦ καὶ τοῦ ὀνόματος Ἰησοῦ Χριστοῦ (v. 12) which would suggest that the Samaritans misunderstood Philip's message. The phrase τὸν Χριστόν *simpliciter* appears frequently in Christian proclamation in Acts and with reference to the central elements of the kerygma: Christ's death (e.g. 3.18) and resurrection (e.g. 2.31).[3] In v. 5, as elsewhere in Acts (9.22; 17.3; 26.23; cf. 18.5, 28), the phrase serves as a summary of the kerygma.[4] Similarly, the phrase τῆς βασιλείας τοῦ θεοῦ καὶ τοῦ ὀνόματος Ἰησοῦ Χριστοῦ can scarcely mean less since it parallels the content of Paul's preaching in Rome (28.31).[5] If the Samaritans had misunderstood Philip, we would expect the apostles to correct the deficiency through additional teaching (cf. 18.26), yet any reference to such activity is conspicuously absent.[6]

(2) Dunn's attempt to dismiss the response of the Samaritans as merely a reflection of their predilection for magic is irreconcilable with the prominent place given to the proclamation of 'the word' in Luke's description of Philip's ministry (vv. 4-8, 12-13; cf. v. 14).[7] Miraculous signs do play an important role in the success of Philip's ministry (vv. 6f., 13), but this emphasis is consistent with Luke's usage elsewhere: 'word and sign are complementary. . . both realities belong together in the missionary endeavour'.[8] Luke's use of

---

1. Roloff, *Die Apostelgeschichte*, p. 133: 'Der Inhalt der verkündigten Heilsbotschaft wird summarisch mit einem terminus technicus der Gemeindesprache umschrieben: "das Wort" (4,4; 10,44; 11,19; 17,11)'.

2. Russell, '"They Believed"', p. 170.

3. ' "They Believed"', p. 170.

4. Roloff, *Die Apostelgeschichte*, p. 133; Turner, 'Luke and the Spirit', p. 163.

5. Russell, '"They Believed"', p. 170. Schneider notes that this phrase is a Lukan description of the content of the proclamation (*Die Apostelgeschichte*, vol. 1, p. 490).

6. Marshall, *Acts*, p. 158; Turner, 'Luke and the Spirit', p. 164.

7. Note the occurrences of εὐαγγελίζομαι (vv. 4, 12); κηρύσσω (v. 5); and ἀκούω (v. 6).

8. O'Reilly, *Word and Sign*, p. 217. The assumption that Luke portrays the Samaritans' faith as defective by connecting it with miraculous signs is particularly dubious when, as Dunn himself notes, 'on a number of occasions Luke makes clear the faith-producing effect of miracles (5.14; 9.42; 13.13; 19.18)'. Indeed, Dunn notes that 'this is the aspect of miracle/faith relation which apparently interests Luke— the publicity, propagandist value of miracle—that which elsewhere in the NT is disparaged' (*Jesus and the Spirit*, p. 168).

προσέχω will hardly bear the weight of Dunn's argument: in v. 6 the Samaritans give heed to Philip's preaching (cf. 16.14);[1] in vv. 10f. their attention is focused on the magician Simon. Also, rather than disparaging this 'attention' as shallow, Luke appears to underline the power of Simon's grip on the people and Philip's resounding triumph over it.[2]

(3) Dunn bases his claim that ἐπίστευσαν τῷ Φιλίππῳ is not descriptive of Christian commitment on two tenets, both of which are without foundation. First, Dunn implies that it is significant that the object of the verb ἐπίστευσαν is the preaching of Philip (τῷ Φιλίππῳ εὐαγγελιζομένῳ περί. . .) rather than κύριος or θεός. However, the description of Lydia's conversion in 16.14 indicates that Luke equates belief in the message of an evangelist with belief in God.[3] Second, Dunn insists that πιστεύειν with a dative object (rather than with the prepositions εἰς or ἐπί) signifies mere intellectual assent to a proposition. Yet Luke uses this construction elsewhere to describe genuine faith in God (Acts 16.34; 18.8).[4] Furthermore, he does not distinguish between πιστεύειν with a dative object and πιστεύειν with εἰς or ἐπί: all three constructions appear with κύριος in descriptions of genuine faith.[5] That ἐπίστευσαν τῷ Φιλίππῳ does indeed refer to genuine faith is confirmed by the report which reached the apostles in Jerusalem: δέδεκται ἡ Σαμάρεια τὸν λόγον τοῦ θεοῦ (8.14). A similar report heralds the conversion of Cornelius and his household (11.1; cf. 2.41, 17.11). Since this latter report is not questioned, 'we should therefore find no reason to question the former'.[6]

---

1. Ervin correctly emphasizes the common elements in the accounts which describe the conversion of the Samaritans (8.6f.) and Lydia (16.14) respectively, 'Lydia "gave heed" (προσέχειν) to what was said by Paul and was baptized. The Samaritans "gave heed" (προσέχειν) to what was spoken by Philip, they believed and were baptized' (*Conversion-Initiation*, p. 32).

2. Russell, ' "They Believed" ', p. 171.

3. Turner, 'Luke and the Spirit', p. 165. Acts 16.14: ἧς ὁ κύριος διήνοιξεν τὴν καρδίαν προσέχειν τοῖς λαλουμένοις ὑπὸ τοῦ Παύλου (cf. 8.6). For the use of πιστεύειν in a similar context see Acts 4.4: πολλοὶ δὲ τῶν ἀκουσάντων τὸν λόγον ἐπίστευσαν.

4. Ervin, *Conversion-Initiation*, p. 31; Marshall, *Acts*, p. 156.

5. Russell, ' "They Believed" ', p. 173. Russell notes that πιστεύειν and the object κύριος occur with the preposition εἰς (14.23), ἐπί (9.42), and simply with the dative object (18.8). He also points out that πιστεύειν is used in relation to the Scriptures with both the simple dative (24.14; 26.27) and the preposition ἐπί (Lk. 24.45). For a similar judgment see J. Taeger, *Der Mensch und sein Heil: Studien zum Bild des Menschen und zur Sicht der Bekehrung bei Lukas* (1982), p. 115.

6. Giles, 'Church Order (Part 1)', p. 197. See also Turner, 'Luke and the Spirit', p. 165.

(4) Dunn's attempt to impugn the faith of the Samaritans by way of analogy with Simon's is also unconvincing, for the premise of Dunn's inference, that Simon's faith was defective, is demonstrably false. Dunn asserts that Simon's behavior reveals the true condition of his heart: he was never really converted.[1] However, the example of Ananias and Sapphira (5.1-11) demonstrates the depth to which believers could sink in Luke's estimation. In all probability, Simon's sin, like that of Ananias and Sapphira, is considered 'so serious precisely because it is committed by a follower of Jesus'.[2] Central to Dunn's argument is Peter's indictment in v. 21: οὐκ ἔστιν σοι μερὶς οὐδὲ κλῆρος ἐν τῷ λόγῳ τούτῳ—a phrase which, according to Dunn, means that Simon 'never had become a member of the people of God'.[3] However, this interpretation is dubious. Two possibilities commend themselves, neither of which accords with Dunn's theory. First, E. Haenchen argues that the phrase forms part of a formula of excommunication[4]—a necessary corollary being that Simon was considered a Christian until this time. Second, noting that Haenchen's explanation fails to account for the demonstrative adjective (τούτῳ), Turner insists that the phrase refers to Simon's misguided attempt to buy the ability to confer the Spirit, and not to Simon's exclusion from the faith.[5] In view of contextual considerations, Turner's interpretation is to be preferred, although other elements within Peter's rebuke (8.20-23) indicate that Simon had apostatized.[6] That Simon's initial faith was sound is confirmed by the absolute use of πιστεύειν in v. 13.

---

1. So also Guthrie, *New Testament Theology*, p. 542: 'There was clearly something defective about both his belief and baptism'.

2. Turner, 'Luke and the Spirit', p. 165. Contra Haenchen, *Acts*, p. 304, 'His [Simon's] subsequent behaviour is incompatible with possession of the Spirit. There is a bad seam in the narrative here.'

3. Dunn, *Holy Spirit*, p. 65. The phrase is reminiscent of Deut. 12.12 (LXX).

4. Haenchen, *Acts*, p. 305; so also G.W.H. Lampe, 'Acts', in *Peake's Commentary on the Bible* (1962), p. 782. Haenchen views the phrase ἐν τῷ λόγῳ τούτῳ as a reference to the Christian message.

5. Turner, 'Luke and the Spirit', p. 166. Turner contends that ἐν τῷ λόγῳ τούτῳ should be translated, 'in this matter', and refers to the apostles' authority to confer the Spirit. See also Russell, ' "They Believed" ', p. 173.

6. The allusions to Ps. 77.37 (LXX: ἡ δὲ καρδία αὐτῶν οὐκ εὐθεῖα μετ' αὐτοῦ, cf. v. 21) and Deut. 29.17f. (LXX: μὴ τίς ἐστιν ἐν ὑμῖν ῥίζα ἄνω φύουσα ἐν χολῇ καὶ πικρίᾳ, cf. v. 23), two OT texts which speak of the unfaithfulness of those within the covenant community, support the contention that Simon was guilty of apostasy, and as such, had abandoned his previous (genuine) profession of faith. See Ervin, *Conversion-Initiation*, p. 34.

Elsewhere in Acts when πιστεύειν is used without an object it refers to genuine faith (2.44; 4.4; 11.21; 15.5).[1]

It has become apparent that the separation of Spirit-reception from baptism/Christian initiation in Acts 8.4f. cannot be explained away as a piece of careless editorial work or disregarded as a unique exception. The former position is based on an implausible tradition-history of the text and the latter on a hypothetical reconstruction of the event; both ignore the significance of the existing narrative for Luke's pneumatology. Neither is it possible to eliminate the contradiction by postulating a 'silent' bestowal of the Spirit at baptism or impugning the faith of the Samaritans: the evidence speaks decisively against both views. Acts 8.4-25 poses an insoluble problem for those who maintain that Luke establishes a necessary link between baptism/Christian initiation and the gift of the Spirit.[2]

---

1. Russell, ' "They Believed" ', pp. 173-74.

2. B.E. Thiering's attempt to explain the Acts 8 account in terms of the stages and conditions of initiation at Qumran must be judged highly improbable ('Qumran Initiation and New Testament Baptism', *NTS* 27 [1981], pp. 615-31). Thiering argues that the stages of initiation at Qumran included four steps within two main grades: provisional and full membership. A rite of water-washing (for the cleansing of the flesh) was associated with provisional membership, and a rite in which the Spirit was conferred (for the purification of the soul) was associated with full membership. These rites were administered at Pentecost, the former by levites, the latter by the higher ranking priests, and separated by a two-year period. According to Thiering, the community anticipated that in the messianic age the two instruments of cleansing (water and Spirit) would merge and the two rites would become one (1QS 4.18-22). Thus Thiering writes: 'The procedure in Acts 8 is consistent with Qumran practice for the present era in several ways. The water-washing is given first, then the Spirit, and they are separated in time. The water-washing is given by a minister whose function is associated with the levitical role of serving in 6.3; the Spirit-giving by superior ministers, the leaders of the Church' (p. 625). The unexpected bestowal of the Spirit (before baptism) on the Gentiles in Acts 10 is explained as divine confirmation that the messianic age had arrived and the two rites had become one (p. 626). Thus in Acts 19 Paul 'practises the full Christian rite, initiation by baptism, followed immediately by the gift of the Spirit, corresponding to the Qumran order' (p. 626). The weaknesses of this novel thesis are apparent. As Thiering notes, the differences between the proposed Qumran practice and Acts 8 are considerable: the two kinds of ministers 'are not called "priests" and "levites", there is not said to be a space of two years between the two events, or that they occurred at Pentecost, and baptism is "into the name of the Lord Jesus" ' (p. 625). In addition, nothing in the Lukan text suggests that the baptism of the Samaritans represented a provisional stage in their initiation into the church. Furthermore, since the gift of the Spirit can precede, accompany, or follow water-baptism in Acts, it is unlikely that Luke's narrative or the practice of the early church was influenced by the proposed Qumran rite. Thiering's attempt to explain the discrepancies in the various accounts by associating them with the initia-

This problem is resolved, however, when we recognize the distinctive character of Luke's prophetic pneumatology: the internal contradictions disappear and Luke is seen to be remarkably consistent. Indeed, it is quite evident that Luke viewed the gift of the Spirit received by the Samaritans (Acts 8.17) as of the same character as the Pentecostal gift; that is, as a prophetic endowment granted to the converted which enabled them to participate effectively in the mission of the church. This conclusion is supported by the following considerations:

First, the inescapable conclusion which emerges from the discussion above is that for Luke the gift of the Spirit does not constitute a Christian. On the contrary, the Spirit is a supplementary gift given to Christians, those who have already been incorporated into the community of salvation.[1]

Second, it is abundantly clear from Luke's choice of language in Acts 8.15f. that he considered the pneumatic gift received by the Samaritans to be identical to the Pentecostal gift. The terms descriptive of the Samaritan experience are also associated with Pentecost: λαμβάνειν πνεῦμα ἅγιον (2.38; 8.15, 17, 19; cf. 1.8); ἐπιπίπτειν τὸ πνεῦμα τὸ ἅγιον (8.16; 11.15). It is also generally recognized that implicit within the narrative is the assumption that the Samaritans, upon reception of the Spirit, began to prophesy and speak with tongues as on the day of Pentecost (8.16-18; cf. 2.4f.; 10.45-46; 19.6).[2] Thus

---

tion procedure of the present (Acts 2; 8) and messianic (Acts 10; 19) ages is incompatible with Lukan eschatology: at Pentecost, Peter, whom in Thiering's view had not yet realized the full messianic age had come, declared that the 'last days' had in fact arrived (Acts 2.17). Also it is unlikely that Luke attempts to obscure Peter's under-realized eschatology and yet unwittingly traces the gradual development of the Jerusalem church's eschatological perspective in his accounts of baptism as Thiering suggests. Luke is too competent, and the eschatology of Peter and the Jerusalem community cannot be so easily pitted against that of Paul. In any event, Thiering's analysis of the 'messianic rite' at Qumran is suspect. It is unlikely that 1QS 4.18-22 refers to an initiatory rite in which the 'two instruments of cleansing, water and spirit, will be merged' (p. 615). This text refers to the final victory of the spirit of truth over the spirit of falsehood in *metaphorical language drawn from water rites*: a future, messianic rite of cleansing through water and Spirit is not in view.

1. Schweizer, 'πνεῦμα', p. 412 and 'The Spirit of Power', pp. 267-68; Haya-Prats, *Force*, pp. 121-38; Bovon, *Luc le théologien*, p. 253; H. Flender, *Saint Luke: Theologian of Redemptive History* (1970), p. 138.

2. See for example Derrett, 'Simon Magus', p. 54; Haenchen, *Acts*, p. 304; Dunn, *Holy Spirit*, p. 56 and 'I Corinthians 15.45: Last Adam, Life-giving Spirit', in *Christ and Spirit in the New Testament* (1973), p. 132; Pesch, *Die Apostelgeschichte (Apg 1-12)*, p. 276; Lampe, 'Acts', p. 782; Bruce, *Book of Acts*, p. 181; Schweizer, 'πνεῦμα', p. 407 n. 488; Kremer, *Pfingstbericht*, p. 201.

the prophetic character of the gift received by the Samaritans is substantiated by the parallels with the Pentecostal gift, which we have already seen to be a prophetic endowment, and by the phenomena which Luke associated (implicitly) with its reception.

Third, the association of the gift of the Spirit with the laying on of hands in Acts 8.17 suggests that Luke viewed the gift as an endowment for service in the mission of the church. There are two unambiguous contexts in which the laying on of hands occurs in the book of Acts: it is associated with healing (9.12, 17; 28.8) and with the commissioning of believers for service in the church's mission (6.6; 13.3; cf. 9.17).[1] The laying on of hands also appears in conjunction with the bestowal of the Spirit in Acts 8.17; 19.6; and probably 9.17. However, it must be noted that the gift is often granted apart from the rite (2.38; 10.44) and the rite does not always confer the gift (6.6; 13.3).[2] This fact suggests that reception of the Spirit is not integral to the rite, but is rather a supplementary element. It appears that the primary focus of the rite can be either healing or commissioning, or, as in the case of Paul, both (9.17; cf. 22.14-15; 26.16-18). Since the rite is clearly not related to healing in Acts 8.17 and 19.6, it is not unreasonable to assume that in these instances it forms part of a commissioning ceremony.[3] I therefore suggest that Peter and John incorporate the Samaritans, not into the church, but into the missionary enterprise of the church.[4] This

1. See also 1 Tim. 4.14; 5.22; 2 Tim. 1.6 (cf. Heb. 6.2). The significance of Acts 6.6 for the missionary enterprise cannot be disputed in view of the summary which immediately follows in 6.7 (καὶ ὁ λόγος τοῦ θεοῦ ηὔξανεν. . .) and the subsequent accounts of the missionary exploits of Stephen (6.8-8.1) and Philip (8.4-40).

2. The laying on of hands which confers the Spirit is not limited to the apostles or to representatives of Jerusalem (cf. 9.17).

3. The laying on of hands as a Jewish rite was frequently used in the commissioning of a person for a special task: e.g. Num. 8.10; 27.19; Deut. 34.9 (Joshua is filled with the spirit of wisdom as a result of the rite); *Asc. Isa.* 6.3-5 (the rite results in prophetic speech); and *j. Sanh.* 1.19a (the rite is employed in the ordination of rabbis). On the Jewish background to the rite see D. Daube, *The New Testament and Rabbinic Judaism* (1956), pp. 224-33; Coppens, 'L'imposition des mains', pp. 433-37; Ysebaert, *Baptismal Terminology*, pp. 227-38; Lampe, *Seal*, p. 71; J.K. Parratt, 'The Laying On of Hands in the New Testament', *ExpTim* 80 (1968-69), pp. 210-14; F. Pereira, *Ephesus: Climax of Universalism in Luke–Acts* (1983), pp. 92-96; Strack–Billerbeck, *Kommentar*, II, pp. 126f., 647f.; and E. Lohse, 'χείρ', *TDNT*, IX, pp. 428-29.

4. Lampe, *Seal*, pp. 70-78 and 'The Holy Spirit', p. 199; Bruce, *Book of Acts*, p. 183; and Hill, *Greek Words*, p. 264. Lampe argues that 'the laying on of hands. . . is a sign of association in the apostolic or missionary task of the Church' (p. 77) and that special missionary charismata are associated with the rite. See also Coppens, 'L'imposition des mains', p. 431.

involves commissioning the nucleus of Samaritan believers for service in the church's mission through the laying on of hands. In this instance, the gift of the Spirit accompanies the laying on of hands because those commissioned have not yet received the prophetic enabling necessary for effective service (cf. 9.17; 19.6), unlike the seven (6.6) or Paul and Barnabas (13.3). Thus the Samaritans are commissioned and empowered for the missionary task which lay before them. A prophetic community has been formed.[1] A new center of missionary activity has been established (cf. 9.31).[2]

2.3. Acts 9.17-18

In the climax to Luke's account of Paul's conversion/call in Acts 9.1-19, Ananias lays his hands upon Paul and declares: Σαοὺλ ἀδελφέ, ὁ κύριος ἀπέσταλκέν με. . . ὅπως ἀναβλέψῃς καὶ πλησθῇς πνεύματος ἁγίου (9.17). Paul is immediately healed and subsequently baptized (9.18). Although the account fails to describe the actual bestowal of the Spirit, it is evident from Ananias' comment in 9.17 that Paul received the gift. In assessing the significance of the pericope for this inquiry, I shall seek to answer the vital question: is the gift of the Spirit presented here as the principal element in Paul's conversion, or is it rather an endowment which enables Paul to fulfill his missionary call?[3] I shall begin our discussion with a few comments concerning methodology.

Paul's conversion/call was, without question, of great importance to Luke, for he recounts the event on three different occasions in Acts

1. G. Dix argues that the laying on of hands in Acts was a rite of ordination for prophets: 'The rite in Acts was in fact historically a totally different rite (from confirmation) for the Ordination of prophets' (*Confirmation, or Laying on of Hands?* [1936], p. 23; see also pp. 18-19).

2. Lampe, *Seal*, p. 72: 'It may not be too much to assert that this event [the bestowal of the Spirit on the Samaritans through the laying on of hands] is meant to demonstrate that a new nucleus of the missionary Church has been established, and to suggest that Luke's readers are intended to infer that the Gospel proceeded to radiate outwards from this new centre of the Spirit's mission'. See also Stronstad, *Charismatic Theology*, p. 65. This conclusion is confirmed by the important summary in Acts 9.31: ἡ μὲν οὖν ἐκκλησία καθ' ὅλης τῆς Ἰουδαίας καὶ Γαλιλαίας καὶ Σαμαρείας. . . τῇ παρακλήσει τοῦ ἁγίου πνεύματος ἐπληθύνετο.

3. Guthrie is illustrative of the former position. With reference to Acts 9.17, he writes, 'The main feature of importance in Luke's account is the indispensable activity of the Spirit in the conversion of Saul' (*New Testament Theology*, p. 543). Note also Dunn, *Holy Spirit*, pp. 73-78. Hill is representative of the latter position: 'Paul . . . is filled with Holy Spirit to fulfil his task of proclamation (9:17)' (*Greek Words*, p. 260). Note also Lampe, *Seal*, pp. 72-75 and Stronstad, *Charismatic Theology*, p. 66.

(9.1-19; 22.4-16; 26.12-18). A comparison of the three texts reveals considerable variation in form and content.[1] These variations led an earlier generation of source critics to postulate the existence of two or more underlying sources for the various accounts.[2] However, these theories have been largely rejected by contemporary critics.[3] It is now generally accepted that all three accounts are based on a single source and that the variations in the accounts are principally the result of Luke's literary method.[4] The various accounts supplement and complement one another.[5] Thus, any attempt to reconstruct the theological

1. For a summary of the main differences in the three accounts see K. Lönig, *Die Saulustradition in der Apostelgeschichte* (1973), p. 14.

2. See Spitta, *Die Apostelgeschichte*, pp. 137-45, 270-77; J. Jüngst, *Die Quelle der Apostelgeschichte* (1895), pp. 83-95, 223f; H.H. Wendt, *Die Apostelgeschichte* (1913), pp. 166-68; E. Hirsch, 'Die drei Berichte der Apostelgeschichte über die Bekehrung des Paulus', *ZNW* 28 (1929), pp. 305-12; K. Lake, 'The Conversion of Paul', in *The Beginnings of Christianity*, V, pp. 188-95; and E. Trocmé, *Le 'Livre des Actes' et l'histoire* (1957), pp. 174-79. Hirsch, for example, attributed the account in Acts 9 to a source deriving from the Damascus community and the account in Acts 26 to a more authentic Pauline source. The remaining account in Acts 22 was the result of Luke's attempt to reconcile the two sources.

3. See Dibelius, *Studies*, p. 158 n. 47; Cadbury, *The Making of Luke–Acts*, pp. 213-38; Haenchen, *Acts*, pp. 108-10; 325-29; Conzelmann, *Acts*, pp. 72-73; Lönig, *Die Saulustradition*, pp. 15-19; G. Lohfink, *The Conversion of St. Paul: Narrative and History in Acts* (1976), pp. 40-46, 81; C. Burchard, *Der dreizehnte Zeuge. Traditions- und kompositionsgeschichtliche Untersuchungen zu Lukas' Darstellung der Frühzeit des Paulus* (1970), p. 121; Schneider, *Die Apostelgeschichte II. Teil*, p. 22.

4. Note, however, that this conclusion does not rule out the possibility that Luke had access to and utilized other items of traditional information. For example, Lohfink writes, 'While we reject the idea of distinct sources for the Damascus account, we do not exclude the possibility that individual traditional items of various origin were contained in the material Luke had about Paul's conversion' (*The Conversion of St. Paul*, p. 46). And Burchard argues that there were two traditional perspectives on Paul's Damascus experience: (1) Luke's source (*überlieferte Geschichte*) presented the experience as Paul's conversion; (2) however, in another traditional conception (*überlieferte Auffassung*) of Paul's experience the emphasis is placed on his calling. Burchard maintains that Luke, influenced by this latter traditional conception, modified his source in Acts 9 (vv. 13-14 and minor modifications to vv. 15-18, such as the insertion of the reference to the Spirit in v. 17, are attributed to Lukan redaction) so as to transform a *Bekehrungsgeschichte* into a *Berufungsgeschichte*. This *Berufung*-perspective has influenced to an even greater extent the formation of the parallel accounts in Acts 22 and 26 (*Der dreizehnte Zeuge*, pp. 118-30).

5. C.W. Hedrick, 'Paul's Conversion/Call: A Comparative Analysis of the Three Reports in Acts', *JBL* 100 (1981), p. 432: 'The complete story of Paul's conversion, as Luke understood it, can only be determined by bringing together features from all three narratives. The entire story is not completely narrated in any one of the

perspectives which gave rise to the account of Paul's conversion/call recorded in Acts 9.1-19 must also take into consideration the parallel accounts in Acts 22.4-16 and 26.12-18.

Paul's reception of the Spirit is closely linked to Ananias and, as such, it forms part of the Ananias episode of Acts 9.10-19. When this episode is compared with the parallel version in Acts 22.12-16 it becomes apparent that, in Luke's perspective, it is not the culmination of an account of Paul's conversion; rather, it is principally an account of Paul's commissioning as a missionary (cf. 22.14-15). Acts 26.12-18 confirms my contention that Paul's missionary call was foremost in Luke's mind, for here the Damascus event itself is viewed as the moment at which Paul receives his divine commission to engage in the mission to the Jews *and the Gentiles*.[1]

There is abundant evidence of this perspective within the Ananias episode of Acts 9. The account exhibits many features of the 'commission form' prevalent in the Old Testament and other Ancient Near Eastern texts.[2] And, although there is some question concerning which stage in the development of the tradition vv. 15-16 should be placed, it is evident that Luke penned these verses with reference to Paul's future missionary activity.[3] Furthermore, this commission for-

---

three accounts.' So also Lohfink argues that Luke progressively intensifies the accounts as he moves from one to another (*The Conversion of St. Paul*, pp. 91-95).

1. As Lönig notes, 'Das Lukas an Apg 9.15f. inhaltlich besonderes Interesse hat, ergibt sich daraus, daß die entsprechenden Verse in beiden Redevarianten einen hervorragenden Platz einnehmen' (*Die Saulustradition*, p. 29).

2. Hubbard, 'Commissioning Stories', pp. 103-26; T.Y. Mullins, 'Commission Forms', pp. 603-14; J. Munck, *Paul and the Salvation of Mankind* (1959), pp. 24-35. Munck argues that the three accounts of Paul's conversion/call in Acts are traditional, ultimately going back to the Apostle himself, and modeled after OT prophetic call/commissioning narratives. Munck's thesis has been severely criticized and largely rejected (see Burchard, *Der dreizehnte Zeuge*, pp. 52-54; Lohfink, *The Conversion of St. Paul*, p. 72; Hedrick, 'Paul's Conversion/Call', p. 415; Schneider, *Die Apostelgeschichte II. Teil*, p. 24). Nevertheless, even if all three accounts were not originally modeled after OT call narratives, 'it is obvious that all three do share call/commissioning features' (Hedrick, p. 415).

3. Lönig argues that vv. 13-16 were inserted into a traditional account of Paul's conversion and healing by a pre-Lukan redactor (*Die Saulustradition*, pp. 25-48, esp. pp. 26-28). The insertion was motivated by a desire to encourage Christians facing persecution and therefore emphasized Paul's role as 'a suffering witness', not his future missionary activity (p. 29). Luke reworked this insertion and interpreted it (especially the σκεῦος ἐκλογῆς of v. 15) with reference to Paul's missionary activity (pp. 35-36, 114-15). He also added references to Paul's reception of the Spirit and Baptism in vv. 17-18 (pp. 46-47), as well as the notice concerning Paul's preaching activity in v. 20 (pp. 45-46). Lönig's analysis is quite similar to that of

mula and the reference to the reception of the Spirit in v. 17 are linked to the statement concerning Paul's preaching activity in v. 20 by the preceding καὶ εὐθέως.[1] In all probability the references to Paul's reception of the Spirit (v. 17) and his ensuing preaching activity (v. 20) are Lukan insertions:[2] the former understood to be the necessary prerequisite for the latter.[3] Luke also indicates that Ananias laid his hands upon Paul (v. 17), a gesture which, in view of the considerations outlined above, must be viewed as the occasion for Paul's commissioning by Ananias (cf. Acts 22.14-15), as well as his healing.[4] The text implies that the Spirit was conferred in conjunction with the laying on of hands,[5] thus Paul's reception of the Spirit is associated with his commissioning.

The answer to my question is now apparent. In Acts 9.17 the gift of the Spirit is presented as an endowment which enables Paul to fulfill his missionary call. For Luke, Ananias' reluctant encounter with Paul is the occasion for a monumental event: Paul is commissioned and empowered to proclaim the gospel to, above all, the Gentiles.

Burchard, *Der dreizehnte Zeuge*. Hedrick ('Paul's Conversion/Call', pp. 415-32) also asserts that a traditional miracle story of Paul's conversion forms the basis for Acts 9.1-19. However, unlike Lönig and Burchard, Hedrick argues that vv. 13-16 are the result of Lukan redaction. Luke adapted the miracle-conversion story into a commissioning narrative by inserting vv. 13-16 and the statement about receiving the Spirit (v. 17) into the narrative (pp. 420-22). Although Lönig and Burchard differ with Hedrick on the precise origin of vv. 13-16, they all maintain that Luke has transformed a traditional conversion-healing story into a commissioning narrative.

1. Lampe, *Seal*, pp. 72-73; Shelton, 'Filled with the Spirit', pp. 418-19.

2. Lönig, *Die Saulustradition*, pp. 45-47; Hedrick, 'Paul's Conversion/ Call', p. 422; Burchard, *Der dreizehnte Zeuge*, p. 124.

3. Burchard, *Der dreizehnte Zeuge*, p. 104: 'Der Geist ist die Bedingung der Möglichkeit, daß Paulus predigt, was er alsbald tut (9,19b ff.)' (cf. p. 124).

4. Lampe, *Seal*, pp. 72-76; Kjeseth, 'The Spirit of Power', p. 159.

5. Burchard, *Der dreizehnte Zeuge*, pp. 103-104; Roloff, *Die Apostelgeschichte*, p. 162; Bruce, *The Acts of the Apostles*, p. 202; Parratt, 'The Laying On of Hands', p. 210; Ervin, *Conversion-Initiation*, p. 49. Burchard acknowledges that a literal reading of the text suggests the bestowal of the Spirit is related to the laying on of hands. Nevertheless, he asserts that Luke actually intended to associate Paul's reception of the Spirit with his baptism. Luke could not place the reference to Paul's reception of the Spirit after his baptism because 'er nicht Geistbegabung und Nahrungsaufnahme nebeneinanderstellen wollte' (p. 124). This speculative hypothesis must be rejected in view of Acts 8.17; 10.44f., and 19.6. As Lönig notes, 'Die Trennung der Taufnotiz von der über den Geistempfang und die Umkehr der chronologischen Reihenfolge beider läßt sich also am besten aus lukanischen Prämissen erklären' (*Die Saulustradition*, p. 47). The strange silence concerning the actual bestowal of the gift is probably due to the redactional character of the reference to the Spirit in v. 17. Any further modification of the source would have been awkward.

2.4. *Acts 10.44-48*

The account of the Spirit-baptism of Cornelius' household (10.44-48) and the subsequent summaries of this dramatic event (11.15-17; 15.8-10) are frequently cited as evidence that for Luke, the Spirit is the agent of 'forgiveness, cleansing, and salvation'.[1] For here, it is claimed, Luke equates the historic conversion of this initial band of Gentile Christians with their Spirit-baptism. On the face of it the assertion appears to be justified, for there can be little doubt that the conversion and Spirit-baptism of Cornelius' household are, at the very least, closely related chronologically. However, upon closer examination it becomes apparent that this interpretation is wide of the mark. The prophetic gift received by Cornelius and household is a 'Zeichen der Errettung', but not the 'Mittel'.[2]

Questions of tradition and history, when applied to the Peter-Cornelius episode (10.1–11.18), have elicited a variety of conflicting responses.[3] Nevertheless, there is a general consensus among scholars

---

1. Dunn, *Holy Spirit*, pp. 79-82, quote from p. 82; See also Kremer, *Pfingstbericht*, pp. 196-97; Bruce, 'The Holy Spirit', pp. 171-72.

2. Contra Kremer, who states the gift of the Spirit is received 'als Zeichen und Mittel der Errettung und des Lebens' (*Pfingstbericht*, p. 197).

3. M. Dibelius maintained that Luke transformed a simple conversion-story into an account relating the inception of the Gentile mission through extensive redaction, including composition of much of the narrative (10.27-29, 34-43; 11.1-18) and the insertion of an independent account of a Petrine vision (10.9-16) originally dealing exclusively with Jewish food laws (*Studies*, pp. 109-23). Dibelius's assertion that the account (10.1-11.18) was based on two originally independent traditions, a conversion-story and a vision-source, has been supported by Conzelmann, *Acts*, p. 80; Weiser, *Die Apostelgeschichte. Kapitel 1–12*, pp. 253-62; and Lüdemann with minor modifications, *Das frühe Christentum*, pp. 136-38. F. Bovon affirms the existence of these two independent traditions, yet also argues for an additional source behind Peter's sermon in 10.34-43 ('Tradition et rédaction en Actes 10,1-11,18' in *L'Oeuvre de Luc* [1987], pp. 97-120). Haenchen, even more critical of the historical and traditional basis of the account than Dibelius, rejects the traditional character of Peter's vision and limits the traditional basis of the pericope to a source delineating the founding of the church in Caesarea (*Acts*, pp. 355-63). However, the theories put forth by Dibelius and Haenchen have been criticized at several crucial points. First, Roloff (*Die Apostelgeschichte*, p. 165) and Pesch (*Die Apostelgeschichte [Apg 1–12]*, p. 333) assert that it is unlikely that a simple conversion-story forms the basis for the account since Peter rather than Cornelius is the main figure in the narrative. Second, a number of scholars argue that Peter's vision (10.9-16) is integral to the narrative and therefore cannot be assigned to an independent source or to Luke's creative hand (Schneider, *Die Apostelgeschichte II. Teil*, pp. 61-63; Munck, *Salvation of Mankind*, p. 229; K. Lönig, 'Die Korneliustradition', *BZ* 18 [1974], pp. 1-19; K. Haacker, 'Dibelius und Cornelius: Ein Beispiel formgeschichtlicher Überlieferungskritik', *BZ* 24 [1980], pp. 234-51; Marshall, *Acts*, p. 182; Roloff.

concerning the significance which Luke attached to the account: it demonstrates that the Gentile mission was initiated and validated by divine revelation.[1] The point is made through a profusion of heavenly visions, angelic visitations, and interventions of the Spirit.[2] The decisive sign of God's favor on the Gentiles is their reception of the gift of the Spirit, manifested in inspired speech (10.46, λαλούντων γλώσσαις καὶ μεγαλυνόντων τὸν θεόν).[3] It is this sign which astonishes Peter's circumcised companions (10.45-46) and results in his command to baptize the Gentile converts (10.47-48). It is also through reference to this sign that Peter justifies his table-fellowship with the uncircumcised (11.3, 15-17) and their admission into the church (15.8-9).

This emphasis on Spirit-baptism as a sign of God's acceptance accords well with Luke's distinctive pneumatology. Since according to Luke reception of the Spirit is the exclusive privilege of 'the servants' of God and generally results in miraculous and audible speech,[4] by its very nature the gift provides demonstrative proof that the uncircumcised members of Cornelius' household have been incorporated into the community of salvation. The sign-value of the prophetic gift is also emphasized in the Pentecost account (2.4f., 17-20). Whether from the lips of a Jew in Jerusalem or a Gentile in Caesarea, the manifestation of inspired speech marks the speaker as a member of the end-time prophetic community.

pp. 165-66; Pesch, p. 333; and tentatively, Wilson, *The Gentiles*, p. 174). Third, Bovon's suggestion that Peter's sermon (10.34-43) is based on traditional material is supported by the narrative, which presupposes such a sermon, and by several features within the sermon itself (G.N. Stanton, *Jesus of Nazareth in New Testament Preaching* [1974], pp. 67-85; R.P.C. Hanson, *The Acts* [1967], p. 124; Marshall, *Acts*, pp. 181-82; and Pesch, p. 333).

1. See Dibelius, *Studies*, p. 117 and virtually all of the commentators.

2. Thus Minear, with good reason, suggests that 'we should read the story of Peter and Cornelius (10.1–11.18; 15.6-11) as a clear instance of prophetic revelation' (*To Heal*, p. 142).

3. The phrase λαλούντων γλώσσαις (10.46; cf. 19.6), unlike the λαλεῖν ἑτέραις γλώσσαις of 2.4, refers to unintelligible inspired utterance (cf. 1 Cor. 14.1-28). See Haenchen, *Acts*, p. 354; Schweizer, 'πνεῦμα', p. 410; George, 'L'Esprit', p. 509; Haya-Prats, *Force*, p. 107; J. Behm, 'γλῶσσα', *TDNT*, I, pp. 725-26; Weiser, *Die Apostelgeschichte. Kapitel 1–12*, p. 270; Schneider, *Die Apostelgeschichte II. Teil*, p. 80; and Roloff, *Die Apostelgeschichte*, p. 174.

4. Of the eight instances where Luke describes the initial reception of the Spirit by a person or group, five specifically allude to some form of inspired speech as an immediate result (Lk. 1.41; 1.67; Acts 2.4; 10.46; 19.6) and one implies the occurrence of such activity (Acts 8.15, 18). In the remaining two instances, although inspired speech is absent from Luke's account (Lk. 3.22; Acts 9.17), it is a prominent feature in the pericopes which follow (Lk. 4.14, 18f.; Acts 9.20).

The evidence suggests that Luke viewed the Gentiles' reception of the Spirit as the decisive sign of their acceptance by God. Luke's perspective is based upon the prophetic nature of the pneumatic gift and, as such, is entirely consistent with my description of his distinctive pneumatology. Although in this instance (in contrast to 8.17) reception of the Spirit accompanies conversion, the text does not imply that the gift is the means by which the uncircumcised are actually cleansed and forgiven. This unwarranted assumption is usually based on the summaries of the event recorded in 11.15-17 and 15.8-10.

Pointing to the similarities between 11.17a and 11.18b,[1] J. Dunn argues that the gift of the Spirit is 'God's gift of μετάνοια εἰς ζωήν'.[2] However, Dunn's equation must be rejected since elsewhere μετάνοια is a prerequisite for receiving the Spirit (Acts 2.38f.) and clearly distinguished from the gift itself (cf. 5.31-32).[3] The similarities between vv. 17a and 18b simply reflect the logic of Peter's argument: since God has granted the Gentiles the gift of the Spirit, it follows *a fortiori* that they have been granted μετάνοια εἰς ζωήν and are eligible for the baptismal rite.[4]

Similarly, it is often claimed that 15.8 is synonymous with 15.9:[5]

v. 8: καὶ ὁ καρδιογνώστης θεὸς ἐμαρτύρησεν
αὐτοῖς δοὺς τὸ πνεῦμα τὸ ἅγιον καθὼς καὶ ἡμῖν

v. 9: καὶ οὐθὲν διέκρινεν μεταξὺ ἡμῶν τε καὶ αὐτῶν,
τῇ πίστει καθαρίσας τὰς καρδίας αὐτῶν.

This assumption has led many to conclude that for Luke, 'God's giving of the Holy Spirit is equivalent to his cleansing of their hearts'.[6] But

---

1. Cf: v. 17a: εἰ οὖν τὴν ἴσην δωρεὰν ἔδωκεν αὐτοῖς ὁ θεὸς ὡς καὶ ἡμῖν, . . .
   v. 18b: Ἄρα καὶ τοῖς ἔθνεσιν ὁ θεὸς τὴν μετάνοιαν εἰς ζωὴν ἔδωκεν.
2. Dunn, *Holy Spirit*, p. 81; see also Bruner, *Holy Spirit*, p. 196.
3. Turner, 'Luke and the Spirit', p. 172; see also Haya-Prats, *Force*, pp. 122-25. Acts 5.31-32 is instructive: repentance (μετάνοια) and forgiveness (ἄφεσις) are attributed directly to Jesus, whom God has exalted to his right hand as σωτήρ; the Spirit, given to the obedient, bears witness to Jesus' true identity.
4. See Marshall, *Acts*, p. 197. Marshall notes that the saying in v. 16 probably means: 'John baptized (merely) with water, but you shall be baptized (not only with water but also) with the Holy Spirit.' Thus Peter considered water-baptism to be the normal prerequisite for the gift of the Spirit and the *a fortiori* argument is made. Water baptism implies that the recipient has received 'repentance unto life'.
5. Dunn, *Holy Spirit*, p. 81; Bruce, 'The Holy Spirit', p. 171 and *Book of Acts*, pp. 306-307; Tiede, *Prophecy*, p. 50.
6. Dunn, *Holy Spirit*, pp. 81-82.

again Peter's argument speaks against this equation.[1] Verse 8 is the premise from which the deduction of v. 9 is drawn: God's bestowal of the Spirit bears witness (v. 8) to the reality of his act of cleansing (v. 9).[2] Peter's argument here is similar to that in 11.16-18. In each instance the logical distinction between the premise (gift of the Spirit) and deduction (repentance/cleansing) is apparent. My analysis is supported by the fact that Luke always attributes forgiveness (ἄφεσις), which is granted in response to faith/repentance, to Jesus—never to the Spirit (cf. 10.43).[3]

The decisive objection against the interpretations outlined above is that Luke equates the gift of the Spirit granted to Cornelius' household—not with cleansing and forgiveness, but with the Pentecostal gift of prophetic inspiration.[4] Luke stresses the point through repetition: the Gentiles received the same gift granted to the Jewish disciples on Pentecost (10.47; 11.15, 17; 15.8). As we have noted, the significance which Peter attaches to the gift as a sign of God's acceptance is based on the prophetic nature of the gift. Indeed, the manifestation of the prophetic gift by the Gentiles is the climactic event in a series of divine interventions which serve to initiate and validate the Gentile mission. Since this is Luke's central concern, he does not pursue further at this point the significance of the gift for the missionary activity of this newly formed Christian community. However, we may presume that the prophetic band in Caesarea, like the communities in Samaria and Antioch, by virtue of the pneumatic gift participated effectively in the missionary enterprise (cf. 18.22; 21.8).

---

1. Taeger, *Der Mensch*, p. 108.

2. It is noteworthy that the Spirit falls upon Cornelius and his household immediately after Peter declares that οἱ προφῆται μαρτυροῦσιν, ἄφεσιν ἁμαρτιῶν λαβεῖν διὰ τοῦ ὀνόματος αὐτοῦ . . . (10.43). The conceptual parallels with 10.44f.; 11.17f., and, above all, 15.8-9 are striking: by pouring out the Spirit of prophecy upon the Gentiles, God testifies that they have received ἄφεσιν ἁμαρτιῶν.

3. Forgiveness (ἄφεσις) is attributed to Jesus (Acts 5.31; 13.38); the name of Jesus (Lk. 24.47; Acts 2.38; 10.43); and faith in Jesus (26.18). See also Lk. 1.77; 3.3; 4.18(2×). Note the conclusions reached by Haya-Prats, 'Nous n'avons trouvé aucun indice nous permettant de dire que les Actes attribuent à l'Esprit Saint le pardon des péchés ou une purification progressive' (*Force*, p. 123); 'Luc attribue à Jésus toute l'œuvre du salut' (p. 125).

4. Hill, *New Testament Prophecy*, pp. 96-97: 'That Luke is so careful to record the same signs of Spirit-possession on these two great occasions [Acts 2.4f.; Acts 10.44f.] demonstrates clearly that for him the "prophetic" character of the gift is central: it is the equipment for Gospel proclamation'.

2.5. *Acts 18.24-28; 19.1-7*

Luke's record of the origins of the church in Ephesus includes the enigmatic and closely related pericopes dealing with Apollos (18.24-28) and the Ephesian disciples (19.1-7). The unusual description of Apollos as a powerful evangelist κατηχημένος τὴν ὁδὸν τοῦ κυρίου and yet knowing μόνον τὸ βάπτισμα Ἰωάννου is matched by the peculiar portrait of the twelve Ephesians as μαθηταί who have received neither Christian baptism nor the gift of the Spirit. These perplexing texts have elicited a variety of explanations.

E. Käsemann has suggested that Luke, writing at a time when the church was battling against the heretics, modified his sources in order to present an idealized picture of a church without division, unified under the authority of the apostles.[1] According to Käsemann, Acts 18.24-28 is based on a tradition which recounted the exploits of Apollos, a noted freelance Christian missionary. In order to connect Apollos to the *Una sancta apostolica*, Luke depicted him as deficient in understanding and in need of correction by Paul's associates.[2] The denigration of Apollos was accomplished by the fabrication of 18.25c, a procedure suggested to Luke by the tradition underlying 19.1-7 which chronicled the conversion of members of the Baptist sect who 'knew only the baptism of John'.[3] Luke heightened the parallels between Apollos and the disciples of the Baptist by transforming the latter into immature Christians. This transformation also enabled Luke to smooth over the rivalry which existed in the early days between the Baptist community and the church. Käsemann asserts that Acts 8.14-17 offers a parallel to this *Tendenz* in Luke's composition.

Käsemann's thesis has been criticized by, among others, Eduard Schweizer.[4] Pointing to Acts 15.39; 21.20, 21, and Luke's omission of

---

1. E. Käsemann, 'The Disciples of John the Baptist in Ephesus', in *Essays on New Testament Themes* (1964), pp. 136-48. Similar views are adopted by Conzelmann, *Acts*, pp. 157-60; Haenchen, *Acts*, pp. 554-57; Wink, *John the Baptist*, pp. 84-85.

2. Käsemann, 'The Disciples of John', p. 147: 'Luke has obviously not dared to report the re-baptism of one known to be inspired by the Spirit and a celebrated missionary into the bargain'.

3. Käsemann is followed at this point by Lüdemann, *Das frühe Christentum*, pp. 215-17 and Pesch, *Die Apostelgeschichte (Apg 13–28)*, pp. 159-60, 164.

4. Schweizer, 'Die Bekehrung des Apollos', pp. 71-79. For criticism of Käsemann's thesis see also Bovon, *Luc le théologien*, p. 248; Coppens, 'L'imposition des mains', pp. 426-27; Giles, 'Church Order (Part 1)', p. 197; K. Aland, 'Zur Vorgeschichte der christlichen Taufe' in *Neues Testament und Geschichte* (1972), pp. 7-11; Marshall, *Luke: Historian and Theologian*, pp. 212-15 and *Acts*, pp. 303-

any significant reference to Paul's collection for the Jerusalem church (11.27f.; 24.17; cf. Gal. 2.10), Schweizer challenges Käsemann's contention that Luke presents an idealized picture of the church unified under Jerusalem. Schweizer also questions Käsemann's treatment of Acts 8.14-17; 18.24-28, and 19.1-7. He insists that these pericopes— rather than reflecting a single theological *Tendenz*—have been shaped by a variety of factors. Acts 8.14-17 is the product of a conflation of two sources. The peculiar features of Acts 18.24-28 are explained as a case of misidentification. The original account related the conversion of a Jewish missionary. However, Luke misinterpreted τὴν ὁδὸν τοῦ κυρίου and ζέων τῷ πνεύματι as references to 'the teaching of *Jesus*' and 'the inspiration of the *Holy Spirit*', and thus erroneously presented Apollos as a Christian who simply received further instruction from Priscilla and Aquila.[1] Schweizer notes that if Luke had intended to describe Apollos' incorporation into the *Una sancta*, he would have had Paul baptize him. Schweizer acknowledges that in 19.1-7 Luke has transformed a Baptist group into immature Christians, nevertheless he insists that the error was inadvertent.[2] The primary focus of the text is the displacement of water baptism by Spirit baptism. Thus Schweizer concludes that Luke is not interested in demonstrating that the individual churches in diverse locations form part of the *Una sancta apostolica*. Luke's principal objective, reflected in these pericopes in varying degrees, is to emphasize the temporal continuity which characterizes salvation history as it moves from Judaism to Christianity.

Schweizer's criticism of Käsemann's thesis is telling. However, his own reconstruction of the tradition-history of Acts 18.24-28 and 19.1-7 is improbable.[3] Apollos is described as a Ἰουδαῖος, but this probably indicates that he, like Aquila, was a Jewish Christian (18.2; cf. 10.28). This suggestion is supported by the fact that Paul knows nothing of a conversion of Apollos by Priscilla and Aquila (cf. 1 Cor. 1.12; 3.4-6, 22; 4.6; 16.12). Furthermore, the expression τὴν ὁδὸν τοῦ κυρίου, like much of the narrative, reflects Lukan style rather

---

304; and C.K. Barrett, 'Apollos and the Twelve Disciples of Ephesus', in The *New Testament Age* (1984), I, pp. 35-36.

1. So also Roloff, *Die Apostelgeschichte*, pp. 278-79.
2. Schweizer, 'Die Bekehrung des Apollos', p. 77: 'Lukas kann sich weder eine konkurrenzierende Täufergruppe noch eine erfolgreiche jüdische Mission, die ehrlich die Schrift predigt, denken. Beide werden zur Vorstufe der christlichen Gemeinde.'
3. Lüdemann, *Das frühe Christentum*, p. 216; Weiser, *Die Apostelgeschichte. Kapitel 13–28*, p. 507; and Pesch, *Die Apostelgeschichte (Apg 13–28)*, p. 160.

than a Jewish *Vorlage*.[1] The phrase ἡ ὁδός is frequently used in Acts with reference to Christian belief and practice (9.2; 19.9, 23; 22.4; 24.14, 22),[2] and κύριος naturally suggests the Lord Jesus.[3] The phrase ζέων τῷ πνεύματι, whether Lukan or traditional, also suggests a Christian origin (cf. Rom. 12.11).[4]

It appears that neither Käsemann nor Schweizer has presented a satisfactory explanation of the two accounts. Perhaps Luke has been more faithful to tradition and history than is often assumed. Both accounts have undoubtedly been significantly shaped by Luke, but this fact does not necessitate a negative assessment of the traditional and historical character of the essential elements in the narrative. It is not improbable that there existed, predominantly in Galilee, groups of former disciples of the Baptist who had come to believe in Jesus as the Coming One without receiving Christian baptism (i.e. in the name of Jesus) or instruction concerning the nature and availability of the Pentecostal gift.[5] This being the case, Luke's narrative is plausible: Apollos was converted by a member of such a group; and the twelve Ephesians were probably converted by Apollos. Luke relates the two accounts in order to retrace the origins of the church in Ephesus, the chief achievement of Paul's missionary career. Together, the two accounts emphasize that—while Apollos served as a precursor[6]—Paul was the

---

1. Conzelmann, *Acts*, p. 158: 'The Lucan style of characterization argues against Schweizer's view'.

2. M. Völkel, 'ὁδός', *EWNT*, II, p. 1203: 'singulär im NT ist der der Apg eigene Sprachgebrauch von ὁ[δός] als Bezeichnung für die christl. Lehre insgesamt'.

3. Barrett, 'Apollos and the Twelve', p. 29.

4. Schille, *Die Apostelgeschichte*, p. 374: '"Brennend im Geist" ist eine christliche Wendung (Röm 12,11) mit dem Sinn: Er war Charismatiker'. See also H. Preisker, 'Apollos und die Johannesjünger in Acts 18.24–19.6', *ZNW* 30 (1931), pp. 301-304; Conzelmann, *Acts*, p. 158; and Barrett, 'Apollos and the Twelve', p. 36 n. 26.

5. Aland, 'Zur Vorgeschichte', pp. 5-11; Preisker, 'Apollos', pp. 301-302; Pereira, *Ephesus*, pp. 92, 108-11; Marshall, *Acts*, p. 304; Bruce, *Book of Acts*, pp. 381-82 and *New Testament History* (1982), p. 309; Beasley-Murray, *Baptism*, pp. 109-10; Hull, *Acts*, p. 112; Dunn, *Holy Spirit*, pp. 84-85; Barrett, 'Apollos and the Twelve', pp. 37-38; Carson, *Showing the Spirit*, pp. 148-49.

6. Contra M. Wolter, 'Apollos und die ephesinischen Johannesjünger (Act 18.24–19.7)', *ZNW* 78 [1987], pp. 49-73, Luke's account should not be read as a polemic against Apollos. Wolter argues that Luke's account (Acts 18.24-19.7) is conditioned by the controversy in Corinth between the followers of Apollos, who claimed to be pneumatics, and Paul (cf. 1 Cor. 1–4). Seeking to elevate Paul over Apollos, Luke skillfully crafted the account in order to depict Paul rather than Apollos as the one who is truly able to baptize and bestow the Spirit. However, the positive portrayal of

principal character in the establishment of the church in Ephesus.[1]
Although the Ephesians had come to believe in Jesus (presumably
through the preaching of Apollos) before their encounter with Paul, it
is Paul who persuades them to express their commitment to Jesus
through Christian baptism and subsequently administers the rite. The
baptismal rite, as the normal prerequisite for reception of the Spirit,
leads to the climax of the second pericope: through the laying on of
hands, Paul commissions the Ephesians as fellow-workers in the mission of the church and the twelve are thus endowed with the prophetic
gift.[2]

Two points emerge from this reconstruction which have a direct
bearing on this inquiry into the nature of Luke's pneumatology and
therefore deserve further examination: (1) the twelve Ephesians, like
Apollos, were disciples of Jesus; (2) and, as a result of their encounter
with Paul, they became his fellow-workers in the mission of the
church.

A number of factors suggest that Luke viewed Apollos and the
twelve Ephesians as disciples of Jesus. Apollos' standing can hardly be
questioned, for Luke indicates that he was κατηχημένος τὴν ὁδὸν
τοῦ κυρίου and ἐδίδασκεν ἀκριβῶς τὰ περὶ τοῦ Ἰησοῦ (18.25).
The former phrase indicates that, at the very least, Apollos was
acquainted with the chief points of Jesus' ministry and teaching.[3] The
latter phrase, descriptive of Paul's preaching in 28.31, suggests that
Apollos preached the Christian gospel.[4] Moreover, Apollos' preaching
was delivered under the inspiration of the Spirit (ζέων τῷ πνεύματι).[5]

Apollos in 18.24-28 and the reference to the Ephesians as 'disciples' in 19.1 speak
against Wolter's thesis.

1. Pereira argues that Luke has shaped the narrative in order to bring out the parallels between John the Baptist and Apollos on the one hand, and Jesus and Paul on the
other (*Ephesus*, pp. 58-73). However, my conclusion is not dependent on such
parallels.

2. For similar assessments see Lampe, *Seal*, pp. 75-76 and Pereira, *Ephesus*,
pp. 106-108. O'Toole argues that Luke structures the account so that Paul can appear
here as Peter and John appeared at Samaria ('Christian Baptism', p. 862), 'Paul puts
the finishing touches to Apollos' work in Ephesus much as Peter and John did to
Philip's work in Samaria'.

3. Barrett, 'Apollos and the Twelve', p. 29; A.M. Hunter, 'Apollos the Alexandrian', in *Biblical Studies: Essays in Honour of William Barclay* (1976), p. 148; and
Carson, *Showing the Spirit*, p. 149. Note also the relevant comments in my criticism
of Schweizer's thesis above.

4. Barrett, 'Apollos and the Twelve', p. 30. As Carson suggests, Apollos may
have been aware of Jesus' death and resurrection (*Showing the Spirit*, p. 149).

5. As Preisker notes, the position of ζέων τῷ πνεύματι 'zwischen "dieser war im
Wege des Herrn unterrichtet" und "er lehrt sorgfältig, was Jesus betrifft" ' indicates

Since according to Luke the gift of the Spirit is not bound to the rite of baptism, there is no contradiction in his portrait of Apollos as a Spirit-inspired preacher who had not received Christian baptism. Similarly, Apollos' experience of the Spirit does not presuppose an awareness of the Pentecostal event or promise (cf. Lk. 1–2). Thus it does not preclude his contact with the Ephesian disciples, who had not heard of the availability of the Spirit. On the contrary, Luke has carefully constructed the narrative in order to emphasize the relationship between Apollos and the Ephesians (cf. 19.1), all of whom knew only 'the baptism of John' (18.25; 19.3).[1] The clear implication is that the twelve from Ephesus were converts of the inspired preacher active in the same city. It must therefore be concluded that in Luke's estimation the Ephesians were, like Apollos, disciples of Jesus.[2] This conclusion is supported by Luke's description of the Ephesians as μαθηταί (19.1), for when he employs the term without any further qualification it always refers to disciples of Jesus.[3] Moreover, since πίστις is the essence of discipleship,[4] the description of the Ephesians as 'believers' (19.2) confirms my findings.[5]

Several objections have been raised against the claim that Luke considered the Ephesians to be disciples of Jesus.

'daß mit πνεῦμα hier der Geist Gottes gemeint ist' ('Apollos', p. 301). See also Aland, 'Zur Vorgeschichte', p. 6; Lampe, 'The Holy Spirit', p. 198; Beasley-Murray, *Baptism*, pp. 110-11; Giles, 'Church Order (Part 1)', p. 199; Guthrie, *New Testament Theology*, p. 548; Weiser, *Die Apostelgeschichte. Kapitel 13–28*, p. 509; and the sources cited in.

1. The verb ἐπίσταμαι occurs frequently in Acts (10.28; 15.7; 18.25; 19.15, 25; 20.18; 22.19; 24.10; 26.26) and always with reference to factual knowledge rather than to religious commitment. Thus the phrase in Acts 18.25, ἐπιστάμενος μόνον τὸ βάπτισμα Ἰωάννου, simply indicates that Apollos' knowledge concerning baptismal practice was limited to the teaching of John the Baptist.

2. Wolter emphasizes the literary connections between 18.24-28 and 19.1-7 (pp. 61-62) and thus concludes: 'Über das beide miteinander verbindende Scharnier der Täuferschülerschaft schlägt des Geist- und Taufdefizit der Johannesjünger von Act 19.1-7 auf den Johannesjünger Apollos zurück' ('Apollos', p. 71).

3. See Lk. 9.16, 18, 54; 10.23; 16.1; 17.22; 18.15; 19.29, 37; 20.45; 22.39, 45; Acts 6.1, 2, 7; 9.10, 19, 26, 38; 11.26, 29; 13.52; 14.20, 22, 28; 15.10; 16.1; 18.23, 27; 19.1, 9, 30; 20.1, 30; 21.4, 16. K. Haacker, 'Einige Fälle von "erlebter Rede" im Neuen Testament', *NovT* 12 (1970), p. 75: 'Der absolut Gebrauch von μαθητής wird von allen Auslegern als eine Bezeichnung für Christen erkannt'.

4. See K.H. Rengstorf, 'μαθητής', *TDNT*, IV, p. 447.

5. See for example Bruce, *Book of Acts*, p. 385: 'Paul's question, "Did ye receive the Holy Spirit when ye believed?" suggests strongly that he regarded them as true believers in Christ'.

1.   K. Haacker argues that 19.1-3, which contains one of the many cases of 'erlebter Rede' in Luke–Acts, is written from the perspective of Paul and not reality as Luke perceived it: Paul initially *thought* that the Ephesians were 'disciples' and 'believers', but he quickly found that this was in fact not the case.[1] Haacker's entire argument rests on the supposition that Luke could not conceive of 'disciples' or 'believers' as being without any knowledge of the Spirit. He rejects Acts 8.15-17 as a contradiction to this claim by insisting that 'dort gilt die "Christianisierung" bezeichnenderweise als unabgeschlossen bis zum Empfang der Geistesgabe'.[2] Yet, as we have already noted, Luke explicitly states that the Samaritans 'believed' (8.12) before they received the Spirit—the very point which Haacker must deny in order to put forth his 'erlebter Rede' thesis—and thus Haacker's argument falls to the ground.[3]

2.   J. Dunn also seeks to mitigate the force of Luke's description in 19.1-3. He asserts that Luke uses the relative pronoun (τινας) with μαθητής in 19.1 in order to highlight the Ephesians' lack of relation to the church in Ephesus: 'they are disciples, but they do not belong to *the* disciples'.[4] However, since Luke uses the same pronoun in the singular with μαθητής in order to describe Ananias (Acts 9.10) and Timothy (Acts 16.1), we must reject this attempt to lessen the force of the phrase in 19.1. Dunn also insists that Paul's question in 19.2 is 'one of suspicion and surprise': the Ephesians claimed to be men of faith, but Paul queries whether or not their claim is valid.[5] Dunn's argument at this

---

1. Haacker, 'Erlebter Rede', pp. 70-77.

2. Haacker, 'Erlebter Rede', p. 75.

3. The other examples of 'erlebter Rede' which Haacker adduces from Luke–Acts do not support his case for Acts 19.1-3. In the three instances where ἀνήρ is used of supernatural beings (Lk. 9.30: Moses and Elijah; 24.4: angels; Acts 10.30: angels) the context clearly indicates the intended referent. Similarly, misguided and magical conceptions concerning the bestowal of the Spirit (Acts 8.18: διὰ τῆς ἐπιθέσεως τῶν χειρῶν τῶν ἀποστόλων) are not unexpected coming from the magician Simon and they are exposed as such in the ensuing verses. Neither of these examples parallels the situation in 19.1-3 where the baptism of the Ephesians rather than their faith is called into question and the judgments purported to be inaccurate come from the noted Apostle. Finally, although Julius' reference to Paul's fellow Christians as φίλοι in Acts 27.3 undoubtedly reflects the perspective of the centurion, it is accurate.

4. Dunn, *Holy Spirit*, pp. 84-85; quote from p. 85 (emphasis his).

5. Dunn, *Holy Spirit*, p. 86. See also C.B. Kaiser 'The "Rebaptism" of the Ephesian Twelve: Exegetical Study on Acts 19:1-7', *RefR* 31 (1977–78), p. 59.

point is based on the observation that the Paul of the epistles could not countenance the idea of 'believers' being without the Spirit (Rom. 8.9; 1 Cor. 12.3; Gal. 3.2; 1 Thess. 1.5f.; Tit. 3.5). However, this objection fails to take into account the fact that the narrative as it currently exists (particularly vv. 2-4) has been significantly shaped by Luke. The dialogue between Paul and the Ephesians is a Lukan construction[1] which highlights the Ephesians' need of the Spirit's enablement and its normal prerequisite, Christian baptism.[2] Paul would undoubtedly have related the story differently,[3] for the potential separation of belief from reception of the Spirit *simpliciter* is presupposed by the question, Εἰ πνεῦμα ἅγιον ἐλάβετε πιστεύσαντες (19.2).[4]

3.   J.K. Parratt maintains that the Ephesians had heard the preaching of John second-hand and therefore, although they had received 'the baptism of John', they had not understood its full significance.[5] The thesis is based on Acts 19.4, where Paul recounts the significance of the Johannine rite.[6] Parratt insists that only after Paul's instruction do the Ephesians comprehend that John had proclaimed repentance and faith in Jesus as Messiah. Having grasped the truth at last, the Ephesians are baptized. However, in view of the prior references to the Ephesians as 'disciples' and 'believers', it is unlikely that 19.4 (τοῦτ' ἔστιν εἰς τὸν Ἰησοῦν) represents teaching of which the Ephesians were hitherto unaware.

---

1. Weiser, *Die Apostelgeschichte. Kapitel 13–28*, p. 513: 'Die Formung von Dialogen ist ein von Lukas oft angewandtes Gestaltungsmittel'. Cf. Lk. 1.34f.; Acts 1.6-8; 4.7-12; 8.34-36; 16.30-32.

2. Paul's question in 19.3 implies that instruction concerning the promise of the Pentecostal gift and perhaps the gift itself would normally accompany Christian baptism (cf. Acts 2.38). However, the latter supposition cannot be pressed in view of Luke's usage elsewhere (cf. 8. 16).

3. Perhaps Luke has compressed a more lengthy traditional account of the event. In any event, we need not question the essential features of Luke's account: he simply tells the story from his own theological perspective.

4. As Turner notes, the question 'would appear meaningless unless such a separation were possible' ('Luke and the Spirit', p. 175). See also Pereira, *Ephesus*, p. 89 and Hanson, *Acts*, p. 189.

5. J.K. Parratt, 'The Rebaptism of the Ephesian Disciples', *ExpTim* 79 (1967–68), pp. 182-83.

6. Parratt argues that there is no essential difference between Johannine and Christian baptism. The only distinction is that whereas the Johannine rite was proleptic, the Christian rite looks back to the accomplished work of Christ ('Rebaptism', p. 183)

Rather, the verse should be seen as a summation of Paul's argument for the appropriateness and necessity of baptism in the name of Jesus, an argument which builds on what the Ephesians already knew: the Coming One which John proclaimed is Jesus.[1] For this reason Luke does not say, 'they believed and were baptized' (8.12, 13; 18.8; cf. 2.41; 16.14f., 33f.); he simply states: ἀκούσαντες δὲ ἐβαπτίσθησαν εἰς τὸ ὄνομα τοῦ κυρίου ᾽Ιησοῦ (19.5).[2] Parratt's thesis, like that of Haacker and Dunn, must be rejected in view of the evidence. My conclusion that Luke viewed the Ephesians as disciples of Jesus is sustained.

This conclusion has significant implications for this inquiry into Luke's pneumatology, for it supports my contention that Luke does not view the gift of the Spirit as a necessary element in conversion. In Luke's perspective, conversion centers on God's gracious act of forgiveness (e.g. Acts 5.31-32; 10.43).[3] And, although faith-repentance[4] and water baptism are usually closely linked, in terms of human response, faith-repentance is the decisive element in conversion,[5] for it forms the sole prerequisite for receiving the forgiveness of God (Lk. 5.20; 24.47; Acts 3.19; 5.31; 10.43; 13.38; 26.18).[6] Therefore, since forgiveness is given to faith, and Luke considered the Ephesians to be men of faith (disciples and believers) *before* they received the gift of the Spirit, he cannot have considered the gift to be the means by which God granted forgiveness to the Ephesians. In short, Luke separates the

---

1. Büchsel, *Geist Gottes*, p. 142 (n. 6 from p. 141): 'Er [Paul] redet ihnen nur von der Taufe auf den Namen Jesu, nicht von Jesu Kreuz und Auferstehung, nicht von Jesu Messianität'.

2. Pereira, *Ephesus*, p. 92.

3. Marshall, *Luke: Historian and Theologian*, p. 169: 'Forgiveness is Luke's characteristic word for the content of salvation'.

4. Dunn correctly notes that repentance and faith are 'the opposite sides of the same coin' (*Holy Spirit*, p. 91).

5. Dunn, *Holy Spirit*, pp. 96-98. Dunn concludes that 'the essential characteristic of the Christian and that which matters on the human side is in the last analysis faith and not water-baptism' (p. 98). R.J. Dillon notes that 'the call to repentance is the structural climax of all the missionary discourses' ('The Prophecy of Christ and His Witnesses according to the Discourses of Acts', *NTS* 32 [1986], p. 547). See also Marshall, *Luke: Historian and Theologian*, pp. 192-95.

6. Dunn notes that whereas water baptism is never spoken of as the sole prerequisite to receiving forgiveness, Luke frequently speaks of repentance or faith as the sole prerequisite (*Holy Spirit*, p. 97).

conversion (forgiveness granted in response to faith) of the twelve Ephesians from their reception of the Spirit.[1]

This judgment, coupled with the prophetic manifestations associated with the Ephesians' reception of the Spirit (19.6, ἐλάλουν τε γλώσσαις καὶ ἐπροφήτευον),[2] indicates that Luke viewed the gift as a prophetic endowment granted to the converted. Furthermore, the association of the gift with the laying on of hands suggests that, according to Luke, the prophetic gift enabled the Ephesians to participate effectively in the mission of the church. The bestowal of the Spirit is God's response to Paul's incorporation of the Ephesians into the missionary enterprise of the church (accomplished through the laying on of hands). The prophetic gift enables the Ephesians, like the Samaritans and Paul, to fulfill the task for which they have been commissioned and, in the prophetic manifestations which it inspires, it provides a sign that the twelve are members of the prophetic community.

My analysis is substantiated by the way in which Luke highlights the strategic role played by the Ephesian disciples in the missionary enterprise. The disciples remain in close company with Paul in Ephesus (19.9, 30; 20.1)[3] and were undoubtedly active in the remarkable missionary effort which took place during the two years Paul remained in Ephesus (19.10). In view of the charge given in 20.28, we may assume that the Ephesian twelve formed, at the very least, part of the πρεσβυτέρους τῆς ἐκκλησίας in Ephesus (20.17) who traveled to Miletus to hear Paul's farewell address.[4] The charge itself, προσέχετε. . . ἐν

---

1. Thus Dunn's contention that 'one cannot separate the act of faith from the gift of the Spirit' (*Holy Spirit*, p. 93-96, quote from p. 96) must be rejected. This is precisely what Luke does.

2. The term ἐλάλουν τε γλώσσαις denotes unintelligible inspired speech and, in Luke's perspective, constitutes a special type of prophecy (see also Acts 2.17). Nevertheless, since προφητεύω designates a broad range of speech activity embracing both intelligible (cf. Lk. 1.67) and unintelligible inspired speech, the two terms should not be simply equated (so also Schneider, *Die Apostelgeschichte II. Teil*, p. 264). In this instance ἐπροφήτευον may imply that additional forms of inspired speech (intelligible) accompanied the manifestation of tongues-speech.

3. Pereira, *Ephesus*, p. 112: 'It may be reasonably assumed that when Paul went to the synagogue in Ephesus, the twelve disciples, specially endowed with the "Pentecostal" gift of the Holy Spirit, accompanied him (cf. 19:9b. . . τοὺς μαθητάς)'. See also pp. 107-108, 253-54.

4. This suggestion is supported by the fact that Paul addresses the elders from Ephesus 'as those first converted, who have been with Paul from the first day' (Haenchen, *Acts*, p. 590; see 20.18). It is also possible that the reference in 19.7 to the number of disciples being about twelve (ὡσεὶ δώδεκα) is Luke's way of emphasizing that these men formed the nucleus of the church in Ephesus.

ᾧ ὑμᾶς τὸ πνεῦμα τὸ ἅγιον ἔθετο ἐπισκόπους (v. 28), suggests that the Spirit came upon the Ephesian twelve (19.6) in order to equip them for the task which lay ahead—a task which in their case included sustaining the work in the region of Ephesus that Paul had initiated.

Therefore Luke's perspective is that the gift of the Spirit received by the Ephesians was of the same character as the gift received by the Samaritans, Paul, the household of Cornelius, and the disciples in Jerusalem on the day of Pentecost. In each instance the Spirit comes upon the individual or group as a prophetic endowment enabling the recipient(s) to participate effectively in the mission which has been entrusted to the prophetic people of God.

CONCLUSION

This analysis of Luke–Acts has revealed that Luke consistently portrays the gift of the Spirit as a prophetic endowment which enables its recipient to fulfill a divinely ordained task. From the very outset of his two-volume work, Luke emphasizes the prophetic dimension of the Spirit's activity. The profusion of Spirit-inspired pronouncements in the infancy narratives herald the arrival of the era of fulfillment (Lk. 1.41f., 67f.; 2.25f.). This era is marked by the prophetic activity of John, the ministry of Jesus, and the mission of his church, all of which are carried out in the power of the Spirit. Filled with the Spirit from his mother's womb (Lk. 1.15, 17), John anticipates the inauguration of Jesus' ministry. By carefully crafting his narrative, Luke ties his account of Jesus' pneumatic anointing (Lk. 3.22) together with Jesus' dramatic announcement at Nazareth (Lk. 4.18f.), and thus indicates that the Spirit came upon Jesus at the Jordan in order to equip him for his task as messianic herald. Literary parallels between the description of Jesus' anointing at the Jordan and that of the disciples at Pentecost suggest that Luke interpreted the latter event in light of the former: the Spirit came upon the disciples at Pentecost to equip them for their prophetic vocation. This judgment is supported by the Baptist's prophecy concerning the coming baptism of Spirit and fire (Lk. 3.16), for Luke interprets the sifting activity of the Spirit of which John prophesied as being accomplished in the Spirit-directed and Spirit-empowered mission of the church (Acts 1.5, 8). It is confirmed by Luke's narration of the Pentecost event (Acts 2.1-13), his interpretation of this event in light of his slightly modified version of Joel 3.1-5a (LXX), and his subsequent description of the church as a prophetic community empowered by the Spirit. Whether it be John in his mother's womb, Jesus at the Jordan, or the disciples at Pentecost, the Spirit comes upon them all as the source of prophetic inspiration, granting special insight and inspiring speech.

The distinctive character of Luke's prophetic pneumatology is particularly evident in his modification of primitive church tradition. Luke's nuanced use of δύναμις, particularly his integration of the term into the tradition of Jesus' birth by the Spirit, his omission of the phrase, ἰάσασθαι τοὺς συντετριμμένους τῇ καρδίᾳ, from the quotation of Isa. 61.1-2 (LXX) in Lk. 4.18f., and his redaction of the Beelzebub Controversy tradition (Lk. 11.20; 12.10), all reflect his conviction that the activity of the Spirit is inextricably related to prophetic inspiration. Whereas the primitive church, following in the footsteps of Jesus, broadened the functions traditionally ascribed to the Spirit in first-century Judaism and thus presented the Spirit as the source of miracle-working power, Luke retained the traditional Jewish understanding of the Spirit as the source of special insight and inspired speech.

Luke, in accordance with the primitive church, does not present reception of the Spirit as necessary for one to enter into and remain with the community of salvation. Thus, in Luke's perspective, the disciples receive the Spirit, not as the source of cleansing and a new ability to keep the law, nor as the essential bond by which they (each individual) are linked to God, not even as a foretaste of the salvation to come; rather, the disciples receive the Spirit as a prophetic *donum superadditum* which enables them to participate effectively in the missionary enterprise of the church. As such, the gift of the Spirit is received principally for the benefit of others.

Therefore, with reference to pneumatology, Luke has more in common with the primitive church than with Paul or later Christian writers who reflect contact with Paul's perspective on the soteriological dimension of the Spirit's work (e.g. John and some of the Apostolic Fathers).[1] This fact, coupled with the Jewish nature of Luke's pneumatology, suggests that Luke–Acts was written at a relatively early date (70–80 AD). This judgment is also supported by the enthusiastic character of Luke's pneumatology. Far from representing an 'early catholic' perspective and institutionalizing the Spirit, in Luke's perspective the Spirit, frequently bestowed sovereignly by God or by figures outside of the apostolic circle, transforms the entire Christian community into a band of prophets.

Luke also anticipated that the prophetic Spirit would inspire the church of his day (Lk. 11.13; 12.10-12; Acts 2.38-39), as it had the church of the past (e.g. Acts 2.4). In light of this fact, I have suggested that one of the reasons Luke wrote was to offer theological and methodological direction for the ongoing Christian mission. This thesis explains Luke's emphasis on the validity of the mission to the Gentiles, and the necessity of the Spirit's enabling.

---

1. See for example 2 *Clement* 14.3-5; Ignatius to the *Ephesians* 9.1; *Polycarp* 14.2; *Barnabas* 11.11; 19.7; *Shepherd of Hermas* 1.3-5; 6.5-7.

PART III

THE ORIGIN OF PAUL'S
SOTERIOLOGICAL PNEUMATOLOGY

No-one would deny that Paul attributes soteriological functions to the Spirit. According to Paul, the Spirit mediates (to the recipient of the pneumatic gift) the knowledge of and ability to comply with those aspects of the divine will necessary to enter into and remain within God's covenant people—the community of salvation (1 Cor. 2.6-16; 2 Cor. 3.3-18; Rom. 8.1-17; Gal. 5.16-26). More specifically, this means that, above all, the Spirit reveals to each Christian the supreme significance of the death and resurrection of Jesus Christ in God's redemptive plan (1 Cor. 2.6-16; 12.3; Rom. 8.9) and progressively transforms him/her into the image of Christ (2 Cor. 3.18)—a process which culminates in the resurrection and ultimate transformation into σῶμα πνευματικον (Rom. 8.11; 1 Cor. 15.45f.; Gal. 6.8).[1] Thus while Paul describes the Spirit as the source of the Christian's cleansing (1 Cor. 6.11; Rom. 15.16), righteousness (Gal. 5.5; Rom. 2.29; 14.17; cf. Gal. 3.14), and intimate fellowship with God (Gal. 4.6; Rom. 8.14-17), he nonetheless maintains that in this present age the gift of the Spirit remains the 'initial-installment' or 'first-fruit' (ἀρραβών: 2 Cor. 1.22; 5.5; Eph. 1.14; ἀπαρχήν: Rom. 8.23) of a more glorious transformation to come.

This is particularly significant when one compares Paul with his close contemporaries in Judaism and the early church. If my conclusions in the previous sections are correct, the soteriological dimension of the Spirit's activity which is so prominent in Paul's epistles[2] appears

---

1. J. Dunn correctly notes that this process is characterized by tension and warfare: 'Paul. . . sees the Christian as living in "the overlap of the ages". . . where once he lived only in the power of the σάρξ, now he experiences the power of the πνεῦμα as well. . . The Christian has indeed entered the new sphere of power (πνεῦμα), but not entirely; he still belongs to the old sphere of power (σάρξ) at the same time—simul-peccator et justus' ('Jesus-Flesh and Spirit: An Exposition of Romans 1. 3-4', *JTS* 24 (1973), p. 52; see pp. 51-54 for a good overview of Paul's soteriology).

2. Although for the purposes of this study I shall include in this category the ten epistles most frequently attributed to Paul (thus excluding only the Pastoral epistles), it should be noted that the evidence significant to this inquiry is contained in those epistles which are (virtually) universally accepted as Pauline (Romans, 1 and 2

infrequently in intertestamental Judaism (cf. Wisdom and the Hymns of Qumran) and is wholly lacking in the pneumatologies of Luke and the primitive church.[1] The latter judgment has profound implications for the development of pneumatological thought in the early church. It suggests that Paul was the first Christian to attribute soteriological functions to the Spirit; and that this original element in Paul's theology did not significantly influence wider (non-Pauline) sectors of the early church until after the writing of Luke–Acts (70–80 AD). Although a definitive defense of this thesis would necessitate providing tradition-histories of relevant Spirit-passages from numerous New Testament documents not yet treated[2]—a procedure clearly beyond the scope of this study—there is justification, given the fact that Paul's epistles represent the earliest written stage in the development of Christian thought, for an examination of the pneumatological content of the early Christian traditions utilized by Paul. Indeed, if it can be established with a high degree of probability that the Christian traditions (hymns, liturgical formulations, etc.) taken up by Paul do not attribute soteriological functions to the Spirit, then my our thesis concerning the originality of Paul's soteriological pneumatology will have been significantly advanced. Moreover, in view of the conclusions offered by

Corinthians, Galatians, Philippians, 1 Thessalonians and Philemon) and therefore my conclusions are not dependent upon or influenced by any of the various options commonly held pertaining to the limits of the Pauline corpus.

1. However, the prophetic pneumatology of Luke and particularly the charismatic pneumatology of the primitive church find their counterparts in Paul's concept of spiritual gifts (cf. N.Q. Hamilton, *The Holy Spirit and Eschatology in Paul* (1957), p. 85, 'The Synoptic doctrine [of the Spirit] finds its continuation in Paul in the equipment of each member of the body of Christ with gifts to fulfil his appointed function'). E. Ellis has argued that in 1 Cor. 12–14 Paul uses the term πνευματικά to denote a special category of χαρίσματα consisting of prophetic gifts of inspired speech and discernment (' "Spiritual Gifts" ', pp. 128-33; *Prophecy and Hermeneutic in Early Christianity* [1978], pp. 24-27; 'Prophecy', p. 49; and 'Christ and Spirit in 1 Corinthians', in *Christ and Spirit in the New Testament* [1973], p. 274). Although an important element in Ellis's argument—his interpretation of 1 Cor. 2.6-16 as distinguishing pneumatics from believers in general—is highly improbable (see Wilkinson, 'Tongues', pp. 14-15 and Fee, *1 Corinthians*, pp. 97-120); nevertheless, his thesis remains plausible with respect to Paul's usage in 1 Cor. 12–14 (note, however, the objections raised by Carson, *Showing the Spirit*, pp. 23-24 and S. Schatzmann, *A Pauline Theology of Charismata* [1987], p. 7). If Ellis is correct at this point, then the Pauline category of πνευματικά is strikingly similar in function to the Lukan gift of the Spirit.

2. Most notable in this regard, apart from the Pauline epistles, is the Gospel of John.

J.S. Vos,[1] such an inquiry is essential if I am to demonstrate that my thesis is historically credible. I shall take up this task in Chapter 12.

Seyoon Kim has recently pointed out the strategic role which the Damascus road Christophany played in the formation of Paul's theological perspective.[2] Yet all experience, even profound religious experience, must be interpreted in language, concepts, and categories with which one is familiar. How is it then that Paul describes the dynamics of Christian life, particularly as it pertains to the work of the Spirit, in such a unique fashion? In Chapter 13 I shall address this question and attempt to place the distinctive soteriological dimension in Paul's pneumatology against the backdrop of Jewish wisdom traditions.

1. Vos, *Untersuchungen*. See Chapter 1 §2.2.3 above for a brief summary of Vos's thesis.
2. S. Kim, *The Origin of Paul's Gospel* (1981).

Chapter 12

SOTERIOLOGICAL PNEUMATOLOGY
AND PRE-PAULINE TRADITION

The major difficulty in attempting to evaluate the pneumatology of the primitive-church traditions utilized by Paul, is of course, separating the traditional elements from that which is uniquely Pauline.[1] In the 'formula-hungry' atmosphere of present-day research one cannot hope to deal with all of the possibilities: the passages purported to contain pre-Pauline formulae are ever-increasing and the relentless, often overly zealous search for more appears to have no end.[2] Nevertheless, there is general agreement concerning the traditional character of a number of formulae,[3] hymns,[4] and dominical sayings[5] found within

---

1. I use the term 'tradition' here to refer to a statement formed in oral or written usage before Paul incorporated it into one or more of his epistles (cf. E.E. Ellis, 'Traditions in 1 Corinthians', *NTS* 32 [1986], p. 481).

2. Kim, *Origin*, p. 149: 'The search for pre-Pauline formulae seems to have gone too far, and, if it progresses at the present rate, one wonders whether before long all the sentences written in exalted language and style in the Pauline corpus will not be declared pre-Pauline or at least non-Pauline, just as some critics in the 19th century managed to declare that all the letters of the Pauline corpus were non-Pauline'. See also Hans F. von Campenhausen, 'Das Bekenntnis im Urchristentum', *ZNW* 63 (1972), p. 231.

3. I include in this category those passages from the Pauline corpus cited as containing traditional formulae in any of the works listed below. Although the same texts are generally cited in each of the works listed below, I have intentionally included references cited in any of these standard works in an effort not to exclude a text which might be recognized by a significant portion of the scholarly community as belonging to this category. The standard works consulted are: A.M. Hunter, *Paul and His Predecessors* (1961), pp. 15-36, 117-22; L. Goppelt, 'Tradition nach Paulus', *KuD* 4 (1958), pp. 213-33; V.H. Neufeld, *The Earliest Christian Confessions* (1963), pp. 42-68; K. Wegenast, *Das Verständnis der Tradition bei Paulus und in den Deuteropaulinen* (1962), pp. 51-92; and K. Wengst, *Christologische Formeln und Lieder des Urchristentums* (1972), pp. 27-143. Thus the category includes: Rom. 1.3-4; 3.24-25; 3.30; 4.24-25; 8.34; 10.9; 14.9; 1 Cor. 8.5-6; 10.16; 11.23-25; 12.3 ('Ανάθεμα 'Ιησοῦς/Κύριος 'Ιησοῦς; both O. Cullmann [*The Earliest Christian Confessions* (1949), pp. 28-30] and Neufeld interpret this passage, at least in its pre-

the Pauline corpus. A review of these texts reveals that only one passage, Rom. 1.3-4, contains material closely related to Paul's soteriological pneumatology; and, as I shall seek to establish, this material—the κατὰ σάρκα–κατὰ πνεῦμα antithesis—represents the redaction of Paul rather than primitive church tradition.

There is also considerable speculation that various aspects of Paul's paraenesis originate from catechetical and liturgical (baptismal) traditions of the primitive church. Although there appears to be little consensus concerning the specific elements from Paul's texts which should be placed in this category,[1] J.S. Vos has argued for the inclusion of references to the soteriological dimension of the Spirit's activity contained in 1 Cor. 6.9-11, Gal. 5.19-24, and 1 Cor. 15.44-50.[2] In the final portion of this chapter I shall demonstrate the improbable nature of Vos's claims.

Thus, by first examining a recognized core of pre-Pauline texts and then demonstrating the tenuous nature of the catechetical-baptismal hypothesis of Vos, I hope to offer evidence from the Pauline epistles which, when coupled with my analysis of Luke–Acts, shifts the burden

Pauline form, against the background of persecution and thus in terms of Mt. 10.17-20/Lk. 12.11-12); 15.3-7; 16.22; 2 Cor. 13.4; Gal. 3.20; Eph. 4.5-6, 8-10; 1 Thess. 1.9f.; 4.14; numerous passages which contain formulae referring to the death (e.g. Rom. 5.6) or resurrection of Jesus (e.g. Rom. 4.24); and those passages which contain the 'faith, hope, love' triad.

4. I include in this category those passages from the Pauline corpus cited as containing traditional hymns from any of the following works: Goppelt, 'Tradition', pp. 213-33; R. Deichgräber, *Gotteshymnus und Christushymnus in der frühen Christenheit* (1967); J.T. Sanders, *The New Testament Christological Hymns: Their Historical Religious Background* (1971); Wengst, *Formeln*, pp. 144-208. This category includes: Rom. 11.33-36; 2 Cor. 1.3f.; Eph. 1.3-12; 2.4-10, 14-18; 5.14; Phil. 2.6-11; Col. 1.12-14, 15-20; 2.13-15.

5. See 1 Cor. 7.10; 9.14; 11.23; and 1 Thess. 4.16. Hunter also points to almost two dozen passages which 'echo' dominical sayings (*Paul*, pp. 47-52; 126-128). In two of these 'echoes' (Rom. 14.17 = the Beatitudes; 1 Thess. 4.8 = Lk. 10.16) Paul has added a reference to the Spirit to the original saying.

1. Thus von Campenhausen sarcastically refers to what 'we presume to know' about the early church's *Taufunterricht* and quotes with approval the words of E. Molland ('A Lost Scrutiny in the early Baptismal Rite', *Opuscula Patrist* [1970], p. 232): 'In the NT there is no trace of a catechumenate' ('Das Bekenntnis', pp. 227-28, quote from p. 228 n. 111). The judgment of Goppelt is still valid: 'Die Forschung ist hier noch sehr im Fluß' ('Tradition', p. 227). However, two points merit comment: the traditional character of aspects of the lists of vices and virtues (as well as the household codes) is generally acknowledged; and the similarities between Col. 3.18-4.1; Eph. 5.22-6.9; and 1 Pet. 2.11-3.7 are often noted.

2. Although Vos's study is not limited to these texts, they form the cornerstone of his thesis. See Chapter 1 §2.2.3 above.

of proof to those who argue for the traditional character of Paul's soteriological pneumatology.

1. *Romans 1.3-4*

. . . περὶ τοῦ υἱοῦ αὐτοῦ
τοῦ γενομένου ἐκ σπέρματος Δαυὶδ κατὰ σάρκα,
τοῦ ὁρισθέντος υἱοῦ θεοῦ ἐν δυνάμει κατὰ πνεῦμα ἁγιωσύνης
ἐξ ἀναστάσεως νεκρῶν,
Ἰησοῦ Χριστοῦ τοῦ κυρίου ἡμῶν.

It is generally acknowledged that Rom. 1.3-4 contains a pre-Pauline confessional formula.[1] The chief arguments advanced in support of this judgment are: the parallelism of participial and relative clauses characteristic of fixed formulae; the occurrence of Semitically styled expressions normally not used by Paul; the untypically Pauline emphasis on Jesus' descent from David; the absence of any reference to the cross, so prominent in Paul's thought elsewhere; and the emphasis on Christ's exaltation at his resurrection (τοῦ ὁρισθέντος υἱοῦ θεοῦ) rather than his pre-existence.[2] There is, however, considerable disagreement concerning the extent to which Paul has modified the formula. Most would agree that Paul has added both the introductory reference to the 'Son' (περὶ τοῦ υἱοῦ αὐτοῦ) and the closing phrase Ἰησοῦ Χριστοῦ τοῦ κυρίου ἡμῶν.[3] Yet debate continues over the origin of the phrases ἐν δυνάμει[4] and κατὰ πνεῦμα ἁγιωσύνης.[5]

---

1. See the extensive list of proponents of this view offered by H. Zimmermann, *Neutestamentliche Methodenlehre—Darstellung der historisch-kritischen Methode* (3rd edn, 1970), pp. 193-94 n. 187.
2. See the summaries provided by V.S. Poythress, 'Is Romans 1.3-4 a Pauline Confession after All?', *ExpTim* 87 (1975–76), p. 180; Dunn, 'Flesh and Spirit', p. 40; and Zimmermann, *Methodenlehre*, pp. 193-94; and the literature they cite.
3. Hahn, *Titles*, p. 246; J. Becker, *Auferstehung der Toten im Urchristentum* (1976), pp. 18-20; and Dunn, 'Flesh and Spirit', p. 41.
4. The thesis that Paul has added ἐν δυνάμει to the formula in order to soften the adoptionism of τοῦ ὁρισθέντος υἱοῦ θεοῦ has received considerable support: E. Schweizer, 'Röm. 1,3f, und der Gegensatz von Fleisch und Geist vor und bei Paulus', in *Neotestamentica* (1963), p. 180; Wegenast, *Tradition*, p. 71; W. Kramer, *Christ, Lord, Son of God* (1966), p. 110; R.H. Fuller, *The Foundations of New Testament Christology* (1965), p. 165; Schlier, 'Zu Röm 1,3f', pp. 210, 215-16; H.-J. van der Minde, 'Wie geht Paulus mit der Tradition um?', *BiKi* 37 (1982), p. 8. C.K. Barrett argues on the basis of structure that the phrase is a Pauline interpolation: it breaks the antithetic parallelism of the clauses (*The Epistle to the Romans* [1957], p. 18).

The origin of the latter phrase is particularly important for this inquiry; for, by virtue of its inclusion, the text portrays the Spirit as the agent of Jesus' resurrection and the source of his exalted existence,[1] thereby giving voice to a central element in Paul's soteriological pneumatology.

5. Those who view the κατὰ σάρκα–κατὰ πνεῦμα ἁγιωσύνης antithesis as Pauline include: R. Bultmann, *Theology of the New Testament* (1952), I, p. 49; N.A. Dahl, 'Die Messianität Jesu bei Paulus', in *Studia Paulina* (1953), p. 90; O. Michel, *Der Brief an die Römer* (1963), p. 38; O. Kuß, *Der Römerbrief* (2nd edn, 1963), I, p. 8; A. Sand, *Der Begriff 'Fleisch' in den paulinischen Hauptbriefen* (1967), p. 161; Wengst, *Formeln*, pp. 112-13. H. Schlier argues that the κατὰ σάρκα–κατὰ πνεῦμα antithesis was not a part of the original formula, but was added to the formula in the pre-Pauline stage by the hellenistic community ('Zu Röm 1,3f ', pp. 207-18). R. Jewett also views the antithesis as an interpolation of the hellenistic church (*Paul's Anthropological Terms* [1971], pp. 136-39). However, Jewett argues that Paul created the σάρξ–πνεῦμα antithesis 'out of exegetical materials in response to the threat posed by the Judaizer movement' (p. 108; see pp. 108-14) and thus insists that 'there are no grounds whatever for the assertion that the confession in its interpolated form was "pre-Pauline" in a strictly chronological sense. The probability is that it emerged in the Pauline congregation sometime after the development of the technical "flesh" category [by Paul] in the year 52' (p. 139). E. Linnemann asserts that Paul sought to harmonize the original formula with his pre-existence Christology; thus he inserted the κατά contrast and placed πνεῦμα, which originally stood in the genitive case (πνεύματος ἁγιωσύνης), in the accusative case ('Tradition und Interpretation in Röm. 1,3f.', *EvTh* 31 [1971], pp. 264-75).

1. The Spirit's role as the agent of Jesus' resurrection is explicitly expressed in Rom. 1.4 if one interprets κατὰ πνεῦμα ἁγιωσύνης with instrumental ('by means of ') force (e.g. Linnemann, 'Röm 1,3f.', pp. 274-75). However, it is more probable that the agency of the Spirit in Jesus' resurrection is implicit in the more general notion that the Spirit is the source of Jesus' exalted existence (see the discussion in §1.2 below). As Vos notes, 'Die Erwähnung des Geistes in diesen Aussagen [Rom. 1.4] bezieht sich nicht nur auf den Akt der Auferweckung als solchen, sondern auch auf die durch diesen Akt eröffnete neue Daseinsweise und Funktion Christi' (*Untersuchungen*, p. 80). Although the agency of the Spirit in Jesus' resurrection is never explicitly expressed in the NT (see Dunn, *Christology in the Making*, p. 144 and 'Flesh and Spirit', p. 67), the concept is presupposed elsewhere by Paul and those in the Pauline tradition (e.g. Rom. 6.4; 8.11; 1 Cor. 15.44f.; 1 Tim. 3.16; 1 Pet. 3.18). The ambiguity of the various NT authors on this point, particularly Paul in Rom. 1.3-4, is attributable to the complexity of their conviction concerning the relationship between Jesus and the Spirit: the Spirit who inspired Jesus during his earthly ministry was instrumental in his resurrection and is now constitutive of his exalted existence.

A.M. Hunter has proposed a triadic division of the text which associates Jesus' appointment as Son of God according to the Holy Spirit with his baptism (*Paul*, p. 25). But, as P. Beasley-Murray notes, 'the fatal objection to this arrangement. . . is the lack of a corresponding participle in the third clause' ('Romans

Three arguments have been offered in support of the thesis that πνεῦμα ἁγιωσύνης forms part of the pre-Pauline formula: (1) the phrase πνεῦμα ἁγιωσύνης is not characteristic of Paul;[1] (2) the κατὰ σάρκα–κατὰ πνεῦμα ἁγιωσύνης antithesis is used in a non-Pauline way;[2] and (3) similar references to the Spirit occur in the formulae contained in 1 Tim. 3.16 and 1 Pet. 3.18.[3] I shall examine each of these arguments separately.

1.1. *πνεῦμα ἁγιωσύνης*
The phrase πνεῦμα ἁγιωσύνης occurs only once in the New Testament (Rom. 1.4) and is entirely absent from the LXX.[4] Thus while the term is unusual for Paul, it is no less so for the rest of the New Testament and, we may presume, the traditions of the primitive church. Furthermore, the noun ἁγιωσύνη occurs only twice in the New Testament and in each instance in an epistle penned by Paul (1 Thess. 3.13; 2 Cor. 7.1).[5] It would appear that the antecedents of πνεῦμα ἁγιωσύνης are to be found in the epistles of Paul rather than in the tradition of the primitive church. Indeed, in view of Paul's unique usage of ἁγιωσύνη prior to the writing of Romans, it is entirely probable that Paul is responsible for the phrase. In the process of editing a

---

1.3f.: An Early Confession of Faith in the Lordship of Jesus', *TB* 31 [1980], p. 149).

1. O. Betz, *What Do We Know about Jesus?* (1968), p. 95; G. Bornkamm, *Paul* (1969), p. 248; Dunn, 'Flesh and Spirit', p. 60; Müller, 'Geisterfahrung', p. 263; J. Beker, *Auferstehung der Toten im Urchristentum* (1976), p. 21; P.W. Meyer, 'The Holy Spirit in the Pauline Letters: A Contextual Exploration', *Int* 33 (1979), p. 14; see also those cited in the note which follows.

2. This viewpoint was forcefully put forth by Schweizer, 'Fleisch und Geist', pp. 180-89 (cf. *Erniedrigung und Erhöhung bei Jesus und seinen Nachfolgern* [1962], pp. 91-92) and subsequently adopted by numerous scholars: Barrett, *Romans*, p. 18; Wegenast, *Tradition*, p. 71; F.J. Leenhardt, *The Epistle to the Romans* (1961), pp. 35f.; Hahn, *Titles*, pp. 247, 249; Kramer, *Christ*, p. 109; R.H. Fuller, *Christology*, pp. 165f., 187; Hill, *Greek Words*, pp. 280-81; B. Schneider, 'Κατὰ Πνεῦμα Ἁγιωσύνης', *Bib* 48 (1967), p. 369; Beasley-Murray, 'Romans 1.3f', pp. 149, 151; van der Minde, 'Tradition', p. 8.

3. Schweizer, 'Fleisch und Geist', p. 181; cf. Dunn, 'Flesh and Spirit', pp. 63-65.

4. The term is found only in *T. Levi* 18.7 and perhaps an inscription from an 'Amulett von Acre' (see E. Peterson, *Frühkirche, Judentum und Gnosis* [1959], pp. 351-52 concerning *Corpus inscriptionum graecarum*, ed. G. Kaibel [Berlin, 1873], XIV, no. 2413, 17).

5. Note also the frequency which Paul uses the terms ἁγιασμός (Rom. 6.19, 22; 1 Cor. 1.30; 1 Thess. 4.3, 4, 7; 2 Thess. 2.13 [1 Tim. 2.15; Heb. 12.14; 1 Pet. 1.20]) and ἁγιότης (2 Cor. 1.12; [Heb. 12.18]).

well-known confession of the primitive church, it would be natural for Paul to include a phrase of elevated and Semitic style in his redaction.[1]

1.2. *The κατὰ σάρκα–κατὰ πνεῦμα ἁγιωσύνης Antithesis*

The κατὰ σάρκα–κατὰ πνεῦμα antithesis is distinctively Pauline (Rom. 1.3-4; 8.4-5; Gal. 4.29).[2] Therefore, the Pauline origin of the antithesis is virtually assured unless substantial evidence to the contrary can be adduced. E. Schweizer sought to provide this sort of evidence by arguing that in Rom. 1.3-4 the antithesis is used in a non-Pauline way: whereas κατὰ σάρκα, when contrasted with κατὰ πνεῦμα, is always used pejoratively by Paul to denote moral inferior-

---

1. Poythress, 'Confession after All?', p. 181: 'One could. . . argue that a confession would be less likely to exhibit peculiarities or idiosyncrasies than an individual writer'.

2. The phrases κατὰ σάρκα (Rom. 1.3; 4.1; 8.4, 5, 12, 13; 9.3, 5; 1 Cor. 1.26; 10.18; 2 Cor. 1.17; 5.16 (2×); 10.2, 3; 11.18; Gal. 4.23, 29; Eph. 6.5; Col. 3.22; and outside of Paul, only in Jn 8.15) and κατὰ πνεῦμα (Rom. 1.4; 8.4, 5; 1 Cor. 12.8; Gal. 4.29) are characteristic of Paul. Furthermore, κατὰ σάρκα is associated with Christ only two times in the entire NT outside of Rom. 1.3 and in each instance by Paul (Rom. 9.5; 2 Cor. 5.16).

The σάρξ–πνεῦμα antithesis in general is also characteristic of Paul (Rom. 1.4; 8.4-6, 9, 13; 1 Cor. 5.5; Gal. 3.3; 4.29; 5.17f.; 6.8 cf. 1 Cor. 6.17; 2 Cor. 7.1; Col. 2.5; πνευματικός–σαρκικός/σάρκινος—Rom. 7.14; 1 Cor. 3.1; cf. Rom. 15.27; 1 Cor. 9.11). The terms are correlated infrequently outside of Paul (Jn 3.6; 6.63; 1 Tim. 3.16; 1 Pet. 3.18; cf. Heb. 12.9; and 1 Pet. 4.6) and several of these references reflect Pauline influence (see §1.3 below). In the only instance where the correlation is found in the synoptic gospels, the terms carry meanings different from Paul's distinctive usage (Mk 14.38 = Mt. 26.41; here πνεῦμα refers to the human spirit or will [cf. Mk 2.8; 8.12] and σάρξ, to the constraints of the body upon the will). Antecedents to the Pauline σάρξ–πνεῦμα antithesis can be found in pagan and Jewish sources. The closest parallels are found in the rabbinic antithesis between הרע יצר and הטוב יצר (cf. Davies, *Paul*, pp. 21-35), the matter-spirit dualism in Philo (cf. Brandenburger, *Fleisch und Geist*, pp. 114-221), and the 'two Spirits' doctrine of Qumran (cf. Jewett, *Anthropological Terms*, pp. 82-94, 100, 108). However, the differences between the Pauline σάρξ–πνεῦμα antithesis and these precedents are significant (cf. Jewett, p. 92; Davies, p. 18; F. Mußner, *Der Galaterbrief* [1974], p. 394; H.D. Betz, *Galatians* [1979], p. 278 n. 64; R. Meyer, 'σάρξ', *TDNT*, VII, p. 114) and indicate that the latter 'merely provided the raw materials for Pauline usage' (Jewett, *Anthropological Terms*, p. 108); Indeed, Jewett has argued persuasively that the σάρξ–πνεῦμα antithesis of the epistles was created by Paul 'in response to the threat posed by the Judaizer movement' (p. 108): 'σάρξ was first used as a technical term in connection with the circumcision problem raised by the Judaizers; it developed through Paul's typological exegesis into a full dialectical counterpart to the spirit; and after having been created as an argument against nomism, it was applied to the problem of antinomianism' (p. 114).

ity or inadequacy, in Rom. 1.3-4 κατὰ σάρκα refers, in a neutral sense, to Christ's physical and earthly existence. This led Schweizer to conclude that the antithesis in Rom. 1.3-4 refers to two distinct spheres (earthly and heavenly) rather than modes of existence determined by the sinful nature and the Spirit of God respectively.[1]

However, Schweizer's argument has been decisively rebutted by J. Dunn.[2] Dunn demonstrates that for Paul, κατὰ σάρκα is a phrase of contrast and that it always 'stands on the negative side of the contrast denoting inferiority or inadequacy'.[3] This remains the case whether the phrase is principally associated with kinship (Gal. 4.23, 29; Rom. 4.1; 9.3) or conduct (e.g. Rom. 8.4f.). For this reason simple distinctions between 'physical and moral and between neutral and pejorative' uses of the phrase are not valid.[4] Moreover, Dunn argues persuasively that κατὰ σάρκα in Rom. 1.3 'carries its normal note of depreciation'[5] and that the antithesis in Rom. 1.3-4 should be interpreted in light of Paul's normal usage. Dunn's argument centers on 'the fact that in Paul's view the Christian's experience of flesh and Spirit is patterned on Christ's'.[6] Just as the Christian is caught in the overlap of ages, and as such experiences the conflict of flesh and Spirit, so also

---

1. Schweizer, *Erniedrigung*, p. 92: 'Sie [flesh and Spirit] bezeichnen die irdische Sphäre, in der das im ersten Satz Ausgesagte gilt, und die himmlische Sphäre, in der erst die vollendete Gottessohnschaft Wirklichkeit geworden ist' (see also Schweizer, 'σάρξ', *TDNT*, VII, p. 126). Kramer, following Schweizer, writes: 'These two concepts are not to be understood in the Pauline sense as descriptions of the domain of sin and the domain of life' (*Christ*, p. 109).

2. Dunn, 'Flesh and Spirit', pp. 40-68. For criticism of Schweizer's thesis see also Linnemann, 'Röm. 1,3f.', pp. 265-68; Wengst, *Formeln*, pp. 112-13; and Jewett, *Anthropological Terms*, pp. 136-39.

3. Dunn, 'Flesh and Spirit', pp. 46-49; quote from p. 49.

4. Dunn, 'Flesh and Spirit', p. 49. Wengst responds to Schweizer, whom he quotes, by pointing to Gal. 4.23: 'Wenn man so will, kann man sagen, Paulus gebrauche κατὰ σάρκα "rein neutral für die menschliche Abstammung" Ishmaels, aber hier ist es ganz deutlich, daß dieses "rein neutral" für Paulus eine theologische Disqualifizerung bedeutet' (*Formeln*, p. 113). The fact that the soteriological inadequacy of birth κατὰ σάρκα (Gal. 4.23; cf. Rom. 4.1) is closely associated with improper conduct in Galatians (Gal. 4.29; 5.16f.; described in Gal. 5.19 as τὰ ἔργα τῆς σαρκός) demonstrates the tenuous nature of distinctions drawn at this point.

5. Dunn, 'Flesh and Spirit', pp. 49-51. Dunn asserts that 'the identification of Jesus as Son of David seems to have been more of an embarrassment and hindrance than a glad and central affirmation' and that Paul never uses the title (p. 50).

6. Dunn, 'Flesh and Spirit', p. 54. Dunn maintains that the strand of *imitatio Christi* is 'firmly embedded in Paul's thought' (cf. Rom. 15.2f.; 1 Cor. 4.17; 11.1; 2 Cor. 8.8f.; Gal. 1.10; Eph. 4.20, 32–5.2; Phil. 2.5-8; Col. 2.6; 1 Thess. 1.6) (p. 55).

Jesus came in the likeness of sinful flesh (ἐν ὁμοιώματι σαρκὸς ἁμαρτίας, Rom. 8.3) and experienced the same tension.[1] Jesus was victorious over the flesh and serves as both the supreme example and source of power for the Christian seeking to live κατὰ πνεῦμα, a process which—as we have noted—culminates in the resurrection (Rom. 8.11) and ultimate transformation into σῶμα πνευματικόν (1 Cor. 15.44f.). Thus Dunn asserts that κατὰ σάρκα and κατὰ πνεῦμα in Rom. 1.3-4 'denote not successive and mutually exclusive spheres of power, but modes of existence and relationships which overlap and coincide in the earthly Jesus'.[2]

Dunn bolsters his argument by pointing to the introductory υἱός in v. 3 and the unusual ἐξ ἀναστάσεως νεκρῶν (rather than ἐξ ἀναστάσεως ἐκ νεκρῶν) in v. 4: the former indicates that Jesus is Son at both stages (earthly and exalted) and suggests further that his Sonship is, at each stage, a function of (or, as I prefer, manifest through) the Spirit; the latter emphasizes that Jesus, by virtue of his resurrection, is the forerunner of the final resurrection of the dead, which in turn implies that Jesus in the flesh is the forerunner of the Christian caught between the ages.[3] The logic of Dunn's argument suggests not only that (in Paul's perspective) Jesus experienced the tension between flesh and Spirit common to every Christian, but also that he, as the forerunner of the final resurrection of the dead, was resurrected by the Spirit (Rom. 8.11) and that his exalted existence is determined by the Spirit (1 Cor. 15.44f.).[4] Indeed, the emphasis in

---

1. Dunn, 'Flesh and Spirit', pp. 52-55, and *Christology in the Making*, p. 139. One need not accept Dunn's analysis of the κατὰ σάρκα–κατὰ πνεῦμα tension at every point, particularly concerning the extent to which the life of the individual Christian is, and the life of the earthly Jesus was (p. 57), determined by the flesh, in order to affirm the reality of the tension and the validity of the essential elements of Dunn's interpretation of Rom. 1.3-4 (p. 53; cf. Dunn, 'Romans 7:14-25 in the Theology of Paul', in *Essays on Apostolic Themes* [1985], pp. 49-70 and the responses by D. Wenham, 'The Christian Life: A Life of Tension? A Consideration of the Nature of Christian Experience in Paul', pp. 80-94 and R.H. Gundry, 'The Moral Frustration of Paul before His Conversion', in *Pauline Studies* [1980], pp. 228-45).

2. Dunn, 'Flesh and Spirit', p. 54.

3. 'Flesh and Spirit', pp. 55-56.

4. As M. Turner notes, with the phrase ὁ ἔσχατος Ἀδὰμ εἰς πνεῦμα ζῳοποιοῦν (1 Cor. 15.45) Paul indicates that Jesus is 'an eschatological "being" vitalised by πνεῦμα which is the life-principle of the age to come' ('The Significance of Spirit Endowment for Paul', *VE* 9 [1975], p. 63). In Paul's view Jesus, resurrected as σῶμα πνευματικόν, became the representative Man for all who will bear his likeness at the final resurrection; and, by virtue of his special status, he also became the source of life κατὰ πνεῦμα, that is πνεῦμα ζῳοποιοῦν (1 Cor. 15.45) or 'Son of God in power' (see Fee, *1 Corinthians*, p. 789; Dunn, 'Last Adam'

Rom. 1.3-4 is placed on the *culmination* of Jesus' experience of the κατὰ σάρκα–κατὰ πνεῦμα tension: his resurrection and enthronement in power wrought in and by the Spirit. The period of conflict between σάρξ and πνεῦμα in Jesus' earthly life is a presupposition of, not the central element within, the formula as it currently stands.[1]

At times Dunn appears to depict the tension itself rather than the culmination and transcendence of the tension as the focal point of the formula; nevertheless, he demonstrates that Rom. 1.3-4 should be interpreted in a manner consistent with Paul's theology in general and his antithetical use of κατὰ σάρκα and κατὰ πνεῦμα in particular. Dunn acknowledged that this interpretation could be taken as support for the view that κατὰ πνεῦμα ἁγιωσύνης was added by Paul.[2] Yet,

p. 132). Since the conceptual movement in Rom. 1.3-4 is from 'existence κατὰ σάρκα and κατὰ πνεῦμα' to 'existence solely κατὰ πνεῦμα', the Spirit must be viewed as integral to both stages (earthly and exalted) of Jesus' Sonship and thus the agent of his resurrection as well as the source of his exalted existence (cf. Hamilton, *Eschatology*, p. 14, 'we are justified in ascribing the resurrection as well as the exaltation life [of Christ] to the Spirit'. Note also the similar conclusions offered by C. Pinnock, 'The Concept of the Spirit in the Epistles of Paul' [1963], p. 108).

1. C.E.B. Cranfield is quite right to criticize Dunn at this point: 'It is surely preferable to understand the times referred to in the two phrases κατὰ πνεῦμα ἁγιωσύνης and ἐξ ἀναστάσεως νεκρῶν as the same, rather than to assume a temporal disjunction between them, as does Professor Dunn' ('Some Comments on Professor J.D.G. Dunn's *Christology in the Making* with Special Reference to the Evidence of the Epistle to the Romans', in *The Glory of Christ in the New Testament* [1987], p. 270).

2. Dunn, 'Flesh and Spirit', p. 60. By demonstrating that the κατὰ σάρκα–κατὰ πνεῦμα antithesis in Rom. 1.3-4 is consistent with Paul's theology, Dunn undermines the thesis put forth by Jewett (*Anthropological Terms*, pp. 136-38). Jewett rejected Schweizer's analysis of Rom. 1.3-4, for he recognized that the formula could not have come from a single source: 'If the congregation were really Hellenistic as the opposition between κατὰ σάρκα and κατὰ πνεῦμα implies, it would scarcely be interested in claiming messianic honors for the fleshly Jesus; if the congregation were Jewish Christian as the messianic interest implies, it would scarcely contradict itself by the addition of the derogatory expression "in the realm of the flesh"' (p. 137). Nevertheless, Jewett concluded that the κατὰ σάρκα–κατὰ πνεῦμα antithesis was added to the formula by the hellenistic community, not by Paul. Two arguments were offered in support of this judgment: (1) the expression πνεῦμα ἁγιωσύνης is unusual for Paul and therefore came from another source (so also Schlier, 'Zu Röm 1,3f.', p. 211); (2) Paul would not have emphasized 'the superiority of Jesus' pneumatic existence at the expense of his earthly existence and status', for such an emphasis would 'conflict with his belief in the centrality of Jesus' earthly suffering as well as with the apocalyptic belief that Jesus was the Messiah who ushered in the new aeon' (*Anthropological Terms*, p. 137). Jewett later acknowledged the weakness of the first argument and affirmed that ἁγιωσύνης was

he rejected this position and argued that the formula reflects the faith of the wider church.[1] I shall examine the validity of this claim in the following section.

1.3. *Romans 1.3-4 and the Non-Pauline Church*

The parallels between the role attributed to the Spirit in Rom. 1.3-4 and similar statements in 1 Tim. 3.16 and 1 Pet. 3.18 have been cited as evidence that the pneumatological ideas present in these texts are based on a well known and early (pre-Pauline) tradition of the primitive church.[2] However, the force of this argument is mitigated by the fact that the parallel texts, if not directly dependent upon Rom. 1.3-4, in all probability originate from a milieu influenced by Paul. This is undoubtedly the case for 1 Tim. 3.16 and, in view of the affinities between 1 Peter and Pauline theology,[3] most likely the case for 1 Pet. 3.18 as well. Furthermore, although the pneumatological ideas present in Rom. 1.3-4 and its parallels (i.e. the Spirit is the agent of Jesus' resurrection and the source of his exalted existence) are found elsewhere in Paul's epistles (e.g. Rom. 8.11; 1 Cor. 15.44f.), they are completely absent from the synoptic gospels and Acts.

Acts 2.33 is particularly instructive. Here the Spirit is not depicted as the agent of Jesus' resurrection (God is the agent, Acts 2.32); rather, the Spirit is given to Jesus *by virtue of* his resurrection-exaltation. Moreover, this endowment of the Spirit is not integral to Jesus' exalted existence: it is given to him 'only for distribution'.[4] Thus Acts 2.33 presupposes a pneumatological perspective significantly different

---

inserted into the interpolated formula by Paul (p. 138). Thus his conclusion concerning the interpolation of the antithesis by the hellenistic church was based entirely on the second argument. However, this argument is valid only if one accepts Schweizer's interpretation of the antithesis. The argument can be turned on its head and adduced in favor of Dunn's contention and the Pauline origin of the antithesis.

1. Dunn, 'Flesh and Spirit', pp. 62-65.

2. Dunn states that the essential content of 1 Pet. 3.18 is given more formalized expression in Rom. 1.3f. and 1 Tim. 3.16: 'Jesus was put to death as flesh: it was because he was flesh that death was possible, indeed necessary for him. But he was brought to life as Spirit: it was because he possessed the Spirit, because the Spirit wrought in him and on him, that ζωοποίησις followed death' ('Flesh and Spirit', p. 65).

3. W.G. Kümmel, *Introduction to the New Testament* (1975), p. 423: 'There can be no doubt that the author of I Peter stands in the line of succession of Pauline theology'.

4. Haenchen, *Acts*, p. 183.

from that of Rom. 1.4 (and parallels).[1] While both texts affirm that the resurrection marks a decisive shift in Jesus' relationship to the Spirit ('from Spirit inspiring Jesus to Spirit of Jesus'),[2] the nature of the transformed relationship is perceived in different ways. This fact, coupled with the other synoptic writers' silence concerning the Spirit's role in Jesus' resurrection, indicates that it is highly improbable that the κατὰ πνεῦμα ἁγιωσύνης of Rom. 1.4 represents primitive-church tradition.

I am now in a position to summarize my argument regarding the Pauline origin of κατὰ σάρκα and κατὰ πνεῦμα ἁγιωσύνης and, by way of conclusion, suggest a motive for Paul's redaction at this point. Paul's unique usage of ἁγιωσύνη prior to the writing of Romans, together with the Pauline nature of the κατὰ σάρκα–κατὰ πνεῦμα antithesis, and the distinctively Pauline character of the pneumatology presupposed by the inclusion of κατὰ πνεῦμα ἁγιωσύνης in Rom. 1.4 indicate that κατὰ σάρκα and κατὰ πνεῦμα ἁγιωσύνης were added to the traditional formula underlying Rom. 1.3-4 by Paul.[3] These insertions, representative as they are of Paul's distinctive theological perspective, were in all probability inspired by his desire to declare a law-free gospel. Through his redactional activity Paul transformed the traditional formula, which affirmed Jesus' Davidic descent as vital to his messianic mission and status, into a declaration which gave expression to his critique of Judaism: the pedigree of Jesus, born of the seed of David, was defective as a basis for his mission and inadequate as an expression of his relationship to God as Son; it was overcome in and through the Spirit—decisively at the resurrection.[4]

---

1. Busse notes the fundamental difference between Acts 2.33 and Rom. 1.4: 'Im Unterschied zu Röm 1,4 ist jener Geist, den der zur rechten Gottes Erhöhte empfängt, kein für ihn notwendiges Geschenk, sondern zur Weitergabe an die Jünger und Glaübigen bestimmt. Jesus leitet von Himmel her die weltweite Mission' (*Das Nazareth-Manifest Jesu*, p. 99). Dunn ('Flesh and Spirit', p. 66) and Schneider ('Κατὰ Πνεῦμα Ἁγιωσύνης', pp. 371-76) fail to acknowledge this point.

2. Dunn, 'Flesh and Spirit', p. 67.

3. Thus, although the origin of ἐν δυνάμει remains uncertain, the original formula may be reconstructed as follows:

> τοῦ γενομένου ἐκ σπέρματος Δαυίδ,
> τοῦ ὁρισθέντος υἱοῦ θεοῦ (ἐν δυνάμει) ἐξ ἀναστάσεως νεκρῶν.

4. See Wengst, *Formeln*, p. 113; and for a more radical elaboration of this idea, see Dunn, 'Flesh and Spirit', p. 57.

2. Tradition and Redaction in 1 Corinthians 6.9-11; 15.44-50, and Galatians 5.19-24

J.S. Vos maintains that Gal. 5.19-24; 1 Cor. 6.9-11, and, to a lesser extent, 1 Cor. 15.44-50 are based upon a baptismal tradition detailing conditions of entrance into the Kingdom of God. According to Vos this baptismal tradition contained a list of positive and negative conditions for entrance into the Kingdom of God in the form of a catalog of vices and virtues. And, most significant for this inquiry, Vos argues that this tradition named both Christ and the Spirit as 'Heilsfaktoren' which made entrance into the Kingdom possible.[1]

Vos supports his thesis by pointing to the similarities between Gal. 5.19-24 and 1 Cor. 6.9-11. Both texts enumerate conditions for entering into the Kingdom of God and name Christ and the Spirit as the agents which make this entrance possible. Moreover, since both texts refer to the baptismal rite as the decisive soteriological moment, 'man darf sogar vermuten, daß die ganze Tradition vom Einlaß in das Reich Gottes in der vorpaulinischen Gemeinde zur Taufverkündigung gehörte'.[2]

Vos asserts that the baptismal tradition underlying 1 Cor. 6.9-11 and Gal. 5.19-24 also stands behind 1 Cor. 15.44-50, although here the tradition is utilized in a different manner. This judgment is based upon the fact that 1 Cor. 15.44-50, like the previous texts mentioned, refers to conditions for entrance into the Kingdom of God and names Christ and the Spirit as 'Heilsfaktoren'. It finds confirmation in the εἰκών-clothing language of v. 49 (cf. v. 53), a motif commonly employed in baptismal tradition.[3]

Vos finds further support for these conclusions in his analysis of the relationship between the Spirit and salvation in the Jewish literature. Pointing to a series of Jewish texts (Ps. 51; Ezek. 36.27; Isa. 44.1-5; 1QS 2.25b–3.12; 1QS 3.13–4.26; Wisdom; Joseph and Aseneth), he argues that pre-Christian Judaism commonly attributed soteriological significance to the Spirit. Therefore Vos does not find it surprising that the primitive church held similar beliefs:[4]

> In light of the Old Testament-Jewish understanding of the Spirit, which we have attempted to elucidate, it is not surprising that the early church not only viewed the Spirit as the source of the miraculous, but attributed salvific significance to the Spirit as well.

1. Vos, *Untersuchungen*, pp. 26-33.
2. *Untersuchungen*, p. 30.
3. *Untersuchungen*, p. 32.
4. *Untersuchungen*, p. 77. ET is my own.

In spite of the vigor with which Vos argues his case, there are numerous reasons to reject his contention that pre-Pauline baptismal tradition named the Spirit alongside Christ as a 'Heilsfaktor' which made entrance into the Kingdom of God possible.[1]

2.1. *The Catalogs of Vices and Virtues*
Although it is quite possible that the catalogs of vices and virtues in Gal. 5.19f. and 1 Cor. 6.9f. were influenced by similar pagan, Jewish, and Christian lists,[2] the *ad hoc* nature of the catalogs in Gal. 5.19f. and 1 Cor. 6.9f.[3] and the diversity of the various Pauline lists in general[4] indicate that Paul was not dependent on a single source or established tradition. For this reason we must be cautious in attributing material from these texts to tradition. Furthermore, since the New Testament catalogs are never associated with the Spirit outside of (and only infrequently within) the Pauline corpus,[5] it is exceedingly improbable that Paul has been influenced by traditional material at this point.

1. This contention is the basis for Vos's claim that the pre-Pauline community attributed 'das gesamte Heil, die Reinigung, Heiligung und Rechtfertigung in der Vergangenheit, der gerechte Wandel in der Gegenwart und die Verwandlung in der Zukunft' to both Christ and the Spirit (*Untersuchungen*, p. 33, see also pp. 131, 144).

2. A. Vögtle, *Die Tugend- und Lasterkataloge im Neuen Testament* (1936); B.S. Easton, 'New Testament Ethical Lists', *JBL* 51 (1932), pp. 1-12; S. Wibbing, *Die Tugend- und Lasterkataloge im Neue Testament und ihre Traditionsgeschichte* (1959); E. Kamlah, *Die Form der katalogischen Paränese im Neuen Testament* (1964); M.J. Suggs, 'The Christian Two Way Tradition: Its Antiquity, Form, and Function', in *Studies in the New Testament and Early Christian Literature* (1972), pp. 60-74. Suggs, following the lead of Kamlah, argues that the form as well as the content of the 'Two Way' tradition has influenced Gal. 5. 17-24: (1) dualistic introduction (Gal. 5.17-18); (2) double catalog (Gal. 5.19-21a, 22-23); (3) eschatological threat/promise (Gal. 5.21b, 24) (p. 69). However, since Gal. 5.17-24 is the only example from the NT which follows this pattern, the hypothesis must be judged unlikely.

3. Easton, 'Ethical Lists', p. 5: 'In Galatians 5.19-21 . . . a real attempt has been made to adapt the list to the context'. See also F.F. Bruce, *The Epistle of Paul to the Galatians* (1982), p. 250. Fee ties elements from the list in 1 Cor. 6.9-10 to the context of the letter (*1 Corinthians*, pp. 242-43). See also E. Schweizer, 'Traditional Ethical Patterns in the Pauline and Post-Pauline Letters and Their Development (Lists of Vices and House-Tables)', in *Text and Interpretation* (1979), p. 196; and C.K. Barrett, *1 Corinthians* (1968), p. 140.

4. Fee, *1 Corinthians*, p. 225 n. 27: 'The search for a "source" is futile. . . The Pauline lists are so diverse as to defy explanation'. See also P. O'Brien, *Colossians, Philemon* (1982), p. 180 and Easton, 'Ethical Lists', p. 5.

5. The only exception, Tit. 3.3-5, is clearly in the Pauline tradition. Catalogs cited by Betz (*Galatians*, p. 281 n. 91) and Conzelman (*1 Corinthians* [1975], p. 101 n. 69) include: Mt. 15.19; Mk 7.22; Rom. 1.29-31; 13.13; 1 Cor. 5.10f.; 6.9f.: 2

This judgment is confirmed by the Pauline nature of the concepts and terms associated with the Spirit in Gal. 5.19f. and 1 Cor. 6.11. The σάρξ–πνεῦμα antithesis in Gal. 5.19f. is characteristic of Paul[1] and integral to the argument of the epistle.[2] 1 Corinthians 6.11 also has a decidedly Pauline ring: Paul frequently concludes on a positive note after a warning such as is found in 1 Cor. 6.9-10;[3] the verse follows the indicative-imperative pattern characteristic of Paul;[4] ἐδικαιώθητε, πνεύματι τοῦ θεοῦ, and the repetition of ἀλλά reflect Paul's hand.[5]

There is also little reason to accept Vos's contention that the catalogs in Gal. 5.19f. and 1 Cor. 6.9f. form part of an early tradition detailing conditions for entrance into the Kingdom of God. Catalogs are never associated with the Kingdom of God in the relevant synoptic texts.[6]

Cor. 6.6f; 12.20f.; Gal. 5.19f.; Eph. 4.2, 31f.; 5.3f.; Phil. 4.8; Col. 3.5, 8, 12; 1 Tim. 1.9f.; 4.12; 6.11; 2 Tim. 2.22; 3.2-5, 10; Tit. 3.3; 1 Pet. 2.1; 3.8; 4.3, 15; 2 Pet. 1.5-7; Rev. 21.8; 22.15. See also *Didache* 2.1–5.2 and *Barnabas* 18–20. The Spirit is associated with the catalogs in Gal. 5.19f; 1 Cor. 6.9f; 2 Cor. 6.6f.; Eph. 4.2,31f.; and Tit. 3.3-5.

1. Contra Vos, *Untersuchungen*, p. 126: 'Gemeinchristlich war die Anschauung von dem Kampf zwischen Fleisch und Geist'. The phrase καρπὸς τοῦ πνεύματος (v. 22) has a close parallel in Eph. 5.9 (καρπὸς τοῦ φωτός) and the language is familiar to Paul (καρπός: Rom. 6.21f.; 15.28; Phil. 1.11, 22; 4.17; καρποφορέω: Rom. 7.4f.; Col. 1.6, 10).

2. Jewett stresses the conceptual and verbal links between Gal. 4.21f.; 5.19f., and 6.11-16 (*Anthropological Terms*, pp. 107-108). Note also the polemic nature of the phrase κατὰ τῶν τοιούτων οὐκ ἔστιν νόμος (v. 23).

3. See Fee, *1 Corinthians*, p. 245 n. 29, who cites numerous examples from 1 Corinthians: 3.22-23; 4.14-17 (as a conclusion to 1.18–4.21); 5.7; 6.20; 10.13; 11.32. Fee writes, 'Paul cannot bring himself to conclude on the note of warning struck in vv. 8-10, especially since it might leave the impression that the Corinthians were actually still among "the wicked"' (p. 245).

4. Fee, *1 Corinthians*, pp. 247-48. So also Conzelmann notes that the verse contains 'an echo of the "once–but now" schema' employed by Paul elsewhere (e.g. Rom. 11.30; Eph. 5.8; Col. 3.5-8; cf. 1 Pet. 2.10) (*1 Corinthians*, pp. 106-107).

5. (1) The verb δικαιόω occurs with the following frequencies in the NT: Matthew, 2×; Luke–Acts, 7×; Paul, 27×; James, 3×. (2) The phrase πνεῦμα (τοῦ) θεοῦ is used frequently by Paul (Rom. 8.9, 14; 1 Cor. 2.11, 14; 3.16; 6.11; 7.40; 12.3; 2 Cor. 3.3; Phil. 3.3) and rarely by the other NT authors (Mt. 3.16; 12.28; 1 Pet. 4.14; 1 Jn 4.2). (3) The threefold repetition of ἀλλά in 1 Cor. 6.11 is closely paralleled by the sixfold repetition in 2 Cor. 7.11. These are the only occasions in the NT where ἀλλά occurs more than two times in a single verse. The term occurs more than once in a single verse with the following frequency in the NT: Mark, 2×; Paul, 18×; 1 Peter 1×; 2 Peter, 1×; Revelation, 1×.

6. See Mk 9.43-48/Mt. 18.8f.; Mk 10.23/Mt. 19.23/Lk. 18.24; Mt. 5.20; Mt. 7.21/Lk. 6.46; Mt. 18.3; cf. Mt. 21.31; 23.13; Lk. 13.24-30 and the comments

The association is found only in the Pauline corpus where a form of the distinctively Pauline phrase, θεοῦ βασιλείαν οὐ κληρονομήσουσιν,[1] is appended to vice-catalogs (Gal. 5.21; 1 Cor. 6.9, 10; Eph. 5.5). The phrase also occurs in 1 Cor. 15.50, but here σάρξ καὶ αἶμα, another Pauline idiom,[2] rather than a catalog of vices excludes one from the Kingdom. In any event, the Spirit is never cited as the agent which makes entrance into the Kingdom of God possible in the synoptics or Acts.[3]

2.2. A Baptismal Setting?

Vos provides a liturgical setting for his hypothetical tradition by arguing that the three texts in question all refer to the baptismal rite. According to Vos, the aorist tense of σταυρόω in Gal. 5.24 and the three verbs in 1 Cor. 6.11, particularly ἀπολούομαι, indicate that the baptismal rite is in view.[4] Vos also asserts that the water rite stands behind 1 Cor. 15.49 since εἰκών and clothing language are commonly employed in baptismal tradition.[5] Yet here again Vos's thesis is tenuous.

The discussion in Gal. 5.16-24 centers on the conflict between the flesh and the Spirit. In v. 24 Paul relates this conflict to the believer's experience of Christ: 'the presence of the crucified Christ means... the crucifixion of the flesh'.[6] The parallels with Gal. 2.15-21 (esp. v. 20), where faith in Christ is related to crucifixion with Christ, confirm that Paul is thinking here of subjective spiritual transformation rather than the objective event of baptism.[7]

The evidence also conflicts with a sacramental interpretation of 1 Cor. 6.11. Paul uses the preposition εἰς rather than ἐν with 'baptism' (cf. 1 Cor. 1.13-15; 12.13; Gal. 3.27). Indeed, he never uses the phrase ἐν τῷ ὀνόματι in conjunction with baptism. Furthermore, Paul never asserts that one is sanctified or justified at baptism; and, in view

offered by Hans Windisch in 'Die Sprüche von Eingehen in das Reich Gottes', *ZNW* 27 (1928), pp. 163-71.

1. The phrase occurs in Gal. 5.21; 1 Cor. 6.9, 10; 15.50; and in a modified form in Eph. 5.5: οὐκ ἔχει κληρονομίαν ἐν τῇ βασιλείᾳ τοῦ Χριστοῦ καὶ θεοῦ.

2. The phrase occurs in Gal. 1.16 and Eph. 6.12.

3. The only instance outside of Paul where this usage is found is Jn 3.5.

4. Vos, *Untersuchungen*, pp. 27, 30.

5. Vos, *Untersuchungen*, p. 32. Vos cites Gal. 3.27; Col. 3.8f.; and Eph. 4.24f. as evidence that 'die Vorstellung vom Eikon-Gewand einen festen Sitz in der Tauf-tradition hat' (p. 32).

6. Betz, *Galatians*, p. 289.

7. Dunn, *Holy Spirit*, pp. 106-107, 115. Thus Betz concludes that ' "sacramental" interpretation is as artificial here as it is elsewhere in Galatians' (*Galatians*, p. 289 n. 172).

of the prior list of vices, the verb ἀπελούσασθε must refer to spiritual cleansing.[1]

With regard to 1 Cor. 15.49, even if the hortatory subjunctive rather than future indicative reading of φορέω is accepted[2] and the text is rendered, 'let us bear (φορέσωμεν) the likeness (εἰκόνα) of the man from heaven', this sort of metaphorical language is characteristic of Paul and employed in a variety of contexts, most of which have nothing to do with baptism.[3] This fact, coupled with the Pauline character of the language in v. 50a,[4] indicates that here, as in Gal. 5.19f. and 1 Cor. 6.11, there is little reason to postulate an underlying baptismal tradition.

2.3. *The Jewish Background: A Critique of Vos's Analysis*

With his contention that pre-Christian Judaism commonly attributed soteriological significance to the Spirit, Vos seeks to lend credibility to his tradition-historical analysis. However, his analysis of the Jewish background is flawed at numerous points.

Vos places considerable emphasis on a number of Old Testament texts which appear to support his thesis (e.g. Ezek. 36.26f.; Ps. 51.13, MT; Isa. 44.3). Yet, he does not examine with sufficient detail how these texts were interpreted in the (first-century) Judaism which gave rise to Christianity. Thus he fails to recognize that the transformation of the heart referred to in Ezek. 36.26f. was viewed as a *prerequisite* for the eschatological bestowal of the Spirit, generally interpreted in

1. These points are discussed by Dunn, *Holy Spirit*, pp. 121-23; Fee, *1 Corinthians*, pp. 246-47; and R.P. Carlson, 'Baptism and Apocalyptic in Paul' (1983), pp. 345-51.

2. Fee, *1 Corinthians*, p. 795: 'The future is found in only a few disparate MSS and is easily accounted for on the very same grounds that it is now adopted by so many, while it is nearly impossible to account for anyone's having changed a clearly understandable future to the hortatory subjunctive so early and so often that it made its way into every textual history as the predominant reading'. Note, however, Metzger, *A Textual Commentary*, p. 569.

3. The verb φορέω occurs elsewhere in Paul, but only once in a metaphorical sense (Rom. 13.4). However, ἐνδύω is used metaphorically in Rom. 13.12, 14; 1 Cor. 15.53, 54; Gal. 3.27; Eph. 4.24; 6.11, 14; Col. 3.10, 12; 1 Thess. 5.8; and outside of Paul only in Lk. 24.49. References to the εἰκών of God or Christ are found exclusively in the epistles of Paul: Rom. 8.29; 1 Cor. 11.7; 15.49; 2 Cor. 3.18, 4.4; Col. 1.15; 3.10. The baptismal rite is clearly in view only in Gal. 3.27. Thus Dunn, with reference to Col. 3.5-17, writes: 'the metaphors are so common and natural that I am not convinced of the necessity to refer them to a common source or occasion' (*Holy Spirit*, p. 158).

4. Fee, *1 Corinthians*, p. 798 n. 12: 'the language "flesh and blood" and "inherit the kingdom of God" are both Pauline'.

light of Joel 2.28f. as restoration of the Spirit of prophecy;[1] and that according to early Jewish tradition, Ps. 51.13 (MT) records David's plea for undeserved retention of the *Spirit of prophecy*.[2] He also fails to recognize that Isa. 44.3 was interpreted by the rabbis as a reference to the outpouring of the *Spirit of prophecy* upon Israel.[3] Furthermore, Vos does not distinguish adequately between those texts which portray the Spirit as the source of prophetic activity, producing righteousness indirectly through the prophetic word; and those which portray the Spirit as the source of inner renewal, mediating righteousness directly to the recipient of the pneumatic gift (e.g. Wis. 9.17).[4] The distinction is important, for the pre-Pauline tradition he postulates clearly falls into the latter category. When this distinction is recognized, the Old Testament antecedents to Vos's hypothetical baptismal tradition appear remote.

Vos also exaggerates the extent to which pre-Christian Judaism attributed soteriological functions to the Spirit by uncritically accepting evidence from *Joseph and Aseneth*, a text marked by Christian interpolation.[5] Moreover, he emphasizes the relationship between the

1. Vos maintains that the Rabbis looked forward to the day when the 'evil impulse' would be conquered through the outpouring of the Spirit (*Untersuchungen*, p. 71). In numerous rabbinic texts, Ezek. 36.26 is interpreted as a prophecy concerning the endtime removal of the evil impulse. However, these texts usually omit any reference to the work of the Spirit. In the rabbinic literature a transformed heart (righteousness) remains a precondition for restoration of the prophetic gift. See the comments on Ezek. 36.26f. in Chapter 5 §2.1 and Chapter 10 §2 above.

2. The Targum on Ps. 51.13 replaces the expression 'holy Spirit' with 'holy Spirit of prophecy'. See also *MHG* Gen. 242 cited in Chapter 5 §1.1.2 above. Thus, although Kaiser asserts that the text does not refer 'to the Spirit's gift of government and administration but rather to his [the pray-er's] personal fellowship with God' ('The Promise of God', p. 122), it appears that Ps. 51.13 was interpreted with reference to the Spirit as *Amtscharisma*. The text reflects the widespread Jewish belief that the Spirit resided only in the righteous.
Vos makes no mention of the Targum on Psalm 51, yet he does acknowledge that the Spirit in Ps. 51.13 functions principally as the 'Vermittler des Heilsorakels' (*Untersuchungen*, p. 40). Nevertheless, he also maintains that the Psalm presents the Spirit as the agent of the pray-er's justification and cleansing.

3. See *Midr. Ps.* 111.1.

4. See for example Vos's treatment of Ps. 51 as outlined above.

5. Vos is undoubtedly correct when he writes: 'Damit Aseneth in die den Auser-wählten bereitete κατάπαυσις eingehen kann, so heißt es in Josephs Gebet...[8.10f], muß sie zunächst durch das göttliche Pneuma neugeschaffen werden' (*Untersuchungen*, p. 69). However, Holtz has argued persuasively for Christian influence on *Joseph and Aseneth* at this point: 'Es ist mir nicht zweifelhaft, daß die Darstellung der Form von Aseneths Aufnahme in die neue Religion durch eine Speisung mit Honig = Mana und ihre Deutung als Neuwerdung oder Wiedergeburt

'spirit of truth' (1QS 3.13–4.6; cf. 2.25b–3.12) and the Spirit of God;[1] although the 'spirit of truth', as the anthropological counterpart to the 'spirit of falsehood', is more closely related to the rabbinic 'good impulse' (יצר הטוב).[2] The picture which emerges from Vos's analysis is distorted further by the limited scope of his inquiry. By focusing on those texts which tend to support his thesis, Vos obscures the fact that the Spirit is almost always portrayed as the source of prophetic inspiration in the relevant Jewish texts. As we have seen, the only Jewish texts which attribute soteriological functions to the Spirit in a manner analogous to the Pauline epistles are the Hymns of Qumran and Wisdom.

It has become apparent that Vos has built his thesis on a foundation of sand. The Pauline character of the principal terms and concepts contained in the three texts, the improbable nature of a common baptismal setting, and the general lack of Jewish parallels indicate that a pre-Pauline baptismal tradition does not form the basis of 1 Cor. 6.9-11; 15.44-50; and Gal. 5.19-24. These texts, together with the distinctive soteriological pneumatology which they reflect, find their origin in the mind of Paul.

(zum ewigen Leben) nicht jüdisch ist, sondern mindestens die christliche Umprägung eines ursprünglich andersartigen jüdischen Berichts' ('Christliche Interpolationen', pp. 482-97; quote from p. 486).

1. Vos, *Untersuchungen*, pp. 61-64, see also pp. 56-58.
2. See Chapter 4 §1 above.

Chapter 13

WISDOM OF SOLOMON
AND PAUL'S SOTERIOLOGICAL PNEUMATOLOGY

In the examination of the Jewish literature in the intertestamental period we found that references to the soteriological dimension of the Spirit's activity were limited to a narrow strand within the wisdom tradition: Wisdom and the Hymns of Qumran. Although these texts are closely related in many respects, they originate from different milieus. Wisdom illustrates how wisdom concepts influential in the Qumran community were appropriated in a hellenistic setting. It is my contention that wisdom traditions from the hellenistic Jewish milieu which produced Wisdom were known to Paul either through this text or related (oral or written) sources and provided the conceptual framework for his distinctive pneumatology. I shall seek to support this judgment by establishing the unique character of the conceptual parallels which unite Wis. 9.9-18 with 1 Cor. 2.6-16 and Gal. 4.4-6, and by noting other striking conceptual and linguistic similarities which suggest Paul's indebtedness to Wisdom or traditions contained within it.

1. *Wisdom 9.9-18 and 1 Corinthians 2.6-16*

In 1 Cor. 2.6-16 Paul discusses the nature of the wisdom of God, previously identified with the crucified Christ (1 Cor. 1.23-24, 30). Paul declares that the wisdom of God is redemptive (v. 7) and stands against the wisdom of this age, which is coming to nothing (v. 6). Furthermore, Paul insists that only those who have received the Spirit of God can understand God's wisdom (i.e. his redemptive purpose in the cross of Christ), for only the Spirit of God knows the mind of God (vv. 11-12).[1] Although the people of this age pursue wisdom, since they do not possess the Spirit it remains hidden from them (vv. 6-10a). They are utterly incapable of understanding true wisdom (v. 14)

---

1. E. Cothenet, 'Les prophètes chrétiens', p. 97: 'L'Ecriture devient lettre morte pour qui n'est pas illuminé par l'Esprit du Seigneur'.

and making valid judgments (v. 15); as a result, their rulers crucified Christ (v. 8). However, in accordance with God's salvific plan, the hidden wisdom of God has been revealed to every Christian by the Spirit of God (vv. 7, 10b-13).[1] Through the Spirit the Christian knows 'the mind of Christ' (v. 16). Paul thus reminds the Corinthians that they are Christians possessing the Spirit of God and implicitly exhorts them to act accordingly.[2]

Although it is quite likely that Paul's language in 1 Cor. 2.6-16 has been influenced by Corinthian usage, the theological perspective which emerges is undoubtedly Paul's.[3] His perspective may be summarized as follows: (1) anthropology—man by nature is utterly incapable of understanding the wisdom of God; (2) pneumatology—only by receiving the gift of the Spirit can man comprehend the wisdom of God; (3) soteriology—the gift of the Spirit, as the transmitter of God's wisdom, is redemptive.

When we turn to Wisdom we find a perspective remarkably similar to that of Paul as outlined above. Chapter 9 records Solomon's description of God's wisdom in the form of a prayer. Verses 9-18 are particularly striking and will form the basis of our comparison.[4]

---

1. Scroggs maintains that Paul is speaking of an 'esoteric wisdom' unrelated to the kerygma and reserved for a spiritual elite ('ΠΝΕΥΜΑΤΙΚΟΣ', pp. 33-55, esp. 37-40, 54; see also Conzelmann, *1 Corinthians*, p. 57, and Ellis as cited in p. 331 n. 2 above). However, Fee argues persuasively that a distinction between a special class of pneumatics and believers in general is not in view in these verses: 'the real contrast is. . . between Christian and non-Christian, between those who have and those who do not have the Spirit' (*1 Corinthians*, pp. 99-103, 122-23, quote from p. 101). Fee notes that: (1) the τέλειοι of v. 6 are those who have received the Spirit (v. 12) and related to the 'spiritual man' (πνευματικός) of v. 15; (2) 'the argument of the whole paragraph, particularly the language "for our glory" (v. 7), "for those who love him" (i.e. "us"; v. 9), "revealed it to us" (v. 10), and "we have received the Spirit who is from God" (v. 12), implies that Paul is. . . addressing the whole Church' (p. 102); and (3) Paul's concern in 3.1-4 is 'not to suggest classes of Christians or grades of spirituality, but to get them [the Corinthians] to stop thinking like the people of this present age' (p. 122). So also Davis argues that in 1 Cor. 2.14-16 Paul 'rede-fines the πνευματικός–ψυχικός antithesis [of his Corinthian opponents] so as to change the nature of the distinction from a qualitative distinction among believers, into an absolute distinction between Christian and pagan' (*Wisdom*, p. 125).

2. See Fee, *1 Corinthians*, pp. 100-101.

3. See Fee, *1 Corinthians*, p. 100 and Brandenburger, *Fleisch und Geist*, p. 106: 'Die positive Verwendung der Verbindung von Pneuma und Sophia [in 1 Cor. 2.6f.]. . . ist kaum nur ein polemisches Produkt'.

4. The influence which Wisdom exerted upon Paul's thought, particularly his pneumatology, was noted as early as 1887 by Pfleiderer in his *Das Urchristenthum*, pp. 158-68, 257. The link which Pfleiderer proposed between the pneumatology of

1.1. *Anthropology*

The author of Wisdom clearly shares Paul's conviction concerning humanity's inability to comprehend the wisdom of God. He contrasts the redemptive power of wisdom with the 'feebleness of human reason' (v. 14).[1] Human thoughts are fallible, 'for the mortal body weighs down the soul and the tent of clay burdens the active mind' (φθαρτὸν γὰρ σῶμα βαρύνει ψυχήν, καὶ βρίθει τὸ γεῶδες σκῆνος νοῦν πολυφρόντιδα, v. 15).

The extreme pessimism characteristic of this anthropological perspective is rarely found in pre-Christian Judaism and is absent from the synoptic gospels and Acts. Although Jewish wisdom theology in the intertestamental period identified wisdom with the Torah,[2] and thus viewed wisdom as a revelatory gift from God,[3] it still emphasized the human capacity to acquire wisdom by rational means through study of the Torah.[4] Humanity's culpability for sin is grounded in its capacity to understand and appropriate the wisdom of the Torah (e.g. Sir. 15.15). Luke and the primitive church also stress humanity's ability to

Wisdom and Paul was subsequently criticized by Gunkel (*Die Wirkungen*, pp. 86-88) and E. Sokolowski (*Geist und Leben bei Paulus* [1903], p. 200). Their criticisms may be summarized with the words of Gunkel: 'Weisheit lernt der Mensch; der Geist ergreift ihn' (p. 87). However, Gunkel and Sokolowski clearly underestimated the power of Spirit-revealed wisdom in Wis. 9.17-18 (cf. Nickelsburg, *Jewish Literature*, p. 184-85: 'Paul's doctrine of the Holy Spirit as. . . God's power for the godly life (e.g. Rom 8) parallels [the author of Wisdom's] understanding of Wisdom'), and the cognitive aspect of the revelation of the Spirit in 1 Cor. 2.6-16. As we shall see, they have also failed to recognize the distinctive nature of the parallels which unite the pneumatological perspectives of the author of Wisdom and Paul. More recently the parallels between Wis. 9.9-18 and 1 Cor. 2.6-16 have been noted by Scroggs: 'content and context are similar in striking ways. . . the least to be said is that ix. 9-18 and I Cor. ii. 6-16 arise out of the same context of wisdom theology' ('ΠΝΕΥΜΑΤΙΚΟΣ', pp. 48-50, quote from p. 49).

1. Cf. Wis. 9.6: 'Even if one is perfect (τέλειος) among the sons of men, without the wisdom that comes from [God] he will be regarded as nothing'.

2. Schnabel notes that the identification of the Law with wisdom is clearly made in Baruch, *1 Enoch, Testaments of the Twelve Patriarchs*, the *Letter of Aristeas*, the Jewish *Third Sibylline Oracle, 4 Maccabees, Pseudo-Philo, 4 Ezra*; and the *Apocalypse of Baruch (Law and Wisdom*, p. 162).

3. Rylaarsdam has shown that a gradual shift occurred in the orientation of Jewish wisdom theology during the late- and post-OT periods: wisdom was increasingly viewed as a revelatory gift from God rather than knowledge acquired through empirical study of nature (see *Revelation*). Rylaarsdam notes that while the wisdom tradition generally identifies this revelatory gift with the Torah, the author of Wisdom equates it with the Spirit (pp. x, 116-18).

4. See for example Sir. 3.22; 6.36; 15.1; 21.11f.; 32.15; Bar. 3.9; *4 Macc.* 1.15-19; 18.1-2. Note also Chapter 2 §2.2 and Chapter 3 §1 above.

grasp the true significance of Christ, renounce sin, and follow him.[1]
The perspective of the author of Wisdom and Paul is quite different:
the wisdom of God expressed in the Torah (Wisdom) or Christ (Paul)
cannot be apprehended by the human mind apart from the illumination
of the Spirit.[2]

The author of Wisdom and Paul not only share similar assumptions
regarding the nature of humankind, they also employ similar
anthropological terms. E. Brandenburger has argued that Paul's
σάρξ–πνεῦμα language reflects the influence of the 'dualistische
Weisheit' found in the Hymns of Qumran, Wisdom, and ultimately in
the writings of Philo;[3] and K.-G. Sandelin and B. Pearson have traced

---

1. Thus R. Mohrlang (*Matthew and Paul: A Comparison of Ethical Perspectives*
[1984], esp. pp. 111-25) and J.W. Taeger ('Paulus und Lukas über den Menschen',
ZNW 71 [1980], pp 96-108; and *Der Mensch*) contrast the pessimistic anthropology
of Paul with the more positive appraisals of man given by Matthew and Luke respectively. Mohrlang notes that for Paul human beings do not have the capacity to live a
moral life; ethical living is made possible by the Spirit (p. 115). Matthew, however,
affirms humanity's capacity for ethical behavior and attributes it to 'an essential inner
goodness' (p. 123). Taeger argues that whereas Paul views the natural human being
as completely dominated by the power of sin, in Luke's perspective the individual is
capable of deciding to follow Christ and renounce sin (*Der Mensch*, esp. pp. 85-103;
184-87; 220-28). He concludes: 'Diese Sicht des Apostles ist mit der lukanischen
sachlich nicht vereinbar' ('Paulus and Lukas', p. 108). I would affirm, however,
that for the purpose of formulating a holistic biblical theology, the differences
between the anthropological and pneumatological perspectives of Luke and Paul are
ultimately reconcilable. They represent different (theological rather than chronological) stages in the progressive and harmonious development of God's revelation:
Luke's understanding of the nature of humanity and its experience of the Spirit must
be augmented by Paul's more pervasive treatment of the Spirit's role in the dynamics
of spiritual life. The task of synthesizing these perspectives into a coherent biblical
theology is beyond the scope of this study. On the issue of theological diversity
within the canon see I.H. Marshall's analysis of *Sachkritik*: 'An Evangelical
Approach to "Theological Criticism"', *Them* 13 (1988), pp. 79-85.

2. Brandenburger notes that 1QH 4.31, *Leg. All.* 1.38, Wisd. 9.17, and 2 Cor.
2.11 all employ variations of the form, 'who/no one can know . . . except (εἰ μή,
כי אם)', and in a context which refers to humanity's inability to known the will or
wisdom of God apart from God's giving of his Spirit (*Fleisch und Geist*, p. 152).
Although these texts probably find their origin in a common tradition, it is important
to note that they represent different trajectories of development: the author of 1QH (in
1QH 4.31) and Philo associate this gift of the Spirit with the act of creation, whereas
the author of Wisdom and Paul do not.

3. See Brandenburger, *Fleisch und Geist*, pp. 24, 119-235 (on Philo); pp. 106-
16 (on Wisdom); and pp. 86-106, 114-16 (on the Hodajot). Brandenburger concludes: 'Die Ergebnisse der vorliegenden Untersuchung zeigen jedenfalls, daß Paulus
gewichtige Partien seiner Theologie im Rahmen dualistisch-weisheitlicher

many of the anthropological terms in 1 Cor. 15 to a similar milieu.[1] The linguistic similarities between Wis. 9.15 and 2 Cor. 5.1-5 are particularly striking: both texts refer to the earthly tent (σκῆνος) which burdens (βαρύνω, Wis. 9.15; βαρέω; 2 Cor. 5.4) humanity and which is overcome by the Spirit of God (Wis. 9.17; 2 Cor. 5.5).[2]

1.2. *Pneumatology*

Like many of the Jewish wisdom teachers of his day, the author of Wisdom associates sapiential achievement with the revelation of the Spirit. However, while the esoteric wisdom of the prophet or sage is frequently attributed to the inspiration of the Spirit in the literature; lower levels of sapiential achievement are ascribed to human effort unaided by the Spirit, such as the study of the Torah.[3] The author of Wisdom breaks from his Jewish contemporaries[4] (excluding the Qumran community) and shows his unique affinity to Paul (1 Cor. 2.11f.)[5] by attributing every level of sapiential achievement, from the lowest to the highest, to the gift of the Spirit: 'Who has learned your will, unless you gave him wisdom, and sent your Holy Spirit from on high? In this

Gedanken—freilich sachlich in höchst kritischer Aufnahme -versteht und entfaltet' (p. 228).

1. K.-G. Sandelin, *Die Auseinandersetzung mit der Weisheit in 1. Korinther 15* (1976) and B.A. Pearson, *The Pneumatikos-Psychikos Terminology in I Corinthians* (1973).

2. The parallels between Wis. 9.15 and 2 Cor. 5.1-5 have been observed by E. Grafe, 'Das Verhältnis der paulinischen Schriften zur Sapientia Salomonis', in *Theologische Abhandlungen* (1892), pp. 274-75; A. Feuillet, *Le Christ Sagesse de Dieu d'après les Épitres Pauliniennes* (1966), p. 333; and Scroggs, 'ΠΝΕΥΜΑΤΙΚΟΣ', p. 49. Note also that the term τέλειος is employed in 1 Cor. 2.6 in a manner quite similar to Wis. 9.6.

3. Davis, *Wisdom*, pp. 9-62. See Sir. 24.23f. and Bar. 4.1-2.

4. D. Winston, *The Wisdom of Solomon* (1979), p. 43: 'When he [the author of Wisdom] insists that unless God send his Wisdom down from on high men would not comprehend God's will (9:17), he is certainly implying that the Torah is in need of further interpretation for the disclosure of its true meaning, interpretation which Wisdom alone is able to provide'.

5. Davis, *Wisdom*, p. 106: 'For Paul, the Spirit alone is a complete and reliable guide to all of divine wisdom'. See also Jaubert, *La notion d'alliance*, p. 372 and Scroggs, 'ΠΝΕΥΜΑΤΙΚΟΣ', p. 54: 'So close is Paul here [1 Cor. 2.6-16] to ideas in Wisd. ix. 9-18 that one must judge this passage figured in an important way in Paul's thinking. Particularly is this so with respect to the close relationship between σοφία and πνεῦμα and the absolute revelatory quality of wisdom.' Although Scroggs correctly notes that the 'absolute revelatory quality of wisdom' is affirmed by Paul, he incorrectly distinguishes this wisdom from the kerygma.

way people on earth have been set on the right path, have learned what pleases you, and have been saved by wisdom' (Wis. 9.17-18).

In addition to the important conceptual parallel outlined above, the author of Wisdom and Paul portray the Spirit as the functional equivalent of wisdom and Christ respectively: wisdom (Wisdom)[1] and Christ (Paul)[2] are experienced through the Spirit. This is particularly significant, since Paul draws upon the wisdom speculation so prominent in Wisdom for many of his christological formulations.[3] Together these facts suggest that Wisdom or related traditions

1. Note the way in which wisdom is equated with πνεῦμα in Wis. 1.4-7; 7.7, 22; and 9.17 (see B.L. Mack, *Logos und Sophia: Untersuchungen zur Weisheitstheologie in hellenistischer Judentum* [1973], p. 64). The author of Wisdom also attributes functions normally reserved for the Spirit, such as the inspiration of rulers (*Amtscharisma*) and prophets, to wisdom (cf. 10.14, 16; 11.1).

2. Pointing to Rom. 1.1-5; 8.9-11; 1 Cor. 6.17; 15.45; and particularly 2 Cor. 3.17, I. Hermann argues for the functional identification of the Spirit and the resurrected Christ by Paul: 'Christus wird erfahrbar als Pneuma' (*Kyrios und Pneuma* [1961], p. 49). See also Dunn, 'Last Adam', pp. 127-41 and *Jesus and the Spirit*, pp. 318-26; Kim, *Origin*, pp. 228-29; Hamilton, *Eschatology*, pp. 3-16; J.L. Leuba, 'Der Zusammenhang zwischen Geist und Tradition nach dem Neuen Testament', *KuD* 4 (1958), pp. 238-39; W. Wright, 'The Source of Paul's Concept of Pneuma', *CovQ* 41 (1983), pp. 23-25; H.S. Benjamin, 'Pneuma in John and Paul', *BTB* 6 (1976), p. 47; and more cautiously, Turner, who speaks of 'some degree of functional identification' ('Spirit Endowment for Paul', p. 64). Note also A. Deissmann's assertion that Paul employs the phrases 'in Christ' and 'in the Spirit' synonymously (*Paul: A Study in Social and Religious History* [2nd edn, 1926], pp. 138-40; cf. E. Ellis, 'Christ and Spirit', p. 273 and Y. Congar, *I Believe in the Holy Spirit* [1983], I, pp. 37-38).

3. Rom. 8.3; 1 Cor. 1.24, 30; 8.6; 10.4; 15.22-28, 44b-59; Gal. 4.4-6; and Col. 1.15f. are often cited in this regard. See H. Windisch, 'Die göttliche Weisheit der Juden und die paulinische Christologie', in *Neutestamentliche Studien* (1914), pp. 220f.; W.L. Knox, *St. Paul and the Church of the Gentiles* (1939), pp. 111-24, 133f., 163f.; Davies, *Paul*, pp. 147-176; three articles by E. Schweizer, 'Zur Herkunft der Präexistenzvorstellung bei Paulus', in *Neotestamentica* (1963), pp. 105-109, 'Aufnahme und Korrektur jüdischer Sophiatheologie im Neuen Testament', in *Neotestamentica* (1963), pp. 110-11, and 'Zum religionsgeschichtlichen Hintergrund der "Sendungsformel"', in *Beiträge zur Theologie des Neuen Testaments: Neutestamentliche Aufsätze (1955–1970)* (1970), pp. 83-95; H. Conzelmann, 'Paulus und die Weisheit', *NTS* 12 (1965–66), pp. 231-44; Feuillet, *Le Christ, passim*; C. Romaniuk, 'Le Livre de la Sagesse dans le Nouveau Testament', *NTS* 14 (1967–68), pp. 511-13; Sandelin, *Weisheit in 1. Korinther 15, passim*; M. Hengel, *The Son of God* (1976), pp. 72-74; Dunn, *Christology in the Making*, pp. 163-96 and ' "A Light to the Gentiles": the Significance of the Damascus Road Christophany for Paul', in *The Glory of Christ in the New Testament* (1987), p. 265; Schnabel, *Law and Wisdom*, pp. 236-64; and Kim, *Origin*, pp. 114-20, 127-28, 258-60, 266-68.

provided the conceptual background for the close connection between Christ and Spirit envisioned by Paul.[1] The striking correlation of light, image, and Spirit/breath motifs in 2 Cor. 3.18; 4.4, 6 and Wis. 7.25-26 lends further support to this thesis.[2] These texts associate Christ/Wisdom with a bright φῶς,[3] the δόξα of the Lord, the εἰκών of God, and the divine πνεῦμα or ἀτμίς.[4]

1.3. *Soteriology*

According to the author of Wisdom, wisdom 'knows and understands all things' (οἶδε γὰρ ἐκείνη πάντα καὶ συνίει, v. 11),[5] including that which pleases God (v. 9). For this reason Solomon can confidently declare that wisdom 'will guard me in her glory' (φυλάξει με ἐν τῇ δόξῃ αὐτῆς, v. 11) and that by her the people of the earth 'are saved' (τῇ σοφίᾳ ἐσώθησαν, v. 18).[6] Although the σῴζω of v. 18, like φυλάσσω in v. 11, may refer principally to physical preservation, the eschatological significance of these verses should not be minimized.[7] For elsewhere the eschatological dimension of wisdom's redemptive

1. Isaacs, *Spirit*, p. 145: 'The close association (and possible identification) of Christ with the spirit which we find in Johannine and Pauline writings, may have arisen out of an identification of Christ with the wisdom figure of Hellenistic Judaism'.

2. See Romaniuk, 'Le Livre', p. 511; Kim, *Origin*, pp. 117, 128-29, 258 and, on the Pauline origin of 2 Cor. 3.18–4.6, pp. 141-44.

3. Cf. ἀπαύγασμα (Wis. 7.26) with αὐγάζω (2 Cor. 4.4). Romaniuk notes that 2 Cor. 4.4 represents the only occurrence of αὐγάζω in the NT, the term occurs infrequently in the LXX, and 'le contexte dans lequel se trouve ce mot chez saint Paul est le même que dans le livre de la Sagesse' ('Le Livre', p. 511). Romaniuk also observes that mirror language appears in both texts: ἔσοπτρον (Wis. 7.26); κατοπτρίζω (2 Cor. 3.18) (p. 511).

4. In view of Wis. 7.22, ἀτμίς should be seen as a synonym for πνεῦμα. The interpretation of 2 Cor. 3.17-18 is problematic. However, even if the text does not explicitly identify the resurrected Christ with πνεῦμα, a functional identification is implicit in the naming of both πνεῦμα (3.18) and Christ (4.4, 6) as the source of God's glory.

5. Cf. 1 Cor. 2.10, τὸ γὰρ πνεῦμα πάντα ἐραυνᾷ, and v. 15a, ὁ δὲ πνευματικὸς ἀνακρίνει [τὰ] πάντα.

6. A. Van Roon notes that in the following chapter (Wis. 10) wisdom is 'presented as God's saving power in the history of mankind and Israel' ('The Relation between Christ and the Wisdom of God according to Paul', *NovT* 16 [1974], p. 209).

7. The term σῴζω appears frequently in the remaining chapters of Wisdom (10.4; 14.4, 5; 16.7, 11; 18.5) and the sense of physical preservation is always paramount. Yet this is due to the fact that the following verses chronicle Wisdom's saving power in history. In view of the passages cited above and in the following note, it is evident that these examples of the salvific power of wisdom drawn from Israel's history are merely symbols which convey a more profound message.

power is given prominence: immortality[1] and authority over the nations[2] are promised to the righteous (3.1-9; cf. 5.1-23), 'his chosen ones' (τοῖς ἐκλεκτοῖς αὐτοῦ, 3.9).[3] Therefore, by presenting the Spirit as the functional equivalent of wisdom, the author of Wisdom affirms with (and in a manner similar to) Paul the soteriological necessity of the pneumatic gift (9.17-18; cf. 1 Cor. 2.7).[4]

We have already noted that the soteriological pneumatology found in Wisdom and the Pauline corpus is absent from the synoptic gospels and Acts. This perspective is also unparalleled in the literature of intertestamental Judaism (excluding the scrolls from Qumran). The precondition for eschatological redemption, righteousness, is elsewhere associated with devotion to the Torah unaided by the inspiration of the Spirit.[5] Philo, with his conception of πνεῦμα as the rational and immortal aspect of the soul, offers the closest Jewish parallel to the perspective outlined above. However, unlike Philo, the author of Wisdom clearly distinguishes the gift of the Spirit which is given to all at creation (15.11) from the gift of the Spirit which enables one to comprehend the wisdom of God and attain immortality (9.17).[6]

---

1. Note also Wis. 6.18, 'to keep her [wisdom's] laws is to be certain of immortality [ἀφθαρσία], and immortality brings a man near to God'; 8.17, 'there is immortality in kinship with wisdom' (cf. 8.13); and 15.3, 'to acknowledge your [God's] power is the root of immortality'.

2. D. Georgi highlights the apocalyptic character of Wis. 3.7-9 (*Weisheit Salomos* [1980], pp. 410-11). It is important to note that the union of wisdom and apocalyptic is found in Wisdom as well as in the writings of Paul (Scroggs, 'ΠΝΕΥΜΑΤΙΚΟΣ', p. 35 n. 3). The close connection between wisdom and apocalyptic is noted by Hengel, *Judaism and Hellenism*, I, p. 206 and *Between Jesus and Paul* (1983), p. 50; G. von Rad, *Old Testament Theology* (1965), II, pp. 306-308; and Manns, *Symbole*, p. 108.

3. Thus Sandelin notes that 'die Erretung des Menschen kann in Sap. sowohl irdisch (Kap. 10-19) als auch himmlisch (5,1ff.; 3,1ff.) aufgefasst werden' (*Weisheit in 1. Korinther 15*, p. 43).

4. Knox notes that according to the author of Wisdom, the gift of the Spirit is needed as the means of attaining immortality rather than as a special gift of government (*St. Paul*, p. 79).

5. See for example *4 Ezra* 7.78-99; *2 Macc.* 7; *4 Macc.* 18; *2 Bar.* 51; *Sib. Or.* 4.25-45; *1 En.* 108; *T. Mos.* 9–10; *Jub.* 23.24-31; *Pss. Sol.* 3; 13; 14; 15. Note also G.W.E. Nickelsburg, *Resurrection, Immortality, and Eternal Life in Intertestamental Judaism* (1972), pp. 93-143.

6. This distinction is presupposed in Wis. 15.11. However, according to Philo the πνεῦμα breathed into every human soul at creation makes the mind (νοῦς) rational and thus capable of knowing God and immortal (e.g. *Leg. All.* 1.31-38; *Op. Mund.* 135; *Det. Pot. Ins.* 80–90; *Plant.* 18–22; *Congr.* 97). See Chapter 2 §5.1 above. Sandelin maintains that Philo (in *Leg. All.*), in a manner similar to the author of Wisdom, refers to two distinct receptions of the Spirit: the first sustains physical life:

My suggestion that Paul was influenced by Wisdom or related traditions is supported by three additional observations. First, the fall of man is described by the author of Wisdom in language reminiscent of Paul. Wisdom 2.24 states that humankind was originally created to live forever, but through the Devil 'death entered into the world' (θάνατος εἰσῆλθεν εἰς τὸν κόσμον, Wis. 2.24). The formula, εἰσῆλθεν εἰς τὸν κόσμον, is also found in Wis. 14.14 with reference to idols. Outside of Wisdom the formula is found neither in the LXX nor in the rabbinic literature.[1] The phrase occurs occasionally in early non-Christian Greek sources, but never in a context pertaining to death.[2] However, Paul employs the formula with reference to the fall of man and death in Rom. 5.12: ἡ ἁμαρτία εἰς τὸν κόσμον εἰσῆλθεν καὶ διὰ τῆς ἁμαρτίας ὁ θάνατος. It is unlikely that the similarities between Rom. 5.12 and Wis. 2.24 are the product of chance.[3]

Second, the book of Wisdom may help explain how Paul came to view the Spirit as the agent of the resurrection. We have already noted

the second enables one to comprehend the wisdom of God and attain immortality (*Weisheit in 1. Korinther 15*, pp. 26-44). However, Sandelin notes that Philo, unlike the author of Wisdom, associates both of these divine inbreathings with the creation event (p. 36). Sandelin summarizes the main points from *Leg. All.* as follows: 'Jeder menschliche νοῦς hat bei der Schöpfung eine göttliche πνοή durch den Logos bekommen. Diese πνοή war aber sehr schwach. Der νοῦς des Menschen ist auch nach der Einhauchung bei der Schöpfung vergänglich. Er kann aber stärker werden, sich von dem Körper zu lösen anfangen durch tugendhaftes Leben. Die Bedingung für das wahrhaftige und unvergängliche Leben ist aber noch eine zweite Einhauchung durch die Sophia, welche den νοῦς vollkommen, unvergänglich und weise macht. Der νοῦς erreicht dadurch dieselbe Stellung wie der himmlische Mensch, der nach dem Abbild des Abbildes Gottes geschaffen worden ist' (p. 37). Sandelin's interpretation, particularly with reference to the second inbreathing of the Spirit, is based on his contention that Philo in *Leg. All.* 1.32, 37-38 describes the creation of the *Pneumatiker* or wise one rather than the creation of the natural person. Although Sandelin's interpretation of *Leg. All.* 1.32-42 is open to question (see the alternative views presented by Brandenburger, *Fleisch und Geist*, pp. 148-54, esp. p. 149 n. 2; Weaver, 'Πνεῦμα in Philo', pp. 75-77, 110-12; Tobin, *The Creation of Man*, esp. pp. 48f., 77f., 102-34 and Runia, *Philo*, pp. 334-40) he correctly recognizes that the text is a 'Mischung von Schöpfungs- und Erlösungslehre' (p. 35, quoting J. Pascher, *Η ΒΑΣΙΛΙΚΗ ΟΔΟΣ. Der Königsweg zu Wiedergeburt und Vergottung bei Philon von Alexandreia* [Paderborn, 1931], p. 127).

1. Romaniuk, 'Le Livre', p. 504.

2. Variations of the formula are found in Anaxagoras Phil. 75; Galen 10.2.122; Marcus Aurelius Antoninus 6.56; Plotinus, *Ennead*, 2.9.12; and Philo, *Op. Mund.* 78; *Spec. Leg.* 1. 294-95 (this information was obtained from the TLG disc by Ibycus [Tyndale House, Cambridge]). Philo utilizes the phrase with reference to humans' entrance into the world.

3. Romaniuk, 'Le Livre', p. 505.

that Paul was probably the first Christian to give voice to this perspective.[1] Jewish precursors to Paul at this point do exist. However they
are exceedingly rare. The intertestamental texts which make a connection between the Spirit and resurrection are limited to *2 Bar.* 23.5 and
a handful of rabbinic citations generally based on Ezekiel 37.[2] Two
significant points of contact suggest that the association between
immortality and the gift of the Spirit found in Wisdom rather than
these Jewish resurrection-texts formed the basis for Paul's thought.
(1) Neither Paul nor the author of Wisdom associates resurrec-
tion/immortality with the divine breath received at creation (Philo) or
after death (Ezek. 37, *2 Bar.* 23.5, and the rabbinic texts). Rather,
both declare that the righteous attain immortality by virtue of the gift
of the Spirit which they have received during their natural life (Rom.
8.11; Wis. 8.17; 9.17).[3] (2) The terminology of Wisdom is employed
by Paul. A survey of the LXX and the New Testament reveals that the
terms ἀφθαρσία, ἄφθαρτος, and ἀθανασία are employed almost
exclusively by the author of Wisdom and Paul.[4] Although the author
of Wisdom never refers to the resurrection of the body, the concept is
not incompatible with his emphasis on immortality.[5]

1. See Chapter 12 above.

2. Müller concludes his survey of the evidence by stating that 'der heilige Geist bei
der Totenauferstehung vor Paulus keine quantitative bedeutende Rolle spielt'
('Geisterfahrung', pp. 111-32, quote from p. 131). See also Sokolowski, *Geist und
Leben*, p. 203. Note that *2 Baruch* was probably penned in the 2nd century AD.

3. The author of Wisdom, like Paul, insists that humans are mortal by nature (Wis.
7.1; 9.15; 15.8, 17; 16.14). Immortality is thus a divine gift reserved for the
righteous (J.M. Reese, *Hellenistic Influence on the Book of Wisdom and Its
Consequences* [1970], p. 64). Furthermore, the indwelling presence of
wisdom/Spirit 'makes the eschatological gift of immortality a reality in the present life
of the righteous' (Nickelsburg, *Jewish Literature*, pp. 176, 181).

4. The frequency with which the terms ἀφθαρσία, ἄφθαρτος, and ἀθανασία
occur in the LXX and the NT are as follows: ἀφθαρσία (LXX: Wisd, 2×—2.23; 6.19;
4 Maccabees, 2×—9.22; 17.12; NT: Paul, 7×), ἄφθαρτος (LXX: Wisdom, 2×—
12.1; 18.4; NT: Paul, 4×; 1 Peter, 3×), ἀθανασία (LXX: Wisdom, 5×—3.4; 4.1;
8.13,17; 15.3; *4 Maccabees*, 2×—14.5; 16.13; NT: Paul, 3×). Josephus never
employs ἀφθαρσία, but ἄφθαρτος (4×) and ἀθανασία (7×) appear occasionally
throughout his works. Philo frequently utilizes all three terms. Pfleiderer, pointing to
2 Cor. 5.1f. and Phil. 1.23, suggested that Paul's doctrine of the resurrection was
influenced by Wisdom (*Das Urchristentum*, pp. 161f.).

5. Reese, *Hellenistic Influence*, p. 68: 'The Sage refrains from going into specific
aspects of this salvation, such as the resurrection. He makes no attempt to exclude it,
but he does not affirm it explicitly'. A number of studies produced in the early part of
this century argued that the resurrection of the body is implied in Wis. 3–5 and
alluded to in 16.13-14 (for bibliography see R.H. Pfeiffer, *History of New Testa-*

Third, the description of the future reign of the righteous in Wis. 3.8, κρινοῦσιν ἔθνη, is closely paralleled by Paul's statement in 1 Cor. 6.2, οἱ ἅγιοι τὸν κόσμον κρινοῦσιν.[1]

2. *Wisdom 9.9-18 and Galatians 4.4-6*

E. Schweizer has argued persuasively that the early Christian formula concerning God's sending of his pre-existent Son (Gal. 4.4-6; Rom. 8.3-4; Jn 3.16-17; 1 Jn 4.9) is rooted in Jewish wisdom speculation.[2] The similarities between Wis. 9.10-17 and Gal. 4.4-6 form a crucial part of Schweizer's argument.[3] He notes two significant points of contact between these texts. First, the only parallel to the double sending of the Son and Spirit in Gal. 4.4-6 is found in the double sending of wisdom and Spirit in Wis. 9.10-17. Second, the verb ἐξαποστέλλω, which Paul employs only in conjunction with the double sending in Gal. 4.4-6, also appears in Wis. 9.10 (and in connection with a ἵνα-clause as in Gal. 4.4): ἐξαπόστειλον αὐτὴν ἐξ ἁγίων οὐρανῶν... ἵνα συμπαροῦσά μοι κοπιάσῃ.[4]

R.H. Fuller has challenged Schweizer's thesis.[5] Fuller contends that the sending of the Son Christology originated in salvation-historical thinking[6] rather than 'the mythological thinking of Jewish wisdom speculation'.[7] An important aspect of Fuller's critique is his suggestion that in Jewish wisdom speculation sophia was never sent: 'She always comes on her own initiative'.[8] However, the explicit references to

---

ment Times with an Introduction to the Apocrypha [1949], p. 339 n. 15), but these views have been largely rejected (Nickelsburg, *Resurrection*, p. 88).

1. Rev. 20.4, Dan. 7.27, and *1 En.* 96.1 express thoughts similar to Wis. 3.8 and 1 Cor. 6.2, but these texts employ different terms. Mt. 19.28 records Jesus' promise that his disciples shall be given authority to judge the twelve tribes of Israel. In contrast, the future authority promised in Wis. 3.8 and 1 Cor. 6.2 extends over the 'nations' and 'the world' respectively.

2. Schweizer, '"Sendungsformel"', pp. 83-95. See also Schnabel, *Law and Wisdom*, pp. 240-42 and Kim, *Origin*, pp. 117-20.

3. See Schweizer, '"Sendungsformel"', pp. 91-92 and 'Zur Herkunft', p. 108.

4. Schweizer's case is strengthened by Philo's identification of the Logos, 'the firstborn Son of God', with the angel sent by God in Exod. 23.30 (*Agr.* 51).

5. Fuller, 'Christological Moment', pp. 42-43.

6. Thus Fuller argues that the sending of the Son schema exhibits a striking affinity to the synoptic parable of the vineyard (Mk 12.1-2 & par.): 'Here the sending of the Son is the last in a series of sendings, and the Son is no more pre-existent than were the Old Testament prophets before him' ('Christological Moment', p. 43).

7. Fuller, 'Christological Moment', p. 43.

8. Fuller, 'Christological Moment', p. 42. In n. 19 Fuller states that M.D. Johnson ('Reflections on a Wisdom Approach to Matthew's Christology', *CBQ* 36

God's sending of wisdom and Spirit in Wis. 9.10-17 reveal the weakness of Fuller's argument and the uniqueness of the parallels between Wis. 9.10-17 and Gal. 4.4-6.

The sending scheme in Wis. 9.10-17 not only confirms Schweizer's contention that the New Testament sending formula is rooted in Jewish wisdom speculation; but also, by virtue of its close affinity to Gal. 4.4-6, it suggests that Paul, at the earliest stage of his literary activity, had been influenced by Wisdom or related traditions. For the language in Gal. 4.4 concerning God's sending of his pre-existent Son is unparalleled in the synoptic Gospels and Acts, and probably originated with Paul.[1] The Pauline origin of the double sending of the Son and Spirit can hardly be questioned.[2]

3. Conclusion

We have seen that the anthropological, soteriological, and above all, pneumatological perspectives shared by the author of Wisdom and Paul, particularly as they are expressed in Wis. 9.9-18 and 1 Cor. 2.6-16, are unparalleled in intertestamental Judaism and in the non-Pauline church prior to the writing of Luke–Acts. The Hymns of Qumran represent a notable exception. However, the reference to God's double sending of wisdom/the Son and Spirit in Wis. 9.10, 17 and Gal. 4.4-6, along with many striking linguistic parallels, suggests that Wisdom or related sources rather than the Hodajot provided the framework for Paul's distinctive thought.

This conclusion is consistent with the large body of scholarship which affirms that Paul knew either Wisdom or traditions contained within it. The question of Paul's knowledge and use of Wisdom has been the source of lively debate since the publication of E. Grafe's influential work, 'Das Verhältnis der paulinischen Schriften zur Sapientia Salomonis', in 1892.[3] Although it would be premature to speak

---

[1974], pp. 44-64) 'demonstrated that the sending of wisdom is foreign to Jewish wisdom speculation, where wisdom always comes on her own initiative'. However, Johnson's discussion centers on wisdom's sending of envoys rather than the actual sending of wisdom herself.

1. Kim, *Origin*, pp. 111-36, 258-60, contra Fuller, 'Christological Moment', pp. 41-45; see also Hengel, 'Christologie und neutestamentliche Chronologie: Zu einer Aporie in der Geschichte des Urchristentums', in *Neues Testament und Geschichte* (1972), pp. 62f., 66.

2. See Chapter 12 above.

3. Published in *Theologische Abhandlungen* (1892), pp. 251-86.

of any established conclusions,[1] the more negative appraisals of H. Gunkel, E. Gärtner, and F. Focke have been largely rejected.[2] It is generally recognized that Paul was, at the very least, aware of traditions which had a profound impact on the author of Wisdom;[3] and, following Grafe, it is frequently asserted that Paul had direct contact with the book.[4]

---

1. Brief surveys of scholarly opinion on the question are provided by Romaniuk, 'Le Livre', pp. 503-504 and E. Ellis, *Paul's Use of the Old Testament* (1957), pp. 77-80.

2. Gunkel, *Die Wirkungen* (1899 edn), p. 76; E. Gärtner, *Komposition und Wortwahl des Buches der Weisheit* (1912), pp. 37-46; F. Focke, *Die Entstehung der Weisheit Salomos* (1913), pp. 113-26.

3. See G. Kuhn, 'Beiträge zur Erklärung des Buches der Weisheit', *ZNW* 28 (1929), pp. 334-41; J. Fichtner, 'Die Stellung der Sapientia Salomonis in der Literatur und Geistgeschichte ihrer Zeit', *ZNW* 36 (1937), pp. 113-32; and several other works cited by Romaniuk, 'Le Livre', p. 503. Note also Ellis, *Paul's Use*, p. 80; Conzelmann, 'Paulus und die Weisheit', p. 244; Nickelsburg, *Jewish Literature*, p. 185; Schnabel, *Law and Wisdom*, p. 232; and Kim, *Origin*, pp. 118-19.

4. Grafe, 'Das Verhältnis', esp. p. 285; F.W. Farrar, *Life and Work of Paul* (1879), II, pp. 643f.; H.J. Thackeray, *The Relation of Paul to Contemporary Jewish Thought* (1900), p. 78; R.B. Hoyle, *The Holy Spirit in St. Paul* (1927), p. 213; A.E.J. Rawlinson, *The New Testament Doctrine of Christ* (1949), pp. 133f.; S. Lyonnet, *Saint Paul. Épître aux Romains* (1959), p. 90; W. Sanday and A.C. Headlam, *A Critical and Exegetical Commentary on the Epistle to the Romans* (2nd edn, 1896), pp. 51-52; L. Ligier, *Péché d'Adam et péché du monde* (1961), II, p. 268; Romaniuk, 'Le Livre', pp. 503-14; Feuillet, *Le Christ*, pp. 150-52. Significant parallels between Wisdom and Paul frequently cited in the literature and not mentioned above include: Rom. 1.18-27 and Wis. 13–15; Rom. 2.4 and Wis. 11.23-24 (cf. 12.10, 19-21; 15.1); Rom. 3.25 and Wis. 11.23; Rom. 9.20f. and Wis. 15.7; 1 Cor. 10.1-4 and Wis. 10.17f.; 11.4.

Chapter 14

CONCLUSION

We have noted that Paul attributes soteriological significance to the gift of the Spirit. According to Paul, reception of the Spirit enables one to enter into and remain within the community of salvation. For, in Paul's perspective, the Spirit reveals to each Christian the true meaning of the death and resurrection of Jesus Christ, and progressively transforms him/her into the image of Christ. Thus Paul declares that the Spirit is the source of the Christian's cleansing, righteousness, intimate fellowship with God, and ultimate transformation through the resurrection.

We have also noted that the soteriological dimension of the Spirit's activity which forms such a prominent part of Paul's pneumatology appears infrequently in the literature of intertestamental Judaism. The literature is united in its description of the Spirit as a prophetic endowment. As the source of special insight and inspired speech, the Spirit enables the prophet, sage, or messiah, to fulfill special tasks. Thus the gift of the Spirit is presented as a *donum superadditum* rather than a soteriological necessity. The only significant exceptions to this perspective are found in later sapiential writings: Wisdom and the Hymns of Qumran.

The soteriological dimension is entirely absent from the pneumatology of Luke. In accordance with the Jewish perspective outlined above, Luke consistently portrays the gift of the Spirit as a prophetic endowment which enables its recipient to fulfill a particular task. The Spirit equips John for his role as the prophetic precursor, Jesus for his task as messianic herald, and the disciples for their vocation as witnesses. Furthermore, we have seen that Luke not only fails to refer to soteriological aspects of the Spirit's work, his narrative presupposes a pneumatology which excludes this dimension. Therefore, it cannot be maintained that Luke recognized the soteriological significance of the pneumatic gift, but simply chose to emphasize the prophetic and missiological implications of the gift. Luke's 'prophetic' pneumatology must be distinguished from the 'soteriological' pneumatology of Paul.

We have observed that the traditions of the primitive church utilized by Luke and Paul also fail to attribute soteriological functions to the Spirit. Although the primitive church, following the lead of Jesus, broadens the functions traditionally ascribed to the Spirit in first-century Judaism and thus presents the Spirit as the source of miracle-working power (as well as prophetic inspiration), the 'charismatic' pneumatology of the primitive church is otherwise essentially the same as the 'prophetic' pneumatology of Luke. The gift of the Spirit is viewed as an endowment for special tasks granted to those already within the community of salvation.

These observations have led me to conclude that Paul was the first Christian to attribute soteriological functions to the Spirit. Although Paul's unique insight into the work of the Spirit was undoubtedly stimulated by his experience on the Damascus road, I have suggested that wisdom traditions from the hellenistic Jewish milieu which produced Wisdom provided the conceptual framework for his distinctive thought. Reflecting upon his own experience in light of these traditions, Paul came to the realization that Christ, the embodiment of divine wisdom, is experienced in and through the Spirit. Indeed, according to Paul the existence of the exalted Christ is shaped by the Spirit, and the true significance of the person and mission of Christ cannot be ascertained apart from the illumination of the Spirit. Thus Paul associated Christ with the Spirit as no other Christian before him, and came to view the Spirit as a soteriological agent.

A further implication of these findings is that this original element of Paul's pneumatology did not influence wider (non-Pauline) sectors of the early church until after the writing of Luke–Acts (70–80 AD). This should not surprise us given the striking fact that Luke apparently was not acquainted with Paul's epistles.[1] And, since other distinctive aspects of Paul's theology have not significantly influenced Luke or the other synoptic evangelists,[2] this suggestion is all the more credible.[3]

---

1. Hengel, *Acts*, pp. 66-67; J.C. O'Neill, *The Theology of Acts in Its Historical Setting* (1970), p. 135; C.K. Barrett, 'Acts and the Pauline Corpus', *ExpTim* 88 (1976), pp. 2-5; and Maddox, *Purpose*, p. 68: 'It is today generally recognized that Luke did not know the Pauline letters'. A. Lindemann, however, suggests that Luke did know a few of Paul's letters (Romans, 2 Corinthians, and perhaps Galatians), but that Luke, like Matthew and Mark, was not significantly influenced by Paul's theology (*Paulus im ältesten Christentum* [1979], pp. 171-73).

2. See for example Lindemann, *Paulus*, pp. 149-73.

3. Nevertheless, some who identify the author of Luke–Acts as the traveling companion of Paul might question whether Luke could have remained untouched by the influence of the Apostle at this point. It is therefore worth noting that Luke's summaries of Paul's preaching—generally viewed as accurate representations of Paul's

The exclusion of the Johannine corpus from our study does not lessen the force of these conclusions. Since these writings originate from a geographical environment in which Paul was active and an era considerably later than the period under discussion, I am justified in assuming that the soteriological elements of John's pneumatology reflect Pauline influence.[1]

One must therefore affirm that the pneumatology of the early church was not as homogeneous as most of the major post-Gunkel studies have maintained. On the contrary, the texts of the formative period from the church's inception to the writing of Luke–Acts indicate that three distinct pneumatological perspectives co-existed: the 'charismatic' pneumatology of the primitive church; the 'prophetic' pneumatology of Luke; and the 'soteriological' pneumatology of Paul. The differences between the pneumatologies of the primitive church and Luke on the one hand, and the perspective of Paul on the other, are particularly acute.

This conclusion has important implications for the theological reflection of the contemporary church. It indicates that the task of articulating a holistic biblical theology of the Spirit is more complex than is often assumed. More specifically, it calls into question attempts at theological synthesis which do not adequately account for the distinctive pneumatological perspectives of the primitive church (Mark, Matthew), and particularly Luke–Acts. Indeed, as we re-examine the foundations upon which our theologizing is built, we are reminded that the church, by virtue of its reception of the Pentecostal gift, is a prophetic community empowered for a missionary task.

gospel by those who affirm that Luke traveled with Paul—do not contain any traces of Paul's soteriological pneumatology. This indicates that if indeed Luke heard Paul preach or entered into discussions with the Apostle and thereby came to an accurate understanding of his gospel, it is entirely possible, indeed probable, that he did so without coming to terms with Paul's distinctive pneumatological perspective. In any event, assumptions concerning the extent to which Luke was influenced by Paul must be judged in light of the evidence we have available to us.

1. See U. Schnelle, 'Paulus und Johannes', *EvTh* 47 (1987), pp. 212-28. In view of the similarities in the theological perspectives of Paul and John (e.g. the Spirit as the controlling factor of the new life), Schnelle argues that the Pauline tradition reached John's school through oral tradition and that this transmission of tradition reflects a dominant geographical environment, probably Ephesus.

BIBLIOGRAPHY

Abelson, J., *The Immanence of God in Rabbinic Literature* (London: Macmillan, 1912).

Achtemeier, Paul J., 'The Lukan Perspective on the Miracles of Jesus: A Preliminary Sketch', in *Perspectives on Luke–Acts* (ed. Charles H. Talbert; Edinburgh: T. & T. Clark, 1978), pp. 153-67.

Adler, N., *Das erste christliche Pfingstfest: Sinn und Bedeutung des Pfingstberichtes Apg. 2,1-13* (Münster: Aschendorff 'sche Verlagsbuchhandlung, 1938).

Aker, Ben, 'New Directions in Lucan Theology: Reflections on Luke 3:21-22 and Some Implications', in *Faces of Renewal: Studies in Honor of Stanley M. Horton* (ed. P. Elbert; Peabody, Mass.: Hendrickson, 1988), pp. 108-27.

Aland, K., 'Zur Vorgeschichte der christlichen Taufe', in *Neues Testament und Geschichte: Historisches Geschehen und Deutung im Neuen Testament* (FS for O. Cullmann; ed. H. Baltensweiler and B. Reicke; Tübingen: J.C.B. Mohr, 1972), pp. 1-14.

Albertz, R., 'Die "Antrittspredigt" Jesu im Lukasevangelium auf ihrem alttestamentlichen Hintergrund', *ZNW* 74 (1983), pp. 182-206.

Alexander, P.S., 'Rabbinic Judaism and the New Testament', *ZNW* 74 (1983), pp. 237-46.

Allen, Leslie C., *The Books of Joel, Obadiah, Jonah and Micah* (NICOT; Grand Rapids: Eerdmans, 1976).

Andersen, F.I., '2 (Slavonic Apocalypse of) Enoch', in *The Old Testament Pseude-pigrapha*, I (ed. J.H. Charlesworth; London: Darton, Longman, & Todd, 1983), pp. 91-221.

Anderson, A.A., 'The Use of "Ruah" in 1QS, 1QH, and 1QM', *JSS* 7 (1962), pp. 293-303.

Anderson, H., '4 Maccabees', in *The Old Testament Pseudepigrapha*, II (ed. J.H. Charlesworth; London: Darton, Longman, & Todd, 1985), pp. 531-64.

Aune, David E., *Prophecy in Early Christianity and the Ancient Mediterranean World* (Grand Rapids: Eerdmans, 1983).

—'Magic in Early Christianity', in *ANRW* II 23.2, pp. 1507-57.

Avigad, Nahman. *Discovering Jerusalem* (Oxford: Blackwell, 2nd edn, 1984; 1st edn, 1980).

Bachmann, M., *Jerusalem und der Tempel: Die geographisch-theologischen Elemente in der lukanischen Sicht des jüdischen Kultzentrums* (BWANT, 109; Stuttgart: Kohlhammer, 1980).

Baer, Heinrich von, *Der heilige Geist in den Lukasschriften* (Stuttgart: Kohlhammer, 1926).

Barrett, C.K., *The Holy Spirit and the Gospel Tradition* (London: SPCK, 1947).

—*A Commentary on the Epistle to the Romans* (HNTC; New York: Harper & Row, 1957).

—*A Commentary on the First Epistle to the Corinthians* (London: A. & C. Black, 1968).

—'Acts and the Pauline Corpus', *ExpTim* 88 (1976), pp. 2-5.

—'Light on the Holy Spirit from Simon Magus', in *Les Actes des Apôtres* (ed. J. Kremer; BETL, 68; Gembloux: Leuven University Press, 1979), pp. 281-95.

—'Apollos and the Twelve Disciples of Ephesus', in *The New Testament Age: Essays in Honor of Bo Reicke*, I (ed. W.C. Weinrich; Macon, GA: Mercer University Press, 1984), pp. 29-39.

Barth, M., *Die Taufe: ein Sakrament?* (Zollikon-Zürich: Evangelischer Verlag, 1951).

Basset, Jean-Claude, 'Dernières paroles du ressuscité et mission de l'Église aujourd'hui (à propos de Mt 28, 18-20 et parallèles)', *RTP* 114 (1982), pp. 349-67.

Bauernfeind, O., *Die Apostelgeschichte* (THNT, 5; Leipzig: Deichert, 1939).

Beasley-Murray, G.R., *Baptism in the New Testament* (Exeter: Paternoster Press, 1962).

—'Jesus and the Spirit', in *Mélanges Bibliques* (ed. A. Déscamps and A. de Halleux; Gembloux: Duculot, 1970), pp. 463-78.

Beasley-Murray, P., 'Romans 1.3f: An Early Confession of Faith in the Lordship of Jesus', *TB* 31 (1980), pp. 147-54.

Becker, J., *Auferstehung der Toten im Urchristentum* (SBS, 82; Stuttgart: KBW, 1976).

Benjamin, H.S., 'Pneuma in John and Paul', *BTB* 6 (1976), pp. 27-48.

Bennett, Dennis and Rita, *The Holy Spirit and You* (Plainfield, NJ: Logos, 1971).

Bertrams, H., *Das Wesen des Geistes* (Münster: Aschendorff'sche Verlagbuchhandlung, 1913).

Best, E., 'The Use and Non-Use of Pneuma by Josephus', *NovT* 3 (1959), pp. 218-25.

—'Spirit-Baptism', *NovT* 4 (1960), pp. 236-43.

Betz, Hans Dieter, *Galatians: A Commentary on Paul's Letter to the Churches in Galatia* (Herm; Philadelphia: Fortress Press, 1979).

—(ed.), *The Greek Magical Papyri in Translation: Including the Demotic Spells* (Chicago: The University of Chicago Press, 1986).

Betz, Otto, 'Die Proselytentaufe der Qumransekte und die Taufe im Neuen Testament', *RQ* 1 (1958-59), pp. 213-3.

—'φωνή', *TDNT*, IX, pp. 2 8-309.

—'The Eschatological Interpretation of the Sinai-Tradition in Qumran and in the New Testament', *RQ* 6 (1967), pp. 89-107.

—*What Do We Know about Jesus?* (trans. M. Kohl; London: SCM Press, 1968).

—'Jesu Evangelium vom Gottesreich', in *Das Evangelium und die Evangelien* (ed. P. Stuhlmacher; WUNT, 28; Tübingen: J.C.B. Mohr, 1983), pp. 55-77.

Beyer, Hans, 'ἕτερος', *TDNT*, II, pp. 702-704.

Bieder, W., 'πνεῦμα', *TDNT*, XI, pp. 68-75.

Billerbeck, P., 'Ein Synagogengottesdienst in Jesu Tagen', *ZNW* 55 (1965), pp. 143-61.

Black, Matthew (ed.), *Apocalypsis Henochi Graece* (PVTG, 3; Leiden: Brill, 1970).

—*The Book of Enoch* (Leiden: Brill, 1985).

Blass, F. and A. Debrunner, *A Greek Grammar of the New Testament and other Early Christian Literature* (trans. and rev. R.W. Funk; Chicago: Chicago University Press, 1961).

Bloch, Renée, 'Methodological Note for the Study of Rabbinic Literature', in *Approaches to Ancient Judaism: Theory and Practice* (ed. W.S. Green; Missoula, MT: Scholars Press, 1978), pp. 51-75.

Böcher, O., *Dämonenfurcht und Dämonenabwehr: Ein Beitrag zur Vorgeschichte der christlichen Taufe* (Stuttgart: W. Kohlhammer, 1970).

Bock, Darrell L., *Proclamation from Prophecy and Pattern: Lucan Old Testament Christology* (JSNTSS, 12; Sheffield: JSOT Press, 1987).

Boring, M.E., ' The Unforgivable Sin Logion Mark III 28-29/Matt XII 31-32/Luke XII 10: Formal Analysis and History of the Tradition', *NovT* 18 (1976), pp. 258-79.

Bornkamm, G., *Jesus of Nazareth* (trans. Irene and Fraser McLuskey with J.M. Robinson; London: Hodder & Stoughton, 1960).

—*Paul* (trans. D.M.G. Stalker; London: Hodder & Stoughton, 1985).

Borremans, J., 'The Holy Spirit in Luke's Evangelical Catechesis: A Guide to Proclaiming Jesus Christ in an Secular World', *LV* 25 (1970), pp. 279-98.

Bovon, François, *Luc le théologien: Vingt-cinq ans de recherches (1950–1975)* (Paris: Delachaux & Niestlé, 1978).

—'Aktuelle Linien lukanischer Forschung', in *Lukas in neuer Sicht* (BTS, 8; Neukirchen-Vluyn: Neukirchener Verlag, 1985), pp. 9-43.

—'Tradition et rédaction en Actes 10,1-11,18', in *L'Oeuvre de Luc: études d'exégèse et de théologie*, pp. 97–120 (Paris: Cerf, 1987).

Bowker, J., *The Targums and Rabbinic Literature* (Cambridge: Cambridge University Press, 1969).

Brandenburger, Egon, *Fleisch und Geist: Paulus und die dualistische Weisheit* (WMANT, 29; Neukirchen-Vluyn: Neukirchener Verlag, 1968).

Braude, William G., *The Midrash on Psalms* (2 vols.; New Haven: Yale University Press, 1959).

—*Pesikta Rabbati: Discourses for Feasts, Fasts, and Special Sabbaths* (2 vols.; New Haven: Yale University Press, 1968).

Braumann, G., 'Das Mittel der Zeit', *ZNW* 54 (1963), pp. 117-45.

Braun, H., *Qumran und das Neue Testament* (2 vols.; Tübingen: J.C.B. Mohr, 1966).

Broer, Ingo, 'Der Geist und die Gemeinde: Zur Auslegung der lukanischen Pfingstgeschichte (Apg 2,1-13)', *BL* 13 (1972), pp. 261-83.

Brown, Raymond E., *The Birth of the Messiah: A Commentary on the Infancy Narratives in Matthew and Luke* (London: Geoffrey Chapman, 1977).

—'Luke's Method in the Annunciation Narratives of Chapter One', in *Perspectives on Luke–Acts* (ed. Charles H. Talbert; Edinburgh: T. & T. Clark, 1978).

Brown, Schuyler, ' "Water Baptism" and "Spirit-Baptism" in Luke–Acts', *ATR* 59 (1977), pp. 135-51.

Bruce, F.F., *The Acts of the Apostles: The Greek Text with Introduction and Commentary* (London: Tyndale Press, 1951).

—*Commentary on the Book of Acts* (NICNT; Grand Rapids: Eerdmans, 1984 [reprint of 1954 1st edn]).

—'The Holy Spirit in the Acts of the Apostles', *Int* 27 (1973), pp. 166-83.

—'The Speeches in Acts: Thirty Years After', in *Reconciliation and Hope* (ed. R. Banks; Grand Rapids: Eerdmans, 1974), pp. 53-58.

—*Second Thoughts on the Dead Sea Scrolls* (Grand Rapids: Eerdmans, 5th edn, 1975).

—*New Testament History* (Basingstoke: Pickering & Inglis, 1982).

—*The Epistle of Paul to the Galatians: A Commentary on the Greek Text* (NIGTC; Exeter: Paternoster Press, 1982).

Bruner, F.D., *A Theology of the Holy Spirit: The Pentecostal Experience and the New Testament Witness* (Grand Rapids: Eerdmans, 1970).

Buber, S., *Midrasch Tanchuma* (Wilna, 1885).

Büchsel, Friedrich, *Der Geist Gottes im Neuen Testament* (Gütersloh: C. Bertelsmann, 1926).

Bultmann, R., *Theology of the New Testament* (trans. K. Grobal; 2 vols.; London: SCM Press, 1952, 1955).

—*The History of the Synoptic Tradition* (trans. J. Marsh; Oxford: Blackwell, 1968).

—'ἀγαλλιάομαι', *TDNT*, I, pp. 19-21.

Burchard, Christoph, *Der dreizehnte Zeuge: Traditions- und kompositionsgeschichtliche Untersuchungen zu Lukas' Darstellung der Frühzeit des Paulus* (FRLANT, 103; Göttingen: Vandenhoeck & Ruprecht, 1970).

Burge, Gary M., *The Anointed Community: The Holy Spirit in the Johannine Tradition* (Grand Rapids: Eerdmans, 1987).

Burrows, M., *More Light on the Dead Sea Scrolls* (New York: Viking, 1958).

Busse, Ulrich, *Das Nazareth-Manifest Jesu: Eine Einführung in das lukanische Jesubild nach Lk 4,16-30* (SBS, 91; Stuttgart: Katholisches Bibelwerk, 1977).

Cadbury, H.J., *The Making of Luke–Acts* (London: Macmillan, 1927).

—'The Speeches in Acts', in *The Beginnings of Christianity*, V (ed. F.J. Foakes-Jackson and K. Lake; London: Macmillan, 1933), pp. 402-27.

Calvin, John, *The Acts of the Apostles 1–13* (ed. D.W. & T.F. Torrance; Grand Rapids: Eerdmanns, 1965).

Campenhausen, Hans F. von, 'Das Bekenntnis im Urchristentum', *ZNW* 63 (1972), pp. 210-53.

Carlson, R.P., 'Baptism and Apocalyptic in Paul', unpublished PhD dissertation; Union Theological Seminary, 1983.

Carson, Don, *Showing the Spirit: A Theological Exposition of 1 Corinthians 12–14* (Grand Rapids: Baker Book House, 1987).

Cerfaux, Lucien, *The Christian in the Theology of Paul* (trans. L. Soiron; London: Geoffrey Chapman, 1967).

Charles, R.H., *The Book of Jubilees* (London: A. & C. Black, 1902).

—*The Book of Enoch* (Oxford: Clarendon, 1912).

Charlesworth, J.H. (ed.), *The Old Testament Pseudepigrapha* (2 vols.; London: Darton, Longman, & Todd, 1983, 1985).

Chase, F.H., *The Credibility of the Book of the Acts of the Apostles* (London: Macmillan, 1902).

Chevallier, M.A., *L'Esprit et le Messie dans le Bas-Judaïsme et le Nouveau Testament* (EHPR, 49; Paris: Presses Universitaires de France, 1958).

—*Souffle de dieu: Le Saint-Esprit dans le Nouveau Testament* (PTh, 26; Paris: Éditions Beauchesne, 1978).

—'Luc et l'Esprit Saint à la Mémoire du P. Augustin George (1915–1977)', *RSR* 56 (1982), pp. 1-16.

—'L'Apologie du baptême d'eau à la fin du premier siècle: introduction secondaire de l'etiologie dans les récits du baptême de Jesus', *NTS* 32 (1986), pp. 528-43.

Chilton, B., 'Announcement in Nazara: An Analysis of Luke 4.16-21', in *Gospel Perspectives: Studies of History and Tradition in the Four Gospels*, II (ed. R.T. France and D. Wenham; Sheffield: JSOT Press, 1981), pp. 147-72.

Collins, J.J., 'Artapanus', in *The Old Testament Pseudepigrapha*, II (ed. J.H. Charlesworth; London: Darton, Longman, & Todd, 1985), pp. 889-903.

Collins, Raymond F., 'Luke 3.21-22, Baptism or Anointing', *BibT* 84 (1976), pp. 821-31.

Colson, F.H. and G.H. Whitaker, *Philo* (10 vols. and 2 suppl. vols.; ed. R. Marcus; LCL; London: Heinemann, 1929–1962).

Combrink, H.J.B., 'The Structure and Significance of Luke 4:16-30', *Neo* 7 (1973), pp. 27-47.

Congar, Yves M.J., *I Believe in the Holy Spirit*, I (trans. D. Smith; New York: Seabury, 1983).

Conzelmann, Hans, *The Theology of St. Luke* (trans. G. Buswell; Philadelphia: Fortress Press, 1961).

—'Paulus und die Weisheit', *NTS* 12 (1965–66), pp. 231-44.

—*1 Corinthians: A Commentary on the First Epistle to the Corinthians* (Herm; Philadelphia: Fortress Press, 1975).

—*Die Apostelgeschichte* (HNT, 7; Tübingen: J.C.B. Mohr, 1963; ET; *Acts of the Apostles*; Herm; Philadelphia: Fortress Press, 1987).

Coppens, J., 'L'imposition des mains dans les Actes des Apôtres', in *Les Actes des Apôtres* (ed. J. Kremer; BETL, 68; Gembloux: Leuven University Press, 1979), pp. 405-38.

Cothenet, É., 'Les prophètes chrétiens comme exégètes charismatiques de l'Écriture', in *Prophetic Vocation in the New Testament and Today* (ed. J. Panagopoulos; SNT, 45; Leiden: Brill, 1977), pp. 77-107.

Cranfield, C.E.B., *The Gospel According to Saint Mark* (CGTC; Cambridge: Cambridge University Press, 5th edn, 1977).

—'Some Comments on Professor J.D.G. Dunn's *Christology in the Making* with Special Reference to the Evidence of the Epistle to the Romans', in *The Glory of Christ in the New Testament* (FS for G.B. Caird; ed. L.D. Hurst and N.T. Wright; Oxford: Clarendon, 1987), pp. 267-80.

Creed, J.M., *The Gospel According to St. Luke* (London: Macmillan, 4th edn, 1953).

Crockett, L., 'Luke IV. 16-30 and the Jewish Lectionary Cycle: A Word of Caution', *JJS* 17 (1966), pp. 13-46.

Cullmann, O., *The Earliest Christian Confessions* (trans. J.K.S. Reid; London: Lutterworth, 1949).

Dahl, N.A., 'Die Messianität Jesu bei Paulus', in *Studia Paulina* (FS for J. de Zwaan; ed. J.N. Sevenster and W.C. van Unnik; Haarlem: Bohn, 1953), pp. 83-95.

Danby, Herbert, *The Mishnah* (Oxford: Clarendon, 1933).

Daube, D., *The New Testament and Rabbinic Judaism* (JL, 2; London: Athlone Press, 1956).

Dautzenberg, G., *Urchristliche Prophetie: Ihre Erforschung, ihre Voraussetzungen im Judentum, und ihre Struktur im ersten Korintherbrief* (BWANT, 104; Stuttgart: Kohlhammer, 1975).

Davies, P.E., 'Jesus and the Role of the Prophet', *JBL* 64 (1945), pp. 241-54.

Davies, W.D., *Paul and Rabbinic Judaism. Some Rabbinic Elements in Pauline Theology* (London: SPCK, 1948).

—'Paul and the Dead Sea Scrolls: Flesh and Spirit', in *The Scrolls and the New Testament* (ed. K. Stendahl; London: SCM Press, 1958), pp. 157-82.

—'Reflections on the Spirit in the Mekilta', in *The Gaster Festschrift* (ed. D. Marcus; JANES, 5; New York: Columbia University, 1973).

Davis, J.A., *Wisdom and Spirit: An Investigation of 1 Corinthians 1.18–3.20 against the Background of Jewish Sapiential Tradition in the Greco-Roman Period* (Lanham, MD: University Press of America, 1984).

Deichgräber, R., *Gotteshymnus und Christushymnus in der frühen Christenheit* (SUNT, 5; Göttingen: Vandenhoeck & Ruprecht, 1967).

Deissmann, A., *Light from the Ancient East* (London: Hodder & Stoughton, 1910).

—*Paul: A Study in Social and Religious History* (London: Hodder & Stoughton, 2nd edn, 1926).

de la Potterie, I., 'L'onction du Christ: Étude de théologie biblique', *NRT* 80 (1958), pp. 225-52.

Delobel, J., 'La rédaction de Lc., IV, 14-16a et le "Bericht vom Anfang" ', in *L'Évangile de Luc: Problèmes littéraires et théologiques* (Mémorial Lucien Cerfaux; ed. F. Neirynck; Gembloux: J. Duculot, 1973), pp. 203-23.

Denis, A.M. (ed.), *Fragmenta Pseudepigraphorum Quae Supersunt Graeca* (PVTG, 3; Leiden: Brill, 1970).

Derrett, J.D.M., 'Simon Magus (Act 8.9-24)', *ZNW* 73 (1982), pp. 52-68.

de Vaux, Roland, *Ancient Israel: Its Life and Institutions* (trans. J. McHugh; London: Darton, Longman, & Todd, 1961).

Dibelius, Martin, *A Fresh Approach to the New Testament and Early Christian Literature* (Hertford: Stephen Austin & Sons, 1936).

—*Studies in the Acts of the Apostles* (trans. Mary Ling; London: SCM Press, 1956).

—'The Speeches in Acts and Ancient Historiography', in *Studies in the Acts of the Apostles* (London: SCM Press, 1956).

—*From Tradition to Gospel* (trans. B. Woolf; Greenwood, SC: Attic Press, 1971).

Diez Macho, Alejandro, 'The Recently Discovered Palestinian Targum: Its Antiquity and Relationship with the other Targums', VTSup 7 (1959), pp. 222-45.

—*Neophyti I* (6 vols.; Madrid: Consejo Superior de Investigaciones Cientificas, 1968).

Dillon, R.J., *From Eye-Witness to Ministers of the Word: Tradition and Composition in Luke 24* (AnBib, 82; Rome: Biblical Institute Press, 1978).

—'The Prophecy of Christ and His Witnesses according to the Discourses of Acts', *NTS* 32 (1986), pp. 544-56.

Dix, Gregory, *Confirmation, or Laying on of Hands?* (ThOP, 5; 1936).

Dömer, M., *Das Heil Gottes: Studien zur Theologie des lukanischen Doppelwerkes* (BBB, 51; Köln-Bonn: Peter Hanstein, 1978).

Drumwright, H.L., 'The Holy Spirit in the Book of Acts', *SwJT* 17 (1974), pp. 3-17.

Dunn, James D.G., *Baptism in the Holy Spirit: A Re-examination of the New Testament Teaching on the Gift of the Spirit in Relation to Pentecostalism Today* (London: SCM Press, 1970).

—'Spirit-Baptism and Pentecostalism', *SJT* 23 (1970), pp. 397-407.

—'Spirit and Kingdom', *ExpTim* 82 (1970), pp. 36-40.

—'Spirit-and-Fire Baptism', *NovT* 14 (1972), pp. 81-92.

—'Jesus—Flesh and Spirit: An Exposition of Romans I. 3-4', *JTS* 24 (1973), pp. 40-68.

—'I Corinthians 15.45: Last Adam, Life-giving Spirit', in *Christ and Spirit in the New Testament: In Honour of Charles Francis Digby Moule* (ed. B. Lindars and S.S. Smalley; Cambridge: Cambridge University Press, 1973), pp. 127-42.

—*Jesus and the Spirit: A Study of the Religious and Charismatic Experience of Jesus and the First Christians as Reflected in the New Testament* (London: SCM Press, 1975).

—'The Birth of a Metaphor: Baptized in the Spirit', *ExpTim* 89 (1977), pp. 134-38, 173-75.

—*Unity and Diversity in the New Testament: An Inquiry into the Character of Earliest Christianity* (London: SCM Press, 1977).

—' "They Believed Philip Preaching (Acts 8.12)": A Reply', *IBS* 1 (1979), pp. 177-83.

—*Christology in the Making: A New Testament Inquiry into the Origins of the Doctrine of Incarnation* (London: SCM Press, 1980).

—'Romans 7:14-25 in the Theology of Paul', in *Essays on Apostolic Themes: Studies in Honor of Howard M. Ervin* (ed. Paul Elbert; Peabody, MA: Hendrickson, 1985), pp. 49-70.

—' "A Light to the Gentiles": the Significance of the Damascus Road Christophany for Paul', in *The Glory of Christ in the New Testament* (FS for G.B. Caird; ed. L.D. Hurst and N.T. Wright; Oxford: Clarendon, 1987), pp. 251-66.

Dupont, Jacques, *The Sources of Acts: The Present Position* (trans. K. Pond; London: Darton, Longman & Todd, 1964).

—'The First Christian Pentecost', in *The Salvation of the Gentiles* (New York: Paulist Press, 1979; French edn, 1967), pp. 35-59.

—*Les Tentations de Jésus au Désert* (SN, 4; Paris: de Brouwer, 1968).

—*Nouvelles études sur les Actes des Apôtres* (LD, 118; Paris: Cerf, 1984).

—'La nouvelle Pentecôte (Ac 2, 1-11)', in *Nouvelles études sur les Actes des Apôtres* (LD, 118; Paris: Cerf, 1984), pp. 193-98.

—'Ascension du Christ et don de l'Esprit d'après Actes 2,33', in *Nouvelles études sur les Actes des Apôtres* (LD, 118; Paris: Cerf, 1984), pp. 199-209.

Easton, B.S., 'New Testament Ethical Lists', *JBL* 51 (1932), pp. 1-12.

Eisler, R., *The Messiah Jesus and John the Baptist according to Flavius Josephus' Recently Rediscovered 'Capture of Jerusalem' and the Other Jewish and Christian Sources* (London: Methuen, 1931).

Ellis, E.E., *Paul's Use of the Old Testament* (Edinburgh: Oliver & Boyd, 1957).

—'The Role of the Christian Prophet in Acts', in *Apostolic History and the Gospel: Studies in Honor of F.F. Bruce* (ed. W.W. Gasque and R.P. Martin; Exeter: Paternoster Press, 1970), pp. 55-67.

—'Christ and Spirit in 1 Corinthians', in *Christ and Spirit in the New Testament: In Honour of Charles Francis Digby Moule* (ed. B. Lindars and S.S. Smalley; Cambridge: Cambridge University Press, 1973), pp. 269-77.

—' "Spiritual" Gifts in the Pauline Community', *NTS* 20 (1973–74), pp. 128-44.

—*The Gospel of Luke* (NCB; London: Oliphants, Marshall, Morgan, & Scott, 1974).

—'Prophecy in the New Testament Church—And Today', in *Prophetic Vocation in the New Testament and Today* (ed. J. Panagopoulos; SNT, 45; Leiden: Brill, 1977), pp. 46-57.

—*Prophecy and Hermeneutic in Early Christianity: New Testament Essays* (WUNT, 18; Grand Rapids: Eerdmans, 1978).

—' Traditions in 1 Corinthians', *NTS* 32 (1986), pp. 481-502.

Eltester, W., 'Israel im lukanischen Werk und die Nazarethperikope', in *Jesus in Nazareth* (ed. Walther Eltester; Berlin: de Gruyter, 1972), pp. 76-147.

Epp, Eldon. *The Theological Tendency of Codex Bezae Cantabrigiensis in Acts* (Cambridge: Cambridge University Press, 1966).

Epstein, I. (ed.), *The Babylonian Talmud* (35 vols.; London: Soncino, 1935–1952).

Ernst, J., *Das Evangelium nach Lukas* (RNT; Regensburg: Pustet, 1977).

Ervin, Howard, *'These Are Not Drunken as Ye Suppose'* (Plainfield, NJ: Logos, 1968).

—*Conversion-Initiation and the Baptism in the Holy Spirit* (Peabody, MA: Hendrickson, 1984).

Esler, Philip F., *Community and Gospel in Luke–Acts: The Social and Political Motivations of Lucan Theology* (SNTSMS, 57; Cambridge: Cambridge University Press, 1987).

Etheridge, J.W., *The Targums of Onkelos and Jonathan Ben Uzziel on the Pentateuch* (New York: KTAV, 1968).

Evans, C.A., 'The Prophetic Setting of the Pentecost Sermon', *ZNW* 74 (1983), pp. 148-50.

Evans, C.F., 'The Central Section of St. Luke's Gospel', in *Studies in the Gospels* (ed. D.E. Nineham; Oxford: Blackwell, 1957), pp. 37-53.

Ewert, D., *The Holy Spirit in the New Testament* (Kitchener, Ontario: Herald Press, 1983).

Farrar, F.W., *The Life and Work of St. Paul,* (2 vols.; London: Cassell, Petter, Galpin, 1879).

Farris, Stephen C., 'On Discerning Semitic Sources in Luke 1–2', in *Gospel Perspectives: Studies of History and Tradition in the Four Gospels*, II (ed. R.T. France and D. Wenham; Sheffield: JSOT Press, 1981), pp. 201-37.

—*The Hymns of Luke's Infancy Narratives: Their Origin, Meaning and Significance* (JSNTSS, 9; Sheffield: JSOT Press, 1985).

Fee, Gordon, 'A Text-Critical Look at the Synoptic Problem', *NovT* 22 (1980), pp. 12-28.

—*The First Epistle to the Corinthians* (NICNT; Grand Rapids: Eerdmans, 1987).

Feuillet, A., *Le Christ Sagesse de Dieu d'après les Épitres Pauliniennes* (Paris: J. Gabalda, 1966).

—'Vocation et mission des prophètes, baptême et mission de Jésus. Étude de christologie biblique', *NV* 54 (1979), pp. 22-40.

Fichtner, J., 'Die Stellung der Sapientia Salomonis in der Literatur und Geistgeschichte ihrer Zeit', *ZNW* 36 (1937), pp. 113-32.

Finegan, Jack, *Die Überlieferung der Leidens- und Auferstehungsgeschichte Jesu* (Giessen: Töpelmann, 1934).

Fitzmyer, J.A., ' The Priority of Mark and the "Q" Source in Luke', in *Jesus and Man's Hope*, I (ed. D.G. Miller and D.Y. Hadidian; Pittsburg: Pittsburg Theological Seminary, 1970), pp. 131-70.

—*The Gospel According to Luke* (2 vols.;Ab, 28; New York: Doubleday, 1981, 1985).

Flender, H., *Saint Luke: Theologian of Redemptive History* (trans. R.H. and I. Fuller; London: SPCK, 1970).

Flew, R. Newton, *Jesus and His Church* (London: Epworth Press, 1960; 1st edn, 1938).

Flusser, David, ' The Dead Sea Scrolls and Pre-Pauline Christianity', in *Aspects of the Dead Sea Scrolls* (ed. C. Rabin and Y. Yadin; SH, 4; Jerusalem: Magnes, 1967), pp. 215-66.

Foakes-Jackson, F.J. and K. Lake (eds.), *The Beginnings of Christianity* (5 vols.; London: Macmillan, 1920–33).

Focke, F., *Die Entstehung der Weisheit Salomos: Ein Beitrag zur Geschichte der jüdischen Hellenismus* (FRLANT, 22; Göttingen: Vandenhoeck & Ruprecht, 1913).

Foerster, Werner, 'Der Heilige Geist im Spätjudentum', *NTS* 8 (1961–62), pp. 117-34.

France, R.T., 'Scripture, Tradition, and History in the Infancy Narratives of Matthew', in *Gospel Perspectives: Studies of History and Tradition in the Four Gospels*, II (ed. R.T. France and D. Wenham; Sheffield: JSOT Press, 1981), pp. 239-66.

Franklin, E., 'The Ascension and the Eschatology of Luke–Acts', *SJT* 23 (1970), pp. 191-200.

—*Christ the Lord: A Study in the Purpose and Theology of Luke–Acts* (London: SPCK, 1975).

Freedman, H. and Maurice Simon, *The Midrash Rabbah* (5 vols.; London: Soncino, 1977).

Fridrichsen, A., 'Le péché contre le Saint-Esprit', *RHPR* 3 (1923), pp. 367-72.

Fuller, R.H., *The Foundations of New Testament Christology* (London: Lutterworth, 1965).

—*The Formation of the Resurrection Narratives* (London: SPCK, 1972).

—'The Conception/Birth of Jesus as a Christological Moment', *JSNT* 1 (1978), pp. 37-52.

Gärtner, E., *Komposition und Wortwahl des Buches der Weisheit* (Berlin: Itzkowski, 1912).

Gasque, W.W., 'Did Luke Have Access to Traditions about the Apostles and the Early Christians?', *JETS* 17 (1974), pp. 45-48.

—'The Speeches of Acts: Dibelius Reconsidered', in *New Dimensions in New Testament Study* (ed. R.N. Longenecker and M.C. Tenney; Grand Rapids: Zondervan, 1974), pp. 232-250.

—'A Fruitful Field: Recent Study of the Acts of the Apostles', *Int* 42 (1988), pp. 117-31.

Gaster, T.H., *The Scriptures of the Dead Sea Sect* (London: Secker & Warburg, 1957).

George, A., 'L'Esprit Saint dans l'œuvre de Luc', *RB* 85 (1978), pp. 500-42.

Georgi, Dieter, *Weisheit Salomos* (JSHRZ, 3.4; Gütersloh: Gütersloher Verlagshaus, 1980).

Gero, Stephen, 'The Spirit as a Dove at the Baptism of Jesus', *NovT* 18 (1976), pp. 17-35.

Giblet, J., 'Baptism in the Spirit in the Acts of the Apostles', *OC* 10 (1974), pp. 162-71.

Giles, K., 'Is Luke an Exponent of "Early Protestantism"? Church Order in the Lukan Writings (Part 1)', *EQ* 54 (1982), pp. 193-205.

—'Is Luke an Exponent of "Early Protestantism"? Church Order in the Lukan Writings (Part 2)', *EQ* 55 (1983), pp. 3-20.

—'Salvation in Lukan Theology', *RTR* 42 (1983), pp. 10-16, 45-49.

Ginsberger, M., *Pseudo-Jonathan* (Berlin: Calvary, 1903).

Gloël, J., *Der heilige Geist in der Heilsverkündigung des Paulus* (Halle: Niemeyer, 1888).

Glombitza, Otto, 'Der Schluß der Petrusrede Acta 2:36-40: Ein Beitrag zum Problem der Predigten in Acta', *ZNW* 52 (1961), pp. 115-18.

Glover, R., '"Luke the Antiochene" and Acts', *NTS* 11 (1964–65), pp. 97-106.

Goldberg, A.M., 'Die spezifische Verwendung des Terminus Schekhinah in Targum Onkelos als Kriterium einer relativen Datierung', *Jud* 19 (1963), pp. 43-61.

—*Untersuchungen über die Vorstellung von der Schekhinah in der frühen rabbinischen Literatur* (StJud, 5; Berlin: de Gruyter, 1969).

Goldin, Judah, *The Fathers according to Rabbi Nathan* (YJS, 10; New Haven: Yale University Press, 1955).

Goldschmidt, L. (ed.), *Der Babylonische Talmud* (8 vols.; Leipzig: Otto Harrassowitz, 1897–1922).

Goppelt, Leonhard, 'Tradition nach Paulus', *KuD* 4 (1958), pp. 213-33.

Gourges, M., 'Esprit des Commencements et Esprit des Prolongements dans les Actes: Note sur la "Pentecôte des Samaritains" (Act., VIII, 5-25)', *RB* 93 (1986), pp. 376-85.

Grafe, E., 'Das Verhältnis der paulinischen Schriften zur Sapientia Salomonis', in *Theologische Abhandlungen* (FS for C. von Weizsäcker; ed. G. Heinrici; Freiburg: Akademische Verlagsbuchhandlung, 1892), pp. 251-86.

Green, Michael, *I Believe in the Holy Spirit* (Grand Rapids: Eerdmans, 1975).

Greeven, A., 'περιστερά', *TDNT*, VI, pp. 63-72.

Grundmann, Walter, *Das Evangelium nach Lukas* (THNT, 3; Berlin: Evangelische Verlagsanstalt, 1961).

—'δύναμαι', *TDNT*, II, pp. 284-317.

—'Der Pfingstbericht der Apostelgeschichte in seinem theologischen Sinn', in *Studia Evangelica Vol II: Papers Presented to the Second International Congress on New Testament Studies* (ed. F.L. Cross; TU, 87; Berlin: Akademie Verlag, 1964), pp. 584-94.

Grygelwicz, F., 'Die Herkunft der Hymnen des Kindheitsevangeliums des Lucas', *NTS* 21 (1975), pp. 265-73.

Gundry, Robert H., 'The Moral Frustration of Paul before His Conversion: Sexual Lust in Romans 7:7-25', in *Pauline Studies* (FS for F.F. Bruce; ed. D.A. Hagner and M.J. Harris; Exeter: Paternoster Press, 1980), pp. 228-45.

Gunkel, Hermann, *Die Wirkungen des heiligen Geistes nach der populären Anschauung der apostolischen Zeit und nach der Lehre des Apostels Paulus* (Göttingen: Vandenhoeck & Ruprecht, 1888; ET; trans. R.A. Harrisville and P.A. Quanbeck II; *The Influence of the Holy Spirit: the Popular View of the Apostolic Age and the Teaching of the Apostle Paul*; Philadelphia: Fortress Press, 1979).

Guthrie, Donald, *New Testament Theology* (Leicester: Inter-Varsity Press, 1981).

Haacker, K., 'Einige Fälle von "erlebter Rede" im Neuen Testament', *NovT* 12 (1970), pp. 70-77.

—'Das Pfingstwunder als exegetisches Problem', in *Verborum Veritas* (FS for G. Stählin; ed. O. Böcher and K. Haacker; Wuppertal: Theologischer Verlag Rolf Brockhaus, 1970), pp. 125-31.

—'Dibelius und Cornelius: Ein Beispiel formgeschichtlicher Überlieferungskritik', *BZ* 24 (1980), pp. 234-51.

Habel, N., 'The Form and Significance of the Call Narratives', *ZAW* 77 (1965), pp. 297-323.

Haenchen, Ernst, 'Schriftzitate und Textüberlieferung in der Apostelgeschichte', *ZTK* 51 (1954), pp. 153-67.

—*Der Weg Jesu* (Berlin: Töpelmann, 1966).

—'The Book of Acts as Source Material for the History of Early Christianity', in *Studies in Luke–Acts* (ed. L.E. Keck and J.L. Martyn; London: SPCK, 3rd edn, 1978), pp. 258-78.

—*The Acts of the Apostles* (trans. B. Noble and G. Shinn; Oxford: Blackwell, 1971).

Hahn, F., *The Titles of Jesus in Christology: Their History in Early Christianity* (trans. H. Knight and G. Ogg; London: Lutterworth, 1969).

—'Sendung des Geistes: Sendung der Jünger', in *Universales Christentum angesichts einer pluralen Welt* (ed. A. Bsteh; BeiRT, 1; Mödling: St. Gabriel, 1976), pp. 87-106.

—'Der gegenwärtige Stand der Erforschung der Apostelgeschichte: Kommentare und Aufsatzbände 1980–1985', *TRev* 82 (1986), pp. 177-90.

Hamerton-Kelly, R.G., 'A Note on Matthew XII.28 Par. Luke XI. 20', *NTS* 11 (1964–65), pp. 167-69.

Hamilton, N.Q., *The Holy Spirit and Eschatology in Paul* (SJTOP, 6; Edinburgh: Oliver & Boyd, 1957).

Hanson, R.P.C., *The Acts* (NClarB; Oxford: Clarendon, 1967).

Harrington, D.J., 'Pseudo-Philo', in *The Old Testament Pseudepigrapha*, II (ed. J.H. Charlesworth; London: Darton, Longman, & Todd, 1985), pp. 297-377.

Harrington, D.J. and A.J. Saldarini, *Targum Jonathan of the Former Prophets* (ArBib, 10; Edinburgh: T. & T. Clark, 1987).

Harter, J.L., 'Spirit in the New Testament: A Reinterpretation in Light of the Old Testament and Intertestamental Literature', unpublished PhD dissertation; University of Cambridge, 1965.

Haya-Prats, Gonzalo, *L'Esprit force de l'église. Sa nature et son activité d'après les Actes des Apôtres* (trans. J. Romero; LD, 81; Paris: Cerf, 1975).

Hedrick, Charles W., 'Paul's Conversion/Call: A Comparative Analysis of the Three Reports in Acts', *JBL* 100 (1981), pp. 415-32.

Heinemann, J., 'The Triennial Lectionary Cycle', *JJS* 19 (1968), pp. 41-48.

Heitmüller, Wilhelm, *'Im Namen Jesu': Eine sprach- und religionsgeschichtliche Untersuchung zum Neuen Testament, speziell zur altchristlichen Taufe* (Göttingen: Vandenhoeck & Ruprecht, 1903).

Hengel, Martin, 'Christologie und neutestamentliche Chronologie: Zu einer Aporie in der Geschichte des Urchristentums', in *Neues Testament und Geschichte: Historisches Geschehen und Deutung im Neuen Testament* (FS for O. Cullmann; ed. H. Baltensweiler and B. Reicke; Tübingen: J.C.B. Mohr, 1972), pp. 43-67.

—*Judaism and Hellenism: Studies in their Encounter in Palestine during the Early Hellenistic Period* (2 vols.; trans. J. Bowden; London: SCM Press, 1974.)

—'Zwischen Jesus und Paulus: Die "Hellenisten", die "Sieben" und Stephanus (Apg 6,1-15; 7,54–8,3)', *ZTK* 72 (1975), pp. 151-206.

—*The Son of God: The Origin of Christology and the History of Jewish-Hellenistic Religion* (trans. J. Bowden; London: SCM Press, 1976).

—*Acts and the History of Earliest Christianity* (trans. J. Bowden; London: SCM Press, 1979).

—*Between Jesus and Paul: Studies in the Earliest History of Christianity* (trans. J. Bowden; London: SCM Press, 1983).

Hermann, Ingo, *Kyrios und Pneuma: Studien zur Christologie der paulinischen Hauptbriefe* (StANT, 2; München: Kösel, 1961).

Hill, David, *Greek Words and Hebrew Meanings. Studies in the Semantics of Soteriological Terms* (SNTSMS, 5; Cambridge: Cambridge University Press, 1967).

—'The Rejection of Jesus at Nazareth (Lk 4.16-30)', *NovT* 13 (1971), pp. 161-80.

—'Prophecy and Prophets in the Revelation of St. John', *NTS* 18 (1971–72), pp. 401-18.

—*New Testament Prophecy* (London: Marshall, Morgan, & Scott, 1979).

—'The Spirit and the Church's Witness: Observations on Acts 1:6-8', *IBS* 6 (1984), pp. 16-26.

Hirsch, E., 'Die drei Berichte der Apostelgeschichte über die Bekehrung des Paulus', *ZNW* 28 (1929), pp. 305-12.

Holladay, Carl R. (ed.), *Fragments from Hellenistic Jewish Authors, I: Historians* (Chico, CA: Scholars Press, 1983).

Holm-Nielsen, S., *Hodayot: Psalms from Qumran* (AThD, 2; Aarhus: Universitetsforlaget, 1960).

Holst, R., 'Re-examining Mk 3.28f. and Its Parallels', *ZNW* 63 (1972), pp. 122-24.

Holtz, T., 'Christliche Interpolationen in "Joseph und Aseneth"', *NTS* 14 (1967-68), pp. 482-97.

—*Untersuchungen über die alttestamentlichen Zitate bei Lukas* (TU, 104; Berlin: Akademie Verlag, 1968).

Horsley, R.A., 'Wisdom of Word and Words of Wisdom in Corinth', *CBQ* 39 (1977), pp. 224-39.

Hoyle, R.B., *The Holy Spirit in St. Paul* (London: Hodder & Stoughton, 1927).

Hubbard, B.J., 'Commissioning Stories in Luke–Acts: A Study of their Antecedents, Form and Content', *Sem* 8 (1977), pp. 103-26.

Hull, J.H.E., *The Holy Spirit in the Acts of the Apostles* (London: Lutterworth, 1967).

Hull, J.M., *Hellenistic Magic and the Synoptic Tradition* (SBT, 2.28; London: SCM Press, 1974).

Hunter, A.M., *Paul and His Predecessors* (Philadelphia: Westminster, rev. edn, 1961).

—'Apollos the Alexandrian', in *Biblical Studies: Essays in Honour of William Barclay* (ed. J.R. McKay and J.F. Miller; London: Collins, 1976), pp. 147-56.

Hunter, Harold D., *Spirit-Baptism: A Pentecostal Alternative* (Lanham, MD: University Press of America, 1983).

Isaac, E., '1 (Ethiopic Apocalypse of) Enoch', in *The Old Testament Pseudepigrapha*, I (ed. J.H. Charlesworth; London: Darton, Longman, & Todd, 1983), pp. 5-89.

Isaacs, M., *The Concept of Spirit: A Study of pneuma in Hellenistic Judaism and Its Bearing on the New Testament* (HM, 1; London: Heythrop College, 1976).

Jaubert, A., *La notion d'alliance dans le Judaïsme aux abords de l'ère Chrétienne* (PS, 6; Paris: Seuil, 1963).

Jeremias, Joachim, *Jesus' Promise to the Nations* (trans. S.H. Hooke; SBT, 24; London: SCM Press, 1958).

—*The Prayers of Jesus* (London: SCM Press, 1967).

—*New Testament Theology: The Proclamation of Jesus* (trans. J. Bowden; London: SCM Press, 1971).

—*Die Sprache des Lukasevangeliums: Redaktion und Tradition im Nicht-Markusstoff des dritten Evangeliums* (KEKNT, Sonderband; Göttingen: Vandenhoeck & Ruprecht, 1980).

Jervell, J., *Luke and the People of God: A New Look at Luke–Acts* (Minneapolis: Augsburg, 1972).

—*The Unknown Paul. Essays on Luke–Acts and Early Christian History* (Minneapolis: Augsburg, 1984).

Jewett, Robert, *Paul's Anthropological Terms: A Study of Their Use in Conflict Settings* (AGAJU, 10; Leiden: Brill, 1971).

Johnston, G., ' "Spirit" and "Holy Spirit" in the Qumran Literature', in *New Testament Sidelights* (FS for A.C. Purdy; ed. H.K. McArthur; Hartford, Conn: Hartford Seminary Foundation Press, 1960), pp. 27-42.

Johnson, M.D., 'Reflections on a Wisdom Approach to Matthew's Christology', *CBQ* 36 (1974), pp. 44-64.

Jüngst, J., *Die Quelle der Apostelgeschichte* (Gotha: Friedrich Andreas Perthes, 1895).

Kahle, P., *The Cairo Geniza* (Oxford: Blackwell, 2nd edn, 1959).

Kaiser, C.B., 'The "Rebaptism" of the Ephesian Twelve: Exegetical Study on Acts 19:1-7', *RefR* 31 (1977–78), pp. 57-61.

Kaiser, W., 'The Promise of God and the Outpouring of the Holy Spirit: Joel 2.28-32 and Acts 2.16-21', in *The Living and Active Word of God* (FS for S.J. Schultz; ed. M. Inch and R. Youngblood; Winona Lake, IN: Eisenbrauns, 1983), pp. 109-22.

Kamlah, E., *Die Form der katalogischen Paränese im Neuen Testament* (WUNT, 7; Tübingen: J.C.B. Mohr, 1964).

Käsemann, Ernst, 'Geist und Geistgaben', *RGG* 2, pp. 1272-79.

—'Amt und Gemeinde im Neuen Testament', in *Exegetische Versuche und Besinnungen*, I (Göttingen: Vandenhoeck & Ruprecht, 6th edn, 1970), pp. 109-34.

—'Die Johannesjünger in Ephesus', in *Exegetische Versuche und Besinnungen*, I (Göttingen: Vandenhoeck & Ruprecht, 6th edn, 1970; ET; 'The Disciples of John the Baptist in Ephesus', in *Essays on New Testament Themes*; SBT, 41; London: SCM Press, 1964).

—'The Cry for Liberty in the Worship of the Church', in *Perspectives on Paul* (trans. M. Kohl; London: SCM Press, 1971), pp. 122-37.

Keck, L.E., 'The Spirit and the Dove', *NTS* 17 (1970), pp. 41-68.

Kee, Howard C., *Medicine, Miracle and Magic in New Testament Times* (SNTSMS, 55; Cambridge: Cambridge University Press, 1986).

Kelsey, M., *Speaking with Tongues* (London: Epworth Press, 1965).

Kilpatrick, G.D., 'An Eclectic Study of the Text of Acts', in *Biblical and Patristic Studies in Memory of Robert Pierce Casey* (ed. J. Neville Birdsall and Robert W. Thomson; Freiburg: Herder, 1963), pp. 64-77.

—'The Greek New Testament Text of Today and the Textus Receptus', in *The New Testament in Historical and Contemporary Perspective* (FS for G.H.C. Macgregor; ed. H. Anderson and W. Barclay; Oxford: Blackwell, 1965), pp. 189-208.

—'Some Quotations in Acts', in *Les Actes des Apôtres* (ed. J. Kremer; BETL, 68; Gembloux: Leuven University Press, 1979), pp. 81-97.

Kim, Seyoon, *The Origin of Paul's Gospel* (WUNT, 2.4; Tübingen: J.C.B. Mohr, 1981).

Kjeseth, Peter L., 'The Spirit of Power: A Study of the Holy Spirit in Luke–Acts', unpublished PhD dissertation; The University of Chicago, 1966.

Klein, Michael L., *The Fragment-Targums of the Pentateuch according to their Extant Sources* (2 vols.; AnBib, 76; Rome: Biblical Institute Press, 1980).

Klostermann, E., *Das Lukasevangelium* (HNT, 5; Tübingen: J.C.B. Mohr, 1975).

Knibb, M.A., 'Martyrdom and Ascension of Isaiah', in *The Old Testament Pseudepigrapha*, II (ed. J.H. Charlesworth; London: Darton, Longman, & Todd, 1985), pp. 143-76.

—*The Qumran Community* (Cambridge: Cambridge University Press, 1987).

Knox, W.L., *St. Paul and the Church of the Gentiles* (Cambridge: Cambridge University Press, repr., 1961).

—*The Acts of the Apostles* (Cambridge: Cambridge University Press, 1948).

Kodell, J., 'Luke's Gospel in a Nutshell (Lk 4:16-30)', *BTB* 13 (1983), pp. 16-18.

Koch, Dietrich-Alex, 'Geistbesitz, Geistverleihung und Wundermacht: Erwägungen zur Tradition und zur lukanischen Redaktion in Act 8.5-25', *ZNW* 77 (1986), pp. 64-82.

Kraeling, C.H., *The Christian Building, The Excavations at Dura-Europos. Final Report VIII.2* (New Haven: Dura-Europos Publications, 1967).

Kraft, H., 'Vom Ende der urchristlichen Prophetie', in *Prophetic Vocation in the New Testament and Today* (ed. J. Panagopoulos; SNT, 45; Leiden: Brill, 1977), pp. 162-85.

Kramer, W., *Christ, Lord, Son of God* (London: SCM Press, 1966).

Kremer, J., 'Die Voraussagen des Pfingstgeschehens in Apg 1,4-5 und 8: Ein Beitrag zur Deutung des Pfingstberichts', in *Die Zeit Jesu. Festschrift für Heinrich Schlier* (ed. G. Bornkamm and K. Rahner; Freiburg: Herder, 1970), pp. 145-68.

—*Pfingstbericht und Pfingstgeschehen: Eine exegetische Untersuchung zur Apg 2,1-13* (SBS, 63-64; Stuttgart: KBW, 1973).

Kretschmar, G., 'Himmelfahrt und Pfingsten', *ZKG* 66 (1954–55), pp. 209-53.

Krodel, G., 'The Functions of the Spirit in the Old Testament, the Synoptic Tradition and the Book of Acts', in *The Holy Spirit in the Life of the Church* (ed. Paul D. Opsahl; Mineapolis: Augsburg, 1978), pp. 10-46.

Küchler, M., *Frühjüdische Weisheitstraditionen: zum Fortgang weisheitlichen Denkens im Bereich des frühjüdischen Jahweglaubens* (OBO, 26; Freiburg/Göttingen: Universitätsverlag/Vandenhoeck & Ruprecht, 1979).

Kuhn, G., 'Beiträge zur Erklärung des Buches der Weisheit', *ZNW* 28 (1929), pp. 334-41.

Kuhn, H.W., *Enderwartung und gegenwärtiges Heil: Untersuchungen zu den Gemeindeliedern von Qumran* (SUNT, 4; Göttingen: Vandenhoeck & Ruprecht, 1966).

Kuhn, K.G., 'πειρασμός–ἁμαρτία–σάρξ im Neuen Testament und die damit zusammenhängenden Vorstellungen', *ZTK* 49 (1952), pp. 200-22.

—*Konkordanz zu den Qumrantexten* (Göttingen: Vandenhoeck & Ruprecht, 1960).

Kümmel, W.G., 'Lukas in der Anklage der heutigen Theologie', *ZNW* 63 (1972), pp. 149-65.

—*Introduction to the New Testament* (trans. H.C. Kee; Nashville: Abingdon Press, 1975).

Kuß, Otto, *Der Römerbrief*, I (Regensburg: Pustet, 2nd edn, 1963).

Lake, K., ' The Conversion of Paul and the Events Immediately Following It', in *The Beginnings of Christianity*, V (ed. F.J. Foakes-Jackson and K. Lake; London: Macmillan, 1933), pp. 188-95.

Lampe, G.W.H., *The Seal of the Spirit* (London: Longmans, Green & Co., 1951).

—'The Holy Spirit in the Writings of St. Luke', in *Studies in the Gospels* (ed. D.E. Nineham; Oxford: Blackwell, 1957), pp. 159-200.

—'Acts', in *Peake's Commentary on the Bible* (ed. M. Black and H.H. Rowley; London: Thomas Nelson & Sons, 1962), pp. 882-926.

—*God as Spirit: The Bampton Lectures, 1976* (Oxford: Clarendon, 1977).

Langston, E., *Essentials of Demonology. A Study of Jewish and Christian Doctrine: Its Origin and Development* (London: Epworth Press, 1949).

Laporte, J., 'Philo in the Tradition of Biblical Wisdom Literature', in *Aspects of Wisdom in Judaism and Early Christianity* (ed. R.L. Wilken; UNDCSJCA, 1; Notre Dame: University of Notre Dame Press, 1975), pp. 103-41.

Laurentin, A., 'Le Pneuma dans la doctrine de Philon', *ETL* 27 (1951), pp. 390-437.

Laurentin, René, *Structure et Théologie de Luc I–II* (Paris: J. Gabalda, 1964).

—*Les évangiles de l'enfance du Christ: Vérité de noël au-delà des mythes* (Paris: Desclée, 1982).

Le Déaut, R., 'Pentecost and Jewish Tradition', *DL* 20 (1970), pp. 250-67.

—*The Message of the New Testament and the Aramaic Bible (Targum)* (trans. S.F. Miletic; SubB, 5; Rome: Biblical Institute Press, 1982).

Leenhardt, F.J., *Le baptême chrétien, son origine, sa signification* (Neuchatel: Delachaux & Niestlé S.A., 1946).

—*The Epistle to the Romans: A Commentary* (trans. H. Knight; London: Lutterworth, 1961).

Legrand, L., 'L'Arrière-plan néotestamentaire de Lc. 1,35', *RB* 70 (1963), pp. 161-92.

Leisegang, Hans, *Der Heilige Geist. Das Wesen und Werden der mystich-intuitiven Erkenntnis in der Philosophie und Religion der Griechen* (Leipzig: B.G. Teubner, 1919).

—*Pneuma Hagion. Der Ursprung des Geistbegriffs der synoptischen Evangelien aus der griechischen Mystik* (Leipzig: J.C. Hinrichs, 1922).

Leivestadt, R., 'Das Dogma von der prophetenlosen Zeit', *NTS* 19 (1973), pp. 288-300.

Lentzen-Deis, F., *Die Taufe Jesu nach den Synoptikern: Literarkritische und gattungsgeschichtliche Untersuchungen* (Frankfurt am Main: Josef Knecht, 1970).

Leuba, J.L., 'Der Zusammenhang zwischen Geist und Tradition nach dem Neuen Testament', *KuD* 4 (1958), pp. 234-50.

Levey, S.H., *The Targum of Ezekiel* (ArBib, 13; Edinburgh: T. & T. Clark, 1987).

Lewy, H., *Sobria Ebrietas. Untersuchungen zur Geschichte der antiken Mystik* (BZNW, 9; Gießen: Töpelmann, 1929).

Liebermann, Saul, *Midrash Debarim Rabbah: Edited for the first time from the Oxford ms. No. 147 with an Introduction and Notes* (Jerusalem: Bamberger & Wahrmann, 1940).

Ligier, L., *Péché d' Adam et Péché du monde* (2 vols.; Théo, 48; Paris: Aubier, 1960, 1961).

Lincoln, A.T., 'Theology and History in the Interpretation of Luke's Pentecost', *ExpTim* 96 (1984–85), pp. 204-209.

Lindars, B., *New Testament Apologetic* (London: SCM Press, 1961).

Lindemann, Andreas, *Paulus im ältesten Christentum: Das Bild des Apostels und die Rezeption der paulinischen Theologie in der frühchristlichen Literatur bis Marcion* (BeiHT, 58; Tübingen: J.C.B. Mohr, 1979).

Linnemann, Eta, 'Tradition und Interpretation in Röm. 1,3f.', *EvTh* 31 (1971), pp. 264-75.

Lohfink, Gerhard, *Die Himmelfahrt Jesu: Untersuchungen zu den Himmelfahrts- und Erhöhungstexten bei Lukas* (StANT, 26; München: Kösel, 1971).

—*The Conversion of St. Paul: Narrative and History in Acts* (trans. B.J. Malina; Chicago: Franciscan Herald Press, 1976).

Lohmeyer, E., *Das Evangelium des Markus* (Göttingen: Vandenhoeck & Ruprecht, 1959).

Lohse, Eduard, 'Lukas als Theologe der Heilsgeschichte', in *Die Einheit des Neuen Testament* (Göttingen: Vandenhoeck & Ruprecht, 1973), pp. 145-64.

—'πεντηκοστή', *TDNT*, VI, pp. 44-53.

—'χείρ', *TDNT*, IX, pp. 429-37.

—'Missionarisches Handeln Jesu nach dem Evangelium des Lukas', in *Die Einheit des Neuen Testament* (Göttingen: Vandenhoeck & Ruprecht, 1973), pp. 165-77.

—'Die Bedeutung des Pfingstberichtes im Rahmen des lukanischen Geschichtswerkes', in *Die Einheit des Neuen Testament* (Göttingen: Vandenhoeck & Ruprecht, 1973), pp. 178-92.

—(ed.), *Die Texte aus Qumran: hebräisch und deutsch* (München: Kösel, 1971).

Loisy, A., *L'Évangile selon Luc* (Paris: Minerva GMBH, 1924).

Longenecker, R., *Paul: Apostle of Liberty* (New York: Harper & Row, 1964).

—*Biblical Exegesis in the Apostolic Period* (Grand Rapids: Eerdmans, 1975).

Lönig, K., *Die Saulustradition in der Apostelgeschichte* (NTA NF, 9; Münster: Verlag Aschendorff, 1973).

—'Die Korneliustradition', *BZ* 18 (1974), pp. 1-19.

Lüdemann, Gerd, *Das frühe Christentum nach den Traditionen der Apostelgeschichte* (Göttingen: Vandenhoeck & Ruprecht, 1987).

Lyonnet, S., *Saint Paul. Épître aux Romains* (BJ, 37; Paris: Cerf, 2nd edn, 1959).

Mack, B.L., *Logos und Sophia: Untersuchungen zur Weisheitstheologie in hellenistischer Judentum* (SUNT, 10; Göttingen: Vandenhoeck & Ruprecht, 1973).

Maddox, Robert, *The Purpose of Luke–Acts* (FRLANT, 126; Göttingen: Vandenhoeck & Ruprecht, 1982).

Maier, G., *Mensch und freier Wille: Nach den jüdischen Religionsparteien zwischen Ben Sira und Paulus* (WUNT, 12; Tübingen, J.C.B. Mohr, 1971).

Maile, J.F., 'The Ascension in Luke–Acts', *TB* 37 (1986), pp. 25-59.

Mandelbaum, B., *Pesikta de Rab Kahana* (New York: The Jewish Theological Seminary of America, 1962).

Mánek, J., 'The New Exodus in the Books of Luke', *NovT* 2 (1958), pp. 8-23.

Manns, Frédéric, *Le Symbole Eau-Esprit dans le Judaïsme Ancien* (SBF, 19; Jerusalem: Franciscan Printing Press, 1983).

Mansfield, M. Robert, *'Spirit and Gospel' in Mark* (Peabody, MA: Hendrickson, 1987).

Manson, T.W., *The Sayings of Jesus* (London: SCM Press, 2nd edn, 1949).

—*The Teaching of Jesus* (Cambridge: Cambridge University Press, 1952).

Mansoor, M., *The Thanksgiving Hymns: Translated and Annotated with an Introduction* (STDJ, 3; Leiden: Brill, 1961).

Margulies, Mordecai, *Midrash Haggadol on the Pentateuch, Genesis* (Jerusalem: Mossad Harev Kook, 1947).

Marmorstein, A., *The Old Rabbinic Doctrine of God* (London: Oxford University Press, 1927).

—*Studies in Jewish Theology* (ed. J. Rabbinowitz and M.S. Lew; London: Oxford University Press, 1950).

Marsh, Thomas, 'Holy Spirit in Early Christian Thinking', *ITQ* 45 (1978), pp. 101-16.

Marshall, I.H., 'Hard Sayings: VII. Lk 12.10', *Th* 67 (1964), pp. 65-67.

—'Son of God or Servant of Yahweh? A Reconsideration of Mark 1.11', *NTS* 15 (1968–69), pp. 326-36.

—'"Early Catholicism" in the New Testament', in *New Dimensions in New Testament Study* (ed. W. Ward Gasque and Ralph P. Martin; Exeter: Paternoster Press, 1970), pp. 217-31.

—*Luke: Historian and Theologian* (Grand Rapids: Zondervan, 1970).

—'The Meaning of the Verb "to Baptize"', *EQ* 45 (1973), pp. 130-40.

—*The Origins of New Testament Christology* (Leicester: Inter-Varsity Press, 1976).

—'The Significance of Pentecost', *SJT* 30 (1977), pp. 347-69.

—*The Gospel of Luke: A Commentary on the Greek Text* (NIGTC; Grand Rapids: Eerdmans, 1978).

—*The Acts of the Apostles: An Introduction and Commenatry* (TynNTC, 5; Leicester: Inter-Varsity Press, 1980).

—'Luke and His "Gospel"', in *Das Evangelium und die Evangelien* (ed. P. Stuhlmacher; WUNT, 28; Tübingen: J.C.B. Mohr, 1983), pp. 289-308.

—'How to Solve the Synoptic Problem: Luke 11:43 and Parallels', in *The New Testament Age: Essays in Honor of Bo Reicke* (2 vols.; ed. W.C. Weinrich; Macon, GA: Mercer University Press, 1984).

—'An Evangelical Approach to "Theological Criticism" ', *Them* 13 (1988), pp. 79-85.

Martin, R.A., 'Syntactical Evidence of Aramaic Sources in Acts I–XV', *NTS* 11 (1964–65), pp. 38-59.

Martin, Ralph P., 'Salvation and Discipleship in Luke's Gospel', *Int* 30 (1976), pp. 366-80.

März, Claus-Peter, *Das Wort Gottes bei Lukas: Die lukanische Worttheologie als Frage an die neuere Lukasforschung* (ErTS, 11; Leipzig: St. Benno-Verlag, 1974).

Mattill, A.J., *Luke and the Last Things* (Dillsboro, NC: Western North Carolina Press, 1979).

McNamara, M., *Palestinian Judaism and the New Testament* (GNS, 4; Wilmington, DE: John Carroll University Press, 1983).

Meagher, G., ' The Prophetic Call Narrative', *ITQ* 39 (1972), pp. 164-77.

Meeks, Wayne, *The Prophet-King: Moses Traditions and the Johannine Christology* (SNT, 14; Leiden: Brill, 1967).

Menoud, Philippe H., 'La Pentecôte lucanienne et l'histoire', *RHPR* 42 (1962), pp. 141-47.

Merk, O., 'Das Reich Gottes in den lukanischen Schriften', in *Jesus und Paulus: Festschrift für Werner Georg Kümmel zum 70. Geburtstag* (ed. E.E. Ellis and Erich Gräßer; Göttingen: Vandenhoeck & Ruprecht, 1973), pp. 201-20.

Merrill, E.H., *Qumran and Predestination: A Theological Study of the Thanksgiving Hymns* (STDJ, 8; Leiden: Brill, 1975).

Metzger, Bruce, *A Textual Commentary on the Greek New Testament* (London: United Bible Societies, 2nd edn, 1975).

—' The Fourth Book of Ezra', in *The Old Testament Pseudepigrapha*, I (ed. J.H. Charlesworth; London: Darton, Longman, & Todd, 1983), pp. 517-59.

Meyer, P., 'The Holy Spirit in the Pauline Letters: A Contextual Exploration', *Int* 33 (1979), pp. 3-18.

Meyer, R., *Der Prophet aus Galiläa* (Darmstadt: Wissenschaftliche Buchgesellschaft, 1970).

—'προφήτης', *TDNT*, VI, pp. 812-28.

—'σάρξ', *TDNT*, VII, pp. 110-19.

Michel, O., *Der Brief an die Römer* (KEKNT, 4; Göttingen: Vandenhoeck & Ruprecht, 1963).

Migne, J.P., *Patrologiae Cursus Completus: Series Graeca* (Paris, 1857).

Milik, J.T., *Ten Years of Discovery in the Wilderness of Judaea* (trans. J. Strugnell; SBT, 26; London: SCM Press, 1959).

Minear, Paul S., 'Luke's Use of the Birth Stories', in *Studies in Luke-Acts* (ed. L.E. Keck and J.L. Martyn; London: SPCK, 3rd edn, 1978), pp. 111-30.

—*To Heal and to Reveal—The Prophetic Vocation According to Luke* (New York: Seabury, 1976).

Miyoshi, M., *Der Anfang des Reiseberichts Lk. 9,51–10,24: Eine redaktionsgeschichtliche Untersuchung* (AnBib, 60; Rome: Biblical Institute Press, 1974).

Moessner, D.P., '"The Christ Must Suffer": New Light on the Jesus-Peter, Stephen, Paul Parallels in Luke–Acts', *NovT* 28 (1986), pp. 220-56.

Mohrlang, Roger, *Matthew and Paul: A Comparison of Ethical Perspectives* (SNTSMS, 48; Cambridge: Cambridge University Press, 1984).

Montague, G.T., *The Holy Spirit: Growth of a Biblical Tradition* (New York: Paulist Press, 1976).

Moore, Carey A., *Daniel, Esther, and Jeremiah: The Additions* (AB, 44; New York: Doubleday, 2nd edn, 1978).

Moore, G.F., *Judaism in the First Centuries of the Christian Era: The Age of the Tannaim* (2 vols.; Cambridge, MA: Harvard University Press, 1927).

Morgenthaler, R., *Die lukanische Geschichtsschreibung als Zeugnis: Gestalt und Gehalt der Kunst des Lukas* (2 vols.; ATANT, 15; Zurich: Zwingli, 1949).

Morrice, W.G., *Joy in the New Testament* (Exeter: Paternoster Press, 1984).

Morris, Leon, *The New Testament and Jewish Lectionaries* (London: Tyndale Press, 1964).

—'Luke and Early Catholicism', *WTJ* 35 (1973), pp. 121-36.

Moule, C.F.D., *The Holy Spirit* (London: Mowbrays, 1978).

—*The Birth of the New Testament* (New York: Harper & Row, 3rd edn, 1981).

Mulholland, M.R., 'The Infancy Narratives in Matthew and Luke—of History, Theology and Literature: A Review Article of Raymond E. Brown's Monumental *The Birth of the Messiah*', *BAR* 7 (1981), pp. 46-59.

Müller, Dieter, 'Geisterfahrung und Totenauferweckung: Untersuchung zur Totenauferweckung bei Paulus und in den ihm vorgegebenen Überlieferungen', unpublished PhD dissertation; Christian-Albrecht-Universität zu Kiel, 1980.

Mullins, Terence Y., 'New Testament Commission Forms, Especially in Luke–Acts', *JBL* 95 (1976), pp. 603-14.

Munck, Johannes, *Paul and the Salvation of Mankind* (Atlanta: John Knox, 1959).

Mußner, F., 'In den letzten Tagen (Apg 2,17a)', *BZ* 5 (1965), pp. 263-65.

—*Der Galaterbrief* (HTK, 9; Freiburg: Herder, 1974).

Neufeld, Vernon H., *The Earliest Christian Confessions* (Leiden: Brill, 1963).

Neusner, J., ' The Teaching of the Rabbis: Approaches Old and New', *JJS* 27 (1976), pp. 23-35.

—'The History of Earlier Rabbinic Judaism: Some New Approaches', *HR* 16 (1977), pp. 216-36.

—*The Tosefta: Translated from the Hebrew* (6 vols.; New York: KTAV, 1977–86).

Nickelsburg, George W.E., *Resurrection, Immortality, and Eternal Life in Intertestamental Judaism* (HTS, 26; Cambridge, MA: Harvard University Press, 1972).

—*Jewish Literature between the Bible and the Mishnah: A Historical and Literary Introduction* (London: SCM Press, 1981).

Nielsen, H.K., *Heilung und Verkündigung* (AThD, 22; Leiden: Brill, 1987).

Noack, B., 'The Day of Pentecost in Jubilees, Qumran, and Acts', *ASTI* 1 (1962), pp. 73-95.

Nötscher, F., 'Heiligkeit in den Qumranschriften', *RQ* 2 (1960), pp. 315-44.

O'Brien, Peter, *Colossians, Philemon* (WBC, 44; Waco, Texas: Word Books, 1982).

Oliver, H.H., 'The Lucan Birth Stories and the Purpose of Lk–Acts', *NTS* 10 (1964), pp. 202-26.

O'Neill, J.C., *The Theology of Acts in Its Historical Setting* (London: SPCK, 2nd edn, 1970).

O'Reilly, L., *Word and Sign in the Acts of the Apostles: A Study in Lucan Theology* (AnGreg, 243; Rome: Editrice Pontificia Università Gregoriana, 1987).

Origen, *Origen contra Celsum* (trans. F. Crombie; ANCL, 23; Edinburgh: T. & T. Clark, 1872).

O'Toole, Robert F., 'Christian Baptism in Luke', *RevRel* 39 (1980), pp. 855-66.

—'Acts 2:30 and the Davidic Covenant of Pentecost', *JBL* 102 (1983), pp. 245-58.

Ott, Wilhelm, *Gebet und Heil: Die Bedeutung der Gebetsparänese in der lukanischen Theologie* (StANT, 12; München: Kösel-Verlag, 1965).

Otzen, B., 'יצר', *TWAT*, III, pp. 830-39.

Oulton, J.E.L., 'The Holy Spirit, Baptism, and Laying on of Hands in Acts', *ExpTim* 66 (1955), pp. 236-40.

Panagopoulos, J., 'Die urchristliche Prophetie: Ihr Charakter und ihre Funktion', in *Prophetic Vocation in the New Testament and Today* (ed. J. Panagopoulos; SNT, 45; Leiden: Brill, 1977), pp. 1-32.

Parratt, J.K., 'The Rebaptism of the Ephesian Disciples', *ExpTim* 79 (1967–68), pp. 182-83.

—'The Laying On of Hands in the New Testament', *ExpTim* 80 (1968–69), pp. 210-14.

Pearson, B.A., *The Pneumatikos-Psychikos Terminology in 1 Corinthians: A Study in the Theology of the Corinthian Opponents of Paul and Its Relation to Gnosticism* (SBLDS, 12; Missoula, MT: SBL, 1973).

—'Hellenistic-Jewish Wisdom Speculation and Paul', in *Aspects of Wisdom in Judaism and Early Christianity* (ed. R.L. Wilken; UNDCSJCA, 1; Notre Dame, IN: University of Notre Dame Press, 1975), pp. 43-66.

Pereira, F., *Ephesus: Climax of Universalism in Luke–Acts. A Redaction-Critical Study of Paul's Ephesian Ministry (Acts 18.23–20.1)* (JTF, 10.1; Anand, India: Gujarat Sahitya Prakash, 1983).

Perrot, C., 'Luc 4, 16-30 et la lecture biblique de l'ancienne Synagogue', *RSR* 47 (1973), pp. 324-40.

Pesch, R., *Das Markusevangelium* (2 vols.; HTK, 2; Freiburg: Herder, 1976).

—*Die Apostelgeschichte* (2 vols.; EKK; Zürich: Benzinger Verlag, 1986).

Peterson, E., *Frühkirche, Judentum und Gnosis: Studien und Untersuchungen* (Freiburg: Herder, 1959).

Petersen, Norman, *Literary Criticism for New Testament Critics* (Philadelphia: Fortress Press, 1978).

Pfeiffer, R.H., *History of New Testament Times with an Introduction to the Apocrypha* (New York: Harper & Row, 1949).

Pfleiderer, Otto, *Paulinism: A Contribution to the History of Primitive Christian Theology* (trans. Edward Peters; 2 vols.; London: Williams & Norgate, 1877).

—*Das Urchristenthum: seine Schriften und Lehren in geschichtlichem Zusammenhang* (Berlin: Georg Reimer, 1887).

Pinnock, C., 'The Concept of the Spirit in the Epistles of Paul', unpublished PhD thesis; University of Manchester, 1963.

Potin, J., *La fête juive de la Pentecôte* (LD, 65; Paris: Cerf, 1971).

Poythress, V.S., 'Is Romans 1.3-4 a Pauline Confession after All?', *ExpTim* 87 (1975–76), pp. 180-83.

Preisendanz, Karl (ed.), *Papyri Graecae Magicae: Die griechischen Zauberpapyri* (2 vols.; Leipzig: Teubner, 1928, 1931).

Preisigke, F., 'Die Gotteskraft der frühchristlichen Zeit', in *Der Wunderbegriff im Neuen Testament* (ed. A. Suhl; WF, 295; Darmstadt: Wissenschaftliche Buchgesellschaft, 1980), pp. 210-47.

Preisker, H., 'Apollos und die Johannesjünger in Acts 18.24–19.6', *ZNW* 30 (1931), pp. 301-304.

Pryke, J., '"Spirit" and "Flesh" in the Qumran Documents and Some New Testament Texts', *RQ* 5 (1965), pp. 345-60.

Pulver, Max, 'Das Erlebnis des Pneuma bei Philon', *EJ* 13 (1945), pp. 111-32.

Rad, G. von (trans. D.M.G. Stalker), *Old Testament Theology*, II (Edinburgh: Oliver & Boyd, 1965).

Rahlfs, A. (ed.), *Septuaginta* (Stuttgart: Deutsche Bibelgesellschaft, 2nd edn, 1979).

Rawlinson, A.E.J., *The New Testament Doctrine of Christ* (BamL, 1926; London: Longmans, Green, 1949).

Reese, J.M., *Hellenistic Influence on the Book of Wisdom and Its Consequences* (AnBib, 41; Rome: Biblical Institute Press, 1970).

Reicke, Bo, 'Jesus in Nazareth—Lk 4,14-30', in *Das Wort and die Wörter* (FS for Gerhard Friedrich; ed. H. Balz and S. Schulz; Stuttgart: W. Kohlhammer, 1973), pp. 47-55.

Reiling, J., 'Prophecy, the Spirit and the Church', in *Prophetic Vocation in the New Testament and Today* (ed. J. Panagopoulos; SNT, 45; Leiden: Brill, 1977), pp. 58-76.

Rengstorf, K.H., *Das Evangelium nach Lukas* (NTD, 3; Göttingen: Vandenhoeck & Ruprecht, 1937).

—'σημεῖον', *TDNT*, VII, pp. 200-68.

—'μαθητής', *TDNT*, IV, pp. 390-461.

Rese, Martin, *Alttestamentliche Motive in der Christologie des Lukas* (StNT, 1; Gütersloh: Gütersloher Verlagshaus, 1969).

Ringgren, H., *The Faith of Qumran* (Philadelphia: Fortress Press, 1963).

—'Luke's Use of the Old Testament', *HTR* 79 (1986), pp. 227-35.

Robinson, W.C., *Der Weg des Herrn* (trans. by G. & G. Strecker; WBKEL, 36; Hamburg: Herbert Reich Evangelischer Verlag, 1964).

Rodd, C.S., 'Spirit or Finger', *ExpTim* 72 (1960–61), pp. 157-58.

Rodgers, Margaret, 'Luke 4.16-30: A Call for a Jubilee Year?', *RTR* 40 (1981), pp. 72-82.

Roebeck, Cecil M., 'The Gift of Prophecy in Acts and Paul, Part I', *StBT* 5 (1975), pp. 15-38.

Roloff, Jürgen, *Die Apostelgeschichte* (NTD; Göttingen: Vandenhoeck & Ruprecht, 1981).

Romaniuk, C., 'Le Livre de la Sagesse dans le Nouveau Testament', *NTS* 14 (1967–68), pp. 498-514.

Runia, David T., *Philo of Alexandria and the Timaeus of Plato* (PA, 44; Leiden: Brill, 1986).

Russell, D.S., *The Method and Message of Jewish Apocalyptic* (London: SCM Press, 1964).

Russell, E.A., ' "They Believed Philip Preaching" (Acts 8.12)', *IBS* 1 (1979), pp. 169-76.

Russell, Walt, 'The Anointing with the Holy Spirit in Luke–Acts', *TJ* ns 7 (1986), pp. 47-63.

Rylaarsdam, J.C., *Revelation in Jewish Literature* (Chicago: The University of Chicago Press, 1946).

—'Feast of Weeks', *IDB*, IV, pp. 827-28.

Safrai, S. and Stern, M. (eds.), *The Jewish People in the First Century* (2 vols.; Assen: Van Gorcum, 1976).

Sand, A., *Der Begriff 'Fleisch' in den paulinischen Hauptbriefen* (Regensburg: Pustet, 1967).

Sanday, W. and Headlam, A.C., *A Critical and Exegetical Commentary on the Epistle to the Romans* (ICC; Edinburgh: T. & T. Clark, 2nd edn, 1896).

Sandelin, Karl-Gustav, *Die Auseinandersetzung mit der Weisheit in 1. Korinther 15* (MFSAAF, 12; Åbo: Åbo Akademi, 1976).

Sanders, E.P., *Paul and Palestinian Judaism: A Comparision of Patterns of Religion* (London: SCM Press, 1977).

—*Jesus and Judaism* (London: SCM Press, 1985).

Sanders, J.T., *The New Testament Christological Hymns: Their Historical Religious Background* (SNTSMS, 15; Cambridge: Cambridge University Press, 1971).

Sandmel, S., 'Parallelomania', *JBL* (1962), pp. 1-13.

Sauvagant, B., 'Se repentir, être baptisé, recevoir l'Esprit, Actes 2,37 ss.', *FV* 80 (1981), pp. 77-89.

Schäfer, P., 'Die Termini "Heiliger Geist" und "Geist der Prophetie" in den Targumim und das Verhältnis der Targumim zueinander', *VT* 20 (1970), pp. 304-14

—*Die Vorstellung vom heiligen Geist in der rabbinischen Literatur* (StANT, 28; Münich: Kösel-Verlag, 1972).

Schatzmann, Siegfried S., *A Pauline Theology of Charismata* (Peabody, MA: Hendrickson, 1987).

Schille, G., *Die Apostelgeschichte des Lukas* (THNT, 5; Berlin: Evangelische Verlagsanstalt, 2nd edn, 1984).

Schlier, H., 'Zu Röm 1,3f ', in *Neues Testament und Geschichte: Historisches Geschehen und Deutung im Neuen Testament* (FS for O. Cullmann; ed. H. Baltensweiler and B. Reicke; Tübingen: J.C.B. Mohr, 1972), pp. 207-218.

Schmeichel, Waldemar, 'Christian Prophecy in Lukan Thought: Luke 4:16-30 as a Point of Departure', in *Society of Biblical Literature 1976 Seminar Papers* (ed. G. MacRae; Missoula, MT: Scholars Press, 1976), pp. 293-304.

Schmitz, O., 'Der Begriff δύναμιά bei Paulus', in *Festgabe für Adolf Deissmann* (Tübingen: J.C.B. Mohr, 1927), pp. 139-67.

Schnabel, Eckhard J., *Law and Wisdom from Ben Sira to Paul: A Tradition Historical Enquiry into the Relation of Law, Wisdom, and Ethics* (WUNT, 2.16; Tübingen: J.C.B. Mohr, 1985).

Schneider, B., 'Κατὰ Πνεῦμα ὁ 'Αγιωσύνης', *Bib* 48 (1967), pp. 359-87.

Schneider, G., 'Jesu geistgewirkte Empfängnis (Lk 1,34f)', *TPQ* 119 (1971), pp. 105-16.

—'Lk 1,34.35 als redaktionelle Einheit', *BZ* 15 (1971), pp. 255-59.

—*Das Evangelium nach Lukas* (2 vols.; ÖTKNT, 3; Gütersloh: Gütersloher Verlagshaus, 1977).

—*Die Apostelgeschichte* (2 vols.; HTK, 5; Freiburg: Herder, 1980, 1982).

—'Die Bitte um das Kommen des Geistes im lukanischen Vaterunser (Lk 11,2 v.1)', in *Studien zum Text und zur Ethik des Neuen Testaments: Festschrift zum 80. Geburtstag von Heinrich Greeven* (ed. Wolfgang Schrage; Berlin: de Gruyter, 1986), pp. 344-73.

Schnelle, U., 'Paulus und Johannes', *EvTh* 47 (1987), pp. 212-28.

Schramm, Tim, *Der Markus-Stoff bei Lukas: Eine Literarkritische und Redaktion-sgeschichtliche Untersuchung* (SNTSMS, 14; Cambridge: Cambridge University Press, 1971).

Schulz, S., *Q: Die Spruchquelle der Evangelisten* (Zürich: Theologischer Verlag, 1972).

Schürer, Emil., *The History of the Jewish People in the Age of Jesus Christ* (rev. and ed. Geza Vermes, Fergus Millar, and Matthew Black; 3 vols.; Edinburgh: T. & T. Clark, 1973–1986).

Schürmann, Heinz, *Traditionsgeschichtliche Untersuchungen zu den synoptischen Evangelien* (Düsseldorf: Patmos, 1968).

—'Der "Bericht vom Anfang": Ein Rekonstruktionsversuch auf Grund von Lk 4,14-16', in *Traditionsgeschichtliche Untersuchungen zu den synoptischen Evangelien* (Düsseldorf: Patmos, 1968), pp. 69-80.

—'Zur Traditions- und Redaktionsgeschichte von Mt 10,23', in *Traditionsgeschichtliche Untersuchungen zu den synoptischen Evangelien* (Düsseldorf: Patmos, 1968), pp. 150-56.

—*Das Lukasevangelium, 1. Teil: Kommentar zu Kap. 1,1–9,50* (HTK, 3; Freiburg: Herder, 1969).

—'Zur Traditionsgeschichte der Nazareth-Perikope Lk 4,16-30', in *Mélanges Bibliques* (ed. A. Déscamps and A. de Halleux; Gembloux: Duculot, 1970), pp. 187-205.

—'Die geistgewirkte Lebensentstehung Jesu', in *Einheit in Vielfalt* (FS for Hugo Aufderbeck; ed. W. Ernst and K. Feiereis; Leipzig: St Benno, 1974), pp. 156-69.

Schweizer, Eduard, ' The Spirit of Power: The Uniformity and Diversity of the Concept of the Holy Spirit in the New Testament' (trans. J. Bright and E. Debor), *Int* 6 (1952), pp. 259-78.

—'πνεῦμα', *TDNT*, VI, pp. 389-455.

—'σάρξ', *TDNT*, VII, pp. 98-105, 119-51.

—'Röm. 1,3f, und der Gegensatz von Fleisch und Geist vor und bei Paulus', in *Neotestamentica* (Zürich: Zwingli, 1963; reprint of an article in *EvTh* 15 [1955]), pp. 180-89.

—'Zur Herkunft der Präexistenzvorstellung bei Paulus', in *Neotestamentica* (Zürich: Zwingli, 1963), pp. 105-109.

—'Aufnahme und Korrektur jüdischer Sophiatheologie im Neuen Testament', in *Neotestamentica* (Zürich: Zwingli-Verlag, 1963), pp. 110-21.

—'Zum religionsgeschichtlichen Hintergrund der "Sendungsformel": Gal 4.4f, Röm 8.3f, Joh 3.16f, 1 Joh 4.9', in *Beiträge zur Theologie des Neuen Testaments: Neutestamentliche Aufsätze (1955–1970)* (Zürich: Zwingli-Verlag, 1970), pp. 83-95.

—*Erniedrigung und Erhöhung bei Jesus und seinen Nachfolgern* (ATANT, 28; Zürich: Zwingli-Verlag, 1962).

—'Concerning the Speeches in Acts', in *Studies in Luke–Acts* (ed. L.E. Keck and J.L. Martyn; London: SPCK, 3rd edn, 1978), pp. 208-16.

—'Die Bekehrung des Apollos, Apg 18,24-26', in *Beiträge zur Theologie des Neuen Testaments: Neutestamentliche Aufsätze (1955–1970)* (Zürich: Zwingli Verlag, 1970), pp. 71-79.

—*Das Evangelium nach Matthäus* (NTD 2; Göttingen: Vandenhoeck & Ruprecht, 1973).

—' Traditional Ethical Patterns in the Pauline and Post-Pauline Letters and Their Development (Lists of Vices and House-Tables)', in *Text and Interpretation: Studies in the New Testament Presented to Matthew Black* (ed. E. Best and R. McL. Wilson; Cambridge: The University Press, 1979), pp. 195-209.

—*The Holy Spirit* (trans. R.H. and Ilse Fuller; Philadelphia: Fortress, 1980).

Scroggs, R., 'Paul: ΣΟΦΟΣ and ΠΝΕΥΜΑΤΙΚΟΣ', *NTS* 14 (1967), pp. 33-55.

Seccombe, D.P., 'Luke and Isaiah', *NTS* 27 (1981), pp. 252-59.

—*Possessions and the Poor in Luke–Acts* (SNTU 6; Linz: SNTU, 1982).

Seidelin, P., 'Der 'Ebed Jahwe und die Messiasgestalt im Jesajatargum', *ZNW* 35 (1936), pp. 194-231.

Shelton, James, ' "Filled with the Holy Spirit": A Redactional Motif in Luke's Gospel', unpublished Ph.D. dissertation; University of Stirling, 1982.

—' "Filled with the Holy Spirit" and "Full of the Holy Spirit": Lucan Redactional Phrases', in *Faces of Renewal: Studies in Honor of Stanley M. Horton* (ed. P. Elbert Peabody, Mass.: Hendrickson, 1988), pp. 80-107.

Sherrill, J.L., *They Speak with Other Tongues* (London: Hodder & Stoughton, 1965).

Shoemaker, W.R., ' The Use of רוח in the Old Testament, and of Pneûma in the New Testament', *JBL* 23 (1904), pp. 13-67.

Simon, Marcel, *Verus Israel: A Study of the Relations between Christians and Jews in the Roman Empire (135–425)* (trans. H. McKeating; Oxford: Oxford University Press, 1986).

Sjöberg, E., 'πνεῦμα', *TDNT*, VI, pp. 375-89.

Sloan, Robert Bryan, *The Favorable Year of the Lord: A Study of Jubilary Theology in the Gospel of Luke* (Austin, TX: Schola Press, 1977).

Smalley, S.S., 'Spirit, Kingdom, and Prayer in Luke–Acts', *NovT* 15 (1973), pp. 59-71.

—'Redaction Criticism', in *New Testament Interpretation: Essays on Principles and Methods* (ed. I.H. Marshall; Grand Rapids: Eerdmans, 1977), pp. 181-95.

Smith, Morton, 'What is Implied by the Variety of Messianic Figures?', *JBL* 78 (1959), pp. 66-72.

—*Jesus the Magician* (London: Victor Gollancz, 1978).

Sokolowski, Emil, *Die Begriffe Geist und Leben bei Paulus* (Göttingen: Vandenhoeck & Ruprecht, 1903).

Sperber, Alexander, *The Bible in Aramaic* (4 vols.; Leiden: Brill, 1959–68).

Spitta, F., *Die Apostelgeschichte: Ihre Quellen und deren geschichtlicher Wert* (Halle: Waisenhaus, 1891).

Spittler, R.P., ' Testament of Job', in *The Old Testament Pseudepigrapha*, vol. 1 (ed. J.H. Charlesworth; London: Darton, Longman, & Todd, 1983), pp. 829-68.

Stadelmann, H., *Ben Sira als Schriftgelehrter: Eine Untersuchung zum Berufsbild des vormakkabäischen Sofer unter Berücksichtigung seines Verhältnisses zu Priester-, Propheten- und Weisheitslehrertum* (WUNT 2.6; Tübingen: J.C.B. Mohr, 1980).

Stählin, G., *Die Apostelgeschichte* (NTD 5; Göttingen: Vandenhoeck & Ruprecht, 1970).

Stanton, G.N., *Jesus of Nazareth in New Testament Preaching* (SNTSMS 27; Cambridge: Cambridge University Press, 1974).

Stein, R.H., 'What is Redaktionsgeschichte?', *JBL* 88 (1969), pp. 45-56.

Stemberger, Günter, *Der Leib der Auferstehung: Studien zur Anthropologie und Eschatologie des palästinischen Judentums im neutestamentlichen Zeitalter (ca. 170 v. Chr.- 100 n. Chr.)* (AnBib 56; Rome: Biblical Institute Press, 1972).

Stenning, J.F., *The Targum of Isaiah* (Oxford: Clarendon, 1953; reprint of 1949 1st edn).

Strack, Hermann L., *Introduction to the Talmud and Midrash* (Philadelphia: Jewish Publication Society of America, 1931).

Strack, Hermann L. and Paul Billerbeck, *Kommentar zum Neuen Testament aus Talmud und Midrasch* (4 vols.; München: Becksche, 1922–1928).

Streeter, B.H., *The Four Gospels: A Study in Origins* (London: Macmillan, 1924).

Strobel, A., 'Die Ausrufung des Jobeljahres in der Nazarethpredigt Jesu: Zur apokalyptischen Tradition Lc 4.16-30', in *Jesus in Nazareth* (ed. Walther Eltester Berlin: de Gruyter, 1972), pp. 38-50.

Stronstad, R., *The Charismatic Theology of St. Luke* (Peabody, MA: Hendrickson, 1984).

Styler, G.M., 'The Priority of Mark' (Excursus 4), in *The Birth of the New Testament* (C.F.D. Moule; New York: Harper & Row, 3rd edn, 1981), pp. 285-316.

Suggs, M.J., 'The Christian Two Way Tradition: Its Antiquity, Form, and Function', in *Studies in the New Testament and Early Christian Literature: Essays in Honor of A.P. Wikgren* (ed. D.E. Aune; Leiden: Brill, 1972), pp. 60-74.

Surburg, R.F., 'Rabbinical Writings of the Early Christian Centuries and New Testament Interpretation', *CTQ* 43 (1979), pp. 273-85.

Tachau, P., 'Die Pfingstgeschichte nach Lukas: Exegetische Überlegungen zu Apg. 2,1-13', *EE* 29 (1977), pp. 86-102.

Taeger, Jens W., 'Paulus und Lukas über den Menschen', *ZNW* 71 (1980), pp. 96-108.

—*Der Mensch und sein Heil: Studien zum Bild des Menschen und zur Sicht der Bekehrung bei Lukas* (StNT, 14; Gütersloh: Gütersloher Verlagshaus, 1982).

Talbert, Charles H., *Literary Patterns, Theological Themes, and the Genre of Luke–Acts* (SBLMS, 20; Missoula, MT: SBL and Scholars Press, 1974).

—'Shifting Sands: The Recent Study of the Gospel of Luke', in *Interpreting the Gospels* (ed. J.L. Mays; Philadelphia: Fortress Press, 1981), pp. 197-213.

Talmon, S., 'The Calendar Reckoning of the Sect from the Judaean Desert', in *Aspects of the Dead Sea Scrolls* (ed. C. Rabin and Y. Yadin; SH 4; Jerusalem: Magnes, 1967), pp. 162-99.

Tannehill, R.C., 'The Mission of Jesus according to Luke 4.16-30', in *Jesus in Nazareth* (ed. Walther Eltester; Berlin: de Gruyter, 1972), pp. 51-75.

—*The Narrative Unity of Luke–Acts: A Literary Interpretation, I, The Gospel according to Luke* (Philadelphia: Fortress, 1986).

Tatum, W. Barnes, 'The Epoch of Israel: Luke I–II and the Theological Plan of Luke–Acts', *NTS* 13 (1966–67), pp. 184-95.

Taylor, Vincent, *The Gospel According to Mark* (London: Macmillan, 1952).

—*The Passion Narrative of St Luke: A Critical and Historical Investigation* (SNTSMS, 19; Cambridge: Cambridge University Press, 1972).

Thackeray, H.J., *The Relation of Paul to Contemporary Jewish Thought* (London: Macmillan, 1900).

—and R. Marcus, (eds.), *Josephus with an English Translation* (9 vols.; LCL; London: W. Heinemann, 1926–65).

Thiering, B.E., 'Qumran Initiation and New Testament Baptism', NTS 27 (1981), pp. 615-31.

Tiede, D.L., *The Charismatic Figure as Miracle Worker* (SBLDS, 1; Missoula, MT: Society of Biblical Literature, 1972).

—*Prophecy and History in Luke–Acts* (Philadelphia: Fortress Press, 1980).

—'The Exaltation of Jesus and the Restoration of Israel in Acts 1', *HTR* 79 (1986), pp. 278-86.

Tobin, Thomas, *The Creation of Man: Philo and the History of Interpretation* (CBQMS, 14; Washington: Catholic Biblical Association, 1983).

Treves, M., 'The Two Spirits of the Rule of the Community', *RQ* 3 (1961), pp. 449-52.

Trites, A.A., *The New Testament Concept of Witness* (SNTSMS, 31; Cambridge: Cambridge University Press, 1977).

Trocmé, E., *Le 'Livre des Actes' et l'histoire* (Paris: Presses Universitaires de France, 1957).

Tuckett, C., 'Luke 4,16-30, Isaiah and Q', in *Logia: Les Paroles de Jésus—The Sayings of Jesus* (ed. J. Delobel; BETL, 59; Leuven: Leuven University Press, 1982), pp. 343-54.

Turner, M.M.B., ' The Significance of Spirit Endowment for Paul', *VE* 9 (1975), pp. 56-69.

—'Luke and the Spirit: Studies in the Significance of Receiving the Spirit in Luke–Acts', unpublished Ph.D. dissertation; University of Cambridge, 1980.

—' The Significance of Receiving the Spirit in Luke–Acts: A Survey of Modern Scholarship', *TJ* 2 (1981), pp. 131-58.

—'Spirit Endowment in Luke–Acts: Some Linguistic Considerations', *VE* 12 (1981), pp. 45-63.

—'Jesus and the Spirit in Lucan Perspective', *TB* 32 (1981), pp. 3-42.

—' The Spirit of Christ and Christology', in *Christ the Lord* (ed. H.H. Rowdon; Leicester: Inter-Varsity Press, 1982), pp. 168-90.

—' The Sabbath, Sunday, and the Law in Luke–Acts', in *From Sabbath to Lord's Day: A Biblical, Historical, and Theological Investigation* (ed. D.A. Carson; Grand Rapids: Zondervan, 1982), pp. 99-157.

—'Spiritual Gifts Then and Now', *VE* 15 (1985), pp. 7-64.

Turner, Nigel, *A Grammar of New Testament Greek*, III (Edinburgh: T. & T. Clark, 1963).

Tyson, J.B., 'Source Criticism of the Gospel of Luke', in *Perspectives on Luke–Acts* (ed. Charles H. Talbert; Edinburgh: T. & T. Clark, 1978), pp. 24-39.

Urbach, E.E., '?מתי פסקה הנבואה' ('When Did Prophecy Disappear?'), *Tarb* 17 (1945-46), pp. 1-11.

Van Cangh, Jean-Marie, ' "Par l'esprit de Dieu—par le doigt de Dieu" Mt 12,28 par. Lc 11,20', in *Logia: Les Paroles de Jésus—The Sayings of Jesus* (ed. J. Delobel; BETL, 59; Leuven: Leuven University Press, 1982), pp. 337-42.

van der Horst, P.W., 'Pseudo-Phocylides', in *The Old Testament Pseudepigrapha*, II (ed. J.H. Charlesworth; London: Darton, Longman, & Todd, 1985), pp. 565-82.

van der Loos, H., *The Miracles of Jesus* (SNT, 9; Leiden: Brill, 1965).

van der Minde, H.-J., 'Wie geht Paulus mit der Tradition um?', *BiKi* 37 (1982), pp. 6-13.

Van Roon, A., ' The Relation between Christ and the Wisdom of God according to Paul', *NovT* 16 (1974), pp. 207-39.

van Unnik, W.C., 'Jesus the Christ', *NTS* 8 (1961–62), pp. 101-16.

Verbeke, G., *L'évolution de la doctrine du Pneuma du Stoicisme à S. Augustin* (Paris: Desclée de Brouwer, 1945).

Vermes, Geza, *Scripture and Tradition in Judaism: Haggadic Studies* (SPB, 4; Leiden: Brill, 2nd edn, 1973).

—*Jesus the Jew: A Historian's Reading of the Gospels* (London: Collins, 1973).

—' The Impact of the Dead Sea Scrolls on the Study of the New Testament', *JJS* 27 (1976), pp. 107-16.

—'Jewish Studies and New Testament Interpretation', *JJS* 31 (1980), pp. 1-17.

—*The Dead Sea Scrolls in English* (Sheffield: JSOT Press, 3rd edn, 1987).

Violet, Bruno, *Die Esra-Apokalypse (IV. Esra)* (GCS, 18; Leipzig: Hinrichs, 1910).

Vögtle, A., *Die Tugend- und Lasterkataloge im Neuen Testament* (NTA, 16.4-5; Münster: Aschendorff, 1936).

Völkel, M., 'ὁδός', *EWNT*, II, pp. 1200-1204.

Vos, Johannes Sijko, *Traditionsgeschichtliche Untersuchungen zur paulinischen Pneumatologie* (Assen: Van Gorcum, 1973).

Watts, John D.W., *Isaiah 1–33* (WBC, 24; Waco, Texas: Word Books, 1985).

Weaver, M.J., 'Πνεῦμα in Philo of Alexandria', unpublished Ph.D. dissertation; University of Notre Dame, 1973.

Wedderburn, A.J.M., *Baptism and Resurrection: Studies in Pauline Theology against Its Graeco-Roman Background* (WUNT, 44; Tübingen: J.C.B. Mohr, 1987).

Wegenast, Klaus, *Das Verständnis der Tradition bei Paulus und in den Deuteropaulinen* (WMANT, 8; Neukirchen: Neukirchener Verlag, 1962).

Weiser, Alfons, *Die Apostelgeschichte* (2 vols.; ÖTKNT, 5; Gütersloh: Gütersloher Verlagshaus, 1981).

Weiss, Bernhard, *Lehrbuch der biblischen Theologie des Neuen Testaments* (Berlin: Hertz, 2nd edn, 1873).

Wellhausen, J., *Das Evangelium Lucae* (Berlin: Reimer, 1904).

Wenham, David, ' The Christian Life: A Life of Tension? A Consideration of the Nature of Christian Experience in Paul', in *Pauline Studies; FS for F.F. Bruce* (ed. D.A. Hagner and M.J. Harris; Exeter: Paternoster Press, 1980), pp. 80-94.

Wendt, H.H., *Die Begriffe Fleisch und Geist im biblischen Sprachgebrauch* (Gotha, 1878).

—*Die Apostelgeschichte* (KEKNT, 3; Göttingen: Vandenhoeck & Ruprecht, 1913).

Wengst, K., *Christologische Formeln und Lieder des Urchristentums* (StNT, 7; Gütersloh: Gütersloher Verlagshaus, 1972).

Wernberg-Møller, P., *The Manual of Discipline Translated and Annotated with an Introduction* (STDJ, 1; Leiden: Brill, 1957).

—'A Reconsideration of the Two Spirits in the Rule of the Community', *RQ* 3 (1961), pp. 413-41.

White, L.M., 'Domus Ecclesiae—Domus Dei: Adaptation and Development in the Setting for the Early Christian Assembly', unpublished PhD dissertation; Yale University, 1982.

Wibbing, S., *Die Tugend- und Lasterkataloge im Neuen Testament und ihre Traditionsgeschichte* (BZNW, 25; Berlin: Töpelmann, 1959).

Wilckens, U., *Die Missionsreden der Apostelgeschichte: Form- und traditionsgeschichtliche Untersuchungen* (WMANT, 5; Neukirchen-Vluyn: Neukirchener Verlag, 3rd edn, 1974).

—'Empfangen von Heiligen Geist, geboren aus der Jungfrau Maria—Lk 1,26-38', in *Zur Theologie der Kindheitsgeschichten: Der heutige Stand der Exegese* (ed. R. Pesch; München: Schnell & Steiner, 1981), pp. 49-73.

Wilkinson, T.L., ' Tongues and Prophecy in Acts and 1st Corinthians', *VR* 31 (1978), pp. 1-20.

Williams, C.G., 'Glossolalia as a Religious Phenomenon: "Tongues" at Corinth and Pentecost', *Rel* 5 (1975), pp. 16-32.

Williams, G.O., ' The Baptism in Luke's Gospel', *JTS* 45 (1944), pp. 31-38.

Wilson, S.G., 'Lukan Eschatology', *NTS* 16 (1970), pp. 330-47.

—*The Gentiles and the Gentile Mission in Luke–Acts* (SNTSMS, 23; Cambridge: Cambridge University Press, 1973).

Windisch, Hans, 'Die göttliche Weisheit der Juden und die paulinische Christologie', in *Neutestamentliche Studien, FS for G. Heinrici* (ed. A. Deissmann; Leipzig: Hinrichs, 1914), pp. 220-34.

—'Die Sprüche von Eingehen in das Reich Gottes', *ZNW* 27 (1928), pp. 163-71.

Wink, W., *John the Baptist in the Gospel Tradition* (SNTSMS, 7; Cambridge: Cambridge University Press, 1968).

Winston, David, *The Wisdom of Solomon: A New Translation with Introduction and Commentary* (AB, 43; Garden City, New York: Doubleday, 1979).

Wintermute, O.S., 'Jubilees', in *The Old Testament Pseudepigrapha*, II (ed. J.H. Charlesworth; London: Darton, Longman, & Todd, 1985), pp. 35-142.

Wojciechowski, M., 'Le don de l'Esprit Saint dans Jean 20.22 selon Tg. Gn. 2.7', *NTS* 33 (1987), pp. 289-92.

Wolff, Hans Walter, *Joel and Amos* (ET; Herm; Philadelphia: Fortress, 1977).

Wolfson, A., *Philo* (2 vols.; Cambridge, MA: Harvard University Press, 1948).

Wolter, M., 'Apollos und die ephesinischen Johannesjünger (Act 18.24–19.7)', *ZNW* 78 (1987), pp. 49-73.

Worrell, J.E., 'Concepts of Wisdom in the Dead Sea Scrolls', unpublished Ph.D. dissertation; Claremont Graduate School, 1968.

Wrege, Hans-Theo, 'Zur Rolle des Geisteswortes in frühchristlichen Traditionen (Lc 12,10 parr.)', in *Logia: Les Paroles de Jésus—The Sayings of Jesus* (ed. J. Delobel; BETL, 59; Leuven: Leuven University Press, 1982), pp. 373-77.

Wright, R.B., 'Psalms of Solomon', in *The Old Testament Pseudepigrapha*, vol. 2 (ed. J.H. Charlesworth; London: Darton, Longman, & Todd, 1985), pp. 639-70.

Wright, Walt, 'The Source of Paul's Concept of Pneuma', *CovQ* 41 (1983), pp. 17-26.

Wurm, K., 'Rechtfertigung und Heil: eine Untersuchung zur Theologie des Lukas unter dem Aspekt "Lukas und Paulus"', unpublished Ph.D. dissertation; Universität Heidelberg, 1978.

Yadin, Yigael. *The Temple Scroll: The Hidden Law of the Dead Sea Sect* (London: Weidenfeld & Nicolson, 1985).

Yates, J.E., *The Spirit and the Kingdom* (London: SPCK, 1963).

—'Luke's Pneumatology and Luke 11.20', in *Studia Evangelica Vol II: Papers Presented to the Second International Congress on New Testament Studies* (ed. F.L. Cross; TU, 87; Berlin: Akademie Verlag, 1964), pp. 295-99.

Yoder, John Howard, *The Politics of Jesus* (Grand Rapids: Eerdmans, 1972).

Ysebaert, J., *Greek Baptismal Terminology: Its Origins and Early Development* (Nijmegen: Dekker & Van de Vegt N.V., 1962).

Zehnle, F., *Peter's Pentecost Discourse: Tradition and Lukan Reinterpretation in Peter's Speeches of Acts 2 and 3* (SBLMS, 15; New York: Abingdon Press, 1971).

Ziegler, Joseph (ed.), *Duodecim prophetae. Septuaginta Vetus Testamentum Graecum*, XIII (Göttingen: Vandenhoeck & Ruprecht, 1967).

Zimmermann, H., *Neutestamentliche Methodenlehre: Darstellung der historisch-kritischen Methode* (Stuttgart: Verlag Kath. Bibelwerk, 3rd edn, 1970).

Zuckermandel, M.S., *Tosefta unter Zugrundelegung der Erfurter und Wiener Handschriften* (Trier: Fr. Lintz'schen Buchhandlung, 1882).

INDEXES

INDEX OF BIBLICAL REFERENCES

OLD TESTAMENT

RABBINIC LITERATURE

Burchard, D., 261-63
Burge, G., 129
Burrows, M., 78
Busse, U., 134, 160-62, 165, 166, 295

Cadbury, H.J., 161, 203, 220, 230, 261
Calvin, J., 252
Campenhausen, H.F. von, 185, 186
Carlson, R.P., 300
Carson, D., 204, 209, 224, 228, 270, 271
Cerfaux, L., 27
Charles, R.H., 71, 75
Charlesworth, J.H., 53, 55, 56, 68, 72, 74, 75, 238
Chase, F.H., 230
Chevallier, M.A., 26, 31, 59, 65, 72, 108, 123, 135, 138, 140, 149, 150, 154, 156, 161, 162, 293, 201, 221, 243, 250
Chilton, B., 161-63, 165
Collins, J.J., 57
Collins, R.F., 154
Colson, F.H., 64
Combrink, H.J.B., 161, 163, 166
Congar, Y., 308
Conzelmann, H., 32, 37, 39, 131, 133, 134, 143, 147, 148, 153, 183, 215, 218, 233, 234, 239, 243, 246, 249, 261, 264, 268, 270, 297, 298, 304, 308, 315
Coppens, J., 247, 251, 259, 268
Cothenet, E., 89, 101, 303
Cranfield, C.E.B., 191, 192, 293
Creed, J.M., 136, 199
Crockett, L., 165
Cullman, O., 185

Dahl, N.A., 288
Danby, H., 108
Daube, D., 159
Dautzenberg, G., 88
Davies, P.E., 176
Davies, W.D., 22, 27, 52, 78, 83, 87, 96, 107, 122, 290, 308
Davis, J., 64-66, 68, 69, 84, 89, 304, 307
Debrunner, A., 149, 201

Deichgräber, R., 186
Deissmann, A., 189, 308
de la Potterie, I., 153, 154, 206
Delobel, J., 158-60
Denis, A.-M., 55-58, 75
Derrett, J.D.M., 249, 250, 258
de Vaux, R., 232, 243
Dibelius, M., 115, 197, 214, 249, 261, 264, 265
Diez Macho, A., 99, 100
Dillon, R.J., 176, 198, 275
Dix, G., 160
Dömer, M., 154, 205, 211, 243
Drumwright, H.L., 155
Dunn, J.D.G., 31-36, 39, 42, 43, 47, 48, 62, 88, 128, 134-39, 143, 146, 149, 150, 152, 153, 183, 184, 186-91, 204-208, 212, 216, 217, 219, 224, 228, 229, 230, 241, 245, 246, 248-56, 258, 260, 264, 266, 270, 273-76, 282, 287-89, 291-95, 299, 300, 308
Dupont, J., 115, 160, 161, 183, 208, 209, 211, 229, 230, 231, 242

Easton, B.S., 297
Eisler, R., 140
Ellis, E.E., 91, 131, 132, 135, 181, 182, 215, 228, 283, 285, 304, 308, 315
Eltester, W., 161
Epp, E., 213
Epstein, I., 240
Ernst, J., 186
Ervin, H., 152, 183, 219, 253, 255, 256, 263
Esler, P.F., 162, 184
Etheridge, J.W., 237
Evans, C.F., 189, 207
Ewert, D., 250, 253

Farrar, F.W., 315
Farris, S., 117
Fee, G., 115, 228, 283, 292, 297, 298, 300, 304
Feuillet, A., 154, 307, 308, 315
Finegan, J., 198
Fitchner, J., 315

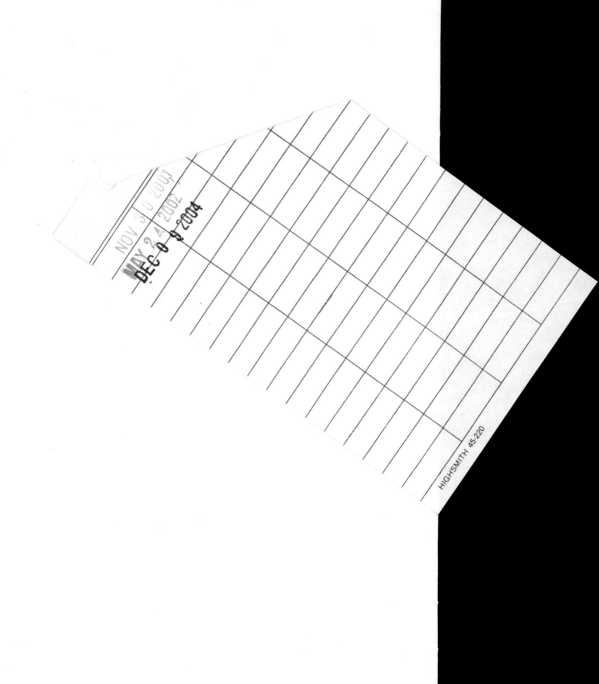